# ROBERT

MW00583554

Michael Penman is Senior
Stirling. He has published a nu
the politics and culture of Scotland in medieval Europe and on the reigns
of the Bruce kings of Scotland. He is the author of *The Scottish Civil War:
The Bruces and the Balliols and the War for Control of Scotland 1286–1356*
(2002) and *David II, 1329–71: The Bruce Dynasty in Scotland* (2004).

# Robert the Bruce

## KING OF THE SCOTS

MICHAEL PENMAN

YALE UNIVERSITY PRESS
NEW HAVEN AND LONDON

*With love,*
*for Angela and Rosie*

Copyright © 2014 Michael Penman

First published in paperback in 2018

The right of Michael Penman to be identified as the author of this work has been asserted by him in accordance with the Copyright, Designs and Patents Act 1988.

For information about this and other Yale University Press publications, please contact:
U.S. Office: sales.press@yale.edu  yalebooks.com
Europe Office: sales@yaleup.co.uk  yalebooks.co.uk

Set in Adobe Caslon Pro by IDSUK (DataConnection) Ltd
Printed in Great Britain by Hobbs the Printers Ltd, Totton, Hampshire

Library of Congress Cataloging-in-Publication Data

Penman, Michael A.
  Robert the Bruce: King of Scots / Michael Penman.
    pages cm
  Includes bibliographical references and index.
  ISBN 978-0-300-14872-5 (cl : alk. paper)
  1. Robert I, King of Scots, 1274–1329. 2. Scotland—History—Robert I, 1306–1329.
  3. Scotland—Kings and rulers—Biography. I. Title.
  DA783.4.P46 2014
  941.102092—dc23
  [B]

2014007172

ISBN 978-0-300-24031-3 (pbk)

A catalogue record for this book is available from the British Library.

10 9 8 7 6 5 4 3 2 1

# Contents

*List of Illustrations and Maps*   vi
*Genealogical Tables*   viii
*A Note about Distances, Money and Bibliography*   x

Introduction: Re-opening the 'Book on Bruce'   1

**Part One: To Be King**

1 *Body and Soul*: Formative Years, 1274–92   13
2 *Conflict*: Earl of Carrick, 1293–99   38
3 *Dead End*: Vacillation, 1300–6   64
4 *You Can't Get Away with Murder*: King Robert, 1306–10   92
5 *The Harder they Fall*: Victory in Scotland, 1310–14   118

**Part Two: After Bannockburn**

6 *The Desperate Hours*: War and Famine, 1314–17   149
7 *Dark Victory*: The Price for Berwick, 1317–19   177
8 *Dark Passage*: In Search of Respite, 1319–22   209
9 *To Have and Have Not*: King of Scotland, 1322–26   235
10 *Dead Reckoning*: Peace and Piety, 1326–28   266
11 *Beat the Devil*: Preparing for the End, 1328–29   296

Conclusion:
Bruce Kingship and the Legacy of Scotland's Wars, c.1286–c.1329   309

*Appendix: Councils and Parliaments of Robert I, 1306–29*   332
*Abbreviations*   334
*Notes*   337
*Acknowledgements*   406
*Index*   408

# Illustrations and Maps

**Plates**

1. All Souls church, Writtle, Essex. Photograph by John Whitworth.
2. Edward I and Alexander III in parliament at Westminster, 1278. © De Agostini/The British Library Board.
3. Ruins of Turnberry castle, Carrick, Ayrshire.
4. Recreation of Portencross castle, Ayrshire, with war galley. Illustration by Bob Marshall; with the permission of Friends of Portencross castle.
5. Wall painting of Judas Maccabeus from the Painted Chamber, Palace of Westminster. © Westminster Palace.
6. The Great Hall and Round Table, Winchester. Photograph by Graham Horn.
7. King John (Balliol) submits to Edward I, 1292. © The British Library Board, Royal 20 C. VII, f.28.
8. Coronation of an English King, c.1308. By permission of the Master and Fellows of Corpus Christi College, Cambridge.
9. Plaque commemorating Bruce's murder of Comyn of Badenoch, Dumfries, 1306. Photograph by Darrin Antrobus.
10. Seal of Scone Abbey.
11. Plaque commemorating Bruce's exile to Rathlin, 1306–7. Photograph by Ross.
12. a), b), c). Cults and relics venerated by Robert I. a) © National Museums Scotland; b) © National Museums Scotland; c) © The Metropolitan Museum, New York.
13. a), b). Arbroath abbey and seal. Kind permission of Angus Council Museums and Galleries.

14. Robert I kills Henry de Bohun at Bannockburn, 1314. By permission of the Master and Fellows of Corpus Christi College, Cambridge.
15. Bothwell castle, Lanarkshire. Photograph by Otter.
16. a), b). Robert I's second great seal. Author's collection.
17. Cambuskenneth Abbey, south of Stirling castle. © National Library of Scotland.
18. Robert I's parliamentary forfeiture of his opponents, 1314. © The National Archives of Scotland.
19. The Bute Mazer. © National Museums Scotland, on loan from The Bute Collection at Mount Stuart.
20. The Savernake horn and baldric. © The British Museum.
21. The *Luttrell Psalter*: a) agriculture; b) a wild Scot; c) the execution of the earl of Lancaster, 1323. a) © The British Library Board, Add. 42130, f.170; b) © The British Library Board, Add. 42130, f.70; c) © The British Library Board, Add. 42130, f.56.
22. Recreation of St Andrews Cathedral, Fife. Courtesy of the Virtual St Andrews project.
23. Tarbert castle, Argyll. Photograph by Alasdair Ross.
24. Mains of Cardross farm, Dunbartonshire. Photograph by Lairich Rig.
25. Robert I's defiance to Edward III, 1327. © Bibliothèque nationale, Paris FR 2643, f.13v.
26. Tomb of St Margaret, Dunfermline Abbey.
27. a) Fragments of the tomb of Robert I (Dunfermline Abbey) and b) his heart casket (Melrose Abbey). a) © Society of Antiquaries of Scotland; b) © Crown Copyright Historic Scotland, reproduced courtesy of Historic Scotland, www.historicscotlandimages.gov.uk.

## Maps                                                          *page*

1. Scotland during the Wars 1296–1329.                            xi
2. Robert I's resettlement: Scotland, north of Forth.            146
3. Robert I's resettlement: Scotland, south of Forth.            147
4. Raiding of the north of England and of Ireland, c.1311–27.    148

Maps 2, 3 and 4 are extrapolated from P. G. B. McNeill and H. L. MacQueen, eds, *Atlas of Scottish History to 1707* (Edinburgh, 1996), 101, 202–5.

# Table 1: Scottish Royal Succession c.1152–c.1292

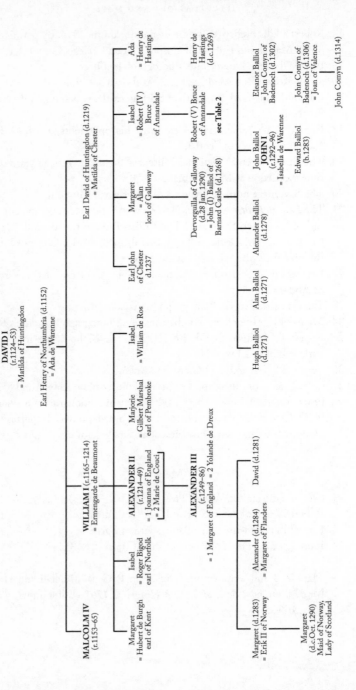

**Table 2: Bruce Succession**

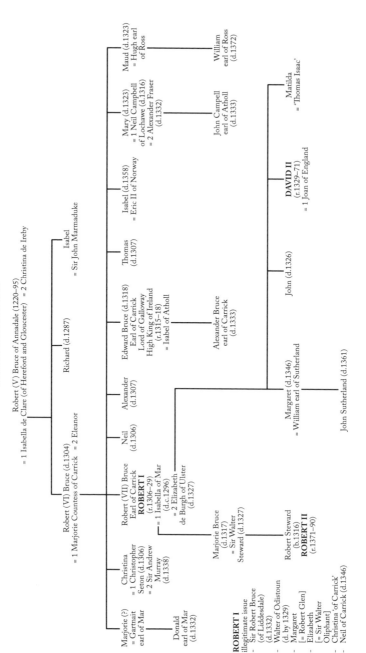

# A Note about Distances, Money and Bibliography

The Scots mile was equivalent to 1.12 English miles in this period, but all distances cited in the text are modern measurements (as the crow flies over land, taking account of rivers and ferries crossing water).[1]

Scottish and English pounds remained roughly equivalent until c.1350. All fiscal amounts cited in the text are direct citations from contemporary sources (but readers must bear in mind that a medieval £1 contained 240 silver pennies of the period). A Scots merk (English mark) was worth two-thirds of a pound, at 13s 4d.[2]

Finally, in the interests of space, I have reduced my original footnoting, and a full bibliography of manuscripts, printed primary sources, books, articles, theses and web materials consulted can be found in a listing for students and teachers (updated annually) held under Research Output at: http://rms.stir.ac.uk/people/11182.

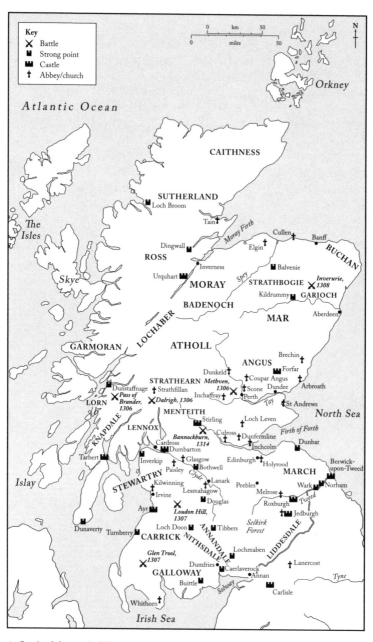

**Key**
- ✕ Battle
- ◼ Strong point
- ⌘ Castle
- ✝ Abbey/church

km 0 — 50
miles 0 — 50

N

Atlantic Ocean

Orkney

CAITHNESS

SUTHERLAND
Loch Broom

The Isles

Tain

Moray Firth

Cullen    Banff

Dingwall    Elgin    BUCHAN

Skye    ROSS    Inverness    Balvenie

Urquhart    MORAY    Spey    STRATHBOGIE    *Inverurie, 1308*

Kildrummy    GARIOCH

BADENOCH    Aberdeen

MAR

GARMORAN    LOCHABER    ATHOLL

Brechin

ANGUS    Forfar

Dunkeld    *Methven, 1306*    Coupar Angus

STRATHEARN    Strathfillan    Arbroath

Dunstaffnage    Scone    Dundee

LORN    *Pass of Brander, 1306*    Inchaffray    Perth

✕ *Dalrigh, 1306*    Tay    St Andrews

MENTEITH    North Sea

Stirling    Loch Leven

MENTEITH    Firth of Forth

LENNOX    Culross    Dunfermline

*Bannockburn, 1314*    Inchcolm    Dunbar

Cardross    Dumbarton

Tarbert    Glasgow    Edinburgh    Holyrood    Berwick-upon-Tweed

KNAPDALE    Inverkip    Bothwell

Paisley    Clyde    MARCH

Islay    Lanark    Wark    Norham

STEWARTRY    Kilwinning    Lesmahagow    Peebles    Melrose

Irvine    Douglas    Roxburgh    Jedburgh    Tweed

Ayr    *Loudon Hill, 1307*    Tibbers    *Selkirk Forest*    LIDDESDALE

Dunaverty    Turnberry    Loch Doon    Lochmaben

CARRICK    NITHSDALE

✕ *Glen Trool, 1307*    Dumfries    Lanercost

GALLOWAY    Caerlaverock    Annan    Tyne

Buittle    Carlisle

Whithorn    Solway

Irish Sea

1. Scotland during the Wars, 1296–1329.

# Introduction

## Re-opening the 'Book on Bruce'

*And to record maire of this taill*
*It nedis nocht now, for ye alhaill*
*May find it in the Bruss buke*
Prior Andrew Wyntoun's *Original Chronicle* (c.1420)[1]

Between 6 and 14 November 1314 a Scottish parliament was held at the Augustinian abbey of Cambuskenneth, nestled between bends in the river Forth and overlooked by the crag-top royal castle of Stirling.[2] We do not know how many people were in attendance but it is easy to imagine that the monastic facilities were overwhelmed. Nobles, churchmen, burgh officials and curious crowds of ordinary locals surely felt compelled to be present even as winter set in. They came in the wake of the great victory in battle over an English royal army achieved on 24 June 1314 less than three miles to the south, at Bannockburn, by forces led by Robert Bruce – King Robert I since 1306.

Traces of that awful slaughter of thousands of English troops – routed by Scottish spears, crushed by their own retreating horses or drowned in the marshy streams of Stirling's estuarial carse – must still have been visible.[3] It had been a bloody defeat from which the English king, Edward II, had only narrowly escaped. Thus Robert may have chosen the abbey as a convenient location with room for conferral in central Scotland because of its proximity both to the battlefield and the symbolic gateway to the north that was Stirling castle, over which Scottish colours flew once more. In private, the king may also have favoured Cambuskenneth as the site of his secret indenture a decade before (when the castle last fell to English control) with Bishop William Lamberton of St Andrews, Scotland's leading prelate: the two men had pledged mutual support in the name of God, the Church and crusade, in anticipation of a Bruce revival of Scotland's kingship.[4]

However, in late 1314 public expectation held that the most important item of business of the Cambuskenneth assembly was to be a general act of forfeiture upon Robert's enemies: a formal deprivation 'in perpetuity' of the lands and goods of those holders of Scottish titles who remained (or had died) outside the faith of their king.[5] If exploited to the full, this would see the Bruce regime seize formal control of no fewer than six of the Scottish kingdom's (thirteen) ancient earldoms and several associated lordships of comparable size and wealth, all told almost half of the realm's lands: this would confirm Robert's revolutionary shake-up of Scottish elite society.[6]

Yet this watershed moment had by no means been predicted confidently just a year before. It is now generally accepted that the parliamentary forfei-ture of 6 November 1314 brought to an end a twelve-month ultimatum pronounced by King Robert and his councillors, probably in October 1313 at a much smaller parliament or council held in the burgh of Dundee.[7] This had surely not been Bruce's first such demand for all holders of Scottish lands to recognise his authority. However, the military and polit-ical landscape of Scotland was radically altered over the course of 1314: first by the Scots' capture from English garrisons of the major royal castles of Roxburgh and Edinburgh; then by Robert's unexpected triumph over the army of Edward II at Bannockburn, leading to the fall of further occu-pation strongholds including Stirling, Bothwell and Dunbar castles. Thus, those who formed the parliament that met at the abbey almost five months after the battle surely did so as subjects of a regime undeniably blessed by God, in a mood of awe and hope of royal acts to be applied by King Robert with vigour across the realm.

Bannockburn meant that Robert was also able to demand the exchange of English noble prisoners for the release of his past mentor, Bishop Robert Wishart of Glasgow, as well as for his own queen, Elizabeth de Burgh of Ulster, and only legitimate child (by his first wife, Isabella of the house of Mar), his daughter Marjorie.[8] Robert could now look to father a male heir and determine his succession. In addition, victory had brought large rewards of spoil from the English baggage train and prospects of further ransoms and border plunder. These were badly needed resources that could be directed both to rebuilding Scotland and to military and diplomatic campaigns on a number of fronts, plans surely discussed at Cambuskenneth. But, most importantly, Robert could now undertake in earnest a territorial and governmental resettlement through grants of lands, resources and office, and the dispensation of justice. Thus the Cambuskenneth parliament was surely marked by vociferous lobbying by parties seeking both new patronage and confirmation of past rights from their battle-anointed king.

Robert's surviving grants give the impression that this was something the king had begun only hesitantly before his victory at Bannockburn, a caution which persisted even after November 1314.[9] The only extant royal acts issued in the weeks after the battle included a letter of 5 September seeking peace talks with Edward II; this followed further Scottish raids into the unprotected marches of northern England which had seen Robert I grant the manor of Wark in Tynedale (Northumberland) to Sir William Soules of Liddesdale, a former enemy now re-admitted to the king's peace.[10] But some of the surviving acts of the Cambuskenneth parliament confirm Robert I's new mandate. On 12 November, Sir Gilbert Hay of Errol was awarded the hereditary office of Constable, responsible for royal household security and musters of the army, replacing a forfeited defector who had chosen the wrong side at Bannockburn, the powerful earl of Atholl, David Strathbogie.[11] It may have been about this time, too, that the Atholl title was promised to another Bruce supporter, the king's brother-in-law, Neil Campbell of Lochawe, whose son would receive Argyllshire lands in barony on 10 February 1315 in return for the services of a forty-oared ship.[12] Nonetheless, this marked only the tentative beginnings of Bruce patronage distribution, remaining within the immediate circle of his closest supporters, a group recorded as witnesses to his Cambuskenneth charters and headed by the king's only surviving brother and heir, Edward Bruce, as earl of Carrick and lord of Galloway, Thomas Randolph as earl of Moray, James lord Douglas, Walter the hereditary Steward and Robert Keith now hereditary Marischal (Marshal).

At the same time Robert also used this parliament to further associate his kingship and victory with the spiritual lights of royal Scotland. On 14 November 1314 he granted the church of Kinross to the Benedictine abbey of Dunfermline in Fife in thanks for the support of the royal St Margaret (d.1093) and her relics interred there, alongside the tombs of six of Scotland's Canmore kings, including her husband Malcolm III (r.1058–93) and son David I (r.1124–53) – both of whom the monks also regarded as saintly – and Alexander III (r.1249–86), whose untimely death had precipitated Scotland's wars of succession.[13] These relics were tokens of faith and identity that had been brought to Bannockburn along with those of other 'national' cults to bless Robert's forces.[14] Two days later on 16 November – the chief feast day of St Margaret – Robert journeyed 20 miles east to gain an indulgence for his soul by visiting Dunfermline in person.[15] Here he gave the first indication that he intended to build his own tomb there, next to the sepulchres of his dynastic predecessors.[16]

Two generations later, Archdeacon John Barbour of Aberdeen, author of an epic poetic history of Robert's reign in vernacular Scots, *The Bruce* (c.1371–5), still remembered Bannockburn and the proclamation of the Cambuskenneth parliament as historic turning points.[17] Yet in doing so, Barbour and his 'Bruss buke' must bear a large measure of blame for the battle of 1314 serving as a false, heavily abridged climax to popular memory of the events of Robert's reign. For Barbour drew upon a variety of now lost works in verse and prose celebrating the deeds of Robert and several of his close supporters, some undoubtedly composed just after Bannockburn or Robert's death. Thus Barbour glossed the already biased family histories of the victors of Bannockburn, and then added his own courtly veneer for the political and chivalric sympathies of their descendants, especially the later fourteenth-century Stewarts and Douglases.[18]

The result was often quite extreme historical distortion or omission. For example, coverage of 1318 in *The Bruce* makes no connection between the Scots' recapture from the English in April–June of their realm's most valuable port, Berwick-upon-Tweed, and the destruction in October of Edward Bruce's invasion forces then in English-held Ireland: the latter provoked a crisis of succession and politics for Robert I played out in his parliament at Scone in December that year. Similarly, a noble conspiracy against Robert in 1320, tightly bound to all the foregoing, was blamed by Barbour upon the pathetic royal ambitions of Sir William Soules of Liddesdale without a hint at the reality of wider, lingering aristocratic sympathies for the alternative kingship claims of exile Edward Balliol, son of King John (r.1292–96), the Bruces' main dynastic rival yet a monarch of Scotland who is mentioned only once in the poem as having 'ruled bot a lytill quyle'.[19] Overall, Robert I's real difficulties of succession, patronage, finance and foreign relations in the later part of his reign are telescoped all too neatly by Barbour into a single, joyous parliament (fusing actual sessions of 1326, 1328 and 1331). This merged Anglo-Scottish peace, Franco-Scottish alliance, domestic consensus and full coronation of the infant Prince David Bruce as king within his father's own lifetime alongside recognition of a presumptive Stewart inheritance.[20]

It is thus both fascinating and problematic that Barbour's poem continues to be cited as a *historical* source for much of the period 1306–29. This is a particular quandary for the two-thirds of Robert I's reign that fall after Bannockburn. Barbour reaches the end of 1314 two-thirds of the way through his 13,000-line narrative. It is striking that most modern histories of Robert have echoed this structure. Even Geoffrey Barrow's classic *Robert the*

*Bruce and the Community of the Realm of Scotland* (1965, 5th edn 2013) leaves only two condensed, thematic chapters for the last fifteen years of the reign of 'Good King Robert'.[21] As such, an alternative title for the present volume might have been *After Bannockburn*. It attempts a detailed account of that crucial period, especially in terms of domestic politics and Robert I's resettlement of political and landed society year-by-year, in search of both his regime's long-term plans and real-time reactions to wider crises and events.

However, this does not come at the expense of a re-evaluation of Bruce's earlier, formative years. A well-known story, it is often told within the context of general histories of the wars (and William Wallace). It is headlined by Robert's murder of rival John Comyn of Badenoch in the Greyfriars church at Dumfries on 10 February 1306 and his rushed seizure of the throne a few weeks later. This was the start of a long, hard high-road of civil conflict and guerrilla warfare leading up to Bannockburn. Yet here the concern must be to investigate key influences upon the future king, not least the intimidating English monarch Edward I ('Longshanks'), who first exploited Scotland's succession crisis to assert his rule; but also Robert's own grandfather and father, nobles like James the hereditary royal Steward of Scotland and prominent prelates like Wishart of Glasgow, Lamberton of St Andrews and Bernard, abbot of Arbroath (and Robert's Chancellor). However, such personal networks must also speak to the influence of political ideas, piety and a mixed cultural and geographical identity.

Indeed, a chronological study of all of this reign must explore the competing, often contradictory currents of politics and social change acting upon King Robert and his subjects as well as upon their counterparts in other European realms.[22] Growing to maturity, first as earl of Carrick in the Gaelic south-west of Scotland then as a potential claimant to the Scottish kingship, Robert Bruce cannot have been unaware of developments and tensions of political representation and lordly authority between the Crowns, political classes and institutions of England and Scotland, the realms in which his family held lands before 1306. This period provided the backdrop across north-western Europe for the complex, interwoven expansion of royal and lordly power, of increasingly bureaucratic government, of the definition and assertion of legal rights, and of the development of powers of representative assembly and right-to-redress of overlapping communities large and small, communities that were regnal (or 'national'), regional (and thus sometimes ethnic and linguistic, cultural as well as economic or geographic), aristocratic, ecclesiastical and urban, institutional and professional, and, of course, familial and dynastic. For the Scottish kingdom and subjects, the experience of these continuously evolving forces was unavoidably accelerated by their royal succession crisis and repeated occupations by the stronger 'imperial' neighbour, England.

This was a crucible forged by a failed ruling lineage, a fate that Scotland shared with a number of other European realms across the period c.1275–c.1330. They included the various duchies of the contested Low Countries (Flanders, Brabant, Holland and Hainault) as well as the kingdoms of Sweden, Denmark, Castile, Sicily, Hungary, Bohemia and Poland, and, in its own way, Ireland.[23] The heads of a number of otherwise stable dynasties also had to muster their realms to resist the territorial and jurisdictional demands of ambitious, aggressive rivals as well as of traditional hegemonic powers, not least the claims of the Holy Roman Empire and the Papacy. Such rulers sought at the same time to assert their superiority over their own subjects or peripheral regions and peoples and lesser neighbour 'states'. These were powerful competing tides certainly felt by England, France, Burgundy, Aragon and Naples in this period.[24] But within these struggles, as we shall see, the efforts to define and defend a kingship, territorial borders or polity at a 'national' level through war and diplomacy, and allied innovations in law, worship, military organisation or economic and cultural activity, all had inescapable consequences. These were in turn shaped by the concerns and actions of lesser communities and individual subjects.

How Robert Bruce and his supporters interacted with this emerging dynamic of politics and lordship is also a focus of this book. In England, representatives of the nobility, Church, shires and towns in parliament acted as the 'community of the realm' in coordinated moves to limit and manage the authority of an increasingly intrusive Crown, often as the voice of opposition and in the context of sustained royal demands for war taxation.[25] By contrast, in Scotland the responsible men of the kingdom (earls, barons and clergy) acted rather as the 'community of the realm' in the absence of an active monarch after 1286, so as to protect the sovereign kingdom and its customary laws and institutions against both internal factionalism and an external threat from its neighbouring kingdom, England.[26] As a noble, before his seizure of the Scottish throne in 1306, Robert would be compelled to work within several overlapping and often competing communities: familial, regional, economic, spiritual, cultural and political. But to take that extra step and to establish his own *royal* legitimacy in Scotland he would have to work with and wield the very power of the 'community of the realm' that had frequently been used to obstruct his family's claims and that, once fully recovered, might seek to check his authority as king.

Within this increasingly difficult framework Robert I found common cause with leading Scottish churchmen. The clergy formed a community within the realm that could understand the value of a strong king, just as they could a strong Pope, to protect the *Ecclesia Scoticana* as a 'special daughter' (since 1192) from the predation of English supremacy (and even from the power of Scotland's own monarchy). However, Scottish clerics schooled in Oxford as well as France, Italy and at other continental universities before 1286 would also have been aware of the growing power of conciliar checks upon high authority (papal, imperial, royal, prelatical). Thus, such clerics could also seek to control and mould a king and his policies, not merely through the power of the pulpit but also through daily counsel to the Crown, or an assembly of subjects' representatives, or via an otherwise well-managed government bureaucracy.[27] At the same time, the laity – from the titled nobility and lesser freeholders on the land to merchant and craft communities in the burghs – all rallied at times behind the restoration of a strong monarchy to defend an independent Scottish realm and customs. But, in return for their support, they might expect greater local autonomy and/or input as to the formulation and supervision of royal government and policy. Such scope for both cooperation and confrontation contributed much to a politics of control and compromise in Scotland after 1306, with institutions, resources and community consent closely managed by the king and his councillors, often to the exclusion of others.

It is essentially the more factional, practical stresses of such domestic politics that this book seeks to explore in detail, over and above the more idealistic, consensual thread of the 'community of the realm' presented by Barrow.[28] Here, the new edition of the *Records of the Parliaments of Scotland* provides an important starting point.[29] To this must be added studies exploring the recodification of law undertaken post-Bannockburn in Bruce's Scotland, in such celebrated working treatises as *Regiam Majestatem*.[30] However, as part of this volume's wider attempt to evaluate Robert's reign, especially after 1314, there remain severe source limitations.

Some contemporary Scottish comment is preserved in some of the Latin annals collected (and glossed) by cleric John of Fordun c.1383 and by his fifteenth-century continuator, Abbot Walter Bower of Inchcolm in the Forth (d.1449). Both Fordun and Bower had access to chronicles compiled by clerics at St Andrews, which sustained coverage of events through from the thirteenth century. Bower also had access to government records, including parliamentary rolls and diplomatic correspondence, as well as to other now lost narrative accounts. However, these Scottish chronicles very often have more to reveal about the politics of their authors' generations. Others, including the vernacular verse of the *Original Chronicle* (c.1410–20) of Prior Andrew Wyntoun from the Augustinian priory of St Serf's, Lochleven (Fife), simply referred their readers to Barbour's *Bruce* for coverage of 1306–29.[31]

Genuine contemporary comment about Robert and the events of his lifetime must instead be found in English monastic annals and Anglo-French chronicles. On the whole such works focus upon military events. For example, the scribes of the priory of Lanercost in Cumbria poured scorn upon Bruce and his nobles for their repeated plunder of the Borders and their house. But works such as Walter of Guisborough's chronicle (c.1305) from a North Yorkshire Augustinian priory actually founded by the Bruces or the royal household source of the *Vita Edwardi Secundi* (c.1307–26) or the *Scalacronica* from the 1350s by the Northumbrian nobleman Sir Thomas Gray, do provide important testimony about Scottish figures and politics, drawing on eyewitness accounts of Edward II's court and parliaments as well as the wars.[32] Further first-hand evidence is also preserved by Flemish chronicler Jean le Bel (c.1290–1370) and collected in the various recension *Chroniques* of his countryman, Jean Froissart (c.1337–c.1407).[33]

Turning to record sources, seventeenth-century indices of lost royal patronage rolls provide listings of almost seven hundred 'lost' acts of Robert I, only in part duplicating the more than five hundred remaining acts identifiable as fuller texts from original charters or later transcripts.[34] Very often, though, Robert's charters indicate not the itinerary of the king but of his busy Chancellor, Abbot Bernard of Arbroath (c.1308–28).[35] Far more painful, however, is the complete loss of Robert I's exchequer rolls of summarised royal income and expenditure for all but the last two years of his reign (1327–28, 1328–29) and some earlier fragments.[36] Nevertheless, historians still have a wealth of material with which to work, both published and unpublished, in the various 'Scottish rolls' that recorded the occupation administration of the English Crown, as well as in papal supplications and correspondence, fragmentary Scottish church cartularies and Scottish noble family archives.

By integrating all of the foregoing material this book seeks to illustrate two further themes, especially for the period after 1314. First, Robert I's assertion of his legitimacy as king by building a royal image that included the sacred power of monarchy: his association through patronage, itinerary and ritual with a number of the churches, saints' cults and holy relics closely linked with the Scottish royal house.[37] Second, another universal experience: the impact of natural environmental crises exacerbated by war. This last goes beyond any sweeping view of the 'long fourteenth century' as a period of sustained social and economic crises across Europe, often linked to models of political upheaval, collapse and stagnation in particular realms.[38] However, some understanding of extreme weather and widespread harvest failures in the 1290s and 1310s, of devastating animal pandemics and price fluctuations, brings in to focus further elements of Robert I's policies after Bannockburn.

Examination of all these interlinked themes, across all of Robert's life and reign, also affords us glimpses of the king's character that go beyond his traditional, inherited image as a figure of deep dynastic ambition, chivalry and, for later commentators, patriotism. Much of this Bruce image can be exploded as myth, propaganda or anachronism, inflated by Robert and his government as well as by their successors. But in truth, in seeking to understand the wider experience of Robert's kingship and reign – especially his political problems and dealings with his subjects and foreign powers after 1314 – we can actually come far closer to appreciating just why he became the standard for Scottish kingship throughout the later fourteenth and fifteenth centuries. We can also better grasp why Robert Bruce has remained a political and cultural icon for Scots through seven hundred years of profound change since Bannockburn.

## Part One

# TO BE KING

*'There the pride will be seen that parches and makes the Scots and Edward's English mad, so that they cannot keep the proper borders.'*

Dante Alighieri, *Paradiso*, Canto xix: 91–148, c.1308/21

# CHAPTER ONE

# Body and Soul
## Formative Years, 1274–92

*If I can obtain the aforesaid kingdom by way of law and a trustworthy jury, it is well indeed: but if not, I shall never in gaining it for myself reduce to servitude the aforesaid kingdom which all its kings with great toil and trouble have until now preserved and held without servitude in firmly-rooted freedom.*

Bruce of Annandale replies to Edward I, November 1292[1]

### Family and Childhood

What can be identified of the early life of Robert (VII) Bruce, future lord of Annandale and earl of Carrick of that ilk, serves to underline just how limited are the labels of such modern constructs as 'Anglo-Norman', 'Celtic' or even 'Scottish' or 'English'.[2] Tradition has long supposed that Robert was born at Turnberry, the sea-castle of the ancient earldom of Carrick in southern Ayrshire.[3] However, a later fourteenth-century English chronicle by Geoffrey 'the Baker' of Swinbroke (d.c.1360), a man with connections to the de Bohun earls of Hereford, asserts that Robert was born in the former English royal manor of Writtle in Essex.[4] This may indeed mistake Robert's birthplace for that of his namesake and father, Robert VI, who between 1295 and his death in April 1304 would certainly reside for the most part on this holding and neighbouring Hatfield Regis.[5] However, the possibility that the future king of Scots was not in fact born in the Scottish realm should not really surprise us.[6] Later fourteenth-century Scottish chroniclers and Archdeacon Barbour might be said conspicuously to have avoided stating where the hero king was born (or simply not to have regarded it as important).[7] Moreover, even if incorrect, the Writtle claim merely reflects the cross-border estates and multi-community outlook of the Bruces by the late thirteenth century.[8]

Writtle, Hatfield and Midlands possessions in England had come into the Bruce family after 1237 thanks to the very marriage (c.1219) that would allow them to claim the Scottish throne in 1290–92: that of Robert's great-grandfather, Robert IV of Annandale, to Isabel, second daughter of David, earl of Huntingdon (d.1219), brother of King William I (William the Lion) of Scotland (r.1165–1214).[9] However, it was not until Isabel's death in 1252 that her eldest son, Robert V of Annandale (c.1220–95), the Competitor (or 'Noble'), came in to full sasine (legal possession) of this share of the Huntingdon–Chester lands, perhaps adding as much as £170 to his annual income by acquiring these manors. By then the eldest of his two sons, Robert (VI), had already been born, in about 1243 (with a brother, Richard, to follow) of a de Clare mother, Isabella, daughter of the earl of Gloucester and lord of Thomond in Ireland.[10]

The Scottish annals collated and glossed by John of Fordun c.1383, drawing on a St Andrews source of the late thirteenth century, embrace the famous romantic tale of the recently widowed Marjorie, daughter of Neil, the last Gaelic earl of Carrick, 'kidnapping' her prospective husband, Robert VI, and holding him in Turnberry until their nuptials. Historians have generally accepted the report, too, that this love-match occurred c.1272–73 in defiance of Alexander III (or perhaps his Comyn advisors serving as justiciars of Galloway and sheriffs of Wigtown), who nonetheless relented, probably as this was not at odds with Crown plans to absorb the formerly autonomous south-west.[11] However, the Bruce–Carrick marriage and its advantages may also have grown out of the crusading network of Princes Edward and Edmund of England of c.1271–74 (inspired by Louis IX of France's own expedition of 1270–71). These retinues had included Robert V of Annandale and Adam of Kilconquhar, earl of Carrick (Marjorie's first husband, killed on the trip), and should also have seen Robert VI take up the cross.[12] In addition, the acquisition by marriage of the Carrick estates (valued c.1260 at £168 annually) effectively doubled the income of the Bruces in Scotland, if only to a modest English baronial level.[13] The importance and status of the rank of earl, however, only the third such title held in Scotland by a family of Norman origin, would seem to have guaranteed the usual presence of Robert VI and his growing family in that realm, where aristocratic living was perhaps more affordable, and with Turnberry, Loch Doon and Lochmaben as their chief residences.[14] Yet in doing so, Robert VI would by no means have deprived his several sons of the experiences open to them in other parts of the family's patrimony: from their Tottenham lands near London to their Hartness manors and other holdings in Yorkshire, Northumberland and Cumberland; from their Scottish border lordship and south-western earldom to inherited lands in the Garioch and the burgh of Dundee; and across the Irish Sea to Olderfleet and Upper Glenarm in Larne, and smaller holdings near Coleraine and Port Stewart, part of a reduced Carrick inheritance.[15]

Recent research has highlighted the record of English royal service that bound John (I) Balliol (d.1268), lord of Barnard castle, Buittle and Galloway, to Henry III and Edward I; this goes a long way to explaining the inherited political behaviour and choices of John (II) Balliol (born in Bailleul, Picardy), the Bruces' main rival for the Scottish throne, both before and after his ascension to that title in 1292.[16] Yet it must be acknowledged that a similar record of service and loyalty can also be described for the Bruces of Annandale, albeit one punctuated by a stronger physical lordship presence in Scotland at key moments.

Just as King Henry attempted in 1251 – with disastrous results – to use John (I) Balliol as an officer in northern England and a representative in Scotland during the factional minority of his son-in-law, Alexander III, so he had also sent Robert V of Annandale north in 1255 and 1257, to displace the domination of the Scottish royal council by the Comyns of Buchan and Badenoch and their allies; Henry also employed Bruce briefly as sheriff of Cumberland.[17] In later years, Robert V may have instilled in his son and grandsons a sense of his frustrations in this period at exclusion from greater influence and reward in Alexander's government after 1260. Yet uncertain Bruce–Comyn relations did not prevent those families serving together in the 1260s in support of Henry III and Prince Edward against baronial rebellion in England. Just as for John (I) Balliol, this display of loyalty in the civil war of 1263–64, with Robert V captured in battle, gained the Bruces lands and office and a further role as the English Crown's spokesman in Scotland in 1269; Robert VI in turn would serve as Alexander III's envoy to England in 1277 and overseas in 1281 but become sheriff of Cumberland and constable of Carlisle in May 1283.[18] This record of service also confirmed good relations with the heir to the English throne and his brother, Edmund, culminating in Robert V's participation in the crusade venture of 1271–74. These strong bonds of English lordship were surely echoed in Robert VI's choice of name for his second (?) son, 'Edward' (born c.1276–78?), just as John (II) Balliol would name his only son (born 1283) by a de Valence wife after the then English king (who also became his godfather).[19]

The Bruces' efforts in English circles may also reflect their apparent facility in Anglo-Norman French, whereas most other mainland noble families of Scotland tended to favour vernacular Scots. In 1270, Robert V received royal letters confirming his family's rights in the churches of Annandale which the Bruces had granted to their foundation of Guisborough Priory in North Yorkshire: these survive as the only Scottish royal letters of that period dealing with domestic matters in French rather than Latin.[20] Then in 1278, according to both English and Scottish sources that were subject to editing in the 1290s, it was Robert VI of Carrick who was selected to perform Alexander III's homage by proxy at Westminster to Edward I for lands held in England. This oath was spoken in French, which persisted as the language of diplomacy, chivalry and court in the Edwardian realm.[21] If Robert VI did fulfil this latter role he presumably also had to translate and reply when, according to the notarised English account, Edward I's ministers reserved the English king's right to raise the issue of homage for the Scottish kingdom itself in the future; or, according to the Scottish record, Alexander III retorted that 'God alone!' had a right to submission for his realm.[22]

As a child Robert VII was thus schooled to speak, read and possibly write in French. As the heir to a considerable estate and a pious layman he would also have been given working knowledge of Latin, the language of charter lordship, liturgy and prayer. This would have afforded Robert and his brothers access to basic education in the law, politics, scripture, saints' Lives (*vitae*), philosophy, history and chivalric instruction and romance.[23] That Robert took personal pleasure in such learning and leisure is suggested in a number of ways. Barbour, of course, reported that the new king read aloud to his band of supporters on the run in 1306, reciting from memory tales from a twelfth-century romance of Charlemagne, *Fierabras*, as well as relating examples from history such as Hannibal's defiance of Rome.[24] As king, Robert certainly commissioned verse to commemorate Bannockburn and his subjects' military deeds.[25] Contemporary chroniclers Jean le Bel and Thomas Gray would both assert that they had read a history of his reign 'commissioned by King Robert himself'.[26] In his last years, Robert would pay for Dominican friars to tutor his son, David, for whom he would also purchase books.[27] A parliamentary briefing document of c.1364 would also assert that Robert 'used continually to read, or have read in his presence, the histories of ancient kings and princes, and how they conducted themselves in their times, both in wartime and in peacetime; from these he derived information about aspects of his own rule'.[28] Finally, verse epitaphs composed for King Robert celebrated his acumen in law and the cultured arts.[29]

Tutors for Robert VII and his brothers were most likely drawn from unbeneficed clergy or mendicant friars associated with the churches patronised by their family. These connections may also speak to the important spiritual influences of cult and relic in Robert's formative years, which he would return to throughout his reign. As Marcher lords, the Bruces of Annandale had long-established links not only to the Augustinians of Guisborough (Yorkshire) but also to the Cistercian houses, mother and daughter, at Melrose (Roxburghshire, itself a daughter of Rievaulx, Yorkshire) and Holm Cultram (Cumbria). Within Carrick and Annandale, dedications to St Cuthbert (Straiton, Ewesdale) and St Ninian (Lochmaben) also suggest an inherited family veneration for these two popular cross-border cults, reaching out to the pilgrimage shrines that held their bodies at the cathedral priories of Benedictine Durham and Premonstratensian Whithorn.[30] Worship of St Ninian in particular may reflect the influence of Robert VII's mother, Marjorie of Carrick. The Huntingdon inheritance brought the Bruces into contact with the Tironensian abbey of Lindores in Fife (Earl David's burial place and also associated with the ancient earls of Fife) as well as churches in the Midlands English honour.[31] Further afield, the Bruces maintained penitential devotion to the cult of St Malachy, a twelfth-century bishop of Armagh whose cult was first offended by Robert II of Annandale in the 1140s: Robert V felt duty bound to establish perpetual lights at Malachy's tomb at Clairvaux Abbey in France on his return from crusade in 1273.[32]

However, arguably it is early evidence for Bruce attachment to the cult of St Thomas Becket that is most striking. Robert V's parents seem to have associated his birth c.1220 with pilgrimage to Canterbury and a gift of annuity in return for indulgences in Becket's jubilee and (second) Translation year of 1220, a journey that confirmed Bruce links with Becket's own kin as well as the importance of Becket's Translation feast, 7 July, as a significant day of worship.[33] The inheritance of valuable lands in Essex after 1237 (really 1252) gave the Bruces access to Canterbury Cathedral Priory and Becket's shrine, with Robert VI notably naming his fourth (?) son Thomas and his second (Kentish) wife displaying devotion towards the saint's shrine.[34] In the context of Anglo-Scottish relations before 1296, honour to Becket may have afforded the Bruces, as it did many other noble houses, an opportunity for further association with the royal families and foundation churches of both England and Scotland, with Henry III and Edward I in particular continuing Plantagenet veneration of the martyr, and their in-laws, Alexander II and Alexander III, both visiting Canterbury on visits south with their English royal wives. The Bruces responded, too, by supporting the Scottish Crown's patronage of the Tironensian abbey of Arbroath in Angus, dedicated to Becket, its blood-red sandstone church founded by William I of Scotland as an act of penance for invading England in 1174. This had been a war in which William had been captured and forced to recognise (until 1189) English feudal superiority over the Scottish kingdom and Church, as well as one in which the Bruces of Annandale had, as during Anglo-Scottish conflict in 1138 during the reign of David I (r.1124–53), protected their cross-border lands by remaining loyal to the English monarch.[35] Bruce favour had begun with a gift to Arbroath Abbey of Haltwhistle church in Northumberland, originally part of a marriage dower to Robert (III) of Annandale (died before 1191) when he took William I's illegitimate daughter to wife: notably, Haltwhistle would be among the properties which King Robert I sought to restore to Scottish control through peace with Edward III in 1328.[36]

However, as growing noble youths it was surely outdoor pursuits and great events that held a stronger fascination for Robert VII and his brothers than did churchly matters. They would have had masters drawn from their parents' household to school them in the arts of horsemanship, swordsmanship, the joust, hunting and perhaps aspects of courtly behaviour, including dress, protocol, speech, table etiquette, music and dance, some of which may have been learned before the age of ten while serving as pages in their father's (or grandfather's) household.[37] As many of these personal and leadership skills were bound up within a code of chivalry, Robert's chief tutor was surely a reputable, experienced knight, drawn from his grandfather's crusade retinue.[38] Robert's later performance in war certainly underlines his skills in tactics and single combat. His expert exploitation of the terrain of the royal park at Stirling prior to Bannockburn hints at his familiarity with this environment and the necessities of outdoor living, just as Barbour reports his and his supporters' survival by stalking deer in the south-west c.1307–8.[39] The exchequer rolls from King Robert's final years provide further proof of his knowledge of the hunt. After 1326 his newly built manor house at Cardross in Dumbartonshire included stables, a park and falcon aviary, but also evidence of an understanding of estate and household management.[40] In the same fashion, at age twenty-eight, Robert's attendance at the post-mortem inquest in May 1304 on his father's lands at Writtle and Hatfield illustrate his awareness of the practical necessities of estate labour, husbandry, crops, waterways and mills.[41]

However, a significant and profound part of the childhood experience of Robert, Edward and possibly the other Bruce brothers (Neil, Thomas and Alexander) was also gained through being fostered to allied Gaelic kindreds, a traditional practice in Carrick, south-west and western Scotland, the Isles and Ireland.[42] There were a number of Carrick and Ayrshire families, many of them from incomer families of the twelfth century, who might perform such a service, including the Carruthers, Carricks, Carlisles, Flemings, de Boscos, Corrys, Torthorwalds and Boyds, who would also feature c.1324–32 in the (admittedly royal) Carrick household of Robert's son, Prince David.[43] Barbour writes of Robert in 1307–8 on the run through Carrick in the company of an unnamed foster-brother.[44] It is possible this figure had accompanied the then king's return to his earldom from exile and that Robert had been fostered as a youth to an Irish or Western Isles kindred affiliated with the Bruces. A contemporary chronicle fragment of northern English provenance explained Edward Bruce's later campaign (1315–18) for the High Kingship of Ireland as being at the invitation of a Gaelic Irish lord who had educated him in his youth.[45] Recent studies have concurred in emphasising the possibility that Marjorie of Carrick's father, Earl Neil, had wed a daughter of the Ó Néill kings of Tyrone in Ireland.[46] Fosterage to such a family as the Ó Néills in the 1280s lends weight to Robert and Edward Bruces' links with the 'Gaels' of Ireland in 1306–7 and 1315–18, and would have imbued the brothers with knowledge of Gaelic language, poetry, song and – more importantly – politics and military tactics throughout the Irish Sea world. It might be cited to explain the choice of Neil as the name of another Bruce brother and Robert VII's apparent affinity for 'hobelar' warfare, using smaller sturdy ponies in mounted raids, as well as for sea-power, ranging from oared war-galleys ('birlings') to boats.[47]

The Bruces' aristocratic upbringing therefore was certainly not merely Anglo-Norman in nature and reflected their hybrid family history.[48] Nevertheless, it must at least be acknowledged that much of this empathy for the Gael might also have been learned from fosterage to an associate Western Isles or Argyllshire family like the MacDonalds or MacRuaridhs, both involved in mercenary 'galloglass' fighting in Ireland for successive genera-tions, or even the Campbells of Lochawe.[49] Indeed, Robert VII first appears in the historical record as a witness to an undated (c.1284–85?) gift by Alexander MacDonald of Islay to the Cistercian abbey of Paisley (founded by the Stewarts), alongside his father, Robert VI, the bishop of Argyll, and minor figures from Carrick, Kintyre and Arran.[50] Similarly, Bruce knowledge of the west might have been gained from fostering with originally 'Anglo-Norman' noble houses in Ireland, notably the de Burgh earl of Ulster or Robert V's in-laws the de Clares of Thomond. Indeed, the Competitor may have felt that such association afforded the opportunity to recover the former Carrick 'lands of Galloway' in what is now County Antrim: by supporting the Anglo-Normans in Ireland against the galloglass predations of the MacDonalds and their Mac Domnaill kin and Ó Néill, Ó Conor and Ó Donnell allies.[51]

By the same token, as they reached the male age of consent of twelve and began training for full knighthood, placement of Robert VII and his brothers in allied noble households was surely undertaken with a view to potential marriages and political connections. Thus it is likely that at least brothers Robert and Edward were sent for polish to reside with one or more English noble families such as the de Clares of Gloucester or in the English royal household. Writing in the 1350s, Sir Thomas Gray (d.1363), whose father fought throughout the Anglo-Scottish wars after 1296, asserted in his *Scalacronica* that in about 1292 Robert (VII) Bruce, aged eighteen, was a 'young bachelor of King Edward's Chamber'.[52] In such a position Robert would have followed (and perhaps even replaced) both his (sonless) uncle Richard Bruce (died late 1286), a waged and robed banneret with a retinue of squires and yeoman in Edward I's household c.1285–86, and his own father, Robert (VI) of Carrick, who served Edward in his successful military campaigns of conquest in Wales in 1277 and 1282–83.[53]

Robert VII was perhaps too young to participate in these events (although he was sixteen in 1290) and there remains little firm evidence of his presence at Edward's court.[54] But on 8 April 1296 both Robert and his father would be pursued through the English Chancery for their private household debts of £60 by several merchants of Winchester.[55] This raises the possibility that young Robert was on occasion resident in a royal centre which Edward I himself would visit some ten times during his reign.[56] The English king undertook substantial building works and held important tournaments there in September–October 1285 and April 1290, both marked by mass knighting ceremonies for royal kin and retainers (including Richard Bruce in 1285), gathered around a specially constructed Arthurian Round Table.[57] Robert VII may thus have continued a family tradition. English rolls evidence from 1304 also places Edward Bruce, then in his early twenties, in the retinue of Edward of Caernarfon, the future Edward II.[58] It had perhaps been the hope of Robert V or VI all along that such high service would advance their issues' careers from an early age. However, in 1286 the Bruce brothers' young lives suffered major disruption as calamitous events began to unfold in Scotland.

## Youth in the Interregnum of Guardians

Robert VII's first substantial participation in a major public event in Scotland may have seen him gather at Dunfermline Abbey in Fife with his grandfather, father and the rest of the Scottish lay and clerical magnates for the funeral of Alexander III, killed ten days earlier on 19 March 1286 in a night-time fall from his horse at Kinghorn. The solemnity of the occasion, the array of royal tombs within the recently extended choir and the magnificence of St Margaret's feretory shrine may have had a deep effect upon the young Bruce. This was perhaps far more profound than any impression he may have formed of the bubbling tensions at this gathering between his family elders on the one hand and John Balliol and his Comyn allies on the other, all watched warily by clerical leaders like Bishops William Fraser of St Andrews and Robert Wishart of Glasgow.[59]

It is impossible to gauge precisely when Robert V gave serious thought to a Bruce claim to the throne given the successive deaths of Alexander's children before the king himself: Prince David by c.late 1280–June 1281 (aged eight), Princess Margaret in April 1283 (aged twenty-two), and Prince Alexander in January 1284 (aged nineteen).[60] It is clear, however, that Robert of Annandale dared not act during the lifetime of an adult king who would soon remarry and could otherwise manage the succession to suit his immediate concerns, anticipating further sons and with no intention of designating heirs to the third or fourth degree.[61] Hence in February 1284 the Bruces had joined the rest of the community of the realm in a parliament at Scone in pledging their collective oath to recognise Alexander III's granddaughter, Margaret (the Maid of Norway), daughter of Eric II of Norway, as his heir until a new royal son might be born.[62]

Alexander's accidental death overturned this situation dramatically and threatened the same for the wider balance of political power within the Scottish realm. It was Robert V, the Competitor, who made the first move. According to later annals, in parliament at Scone from 2 April 1286 Bruce apparently objected to the actual inauguration of a female, though not of course to his own succession through a related female line as the nearest living male heir of the royal line by generational degree.[63] This outburst and the violence that followed have often been cited as proof of Robert of Annandale's awareness of the weakness of his claim. Nevertheless, recent scholarship has come closer than ever to arguing that in fact Robert V may have had a right to be heard and a legitimate claim in law to be king.

Before 1281 there had not been, in living memory or indeed past centuries, a severe succession crisis in the Scottish realm sufficient to provoke a definitive legal (or regal) ruling and thus to establish normative royal custom beyond obvious male primogeniture – father to son (1093, 1214, 1249) or to son's son (1153) or to brother (1165) or brother/nephew (as was William I's plan until the birth of Alexander [II] in 1198). It might thus indeed be argued that there was more than enough doubt about the legal choice of heir when at the unexpected, early death of Alexander III in 1286 there remained a choice between only a minor female heir of that king's direct body and blood (a granddaughter) or several male adult heirs across more than one generation, but descended from an earlier king and his cognate relatives (through the three daughters of Earl David of Huntingdon, brother of William I, grandson of David I).

Nevertheless, Bruce of Annandale may have been encouraged by the attempts of Alexander III's government to deal with some succession issues in 1281, after the death of the child Prince David, a fact that should serve to underline the very ad hoc nature of such inheritance politics, reacting to an immediate situation. The Scots' marriage indenture with Norway of August 1281 guaranteed a place in the succession for Princess Margaret and her issue, both male and female.[64] Then on 4 December 1281, as part of the marriage agreements for Prince Alexander's match to Marguerite, daughter of Guy, Count of Flanders, it was agreed that if the prince predeceased his father then any of his sons by Marguerite became heir to the throne – ahead of their paternal uncle(s) or aunt(s) who would be nearer by degree – at once affirming the primacy of inheritance of the Crown by male primogeniture through a senior line and providing the closest 'representation' of the previous king. At the same time, as in the treaty with Norway, the Flanders agreement stipulated that a king's living second son and his male heirs should succeed before the daughter(s) of the predeceased first son (and her issue), again favouring male nearness by degree. All of this was enshrined in the contract with Flanders as 'the custom and practice used in the kingdom [of Scotland] since time immemorial' and through an oath pledged by an embassy of sixteen magnates, including Robert Bruce of Carrick, and which the Pope was to notarise.[65]

This much was relatively straightforward, but the 1281 contract also acknowledged that failing any male issue amongst or by all of Alexander III's children, already born or to be born if he made a second marriage (which he did in November 1285), then the succession would revert to any daughters of Prince Alexander or his siblings or by that second marriage for Alexander III. This general recognition of female blood succession did seem to confirm the inheritance as queen of Margaret, the Maid of Norway, a truth accepted by the Scottish parliamentary oath of February 1284. However, where there was considerable ambivalence and uncertainty in the 1281 succession clauses was in how these predicted patterns would have been affected by the (unmentioned and no matter how brief) succession of Prince Alexander or his younger half-brother Prince David as king, displacing the 'representation' of the last king; similarly, although the 1281 terms did indeed seem to suggest that nearness by degree should distinguish between female heirs of different generations, it was not clear that this applied between living males.[66]

These were undeniably complex legal arguments which the Scots, and Edward I, would only really scrutinise in 1291–92, and then not comprehensively, by which time, besides, two more significant heirs' deaths would have occurred: Countess Dervorguilla of Galloway (mother of John Balliol) on 28 January 1290, and the Maid of Norway around September 1290.[67] In April 1286, however, it is most relevant that Robert V, by perhaps trying to apply the 1281 agreement to cancel out Alexander III's quick, troubleshooting parliamentary recognition of the Maid in April 1284, was surely attempting to transfer these (inconsistent) principles from application to Alexander III's direct family line across to the parallel issue of Earl David of Huntingdon and to compare the two. In that regard he had no real claim while the Maid, of Alexander III's blood, lived, and as such the ambitious and highly disruptive nature of what Bruce was attempting should be remarked.

Indeed, in 1286 Robert V may have been trying, quite desperately, to forestall any progress at all in the Maid of Norway's formal accession and thus any chance of a marriage she might make producing children (male or female) to whom the 1281 and 1284 succession criteria might be applied. If he could do so, Robert might force the community to consider instead the Huntingdon alternatives, although crucially at a moment when the ages, degrees and sex of living heirs favoured Bruce of Annandale (just as the 1284 act had favoured the Maid and Alexander III's plans to remarry but looked no further ahead in time). That Robert V may have had some initial success in doing so, perhaps even aided by his main rival's anxiety to at least register the Balliol interest before an unfamiliar Scottish community, is suggested by the fact that when the Scottish parliament regrouped at the end of April 1286 John Balliol also lodged a counter-claim as the nearest living male heir in the senior line. However, the 'keenly contested' debate (*acriter placitatum*) that ensued, and then the withdrawal of the Bruces of Annandale and Carrick to the south-west and to arms, at once confirmed the exclusion of both the sextuagenarian Competitor and the middle-aged Balliol from that parliament's selection of six 'custodes', or Guardians of the Realm.[68]

Far from being a careful balance of just two rapidly emerging factional loyalties – with the Comyn earl of Buchan, Comyn lord of Badenoch and Bishop Fraser tied to Balliol, whereas James the Steward, Bishop Wishart and, to a lesser extent, the young and controversial Duncan, earl of Fife, were linked to Bruce – the Guardians represented continuity of royal government and a geographical spread of the key lay and spiritual magnates of the day: two from each 'estate' of earls, barons and prelates, all prominent in judicial office and the royal household before 1286. All but Steward had sworn an oath to the 1281 Flanders succession clauses; all had given their oath to the Maid of Norway in 1284.[69] By contrast, neither Robert V nor John Balliol had been active regularly in Scottish affairs or office. Moreover, the fresh parliamentary oath pledged at the close of the tense April 1286 assembly to whosoever by 'nearness of blood to King Alexander' would inherit the throne, also recognised the probable pregnancy of that late monarch's second wife, the French noblewoman Yolande of Dreux, due to give birth probably in October–November that year at the latest, failing whom the Maid of Norway remained heir presumptive.[70] In other words, at this stage no one was really interested in a Bruce or Balliol claim beyond suppressing any conflict it might provoke.

Still, this is not to downplay too far the very real possibility of unrest that threatened the Scottish community. The election of not one but six Guardians may itself have been a compromise or expediency to smooth over disagreements and reflect a variety of political (if not succession) opinion and geography, so as to help quell anticipated confrontation. This worked only in part. The summer of 1286 was marked by Bruce assaults on Balliol and royal castles in the south-west (including Buittle) and a 'Crown' response to stop them led by the Comyns, Steward and Wishart as Guardians. These were exchanges sufficiently violent as to leave that region 'waste' and unable to contribute income through the sheriffships of Dumfries and Wigtown two years later.[71]

It is fair to assume that Robert VII and his brothers were as yet too young to participate in this conflict (or to fully comprehend any legal argu-ments), and it may be to this period that we should date their fosterage to Ireland or the Western Isles. Yet some measure of his elders' impatience and insecurity with regard to their royal claim may have reached the young Robert, not least an understanding of how unpredictable sequences of deaths might alter fortunes. For the aged Competitor must have been sorely aware that his claim of nearness by degree was limited by his lifetime and would be rendered useless if he himself were to die before a judgment in his favour could be secured (from whatever quarter). In that event, not even the prospect of the brief accession as queen of the pensioner Dervorguilla of Galloway (born c.1209/17) – daughter of the eldest daughter of Earl David of Huntingdon (by Alan lord of Galloway) and who had outlived all but her fourth son, John Balliol (II) – could save the Bruce kingship claim: this would be inherited by the somewhat lacklustre

Robert VI. It is by no means clear that the community would have accepted the argument that the throne should still pass through Robert V to his son (born c.1243) because he would have been the eldest male of his claimant generation, the grandchildren of Earl David (in the manner of David I's transmission of the kingship in 1153 to his grandson Malcolm [IV], following the death of Malcolm's father, Earl Henry of Northumbria, in 1152).[72]

However, just as dynastic rivalries threatened to boil over, so the shifts of 1286 also betray the concerns of nobles to protect and advance their own regional concerns of territory and office. Over the autumn and winter of 1286–87 the Guardians were able to contain the Bruce threat in the south-west, with no need of assistance, say, from Edward I to whom the parliament of April 1286 had sent early notice and then an embassy led by Bishop Fraser, William Comyn bishop of Brechin, and Sir Geoffrey Mowbray (whose family's valuable lands included lordships in Fife and Yorkshire).[73] Yet there is no indication of forfeiture or prolonged exile suffered by the Bruces. This was perhaps because although their claims were marginal (with two possible blood heirs of Alexander III living) and their military efforts wholly unconvincing, Roberts V and VI had nonetheless gathered sufficient support within the Scottish political community and beyond, from families anxious to protect or advance their own interests; this proved enough to serve as protection for the Bruces' disaffection. The Bruces themselves had perhaps insisted upon an appeal to Edward or approached him independently. The English king's household expenditures do include prests (loans from the monarch) for private payments in 1286 to 'domini Roberti de Brus' (Annandale?) and his messenger, John, who had come to Edward in France in December 1286; and in 1287 to 'Robert de Bruce, earl of Carrick' (£100) and his messenger John of Bickerton (£50).[74] The famous Turnberry Band of 20 September 1286 must also be reassessed in this context.

As they gathered at the Bruces' chief coastal residence (or caput) in Carrick, the indenture recorded a common pledge by Bruce of Annandale, Bruce of Carrick and his brother Richard; the Competitor's contemporary, Patrick Dunbar, sixth earl of Dunbar, and his three sons; Angus Mór MacDonald of Islay and his eldest(?) son, Alexander; Walter 'Bulloch' (from the Gaelic for 'freckled'), a Stewart, earl of Menteith, and his two sons, Alexander and John; and, perhaps most significant of all, Walter's nephew, Guardian James Steward with his brother, John Stewart of Jedburgh forest (whose offspring included the Stewarts of Bonkle). All present agreed to support Richard the second de Burgh earl of Ulster and Thomas de Clare of Thomond 'in all their affairs, and we shall stand faithfully by them and their associates against all their enemies'.[75] The primary aim here was surely to bind the named lords of Scottish mainland territories to help curtail the galloglass activities of the MacDonalds and their native Irish allies, against whom de Burgh was at that time planning a major campaign in northern Ireland: initiative may indeed have come from Earl Richard along with early proposals of marriages with the Bruces and Stewarts. Carrick, the Clydeside lands and islands (including Bute) of James Steward and Walter of Menteith's lands of Knapdale and the Isle of Arran might easily become embroiled if warfare flared across the Irish Sea.[76] Earl Patrick was a past crusader (with lands in Ayrshire) who had also represented English interests alongside Bruce of Annandale and the Durwards during the factional minority of Alexander III. He had then been heavily engaged in military campaigns to bring the Western Isles into the control of the Scottish Crown, fighting at Largs in 1263 and joining the earl of Atholl and countess Marjorie of Carrick's father in subsequent expeditions to the west.[77]

In addition, however, all the Scottish lords at Turnberry had reasons to worry for their interests under a sustained Guardianship for a minor Queen Margaret from Norway or a posthumous son of Alexander III and Queen Yolande. It was not generally known until about 25 November 1292 that Yolande's pregnancy had failed (or was false), and the spectre of a government still dominated for either child monarch by the Comyns and their allies may already have brought these men together.[78] Walter Bulloch most obviously feared the loss of his title and portion of the full Menteith earldom that Alexander III had awarded to him in 1260 by depriving the Comyns: the latter had already appealed to Edward I in 1282 to extract a substantial pocket of land from this inheritance.[79] The MacDonalds, of course, had an historic antipathy towards the Comyns' in-laws, the Macdougalls of Lorn, and – like James Steward – worried about the repercussions of plans to complete the establishment of west coast sheriffships in Kintyre, Lorn and Skye.[80] The Bruces' lands bordered directly upon Balliol's lordship of Galloway and fell within Comyn office jurisdictions in the south-west.

The Turnberry Band also saw those present reserve 'our faith to the lord king of England and to whoever, by reason of the blood of the lord Alexander, late king of Scotland, of blessed memory, shall be given and put in possession of the kingdom of Scotland according to the ancient customs used and favoured until now'. In Robert V's mind this wording did not perhaps preclude obstructing the Maid of Norway's succession. Thus as well as seeking to expand his holdings for two sons, five grandsons and five granddaughters, Robert may also have hoped to secure promises of support in the event of legal proceedings or a war to determine the royal succession (especially if Yolande had a daughter). He may have hoped that the support of the influential earl of Ulster in particular would aid him in persuading their mutual superior, Edward I, that a Bruce kingship established by law or force was no threat to Plantagenet power.[81]

The Turnberry indenture may not have been the only deal concluded by the elder Bruces at this stage, or the most effective (undermined as it was by the death of Earl Patrick in 1289).[82] Similar imperatives may also have seen Robert V reach understandings between 1287 and 1289 with John Strathbogie, earl of Atholl (d.1306), and Donald, earl of Mar (d.1297), to which might also be added attempts at concord with Duncan, earl of Fife.[83] It was the notorious murder of Duncan on about 10 September 1289 by Sir Hugh Abernethy that surely confirmed the fears of Atholl and Mar that their earldoms and offices north of Forth were at grave risk of encroachment by the Comyns of Buchan and Badenoch and their allies, the Abernethys and Bishop Fraser of St Andrews, who now stepped in to control the Fife earldom and family lordships in Perthshire and Strathtay (and allowed Walter of Menteith to take control of Dumbarton Castle, weakening his band to Bruce).[84] Mar could find common cause with the Bruces who held lands in the adjacent lordship of Garioch: about this time, Donald's eldest son and heir, Gartnait, married one of Robert VI's several daughters producing a son, Donald; just as the senior Donald of Mar's daughter, Marjory, had married John, earl of Atholl, producing a son, David, and daughter, Isabel.[85] As with the Turnberry Band, the subtext of any indentures reached with Mar and Atholl might also have included suggestions of further marriages for Robert VII or his siblings.[86]

Therefore, although the Bruces were effectively contained in the southwest in 1286–87 (and denied their natural territorial role as sheriffs of Ayrshire and Lanarkshire), their opportunism and networking, as well as that of the Comyns and other Scottish magnates, undoubtedly destabilised parts of the Scottish kingdom in 1286–89 and must go some way to explain why both Duncan of Fife and Alexander Comyn, earl of Buchan (who died of natural causes in May 1289), may not have been replaced as Guardians.[87] This intermittent violence was reflected in the terms of the 'treaty' of Salisbury of 6 November 1289, talks about talks that concluded with Edward I of England and Eric II of Norway agreeing that the Scottish kingdom 'shall have been fully settled in quietness and peace, so that the Lady herself [the Maid of Norway] may come there safely'.[88] The initial approaches from the Scots to King Edward while he was in France in 1286–87 had been largely ignored. However, by 1288 the monarch was aware of the opportunity that the crisis in Scotland presented and he responded favourably to fresh appeals by the Guardians. Throughout this period Bruce of Annandale, and others, must also have continued to solicit Edward's involvement by private correspondence. Indeed, pressure from Edward may explain why Robert V would be included in – or rather could not be excluded from – the Scottish embassy of October 1289 to treat with Edward and the Norwegians at Salisbury.[89] However, in truth, all interested parties may have had an even stronger motive at this sensitive juncture for keeping the English king at arm's length. For once it had been confirmed that Queen Yolande had produced no living bodily heir of Alexander III, the Bruces and others may quickly have seen that a family marriage to Margaret, the Maid of Norway, would achieve their ultimate goal.

This was also reflected in the terms of Salisbury, which stipulated that the 'Queen and heir of the kingdom of Scotland shall come ... free and quit of all contract of marriage and espousal'. This has traditionally been interpreted as a Scottish precaution against Edward I's independent conclusion of a match for his heir, Edward of Caernarfon (born in April 1284), with Eric II of Norway's daughter (born in April 1283), a logical solution first hinted at by Alexander III in a letter written in the very month of the English prince's birth.[90] Yet the houses of Bruce, Balliol, Comyn, Fife, Atholl, Mar and perhaps others all had sons of suitable age who might marry Margaret of Norway, securing the kingship *jure uxoris* and settling their family's territorial worries, not least Robert VII (then fifteen) and Edward Balliol (like the Maid, born in 1283). It is not difficult to believe that as talks with Edward I and England proved increasingly worrying for the prospects of the Scottish polity and Church, even the Scottish prelates began to favour such an 'internal' marital solution. That the Bruces went to Salisbury to pursue this possibility is suggested by their consolation prize by 1292 of a marriage for Robert VI's second daughter, Isabel, to the widower Eric II.[91]

Edward I and Eric, of course, cut across all the strained Scottish alternatives by securing a papal dispensation (granted in November 1289) for Edward of Caernarfon and the Maid to marry, forcing the Scots to accept this fait accompli and path to peace by March 1290; King Edward also took custody of the Isle of Man by June.[92] With their hopes dashed it is likely that Annandale and Carrick did not participate in further Anglo-Scottish talks which resulted in the 'treaty' of Birgham-Northampton (July 1290).[93] However, given the Bruces considerable experience of intrusive and expensive English royal government and justice throughout the thirteenth century, they surely sympathised with the dogged efforts of the

Scottish envoys to persuade Edward I to recognise a veritable 'charter of liberties' for the Scottish realm.[94] The Birgham agreement, indeed, enshrined Edward's paper guarantees of Scottish territorial, governmental, ecclesiastical, legal and financial integrity under an anticipated regnal union. Here, the Scots, led by significant cross-border magnates as well as prelates educated at Oxford University in the 1250s and 1260s (including Fraser, Wishart, Comyn of Brechin and Nicholas Balmyle, archdeacon of Lothian), drew on the ideological and practical legacy of Magna Carta (1215) and the Oxford and Westminster provisions for monarchical supervision born of Simon de Montfort's Barons' Wars (1258–67) against Henry III (and his then heir, Prince Edward).[95] Faced with the prospect of innovations in universal taxation, one-off 'tallages' to meet royal 'necessity', war prize and military service, different modes of land conveyance and common-law legal appeals facilitated by the profusion of English royal writs and courts, not to mention the potentially massive costs and delays of increased travel to Westminster, the Scots worked to ensure that their realm's less-developed (and cheaper) governmental institutions would remain intact, leaving considerable customary power in the hands of regional magnates and their franchise courts; royal records and relics were also to be preserved in Scotland. The terms of this marriage agreement thus also reflected a positive identity of historic political and cultural difference for the Scottish realm.[96]

It may have been at this point, in 1290, that the Bruces signalled their return to magnate normality through Robert VII's entry, in his sixteenth year, into Edward I's service as a squire or 'bachelor' knight. He may even have attended a Round Table tournament at Winchester in April of that year held to celebrate the impending royal nuptials or the translation of Henry III's remains to his newly completed tomb in Westminster Abbey in May.[97] If so, Robert's life was soon disrupted once again.

The death of the Maid of Norway en route to Scotland by October 1290 suddenly brought the factionalism of the last four years into sharp relief. Bishop Fraser's famous letter of that month to Edward I reported that when news of the Maid's demise broke, Bruce of Annandale had arrived unexpectedly at Perth

with a large retinue to confer with some who were there. We do not yet know what he intends to do or how he intends to act. But the earls of Mar and Atholl are already collecting their army and some other nobles of the land have been persuaded to join their party. Because of that there is fear of a general and large-scale slaughter unless the Most

High, through your active involvement and good offices, administer a quick cure.[98]

Bruce and his allies may still have been cooperating in active opposition to the Comyn–Balliol party's territorial opportunism since 1286 and now mustered to challenge that group's apparent domination of preparations for the Maid's arrival and post-inauguration government: Fraser was waiting at Perth for the Maid in the company of Edward's representative, Anthony Bek, bishop of Durham, and John Balliol's father-in-law, John de Warenne, earl of Surrey.[99] However, Robert of Annandale quickly reinvested his noble network in a renewed bid for the throne.

Robert V's infamous appeal to Edward of late 1290–early 1291, in the name of a notional seven ancient earls of Scotland, again reflected his canvassing of key magnates, with Atholl, Mar, Sutherland and the infant son of the murdered Fife ranged in his support.[100] This bold missive sought Edward's special protection and protested the actions of Bishop Fraser and John Comyn of Badenoch – 'who are acting and holding [them]selves as guardians of the realm' – in variously colluding with Edward to make John Balliol king, appointing their own 'sub-guardians', devastating royal lands in Moray (according to a complaint of that region's 'men' presented by Donald of Mar) and generally inflicting 'injuries, losses and arsons'. Although clunky in its fabrication of party, this appeal may have had input from two of the remaining Guardians omitted from mention by its text, Bishop Wishart of Glasgow and James Steward. In its claim to represent a significant part of a divided community, the appeal may have only slightly exaggerated both support for Bruce and others' neutrality in the face of the Comyn–Balliol party. It was also a first, awkward absorption of the language of defence of Scottish custom and institutions far more eloquently invoked by the terms demanded by the Scots at Birgham, although nowhere does it absolutely refute the English king's right to assert his overlordship over Scotland as part of his judgement in the matter. This may reflect Edward's summons of the Scots by 21 March 1291 to a joint Anglo-Scottish parliament at Norham in the following May.[101] It is telling that by mid-1301, Scottish envoys in Rome, pleading for support for King John Balliol (r.1292–96), would blame Bruce of Annandale for inviting Edward I to intervene in the succession crisis, describing how, after the Maid's death, Edward 'cunningly attracted the support of one group of the magnates ... belonging to a party which had no right in the kingdom of Scotland at that time', imposing his will through 'force and fear' over the pro-Balliol majority.[102] However, the counter-assertion of the earls' appeal about

Bruce's status as 'true heir designate' to the throne, 'urgently pursuing our right', matched the public collusion in 1290 of John Balliol (whose mother, Countess Dervorguilla, had died in January, thus clearing the way for his own claim to kingship) with Anthony Bek in November of that year: styling himself 'heir of the kingdom of Scotland', John granted the bishop of Durham the holdings of the Scottish Crown in Northumberland.[103]

In this context, it is surely correct to reinterpret Bishop Fraser's advice to Edward I as a warning about, not an endorsement of, Balliol: 'if Sir John Balliol comes to your presence we advise you to take care to deal with him in such a way that your honour and profit are preserved, whatever happens'.[104] Bruce's appeal in the name of the earls also warned against Edward elevating Balliol to the kingship without a full judgment but seems far more open to the notion of English overlordship as a precondition of judgment on the Scottish succession.[105] Yet the uncertainties of the complex legal questions before them may have made both camps hopeful and insecure in equal measure. Not even Edward I's private determination in April 1290 about the English royal succession – favouring male heirs general of his blood, but admitting females should no males survive him (and thus in essence echoing the Scottish agreement with Flanders of 1281) – can have made matters any clearer for the northern realm.[106]

### Daunting at Norham, Pleadings at Berwick, 1291–92

At this juncture the young Robert VII's entry into Edward I's household may have been a strategic choice. Alternatively, the English king may have insisted upon it himself (perhaps also requiring Edward Balliol to join him).[107] If the young Robert did enter the English royal household for the next two or three years he would have encountered a king at the height of his political powers but also still grieving openly for the death of his queen, Eleanor of Castile (d. November 1290).[108] Edward was then in his fifty-first year, a renowned crusader and statesman, the conqueror and keeper of Wales.[109] By 1291 his government had drawn a line under the *Quo Warranto* hearings in England, withdrawing from a general assertion of royal legal rights to use high-profile cases to demonstrate the king's prerogative. In a parliament at Westminster in January 1292, Edward would intervene to halt a feud between the Welsh Marcher lords the earls of Hereford and Gloucester (Robert VII's cousin and the English king's new son-in-law), forfeiting lands and imposing gaol time and fines only then to display his magnanimity by remitting both earls in return for recognition of royal authority.[110] This was a strong example for the young Robert to absorb, but far more impressive would have been the continuing martial nature of Edward's large household (about 50 household knights and as many as 500 to 600 individuals all told) and the splendour of royal residences and hospitality. Robert may have joined the royal establishment just as a marked turnover of bannerets, knights and their retinues ushered out the veterans of the Welsh Wars in favour of new men. As a squire Robert was entitled to £2 a year, a robe and accommodation, to eat in the king's hall and compensation for the loss of any horses. He would have served alongside Englishmen, Marchers, Gascons, Savoyards and adventurers from a smattering of other realms but – before 1297 – few obvious Scottish lords' sons.[111]

Most important of all, however, such a position may have seen Robert participate in the messengering and retinue of the English king as he prepared for legal hearings to determine the Scottish succession.[112] Robert may have been aware, for example, of Edward's search through the government rolls and monastic libraries of England for record and chronicle evidence of his claim to overlordship of Scotland.[113] It is again tempting to speculate that Robert was expected to report what intelligence he could to his Bruce elders. Added together, this experience may also have given him a personal perspective on the armed force of some 1,300 men and a fleet of ships levied to intimidate the Scots into acquiescence in June 1291.[114]

The real damage to the sovereign Scottish kingship and kingdom was done during the so-called 'Process' of Upsetlington-Norham between 10 May and 12 June 1291.[115] The Scots at the border town of Norham were upset by the opening demand of English Chancellor Roger Brabazon that they recognise King Edward's claim of overlordship of Scotland before proceedings began and they withdrew to the Scottish side of the border (13 May).[116] The bishop of Glasgow presented their bold but somewhat disingenuous written response (2 June): that they had 'no knowledge of your right, nor did they ever see it claimed and used by you or your ancestors'.[117] This was to ignore issues raised in 1251 and 1278, just as the insistence that 'they have no power to reply to your statement, in default of a lord [i.e. a king] to whom the demand ought to be addressed' was effectively a relinquishment of responsibility and form of assent to Edward's next shrewd move: to ask all the claimants to recognise his overlordship.[118] Had the Bruces and other claimants suggested this ploy?

The complicity of the Bruces, and the uncertainty of their claim and Scottish support, was signalled by Robert of Annandale's swift submission to Edward (5 June): A. A. M. Duncan argues that Bruce may also have offered advice in countering the historical record and chronicle proofs brought by Wishart's embassy to refute the overlordship claim in the Norham assembly.[119] Balliol and the Comyns arrived late, but once Guardian John Comyn of Badenoch had subordinated his own minor claim to the kingship to that of his brother-in-law John Balliol, and then Balliol too had recognised Edward's superiority (11 June), there was no further need of proofs or force.[120] According to the chronicler of Lanercost Priory in Cumberland, by 17 June, the feast of the Holy Trinity that year, Edward was acknowledged and installed as Scotland's Lord Superior.[121]

Edward then embarked upon an ayre (tour) to collect fealties from Scottish subjects across south-eastern and central Scotland. Significantly, if Robert (VII) Bruce accompanied the English household on this journey, he now enjoyed an impressive tour of royal Scotland's key political and religious sites: through Haddington, Edinburgh, Linlithgow, Stirling, Dunfermline, St Andrews, Perth and back to Roxburgh. At assemblies in these burghs, castles and churches, Edward made sure to publicise the claimants' submissions. Moreover, it is now known that after 1296 the English king would have some of the key concessions of Norham redated to prove the Scots' quick agreement and appointment of auditors (all by 3 June), while records of the Guardians' resistance and English concessions were removed.[122] Such a devastating display of authority and control, combined with ritual and liturgy, cannot have failed to make an impact on the younger Robert Bruce and the men who would later act as his chief counsel and officers. Elements of Robert's own handling of Scottish parliaments, declarations of community consent or support and potential opposition c.1309–29, as well as several occasions of high ceremony, bear strong hallmarks of Edward I's style at Norham and Berwick in 1291–92 as well as of subsequent ayres and assemblies overseen in Scotland.

If it had not been before, a large part of the Scottish political community was now obliged to declare for one side or the other. Immediately after the Norham Process, Balliol (in conjunction with Comyn of Badenoch) and Bruce had to choose forty 'auditors' each for themselves and other claimants for the Berwick succession hearings held from August 1291, with Edward I providing a further twenty-four. The model for this court was Imperial (in a year in which the Holy Roman electoral princes also manoeuvred to secure that vacant title following the death of Rudolf I of Habsburg on 15 July).[123] It is generally agreed that Bruce's bench held a smaller number of significant lords, particularly in terms of support from Scottish prelates.[124] Wishart of Glasgow and Matthew de Crambeth (bishop of Dunkeld) turned out for Bruce with the abbots of Melrose and Jedburgh, the archdeacon of Lothian and a dozen or so minor associate clerics ('Masters') presumably trained in civil law (including a young Master William Lamberton). The Balliol/Comyn jury was headed by Fraser of St Andrews, Henry Cheyne (bishop of Aberdeen), William Comyn (bishop of Brechin), the bishops of the Isles, Galloway and Ross; and the abbots of Dunfermline, Holyrood, Cambuskenneth, Kelso, Tungland, Scone and Coupar-Angus, and the prior of St Andrews.

The noble auditors were, however, more evenly balanced but along lines that confirmed the factionalism of 1286–90: Balliol's bench included John Comyn, earl of Buchan, Gilbert d'Umfraville, earl of Angus, and his brother (Sir Ingram), Malise, earl of Strathearn, William, earl of Ross, Alexander Macdougall of Argyll, Andrew Murray of Avoch and Bothwell, Geoffrey Mowbray of Barnbougle and Dalmeny, members of the Fraser and Graham families, and a number of men of Fife. Bruce presented Donald, earl of Mar, Walter, earl of Menteith, John, earl of Atholl, Malcolm, earl of Lennox, James Steward and his brother John, and Alexander Stewart of Bonkle, alongside knights supportive of other claimants such as William and John Soules and Patrick, earl of Dunbar (who were excluded as jurors). By contrast, Edward I's smaller bench was made up almost entirely of lawyers.[125]

Yet if both Scottish benches contained lukewarm supporters, it was Bruce the Competitor's that would haemorrhage first. The surviving materials suggest that Bruce and his lawyers made no great play of the succession custom detailed in the 1281 marriage contract with Flanders, although it is possible that Edward I's clerks later excised this evidence from the 'Great Roll'. However, in truth, any Bruce claim 'by degree' had now been muddied by the death of John Balliol's mother Dervorguilla of Galloway in early 1290 and the inheritance of John as a *living* male (with a son) in the senior line. The two conservative 'estates' of Scottish earls and barons may besides have favoured a solution that provided stability of inheritance custom for their own family lands.[126] Thus even before Edward I exploited the spurious claim of Count Floris of Holland (through a sister of William the Lion) and adjourned the hearings for ten months to June 1292, the 'safe' claim of Balliol and his lawyers for impartible inheritance of the kingdom through the senior line had won over a majority.[127]

If Sir Thomas Gray is correct about Robert VII's service at this time, the younger Bruce surely returned with Edward to England for the intervening period. After stays at royal residences at Woodstock (5 September) and Devizes (16 September), October 1291 found the royal household in the Welsh Marches to settle the Gloucester–Hereford feud. December 1291 and January 1292 were spent in Westminster but included a pilgrimage to Canterbury for the feast of St Thomas (29 December). Spring 1292 found Edward back in London planning refurbishments of St Stephen's Chapel and the Painted Chamber of Westminster palace. Robert VII's religious education at the English king's hands may then have continued on the journey back north, with stays at Bury St Edmund's in Suffolk (cult home of the martyred Saxon king, Edmund, d.869), Walsingham in Norfolk (with its shrine of Our Lady) and Durham (with the shrine of St Cuthbert).[128]

Meanwhile, Edward's control of Scottish royal castles and resources was consolidated alongside a continued administration of Guardianship still dominated by the Comyns' affinity and from which the Bruces, if not all of their then and later allies, were excluded.[129] The list of sheriffs and castle-keepers c.1288–90, who returned income to the Chamberlain and presumably continued in post in tandem with English officials in 1291–92, provides evidence of no major locality office for Bruce of Annandale or Carrick, Mar, Atholl or Sutherland, although James Steward had replaced Walter, earl of Menteith, as sheriff of Ayr.[130] Thus the adjournment must have been an agonising wait for the Bruce elders, one in which Robert V's 'pragmatism and ambition' quickly outstripped commitment to any single legal position.[131]

All succession hearings took place behind doors closed to all but the king, claimants, their counsel, jurors and expert witnesses. Therefore Robert VII's knowledge of proceedings must have been second-hand through the English court or his own family. We can only speculate as to his reaction then and later to his grandfather's pursuit of further back-room deals with several claimants in 1292. Clearly, the contingencies of a claim in doubt, the Competitor's indentures with the Count of Holland (13 June), Eric II of Norway (with Carrick and his daughter sailing for Bergen on 28 September), John Hastings (7 November) and Sir Nicholas Biggar (over the Garioch inheritance) channelled a range of conflicting legal arguments – partibility of the kingdom under feudal law and the right to exchange, alienate and redeem royal for noble demesne – which further weakened the case for nearness by degree.[132] Similarly, Robert V's repeated but unsubstantiated claims of 1290–92 that about 1237–38 the then childless Alexander II of Scotland had designated Bruce of Annandale (then eighteen) as heir presumptive to the throne, was clever but incredible without written proof; even if true it provided no evidence about whether or not the birth of Dervorguilla's Balliol sons as males in the senior line displaced this claim.[133]

The hearings at Norham resumed on about 1 June 1292 (originally set to run until 15 July), but a three-month adjournment was instead quickly called while legal opinion was sought from the University of Paris and other academies, an inquiry that Edward I initiated with the assumption that English overlordship of Scotland was a precondition of deliberations. The Roman civil law (or 'Imperial') credentials of the various Paris experts and university 'nations' who replied were questionable and their cases of precedent (e.g. Burgundy in 1274) often alarmingly historically inaccurate. Nonetheless, at least part of the expert opinion returned before the hearings in late summer and autumn 1292, from Dominican authorities, did favour Imperial civil law and thus Bruce nearness 'by degree' *if* an absence of established Scottish custom of succession could be shown. These legal opinions survived in Scottish monastic (and perhaps Crown) muniments for later chroniclers to reproduce and gloss.[134]

In this context, Edward I's decision to draw proceedings quickly to a close in October–November 1292 reflected concern over such legal opinion and a desire to install the more familiar and politically acceptable figure of Balliol as vassal king of Scots.[135] Later Scottish propaganda, surely the work of Robert I's early regime after 1306 and later enshrined in the annals collated by Fordun and his continuators, would certainly insinuate such 'subtlety and malice' into their vignette of a judgment by the French-speaking and untrustworthy Edward, counselled by Bishop Bek, to deny Bruce's legal right.[136] Thus the late fourteenth- and fifteenth-century Scottish chroniclers' spin about Edward I first offering Bruce the Competitor the kingship as a vassal in private interview in late 1292 – only for Robert V to refuse to subject the Scottish kingdom to servitude, prompting the English king to then turn to a servile, toady Balliol – is transparent whitewash; the same rewriting of history by Robert I would be embraced by Barbour.[137] Nevertheless, there must have been conviction amongst contemporaries that the correct result in terms of the laws of the day was reached when John Balliol was declared successor to the throne on 6 November 1292.[138]

It may then have been at this dramatic moment that Robert VII was withdrawn from English royal service as his family regrouped. Robert V transferred his claim to the kingdom to his son, Robert VI, antedating this statement to 7 November after a short-lived, last-gasp attempt to argue in law in partnership with Hastings that the Scottish kingdom was indeed partible into three like a noble fief; the earl of Gloucester's seal was attached to this resignation. Robert VI in turn now began proceedings, antedated to 9 November, to resign his earldom of Carrick to his eldest son, Robert VII, so as to protect the Bruces' kingship claim while their middle lord held only English lands.[139]

The Bruces' bid for the throne had thus ended as a long drawn-out and very expensive failure. John Balliol and his young son, Edward (aged nine), offered longevity for a new dynasty. There may also have been a general awareness that, adapting the terms of the marriage contract with Flanders of 1281 and the principles accepted by the Berwick hearings, the succession itself now passed firmly to Balliol's heirs, a fact that brought John Comyn 'the younger' of Badenoch (born c.1270/5), the son of the sister of the recently crowned King John, into prominence as heir presumptive: about this time, Comyn would marry a daughter of William de Valence, earl of Pembroke, and be knighted by the new king of Scots.[140] At the same time, however, it was the Balliol triumph that now propelled the eighteen-year-old Robert Bruce onto the political stage in his own right.

# CHAPTER TWO

# Conflict

## Earl of Carrick, 1293–99

*N'avons-nous pas autres choses à faire qu'à gagner vos royaumes?*
Edward I to Robert Bruce (VI), earl of Carrick, c.23 April 1296[1]

### King John of Scotland, r.1292–96

All three Robert Bruces withdrew and were absent from John Balliol's inauguration as king at Scone on St Andrew's day (30 November) 1292. This avoided any performance of homage by either elder. Yet the Bruces were now subjects of a monarchy behind which real day-to-day power lay with the Comyn affinity; nor could submission of their oath be evaded for long in a realm confirmed as subject to the overlordship of their other superior, Edward I, by King John's concessions at Newcastle on 26 December 1292 and 2 January 1293, ending any hopes that the guarantees of Scottish liberties and customs of Birgham might still hold.[2]

The record of King John's first parliament at Scone in February 1293 confirms the political and regional advantages taken by the Comyn party since 1286, with legal cases advanced or resolved in favour of Bishop Fraser of St Andrews, the Comyn bishop of Brechin, the Macdougalls and Ingram d'Umfraville, and offices for Macdougall and the earl of Ross as new sheriffs of Lorn and Skye respectively.[3] No Bruce appears to have attended this assembly, although only Robert of Carrick – certainly the middle Bruce – was cited for 'default' to appear in response to the 'lord king's letter' of summons, as was another Turnberry Band party, Angus MacDonald. Sheriffs were assigned to oblige all defaulters to attend to perform homage to the new king at Easter 1293. Although James Steward as sheriff of Ayr (and the new sheriff of Kintyre) was successful in arresting one such, his own former brother-in-law Sir William Douglas (who promptly escaped), Robert VI remained absent perhaps dividing his time between either side of the border.[4]

It was, then, his son, Robert VII, who appeared, somewhat chastened, before King John in parliament at Stirling from 2 August 1293, with his father's retrospective resignation of Carrick in hand, to ask the 'magnificent and serene prince the lord John by grace of God King of Scotland' to accept this transfer and the youth's performance of homage. Those magnates recorded as pledging surety for the Bruce approach spoke to political alliances formed during the interregnum. Donald, earl of Mar, and James Steward underwrote the relief casualty owed to the Crown upon the earldom, while Malcolm, earl of Lennox, Sir John Soules and one Gilbert of Carrick confirmed the resignation of 9 November 1292. As sheriff of Ayr, Steward was charged to take the earldom into royal control and assess it for relief and tax (at the hands of John I's new English-style treasury office in Scotland) before the king would 'inspect' its liberties (an introduction from England by John's Chancery) and regrant it to Robert VII.[5]

Yet for the Bruces it was surely the link with Mar that was of the greatest moment as at about this time the younger Robert would marry Earl Donald's daughter, Isabella: the latter's brother, Gartnait of Mar, had already married and sired heirs by one of Robert VII's sisters.[6] This confirms that the Bruces' priority at this time was to secure political support within Scotland to protect their patrimony under King John. To be now belted an earl and marry, though, Robert would have to be a knight. It is possible this rite had already been performed by his own grandfather or by Edward I himself. Alternatively, was Robert's knighting combined as a cautious olive branch with his personal homage for Carrick and thus performed by none other than King John? With his father absent in Norway from autumn 1292, the younger Robert may also have represented his family at such public events as the jubilee feast of St Margaret at Dunfermline Abbey held about 16 November 1293.[7]

In representing his kin, the young, energetic, ambitious, perhaps even idealistic Robert VII, earl of Carrick – whose family had been filled with notions of their royal rights for the last six years – entered upon what must have been an incredibly difficult, confusing period of his life. For the next decade and more he would be caught on the one hand between ostensible loyalty to King John, a troubled (though perhaps a personally engaging and brave) king of Scots controlled by the Bruce family's main political rivals, and on the other by fealty to the intimidating figure of a veteran English king, Edward, whose assertion of his perceived rights over the Scottish realm entailed thwarting anything that might advance a Bruce claim to the throne. For much of this period, Carrick's behaviour would still be guided by the choices of his family elders. He probably remained a spectator at most of the key political events of John's reign, perhaps attending Scottish parliaments but hearing from his grandfather and father of the Balliol king's personal attendance and humiliation at Westminster assemblies in September 1293 and June 1294, where Edward I heard several legal appeals from Scottish courts and subjects.[8] In June 1294, Robert V would be remitted a 100-mark fine for hunting deer in Essex forest while his son may have waited on Edward during his pilgrimage to Canterbury for St Thomas's Translation feast of 7 July 1293.[9] Nonetheless, both senior men may also have made the effort to attend to matters in Scotland. The Bruces may have used such travel to work behind the scenes to facilitate legal appeals to Edward from parties such as MacDuff of Fife, Angus MacDonald and Eric II of Norway.[10] Meanwhile Robert VII's main focus over the next three years may have been to familiarise himself with his earldom and its socio-economic situation in what were increasingly hard times.

Contemporary English and later Scottish chronicles report the severity of winter 1292–93, with 'a long spell of wind and snow [which] pulled up forests and withered the plants it found; it unroofed houses causing much loss, and violently threw some to the ground, thus accomplishing much devastation.'[11] It was the worst of this decade within a series of long, hard winters followed by wet, stormy summers, typical of a Europe-wide climatic deterioration that had begun in the late 1250s. These cooler and more sodden seasons may have contributed to a serious outbreak of sheep scab in Scotland by August 1293 or 1294 and caused the Teviot to flood in August 1294, washing out the castle's mill at Roxburgh and a bridge at Berwick.[12] Marginal (up)land that had supported a growth in population and livestock in better years increasingly fell unproductive. The chroniclers of Lanercost Priory in Cumberland reported a biting 'scarcity of victual' throughout 1293 such that wheat prices tripled.[13] Reports of heavy rains and harvest failure also survive for 1294 for much of England and Wales.[14] Rising prices, falling wages and increased human and animal mortality carried through to 1295–96, the worst crisis detectable since 1256–58 or before the major famines of 1315–17.[15]

Thus 1292–96 and subsequent seasons may have exposed the vulnerability of an earldom like Carrick with its predominantly pastoral economy, sorely reducing its limited arable land and crop production, just as similar regions of Scotland and the British Isles suffered. This hardship cannot have been helped by the simultaneous demands of papal crusading taxation of annual tenths imposed upon the Church, ultimately to be passed on to those engaged in parish crops, livestock and wool production.[16] Indeed, English involvement in collection of Scottish 'Holy Land' tenths, although a familiar administrative arrangement off and on since at least around 1213, must have been a further source of Scots' resentment throughout 1292–96, as it now facilitated direct English oversight, a broader tax base and increased taxable valuations.[17] By mid-1294, indeed, the bishop of Carlisle had cause to write to the bishops of St Andrews and Glasgow to admonish them for two years' of arrears (over £4,000 each, eventually paid in mid-1295) as well as order his collector for Dunkeld diocese, the abbot of Lindores, to excommunicate the non-paying bishop there, Matthew de Crambeth, in his own cathedral.[18] This universal levy amidst wider economic decline may explain Edward I's further grant of a safe conduct to 'Robert de Breus, earl of Carrick' (possibly Robert VI) on 20 April 1294, granting him permission again to travel to Ireland to purchase corn, wine and other victuals; throughout 1293–94 the English king also remitted Carrick's (unspecified) debts.[19]

As the new reign opened, therefore, the Bruces must have combined everyday concerns for the well-being of their estates and tenants with efforts to safeguard their wider interests from marginalisation. The sympathy of Bishop Wishart would have provided some protection for Bruce patronage of churches in Annandale within the Glasgow diocese. By the same token, Bruce success by mid-1294 in defying King John's government to secure the provision of one Thomas de Dalton (from Annandale) as bishop of Whithorn/Galloway, loyal to the archdiocese of York, safeguarded Bruce ecclesiastical and resource interests in the south-west and rewarded the family's efforts to undermine the traditional influence of the lord of Galloway (Balliol) over the popular cult of St Ninian.[20]

Nevertheless, in such a context, the summons by Edward I in late June 1294 of King John, Robert of Annandale and fifteen other magnates of Scotland to serve in arms in an expensive war against France on the continent (following Philip IV's forfeiture of Gascony) was very much an innovation (conceded by an overawed John attending his final English parliament).[21] It threatened to add further demands to the already challenging conditions facing the Scottish nobility, churches and burghs, especially the 'middling sort' of freeholder and their tenants working the land and feeding Scotland's limited economy; war with France would also disrupt Scotland's staple trade with Flanders. These very real questions of livelihood must thus have provided further impetus to the resolve of John's ministers and counsel in 1294–95 to secure papal absolution from their oaths to Edward I followed by a bold alliance with France and armed resistance.[22] The unexpected Welsh revolt against English occupation and taxation that erupted in October 1294 under the popular leadership of

Madog ap Llywelyn also encouraged the Scots, drawing England's Gascony-bound forces and Edward himself in arms into Wales until order was restored there by May–July 1295.[23]

That the danger to the Scottish kingship and community posed by Edward I was of paramount concern by 1294–95, rather than lingering internal factionalism, is suggested by the choice of personnel for a council of twelve magnates appointed by parliament at Stirling in July 1295, to oversee and dispatch an embassy of four to negotiate with Philip IV. Historians have long argued about the nature of this council. Geoffrey Barrow accepts the evidence provided only by two contemporary (and some later) English chroniclers that this reflected Scottish distrust of their weakening monarch and thus a 'sober constitutional revolution' in sidelining his ineffectual person whilst the community fulfilled the responsibilities of the Crown to defy Edward I's tyranny.[24] Others have suggested that this was a working committee of the estates dedicated to the French talks, just as a similar body drawn from the earls, barons and prelates had overseen marriage agreements with Norway and Flanders in 1281. Besides, in 1295 this committee had to rely upon Balliol contacts to secure the prestigious betrothal of the sixteen-year-old heir to the throne Edward Balliol to Philip IV's niece, which was to underscore the military pact.[25] The evidence of what was to follow strongly suggests that John remained king but was indeed no longer in charge (if he ever had been). Yet it should be added that the Capetian–Balliol marriage was really the only clause that favoured the Scots in a treaty in which Philip IV – fearful of England's alliance with the Holy Roman Empire – otherwise applied considerable pressure (even threatening Scottish merchants' vital access to Flanders), only then to reveal the alliance to Edward I so as to draw his fire from France.[26]

For the Bruces, community action to challenge the competency of a (Balliol) king was useful (as were the arguments used to separate Celestine V from his month-long office as Pope in 1294, and the Imperial electoral princes' deposition of Adolf of Nassau in 1298).[27] Yet if King John really had been marginalised by his magnates as a 'rex inutilis' or 'simplex' in 1295 (in the manner of Sancho I of Portugal in 1245 or Henry III in 1258), it remains surprising that the Bruce regime made no use of this decline in its own exchanges with England and the Papacy from 1306.[28] Even Fordun's contemporary annalist places the appointment of such a committee of twelve 'peers or guardians ... to guard and defend the kingdom and the estates thereof' *after* Edward I had conquered Scotland and removed John and his son, Edward Balliol.[29] As we shall see, though, it may be that John's subsequent transfers from English to papal to French custody (1296–1301), and the diplomatic hopes attached to efforts for his recovery and restoration as king, obliged Scots who would later be prominent in Robert I's government subsequently to play down their Montfortian treatment of the Balliol kingship in 1295.[30] The most important point here is that Bishops Wishart and Crambeth as well as Sir John Soules were charged to go to Paris, and joined their fellow former Bruce auditors of 1291–92, the earls of Mar and Atholl, in the larger council. The resulting treaty with France, ratified by the estates of clergy, earls and barons, joined by procurators for the burghs, at a parliament at Dunfermline on 23 February 1296, was also linked to a Franco-Norwegian treaty that for the moment neutralised Bruce influence through Isabel Bruce (Robert VII's sister), wife of Eric II.[31] The rapid pace of events had thus severely isolated the Bruces.

A large part of this sudden loss of influence must be put down to the passing of Robert V of Annandale on 31 March 1295 and the inability of Robert VI to pursue the kind of energetic troubleshooting that the Competitor would surely have identified as required. The whole family must have attended funeral obsequies on 17 April at Guisborough Priory.[32] Yet in their shared grief the Bruces give the impression of drifting purposelessly through the dramas of 1295–96. Even before war broke out with Scotland, Edward I seemed underwhelmed by the new fifty-year-old lord of Annandale and his second, provincial wife. Nevertheless, on 19 September 1295 Robert VI was at Canterbury to secure Edward's permission to remarry and broach the issue of the imminent royal expedition to Scotland and the future of its vassal kingship, promising men and arms from Annandale and Carrick; on 6 October, Edward appointed Bruce captain of Carlisle castle (a post he had last held in 1283 while sheriff of Cumberland).[33] In the same month, the English government would order the seizure of Scots' lands in England and the arrest of Scots resident in the southern realm, a preamble to hostilities which makes it clear that contemporaries could understand or determine a political and ethnic difference between the two peoples.[34] Both Robert Bruces, father and son, were spared internment and forfeiture in England through their personal submission of loyalty, given to Edward as he marched north, at Wark in Northumberland on Easter Sunday in 1296 (25 March, the Annunciation feast of the Virgin), in company with a tellingly styled 'Patrick Dunbar Earl of March' (whose Northumberland lands and Scottish earldom lay directly in the path of the invading English army) and the d'Umfraville earl of Angus (also lord of Prudhoe, Northumberland).[35] Yet what was to follow makes it plain that at no point in 1295–96 did Edward I entertain the notion of revisiting the pleadings of Berwick and now forfeiting Balliol in favour of a vassal Bruce monarchy.

## War and Occupation, 1296–97

When on about 11 March 1296 the Scottish host was summoned to muster in the Middle March, the Bruces of Annandale and Carrick refused to comply and were forfeited *in absentia* by a parliament at Stirling: Annandale would be used as a military base for Comyn of Buchan to raid into the English Borders.[36] At the same time, clerics in Annandale under Bruce patronage may have been amongst those expelled from benefices in southern Scotland for their English connections or blood.[37] Robert of Carrick perhaps joined his father in successfully defending Carlisle from siege and fire-setting by Scots under Buchan on Easter Monday 1296 (26 March), just a day after their homage to King Edward.[38] However, given his recent service in the English royal household, and perhaps if doubts persisted about Bruce ambition, Robert VII may otherwise have served in Edward's East March force and thus witnessed the sack of the burgh of Berwick (30 March) and the defeat and capture of a force of Scottish nobility near Dunbar castle (23 April, St George's Day).[39] One near contemporary Scottish source, a poem of c.1304–6, probably penned at St Andrews, would even go so far as to blame Edward I's bloody seizure of Berwick upon trickery with false banners supplied by an unnamed Scottish earl, a transparent reference to Carrick.[40]

This must have been the twenty-one-year-old Robert, earl of Carrick's first experience of a full royal host in action and he cannot but have been excited and awed by the arrayed ranks of English chivalry and shire levies, including veteran heavy cavalry and archers. Three English earls – Surrey, Norfolk and Warwick – had turned out for Edward I. Their banners and those of many other nobles flew over the tents, fires and siege engines of the army encamped before Scotland's premier trading port, alongside the royal arms and those of the cults of St John of Beverley, St Cuthbert of Durham, St Edward the Confessor and St George.[41] Even falling far short of his requested muster Edward probably still fielded over 20,000 men supported by a fleet of ships for this campaign. However, it is surely not unreasonable to speculate that as Scottish resistance crumbled and Edward progressed unchallenged through Scotland, reaching Elgin in Moray by mid-July 1296, Robert, earl of Carrick began to take a very different view of English power and its emerging treatment of the Scottish kingdom.[42]

Within the context of King John's formal renunciation of fealty in early April 1296, Edward I was entitled to punish the population of Berwick.[43] Yet the slaughter of civilians numbering into the thousands in Easter week (27 March–2 April) brought appalled comment from both contemporary English and later Scottish chroniclers.[44] This had been a deliberate act of terror, in retaliation for Scottish raids into Cumberland and which caused Scottish resistance to collapse to forestall greater loss of life. Yet this did not lessen the horror of many observers. Later Scottish annals would also link Edward's purge of the Scottish burgh with the defeat at Dunbar and the transfer (from 16 May) of a long list of Scottish noble prisoners to the Tower of London, Windsor Castle and elsewhere in southern England.[45] The Bruces may have anticipated and welcomed such punishment of Balliol's noble supporters along with systematic forfeiture of their English lands.[46] But given the nature of the regime which Edward I would soon impose upon Scotland, these gaolings might have been perceived to herald the thorough degradation of two of the estates (earls and barons) of the Scottish realm, just as the third, the Church, would now be filled with English appointments. It is telling that Fordun's annalist (and his continuators) would date Edward I's allegedly indignant breach of promise to Robert VI, refusing to transfer the Scottish kingship to him as head of the Bruce kin, to immediately after the fall of Berwick and Dunbar. The English king's pithy retort, dismissing Bruce opportunism, opens this chapter: thus Robert VI 'discerning from such a response the treachery of the wily king, withdrew to his lands in England and put in no further appearance in Scotland'.[47]

If the timing of this rebuff of the Bruces is correct, then this must have coloured Robert VII's view of what unfolded. Carrick's outlook at this time may also have been influenced by the increasingly bitter ethnic rivalry of Anglo-Scottish conflict. Indeed, a large measure of Edward's actions would be characterised by apparent imperious contempt for his smaller neighbour realm and its inhabitants and customs: to repeat Sir Thomas Gray's report of the king's quip to Surrey, 'He does good business, who rids himself of shit!'[48] This superiority complex was also reflected in contemporary English popular song and verse (and reciprocated by Scots' jibes about English tails) as well as in northern English monastic chronicles (even though it remained difficult to distinguish between the dialects of Marcher tenant-soldiers and cross-border gentry).[49]

True, the submissions to Edward of King John himself and John Comyn, earl of Buchan, and other nobles by about 10 July cannot have troubled Carrick unduly. Nevertheless, in the wake of Berwick's fate the English king's uneven behaviour towards Scottish cult centres and the symbolic persons, institutions and traditions of Scottish kingship and lordship was surely troubling.[50] This reflected Edward's now blatant attitude that Scotland was no longer a kingdom but a conquered 'land'. The king toured his prize to take 'ragman' submissions of fealty (and perhaps the casualty of 're-entry' at a cost of a penny each!) from all men over fifteen years of age shire by shire through June, July and August 1296.[51] During his southward ayre he may have displayed veneration and respect for the apostolic relics of St Andrew in the great (if unfinished) cathedral in Fife, as well as for the tombs of Plantagenet ancestors and his own sister and nephews buried at Dunfermline Abbey (St Margaret and Queen Margaret, consort of Alexander III, and her children).[52] However, Bruce of Carrick must have been aware of how in doing so Edward not only associated these cult sites and figures with his God-given forfeiture of the Scottish realm, but also how on his northwards surge he had already linked King John's general capitulation (2 July), renunciation of the French treaty (7 July, Stracathro), personal surrender (8 July, Montrose) and ritual humiliation (stripped of his muniments as 'Twme-Tabart', or empty surcoat) with the much-favoured Translation feast of St Thomas Becket. Edward must have venerated Thomas at that feast, 7 July, in Arbroath Abbey (18 miles south of Stracathro), which was dedicated to the saint.[53] As well as invoking memories of Henry II's defeat and feudal subjection of William I and Scotland in 1174 through the intercessionary powers of the saint (and the treaty of Falaise), Edward I would also tie his assertion of authority over Balliol of 1296 directly to the Becket cult by sending in that year some plate and jewels, and then in 1299 a gold crown and great seal found on John's person, as gifts to St Thomas's altar at Canterbury Cathedral.[54] The contemporary Lanercost chronicle would certainly associate John's surrender and forfeiture with punishment for the martyrdom of Becket, mistakenly accepting as true the rumour that Balliol was directly descended from one of St Thomas's killers in 1170, Hugh de Moreville.[55]

Of course, this was just one part of King Edward's systematic removal of the political and spiritual emblems of Scottish monarchy. John Balliol and his heir, Edward, were sent posthaste to London. Then between early June and September 1296, Edward I oversaw the removal from Edinburgh castle of the Scottish royal records (re-inventoried by English clerks in 1291) and the Crown's accumulated collection of plate, jewels and, most significant of all, holy relics, including pieces of the True Cross that had once belonged to St Margaret and that were now gifted to St Cuthbert's shrine at Durham.[56] Reaching Perth and Scone Abbey on about 21–24 June, Edward seized and removed the inauguration stone, dispatching it to Westminster Abbey to form part of the English coronation chair, perhaps along with some other (but crucially not all) enthronement materials. It may have been at either Edinburgh or Scone, or on King John's own person along with his royal mantle (*pallium*) and standard of arms, that Edward also located and confiscated the Scottish royal sceptre, known as 'Aaron's rod', the stem of a golden papal rose sent to William I in 1182 (the first such recorded gift to a layman);

Edward I gifted this to St Edward the Confessor's shrine at Westminster along with John's mantle, the golden rose, a silver orb and a sword.[57]

Defeated, neutral and Anglophile Scots alike in 1296 may have been all too aware of this plunder of the muniments of Scottish kingship, as they were required to swear and attach seals to their recorded oaths of fealty to Edward I, often on the Bible or relics of the saints, and at gatherings in important castles, churches and burghs or on royal demesne lands.[58] However, this was merely the preamble to a political settlement that would confirm the loss of independence of the Scottish kingdom, altering the fundamental fabric of the realm's local, regional and 'national' communities and their traditional personnel and practices of governance and justice (as well as worship). The scale and likely cost of English occupation were surely driven home in that same month by the handing over at Carlisle to Italian bankers of three years' worth of Scottish diocesenal crusading tenths – now extended by another six years by Pope Boniface VIII – and probably forcibly removed by English troops in the course of Edward I's victory tour: a total of over £7,400 (although much of this may have been notional 'parchment money').[59] The totality of English control and administration was then confirmed by the parliament called by Edward at *his* new burgh of Berwick from 28 August.[60] Traces of recent bloodshed must have concentrated the Scots' minds to compliance.

The man appointed Royal Lieutenant for Edward I in Scotland was John Balliol's father-in-law, John de Warenne, earl of Surrey, the victor of Dunbar. His supporting administration – both centrally and at shire level – would be almost totally English in make-up, headed by Chancellor Walter of Amersham and the odious Treasurer, Hugh de Cressingham, three justiciars, two escheators and about thirty sheriffs/castle-keepers.[61] What is most striking about this regime, though, is the almost complete absence of office for Scottish magnates who had demonstrated their loyalty to Edward I before conflict erupted. This included the Bruces, who (if kingship was impossible) must have expected their regional status and opposition to the Balliol–Comyn party to see them compensated with the justiciarship of Galloway and/or the sheriffship of Ayr (and perhaps Lanark or Wigtown or Dumfries), as well as perhaps a key royal castle or two. However, on 8 September, the English parliament named Sir Henry Percy of Northumberland in the justiciary post, alongside Sir Reginald Crawford, who had already been appointed to Ayr in May.[62]

Certain named nobles had been invited to parliament by the king, including Patrick, earl of Dunbar, and Gilbert, earl of Angus, the Bruces' submission companions of March 1296; but neither Carrick nor his father was named in the same regard. In this light, Edward's extension of relief from debt granted to 'Robert Bruce earl of Carrick' (seemingly the son) on 15 October 1296, because of the 'great esteem' in which the king held his services, seems like an unconvincing and overstated attempt to placate a disgruntled young knight developing itchy feet, alienated of place and aspiration.[63] What may have given Robert of Carrick further cause for concern was that there was no obvious sign that Edward intended to forfeit the Comyns of Buchan and Badenoch and any of their supporters for their rebellion; true, these men would serve periods of imprisonment or exile-in-service with Edward in France in 1296–97, but there was an expectation of their return to Scotland. The Bruces' homage to Edward I of March 1296 was restated on 28 August so as to become part of the 'permanent record' in the course of the August–September parliament, and was sown into a larger roll of the extracted tour submissions of Scots who had been in arms against the English king as well as urban and clerical communities and their leaders: over 1,764 names (including eleven different Comyns and four Balliols) across more than forty membranes.[64] This was the document of submission which King Robert I would be so at pains to recover by the peace treaty with Edward III's council in 1328.[65] By May 1297, however, the Comyns, Mar, Atholl, Ross, Menteith, the Murrays, Frasers and others captured in 1296 would be summoned to serve again in France, as would Robert of Carrick and Dunbar.[66] Thus Bruce was in effect to be treated little better than if he, too, had broken his fealty in 1295–96, and he may have anticipated the retreat of occupation administrators in Scotland within a short time, restoring the status quo of a dominant and experienced Comyn affinity to act as Edwardian officers.

## Rebellion, 1297

Robert of Carrick's disaffection may have been publicly known. Walter of Guisborough states that at about this time the prelate of the border town under Robert VI's care, the bishop of Carlisle, required Robert VII to demonstrate his loyalty by swearing an oath on a local relic, no less than one of the swords used to slay Thomas Becket in 1170; however, the chronicler may here have drawn mistakenly on submissions extracted from Carrick after his rebellion of spring 1297.[67] Nevertheless, with all these loyalties, calculations, sentiments and resentments churning and competing in his head and heart, it was indeed perhaps at this juncture – over the winter of 1296–97 and the first few months of English control – that Robert, earl of Carrick, came directly under the guiding influence of Robert Wishart, bishop of Glasgow and his associates.

As the most senior prelate of the realm, following the death in exile of Bishop Fraser of St Andrews (1294–c.1297) without replacement, Wishart assumed the mantle of motivating resistance to Edward I and his occupation regime.[68] As the churches of Carrick and Annandale lay within the Glasgow diocese, there may always have been a strong relationship between incumbent bishops and Bruce lords.[69] Wishart himself (born c.1240) was a younger son of an ambitious family of the Mearns (north of the Tay) and his rise to his Glasgow office by 1271–73 had depended upon his political acumen and connections, especially his kinsman William Wishart, bishop of St Andrews (d.1279), while his education at Oxford must have brought him into contact with the ideological currents of the Barons' Wars to limit monarchical authority in England c.1258–67. Wishart's rise was also achieved in opposition to the aspirations of the Comyn affinity at St Andrews and elsewhere, perhaps with Bruce of Annandale's support.[70]

Close personal links and political sympathy between the bishop and the Bruces were confirmed by Wishart's probable role in ensuring they were treated leniently after their insurgence in the south-west of 1286–87, and by his position as first-named auditor for Robert the Competitor in the pleadings at Berwick in 1291–92. It may have been in the wake of this disappointment that Robert VII's younger brother, Alexander Bruce, first received tutelage and patronage under the auspices of Glasgow Cathedral where he would hold significant office by 1306 (although only after his graduation from Cambridge University c.1303, indicating that he was still under the influence of his father, then resident in Essex).[71] Strong bonds between Robert VII and the bishop may have been nurtured c.1295–97 by any support that Wishart and his clergy were able to offer the earl and his young wife through her first pregnancy, perhaps calling upon the intercession of St Kentigern of Glasgow's known favour to expectant mothers (along with St Margaret at Dunfermline). Robert's first child, a daughter Marjorie, would be born sometime in 1296, but he may have had to mourn the loss of her mother, Isabella of Mar, in labour.[72] The real measure of the importance of Wishart and Glasgow's spiritual support in this period would be reflected in King Robert I's later generosity to Kentigern's cult and his anxiety for Wishart's well-being.[73]

However, Wishart's key role for Carrick c.1296–97 must have been in bringing some sense of rationale and direction to his mixed reaction to the fall of Balliol and Edward I's establishment of Scotland as a conquered English political and ecclesiastical province. Wishart had already stood out at Norham in 1291 for his principled defence of the realm in public defiance of the English king.[74] His role in 1286–90 as a Guardian for the Maid of

Norway, containing the Bruces and negotiating her marriage, and as a
council member agreeing to an alliance with France in 1294–95 in the name
of King John, seemed to underline Wishart's commitment to the integrity of
the kingdom above internal political faction. In that sense, as bishop of
Glasgow, Wishart seems to have taken very seriously the historical legacy of
his diocese and the wider *Ecclesia Scoticana* in protecting Scottish royal and
Church interests; these included the twelfth- and thirteenth-century
attempts to secure a metropolitan archbishopric in St Andrews and the full
rite of royal coronation and unction (both unsuccessful), as well as an independent Scottish Church Council (granted in 1225) and papal canonisation
for Alexander II's ancestral royal saint, Margaret (granted in 1249).[75]

The Church's vital contribution to the development of a Scottish realm
with an ever more distinct and unifying political identity was also reflected
in Scottish chronicle writing of the thirteenth century.[76] In particular,
Anglo-Scottish tensions during the reign of Alexander II and in the 1250s
(including Henry III's tricky question about overlordship of Scotland in
1251) prompted St Andrews clerics to elaborate passages about the Scots'
historic freedom, tolerating 'no foreign rule, but to enjoy of one's own
accord only the power of one's own nation in due succession'.[77] It was this
rich corpus of Scottish records and historiographical material that Bishops
Fraser and Wishart and the claimants' clerical lawyers had taken pains to
bring and consult during the succession hearings at Norham and Berwick
in 1291–92. This accumulated evidence in turn would be consulted by
Scottish clerics presenting Scotland's case to the Papacy c.1297–1301.
Therefore Abbot Bower, glossing Fordun's annals in the 1440s, clearly
exaggerated in asserting that 'after all the libraries of the kingdom had been
searched [in 1291] and authentic and ancient chronicles of history had
been placed in [Edward I's] hands, he took some of these away with him to
England, and the rest he contemptibly consigned to be burned in the
flames'.[78] Edward may have removed key treaties and chronicles when he
cleared out archives from Edinburgh castle and some monastic churches in
1296, but copies remained and this material would be inherited by William
Lamberton, chancellor of Glasgow Cathedral for Wishart from c.1293
and, by 7 November 1297, the new bishop of St Andrews.[79]

In sum, as well as his own personal influence and perhaps the power of
the confessional, there was a compelling weight of historical evidence and
corporate identity that Wishart could bring to bear to convince the young
Robert, earl of Carrick, that service to the kingdom, *ecclesia* and Crown of
Scotland was the best course of action in 1296–97: for example, citing
Richard I of England's formal release of Scotland from overlordship (imposed

upon William I in 1174) by the 'Quitclaim of Canterbury' of 1189, an act thus associated with St Thomas.[80] Given the events of July 1297, it is likely that Wishart was also aided in persuading Carrick by Sir James Steward.[81] Like the bishop, Steward had trodden an honourable path through 1286–96. He had acted for the legally recognised heir to the throne or their representatives but had also been openly in favour of Bruce of Annandale when the succession became a matter of political deliberation. Like Wishart, Steward had supported the alliance with France and taken up arms against Edward in 1296, but quickly capitulated (14 May) when resistance proved futile, carefully overseeing the 'ragman' submission of his family, affinity and royal castles (Roxburgh and Ayr), securing a significant marriage to the sister of Richard de Burgh, earl of Ulster, by October 1296.[82] His actions cost him control of the new sheriffship of Kintyre, where the MacDonalds acted as Edward I's agents from 1296, and its neighbouring office as constable of Dumbarton Castle, which was entrusted to an English officer under the regional lieutenancy (from Ross to Rutherglen) of the only Scot seemingly pardoned and employed in a judicial capacity in 1296–97, Alexander (Stewart), earl of Menteith (his father, Walter Balloch, the Competitor's ostensible ally, having died c.1294).[83] And, of course, a large part of Steward's mainland holdings now fell within the jurisdiction of the soon-to-be-notorious Englishman William Hazelrig as sheriff of Lanark.

Whatever their initial or longer-term political aims, the rebellion of Carrick, Steward, Wishart and other magnates was to coalesce and quicken over the winter and early spring of 1296–97 on a tide of separate regional uprisings characterised by both noble action and some apparently spontaneous, grass-roots resistance.[84] If Walter of Guisborough's report of Lieutenant Surrey's complaints and absence due to the 'awful weather' are true, then this was another tough winter.[85] Economic and environmental hardship was aggravated by the taxation of the occupation regime, which generally disrupted and regulated traditional economic and social activity. Collected by sheriffs, troops and the grasping Cressingham's treasury officials, this levy came to the tune of £5,188 by June 1297.[86] This still left a substantial shortfall for the administration to subvent, hinting at tax resistance and deforcement (stealing from the collectors) in the localities, heightening the already existing resentment of English supervision of the collection of papal crusading tenths throughout Scotland in 1295–96. By summer 1297, however, Edward I had already begun to summon Scottish magnates to perform military service in France once more, a conflict that many Scots must have anticipated would also lead to English purveyance of victuals, horses and wool north of the border. For example, consider the heavy toll on Atholl of Earl John's enforced service in France in August 1297 shortly after Cressingham had requisitioned 700 sheep and about 40 oxen from that 'county'; or the loss of wool by the border abbeys of Sweetheart and Melrose after Edward 'took half a merk sterling from each sack of wool in England and Scotland'.[87]

It is striking, too, that when open revolt erupted in April–May 1297, it did so in Gaelic-speaking quarters. Throughout Argyll and the Isles, the Macdougalls of Argyll and MacRuaridhs of Garmoran reacted violently to MacDonald ascendency and the alien Anglo-Norman presence, conflict that threatened to bleed into Clydeside and James Steward's intransigence.[88] In the north-east and around Inverness and Urquhart, Sir Andrew Murray, son of the lord of Avoch, reaped the support of burgesses and tenants loyal to his father, the Comyns of Badenoch, Lochaber and Buchan, the earl of Mar, John, earl of Atholl, and others, to rebel in the name of King John, sweeping out the English administration and retaking Aberdeen by late summer.[89] It was, though, the celebrated revolt of William Wallace, at first in western-central Scotland, that English chroniclers linked without question to the activities of Wishart, Steward and – through them – to Robert of Carrick.

According to the chronicler of Lanercost Priory in Cumbria, Wishart 'ever foremost in treason, conspired with the Steward of the realm, named James ... [and] caused a certain bloody man, William Wallace, who had formerly been a chief of brigands in Scotland, to revolt against the king and assemble the people in his support'.[90] As Wallace's spiritual and lay superiors respectively, it would have been logical for Wishart and Steward to evade, or even remain officially loyal to, Edward's regime while supplying the rebel leader with men, provisions and perhaps objectives, just as the Comyns and Murray of Avoch masked their support of Sir Andrew Murray in the north-east. Modern historians generally concur that Wallace had risen to prominence on the basis of his own violence and success and was fully capable of independent action.[91] Yet after killing Sheriff Hazelrig at Lanark (3 May), Wallace combined with Sir William Douglas (and perhaps the Stewarts) to target the English justiciar at Scone. Carrick's reported deceit by pretending to attack Douglas but in fact aiding Sir William's family, and then Douglas's presence just a month later in Ayrshire with Wishart, Steward and Carrick, certainly suggests a wider collusion in which the former Guardians and the young Earl Robert were the controlling figures.[92]

This was indeed a patriotic cause, but just what Robert of Carrick's objectives were remains highly contentious. It is likely that Wishart had already secreted away some of the accoutrements of royal inauguration (perhaps obtained by Wallace and Douglas at Scone), which he would produce for Carrick's enthronement in 1306. Writing with knowledge of these later events, Walter of Guisborough certainly asserts that in 1297 'Bruce indeed aspiring to the kingdom, as was publicly said, joined a perverse people, and was allied with the bishop of Glasgow and the Steward of Scotland who were the authors of the whole evil. From then on that wicked race and faithless Scots killed all the English whom they could find.'[93] As a result, at least one historian has suggested that at this juncture Bruce hoped to be named (by the community?) as heir to the forfeited and imprisoned King John.[94] However, it is surely highly unlikely that Carrick and his confederates intended or expected any move towards kingship for himself in the immediate or even median future – *unless* there was already contemplation of acting on the basis that Balliol and his line had been imposed unlawfully by Edward I upon the body politic of Scotland when it was without a 'head' (which would be the rationale Robert's royal government would present to the Papacy in 1309–10).

After all, the prospect of Bruce kingship remained extremely problematic, with Balliol's chief supporters, the Comyns and their affinity, and the rest of the patriotic nobility of 1296 still powerful in the realm. Even if the majority of Scots were inclined to view the Balliols as beyond reach in England, removed besides from the succession by the events of July 1296, John, son of Comyn of Badenoch, remained at liberty as King John and Edward Balliol's male heir presumptive.[95] Moreover, in the alternative line, Robert VII's own father remained alive in England, according to Guisborough 'ignorant' of his son's betrayal and unlikely to consider resigning his kingship claim to his son (as the Competitor had done in 1292). No, rather it seems more rational that in this highly uncertain and unpredictable context, what Wishart, Steward and Carrick sought to direct and associate themselves with was an effective uprising that began the recovery of the kingdom of the Scots towards independence. On 24 July 1297, Cressingham would have to report to his king that 'not a penny could be raised in your realm [of Scotland] ... and in some counties the Scots have appointed and established baillies and ministers ...'.[96] It is likely that Carrick and Steward had reclaimed their family's traditional roles as sheriffs of Ayr and Lanark respectively and perhaps moved to act as regional guardians of the west. At best this would allow them to position Carrick as a natural leader, of royal descent, worthy of consideration for kingship if the Balliols could not be recovered and the issue of a successor was reopened in any shape or form. As we shall see, they must also have been encouraged to do so by the mounting political disquiet within England directed towards Edward I's government.

Guisborough reported that Robert of Carrick began his rebellion by breaking his oath and appealing to the ten knights owed in service by his father for Annandale to follow him in arms to 'go to my people and join my nation from which I am born'.[97] This should not be trusted unquestioningly as evidence for the earl's declared motivation (or birthplace), perhaps referring instead to his more immediate sense of lineage or kindred.[98] It is possible, moreover, that Carrick's actions followed a strategic split in Bruce family loyalties (echoing 1138), approved by his father. But if that was the case then their ploy failed, exposing both men as poorly supported, for the Guisborough chronicler reports that the knights of Annandale slipped away, refusing to serve their lord's rebellious son. As such, these events may indeed speak more to an upsurge of aspirations, perhaps even patriotism, on Carrick's part, at odds with his father. Guisborough is predictably hostile towards Carrick's betrayal of and then submission to England, lending weight to what has emerged as a modern popular view of Robert in the period before 1306 as someone whose personal ambition caused him to change sides repeatedly, just like his grandfather. Yet in truth the record evidence of the period actually suggests that Robert VII now embarked upon a remarkably consistent pattern of resistance for the next three or more years, one that must have required a great deal of personal courage and good counsel to persevere in defiance of both Edward I and his own father (who must, though, have retained control of his other sons).

By mid-June 1297 the forces of Sir Henry Percy and Sir Robert Clifford had indeed pinned down the contingent of Carrick, Wishart, James and John Stewart, the latter's brother-in-law Sir Alexander Lindsay (of Barnweill in Ayrshire, Crawford in Lanarkshire and the Byres in Lothian), and William Douglas (perhaps with his young son, James, the Steward's nephew, in tow) at Irvine, some 12 miles north along the Ayrshire coast from the royal burgh of Ayr itself. Negotiations for terms were opened and found the Scots vocal in complaint about the threat to the 'middling sort' posed by Edward I's recent levies for war in France and disregard for Scottish law and custom.[99] As ideological principles, these grievances chimed in neatly with the growing opposition of the clerical and noble estates in England to Edward I's demands for taxation, wool prise (the *maltot*), and unpaid military service in Flanders. These protests about Edward's unconstitutional and economically damaging behaviour, and his neglect of the situation in Scotland, would reach a head in July 1297 with English magnates' refusal to fight on the continent, the presentation at Westminster of written 'Remonstrances' to the king demanding redress and community consent, and an open clash between Edward and Archbishop Winchelsey of Canterbury.[100]

However, Walter of Guisborough suggests far more believably that the Scots' complaints at Irvine were stalling tactics, allowing Wallace time to withdraw north from Selkirk forest with his troops, a force that surely included men of Carrick, the Stewartry, Douglasdale and Bishop Wishart's manors as well as the border woods. Sir Thomas Gray goes further, asserting that Wishart and Douglas sought to denounce Wallace's violence.[101] The formal agreements about submission of the Carrick party that followed, dated to Irvine on 7 and 9 July 1297, once again at about the Translation feast of St Thomas (and, for Wishart's party, just after the centenary anniversary of the dedication of Glasgow Cathedral, 6 July 1197), lend weight to Guisborough's earlier report of Robert being required to re-pledge his oath on a relic of Becket's martyrdom.[102] However, the Scots' original submission deadline of 9 August was ignored and, as late as 14 November 1297, Carrick was still expected to be received to the king's peace by Bishop Halton of Carlisle (who had just taken over control of Carlisle castle from Bruce's father).[103] There is no evidence that this submission actually occurred, or that Robert ever handed over his infant daughter Marjorie as a hostage, which had been required of him as early as 9 July.[104]

Although the bishop was briefly warded in Roxburgh castle, and Lindsay and Douglas were sent to the Tower (where Douglas died in 1298–99), Carrick and Wishart thus apparently remained at, or quickly returned to, liberty.[105] This was surely due to a mixture of their rank and influence, the possible intercession of Robert's father and Steward's brother-in-law, Richard de Burgh, earl of Ulster, and their promises of loyalty and service against the Scottish rebels. Yet in fact Carrick and Wishart continued to play a double game.

For Robert, any qualms he may have had about breaking his oath and honour, incurring the wrath of St Thomas, may have been soothed by the counsel of Bernard, abbot of the Tironensian house of Kilwinning in Ayrshire (3 miles north of Irvine), who seems to have been deprived of his office by Edward I or his Lieutenant at about this time. In the future Bernard would be Chancellor (c.1309–28) for Bruce (as Robert I) as well as abbot of Arbroath (dedicated to St Thomas and, like Kilwinning, where Bernard would be buried in 1331, a daughter house of Kelso Abbey in the Borders).[106] As such, the events of 1297 may have confirmed Robert VII in his belief in the protective powers of the Becket cult and thus in emulating in his own way the martyred archbishop's defiance of English monarchy – this at a time when Edward I had initiated legal proceedings against the present Archbishop of Canterbury and then left for Flanders (leaving echoes of Henry II's historic clash with Becket). Robert's later patronage as king to the *familia* of cults of Saints Thomas, Winnin (Kilwinning) and Convall (Strathclyde and Ayrshire, including Irvine church) may echo his accommodation of the events of summer 1297 with his conscience.[107]

It is therefore likely that Robert of Carrick was still actively aiding the rebellion when Wallace and Murray's war caught fire. The bloody victory of their few thousand men over an English host probably about 6,000 strong at Stirling Bridge on 11 September 1297 can only have encouraged Carrick and other magnates of Scotland in their intransigence at a time when the English kingdom, with Edward still absent in Flanders, seemed on the brink of civil war; the situation was further aggravated by a harvest failure that affected much of England and Wales (though surely Scotland, too). It is interesting to note that the Guisborough and Lanercost chroniclers named James Steward and Malcolm, earl of Lennox, as the magnates who mediated between the opposing forces at Stirling before joining in the rout as the earl of Surrey fled, leaving Cressingham slain behind him; as two former and future Bruce supporters, Steward and the earl of Lennox may provide a link to sustained rebellion by Carrick at this time.[108]

## Guardians for King John, 1298–99

Firm evidence for Robert VII's activities over the next five years now begins to thin. It can be inferred that he continued to support Wallace's rebellion throughout the harsh winter of 1297–98 (following Murray's death from wounds), no longer necessarily at a distance but without assuming an official leadership position. Men from Carrick and Annandale surely joined raids into Northumberland and Cumberland in October–November 1297 led by Wallace as 'leader of the army of the community of the realm of Scotland'.[109] According to Fordun's anonymous contemporary annalist for the period, c.1285–c.1330, perhaps in part William Comyn, provost of St Mary's of the Rock (St Andrews) who could draw upon records of the grange lands of the cathedral,

as the season of autumn [1297] approached there was a threat of a major dearth and shortage of food in the kingdom, since there was a shortage of grain resulting from inclement weather. On this account, once the crops had been brought in to the yards and barns, [Wallace] ordered the summons of all and sundry Scots who were capable of defending their homeland to invade the country of their enemies and find their substance there, and to spend the wintry part of the year there so as to spare their own very limited food supplies.

Although this account exaggerates the length of Wallace's raid, it should not simply be dismissed as 'folklore'.[110] In retaliation, Surrey and Clifford burned Annandale communities in December (about which time Robert VI was also replaced as keeper of Carlisle castle). In the meantime, Robert VII's role may have consisted of a regional lieutenancy in western-central Scotland, perhaps under the senior Steward and based at Ayr, overseeing the restoration of Scottish administration that Cressingham had reported to Edward I as displacing English occupation by July 1297.[111]

However, by late 1297, perhaps even by August when Wallace had first linked up with Murray, it must have become plain to Robert of Carrick that if the patriotic fight was to continue then the weight of loyalties throughout the Scottish magnate community ensured that it would now be fought explicitly in the name of King John. Carrick presumably assented to this, perhaps quite publicly if he was the unnamed Scottish earl who knighted Wallace according to the contemporary St Albans chronicler, William Rishanger.[112] In truth, though, Robert had little choice given the political influence of magnates like the earls of Buchan, Strathearn and Mar. Yet evidence for events just over a year later would seem to suggest that in doing so Carrick, and perhaps his confederates of 1296–97, had by no means abandoned all hope of advancing the notion of Bruce accession to the throne should Balliol's cause prove fruitless.

Ennoblement preceded Wallace's elevation as sole Guardian, perhaps at a parliament in March 1298 or shortly before.[113] By then Wallace had already begun to issue charters and letters in 'the name of the famous prince, the Lord John, by God's grace illustrious king of Scotland'. Acting within Wishart's and Steward's principle of supporting the legitimate authority of the Crown in Scotland, Carrick also presumably assented – or did not object – to the military and diplomatic policies that would be pursued by Wallace's regime in the first half of 1298.[114] The appointment of Wishart's chancellor at Glasgow Cathedral, William Lamberton, to be bishop of St Andrews facilitated intensive Scottish appeals in June 1298 to Philip IV of France to lobby Pope Boniface VIII to oblige Edward I in turn to release King John.[115] It would be this diplomatic lifeline to which the Scots would cling in the months after their devastating defeat by Edward I of 22 July at Falkirk but not perhaps, as we shall see, without a pragmatic concession towards the claims of Bruce of Carrick to shape a revived Scottish kingship.

As a group, Scotland's chief magnates – the earls and provincial lords – clearly feared Edward I's retribution for Stirling Bridge and would absent themselves from Wallace's army at Falkirk. Their followings may indeed have contributed larger numbers of spearmen to Wallace's host than previously recognised, perhaps enabling as many as 15,000 to 20,000 Scots to face Edward Longshanks's army of cavalry, archers and mixed English/ Welsh infantry, around 24,000 strong.[116] But the Scottish magnates' need to protect themselves was heightened by the settlement of political tensions in England in October–November 1297 and the granting of subsidy for a powerful host to muster at York with the English king, who had returned from Flanders in March.[117] Robert VI, styled 'earl of Carrick and lord of Annandale', was expected to provide troops to serve in the flanking force sent into Galloway. He reached Turnberry by 3 July and probably lingered, perhaps with a force that included one or more of Robert VII's younger brothers. This surely explains Robert VI's absence from the Falkirk Roll of Edward's main army.[118]

Robert VII's subsequent behaviour, his submission to Edward I in late 1301 or his murder of Comyn of Badenoch and seizure of the throne in 1306, would cause Fordun's unnamed annalist for the period (probably the aforementioned William Comyn), writing for Balliol's patriotic cause and perhaps as an apologist for the Scots' military collapse of 1303–4, to blacken Carrick's name deliberately:

> Robert Bruce, who was afterwards king of Scotland, but then fought on the side of the king of England, was the means of bringing about [English] victory [at Falkirk]. For, while the Scots stood invincible in their ranks, and could not be broken by either force or stratagem, this Robert Bruce went with one line, under Anthony Bek, by a long road round a hill, and attacked the Scots in the rear ... it is remarkable that we seldom, if ever, read of the Scots being overcome by the English, unless through the envy of the lords, or the treachery and deceit of the natives, taking them over to the other side.[119]

In the midst of civil war in Lowland Scotland in the 1440s, Abbot Bower would spin this account of Falkirk even further, echoing only in part propaganda of the regime of King Robert I, by explaining the patriot Wallace's defeat at Falkirk as the result of a general plot by 'magnates and powerful men of the kingdom' led by the Comyns, jealous of Wallace's power and who thus 'abandoned the field along with their accomplices'. Yet Bower also introduced to Scots elites the compelling vignette of 'Robert Bruce', whom he also reports as serving on the English side at Falkirk, being harangued for his cowardice by Wallace from across the river Carron:

> on account of all this Robert himself was like one awakening from a deep sleep; the power of Wallace's words so entered his heart that he no longer had a thought of favouring the views of the English. Hence, as he became every day braver than he had been, he kept all these words uttered by his faithful friend, considering them in his heart.[120]

Clearly a mirror for princes for Scottish magnates and dealings with England in the fifteenth century, Bower's version of events would nonetheless reflect and fix a central plank of Bruce's later popular image, a link with the victor of Stirling Bridge.[121] The contemporary evidence suggests, however, that Robert VII stuck to his course after the winter of 1296–97. According to Walter of Guisborough, as Edward I's forces pushed west and north after their victory at Falkirk – besieging Jedburgh castle, reducing Lochmaben tower in Annandale, and burning the burghs of St Andrews and Perth – the young earl of Carrick (who had not been at the battle) razed his charge of Ayr castle and withdrew, perhaps into Carrick, the Stewartry or Argyll, or even made a tactical retreat by sea to the Gaelic Isles.[122]

Robert of Carrick and other magnates must soon, however, have returned to their stations as hunger forced King Edward and his host to withdraw, leaving a reinvigorated stronghold of English occupation in the south-east and Borders. Moreover, long before it became apparent that the English king would not be able to mount a further expedition in 1298 or 1299, the Scottish Guardianship was sustained by the remarkable joint appointment, presumably by a parliament held before December 1298 at the latest, of Carrick and John Comyn the younger of Badenoch.[123] Given the perilous state of King John's cause at this point – defeated in battle and thus perhaps abandoned by God, with as yet no substantive outcome from pressure placed by the French king upon a troubled Pope, both of whom undoubtedly had their own agendas – it must be recognised that this joint Guardianship may have represented a pragmatic political compromise within the Scottish community.

Comyn of Badenoch may have had a recognised claim as the Balliols' heir presumptive, but the Bruces' claim would come to the fore if it became necessary, as it all too easily might, to argue to foreign powers that Edward I had coerced the Scottish kingdom into accepting John's accession. The selection of these two young, ambitious knights as Guardians, therefore, may reflect an attempt – perhaps shaped by Bishops Wishart and Lamberton and experienced peers like James Steward, John Comyn of

Buchan and John Strathbogie of Atholl – to keep the rebellion's options as open as possible; perhaps even to lay the basis of a future indenture about a practical division of power and horse-trading of Comyn–Bruce titles, with one man to be chosen as king and the other as his lieutenant, if the Balliols proved lost.[124] From Robert of Carrick's perspective, his open assumption of the office of Guardian in 1298 was arguably of greater personal moment as an act of rebellion against both his own father and Edward I. Yet it made sense. It placed him in a leadership role through which he might hope to influence his peers, probably through the mechanism of consultation of the community in parliament that had become so necessary and frequent since 1286.[125]

In this context, the joint Guardianship of Comyn and Carrick may have operated at an uneasy distance from each other within regional bailiwicks. Bruce seems to have resumed his duties in western-central Scotland, around Carrick, Ayr and Lanark, as well as taking up something of Wallace's national role.[126] On 5 December 1298, Bruce, styled as 'one of the Guardians of the Realm of Scotland', but without mention of King John, ordered 'his sheriffs and baillies of Forfar' to uphold Wallace's original charter of 29 March that year, which *had* been given in John's name, granting lands to Sir Alexander Scrymgeour as royal standard-bearer and keeper of the castle of Dundee (where the Bruces had inherited Earl David's lands).[127] By contrast, where they were recorded as acting together or were addressed by foreign powers, Carrick (listed first by rank) and Comyn were styled as 'Guardians of the kingdom of Scotland in the name of the famous prince, the illustrious King John'.[128] Both Guardians surely oversaw restoration and running of local administration, collecting and distributing revenues and resources from Crown demesne in their control, and perhaps offering judgments in disputes that had emerged since 1296. Much of their energy, however, was focused upon besieging and harassing enemy garrisons, just as Wallace had attempted to take Berwick and Roxburgh in late 1297– early 1298.[129] This was undoubtedly a period in which sustained damage was done by both sides to border lands, including Annandale.[130]

A dramatic fly-on-the-wall report by a spy in English pay, relayed to Edward I by Robert Hastings as keeper of Roxburgh castle, provides compelling if potentially misleading evidence for factional tensions within the Scottish political community under Carrick and Comyn.[131] With Scottish forces under knights Ingram d'Umfraville and William Balliol scouting ahead into Selkirk forest, the Guardians and other magnates had gathered on about Wednesday 19 August 1299 in the burgh of Peebles (which had both a castle and a Trinitarian priory dedicated to the Holy

Cross) to launch an attack on Roxburgh castle's formidable walls, just over 35 miles to the east. In the light of Edward's absence from Scotland that year, this would have been a significant demonstration of Scottish resolve with participation from the earls of Carrick, Buchan, Menteith and Atholl, Comyn of Badenoch and many other lords, possibly coinciding with the start of a siege of Stirling castle.

Moreover, the capture of either major royal stronghold may have been deliberately chosen to punctuate news that had perhaps only just been brought to the Scots from Rome via Paris by the retinue or person of Bishop Lamberton: that on 27–28 June 1299, Boniface VIII, at the urging of Philip IV, had written letters to Edward I, via the Archbishop of Canterbury, to order him to transfer John, 'called king of Scotland', into curial care at Avignon; to release any Scottish clerics made prisoner (such as Wishart of Glasgow); and, most important of all, in response to a papal bull, *Scimus Fili*, to 'send his proctors and envoys to our presence with records of all his rights' as proof of overlordship of Scotland to be presented at the curia within six months.[132]

These papal missives formed a hugely important coping stone for the defence of the Scottish kingdom. That there was a strong and enthusiastic response to them and their potential among the Scots' rebel regime is indicated by their being copied and archived in governmental, diocesenal and monastic records.[133] In retrospect they can be cautiously read to provide a compelling sense of what Scottish clerics in Rome prioritised in their representations, drawing now not only upon historical records and chronicles but also on the Edwardian injustices and atrocities of the last decade. Yet, at the same time, these papal demands also highlight in part just why the Scots remained so divided and on edge.

Naturally, the Scots' lawyers had throughout impressed upon Boniface the status of Scotland as a historic and 'special daughter' of the Roman see, but they had also now clearly emphasised the guarantees of sovereignty secured by both Alexander III and the Guardians in responding to any English royal summons and Edward's later intervention in the Scottish succession, including the promises of Birgham (1290). However, the Scots had also developed Wishart's protests at Norham (1291), condemning Edward's breach of trust and coercion through 'force and fear', followed by invasion and occupation, when the Scots had been 'virtually headless without the support of a leader or pilot'.[134] Before the Pope had shown willing to seek Balliol's release, the Scottish envoys may also have been prepared to argue that John had been imposed upon them illegally by the English king – 'that man [Balliol] to whom you [Edward] are said to have entrusted rule over the said kingdom (though it was not suitable)'.[135] This must explain some of the paranoia that would erupt at Peebles in August 1299. Yet it is probable that the shrewd Scottish clerics in Rome had nonetheless not called explicitly for the Balliols' exclusion, rather that John's status be reviewed alongside Scotland's sovereignty. To that end the Scots had clearly pressed hard for Boniface to insist even at the outset of his dealings with Edward in this regard that 'we call in and reserve to the Holy See the whole business of whatever suits, disputes and controversies have arisen or can in the future arise from any past cases whatever between the king and the aforementioned kingdom of Scotland and the prelates, clerics and secular persons of the same kingdom'.[136] In sum, the Scots hoped to reopen the succession hearings, but in a papal-convened court.[137]

According to Sir Thomas Gray, the papal envoys presented Boniface's demand for Balliol's release while Edward I was actually at prayer at Canterbury Cathedral during the Translation feast of St Thomas (7 July 1299).[138] It had the desired effect not least because John's release was also a term of widower Edward I's recently proposed marriage to Philip IV's sister, a match agreed on to settle peace with France.[139] The order was duly fulfilled on 18 July: as the captive John was transferred to the continent via Dover, Edward had him stripped of his last remaining Scottish royal jewels and donated them to St Thomas's altar in Canterbury Cathedral.[140] Yet *Scimus Fili* would not in fact reach Edward officially until August 1300, delivered to the king while on campaign at the Cistercian abbey of Sweetheart in Galloway (a Balliol foundation) by the out-of-favour Archbishop Winchelsey, much delayed either by an anxious Pope or perhaps by Philip IV.[141] Nonetheless, their king's release was probably known to the Scots as they assembled at Peebles in August 1299.

However, after aborting the Roxburgh assault in August 1299 for fear of meeting a larger English force in battle, the Scottish community fell to fighting amongst themselves over the Guardians' activities and future objectives. That the spy at Peebles reports William Wallace's brother Malcolm as being in Carrick's affinity seems to provide strong suggestive evidence that William himself – then absent on a diplomatic mission to Rome via Paris (where Philip IV would detain him until about 7 November 1300) – was inclined and, since Falkirk, perhaps actively working to forward a Bruce claim so as to revive the kingship and independent realm more quickly, returning to the loyalties and contingencies first shaped by the mentoring of Bishop Wishart and James Steward in 1296–97.[142]

Comyn of Badenoch certainly suspected as much or feared that Robert of Carrick, through Wallace's and Lamberton's embassies, aimed at the complete rejection of John Balliol (and his heirs) as an Edwardian imposition. While Malcolm Wallace engaged Sir David Graham in a knife fight, Graham's lord, John of Badenoch the younger, 'leaped at the earl of Carrick and seized him by the throat, and the earl of Buchan turned on the bishop of St Andrews, declaring that treason and lesé-majesté were being plotted'. Here the spy's testimony is really too cryptic and brief, giving no firm indication whether the Scots were aware of King John's release (as neither Hastings nor his informant were). Yet given the timing, perhaps a more likely explanation is that with word of John's passage to papal care it was in fact Carrick who had begun to agitate amongst the magnates at Peebles, perhaps canvassing this war parliament for personal support as he feared marginalisation.

Here the spy provides a quite believable description of how 'the Stewart and others came between them and quietened them', hinting at the continued principles of Wishart, James Steward, Sir John Soules, Bishop Crambeth of Dunkeld, Bishop David of Moray and, by extension, Lamberton and others unnamed in placing the most immediate interests of the kingdom first: King John's reign had a heartbeat once more. In the end the situation was calmed before blood was shed by a realistic awareness of the Scots' weak military position and their own now obvious divisions (with Comyn and MacRuaridh scions also reportedly attacking patriots in the north-west at that time). Yet all but Bruce were surely given hope by the watershed opportunity towards progress that Balliol's release seemed to represent, together with reassurances from Lamberton that this diplomatic course at the curia and in Paris was his priority.

According to the spy, the bishop of St Andrews was then chosen as 'principal captain' or Guardian-in-Chief, a fact confirmed by records of 1299–1300.[143] New regional responsibilities were perhaps also agreed before the assembly at Peebles broke up on the same day. Bruce withdrew into Annandale and Galloway, his task probably to prosecute the war there in company with Sir David Brechin; the Comyns returned to the north, James Steward and the earl of Menteith to 'Clydesdale' (and Dumbarton Castle?). In addition, 'each lord has left part of his men with [Ingram de] Umfraville' who, as the Scots' sheriff of Roxburghshire, was to raid the English Marches with horsemen and forest archers under Sir Robert Keith.[144] However, as Robert of Carrick rode west, had he already begun to wonder whether there was ever actually to be a moment when he could legitimately forward his own dynastic ambition within the patriotic cause?

# CHAPTER THREE

# Dead End
## Vacillation, 1300–6

*Thus the king of England reduced the whole kingdom of Scotland to his power
and rule, and so obtained absolute power over England, Scotland and Wales,
the former kingdom of Britain, long torn and divided.*

*Chronicle of Bury St Edmunds*[1]

### Frozen Out, 1300–1

In the wake of King John's release and the angry war council at Peebles in
summer 1299, Robert of Carrick found himself squeezed between a rock
and a hard place. He had to continue to fight English occupation of his
family's border lands, depriving him of resources and the armed following
of his tenants. Sir Robert Clifford's forces included knights of Annandale
paid to help successfully resist Earl Robert's own attack on Lochmaben
'pele' between 1 and 25 August: the same troops stood watches against
Carrick at the awkward coastal port of Annan to protect badly needed
supplies of wheat, oats, malt, flour, meat, fish and drink, much of it from
Ireland.[2] Yet despite this patriotic effort in the field Robert was also increasingly distrusted by magnates within the Scottish Guardianship.

This had not meant a sudden end to collaboration. Late that year, the
Scots would take and sack Stirling castle, escorting the starved English
garrison to Berwick for release. On 13 November 1299, from the Torwood
forest south of Stirling, Bishop Lamberton, Carrick and Comyn the
younger attached their joint seal to a letter to Edward I, in the name of the
'famous prince the lord John, by God's grace illustrious king of Scotland',
offering a truce to be mediated by Philip of France.[3] However, six months
later, according to Sir John de Kingston, Edward's keeper of Edinburgh
castle, on 10 May 1300, at Rutherglen in Lanarkshire, the Scots held

another 'parliament' at which Sir Ingram d'Umfraville was chosen as a Guardian 'in place of the earl of Carrick'.[4]

Robert may have been cut off by fighting in the south-west, exhausted or simply late rather than already 'sulking'.[5] The earl of Buchan was also reportedly absent having gone south to raise Galloway forces against an anticipated English expedition which had as its dubious figurehead the aged Thomas, lord of Galloway (gaoled by the Balliols as new lords of that province in 1235).[6] Carrick may thus have looked to his own defence within or against Buchan's forces as well as in the face of Edward I's army, set to muster at midsummer at Carlisle. Yet we have no evidence to show whether Robert was actually voted out and replaced as Guardian by the Rutherglen assembly or whether he resigned his office shortly before.

Either scenario is possible and the outcome was so regrettable as to warrant later pro-Bruce Scottish chronicle accounts to ignore completely Carrick's service as Guardian between 1298 and 1300, just as they would make no mention of Robert's change of allegiance by 1302. According to Kingston, however, the Peebles tensions had by no means dissipated. At Rutherglen 'the bishop of St Andrews and Sir John Comyn were in discord and the Steward and [John] earl of Atholl held to the party of the bishop. And Sir John Comyn said that he did not wish to be Guardian of the kingdom any longer jointly with the bishop . . .'. This suggests that Comyn remained deeply suspicious of Bishop Lamberton's links with Bruce, James Steward and the activities of William Wallace (who was still in France), and the Guardianship's intentions for John Balliol: whether to seek his (and Edward Balliol's) restoration at the hands of the Pope and King Philip; or John's lawful resignation of his family's royal title to their male heir presumptive, Comyn himself; or the pursuit of fresh succession hearings, ideally under papal jurisdiction.

There must have remained considerable uncertainty within the Scottish community about these options. Franco-papal pressure had slowed markedly as Paris and Rome continued to dispute temporal taxation of the clergy; Edward I was yet to be presented with Boniface VIII's formal bull of demands of June 1299. The Pope himself was distracted by thousands of pilgrims to Rome for the curial Jubilee, with 1300 declared a 'holy year' on 22 February.[7] In the meantime, French overtures for a truce allowed England to prepare a large host for a Scottish expedition, the first since 1298. Bishop Lamberton, then, must have demonstrated fulsome public affirmations in order that the 'community of the realm' remained committed to John's restoration with Rome's help, so as to avert a devastating split with Comyn. In addition, the earl of Carrick was replaced with Umfraville, who was a Comyn adherent, descendant of the Balliols of Urr and Redcastle, and an experienced envoy to Paris in 1295 in company with the then Bishop Fraser of St Andrews, Matthew, bishop of Dunkeld and, significantly, Sir John Soules of Liddesdale. However, it should be acknowledged that Umfraville also held lands in Carrick and may have kept channels open to Bruce.[8]

Nevertheless, for Robert VII, in his twenty-sixth year, widowed, with only an infant daughter (Marjorie) as issue and cut off from the rest of his family, this displacement confirmed his marginalisation within the patriotic community (for a second time, arguably the fourth for his family). It is possible that he and his Carrick following did muster within the Guardians' ranks in the south-west as King Edward entered Annandale with a force of over 20,000 men, in part to relieve his garrison at Lochmaben. The king marked 7 July, the Translation of St Thomas, at the saint's altar in the Bruce church of Applegarth.[9] The Scottish army then observed Edward's overblown, redundant showpiece siege of Caerlaverock castle: the garrison there had already been prepared to submit.[10] Thereafter, Bruce may have contributed to the Scottish force that skirmished with the English across the river Cree. However, it is possible that Robert had already withdrawn to a more localised role protecting Carrick and its adjacent sheriffship of Ayr. This may have involved looking west as well as east, guarding against the MacDonalds in English pay in the Clyde and Irish Sea. It is thus perhaps also to this time that we might date early approaches to or from Richard de Burgh, earl of Ulster, about a second marriage for Bruce, to his daughter Elizabeth (born 1289).[11]

It was in this period that the leadership of Scotland's clergy and thus the collective action of the community of the realm was at its most resolute. In unsuccessful peace talks with Edward I at Kirkcudbright in September–October 1300, the new trio of Guardians demanded King John's restoration, the right to succession of Edward Balliol (crucially, still a prisoner in England) and the re-infeftment of Scottish nobles and churches in lands held in England before 1296: all they got was a truce until next 21 May.[12] But by late 1300–early 1301 the Guardianship had been transferred to a single secular figure, Sir John Soules, with acts issued in King John's name directly by a revived Scottish chancery under Nicholas Balmyle, a St Andrews official and close colleague of those who had shaped and presented Scotland's case at the papal curia since 1298, namely Bishop Lamberton, William Frere, archdeacon of Lothian, William of Eaglesham and Baldred Bisset.[13] These men would continue to press Scotland's and John's cases in response to Edward I's own much delayed response to *Scimus*

*Fili* while, in between short truces (negotiated by King Philip), Soules oversaw continued military resistance in south-west Scotland and the marches by forces under the Comyns of Buchan and Badenoch, Umfraville, Steward, Robert Keith and others.[14] The Scots' relative success seems to have encouraged notable defections, too, by Scottish lords hitherto in Edward I's peace, including Sir Simon Fraser and Sir Herbert Morham.[15] Clergy and nobles also cooperated in embassies, preparing for further peace talks, which failed, at Canterbury with English and French representatives once more in April–May 1301; this allegedly angered Edward to the point of growling threats to lay waste to Scotland from coast to coast.[16]

The specific instructions, legal arguments and proofs advanced to the Bologna-trained Baldred Bisset and his team in Rome, and then to a far larger embassy of Scottish clerics and magnates in Paris, must have required a number of councils or parliaments to convene and be continued throughout 1301–2.[17] These were assemblies from which Bruce of Carrick remained absent. It is thus impossible to know what impression (and materials), if any, he gathered from these exchanges. Yet, as with the papal missives of summer 1299, these representations would produce a vital body of arguments and personnel which the royal government of Robert I would later call upon in its own internal and external dealings from c.1309. An undated letter of summer 1299 from Balliol's custodian, the bishop of Vicenza, addressed to 'Robert Bruce', does suggest that Carrick, or his father, gathered intelligence about the negotiations.[18] Thus it is likely that, rather than waiting until matters had reached a definite turning point, Robert of Carrick made precautionary approaches at least to explore the possibility of resubmission to Edward I some time before it became apparent that the Papacy would be persuaded to release King John into French custody.

Some small measure of Robert's final disaffection from the patriotic cause may be signalled by King John's grant, witnessed by Soules as Guardian at Stirling on 10 July 1301, confirming once more Alexander Scrymgeour's privileges as constable of Dundee castle, rights last confirmed by Carrick as Guardian in December 1298.[19] Admittedly, Scrymgeour may simply have desired his office confirmed by King John's new seal in anticipation of his return, perhaps with a French army. In that sense the level of expectation surrounding Bisset's case in Rome should not be underestimated. One crucial measure of its worth would again be the archiving of this documentation in Scottish royal, diocesenal and monastic records, surviving subsequent English invasions, and Bruce kingship, to be read by chroniclers who would include Fordun's source for c.1285–c.1330 and later continuators. However, the Scrymgeour charter may indeed coincide with the beginnings of Bruce alienation, given the apparent inclusion in the Scots' representations to the Papacy by July 1301 of arguments alluding to Bruce (V) of Annandale – head of 'one group of the magnates . . . who had no right in the kingdom of Scotland at that time' (1290), thus acting unlawfully to invite intervention by Edward I.[20]

The Scottish case at Rome seems the more compelling. Edward's responses of May 1301, including a letter sent in the name of his nobility, focused upon some documented and other falsified historic submissions by the Scots for Scotland, including 1174, 1251 and 1278, as well as John Balliol's submissions of 1291–93, followed by his treason and forfeiture and then his subsequent renunciation of the Scottish kingdom and people (dated to London on 1 April 1298).[21] In response, Bisset and others narrated a detailed history of papal protection for Christian Scotland and of Anglo-Scottish relations characterised since the eleventh century by homage for lands held only in England, the coercion of William I in 1174, his cancellation of imposed overlordship through the Canterbury Quitclaim of 1189, and Edward I's use of 'force and fear' in 1296 to remove 'our king, John' who was king of Scotland 'by hereditary right . . . justly and legitimately'.

It was the latter argument that perhaps spoke more directly to a Pope under similar pressures from the French king and who, since his Jubilee year, had sought to depose Philip IV's Habsburg ally, Albert I, as a usurper of the Holy Roman Imperial throne in 1298 without the required papal approbation (and coronation).[22] The Scottish proctors were careful to shape a considerable part of their case before lawyer-Pope Boniface and against Edward I by using the earlier Pope Innocent IV's influential legal opinions which had defined the integrity of nations under their own princes and jurisdictions, principles which that pontiff had used to depose a bellicose Emperor Frederick II in 1245 for his attacks on Rome and Sicily. Indeed, Bisset's materials accuse Edward I of similar crimes of perjury by breach of oaths, sacrilegious destruction of churches, contempt for the officials and jurisdiction of 'that Roman priest' (a phrase recalling the Becket controversy), and even of the heretical Saracen habit of stabling horses in churches.[23] This was allied to a commitment to the common law which denounced Edward's defilement of both this and, by extension, natural law by invading a sovereign (Scot)land that was under the direct lordship of the Papacy.[24] These points, rather than the eloquent academic recitation of the Scottish kingdom's foundation origins through the travels of Gaythelos Glas, a Greek prince, and his queen, Scota, a daughter of the Pharaoh, may have made some impact on Boniface. But the curia was probably not gripped by the Scots' manipulation of their written histories to obliterate shared kingship with the Picts so as to establish a neat line of 112 kings 'of native stock' that had repelled all foreign invaders.[25] Overall, Boniface seemed to be sufficiently satisfied with Edward I's reply.

Therefore, what actually carried the Pope's favour in the direction of John Balliol's release and the Scots once more was surely the practical fact of his possession of Balliol's person, hence an ability to influence Edward I and to please or frustrate Philip IV.[26] Thus when Balliol was transferred in late summer 1301 from Boniface's care to the bishop of Gevrey near Dijon, he was not freed to rejoin his subjects and titular kingdom, but into French royal control.[27]

On 1 October Kingston again wrote from Edinburgh castle to report the circulating news that 'the King of France's people have taken Sir John Balliol from the place where he was sent to reside by the pope to his castle of Bailleul in Picardy, and some people believe that the King of France will send him with a great force to Scotland as soon as possible'. Edward I had thus certainly been informed of Balliol's secondary release before he settled into winter quarters at Linlithgow in late October–early November 1301 (where he was joined by his queen) after a decidedly mixed campaign since July.[28] It was the coincidence of this Edwardian expedition with Balliol's transfer to France that would now, though, oblige Robert Bruce, earl of Carrick, to break cover and change sides once again.

Bruce's resubmission in 1301–2 may have been, as was that of 1297 (which was never completed), a drawn-out, nervous affair. As late as April 1302 letters were intercepted from Philip IV addressed to Bruce and Comyn as Guardians in the name of King John, a delayed response to earlier missives from the Scots lords delivered by Bishop Lamberton.[29] However, on 16 February 1302, at Roxburgh, Edward I pardoned one Hector Askeloc, 'at the instance of Robert de Bruce Earl of Carrick', for murder, robbery and gaol-break in Cumberland; by the end of April the English king would also have restored some Carrick tenants to their lost English lands.[30] Nicholas Trivet (d.1334), a Dominican writing a history in London in the years after Bannockburn, would assert that Robert in fact submitted about Christmas 1301, to Sir John de St John, English warden of Galloway and Annandale and responsible for troops at Dumfries and Lochmaben.[31] This would fit neatly with Robert's abandonment of Turnberry castle by at least 2 September 1301 to an English host led by the Prince of Wales and the earl of Lincoln. This was quickly followed by an unsuccessful assault on Lochmaben (7–8 September) by Scots led by John

Soules and Ingram d'Umfraville, who also burned Annan. By 3 October 1301 much of this force had shifted west to attempt to recover Turnberry, an effort to which Robert VII and his men may still have contributed, as well as to threaten the English garrison at Ayr.[32] In sum, now homeless and with his family lands harried by both sides, Bruce dispatched entreaties to Edward I.

To do so, Robert may have a kept a force of Carrick men-at-arms in the uplands of his earldom, northern Ayrshire or Lanarkshire, while proposing submission through the 'girth' or sanctuary afforded by the priory of Lesmahagow in Lanarkshire, just over 40 miles west of Linlithgow.[33] This Tironensian house, like Arbroath and Kilwinning a daughter of Kelso Abbey in the Borders, was dedicated to St Machutus, a sixth-century saint of Irish, Welsh or English birth with a cult throughout those realms, western Scotland (as a follower of St Brendan during his exile in the Isles) and even stretching to Normandy (as 'St Malo').[34] Edward I is known to have had at least a passing interest in the feast of Machutus (15 November) with alms payments recorded in 1301 and 1302; in 1296 his troops had also removed a relic (a 'key') of Machutus along with the rest of the Scottish Crown's muniments found in Edinburgh castle. The experienced English king was sensitive to the value of venerating local cults during conquest, hence his alms to St Kentigern's tomb in Glasgow Cathedral in 1301 in thanks for the fall of Turnberry, Ayr and Bothwell castles despite the English forces' lack of supplies and high rates of desertion.[35] Once king, Robert would return to Lesmahagow in March 1316 and pay for eight one-pound candles lit on Sundays and all major festivals around the tomb of Machutus, surely in thanks for succour as early as 1301 or in penitence for his rebroken oath that would follow in 1306.[36]

The truce agreed at Newcastle on 26 January 1302 to last until November that year, allied to the Anglo-French truce of Asnières, was surely the occasion of Bruce's homage (after the collapse of the Scots' siege of Ayr around 23 January).[37] This accompanied attachment of Carrick's seal to an indenture in French under Edward's privy seal, which reveals much of the concerns of both men at this time.[38] On paper Robert recovered the most through this arrangement, although this was surely because his situation was so precarious. In return for renewing his homage, the earl and his men were pardoned and Edward promised to protect Robert's landed inheritance in Scotland and England, not least 'if it should happen by a papal ordinance, or by a truce, or by a conditional peace touching the war against Scotland or the war against France, [that] the aforesaid Robert should be at a disadvantage'. However, Edward also promised to support Bruce in legal pursuit of 'the right' of his family (a conveniently ambivalent phrase but certainly in the main their unnamed claim to the Scottish throne) if it were 'brought into dispute, or reversed, or contradicted in a fresh judgement' in the 'king's court' or 'elsewhere' (surely before the Papacy), and in the event that 'the kingdom of Scotland may be removed from out of the king's hands (which God forbid!) and handed over to Sir John Balliol or to his son'.

This, then, was a mutual insurance policy, if one far more desperate for Carrick in terms of ensuring the survival of his family claim through the decidedly outside chance of papal arbitration to determine the fate of Scottish kingship. By now the latter scenario seemed far less likely than Balliol simply landing in Scotland with French troops. In addition, by 1301 Robert may have been unnerved by favour shown by Edward I to descendants of the third daughter of Earl David of Huntingdon, the claimant of 1291–92, John, now Lord Hastings, and his younger brother Edmund.[39] Robert may have worried about his ability to secure even a reduced third (or half) share of the Scottish realm if Edward decided to back the Hastings as loyal followers in any fresh succession hearings. Admittedly, Robert may have looked upon his deal with King Edward as breakable if unfulfilled. Yet it said nothing about the difficulty presented by his father, Robert VI, still alive, in Edward's peace since 1296 and in possession of the succession claim.[40] Nevertheless, it did afford Carrick some immediate protection by confirming his defection before the terms of the Newcastle truce could be applied (16 February). This was a deadline that would have seen the French take control of Edward's recent conquests in Scotland. Hence the king's commitment to winter in Scotland, and to make substantial improvements to fortifications at such points as Linlithgow and Selkirk, so as to forestall this transfer.[41]

Finally, the indenture of 1301–2 would give Robert and his household relief access through Annan, Blackness, Roxburgh, Berwick and Carlisle to the English supply chain from the south, the Midlands and Ireland, during a cruel winter season in which even the household of the English king and prince struggled to source victuals and fodder for their animals. On 4 March 1302 Carrick was in receipt of supplies with others at Linlithgow and may also have been compensated for the loss of a horse (although this was not generally done during a truce); then on 28 May at Roxburgh he would be issued a Wardrobe imprest for £20.[42] In sum, Robert's decision to submit at this time was perhaps as much a practical, material choice as it was a political one driven by ambition for the crown and factional exclusion.[43]

For Edward I, by contrast, the agreement with Carrick may have been far more pragmatic. It did perhaps reflect the English king's lingering fear

of papal intervention first provoked by *Scimus Fili*; in responding to that
missive in 1300–1 Edward had always worked to safeguard against any
irreversible recognition of the Pope's right to judgment in this matter as 'by
undertaking a suit in this way the king of England would cast doubt on his
right to, and possession of, the realm of Scotland'.[44] However, Carrick's was
not the first high-profile defection from the Scottish cause since the turn
of the century: the Macdougalls had submitted in the face of MacDonald
aggression in 1301, the same year as Alexander Balliol of Cavers, and
Bruce's switch would be followed by those of Sir Alexander de Abernethy
(1302) and Hugh, earl of Ross (1302–3).[45] But as a former Guardian,
Carrick's return was a coup and a potential spanner to throw in the Franco-
papal works, along with Edward I's continued custody of Edward Balliol
(and the Hastings back-up).[46] As it transpired, the English king would
surely have come quickly to view the agreement about the Bruce 'right' as
non-binding once the Balliol threat and Franco-papal pressure collapsed, a
short-term convenience at the very least to ensure England an ally with
local knowledge and troops on the ground to help overcome rebels' military
presence in south-west Scotland. Indeed, Robert could now be reconciled
with his retired father's knights and footmen of Annandale in this role.
This came at a time when Edward's problems of personnel, wages, victuals
and morale were most acute (including a mutiny by the unpaid Berwick
garrison in August 1301).[47] Moreover, the marriage of Robert (twenty-
eight) to Elizabeth de Burgh (thirteen), which took place sometime in
1302 (perhaps at Canterbury), may have been offered, approved or even
arranged by Edward I himself as a further inducement and means to
persuade the heavily indebted and highly reluctant Ulster earl finally to
lead troops to participate (with his new son-in-law) in future expeditions
into Scotland; or at least to help eradicate the Macdougall and MacRuaridh
threat in the Irish Sea and around Dumbarton.[48] Indeed, on 23 February
1302 (perhaps again helping date Robert's submission), negotiations with
Earl Richard and other Irish magnates to provide 500 heavy horse, 1,000
hobelars and 10,000 foot soldiers in Scotland were concluded.[49]

Whatever Edward's strategic thinking, it would take time for trust to be
rebuilt between the king and Robert, a fact reflected in the latter's low-key
status throughout much of 1302–3, whereas by contrast the more consistent
loyalty of Patrick, earl of Dunbar, was rewarded with his appointment as
Edward's keeper of Ayr castle.[50] As with other defectors at this time, Bruce
may have been required to submit hostages (his daughter Marjorie?) or
otherwise seek sureties for his loyalty from his father or other influential
individuals (the earl of Gloucester?).[51] A search of Edward I's Wardrobe

and Treasury rolls at this time reveals no gifts to Carrick comparable to the venison sent to his father in 1291.[52] Some measure of Bruce's sense of anticlimax, disappointment and continued ambivalence immediately after his defection is thus surely revealed in his letter, written on 11 March 1302, apparently while 'troubled in conscience': he promised the border abbey of Melrose, which lay well within Edward's peace, not to call out their tenants on granges in Maybole in Carrick to serve within the retinue of his earldom as he had done in the recent past, 'unless the common army of the whole realm is raised for its defence, when all inhabitants are bound to serve', a scenario that spoke to either Edwardian or independent Scottish control.[53]

### The End of the First Patriotic War, 1302–4

Four months later Carrick must have both cursed and thanked the wheel of fortune. The Pope's plans to call a Church Council in Rome to legislate on the power of kings to tax national churches had provoked Philip IV into burning papal bulls (February 1302) and, for the first time, summoning his nobility, clergy and commons to an Estates-General in Paris (April). Letters were sent by each French estate in support of their king and his authority to tax (as with the 1301 letter of the English nobility to Boniface, a valuable model for Bruce's own regime in 1309 and 1320).[54] Yet before the Pope could reply, Philip suffered a knock-down blow. On 11 July 1302 a Flemish force of roughly 9,000 rebel townsmen with spears and 400 nobles wiped out a battle-hardened army of 2,500 French knights and over 5,000 infantry and archers under Robert, count of Artois, at Courtrai. The sequel for the Scots unfolded in sickening slow motion.[55]

Philip was now no longer concerned to aid the Scots and sought peace with Edward I; at no point did the French king even seem to have considered releasing Balliol just to see what time the Scots might buy him. Peace would be agreed in principle at Amiens on 2 December 1302, by which time a defiant Boniface had also issued a bull, *Unam Sanctam*, asserting papal power over spiritual and temporal affairs and thus over any king.[56] Full ratification of the Anglo-French peace would follow in Paris on 20 May 1303, by which time it was agreed that Edward of Caernarfon should marry Philip's daughter, Isabella. These last agreements were observed by a forlorn Scottish super-embassy sent out in October 1302, desperate to see Scotland written in as a sovereign ally of France: the delegation included Guardian Soules, Bishops Lamberton and Crambeth, the earl of Buchan, James Steward and Ingram d'Umfraville.[57] That the patriots still had hope of turning the situation to their advantage is suggested by a further report to Edward I sometime in late 1302 that 'the bishop of St Andrews is showing the people a letter under the king of France's seal ... asserting that there will be no peace between him and the king of England unless the Scots are included. The people are putting their faith in this and in the success which they hope will be obtained by Master Baldred [Bisset], their spokesman at the court of Rome.'[58] However, by the end of the year, Boniface, too, freed from Philip's control, had turned on the Scots, ordering Bishop Wishart and others to submit. As late as 25 May 1303, Lamberton's correspondence would still express hope that a supplementary treaty promised by Philip would include the Scots; but he also began to prepare Scottish knights such as Comyn of Badenoch, William Wallace and Simon Fraser for a hard, uphill fight.[59]

With no prospect of John Balliol's return and many key Scots trapped in France, Edward I was free to concentrate on the reconquest of Scotland. This threw Bruce of Carrick into service in the English army which would overwhelm the realm and subjects he had until recently fought to defend. In the long term 1302–04 would provide Robert with invaluable experience of the English military machine, both its strengths and weaknesses of logistics, tactics, equipment and personnel.[60] Yet, more immediately, Carrick's submission and participation in the English host and occupation settlement of these years would confirm many Scottish lords as his bitter enemies. Right at the outset, for example, Bruce was on the wrong side (but not present) when Comyn of Badenoch and Simon Fraser achieved a notable skirmish victory at Roslin in Midlothian on 24 February 1303.[61]

At Michaelmas 1302 Carrick had reportedly attended a full parliament at Westminster (of which no record of proceedings survives) and would have been privy to preparations for Edward's 1303 campaign.[62] It must have been sometime in the first half of 1303 that Robert hosted an 'inception' graduation feast for his gifted brother, Alexander, at Cambridge University.[63] Sometime in 1302–3 Robert may also have paid for two rings to be placed upon the high altar of St Thomas in Canterbury Cathedral, perhaps in search of Becket's blessing of his marriage to Elizabeth de Burgh.[64] Then in April 1303 Robert was ordered to bring 1,000 foot and 'all the [mounted] men-at-arms he can' from Carrick and Galloway, plus another 1,000 from Kyle, Cunningham and Cumnock (lands of the sheriffdom of Ayr), to the muster at Roxburgh on 12 May.[65] The retinue he turned out with was surely smaller than this figure, part of a reduced English host numbering approximately 7,500 men. It is possible that initially Carrick and his following joined the divisions of Edward of Caernarfon, now aged nineteen, in whose household Robert's brother, Edward Bruce, also served.[66] Yet this would still have seen Carrick serve within the orbit of the English king as his host advanced north from 25 May, via Edinburgh and Stirling, crossing the Forth with prefabricated pontoon bridges and naval support, passing on to Perth, Scone, Arbroath and the scene of triumph over Balliol (in 1296), Stracathro, before besieging Brechin castle until it fell on 9 August 1303. Edward I then made his most northerly advance yet into Scotland via Aberdeen, Banff and Elgin to the Cistercian abbey of Kinloss in Moray by 13 September, wheeling south into the Comyn heartlands to touch at Lochindorb castle. As Edward took submissions his forces stretched out to take Inverness, Urquhart and Cromarty. Thereafter the English king returned south via Kildrummy castle, Dundee, Scone and Perth.[67]

As a participant in this ill-supplied eastern march, devoid of real confrontation, Bruce was absent from more sustained conflict in the south and west until July–August 1303. The Scots in Selkirk forest under Comyn, Fraser, Wallace and others had taken Selkirk tower (January), attempted Linlithgow (February) and turned their attention in late summer to harassing garrisons at Dumfries, Lochmaben, Roxburgh and even Dumbarton, and raiding into Cumberland.[68] In reply, King Edward in July ordered a contingent of his host, including Bruce, to join Aymer de Valence, lieutenant south of Forth, to push west to meet up with an Irish force 4,000 strong under the Ulster earl (whose debts of £16,000 Edward had agreed to remit). This combined force was poorly victualled but persistent in its assault on Stewart lands in Clydesdale, taking Inverkip and Rothesay by early September.[69] It was to this success that Bruce owed his first appointment to office after his defection, emerging as sheriff of Lanarkshire and constable of Ayr castle by December 1303 and January 1304 respectively (although he may have appointed deputies on the ground); he also advised on other appointments in the west.[70] By 1305, moreover, Bruce would have been granted responsibility for the former Scottish Crown forests of Darnaway and Langmorn (both Moray) and Kintore (Aberdeenshire), as well as wardship of his young nephew, Donald, earl of Mar (with control of his remodelled caput castle of Kildrummy).[71] By early 1304 the Guardianship's resistance had started to collapse. As early as 26 September 1303 Edward and his officials were in negotiations with the 'great lords of Scotland' about surrender terms as well as beginning the practical work of once more supplanting Scottish local government.[72] Yet none of this should be taken as firm proof that Carrick now had Edward's full trust.

As in 1296, Robert may have been profoundly impressed by Edward's stays throughout 1303 at sites of political, military and spiritual significance in the Scottish realm. Bruce must have been especially struck by the powerful symbolism of King Edward and a high-powered court wintering at Dunfermline Abbey, from 5 November 1303 to 4 March 1304.[73] According to the records of his son's royal government, Edward I may have sought to use his long stay at the abbey to encourage further Scottish submissions, for he 'ordained at Dunfermline that no man of Scotland would be disinherited, nor would any woman of Scotland lose her dower, by coming into the king's peace'.[74] A considerable amount of royal business was conducted during these weeks from monastic buildings adjacent to the mausoleum of Scotland's monarchy.[75] Edward was resident there for St Margaret's feast day (16 November) and Christmas, and both he and his son gifted gold jewellery to her shrine; the king may also have removed a further Dunfermline relic at this time (listed without detail in the inventory of the household upon Edward's death at Burgh-by-Sands in 1307).[76] In addition, the king entertained a number of significant individuals at Dunfermline, as did his son resident at Perth.[77] Amongst these courtiers we find listed: the English earls of Gloucester, Hereford, Warwick and Lancaster; key officials like Aymer de Valence, John de Brittany and John de St John; Scots loyal to Edward since 1296 or 1298 such as the earls of Atholl and Strathearn and Sir Richard Siward; and others, either longer-term captives or individuals who had submitted only recently such as the earl of Ross, Robert Keith, Alexander Abernethy and Reginald Cheyne. Throughout January–February 1304 a number of these men would participate in talks in and around Perth with Guardian John Comyn of Badenoch and his 'council'.[78]

Bruce of Carrick, however, does not seem to have been invited to top table at Dunfermline or Perth (although his father, then in Scotland, may have been).[79] In truth Carrick may have had very limited access to this circle. On his penultimate day at Dunfermline Edward I would write to 'his loyal and faithful Robert de Brus earl of Carrick, Sir John de Segrave and their company', applauding their actions in making a 'foray on the enemy' in the Lothians and Borders forest, routing a force led by Wallace and Simon Fraser near Peebles: Edward encouraged them to pursue the rebels to finish the job – 'as the cloak is well made, also make the hood'.[80] Yet Bruce would surely have been concerned to learn that while he served on the margins of Edward's trust, John Comyn had submitted on 9 February at Strathord in Perthshire (a lordship of the earls of Fife) and then dined on fish and good 'king's wine' with the Prince of Wales at Perth on 22 February 1304, a year since his victory at Roslin (and presumably also with the king at Dunfermline a few days later).[81]

## The Bruce Inheritance, 1304–6

John Comyn had fought long and hard against Edward I since 1296 (and had not seen his de Valence wife and children since 1298); he did a remarkable job in securing terms for the Scots' submission in 1304.[82] We can detail Comyn's initial demands from fragmentary records, written in French, indicating that these upheld the principles of the community of the realm and of consultative Guardianship through regular parliaments, established since 1286.[83] Comyn sought Edward's guarantee that there would be no forfeitures or ransoming of Scottish subjects and that the king would restore them to 'all their laws, usages, customs and liberties in every particular as they existed in the time of Alexander III'; this was to include representative assembly should there be 'laws to be amended, in which case it should be done with the advise of King Edward and the advice and assent of the responsible men of the land'.[84]

However, Edward I was very much in command, and the surviving evidence for Comyn's submission talks provides no practical detail about how the Scottish realm and its magnate liberties were to be affected by the English Crown's taxation, parliamentary and military summons, or legal and ecclesiastical jurisdiction. As events over the next two years make plain, Edward felt perfectly able to summon Scots to Westminster parliaments. In the end, Comyn and other leading Scottish magnates had to accept periods of exile and hefty fines to redeem their Scottish lands: Bishop Wishart (exiled from Scotland for three years), James Steward (forced to appeal to the courts to recover his lands in 1305), John Soules (who preferred to remain in France) and Ingram d'Umfraville (charged for five years' relief) were particularly hard hit.[85] Yet the Scots must have been aware of the English regime's financial woes and the general unpopularity of the war against Scotland, a feeling now heightened by the confirmation that there would be no landed rewards in that conquered realm for English lords.[86] More importantly, although Edward I would have his revenge in different ways, even these terms allowed Comyn (and others) to begin stabilising and repositioning the Scottish community of the realm, either for a later revival of resistance, perhaps even one led by Comyn as king as the Balliols' male heir presumptive, or for Edward's acceptance of a largely Comyn-led Scottish administration with its limited central government intact on his behalf as lord superior.

That this is how Robert of Carrick may have begun to interpret matters from early 1304 is revealed by his behaviour while Edward I and his court performed a brutal demonstration of authority in besieging the exhausted garrison of Stirling castle in May, June and July.[87] As in 1295–96, the first half of 1304 proved an extremely challenging time for Carrick both personally and politically. He was perhaps affected by further feelings of regret as Edward once more manhandled the Scottish realm most cruelly. Moreover, although Bruce's aristocratic holdings would reach their greatest extent by the end of the year as the head of his kin, he must have been faced with grave material problems within individual elements of his lordship.[88]

The earl of Carrick was undoubtedly present at a Lenten parliament summoned by the English king to St Andrews from 9 March 1304, at which the Scots' terms of submission were probably confirmed and a large number of homages, perhaps on the relics of the Apostle, were performed by men of Perthshire, Angus and Fife.[89] It must have been clear long before then that the English king was going to honour their agreement of late 1301–early 1302 to protect Bruce's 'right' only in so far as this pertained to his existing family titles. However, Carrick's service at Stirling – with Edward thanking him by letter on 16 April for 'sending his engines' – was interrupted by the death of his father, Robert VI of Annandale, sometime between Easter (29 March) and 21 April while en route to Scotland; he was interred in the Cistercian abbey of Holm Cultram in Cumberland. Bruce's next few weeks were taken up with travel and inquests into his father's English lands and goods.[90]

As we have seen, like many nobles of the day, the income and tenants of the lands of Bruce father and son had suffered throughout a decade of climatic fluctuation and recurrent harvest failure (1293–95, 1297). The demands of war on victuals, animals, timber and men had taken their toll, as had six successive years of Edwardian taxation and ecclesiastical tenths. Just after his inheritance, Robert VII would report to the English Crown that he could neither borrow cash nor raise 'a penny of his rents' from Writtle and Hatfield (Essex) to pay for horses and armour.[91] Carrick may thus have found the annual value of his English inheritance reduced by as much as a third (and his tenantry by about 10 per cent), a magnate experience broadly replicated across the southern realm (despite some inflation of income by high grain prices).[92] He would pay less in inheritance tax ('entry') as a result but still appeal for relief from his father's debt of £518 at Edward's grace.[93] The earl may also have petitioned for Ingram d'Umfraville's lands in Carrick in April 1305 in search of further resources.[94]

Worse, by 1 August 1304 Robert of Carrick would also face a necessary inquest by English officials into his father's lordship of Annandale. The intensity of the fighting across the Scottish Borders and south-west inevitably meant these estates were even more injured and depleted, damage that might take seasons to repair.[95] In addition, Edward exploited this opportunity to scrutinise the exemptions of the lords of Annandale from the jurisdiction of royal officers (mainly the sheriff of Dumfries): as late as November 1305 Carrick would appeal to Edward for a favourable conclusion to this inquiry into his authority to collect judicial income from these holdings under terms of regality.[96] In addition, Robert's likely attempts to stabilise the yield from all his Scottish lands throughout 1304–5 (including the wardship of the earldom of Mar) may have formed part of wider landowning strategies that would in turn provoke the 'husbandmen' of the Scottish community of the realm, tenants on demesne of the Scottish Crown, to appeal to Edward I in March 1305 for England's common laws about security of tenure for their class to be extended to the northern realm.[97] Real uncertainties over lordship may thus have added to Robert's motives for contemplating rebellion once again.

Edward I had learned lessons from 1296–97 and surely kept a close eye on Carrick for signs of backsliding.[98] He certainly kept longer-term rebels under surveillance. Comyn and the knights Alexander Lindsay, David Graham and Simon Fraser were bound over to hunt down William Wallace 'and hand him over to the king, who will watch to see how each of them conducts themselves'.[99] Yet for all these strictures Edward seems to have been completely unaware of a secret meeting and agreement between Carrick and Bishop Lamberton of St Andrews, whose cathedral had been the scene of the conquerors' recent parliament.

The pair had the nerve to meet on 4 June 1304 at the Augustinian abbey of Cambuskenneth, yards from the English bombardment of Stirling castle, to which Robert had returned to perform homage for Annandale, Writtle and Hatfield Regis. As with the earl's indenture of 1301–2 with King Edward himself (and the 'Turnberry Band' of 1286), the terms which Carrick and Lamberton concluded were deliberately vague, perhaps to permit deniability if seized (the text survives only through charges brought against the bishop by Edward's officials in August 1306).[100] On pain of a crippling fine of £10,000 towards the cost of crusade, the earl and bishop promised to support each other against all men and to consult one another before undertaking any 'major enterprise'. It is very tempting in the light of subsequent events to interpret this commitment by both men to avoid 'future perils', 'resist prudently attacks by rivals' and warn each other 'of danger and try to obviate it' as measures set in place not merely to pave the way towards kingship for Bruce, but to guard against any rival challenge posed by John Comyn of Badenoch and other Balliol–Comyn adherents.

In that sense, even before the final stronghold fell – as Stirling under Sir William Oliphant's command would hold out 'of the Lion' until 20 July – Carrick was casting about for support for a plan to revive the Scottish kingship in situ and, crucially, before he could be beaten to the punch by John Comyn, a man with a far more inspiring military and political record (as well as 'royal' Balliol blood).[101]

To do so, Robert of Carrick had gone right to the top, drawing on sympathies first shaped during the Guardianships of 1297–99, and persuaded Lamberton, the Scots' past Chief-Guardian and leading envoy to Paris and Rome, to back or at least consider his cause. For his part, the bishop may have been persuaded, too, of the possibility of reviving sympathy for the Scottish kingdom in Rome where, following Boniface VIII's death at Anagni in October 1303 (after he had been seized and beaten by troops of Philip IV), a new pontiff, Benedict XI, was at least making independent noises (although he, too, would die, in July 1304, heralding a year of papal interregnum until the election of the Frenchman, Clement V, in June 1305).[102] As far as who had the best legal claim to the Scottish throne in law – Comyn or Bruce – Lamberton may now have been more inclined to transcend this problem given that Edward Balliol remained in England. In doing so, the bishop was perhaps influenced by one of his former tutors – if before 1292 Lamberton had followed so many Scots into the 'English nation' at the University of Paris – namely the Scottish teacher and philosopher John Duns Scotus (c.1266–1308): in Scotus's lectures and writings of the early fourteenth century, indeed, Scotland's leading prelate could find reassuring justification of a people's right (through their responsible leaders) to choose their own worthy king, even removing an incumbent who had not fulfilled their expected duties (just as an incompetent prelate or Pope might be deposed).[103] This chimed in more generally with growing ecclesiastical sympathies for conciliar control of aspects of papal monarchy.[104] Lamberton may thus have been fully prepared to apply this rationale to find King John's successor after 1304, displaying decisiveness hitherto denied him by the circumstances of 1298–1303. Lamberton's deal with Bruce did not preclude reaching a similar understanding with Comyn: whichever lord emerged as strongest would be acclaimed king. More immediately, though, the 'Cambuskenneth Bond' was concluded at a time when former Guardians William Wallace and John Soules were still at large, and other key men – Buchan, Atholl, Mar, Ross, Strathearn, Fraser and Bishops Wishart, Crambeth and David de Moravia – were drifting back to some freedom of action in Scotland and might be persuaded to act: several of them also found a place in the interim English administration (February 1304–September 1305).[105]

Robert of Carrick may have concluded similar bonds with other significant, sympathetic Scottish leaders at this time, certainly with his old allies Bishop Wishart and James Steward, as well as perhaps one of his grandfather's auditors of 1291, John Soules. By 1306 Robert's brother Alexander would be dean of Glasgow, a position also owing something to the favour of Edward I.[106] Both Wishart and Carrick may have made considerable lobbying efforts to ensure their participation in Edward's process of settling Scotland's governance throughout 1304–5, as would the Comyn camp. Nevertheless, whatever Bruce's plans, it says a great deal about the relative levels of support for Carrick and Comyn, and the effectiveness of Edward's settlement throughout southern Scotland in sustaining the peace, that almost two years would pass before rebellion re-erupted: even then it would be premature, poorly supported and explosively divisive.

Throughout the rest of 1304 Carrick's duties in Lanarkshire and Ayrshire were combined with the final settlement of his inheritance and his father's debts. On 9 November he was at York to confirm his family's gift of Lochmaben lands to the church of St Peter's in York.[107] Then at some point throughout the winter of 1304–5 he was chosen – either by the English king, his officials or an unrecorded Scottish parliament – to attend the Westminster parliament of February–March 1305 and, with Wishart and Sir John Mowbray, to advise Edward I on the governance (*stabilimentum*) of Scotland.[108]

This assembly remains the best-documented gathering of king, Lords and Commons of Edward I's reign and may have informed some of Robert's later strategies for holding parliament in Scotland.[109] As at his last English parliament in October 1302, Bruce may have had a chance to view the newly painted chambers of Westminster palace – with images of Edward's ancestors and his commissioned murals of the life of Judas Maccabeus, liberator of his people – as well as to view the Stone of Destiny under the new coronation chair in the adjacent abbey during Easter worship (18 April).[110] The parliament itself was a full-scale affair of king, 9 earls, 94 barons, 74 knights of the shire, 200 burgesses and freeholders, and enough prelates and lower clergy to bring the total in attendance to over 600 MPs (although King Edward was absent from the opening sessions). Yet after initial discussions the majority were dismissed and matters dealt with in committee.[111] It is likely that at this time Carrick and others confirmed for themselves news that Edward I, now in his sixty-third year, was in variable health and an end to his reign was perhaps in sight. Thus men's actions were governed by some anticipation of the accession of a less intimidating

Prince of Wales as Edward II.[112] Nonetheless, parliament still very much reflected the authority of the old king. The select committee processed over 300 appeals from England, Gascony, Ireland and Wales as well as almost 200 petitions from churches, burghs and individuals of Scotland.[113] It also passed statutes about forest perambulation and itinerant 'trailbaston' commissions to reassert local law and order in the English realm. In many ways, these acts represented Edward's further canny diffusion of issues lingering from the English political crisis of 1297 and, to a lesser extent, 1300: by December 1305 the king would have persuaded Pope Clement to release him from oaths he had sworn to parliament in those years.[114]

However, although Wishart, Carrick and Mowbray were perhaps present at this parliament throughout, their role was limited to a separate 'committee on Scottish affairs'.[115] It should be noted that these sessions gave Bruce his first sustained experience (other than c.1293), beyond his own local lordship, of the give-and-take or petition-and-redress dynamic of subjects' petitions to representative assembly and royal government on a wide range of issues. In 1305 this included requests from a dozen or more Scottish monastic houses and at least three bishops seeking to recover lands and resources on both sides of the border, most often seeking physical replacement of destroyed or lost charters and grants of timber from Scottish royal forests to effect church repairs.[116] The burgesses of Perth also sought redress from predation by their rivals on the Tay in Dundee; the 'poor people' of Roxburgh appealed, deprived of their goods by English prise; the 'community of Galloway' objected to alien laws and exactions; all the (royal) burgesses of Scotland sought confirmation of their rights as established by David I; and there was the remarkable petition from the 'king's husbandmen in Scotland' – freeholders on Scottish royal demesne – for the right to longer periods of landed tenure 'in the manner in which the king's villeins do in England, so that they are not moved every year as they are at present'.[117] The latter may reflect a level of popular protest and organised agitation hitherto unnoticed in late medieval Scotland, a symptom of the socio-economic upheaval of climatic deterioration and seigneurial strategies of response. However, Robert Bruce may have been struck most of all by the large number of petitions from individuals, ranging from the rank of earl to farmer, ferryman or widow, but which seemed to be very much dominated by former patriot lords who had fought for Balliol before 1304. These were headed by John Comyn, earl of Buchan (eight petitions); Hugh, earl of Ross, and his son William, John Mowbray, Alexander Abernethy, Reginald Cheyne, Alexander Balliol of Cavers, William Bisset of Upsetlington, and Gallovidians Donald McCan and Dougal Macdowall (although there were also appeals from Malcolm, earl of Lennox, Sir Gilbert Hay and the dowager countess of Fife).[118]

Frustratingly, no record of the outcome of most of these petitions survives and it is difficult to detect whether Edward I's responses in parliament had any effect upon Robert I's own rule. Besides, the main focus for Carrick, Wishart and Mowbray remained to facilitate Edward's moves towards a statutory settlement for Scotland. On 26 March 1305 Bruce and company spoke the language of community (perhaps following Wishart's lead) in response to Edward's request for advice on when, where and how the Scots should choose their representatives for the next Westminster parliament. The date and venue of a Scottish parliament should be at Edward's pleasure, they replied, but that body could hardly meet before midsummer and should choose ten men, two from each of the bishops, abbots, earls and barons of Scotland along with 'two on behalf of the community', one each from north and south of Forth (and the community should pay their expenses). Edward agreed, setting a mid-July date for a Westminster assembly to discuss Scottish governance.[119]

The extant evidence suggests that a Scottish parliament was ordered to meet about 28 May 1305 at Perth (or Scone).[120] It is tempting to interpret the selection of the ten Scottish representatives as a collective decision of the 'community of the land', which may have deliberately excluded both Wishart and Robert of Carrick, either at the behest of Edward through his officials or by the will of a majority of the Scottish community there assembled, influenced by the Comyns of Badenoch and Buchan and their allies. Yet in truth, Carrick may have been content to remain behind and attend to his affairs, with Bishop Lamberton elected to attend (and sympathetic to Bruce) along with Bishop Crambeth, the abbots of Melrose and Coupar-Angus, the earls of Buchan and Dunbar, and knights John Mowbray (again), Robert Keith, Adam Gordon and John of Inchmartin. Carrick might expect to participate in future delegations, particularly once English plans to review and codify Scottish law – the 'laws of King David I' and thus customary law pertaining to bloodfeud – reached committee and legislative stages. Indeed, the initial discussions and working materials of this Edwardian legal review may have had a direct impact upon law codification, which would be undertaken during Robert I's mature reign (and which took forward compilations of law begun during the reign of Alexander II and III).[121]

However, in 1305 the possibility of the earl of Carrick once more being marginalised by a re-emerging affinity that constituted a majority of the community is further suggested by the lists of officers selected to serve

under John of Brittany as Edward's Lieutenant of Scotland.[122] The minds
of the Scottish delegates who attended the delayed Westminster parliament from 15 September 1305 must have been concentrated on their task
while they waited by witnessing, or at least hearing of, the ghastly ceremonial execution of William Wallace on 23 August. The former Guardian was
found guilty of breaking his fealty, taking up arms and forming alliances
against Edward I, and of committing numerous wartime atrocities, actions
of which in fact eight of the Scottish parliamentary delegates were just as
guilty (more so, indeed, as they had actually submitted in 1296). Yet only
Wallace would be hung, drawn, disembowelled and beheaded, his body
quartered and dispatched for display in Newcastle, Berwick, Perth and
Aberdeen.[123]

Significantly, Wallace's captor, Sir John Menteith of Knapdale and
Arran – son of Walter (Stewart), earl of Menteith (d.1294), the Bruce
Competitor's ally – sheriff and keeper of Dumbarton castle since 1298, was
replaced by the earl of Dunbar as a Westminster delegate.[124] Menteith
would retain his office, unlike Bruce who now appears to have been substi-
tuted as sheriff of both Lanark and Ayr by Sir Henry Sinclair and
Sir Godfrey de Ros, two close Comyn councillors c.1286–1304. It is true
that there was similarly no such high office for Comyn of Buchan or
Badenoch as a sheriff or one of the four named pairs of regional justiciars.
Moreover, in Ayrshire and Lanarkshire, as elsewhere, the new appointees
may have been obliged to rely on experienced local men to fulfil their office,
such as Robert Boyd of Kilmarnock (who served as coroner for both shires
in 1305–6) and Walter Logan of Hartside.[125] Nonetheless, a significant
number of those who were now to hold sheriffships were drawn, like their
local staff, from the extended Comyn affinity.[126] Furthermore, this bias was
certainly true of the twenty Scottish magnates named to an advisory
committee for the Lieutenant: Carrick and Bishops Lamberton and
Crambeth were so enlisted but were to serve alongside the earls of Buchan,
Dunbar, Atholl and Ross, Comyn of Badenoch, John Mowbray, Alexander
Macdougall of Argyll, Robert Keith, Duncan of Frendraught, John
Menteith, Adam Gordon and John of Inchmartin.[127] Thus the 'Ordinance
for the good order of Scotland' agreed at Westminster in September 1305
also seems to have set the community down the path to the restoration of
the pre-1286 or pre-1296 status quo.

This process was also shaped by lobbying in Scotland for the settlement
of local disputes. The Westminster committee stated that 'for removing
from Scotland those by whom the peace might be disturbed, it is ordained

that the king's lieutenant ... shall take counsel and advice on this from the good people of the realm' and send such people to Edward I. Tellingly, this was followed by several specific citations about individuals, including stipulation that 'the earl of Carrick be ordered to put the castle of Kildrummy in the keeping of a man for whom he himself is willing to answer'.[128] This may point to regional opposition to Bruce's lordship in Garioch and his wardship of the minority of his and his first wife's nephew, Donald, earl of Mar, supported in this quarter by such lords as John, earl of Atholl and lord of Strathbogie and Strath'an (Strathavon), Sir Alexander Lindsay, Patrick of Skene, the Frasers of Philorth and Hamelins of Troup. If so, immediate neighbours in the north-east were surely the source of complaint: the Comyns, Alexander Abernethy, Gilbert of Glencarnie, the Cheynes of Duffus (including Bishop Henry of Aberdeen) and Duncan of Frendraught (who was perhaps still sheriff of Banff), along with Scots loyal to Edward I in that region, including the Bissets of Aboyne (with Sir Walter appointed sheriff of Stirling) and Norman Leslie (who became sheriff of Aberdeen); indeed, it may have been at the insistence of the latter that (in the very ordinance clause before that dealing with Kildrummy) Alexander Lindsay – who had rebelled with and then guaranteed the submission of Carrick in 1297 – was ordered into exile south of Trent for six months.[129]

Such evidence for local politics might be used to describe a situation in which, while they waited for the old king to die, both Comyn and Bruce jockeyed for position and support within the framework of the fledgling English occupation administration. Edward's apparently recovered health (with another pregnancy for his queen through the winter of 1305–6) may have frustrated them in one regard, but the Scots can only have been encouraged to manoeuvre by the temporary appointment of Bishop Lamberton, Sir Robert Keith and an English captain, Sir John Kingston, to act in place of the Lieutenant, who remained delayed in the south.[130] The only surviving Bruce charter from about this time suggests as much. Carrick's grant of lands at Longforgan in eastern Perthshire (adjacent to lands held by Sir Edmund Hastings) to Sir Alexander Keith was witnessed by men ranging across the affinities of Carrick/Annandale and James Steward: Steward's son-in-law Sir Alexander Menzies of Weem (Strathtay, Perthshire), Walter Logan of Hartside (former sheriff of Lanark), Reginald Crawford (former sheriff of Ayr), Boyd of Kilmarnock (coroner of Lanark and Ayr), Patrick of Skene, Peter of Graden (Roxburghshire) and a Robert of Annan.[131]

### Murder at Dumfries, 1306

A similar context of ambition for the crown played out in local tensions may lie at the root of Robert's fatal encounter with Comyn of Badenoch on 10 February 1306. This was a date perhaps dictated by a desire for resolution before Edward's new Lieutenant could act.[132] The ordinance had appointed Sir Richard Siward as sheriff of Dumfries. A cousin of Sir John de St John (Edward I's past warden of Galloway and Annandale) and loyal to the English regime since 1297 (while his son was a hostage), Siward held a remodelled Tibbers castle and was responsible for raising men from Nithsdale (running north from Dumfries); but he was otherwise a Comyn adherent and his office (as had that of his predecessor) may have created difficulties for Bruce's lordship in Annandale.[133] This lends weight to the account of Comyn's murder by Walter of Guisborough (at the priory founded by the Bruces of Annandale) that John of Badenoch 'had denounced him [Bruce] to the king of England and worsened his position to his harm'.[134] According to Guisborough, Carrick, travelling from Lochmaben, expected to overturn this situation through a private interview with Comyn (coming in from Dalswinton, east of southern Nithsdale) at the Greyfriars in Dumfries, while the justiciars of Galloway (and presumably Siward) were in session in Dumfries castle. The choice of this occasion may have been due to the fact that the appointee as the Scottish half of this regional justiciary had been Sir Roger Kirkpatrick: later Scottish accounts would name Kirkpatrick as present at the friary in Carrick's retinue aiding in Comyn's final dispatch.[135]

Given their history of violence at Peebles in August 1299, it is perhaps inevitable that matters should come to blows between Robert of Carrick and John Comyn; hence the decision to meet in a church in an attempt to avert such an outcome, only for all involved to come armed.[136] Similarly, it is unthinkable – given the ambition of these men and Edward I's age – that this confrontation would not turn into an argument over the Scottish kingship. Carrick's seizure of the throne six weeks later certainly drew contemporary and near contemporary English accounts to focus upon Bruce's desire to be king. A recent forensic analysis of the killing has shown how the official Edwardian account focused from April 1306 on the Scottish throne as Bruce's motive. But it is the early account of the *Flores Historiarum*, written at Westminster shortly after 1306, that arguably provides the most credible version of events. According to this source Carrick had been 'first secretly and then openly' gathering support from Scottish magnates for his bid for the throne, promising to wage war to recover Scotland if they will 'crown' him: when approached at Dumfries, Comyn had 'firmly replied no . . . so he [Carrick] slaughtered him' in an act of sacrilegious murder.[137]

Subsequent English accounts would embellish this narrative, stressing Comyn's loyalty to Edward I above all, his martyr's death and Carrick's immediate move on the throne. Writing c.1307–12, Walter of Guisborough or his continuators hinted that Bruce had premeditated the killing, sending two of his brothers – Thomas and Neil – to fetch Comyn to Dumfries, only for Carrick to accuse him of treachery and strike him with 'foot and sword', leaving him for his followers, including his brother-in-law, Sir Christopher Seton, to finish off along with Comyn's uncle, Robert. Merging this and earlier accounts in French verse by c.1322, Pierre Langtoft would escalate Carrick's search for support into a full-blown Scottish parliament on 9 December 1305 (for which there is no evidence at all) with an emergency interview afterwards in Dumfries where Comyn refused to break his oath to Edward and was stabbed by Bruce. Bruce's followers slew the wounded lord at the altar and hunted down his retinue.[138]

By the time Sir Thomas Gray came to record his father's (at times muddled and conflated) memories of that period, both English and Scottish accounts of the murder had taken on the romance of lay fireside tales as well as political bias.[139] In Gray's version Thomas and Neil Bruce had been sent on 29 January 1306 to fetch Comyn but to assassinate him en route on the orders of Carrick who at that time 'maintained a force of men of his blood and of his allegiance, hoping always for the establishment of his right to his claim to the succession to the realm of Scotland'. Unable to kill the amiable and unsuspecting Comyn, however, the brothers conducted him to the Greyfriars where Carrick proposed:

Sir . . . this land of Scotland is wholly subjected, put in servitude to the English through the negligence of its leader [John Balliol], who allowed his rights and the freedom of the realm to be lost. Choose one of two ways: either take my inheritance, or help me to be king; or grant me yours, if I will help you to be the same since you are of his blood who has lost the realm, while I hope for it in succession to my forebears who claimed the right to have it, and who were obstructed by yours. For now is the time, in the dotage of this English king.[140]

Comyn again refused to breach his oath to Edward I, so Bruce and company removed him from their path with lethal force (with Comyn's uncle, Robert, striking the armoured Bruce ineffectually with his sword).

Gray was a prisoner in Edinburgh castle c.1355–58, in contact with veterans of Robert I's reign and their descendants as well as able to consult Scottish written accounts including perhaps a *vita* of Robert I subsequently lost.[141] It is thus of note that Gray's reconstruction also includes Carrick's proposal that one take both men's noble lands while helping the other to become king. By the 1350s this explanation for the killing of Comyn in 'hot blood' may also have been extant in the account of events c.1285–1363 by the anonymous St Andrews annalist whom Fordun would gloss c.1383 for his *Chronica Gentis Scotorum*; this would in turn be embellished by later medieval continuators like Abbot Walter Bower, who also had access to another anonymous St Andrews source for c.1285–c.1330 (that perhaps by William Comyn of St Mary of the Rock).[142]

This surely explains the ambivalence of some of the detail left in the accounts of Fordun and his continuators at a time when we might expect Scottish explanations of Comyn's death to whitewash Bruce. Fordun's possibly much reworked annals certainly present Bruce's actions as those of a God-given saviour but still describe his attempt at offering a 'covenant' to Comyn, 'guaranteed by means of sworn pledges, and by their indentures with their seals attached thereto': thereby the two agreed that in return for Bruce lands Comyn would support Carrick's elevation as king to free the realm from servitude.[143] This was probably the account consulted by Gray. However, although Comyn is described as 'then the most powerful man in the country', he took steps to betray this league to Edward I who began to plot Robert's death. Tipped off by the friendship of the earl of Gloucester, who sent him the warning of a pair of spurs, Robert took the sign to flee to Scotland via Carlisle, killing a messenger from Comyn to Edward bearing further proof of their deal. Thus in this Scottish account Carrick simply confronts Comyn in the Greyfriars about his treachery: 'the lie is at once given. The evil-speaker is stabbed', wounded and later dispatched at the altar by parties unnamed.[144]

Archdeacon John Barbour's great poem of the 1370s, *The Bruce*, also drawing on lost accounts commissioned during Robert I's reign, contains a similar narrative but crucially this time it is Comyn who raises the idea of one lord supporting the other, kingship for lands, and Bruce who agrees to be elevated to the throne 'Sen ye will it be swa': and thus 'writyn war/Thair endentris, and ayhtis maid', only for Comyn to betray these documents to King Edward as 'thocht he [Comyn] to have the leding/Off all Scotland but gane-saying/Fra at the Bruce to ded war brocht'.[145] Robert escaped from London and hastened to confront Comyn at the Greyfriars and 'ryhct in that sted hym reft te lyff' along with many others, a justified act of vengence.[146]

In the 1440s, a period of royal minority and factional strife within Scotland, Abbot Bower drew on all previous Scottish accounts to emphasise killing Comyn as the first God-given act of Robert's rise to the throne, 'like a second Maccabeus adopting forceful measures in order to free his fellow-countrymen'.[147] Riding together from Stirling in 1304, it is again Carrick (with Bower here following Fordun's Latin annals) who proposes that Comyn choose whether to take the 'royal honours' for himself and give Bruce his lands, or to support Bruce as king in return for Carrick and Annandale. Comyn agreed to the latter and indentures were drawn up. However, John the Red (named for the red heraldry that distinguished his branch of the Comyn family from the 'Black' line of Buchan) then reneged, acting to remove Bruce from his path to power over the realm, betraying their agreement to Edward I from whom Bruce escaped with Gloucester's help. However, Bower then acknowledges alternative accounts 'found elsewhere' which assert that Comyn offered the throne–land trade off then committed the same betrayal.[148] Either way, the confrontation in the Greyfriars follows Bruce's decision to 'pay him back' as the act of a man driven 'beyond endurance and beside himself' with rage.[149]

All these accounts have their layers of representation. Nevertheless, the possibility of some form of written accord between Carrick and Comyn should not be dismissed as 'so improbable as to be ludicrous'.[150] It may first have been mooted during Bishop Lamberton's period as chief Guardian over Comyn and Carrick c.1299–1300. The two young nobles surely had cause to communicate about such matters after February 1304, not least at parliament in May 1305. The precedents of Robert's privy seal letters from Edward I about the Bruce 'right' in 1301–2 (in public) and his written pact with Lamberton in June 1304 (in secret) underline the value of such indentures where there was a lack of trust. It is possible, indeed, that such an agreement was the result of mediation between the two rivals by Bishops Lamberton and Wishart or other semi-neutral leaders (such as James Steward or Sir John Soules), men who had worked with both lords in the past and were concerned to make the Scottish cause as strong as possible in time for Edward I's death. Wishart and Lamberton were together at Melrose Abbey in early November 1305 and the plans for enthronement that both prelates seem to have had a hand in through March 1306 could just as easily have been rolled out for Comyn (as John II of Scotland).[151]

That there was certainly an awareness of the strength of Comyn's claim upon the throne at St Andrews and within its wider diocese and beyond is suggested by a contemporary poem of c.1304–6 (preserved in one of Bower's fifteenth-century manuscripts). This verse dismissed Robert of

Annandale's claim to succeed Alexander III in 1286/1290–92 by nearness of degree and alluded to the treachery of an earl (Carrick?) in the capture of Berwick in 1296; but it also condemns King John, as 'when a body has an alien head, it is all filth;/so a people is defiled when a foreigner becomes king'.[152] Its loyalties thus clearly elsewhere, the poem then appealed for the emergence and popular approbation of a worthy lord of native stock, like Scotland's kings before 1292, to take up the vacated throne.[153] In addition, variant genealogies of the claimants of 1291–92, sources perhaps also from St Andrews c.1304–6 and later preserved in Prior Andrew Wyntoun's *Original Chronicle* (c.1410–20), highlight Comyn of Badenoch's descent from both Donald III (1093–94 and 1094–97) and King John. This was a royal pedigree that was therefore censored deliberately by the pro-Bruce family trees reproduced in the later syntheses of Fordun and Bower, emphasising the descent of Robert V, VI and VII from Earl David of Huntingdon.[154]

Therefore a far more likely reconstruction of events at Dumfries in February 1306 has the two lords meet by mutual arrangement, perhaps mediation, and John Comyn refuse to subordinate his own claim to the throne and his war record since 1298 to that of Carrick. This seems to be hinted at by charges recorded against Bishop Lamberton by English officials at Berwick on 9 August 1306 that, put simply, 'Comyn did not wish to assent to the treason which the said Robert thought of committing against the said king of England, that is to say, of raising war against him and making himself king of Scotland by force.'[155] It is also perhaps succinctly echoed in Bruce's appeal for papal absolution c.1306–8 from excommunication for the murders in Dumfries, which suggests he had claimed that 'urged by the Devil . . . [he killed the Comyns] because they were strongly opposing him'.[156] At least one contemporary English cleric thought this violent rivalry between Scots chiefs worthy of ridicule, jibing about a hand-me-down invitation to take up the crown which passed through the earls from Buchan to Ross to Dunbar to Carrick, with the latter failing to persuade the loyal Comyn of Badenoch to defy his oath to England.[157] Yet it is surely unthinkable that a lord with Comyn's history would betray any discussions bearing upon the community of the realm to the hated figure of Edward I.

This surely explains why Edward I had no inkling until *after* Bruce assumed the crown (25/27 March) that the meeting at Dumfries and Comyn's death were connected to the issue of Scotland's kingship. Comyn had revealed nothing. Yet in probably declaring – or not denying – his own intention at some point (when Edward I died) to take the throne and resume the fight, Comyn nonetheless provoked a ruthless calculation by

Bruce. For Carrick's cause to advance he needed accommodation, actual support, from the Comyns – or they had to be removed. This presents the very real possibility that the killing was no mere act of 'hot blood' but premeditated slaughter, a 'pre-emptive strike', and ready to be committed if Comyn of Badenoch said the wrong word.[158]

Some proof that it may indeed have been so is suggested not simply by the presence of Robert's armed companions at the Greyfriars but by his lack of penance in subsequent years. As a mature king, Robert I would extend patronage and veneration to a number of cults and churches that his political and military actions c.1297–c.1314 had damaged and offended, including those of St Thomas, St Machutus, St Malachy and St Ninian. He would also oblige some former political opponents to commit alms or pilgrimage in penance for actions that had harmed Bruce kin.[159] Yet by contrast there survives no such penitential regret for the sacrilegious death of Comyn of Badenoch or the abuse of the Greyfriars.[160] Is this because Robert knew this was something that had to be done, a deed that Scotland's clergy would be forced to excuse immediately if they wanted the independent kingship, realm and *Ecclesia* to be revived?

# CHAPTER FOUR

# You Can't Get Away with Murder
## King Robert, 1306–10

> *Thou pillager of many a sacred shrine,*
> *Butcher of thousands, threefold death be thine!*
> *So shall the English from thee gain relief,*
> *Scotland! be wise, and choose a nobler chief.*
> *Chronicle of Lanercost*[1]

### Resurrecting Kingship, February–March 1306

If the killing of Comyn on 10 February 1306 had been a deliberate act, forced on Bruce by the lord of Badenoch's own declared ambition, over the next several weeks it precipitated into motion plans for rebellion that were by no means fully developed. These reveal the limited, regional level of Carrick's support.

According to a quite detailed report from a Berwick official, sent some-time c.15 March 1306, Carrick and his men pushed west to seize the castles of Tibbers (22 February) and Dalswinton, then returned to take Dumfries (3 March) before marching north-west to seize Ayr (which was razed); they arrested such officials as Sir Richard Siward and Sir William Balliol and captured stores they then used to supply Loch Doon in Carrick and Dunaverty in Kintyre, which they seemed to intend to hold 'for a long period'.[2] Sir Robert Boyd of Kilmarnock's reported use of ships filled with men from Cunningham to take Rothesay castle and his subsequent attempt to seize the sea fortress of Inverkip (then held by Sir Adam Gordon, a Lothian Scot and justiciar) underline Bruce's creation of a line of both seaward supply and retreat to the west. This points, as would subsequent events, to prearranged support from Gaelic kindreds with naval power, namely the MacDonalds and MacRuaridhs, alarmed by revived Macdougall control of the west since February 1304.[3]

In the immediate wake of Comyn's murder Bruce had summoned nobles to his cause and charged mounted messengers and preachers to mobilise the general populace of the west and south-west. The Berwick official reports Bruce receiving the 'fealty of the people where he has come, and has charged them [to be ready?] to go with him with rations for nine days, whenever they receive notice of a day and a [night?]'. Archdeacon Barbour would certainly draw on a near contemporary source that detailed such Bruce messages, including letters to Bishop Lamberton of St Andrews to tell him what he had done to Comyn. When interrogated by Edwardian officials at Newcastle in August 1306, Lamberton – confronted at that time with his secret Cambuskenneth indenture with Carrick of June 1304 – would also acknowledge letters from Bruce summoning his presence and the transfer to Carrick's retinue of Andrew, eldest son of James Steward (perhaps then being tutored by the bishop).[4]

Robert of Carrick must have informed a number of key individuals of his intent to be made king at Scone on a definite date; the latter was not, though, a commitment he could generally declare, even in hand-delivered or oral messages, for fear of betrayal and a waiting trap. The Berwick report warned Edward that 'however you are given to understand of the earl of Carrick, [he nevertheless?] is attempting to seize the realm of Scotland and to be [king?] . . .'. Having ignored calls from the Lieutenant's council to surrender his captures Bruce had replied (by letter) 'that he would take castles, towns and people as fast as he could, and strengthen his self as fast as he could, until the king had notified his will concerning his [Bruce's] demand, and if he would not grant it to him, he would defend himself with the longest stick that he had'.[5]

This Carrick 'demand' was surely not a pardon for killing Comyn, or for his family 'right' to claim the kingship at Edward's will and grace as per their agreement of 1301–2, although Robert may have contemplated both such appeals in the days after 10 February 1306.[6] Rather Carrick now surely insisted upon full recognition as king of a sovereign realm, delivered in expectation of Edward I's angry refusal. This reflected not merely Robert's own ambition and awareness of the gravity of what he had done – with Comyn's powerful family and extensive network of allies now baying for Carrick blood – but the guidance of Bishop Wishart. According again to the Berwick official, sometime in late February–early March Robert had reached Glasgow where 'the wicked bishop remains . . .

as his chief advisor', helping him to muster support throughout his diocese: Wishart 'gave him absolution fully for his sins, and made him swear that he would abide under the direction of the clergy of Scotland, and freed him . . . to secure his heritage by all the means that he could'.[7]

As a leading representative of the clerical estate who had taken a principal role in the Guardianships and parliaments since 1286, Wishart took the opportunity of Bruce's need for forgiveness and legitimacy in an emergency to impress upon him the duties required of him once he became king. This may thus have included a solemn promise that he would seek the kingdom's full restoration to sovereignty, not accept the title as a vassal of Edward I. In that sense, Robert's 'demand' to Edward as alluded to by the Berwick official at the very least amounted to an insistence that the English king transfer the realm to Robert as the rightful claimant and then take his forces and leave, as Edward had been expected to do at the outset of the succession hearings of 1291–92.[8] Furthermore, Wishart surely made it clear to the soon-to-be king that his elevation was conditional upon his defence of this position with his life and with the counsel of his significant subjects. If Robert failed to do so he could be removed, just as a cathedral chapter could oust an abusive, incompetent or incapacitated incumbent prelate and just as the Scottish community of the realm must now justify abandonment of King John. To bind him to these principles, Wishart would have had Carrick swear upon the Holy Gospels and the tomb of St Kentigern, whose churches and relics Robert I would do much to venerate in his later reign; Wishart may also have made use of Glasgow Cathedral's relics of Thomas Becket (a shirt and comb), a saint with a powerful hold over the aspirant king.[9]

Such a role for Wishart and Kentigern's cult surely also had an influence on Bishop Lamberton, former treasurer of Glasgow. His St Andrews seal also bore the fish, ring, bell, branch and bird associated with miracles of St Kentigern whose feast remained a major liturgical day in St Andrews' liturgy.[10] Interrogated by English officials later that year both prelates would maintain they were not present at Scone for Bruce's installation as king, Lamberton claiming that he only arrived about 27 March when he agreed to perform mass in fear of Bruce's 'severe threats'.[11] However, although in 1306–7 both bishops admitted their breach of fealty to Edward I, their past record of defiance proves that they were not above obfuscating (i.e. lying) about their relationship with Bruce. Lamberton's insistence that he had 'utterly forgotten' the 'Cambuskenneth Bond' of June 1304 is just as unconvincing and by 1307 Wishart would have sworn/resworn oaths to Edward no fewer than six times. It is surely the case that both leading bishops, and other key clergy, were in fact present at Scone for Robert's ascension to the throne, playing a central role alongside Carrick in shaping the ceremony and the meaning of the formal oaths exchanged.

Leaving Wishart's hospitality, Robert did not linger before the walls of Dumbarton castle, where Sir John Menteith resisted the attack of Bruce knights Alexander Lindsay and Walter Logan, passing on with a reported retinue of '60 men-at-arms' to cross the Forth near the Lake of Menteith en route for Scone.[12] The charges against Wishart included accusations that at this point he sent Bruce suitable robes made from his own pontificals and a banner 'of the *late* king' (i.e. Alexander III) and then 'joined the earl of Carrick and stayed with him'.[13] It is clear, too, that Lamberton had advance word and left his work on the Lieutenant's council at Berwick to travel the 80 miles or so (via the Earlsferry across the Forth) to Scone before Bruce's elevation.[14]

These details become all the more important when we consider just what kind of enthronement ceremony Bruce and his company undertook. Later Scottish accounts, beginning with that of Fordun's anonymous annalist, would state that Robert 'was there crowned (*coronatur*), on the 27th of March 1306 [sic], in the manner wherein the kings of Scotland were wont (i.e. accustomed) to be invested'.[15] The fact that this close source records the wrong date should provide a first note of caution, but that Bruce did indeed try to emulate the traditional Scottish inauguration ceremony as it had evolved over the twelfth and thirteenth centuries is underlined by his enrolment of Isabel, countess of Buchan, aunt of the earl of Fife (then a minor in English ward), to run from her husband to Scone and to fulfil the customary role of the head of her paternal magnatial house in placing the new king on the seat of Scotland's kings (the Stone of Scone).[16]

It seems logical that Bruce's small party would also have adopted ceremonial elements known from an earlier annal account of the inauguration ceremony in 1249 of the minor Alexander III: girding with a sword blessed on the abbey altar; oaths extracted from the king on the Gospels to uphold the Church, justice and laws; the placement of at least a symbolic coronet of gold upon the king's head (probably by the king himself in 1249 and 1292), followed by enrobement and the presentation of a sceptre (orb?) and sword; then a procession (probably following relics) ending with homage and fealty performed by subjects outside Scone Abbey; and the recitation of the king's genealogy in Gaelic back through the generations to kings from the Dark Ages.[17] Notably, in 1249 the fealty element may have involved a conscious attempt by the Scottish minority regime to elevate the ceremony to approach the much sought-after rite of coronation with unction, repeatedly denied by English obstruction at the Papacy: fealty was reportedly given before a cross in the churchyard with subjects spreading their cloaks at their new monarch's feet by way of invoking the Old Testament's Book of Kings and their ruler's elevation as 'God's anointed'.[18]

English supervision of King John's inauguration on the feast of St Andrew in 1292 may also have seen new forms introduced, although there must have been a conscious effort to avoid aggrandising elements adopted from the full English coronation ceremony.[19] Nonetheless, Edward I's installation as king at Westminster Abbey in 1274 must have been a hugely influential event upon Scottish prelates and magnates present at Scone in 1306. Edward's coronation had included many symbolic innovations, creating a major sacramental event with the king in solemn procession, isolation and contemplation in the hours before, then stripped to penitential undershirt before the high altar of the abbey for anointment with holy oil and balm (chrism, which was left on his head for the next seven days), followed by his investiture with robes and regalia (crown and sceptre) and an exchange of oaths by king then subjects (later subjects then king).[20]

As a hunted fugitive in 1306 it might be assumed that Robert of Carrick could not risk the time for such elaborate ritual. Yet the events of late March arguably hint that, with nothing to lose, his company did pause to mark the revival of their independent monarchy with increased symbolic meaning, innovations that may again have approached the historic ambition of the Scottish Crown and *Ecclesia* (last blocked by Henry III of England in 1251 and 1259) of securing papal approval of the rite of full coronation.[21] After all, in 1306 Robert had neither the traditional inauguration stone (which may in fact have been a reliquary base) nor the royal diadem or sceptre, nor crown records (perhaps with a written *ordo* of ceremony) to hand. He was otherwise reliant upon the institutional memory of Scone Abbey.[22] If nothing else, some form of ceremony approaching anointment would obliterate all Robert's past sins, including Comyn's murder.[23] Kings (and their national prelates) in neighbouring realms had certainly appropriated unction and coronation in a search for personal and political legitimacy in the face of internal faction and external challenge, not least the ancestors of Robert's in-laws, the kings of Norway (c.1163 with formal papal approval only secured in 1249).[24] Wishart, Lamberton and Bruce may also have been confident about their ability to extract both a retrospective lifting of Robert's excommunication and a grant of the full rite of coronation from Clement V, finally crowned himself as Pope in November 1305 and seemingly controlled by Philip IV of France.[25]

The actual installation of Robert as king took place on Friday 25 March 1306, the feast of the Annunciation of the Virgin. Crucially, this placed the first day of Robert I's reign within the octave of Passion Week that year with its much sought-after indulgences and veneration of the Resurrection.[26] The alleged arrival of Bishop Lamberton in time to perform high mass on Palm Sunday (27 March) suggests that Robert's following was prepared to risk remaining at Scone for a traditional feasting period, perhaps even until Good Friday (1 April, when a king should prostrate himself before the Holy Cross) or even Easter Sunday itself (3 April).[27] The bishop's sermon would also have been accompanied by prescribed liturgical elements such as the singing of Psalm 24, marking the entry of Christ, the King of Kings, into Jerusalem.[28]

Moreover, if the ceremony performed did involve some approximation of coronation, 'oil' or water that had washed holy relics might have been supplied by the tomb of St Kentigern or even 'St Margaret's well' at Dunfermline Abbey.[29] The majority of English chroniclers may of course have described Robert Bruce's elevation as a 'coronation' simply by way of misplacing their own realm's generic term. However, some of Edward I's brutal fury at Robert's actions may be further explained by his (unrecorded) suspicion that the more prestigious ceremony of the monarchies of England and France had been imitated.[30] On 17 June 1306 Edward certainly ordered his officials with Bishop Lamberton and the abbot of Dunfermline to make an immediate search of Scone for further relics and muniments and, in November, would request of the Pope that Scone Abbey be 'moved to a more defensible place for its own benefit, since it is situated in the midst of a perverse nation'.[31] The aforementioned English comic poem of circa February 1307 also satirised the sacral presumption of Robert I through a biting parody in which the countess of Buchan and Bishops Lamberton and Wishart were gaoled for their role in Bruce's 'unlawful crowning'.[32] Lastly, on 20 March 1307, 'at the request of Margaret Queen of England', Edward pardoned one 'Geoffrey de Coigners for concealing a certain coronet of gold with which Robert de Brus lately caused himself to be crowned in Scotland'.[33] The odds favour Bishop Wishart as the man who may have anointed Robert's head with oil and an improvised crown (perhaps assisted by his dean, Alexander Bruce).[34]

However, for Robert I, 25 March was also ten years to the day since he and his father had submitted to Edward I at Wark (on what had also been Easter Sunday in 1296) on the eve of invasion.[35] Robert himself may have made a speech to those assembled at Scone, perhaps an Edward I-like promise not to rest until he had recovered all of the Crown's rightful patrimony.[36] He may also have issued a similar written proclamation of acclamation to various corners of the realm.

## Put to the Horn, April–October 1306

The English evidence of arrests, forfeitures and executions throughout 1306–7 suggests that as well as the presence of Lamberton and Wishart, Bruce's enthronement was attended by the bishops of Dunkeld, Brechin and Moray, the abbots of Scone and Inchaffray, the earls of Atholl, Lennox, Menteith and Mar (a minor), and a significant cohort of knights and esquires (although some held castles in the field). This included the veteran James Steward (and his eldest son, Andrew); Sir Christopher Seton (and his brother, John); Sir Walter Logan; Sir Alexander Scrymgeour (resuming his role as royal standard-bearer); Alexander Menzies; several Frasers of Philorth and Murrays of Drumsargard; Boyd of Kilmarnock; Lindsay of Crawford/Byres/Barnweill; and numerous men from the followings of Annandale, Carrick and the Stewartry (such as Gilbert Herries, Gilbert of Carrick and Sir Walter Bickerton). Robert's four brothers, three sisters and ten-year-old daughter Marjorie may also have been witnesses as might his second wife, the sixteen-year-old Elizabeth de Burgh, installed as queen of Scots.[37]

Robert may have marked his elevation by knighting a number of young men, including perhaps Edward and Neil Bruce, Andrew and Walter Steward and their cousin James Douglas, and the king's own 'dearest nephew' (whose mother was Robert's half-sister) Thomas Randolph of Morton, Dumfriesshire.[38] This was a time-honoured method of binding men in service that Edward I had certainly deployed himself (e.g. at Winchester in 1285 and 1290) and would do again at Westminster to great effect in May 1306. The celebrated Feast of Swans saw him knight Prince Edward who declared (in homage to Perceval's search for the Grail) that he would not sleep two nights in the same place until revenge was gained against Bruce and in turn knighted 300 'other noble youths of his realm'. Langtoft's contemporary chronicle embellished this ceremony to include invocation of Edward's Arthurian rule of Britain and the aid of Saints John of Beverley, Becket and Cuthbert.[39] Similarly, for Robert, the display of royal banners ahead of an actual king on the move may have brought more men out in arms to his support through the spring and into the summer. That the new king of Scots was about to enter the thirty-third year of his life, the ideal Christian age of chivalry and sacrifice, may also have helped him begin to project something of a royal, martial image. More importantly, however, in the days and weeks after his 'coronation' he may also have begun to issue some grants of land as king, a possibility that suggests the early appointment of at least a provisional Chancellor with makeshift seals.[40]

Amongst the extant but undatable acts of the king – as well as seventeenth-century listings of his patronage rolls subsequently lost – there survives a number of grants to individuals and families of varying rank amongst those who were captured, executed or forfeited-in-absentia by the English for their support of Robert in 1306–7. As a conventional ice-breaker, Robert may also have begun to confirm the possessions and privileges of the major churches he was able to visit such as the abbeys of Scone, Arbroath, Kilwinning and Paisley, and the Blackfriars of Lanark or Ayr.[41] More immediately, the new king may have sought to make quick halts at these churches in search of some of the stockpiled Scottish crusade taxes collected for the Papacy (which included some of Boniface VIII's original levies as well as Clement V's continuations). Admittedly, however, Robert may have found many of these coffers empty or inaccessible, with about £8,000 having been carefully rounded up by the bishop of Carlisle's officials by October 1308.[42] At the same time, the known grantees and lands concerned in Robert's extant charters hail, as we might expect, from the limited geography of his itinerary of March–June 1306, chiefly south-western, western and central Scotland with excursions into Angus and the Mearns. However, the list of almost 150 Scots (and some English born) who can be identified as the laity supporting Bruce in 1306 also included a scattering of men, particularly of the 'middling sort', with holdings in Roxburghshire, Selkirkshire, Fife and further into the north-east, and Moray, where Bishop David de Moravia preached war against England as if it were a just and holy crusade.[43] These included men not hitherto attached to Bruce by personal lordship but motivated rather to act against the general intrusion of English lordship into their lands and offices.[44]

Predictably, a number of the new king's possible grants of this time looked to secure an immediate return in badly needed revenues or military services and perhaps even to enforce early forfeiture upon irreconcilable enemies. For example, there were grants to John of Kirkintilloch (where Bishop Wishart would send engines to besiege the English garrison in May); to Sir Alexander Fraser of Philorth (of Panbride near Arbroath and the feu of the Aberdeenshire thanage of Aboyne); to Malcolm, earl of Lennox (of the right to hold weapons inspections); to Sir John Stewart (of the Banffshire barony of Frendraught, taken from Duncan of that ilk); to Sir Gilbert Hay (perhaps already appointed Constable); to Sir Robert Boyd of Kilmarnock (of the lordship of Noddsdale in Ayrshire); and to the notorious patriot Sir Simon Fraser (of lands in Inverbervie forfeited from Sir Edmund Hastings, Edward I's Constable of Perth).[45] By the same token, a portion of Robert's extant acts dating to 1308–9 (and any undatable 'lost' acts that might be assigned to this period) may also represent reissued charters for patronage first dispensed in the opening weeks of Robert's reign, subsequently lost (or discarded as discredited) when his support collapsed and he had to flee west.[46]

In sum, although Robert issued no grants affecting major titles or new creations (for example, Galloway, Buchan or Badenoch), we should not simply assume that his kingship was so hard pressed that it did not try to begin to function at this basic level, at least in the immediate vicinity of the king. Nevertheless, in hindsight there is no doubting the scale of the opposition he faced and that this in turn made Scots of all estates reluctant to associate with or accept charters from 'King Robert' (or 'Kinge Hobbe of summer', as his queen mockingly called him according to English chronicle and song).[47]

Robert certainly had to apply threats to the baillies of the burghs of Dundee, Perth and Aberdeen to extract revenue to support his early campaigning: the same market towns may also have provided vital supply by prise.[48] Meanwhile the English military presence had been reinforced, led by Aymer de Valence (Comyn's brother-in-law), and such experienced occupation officers as Henry Percy and Robert Clifford, ordered by a furious Edward I to strip and burn the 'lands, goods and gardens' of any rebel.[49] At the same time, King Robert could expect no support from Berwickshire, the Lothians, western Galloway, much of Perthshire and Fife, the far north-east, Badenoch, Lochaber, Invernessshire and Rossshire, Argyll and Lorn. The murder of Comyn had initiated a bloodfeud within the Scottish community and propelled into English allegiance the powerful network of kindreds that had resisted Edward since 1296. The Berwick official had been able to report even before Robert's 'coronation' that the earls of Buchan and Dunbar, Ingram d'Umfraville, Alexander de Abernethy, David (either of Betoigne or Brechin?) and John Mowbray were in arms and regional office 'well and loyally' against the would-be king: the earls of Ross, Angus and Strathearn, the Macdougalls of Argyll and Sir John Menteith of Arran, Knapdale and Dumbarton castle would also lead out followings against Bruce.[50]

Through April and May uncertainty about Scots' allegiance did cause the English regime to hesitate and opened a window in which forces loyal to Robert overran the royal castle at Forfar and a new tower at Tolibothwell, a few miles south-west of Aberdeen. Robert also harried Malise, sixth earl of Strathearn, into a brief submission by attacking (in company with John of Atholl) his lands at Kenmore, some 24 miles west of Dunkeld at the head of Loch Tay, making a hostage of one of his sons, before perhaps turning to make a reinforcing ayre into Lanarkshire and the south-west.[51] However, by early June Valence's force, including 300 cavalry, had left Berwick and captured the bishops of St Andrews (at a hospital-chapel of St Thomas at Scotlandwell, near Lochleven) and Glasgow (besieging or holding Cupar castle in Fife) and then reoccupied Perth.[52] Here Robert I offered him battle with what must have been a force of some few thousands of men he thought capable of bringing victory and further legitimacy to his cause.

Valence's surprise attack and the rout that followed at Methven on 19 June (the Translation feast of St Margaret) reduced Robert's company to a few score now in westward flight. Simon Fraser of Oliver castle (in Selkirk forest), and Thomas Randolph of Morton were among those captured.[53] We now enter into that period of Robert's life where we are more and more dependent upon Barbour's great poem and traces of its fossilised lost sources for a sustained narrative, and thus must pick our way carefully through an increasingly literary and idealised account of Bruce's trials and sufferings.[54] This was an elegy that later Scottish chroniclers would embrace:

> Robert, putting forth his hand unto force, underwent the countless and unbearable toils of the heat of day, of cold and hunger, by land and sea, gladly welcoming weariness, fasting, dangers, and the snares not only of foes, but also of false friends, for the sake of freeing his brethren . . . being attended at times by three followers, at times by two; and more often he was left alone, utterly without help.[55]

Nonetheless, it is still possible to identify incidents, people and places that had a profound effect on Robert. As in 1297 the lands (*parochia*) and network (*familia*) of clergy, tenants and hereditary relic keepers (*dewars*) associated with particular saints would come to his aid.[56] The composite cult of the eighth-century monk St Fillan (feast day 20 June, the day after the defeat at Methven) sheltered Robert's party as it fled from Strathearn and passed the 30 miles into Glendochart. Local traditions also stress the assistance of the tenantry of Sir Alexander Menzies whom Robert would later reward with a grant of the extensive lordships of Fortingall and Glendochart in western Perthshire, marching on the earldoms of Atholl and Strathearn.[57] Fillan's protection may have drawn upon established family patronage connections, as the arms of Annandale bore the image of the saint's arm reliquary (the *mayne*).[58] That the king would extend generous favour to this cult in 1318, re-establishing the priory chapel of Strathfillan and supporting its care by the Augustinian abbey of nearby Inchaffray, has usually been taken as proof of royal gratitude for the presence of Fillan's relics – including a bell (*bernane*) and crosier (*quigrich*) – on the battlefield at Bannockburn.[59] However, Robert may also have thanked Fillan's intercession for his escape with his life and family intact, sometime in late July or the first half of August 1306 (Fordun's source asserts 11 August), from a skirmish at Dalrigh in Strath Fillan, 18 miles east of Loch Tay, where his company was confronted by a force led by John Macdougall of Argyll.[60]

It was at this juncture that King Robert divided his party in two, sending Atholl, Boyd, Alexander Lindsay with his son David, and Neil Bruce east over the mountains to escort the royal womenfolk to Kildrummy castle in Mar.[61] Robert, his remaining three brothers and a few supporters such as Sir Neil Campbell of Lochawe (who may already have married the king's sister, Mary, and fathered a son, John) and Sir Gilbert Hay continued west, crossing Loch Lomond by ship and then through the barony of Kirkintilloch (perhaps already granted to Sir Malcolm Fleming of Biggar) and the Lennox (aided by Earl Malcolm), taking sail again via the Steward's Bute to Dunaverty castle at the southern tip of Kintyre.[62]

Pursuit by Macdougall of Argyll now made the MacDonalds of Islay Robert's natural allies. Yet the king may have had to pay a high price for their shelter and material support, becoming embroiled in internal MacDonald rivalry.[63] The aforementioned seventeenth-century indices of undated royal grants do contain notes of grants to Angus Og MacDonald of the Macdougall's forfeited lordship of Ardnamurchan, along with the former Comyn mainland lordships of Morvern, Duror, Glencoe and, crucially, Lochaber: these may date to 1306–7 or be later reissues/confirmations of c.1308–12.[64] In addition, Barbour, in The Bruce, asserts that Angus Og was 'lord of Kintyre' when he received Robert as one of his most staunch followers in 1306.[65] The latter may be explained by Barbour's knowledge of the marriage (c.1350) of Angus's son John, first 'Lord of the Isles', to a daughter of Robert II, the first Stewart king (Robert I's grandson), which brought the by then much disputed Kintyre lordship as a dowry.[66] Yet the fact remains that Robert I's undated lost acts also include a grant of Macdougall holdings on Mull and Tiree to an 'Alexander de Insula' or 'Alexander the younger', possibly the still-living elder brother of Angus Og, or his or Angus's eldest son in turn. Furthermore, Robert I's first parliament at St Andrews in March 1309 would be attended, as we shall see, by a 'Donald of Islay', who it has been suggested (without any conclusive proof) may have been another elder brother (or, it might be thought, an uncle or cousin?) of both Alexander and Angus.[67]

Rival claims of seniority and degree might therefore have afflicted this Isles lordship at such a time just as they would later, forcing Robert to deal with one or more MacDonald lord or their allies in 1306 and to promise extensive grants of territory and customary dues (or exemptions), acts that he would later have cause to rethink. According to Barbour, once received at Dunaverty, King Robert 'was dredand for tresoun ay'.[68] Nevertheless, a renewed MacDonald association did facilitate timely links with Gaelic Ireland, with access to ships, sea-castles, troops and supplies. It seems to have been in search of refuge and support in or off present-day Ulster, Antrim or Donegal (Barbour's source would assert on the Isle of Rathlin) that Bruce and what remained of his retinue set sail once more from Dunaverty in early September; or to a MacDonald or MacRuaridh stronghold in the Isles, a day away.[69]

As they left, Robert's wider affinity disintegrated. Valence's force captured Neil Bruce, Donald of Mar, Robert Boyd, Alexander and David Lindsay and others by taking Kildrummy (c.10 September 1306).[70] Before they could sail to safety in Orkney or Norway, Atholl and the Bruce women were seized by William, earl of Ross, within the sanctuary of St Duthac near Tain.[71] Loch Doon and Tibbers had long since fallen; Dunaverty would fall within days of Robert's departure to siege forces under Sir John Menteith and Macdougall. The earls of Menteith and Strathearn and James Steward had already submitted. These important men and Randolph were spared, but Atholl, Neil Bruce, Simon Fraser and the Setons would all be ritually executed along with at least twenty more of Robert's minor noble supporters who were quickly hanged without ceremony.[72] Still more remained gaoled as did Bishops Lamberton and Wishart. Infamously, Edward I would order Queen Elizabeth and Christina and Marjorie Bruce to be held in monastic isolation in England while Mary Bruce and the countess of Buchan were to be displayed in cages in castles within the English stronghold of the Scottish south-east.[73] The aged English king had already used the declaration of Bruce's excommunication by papal legates at St Paul's church in London as the same day and venue for the pronouncement of papal bulls of December 1305 confirming his revocation of his political concessions of 1303, granted in the face of English parliamentary complaint since 1297.[74] By October 1305 the Bruce lands of Annandale had been granted to Humphrey de Bohun, earl of Hereford, and the English king was being lobbied for the forfeiture of at least another ninety Scottish estates (including Carrick, sought by Sir Henry Percy).[75] 'Robert I' had lost everything and was a landless fugitive, put to the horn.

### *Regressio de exilio*, October 1306–8

The celebrated legend about Bruce watching a spider, and the lesson that he too had to try, try again, is surely a Post-Reformation rendering of a cult tale involving the renegade king in the winter of 1306–7 seeking shelter in a cave associated with a wandering missionary saint, perhaps Brendan, Ninian, Kentigern, Winnin or Columba.[76] The support of island churches and cults has been underestimated as a component of Robert's exile. A personal connection of geography and faith may explain the transfer of his beloved Chancellor, Bernard Abbot of Arbroath, to be bishop of the Isles in his retirement from 1328. Literate and pious (with Barbour describing the king reciting tales from Roman history as well as a chivalric romance, *Fierabras*, while awaiting ships to escape in 1306), Robert was certainly aware of the difficult exile but triumphant return home of one of his family's favourite saints, Thomas Becket (the special feast of 'regressio de exilio' celebrated at Canterbury and Arbroath on 2 December).[77] Yet although Robert and company surely prayed for a miracle, their plans for armed return to the mainland also reflected considerable practical preparation.

That Robert's force would land in Carrick in late January–early February 1307, and may have drawn revenues from his family lands discreetly throughout the winter, points to his spending a significant portion of his time with sympathetic kindreds in Ireland, perhaps even on his family's or Steward's Antrim lands.[78] MacDonald galloglass allies such as the Bissets of Antrim, Ó Néills of Tyrone, Ó Conors of Connacht and Ó Donnells of Donegal may have supplied ships and troops for this incursion into south-west Scotland.[79] The famous letter from Robert to Irish Gaelic chieftains, now convincingly dated to 1306–7 and empowering Thomas and Alexander Bruce to negotiate an alliance on their king's behalf, speaks to a strategic cast for support and the genuine knowledge of the region shared by Robert and Edward Bruce, Malcolm of Lennox, the Campbells of Lochawe and western clergy.[80] This letter's stress upon common ancestry, ethnicity, customs and language as a basis for a 'special friendship between us and you, so that with God's will our nation may recover her ancient liberty' – a shared sense of identity that does now refer boldly to 'birth' – was surely thus more than a cynical 'fishing' exercise to destabilise English control of northern Ireland through the fleet and forces operating between Ayr and Carlisle.[81] In fact, this tender of alliance and the support Robert received may have formed the basis of a reciprocal commitment he would act to fulfil after Bannockburn. In that regard his debt to Gaelic lords of the Western Isles may reflect material support he received from Angus Og at Dunyvaig, or from Christina MacRuaridh (a Mar widow) on Knoydart or Uist, or the MacSweens in Kintyre.[82] The ailing Edward I certainly believed Robert's refuge to be the 'isles of the Scottish coast'.[83]

According to the contemporary scribe of Lanercost Priory (where Edward I lay gravely ill), about Lent 1307 (8 February) Robert dispatched an advance party to Galloway led again by his brothers Thomas and Alexander and Sir Reginald Crawford, with 'a certain Irish sub-king' and the 'lord of Kintyre' (Malcolm MacQuillan rather than Barbour's Angus Og?). They were routed and captured by Dougal Macdowall, a Balliol vassal, then executed about 17 February. A similar fate almost befell Robert's main force, if Barbour's dramatised depiction of their error-strewn landing from Arran amidst Sir Henry Percy's sleeping troops at Turnberry is based in fact.[84]

Yet after the painful blow of two more brothers killed, Robert's adoption of hit-and-run guerrilla tactics and exploitation of the rugged terrain of the south-west resulted in an impressive sequence of skirmish victories through April and May – from Glen Trool to Loudon Hill and on to the outskirts of Ayr.[85] This hard-fought momentum was combined with powerful propaganda, spread (according to a report from Forfar castle of about 15 May) by 'false preachers from Bruce's army, men who have previously been before the justice for advocating war and have been released on bail, but are now behaving worse than ever'. Through pulpit and market-cross came a self-fulfilling Arthurian prophecy, reflecting Robert's stay in the west and an attempt to spook Welsh Marcher lords in de Valence's forces: that 'after the death of "le Roy Coveytous" the people of Scotland and the Welsh shall band together and have full lordship and live in peace together to the end of the world'.[86] Yet if the Forfar correspondent could report that after his victories 'it appears that God is with him [Bruce]', then the long-anticipated death of Edward I (aged sixty-eight) at Burgh-by-Sands (Cumberland) on 7 July 1307 must have been seized upon by Robert and his growing army and Church as a further sign from the Almighty: for 'Longshanks' had been gathered to God on the Translation feast of St Thomas.[87] As a universal symbol of defiance of Plantagenet tyranny, association with Becket's cult already formed an important part of Robert's spiritual lights; now such faith became central to the development of his image as king.[88]

Bernard, the displaced abbot of Kilwinning (Ayrshire), first appears in the extant record as Robert I's Chancellor in October 1308.[89] However, his appointment may date to as early as the summer or autumn of 1307. Although it would have to await sequestration of the self-exiled Anglophile, John, abbot of Arbroath, by Bishop Lamberton on 1 November 1309, it may long have been Robert's intention to promote his Chancellor to be head of the wealthy house dedicated to St Thomas in Scotland.[90] Certainly, in the second half of 1307 Robert would act to secure the elevation as bishop-elect to the vacant see of Dunblane of the former Chancellor of the

Guardianship c.1298–1304, the septuagenarian Nicholas Balmyle. The latter had drawn his office fee and latterly a pension from the income of Arbroath Abbey and had travelled to Poitiers for consecration by 11 December 1307.[91] It may also have been part of his brief with his proctors at the curia to speak to a formal appeal lodged with Clement V for the lifting of Robert's excommunication for the murder of John Comyn.[92] This would be granted by the Pope through his chief penitentiary on 23 July 1308 when letters were dispatched to the abbot of Paisley (in lieu of Wishart of Glasgow) to hear the confession of Bruce and his associates and, if 'appropriate satisfaction' had been made to Dumfries Greyfriars, to offer absolution and impose further suitable penance.[93]

As we shall see, by the time of Bannockburn, it was perhaps natural for the Scottish host to pray to 'St Andrew and St Thomas who shed his blood along with the saints of the Scottish Fatherland'.[94] Thus invocation of Becket may also have been deployed by Robert's forces and preachers as they stepped up his military campaign from the summer of 1307.[95] The Forfar report of 15 May had spotted the danger posed if Bruce and his men, with their beachhead in the south-west, could push beyond the Mounth and incite to revolt the volatile people of the north-east. However, the accession of the twenty-three-year-old Edward II, his curtailment of the expedition of his father's host into Scotland by the end of August (when the new king left Ayrshire for England), and then the replacement of Aymer de Valence as Lieutenant, allowed King Robert to do just that.[96]

Over the next twelve months, Robert's success against his Scottish opponents testified to his inspiring physical courage and adaptable tactics as well as to the absence of substantive English intervention. With Sir James Douglas leading a separate force to recover western central Scotland and the forest marches, Robert and Edward Bruce marched north through the Great Glen with a mixed company of Carrick, Stewartry, Clydesdale, Lennox and Irish/Isles galloglass divisions, mostly on foot.[97] After obliging John Macdougall of Argyll to accept the first of a series of short truces, a remarkable succession of royal and pro-Comyn castles would be taken and razed by spring 1308 – Inverlochy, Urquhart, Inverness, Nairn, Balvenie, Lochindorb, Duffus, Tarradale, Skelbo and, perhaps, Ruthven.[98] This run of victories – reported in part in a fragmentary extant letter sent to Edward II's administration by his Scots sheriff in Banff, Duncan de Frendraught (who would be 'slain in the king's service' by May 1310) – surely caused the Bruce ranks to swell, encouraging spontaneous rebellion in other quarters (as had happened with the patriot cause in 1297).[99] Macdougall and William, earl of Ross, were isolated from their allies with the latter obliged to take a truce, too, until 2 June 1308, for his own earldom, Sutherland and Caithness.[100] Able to find supplies and shelter in the royal demesne estates of Moray (where he had overseen forests c.1304–6) and Mar/Garioch, Robert's host – reported by Macdougall about this time as '10,000 men, they say, or 15,000' – terrorised Buchan, Strathbogie and Banffshire.

A sustained guerrilla campaign of rapid movement in all weathers, living off northern lands while harrying nonetheless determined and numerous foes, reaped its costs in what was another severe Scottish winter.[101] A number of Scottish sources report King Robert's outnumbered forces about Christmas as starving and the king as gravely ill (perhaps wounded?) and litter-bound.[102] It was now that Edward Bruce, his only surviving brother and male heir presumptive, arguably grew into his role. It may have been in large part under his leadership in the field that the Bruce host engineered a decisive encounter with the forces of John Comyn, earl of Buchan, David Strathbogie, earl of Atholl, Reginald Cheyne of Duffus (then warden of Moray) and Duncan Frendraught, sheriff of Banff.[103] According to a later verse chronicle by Abbot Bernard, this battle at Old Meldrum or Inverurie, about 15 miles north-west of Aberdeen on the boundary of Garioch and Mar, took place on 23 May 1308.[104] The victory was followed by the systematic burning and laying waste of Buchan in June, a dreadful 'herschip' that etched itself into folk memory and left the ground barren for over a generation. Abbot Bernard would emphasise this victory and its devastating aftermath as a turning point in Robert's fortunes.[105] In the summer of 1308 Edward Bruce and Donald of Islay led a force south to inflict similar punishment on enemies' lands in Galloway, routing a company led by Donald McCan and probably taking Rutherglen castle by January 1309.[106] Meanwhile Robert, the MacDonalds, MacRuaridhs and perhaps James Douglas (although Barbour may simply have inserted his hero knight here) pushed back down the Great Glen and Inverlochy to achieve a brilliant tactical upset c.15–23 August 1308 over the Macdougalls at Ben Cruachan (the Pass of Brander), near Loch Awe, pursuing their defeated forces by sea to Dunstaffnage castle, which may then have surrendered (only to require reduction once again in summer 1309). Remarkably, although John Macdougall seems to have fled into Edward II's service in the Irish Sea, Robert did reach an initial accommodation with John's father, Alexander of Argyll, appointing him as custodian 'of the Isles and other lands there' in late 1308–early 1309; but MacDonald antipathy would ensure that this arrangement lasted barely a few months.[107]

Robert's northern incursion was not merely destructive or undertaken in search of submissions of fealty. He punctuated his itinerary, certainly after Inverurie, with the restoration of local government through the appointment of officers and the issue of patronage. The main beneficiaries of this royal favour would logically have been his noble allies in the region, a number of whom witnessed the handful of charters that survive from 1308–9: Robert Keith (who came into Robert's peace about Christmas 1309 according to English records) and his brother Edward, Gilbert Hay, Norman Leslie, Alexander Menzies, Mogund of Glenesk and Hamelin de Troup (who was perhaps made sheriff of the still-resistant Banff); the MacDonalds and MacRuaridhs may also have been in receipt of conquered Macdougall lands and castles at this time.[108] By late summer the king also clearly had the active support of the bishops of Moray, Ross and Caithness and their tenants. Yet Robert's fledgling regime also needed to win over and work with lesser, local men, past patriots and enemies alike such as Alexander Pylche (appointed sheriff of Inverness?) and William Wiseman (sheriff of Elgin?).[109] A similar mixture of pressure, pardon and patronage may have been applied to the officials of the burgh of Aberdeen when its castle fell to Robert in June–July, significantly increasing his revenues and providing crucial access to European shipping; Sir Alexander Fraser or Sir Walter Barclay was perhaps installed as sheriff there.[110]

In the face of this regional dominance, and with the earl of Buchan's death by the end of the year, William of Ross had no option but to submit. It is a vital measure of Robert I's need for support and legitimation that he accepted the earl's homage and fealty and granted him pardon and patronage in a ceremony performed at Auldearn, between Nairn and Elgin, in what may have been a formal council on 31 October 1308:

Because the magnificent prince the lord Robert by the grace of God king of Scots, out of his innate goodness and inspired mercy and special grace, has remitted to me purely his rancour of spirit and loosed and forgiven me of all manner of transgressions of offences against him and his men ... and graciously granted all my lands and tenements [to me], and, notwithstanding, has undertaken to infeft me heritably in the lands of Dingwall and Ferincoskry in the earldom of Sutherland by his benign generosity ...[111]

This submission was no doubt widely publicised by Robert's growing network, in hope of further defections before Buchan and Atholl and their associated lordships could be forfeited; Earl William and his sons, Hugh and John, also brought their ward, the young William, earl of Sutherland, into Robert's camp.[112] Although in 1321 the king would oblige Ross to assign Dingwall thanage and 'Ferincoskry' to support six chaplains at St Duthac's shrine at Tain, praying for the souls of Alexander III and John, earl of Atholl, lord of Strathbogie (d.1306), the original grant of 1308 may have secured specified military services rather than simply re-established the feu-ferme rental terms by which Ross's father had held the thanage from Alexander III. This highlights Robert's alienation from the outset of such former royal demesne so as to enhance his host (although war damage may otherwise have made it difficult to raise revenues from these lands).[113] But these very public acts of pardon and lordship amounted to a genuine effort of reconciliation with a regionally significant former enemy, one which satisfied Ross territorial ambition and would bring that kindred into Robert's family through marriage to his sister, Maud, by c.1315–16.[114]

Robert now pushed these strategies south into the shires of Perth, Kincardine, Forfar and Fife, embracing the earldoms of Atholl, Menteith, Strathearn, Angus and Fife. He was at Inchmahome, the caput of Menteith, on 28 September.[115] A week later he issued a charter to Coupar-Angus Abbey while stopped at Dunkeld (where some of the chapter may have helped him in summer 1306), seemingly to help determine the election of a new bishop in defiance of an Edward II appointee. Robert's choice was William Sinclair, later known as '[my] fighting bishop', a canon of patriotic stock as a son of the Sinclairs of Roslin in Lothian, kinsman of Baldred Bisset and a man captured in Dunbar in 1296.[116] In supporting his candidacy we find further evidence of Robert's need to exaggerate his support to garner more of the same, and of collusion by sympathetic diocesenal officials in helping him present a community mandate: for his confirmation of grants to Coupar-Angus (including gifts by friend and foe alike) was witnessed with the seals of the imprisoned senior bishops of St Andrews and Glasgow.

A week later, Robert was before the walls of English-held Perth or nearby, collecting homages and revenues. He ordered his 'sheriffs' of Forfar (perhaps headed by a member of the Straton family) to take possession in the king's name of lands recently alienated by Arbroath Abbey. This signalled Robert's intention to sequester the exiled and pensioned John, abbot of Arbroath, and to appoint Chancellor Bernard in his place.[117] The royal castle at Forfar fell and was razed by the end of the year when Sir Alexander Abernethy and an English garrison were expelled at the hands of Philip, a keeper of the nearby royal forest of Plater, who was inspired and rewarded by his king.[118] The Crown's Forfar demesne of a dozen thanages was traditionally a rich region of supply for the royal household.[119] This seizure in turn permitted Robert's itinerant government to make a more permanent home for his chancery, muniments (and even treasury) in the abbey dedicated to St Thomas.[120]

### Forging a Community, 1309

Over the winter of 1308–9 Robert was able to consolidate his achievements when Edward II, already mired in controversy with a large number of his magnates over his association with Piers Gaveston, agreed to a truce from 2 February until 1 November 1309; this extended an initial ceasefire agreed in November 1308 and confirmed the wastage of two successive years of English purveyance for planned campaigns in Scotland.[121] This ceasefire was semi-official recognition of Robert's authority. Its terms were negotiated by French and papal envoys seeking peace to promote Philip IV's plans for a crusade, by mediating between Edward II and his disgruntled nobility, and Pope Clement V's desire for an allied Church Council at Vienne in October 1310; truce talks had also perhaps been aided by Robert's support of visits to the relocated curia in Poitiers/Avignon by the electees of Dunblane and Dunkeld.[122] Significantly, Robert must have decided almost immediately to call his first full parliament for just after Lent 1309. The choice of St Andrews for this meeting in the weeks before Easter (31 March) was a symbolic emulation of Edward I's parliament there in March 1304 (which Bruce as earl of Carrick had attended).[123] Preparations for Robert's assembly involved further receipt of fealties and the dispensation of royal patronage in turn.

Such activity is suggested by the witness list and extant seals of nobles appended to two of the three fragmentary documents that can be assigned to this gathering (albeit in one instance from much later transcriptions). Edward Bruce had in fact struggled in the second half of 1308 to make headway in the south-west, but he was present at St Andrews and perhaps already styled 'lord of Galloway'.[124] At the same time Gilbert Hay was confirmed as Constable, Robert Keith as Marischal, and the king's nephew, Thomas Randolph of the Dumfriesshire barony of Morton (between the Comyn lordships of Dalswinton and Tibbers), was now raised to be lord of Nithsdale, the glen running north–south through Dumfriesshire.[125] These Bruce stalwarts appear within a larger list of nobility who attached their seals on 16 March (Passion Sunday) to two collective letters of reply to Philip IV who had invited the Scots to join his crusade:

William, earl of Ross, Malcolm, earl of Lennox, William, [earl of Suther-land], and the communities of the earldoms of Fife, Menteith, Mar, Buchan and Caithness, the heirs of which are in ward, likewise the communities of all the other earldoms of the kingdom of Scotland [except] [D]unbar . . . James the steward of Scotland, Alexander de Argyll, Donald de Islay, John de Menteith, Hugh, the son and heir of the earl [of Ross] . . . James, lord of Douglas, Alexander de Lindsay, Alexander de [Fraser], [William] Wiseman, David de Barclay, Robert Boyd, barons; and also all of Argyll and the Hebrides and the inhabitants of all the kingdom of Scotland recognising the fealty of the lord Robert by the grace of God king of Scotland.[126]

Two letters were required as Philip had apparently taken to sending Robert duplicate communications, by the same courier through England, the first in the open and addressed to the 'earl of Carrick', the second hidden and addressed to Robert as king.[127] Nonetheless, both replies in the name of the nobility betray the Bruce Scots' concerns about Philip's intentions, chiefly their fear that he might yet make further use of pensioner John Balliol, resident in Picardy, and interfere in the Scottish succession, again enlisting the help of a malleable Pope as a means of influencing Philip's new brother-in-law, Edward II.[128]

Therefore, at St Andrews, these representatives of the noble estates, in a text though authored by Robert and his prelates, thanked Philip IV for his invitation and his good memory of the historic Franco-Scots alliance, but took pains to make it clear that their first priority must be to follow 'our lord Robert by the grace of God king [of Scots . . . whom] justice and truth and the grace of the King of Kings has raised up as our prince and leader . . . [and to see that] the kingdom of Scotland returns to its former free condition, the tempests of war having been quelled and secure peace having been granted'. Only then could they contemplate crusade to recover the Holy Land.

In short, Robert I was 'the true, undoubted and nearest heir of King Alexander III who last died': his kingship was already an established reality, assented to by his subjects, and the Scots had no need of French or papal intervention to restore an exiled king (unlike in 1299–1302). Nobles' seals were to be attached to this formal statement perhaps in a manner akin to the 'Ragman' rolls of Edward I. Thus it was the proclamation of Robert I's legitimacy as king that was this parliament's greatest concern, perhaps for a general domestic as well as an elite, external audience. However, to effect this, the king and his close counsel were not above 'a combination of extorted seals, coerced enemies and falsified names'. The young earl of Sutherland was certainly hostile (or at best indifferent) to the Bruce regime, as were the absent heads of the communities of the earldoms of Buchan, Menteith and Fife (with the latter earl, Duncan, a ward and grandson-in-law of Edward I); nevertheless, their seals were attached. Alexander of Argyll almost instantly rejoined his son, John, in arms to defy Bruce and the MacDonalds of Islay in the west (perhaps encouraged by signs at St Andrews of disquiet about Robert's methods).[129]

This attempt to choreograph loyalty is demonstrated even more clearly by a simultaneous parliamentary letter compiled in the name of the Scottish clergy, dated to 17 March.[130] This was designed as a parallel response to Clement V's summons in August 1308 of bishops and secular rulers to his intended Church Council at Vienne, an invitation which – like one of Philip IV's letters – had surely not styled Bruce as king (and had perhaps been sent to Balliol in Picardy).[131] As such, this second parliamentary state-ment, also probably prepared in two variant forms, drew not only on the known precedents of English (1301) and French (1302) estates' addresses to the Pope, but on the personnel and materials of the Scottish presenta-tions to Boniface VIII of the same time.[132]

Crucially, these Scottish arguments had been carefully reworked since 25 March 1306. The St Andrews clerical declaration thus opened with the assertion that 'the faithful people (*gens*) [of Scotland] without doubt always held, as it had understood and believed to be true from their ancestors and forefathers, that the said Lord Robert, the grandfather, was the true heir after the death of King Alexander [III] and his granddaughter'; thus not the lord John Balliol who had been imposed 'de facto' by Edward I who then deposed him and reduced the Scottish kingdom to slavery 'by force and violence'. Yet through Divine Providence, the clerics continued, the people of the 'disfigured and desolated kingdom'

> ... agreed on the said Lord Robert, the present king ... by the knowledge and consent of the same people he was received as king so he might restore the defects of the kingdom and correct things needing to be corrected, and might steer those that lacked guidance. And by their authority the aforesaid king of Scots was solemnly endowed with the kingdom, with whom the faithful people of the kingdom wish to live and die as with he who, by the right of blood and the other cardinal virtues, is fit, [as] aforesaid, to govern, and is worthy of the name of king and the honour of the kingdom ...[133]

This stirring statement was designed to speak to a Pope who reputedly had been chosen of all the Cardinals as worthy to reform and 'correct' the Church.[134] It asserted Robert's legitimacy and his restoration and governance of the kingdom (*reparatio et regimen*), both by legal right of inheritance and the assent of his subjects to both that right and his suitability, entertaining no need whatsoever for papal jurisdiction to intervene in its 'special daughter's' succession dilemma. This emphasis upon community consent (acclamation or even 'election') for the legitimate authority of a ruler who besides held a legal claim reflected much of the competing contemporary currents of political thought and polemic being expounded in continental royal, academic and curial circles, between secular and papal monarchy, the Papacy and prelates, kings and subjects.[135] It was surely a simplified version of this account which prelates charged Scottish parochial clergy to disseminate to their flocks: that the rightful claimant Robert had been made king by popular acclamation and would restore the liberty of the realm and its people against the church-burning, slaughter of innocents and disruption to agriculture and commerce of England's arrogant kings.

Nevertheless, at least four of the twelve bishops' seals that were originally appended to this declaration belonged to prelates hostile to Robert – Aberdeen (Henry Cheyne, perhaps at St Andrews under duress?), Argyll, Galloway and Caithness. Wishart of Glasgow remained in England (under the supervision of the bishop of Poitiers since November 1308) though perhaps in contact through a proctor; Crambeth of Dunkeld was dying or dead.[136] Meanwhile, Bishop Lamberton, released into Edward II's employ as a go-between on surety of 6,000 merks in August 1308, may have travelled on parole to this parliament in his own diocesenal burgh (with instructions to initiate an inquiry into Templar activities in Scotland); but he may not have been able subsequently to deliver the clergy's letter to Pope Clement at Vienne as was planned.[137] As is shown by a list or *gravamina* of ecclesiastical matters for redress forwarded from Scotland by its clergy to the papal Council by 1312, a number of prelates and their officials were clearly being coerced about this time by Robert, his captains and supporters, into accepting pro-Bruce provisions to vacant and forcibly vacated church benefices.[138] In that light, the 1309 parliamentary letter had clearly been engineered deliberately by Robert in close consultation with the bishops of Moray, Brechin, Ross, Dunblane (Balmyle) and perhaps William Sinclair as elect of Dunkeld, assisted by experienced 'patriotic' officials of St Andrews and Glasgow and Chancellor Bernard.[139]

Thus Robert and his council strove to control and project the voice of the 'community of the realm', for the clergy as a means to influence their king and guard against external threats, for Robert as a legitimating force from which his family (1286–92) and then he himself (1299–1302, 1304–5) had been excluded by a Balliol–Comyn political affinity. Yet this does not mean that the St Andrews parliament – even as a really quite limited gathering – was an acquiescent body without voices of dissent. On the contrary, this very behaviour by Robert's regime may have provoked controversy.

No further record of business at this assembly survives; no evidence of estates' activity is extant again until the celebrated parliament at Cambuskenneth in November 1314, five months after the battle of Bannockburn.[140] Nonetheless, a number of difficult issues may have been debated at St Andrews in Lent–Easter 1309. Not least, the retrospective insistence of both the clergy's and nobility's letters that Robert of Annandale's claim to the kingship was believed by a majority to have been best in law, as the rightful male heir to Alexander III by nearness of degree, might easily have turned men's thoughts to clarification of Edward Bruce's position as Robert I's heir presumptive ahead of the king's daughter, Marjorie, who remained an English captive. If so, this proved abortive, perhaps unworkable, and pointless without a real majority of the community present to give formal assent. Scotland south of the Forth, including its wealthiest burghs and monastic estates, was still under English control, as were Perth and Dundee, supported by a substantial portion of the Scottish estates. Even St Andrews castle may have remained under occupation, with Robert's modest assembly gathering nervously over a few days in cathedral priory buildings while the truce held.[141]

By the same token, the St Andrews gathering may have seen lobbying from nobles present for forfeiture of lands from Robert's more irreconcilable enemies (Buchan, Badenoch, Lochaber, Atholl/Strathbogie, Angus and English lords' Scottish lands such as those of Hastings, Ferrers or Wake); perhaps even requests for lands/redress by former opponents who had recently entered Robert's peace (Ross, Macdougall). Extant but undated royal letters of remission to Gilbert de Carrick, a grant of Eskdale in the Borders to the abbey of Melrose (bypassing their original owner, Sir John Graham, then with the English) and grants dealing with the income of Dumbarton castle (following the defection to Bruce of Sir John Menteith in late 1308) may also have been issued during the parliament; after his submission Menteith was confirmed in control of Arran, Knapdale, Dumbarton and, probably, his brother's earldom of Menteith.[142] However, Robert seems to have stuck fast to a principle of avoiding wholesale forfeitures in the hope of persuading more important kindreds and communities to join him; in the same way, his appropriation of the seals of absent nobles and prelates was arguably undertaken in anticipation of future submissions. This was also the middle way that might recover the lands and resources in England belonging to Scottish nobles and churches (including the Bruces' Yorkshire, Huntingdon and Essex holdings).

The king is unlikely to have allowed the kind of open petitioning from all estates he had observed at Edward I's parliament of 1305. Nonetheless, the St Andrews parliament (and subsequent assemblies) may also have discussed appeals from Scots of varying ranks and all estates that addressed current economic and agricultural conditions after two decades of war and hardship: this surely included a growing number of petitions concerned with quite specific burgh, freeholder and Church properties and privileges badly disrupted and disputed since 1306, even 1296, including provisions to benefices in the sees of St Andrews and Glasgow.[143] It may have been about this time that, in response to the summons of three bishops to Vienne, inquiries were made in the Scottish dioceses about issues requiring redress. Of the resulting twenty or more complaints that would be forwarded to the Church Council by c.1311–12, details of two are known from a papal summary. Tellingly, these focused upon lay interference in Church provisions and trials of clerics accused of crimes (presumably aiding the enemy), particularly by captains of war who had even reportedly threatened bishops with charges of treason placed before King Robert if they refused to oust unacceptable incumbents and confirm new provisions.[144]

Such formal complaints may have reached Robert I through the processes of a Scottish Church Council active c.1309–10. Yet even if unsolicited these appeals were surely welcome in confirming the acceptance by a growing proportion of the populace of Bruce jurisdiction. Admittedly, without any surviving exchequer rolls before 1327–28 it is not possible for historians to confirm the real extent of the Bruce administration's recovery in 1309: some of Robert's appointments may thus have been presumptive (or motivational). By this juncture he had appointed Stephen de Donydouer, a canon of Glasgow, as Chamberlain; but he would be replaced by October that year with William Lindsay, canon of Glasgow and younger son of prominent loyalist Sir Alexander Lindsay of Barnweill.[145] Finally, that the March 1309 parliament saw some discussion, too, of the war's progress and how to improve the Scottish host is suggested by Robert's only extant dated charter from this parliament, of 16 March, to an Adam Marshall (a rebellious son of Sir John Marshall of Hilton in south-east Berwickshire), of the Peeblesshire barony of Manor for the service of ten archers (rather than its original one knight's fee) after its forfeiture from Alexander Baddeby: this

was a grant that promised to take the fight south of Forth with more effective weapons, into the economic hub of the Lothians and marches.[146]

Robert's activities throughout the remaining seven months of truce
further reflected the complexity of royal obligations thus highlighted at
St Andrews and found him dealing with matters in several quarters of his
realm. By 20 March 1309 he had moved to Dunfermline Abbey with key
supporters. He may have gone there to visit the tomb and mark the obsequies of Alexander III (d.19 March 1286), whom he had just claimed very
publicly to have succeeded (and to initiate an inquest with his officers).
While there he granted the royal thanage of Downie in Angus, in free
barony, to the Bruce's family retainer Sir Walter Bickerton of nearby Craigie
(Fife) in return for service by a knight.[147] By late June, however, Robert and
a host had returned north to consolidate his achievements of the previous
year.[148] From Cromarty on 1 July, the furthest north Robert ever ventured
throughout his reign, he ordered his sheriff of Forres (perhaps Sir David
Barclay) not to impede the Cistercian abbey of Kinloss (Moray) in plans to
divert a water course to its precinct.[149]

Then on 16 July the veteran James Steward passed away, depriving the
king of the guidance of an experienced lord who had done much to shape
and steer his choices and affinity over the past twelve years and more;
Robert must have travelled to the Cistercian abbey at Paisley for his
funeral.[150] But 8 August found the king back as far into the north-west as
he would ever issue a charter, on the sea-loch of Broom where he paused
to convert the Nairnshire thanage of Cawdor into an annual rent of
12 merks.[151] This was an act witnessed by Chancellor Bernard, Malcolm of
Lennox, John Menteith and a Nigel Campbell, a company that suggests
pursuit of the Macdougalls or their allies into Wester Ross. Two months
later, the king had only travelled south as far as Dunstaffnage castle in
Argyll with a retinue including knights Robert Keith, David Barclay,
Walter the new young hereditary Steward, James Lindsay and his kinsman
William, now Chamberlain, and Henry of Annan; but while there
confirming the expulsion of the Macdougalls (into English naval service in
the Irish Sea), Robert dealt with business in Lothian and Berwickshire,
confirming three baronies to the de Viponts, father and son, surely as a
promise pending their future recovery.[152]

By All Souls', 2 November, the last day of the truce, Robert was back at
St Andrews (perhaps for talks through Bishop Lamberton about extending
the ceasefire) where he appointed Malcolm, earl of Lennox, as sheriff of
Clackmannan.[153] The king's presence in Fife (over Christmas) may also
have prompted further approaches from local officials. After he had crossed

the country to Dumbarton castle by 5 March 1310 – perhaps to receive continental supplies and arms by sea – he would order his justiciar of Scotia (now Sir Robert Keith) to inquire into the privileges of the office of constable of Crail castle and its valuable royal manors.[154] A lord with similar experience, gravitas and widespread lands had surely been appointed to begin work as Robert's Justiciar of Lothian, perhaps Sir Alexander Lindsay of Barnweill, Crawford and the Byres or, when he died c.1309, his son David.[155]

In sum, although surviving evidence suggests that Robert's immediate counsel remained the same tight-knit group close to him in 1307–8, new faces had appeared and been rewarded and some key men turned. His party did remain an 'uncertain factional rising', unable to risk a large-scale encounter with a substantial Anglo-Scottish force or to make real gains against the network of garrisons in the Lothians, marches and south-west.[156] Yet Robert was undeniably conducting himself as king of Scots. In response, a number of local communities and institutions, mostly north of the Forth – but by the summer of truce of 1309 as far south as Melrose Abbey – had sought his lordship. King Robert, as he now was for many, had already come a long way since the dark days of 1306.

# CHAPTER FIVE

# The Harder they Fall
## Victory in Scotland, 1310–14

*Let the retaliation of Scotland depend on her foot-soldiers, her mountains, her mosses, her countryside;*
*Let woods, bow and spear serve as secure walls.*
*Let her warbands threaten among the narrow places, and let her plains be so kindled with fires that they are abandoned by the enemy . . .*
*Thus thrown into disorder the enemy will retire, put to flight by the sword of hunger;*
*It is a certainty, so King Robert assures us.*

Verse chronicle of Bernard of Arbroath[1]

### King *versus* King, 1310–11

If Edward II hoped that his coronation would be a triumph of reconciliation, he was quickly disappointed. Planned for Westminster Abbey on the Translation feast of St Edward the Confessor (18 February) in early 1308, the ceremony was delayed (with Archbishop Winchelsey of Canterbury unable to officiate).[2] Although the earls, including Aymer de Valence, newly belted as earl of Pembroke, took significant roles in the ritual, the negative reaction of contemporaries focused upon the prominence of Piers Gaveston, now earl of Cornwall, who carried the Confessor's crown and sword and monopolised the king.[3]

Much debate has latched onto perceived innovations within the coronation oath that Edward swore – 'to uphold the rightful laws and customs which the community of the realm shall have chosen' – as proof of mounting opposition to the king and his favourite; that, rather than a willing pledge to work with parliament, and especially the Lords, to reform a legacy of faults of government and accumulated war debt (over £200,000).[4] In the face of pressure from his magnates and Philip IV, Edward II had to agree to Gaveston's exile from court once more. However, Edward's imme-diate efforts to restore his friend – appointing him Lieutenant of Ireland on 16 June 1308, just a day after Richard, earl of Ulster, had been assigned this role – would badly undermine plans to mount a fresh royal expedition to Scotland.[5] A muster ordered on 21 June for Carlisle on 22 August never happened. As we have seen, by year's end French and papal intervention, which Edward hoped to turn to favour Gaveston's restoration, had mediated an Anglo-Scottish truce from 2 February to 1 November 1309; by 3 August Edward would feel obliged to complain to Philip IV that his recent letters to the Scots had even styled Bruce as king.[6]

While Robert I was free to consolidate his position in Scotland, Edward faced the demands of his parliament at Westminster in April 1309 which, in return for Gaveston's rehabilitation, called for substantial reform of the royal prerogative of war prise and purveyance as well as redress of numerous other grievances. Edward's reluctant concession to these demands enabled another muster for war in Scotland, called to Newcastle for 29 September; a force of 3,000 Irish foot under the earl of Ulster was also expected against Bruce supporters in the Western Isles.[7] Yet again this campaign failed to materi-alise, with Edward now locked in a vicious cycle of subjects' complaints about the burdens of two aborted expeditions. A further parliament originally summoned on 26 October to assemble at the northern base of York on 8 February 1310 had to be redirected to Westminster. Here the English king faced definitive demands that a committee of 'Ordainers' be appointed to reform his government, or else he would face deposition as the 'community of the realm' acted to uphold the Crown and common good.[8] By then Edward had already ordered his garrisons at Banff, Perth, Dundee, Ayr, Berwick and, significantly, Carlisle, to take separate truces from the Scots, agreements for which Walter of Guisborough reported the Scots extracted large sums of money, rolled into a general ceasefire until Whitsun–Midsummer 1310.[9]

Robert I's extant acts provide only minimal evidence for his activities during this truce in the first half of 1310. About 24 February a Scottish Church Council, chaired by Bishop Lamberton – again on parole – met in Dundee, under the watchful eye of another beleaguered English garrison.[10] On 19 February 1310 a royal party seems to have met just across the Tay river at the Tironensian abbey of Lindores in Fife (the foundation and burial church of Earl David of Huntingdon and, like Kilwinning, Lesmahagow and Arbroath, a daughter house of Kelso), where Sir Thomas Randolph, already demonstrating his abilities, was described as the 'king's lieutenant between Forth and Orkney' (a brief that may have anticipated his sweeping northern regality of the earldom of Moray).[11] A royal presence around Dundee is likely, as the business of the Church Council was both to report on Bishop Lamberton's inquiry into valuable Templar lands in Scotland (which had taken place at Holyrood Abbey outside Edinburgh in November 1309 before a papal inquisitor) and to seal a revised version of the clergy's parliamentary declaration of the previous March (with the Vienne Council now postponed until September 1310); these statements must have been dispatched with appeals about Wishart's continued confinement in England (albeit under papal supervision) and impediments to William Sinclair's consecration as bishop-elect of Dunkeld. The Crown and *Ecclesia Scoticana* may have hoped for an increasingly favourable hearing from Clement V, given Franco-papal involvement with Edward II's difficulties over Gaveston and English protests over curial control of benefice provisions.[12]

King Robert also required Lamberton's assistance to secure Chancellor Bernard's elevation to the abbacy of Arbroath, and 15 April 1310 found the king back once more at the Augustinian island priory of Inchmahome in Menteith from where he granted Arbroath the forfeited goods of an enemy taken on the abbey's lands.[13] Banff castle seems to have fallen about this time and Robert – or Randolph – may have made another ayre north to reinforce royal authority. In a similar fashion, much of the summer was taken up with preparations to besiege isolated English garrisons at Ayr, Perth and Dundee.[14] Robert surely laid the groundwork by making further promises or grants of patronage, including perhaps to the merchants, churches and hinterland freeholders of the royal burghs around these strongholds.

Summer also saw Robert and Edward Bruce dispatch ships to Ireland where the truce allowed them to purchase corn, meat, wine, armour and weapons.[15] Ireland was a vital source of supply in this and subsequent years, as wet, windy summers compounded the effects of war. By late 1310, there were English reports, too, of a planned assault by Bruce forces aboard MacDonald galleys to capture the strategically vital Isle of Man (recently reinforced by the earl of Ulster).[16] It has been suggested that a previously misdated letter (surviving in a fifteenth-century English transcription) written in papal Latin and offering peace talks to Edward II may place Robert I at Kildrum (now part of Cumbernauld in present-day North Lanarkshire) on 1 October 1310, thus perhaps returning east from Dumbarton from preparations for a seaborne campaign.[17] However, it is far more likely that this olive branch from Bruce (and its submissive tone) in fact belongs to October 1320 and diplomatic stratagems of that year

(when papal legates were on the border engaged in Anglo-Scottish mediation); by this date in 1310, besides, Edward II was already well advanced
into central Scotland with his army, reaching Biggar by c.26 September
(and would surely have been addressed directly in French).[18]

Robert's next datable letter places him (or Chancellor Bernard) at
Montrose on 3 December 1310, acting to inhibit the outgoing abbot of
Arbroath from drawing a pension from the house intended for the royal
Chancery (and still rebuilding after a fire of 1272).[19] By this juncture
Robert I had withdrawn his main army to the north or west to evade the
advancing English host. It is indicative of Robert's still limited level of
support and the strength of the remaining network of Anglo-Scots garrisons
that he still declined a decisive reckoning in battle. Yet in retrospect,
Edward II was perhaps at times far more vulnerable in 1310 than he would
be at the outset of his ill-fated 1314 campaign. Having agreed in March to
the appointment of twenty-one Ordainers to oversee reform of his government in the year from 29 September 1310, Edward had summoned a host to
Berwick for 8 September. He persisted in his plans despite the cancellation
of the aforementioned Ulster force and knowledge that many English
magnates – headed by the earls of Lancaster, Hereford, Warwick and the
experienced Pembroke (de Valence) – would refuse to participate in person,
sending only their minimal feudal levy. It was thus a force of barely 4,000
Welsh infantry with a few hundred English horse and archers that joined the
available southern garrisons for a winter campaign which certainly failed to
live up to the reinforcing efforts of Edward I in 1301–2 and 1303–4.[20] Once
this became clear, might not Robert have risked all to defeat, capture or kill
the enemy king, or seek an alliance with Edward's domestic opponents that
included recognition of a Bruce monarchy over a sovereign Scottish realm?

In fact, Robert did not have a clear opportunity to pursue any of these
possibilities. Edward II may have been motivated to journey north with
Gaveston to distance his household from the Ordainers' scrutiny. Yet he
was at least aware, too, just as he would be in 1314, of the need finally to
show some personal support to Scots loyal to England. At Westminster on
16 June 1310 Edward had received a delegation of Sir Alexander Abernethy,
Ingram d'Umfraville and the Macdougalls, who chided that he would 'lose
both the land and those who still remain faithful to him by reason of [y]our
default and laxity'.[21] But, heeding this to the minimum degree, Edward
confined his operations in September and October 1310 to resupplying his
garrisons only as far north as Linlithgow. By 11 November he was back at
Berwick to oversee fresh castle-keeper and regional lieutenancy appointments: this still included an English warden of Annandale (Sir John de

Segrave) but not of Galloway and Carrick, now lost to Bruce destabilisation.[22] However, Edward would remain at Berwick for the next six months, hamstrung by a lack of funds and supplies during another hard winter in which, typically, the English found 'no food for their horses'; but also, remarkably, because he remained anxious to draw up a line of defence against his own magnatial critics.[23]

A raid by Robert into the Lothians about this time, in which the Scots 'inflicted much damage upon those who were in the king of England's peace', may have been designed to tempt the English out.[24] Yet Edward only pursued his rival a short distance – probably into the Selkirk forest – before returning to Berwick. When English forces did make forays in search of the enemy, the task fell on the one hand to Gaveston, whom Edward sent to winter at Perth until late March 1311 with a mounted contingent 'in case Robert de Brus, who was then marching towards Galloway, should go beyond the said sea [the Forth] to collect troops'; or to the earls of Gloucester and Surrey, charged to take homages from forest and Marcher tenantry in February.[25] As an anonymous report of April 1311 had it: 'it was said that Robert de Brus meant to fight the Earl of Cornwall (Gaveston): but he did not believe he was able to meet the King's forces in a plain field', preferring to let them fend off his raids while they awaited 'the grass, when the [English] host may foray and get supplies for the horses'.[26] In truth hunger kept both sides at bay: according to Fordun's annalist, 'there was such a shortage of bread and such a high price of food in Scotland that in most places through force of necessity many fed on the flesh of horses and other unclean animals'.[27]

Then in early February there was a tense stand-off across the border between Edward and Thomas, earl of Lancaster, who had come north to perform homage for his inheritance of the earldom of Lincoln but refused to cross over to his king: Edward blinked first.[28] On 19 February an English official reported that on about 17 December 1310 talks had taken place at Selkirk, with Edward II's knowledge, between Sir Robert Clifford and 'Robert de Brus'.[29] This may have been for a simple truce but it may also add fire to smoky chronicle rumours that at this time Edward was prepared to make peace with Robert in return for Gaveston's safety.[30] A further reported meeting set 'for a place near Melrose' between the young Gloucester, Gaveston (who was married to a de Clare, the king's niece) and Bruce, suggests talks were indeed escalating to more serious matters.[31]

Yet accusations of collusion with Bruce were surely the tactic of Edward II's opponents and later critics. Edward was not so enamoured of Gaveston as to give up his father's conquest of Scotland and betray his

Scottish supporters: that would have been to play directly into the Ordainers' hands. Crucially, Robert stayed away from the supposed Melrose talks, because 'it was said he had been warned by some he would be taken, and therefore departed, so they have had no parley'.[32] This hints at the far greater likelihood that the English king and his councillors rather intended the success that Robert's capture and destruction would bring to bolster their political position against the Ordainers.

This suspicion of a trap may explain why no further negotiations seem to have taken place in the next six months. Robert can be found at Elgin in June, overseeing by royal brieve his sheriff of Forres' restoration of thanage resources to Dunfermline Abbey's daughter house of Pluscarden Priory.[33] That Edward's intent was besides always war not peace with Robert is confirmed by his orders of late February for a fleet of over sixty Irish and west-coast English ships to transport John Macdougall and a force of about 4,000 men – including 500 hobelar horsemen – for landings along the Scottish coast, from Ayr to Argyll.[34] Once again, this ambitious expedition failed to materialise, just as Edward II's summons of footmen and cavalry from the English shires of April–May 1311, without parliamentary consent, came to nought. So, too, did a royal plan to send Gaveston out against the Scots with a force from Dundee in May while Sir Henry Percy and Robert d'Umfraville, earl of Angus, held Perth.[35] On 16 June Edward relented and summoned parliament to Westminster for 8 August, a gathering delayed long enough for the king to visit Becket's shrine at Canterbury.[36] Yet within a fortnight of Edward's departure from Berwick, Robert and his lieutenants bypassed the restocked border garrisons and launched a series of devastating raids from Annandale and Selkirk forest into Westmorland and Northumberland between 12 and 20 August, with an emboldened, ruthless return between 8 and 23 September.[37]

As well as avenging recent deceit, these raids fulfilled a number of objectives. Penetrating some 70 miles into English territory, the greater scale and duration of these chevauchées brought a significant return in supply and plunder, seizing newly harvested crops from grange barns and a 'very large booty of cattle'. After a poor summer this would help see the Scots through to spring. Such raids could also target quite specific gains: that of August hit the former Bruce/Arbroath holding at Haltwhistle where the uncooperative John, abbot of Arbroath, was taken prisoner; the follow-up in September marched through Corbridge with its lead mines and as far as Ovingham near Prudhoe, lands of the d'Umfravilles. The Scots may even have hoped to hit the granges of Durham Cathedral in Weardale where their old foe, Bishop Bek, who died in March 1311, had kept a stud of over 200 horses.[38]

In such straitened times, the Scots had often sent small forces across the border in recent years. But 1311 saw the beginning of a systematic exploitation of Edward II's inability to defend his northern shires by the Scots who could thus at once worsen the English king's political situation and subsidise their own domestic government and warfare. According to the Lanercost chronicler, in the face of these autumn raids the Northumbrians bought a short truce from Bruce, until 2 February 1312, for the steep sum of £2,000.[39]

## Wondrous Times, 1312-13

In September 1311 the earldom of Dunbar also bought a truce from Robert's Scots until February 1312. Unable to rely on the garrisons of Edinburgh, Jedburgh, Roxburgh and Berwick, Earl Patrick (VIII) had no option against Bruce forces able to move about increasingly freely in the south-east.[40] Indeed, an inquest held at York on 20 February 1312 under the English sheriff of Edinburgh reveals the growing extent of Bruce's south-eastern support (as well as the deterioration of land values).[41] Dunbar's choice was vindicated after 9 October when the Ordainers revoked all recent grants, including offices, made in Scotland and Ireland and moved to purge England of the influence of the now exiled Gaveston; Robert's forces took and razed Ayr castle sometime after December.[42] This was only one of several castles which the Bruce Scots by now sought to take by stealth or blockade. Passion Sunday (12 March) 1312 found Robert at Cambuskenneth Abbey issuing letters to free Scone Abbey from royal exactions for a year, but surely while his forces scouted around Stirling castle.[43] On 7 April he was on the road to Dundee, at Inchture, where he continued compensating Scone Abbey for its losses. Significantly, this charter provides the first extant witness list to a Bruce royal act since November 1309 and includes Chancellor Bernard's debut as abbot of Arbroath at what may have been a short wartime council.[44]

By 12 April the king was at Dundee where the castle and port had just fallen to his siege. Several important charters were processed in what was a continuation of business from Inchture to a formal council or parliament where appeals from a number of individuals and communities may have been presented.[45] Significantly, among the witnesses recorded to two acts on 12 April confirming the regality lands and rights of Arbroath Abbey north of Tay were (for the first time on an extant royal charter) Edward Bruce 'lord of Galloway, our brother' and Thomas Randolph 'lord of Annandale, our nephew'.[46] This was a clear sign of the resolve of Robert's forces in their assault on their enemies in the south-west where the Anglo-Scottish occupation had been pushed back to Buittle, Dumfries and Caerlaverock, a trio of fortresses which Robert himself would lead troops to attack in July. However, Robert's favour to his brother and heir, and his, really prospective, grant of the historic Bruce lordship to Randolph (held in return for ten knights' service), may also be related to the difficult question of the royal succession, an issue the king would soon have to broach. Robert's other extant act from this assembly saw him issue letters patent asserting that burghs should negotiate their military services and other exactions only with his Chamberlain, perhaps a reflection of burgesses' petitions about dealing with local lords and castle-keepers or offsetting purveyance and war service by financial composition.[47]

Robert's energy and intelligence in beginning to prosecute a number of theatres of war simultaneously throughout 1311–12 whilst continuing to oversee the realm's administrative recovery have been understandably praised, not least as they demonstrated his ability to exploit Edward II's own growing political and military problems.[48] By 16–20 January 1311, indeed, Edward had travelled north to York where he denounced the Ordinances, began to gather baronial support and restored Gaveston to his lands. Predictably enraged, at Westminster the Ordainer earls – Lancaster, Hereford, Pembroke, Warwick, Arundel and a reluctant Gloucester – began to muster troops and swore oaths to capture the Gascon 'traitor' while the Archbishop of Canterbury excommunicated him for a second time.[49] According to the contemporary *Vita Edwardi Secundi*, Edward now 'feebly' sought 'Piers' residence in Scotland until the baronial attack should cease'.[50] It is possible that Robert gathered another short council or parliament to discuss this offer, perhaps after Easter 1312: according to a report that reached Edward II by 14 July, Bruce held 'a parliament at Ayr' sometime after Edward's arrival at York (16–20 January or 23 May 1312).[51] An English royal clerk, none other than John Walwayn, a possible author of the *Vita*, had been arrested in February 1311 having made a sudden passage to speak to 'Robert de Brus' near Perth; he may have been privy to similar talks in the following year.[52] Moreover, according to the contemporary *Annales Londonienses*, which are well informed about the English parliament's counter-moves, in March 1312 Clifford and Percy had been given captainship of the Anglo-Scottish Marches by the Ordainers to prevent contact between Edward and Bruce.[53]

However, the *Vita*'s insistence that Robert rejected Edward's offers out of hand again reads more like an imagined speech that further confirms the English monarch's untrustworthiness in the eyes of his English critics:

... finally the kingdom of Scotland itself was offered to Lord Robert freely and for ever, he is said to have replied to the king's message in this manner: 'How shall the king of England keep faith with me, since he does not keep the sworn promises made to his liege men, whose homage and fealty he has received, and with whom he is bound in return to keep faith?'[54]

No Scottish annals (or Barbour) mention any such approach. Moreover, about February–March 1312 talks were afoot for the exchange of Robert's sister, Mary, for Sir Philip Mowbray's brother, but these may have stalled.[55] Thus, if based in truth, Robert's refusal to aid Gaveston may have been influenced by his experience of broken Plantagenet promises of 1296 and 1301–2 as well as by his reading of the political and military situation in 1312. The terms offered would have had to include recognition of Scottish sovereignty and return of territory to the 1286 position (including the Isle of Man and economic hubs of Roxburgh and Berwick), as well as the release of Robert's queen, daughter, three sisters and captive allies. However, the latter points could have been far more quickly resolved than Robert's reconciliation with owners of lands in Scotland who had been his enemies since 1306 (an issue that would prove intractable in the eventual Anglo-Scottish peace process of 1327–28). Both Edward II and Robert, besides, must have reasoned that in 1312 this group of cross-border 'Scottish' lords – headed by the remaining Comyns, Atholl, Dunbar, Angus, the latter's brother Ingram d'Umfraville, Alexander Abernethy, David de Brechin, the Mowbrays, Macdowalls, McCans and Macdougalls – would in turn surely throw their support behind the Ordainers (just as the 'Disinherited' would back Isabella and Mortimer against Edward II in 1326), who included such familiar faces as Valence, Percy and Clifford, a number of whose families had held lands in Scotland before 1296 or who had been rewarded with Scottish titles by Edward I in 1306–7. They would thus immediately surround Edward II at York, holding fast until war in Scotland could be resumed and the titles of Bruce and his supporters could be claimed.

In short, if talks did occur, they represented a last resort for Edward II, his pregnant sixteen-year-old queen, and Gaveston: a similar context might be suggested for the *Vita*'s assertion that Edward was also willing to give up Gascony if Philip IV and Clement V intervened to save Gaveston.[56] In fact, as late as 1 April Edward wrote to Philip IV informing him of his intention to move troops towards Scotland in anticipation of a Bruce attack.[57] According to the anonymous report of July 1312, Robert 'intended to send Sir Edward his brother, with the greater part of his forces, into England, while he himself attacked the castles of Dumfries, Buittle and Caerlaverock, remaining there, and sending his light troops to plunder the north for their support.'[58] Thus in the end it made far more sense for Robert to continue to wait upon events, overrun what he could of a weakening occupation force in Scotland and plunder the northern English counties in the meantime, and then negotiate with whatever regime emerged in Westminster.

This Bruce strategy nearly paid off. In early May much-anticipated civil war broke out in England, with the earl of Lancaster and his allies pursuing Edward and Gaveston from Newcastle, then besieging the latter in Scarborough castle until his surrender on 19 May. The Ordainers opened talks with Edward at York but more hard-line elements – Lancaster, Warwick, Hereford and Arundel – seized Gaveston as he was escorted south under safe-conduct: on 19 June the hated favourite was executed. Just as had Comyn's slaughter in 1306, Gaveston's death polarised a tense situation. Surrey and Pembroke realigned themselves with the king as – at least nominally – did London and the Cinque Ports. Throughout August, as Lancaster and his allies moved towards London, Edward prepared for a parliament at Westminster and marshalled French and papal help to confront the earls and annul the Ordinances. September saw another armed standoff in London while papal envoys sought to facilitate negotiations.[59]

Given the complete distraction of the English political community, Robert I may have felt he had been over-cautious in the late spring/early summer of 1312, focusing his energies on a largely unsuccessful attack on castles in south-west Scotland.[60] Sometime in that summer Bruce may have burned the town of Norham in revenge for damage done to his cause by the castle there, removing cattle and ransoming prisoners.[61] Thereafter, Robert himself reportedly led an even deeper plunder and tribute raid into Northumberland (again hitting Hexham and Corbridge) and now the palatinate see of Durham. Indeed, the rich weekly market of the cathedral priory was stripped and parts of the city put 'to the flames' on the Annunciation feast of the Virgin. A day later, 16 August, County Durham purchased a year's truce from 'Robert par le grace de Dieu roi Descoce' for 450 merks until 24 June 1313, and Westmorland, Cumberland and Copeland may have followed suit; in describing these raids the Lanercost chronicler for the first time, too, styles Robert as 'King of Scotland'.[62]

It was at this juncture that a number of key opponents now entered King Robert's peace. It may have been sometime before 15 October 1312, indeed, that David, earl of Atholl, lord of Strathbogie and Strath'an – the son (born c.1290) of Robert's great ally executed by Edward I in 1306 – submitted to the king: a charter of that date survives to Sir Gilbert Hay who now had to be compensated for loss of the office of hereditary royal constable which was transferred to Earl David.[63] Atholl had served in the Dundee and Roxburgh garrisons of 1311–12.[64] However, his last appearance in the English records dates to 4 December 1312, when it was ordered that he should receive a payment of 100s for attending the Westminster parliament of August that year in company with Ingram d'Umfraville, John Macdougall of Argyll, Alexander Abernethy, David Graham, John Comyn of Badenoch and Edmund Comyn of Cavers.[65] These men were well aware of Edward II's inability to focus upon Scottish affairs. English attention was so poor, indeed, that the regime was unaware as yet of Atholl's switch. The latter might have been predicted if only because of his heavy debts to the English Crown. In June 1307, David had agreed to purchase his forfeited earldom back from Ralph de Monthermer, then earl of Gloucester and Hertford by right of his wife (thus Edward II's brother-in-law), for 5,000 merks over ten years; however, at Cumnock in Ayrshire in March 1311 David had been issued with a writ for arrears with none of this sum yet paid.[66]

Robert had thus probably exploited expertly Atholl's worries over patrimony by promising him his family lands without fine. The resulting defection was a major coup given Atholl influence over landed society in central Scotland.[67] Nevertheless, it may not have been one that the king of Scots fully trusted to last, not least because David's wife Joan, daughter of the murdered John Comyn of Badenoch, and their teenage son probably remained in England on his family's estates at Chilham near Canterbury.[68] Thus at about this time Robert put in place an important counter-balance to restored Strathbogie power by elevating Thomas Randolph, his 'lieutenant from Forth to Orkney', as earl of Moray, now defined as a sweeping regality in northern Scotland, including royal demesne and the forfeited Comyn lordship of Badenoch and thus the Marches of Strathbogie and northern Atholl. (The Moray earldom would now embrace Sir Gilbert of Glencarnie's forfeited lordship, the Speyside royal thanages of Fochabers and Rathenach and the adjacent lordship of Rothes; across Nairn to Inverness and the bounds of the earldom of Ross and then down the Great Glen to include ex-Comyn Lochaber (made up of Mamore, Locharlcaig, Glengarry and Glenelg) and on to march with ex-Macdougall (now MacDonald) lands in Argyll, the whole to be held for eight knights' service (plus customary common army service for Moray holdings).)[69] By the same token, some of Robert's 'lost acts' – preserved as early modern listings without date – may have been issued at this time, including grants of the extensive lordships of Fortingall and Glendochart, embracing the west March of the Atholl earldom, to Sir Alexander Menzies.[70]

In undertaking this landmark act of patronage to Randolph (the first creation of an earl in Scotland since 1230) whilst also going to considerable lengths nonetheless to pardon and accommodate another powerful former foe (David of Atholl), it should be recognised that Robert may also have had to take time in 1312–13 to rework other aspects of his early settlement north of the Forth. Not least, by including Lochaber in Moray's regality, the king may have reversed an early speculative grant of this mainland lordship to the MacDonalds of c.1306–8.[71] Admittedly, the Moray regality was far too large a province for one man and his young affinity to control on the ground, and MacDonald control of Lochaber surely persisted. Yet in 1312 this may have marked the beginnings of a cooling in personal relations between the king and his Western Isles allies, with Robert turning instead to favour William, earl of Ross, the Campbells of Lochawe and Walter Steward as policemen for the north-west.

Therefore it was perhaps now that Ross first received a portion of the Comyn earldom of Buchan (as did his heir, Hugh) and further royal thanages along the Moray Firth, while his second son, John, gained Buchan lands through marriage to one of Earl John Comyn's sisters.[72] Certainly, 6 November 1312 found the king at Elgin offering judgment in a dispute over the Moray castle-barony of Duffus between the widow of his enemy Reginald Cheyne and another Bruce loyalist, Sir Alexander Fraser of Touch-Fraser/Philorth (another Atholl neighbour).[73] Then 24 January 1313 would find the king granting (probably from Perth) significant Argyll lands to Dugall Campbell of Lochawe in return for a 'ship of 26 oars to be imployed in the king's army furnished with men and victuall'.[74]

Favour to William, earl of Ross, may also have secured another check upon David of Atholl, yet Robert extended his lordship ideally in the hope of a strong working relationship between a triumvirate of northern earls, alongside other regional lords and, of course, prelates. Strikingly, on 29 October 1312 Robert would travel with a court to Inverness to seal a treaty with King Håkon V of Norway, easing recent tensions between Scots and Norse baillies in Orkney (where the earl was just emerging from a minority) and Shetland.[75] Robert's first diplomatic agreement with a foreign realm, aided by his sister's status as Dowager Queen of Norway (as Håkon's widowed sister-in-law), settled a number of mutual claims for compensation (with the king of Scots agreeing to pay some 600 merks to St Magnus Cathedral in Orkney) and was witnessed by those Scottish magnates regionally responsible for enforcing these redefined relations: Henry Cheyne, bishop of Aberdeen; David de Moravia, bishop of Moray; Thomas, bishop of Ross; Ferchard, bishop of Caithness; William, earl of

Ross (who also administered the wardship of the earldom of Sutherland); David, earl of Atholl; and Thomas, newly earl of Moray.[76]

Emboldened by this new coalition, as well as by Edward II's ongoing problems, Robert now swept south back to the other end of his realm and launched a surprise attack on Berwick. On the night of 6 December 1312 a sneak assault by men deploying grappling irons and rope ladders was reportedly only foiled by a barking dog.[77] Yet, in truth, this and other operations in the south-east may have been diversionary, designed to bleed men, resources and morale away from northerly garrisons. On the night of 7–8 January, indeed, Barbour (resuming his chronological coverage) relates that Robert himself led his men through the freezing waters of the defensive moats around Perth and up ladders over the burgh's castellated stone walls: this was a feat also celebrated in verse by Chancellor Bernard.[78] Such an inspiring personal example by Robert is at once believable yet questionable for a man periodically ill and as yet without a son to succeed him. Starved of supplies and pay since the Scots had taken Dundee almost a year before, Perth castle itself fell shortly thereafter, bringing such Scottish opponents as Sir William Oliphant (the patriot 'of the Lion' at Stirling in 1304), Alexander Abernethy and, most significantly, the unlucky Malise, the aged sixth earl of Strathearn, into Robert's hands and peace.[79] Yet a retrospective Bruce desire to blacken David of Atholl's name (given his defection back to the English halfway through the battle of Bannockburn in 1314) is suggested by the fact that whereas the later Scottish annals also emphasise King Robert's leadership at Perth, Sir Thomas Gray, with access to both his father's memories and other Scottish accounts, insists instead that 'the Earl of Atholl had taken the town of Perth from William Oliphant, the King of England's captain, for the benefit of Robert Bruce'.[80] This would make sense given Atholl's Perthshire lordship yet, if accepted, calls into serious doubt Barbour's narrative and Robert I's inherited image. However, in 1312, despite the new allegiance of David of Atholl, the king did not plan to garrison 'St John's town' in turn, apparently razing both Perth castle and the burgh walls to the ground while taking fealty from the burgesses and confirming their privileges held of the Crown, but also hanging some identifiable collaborators.[81] It is likely, too, that the sheriffship of Perth was now entrusted not to Atholl, but to Malise, son of the earl of Strathearn, or to one of Robert's lesser regional adherents such as Sir Alexander Menzies or Malcolm of Innerpeffray.

Carrying forward this momentum, Bruce's forces – probably under Edward Bruce and Sir James Douglas – overran the starving garrison in Dumfries castle just a month later (7 February 1312), heralding the domino-effect collapse of any remaining smaller garrisons at Buittle, Tibbers,

Dalswinton, Annan and Caerlaverock; the Bruce family seat of Lochmaben seems, however, to have held out until at least October 1313 (as perhaps did eastward peels at Liddel and Cavers).[82] It is likely that Robert visited Dumfries himself in February for a settlement of the burgh and appointment of a sheriff (Robert Boyd of Kilmarnock/Noddsdale?); the castle's captain, Dougal Macdowall, had been allowed to leave under favourable terms despite his role in the capture and executions of Thomas and Alexander Bruce in 1307. Furthermore, if he had not already been rewarded about the time that Edward Bruce received Galloway, Douglas was perhaps now in receipt of royal favour with prospective grants of lands in Eskdale.[83]

However, Douglas's reward may in fact have been presented at what seems to have been a brief formal council held about 1 March 1313 at Scotlandwell, a property of St Andrews Cathedral Priory in Kinrossshire, home to a hospice dedicated to Thomas Becket and adjacent to St Serf's island priory (Portmoak) on Lochleven, just off the pilgrims' road past Dunfermline Abbey and St Margaret's Queensferry across the Forth.[84] It is possible that this stay reflected a health relapse for Robert after a vigorous winter campaign. But neighbouring Fife had essentially been cleared of enemy garrisons by 1311 and this venue afforded a convenient midway point for a number of important men to gather from all quarters. The king sustained a genuine belief in the intercessionary powers of Serf, a composite missionary and/or episcopal saint of the sixth century. His cult dedications extended from the parishes of Logie, Alva, Tillicoultry and Clackmannan (all east along the road from Stirling) through western coastal Fife from the Cistercian abbey at Culross said to host Serf's body shrine, past Dunfermline and on to Dysart and Burntisland, then north to Kinross parish (also dedicated to Serf) and the priory at Lochleven.[85] Serf's extended *familia* thus seems to have embraced strong associations with its intruded royal neighbour, the Benedictine house dedicated to the Trinity and Queen Margaret at Dunfermline (which also held property at Clackmannan and Dollar), with Portmoak having been founded by King David I in the same year as Dunfermline Abbey's dedication, 1150.[86] In November 1314 Robert would grant Dunfermline the church of Kinross, dedicated to Serf on the shores of Lochleven (in part to support plans for his own tomb in Dunfermline Abbey).[87] In his later years, too, Robert's new manor house at Cardross in Dumbartonshire lay close to a well and chapel dedicated to Serf and it was here that the king's entrails would be interred on his death.[88]

The seven surviving records of the Scotlandwell assembly, if such it was, are all royal grants and confirmations for Arbroath Abbey. Thus Robert I's favour to the cult of St Thomas (and the income of his Chancellor's house) was well served just when Edward II was criticised for using Canterbury's temporalities to cover Crown debts and then intruding his own choice of successor to the vacant archbishopric.[89] However, the Scotlandwell meeting is otherwise significant as a gathering of at least four earls and eight prelates, in many ways a far more confident display of Robert's growing authority over the community of the realm than the St Andrews parliament of March 1309. Robert and his close councillors undoubtedly still strove to retain tight control over the agenda and decisions made by this select assembly. Moreover, that the clergy present included William Lamberton, bishop of St Andrews (in the year in which he would finally break his parole), as well as Prior Adam of St Andrews and Hugh, abbot of Dunfermline, underlined the collapse of Edward II's regime in Scotland north of the Forth.[90] But the consultation at Scotlandwell, like that at St Andrews, may not have passed without controversy. These magnates may have discussed such weighty and potentially divisive matters as war strategy, diplomatic relations, noble patronage and the Scottish estates of the king's enemies, vacant church benefices and even the royal succession, carrying these issues forward to a parliament at Dundee in October 1313.

One item over which the king and his counsel may have wrangled was who would take up lordship of the Isle of Man from the king's hand once it was conquered, as plans for a naval landing must already have been well under way. Title to the Isle of Man may have been a source of later tension between Edward Bruce and Thomas Randolph requiring royal mediation in 1316–17. However, between 18 May and 12 June 1313 Robert's forces cooperated to great effect, the ships of Captain Thomas Dun and MacDonald galleys landing the king and troops who crossed the island to force the unfortunate Dougal Macdowall to surrender yet another castle, Rushen.[91] Together with castle-ports at Dumbarton, Ayr and Annan, this confirmed Bruce dominance of the seaways of the eastern Irish Sea and Clyde and Solway Firths, bolstering control of the western March. As if to drive this point home, Robert is reported to have sent some of the galleys that landed on the Isle of Man to raid nearby Ulster.[92]

It was through the border passes of the western March that Robert's forces began to threaten northern English communities once more in spring and summer 1313, as they struggled to maintain tribute instalments and the end of the border truce loomed. Edward II was preoccupied after 20 December 1312 with negotiations to finalise a settlement with the Ordainers through French and papal envoys, even absenting himself to the court of Philip IV in France from 23 May until about 26 July 1313.[93] As a result, several communities of the English Marches 'apprehending this, and

neither having nor hoping for any defence or help from their king . . .
offered to the said Robert no small sum of money, indeed a very large
one, for a truce to last till the feast of St Michael in the following year (29
September 1314)'; the Dunbar earldom, Berwickshire and Roxburghshire
also bought respite by surrendering '1000 quarters of corn'.[94]

## The Road to Stirling, October 1313 to May 1314

During his stay in France, Edward II had also been persuaded to accept an
extended general truce with the Scots until midsummer 1314.[95] It must
have been shortly after this agreement that Robert I summoned a parliament to Dundee on or about 21 October 1313.[96] This may have been a more
relaxed and open meeting of the estates of earls, barons and clergy than
Robert had hitherto held. For example, it saw the king issue two grants in
free alms from royal demesne to the Blackfriars of Inverness and Elgin. The
parliament may also have been combined with an exchequer audit of royal
officials' accounts from the growing number of shires and burghs now
within Robert's peace; after a wet, unproductive summer this may have been
a vital exercise for identifying resources for the coming winter.[97]

A number of difficult issues may have been discussed at this meeting
and it should not simply be assumed that Robert and his councillors had
everything their way in another stage-managed forum. The Bruce Scots
had now undergone six years of hard fighting since Robert's return from
exile, and the last year had witnessed the beginnings of a substantial realignment of aristocratic power by royal charter, including the creation of Moray,
the alienation of Lochaber, Badenoch and perhaps parts of Buchan, the
return of Atholl, and the capture of the earl of Strathearn (as well as perhaps
redistribution of titles in the south-west in addition to Galloway). In this
context, there may have been renewed calls for Crown forfeiture of other
enemies' lands and decisions on important titles whose hereditary chiefs
were in ward in England, not least the earldoms of Fife, Angus, Menteith
and Mar; a more general need for inquests and judgments (with enforcement) on lands and resources that had fallen into dispute in the course of
war since around 1296 may also have been voiced.

At the same time there might naturally have been concerns raised about
the state of Robert's succession. Now in his fortieth year and intermittently
ill, Robert had no hope of a legitimate male heir while his queen, Elizabeth,
remained a prisoner in England together with his one direct heir, his
daughter Marjorie by his first, Mar wife. Between 1296 and 1312 Robert
seems to have had more than one illegitimate child, including a son, Robert,

to whom he would later show considerable favour; but this was a 'natural' child and in the meantime younger, healthier lords all around him were siring sons, not least Edward II himself, with the birth of the future Edward III celebrated at Windsor on 13 November 1312 (as well as with Philip IV at the knighting of his three sons in June 1313).[98]

Nevertheless, by the legal claim of nearness by (male) degree that the Bruces had at least at first espoused in the succession hearings of 1291–92, Edward Bruce was present as a vigorous, adult male heir presumptive who might be recognised as such by a formal act solemnised by subjects in parliament (something Robert's regime would put in place in April 1315). However, Edward, like his brother Robert, was constantly in physical danger, and in 1312–13 questions may also have been asked about the inheritance of the Scottish throne in the event of both their deaths without issue (i.e. children who were not otherwise in an English gaol). Thus alternative Scottish lords may have been discussed in terms of the succession even at this early stage.

Thanks to their family intermarriages, young Donald of Mar (born 1293), King Robert's nephew (by an older sister), may have been generally known to be the Bruces' male heir presumptive. However, contemporaries may have been persuaded that Donald's likely inability to return from England (where he was a page in the household of Edward II) would see his title and claims pass to none other than David, earl of Atholl, like Donald also a grandson of the older Donald, earl of Mar (d. 1297), and thus another nephew of King Robert (who had married the sister of David's mother).[99] Both Donald of Mar senior and Earl David's father, John of Atholl, had aligned themselves with Robert Bruce of Annandale between 1286 and 1292; Earl John, of course, died in Robert I's service in 1306. In addition, David of Atholl's (inherited) aspirations may also have extended to hoping to gain title to the vacant earldom of Menteith (causing tension with Sir John Menteith, now Bruce's sheriff of Dumbarton) and the most ancient earldom of Fife with its valuable Perthshire lordships adjacent to Atholl (Strath Braan and Strathord).[100] Interestingly, David of Atholl's attempt to mortgage his Scottish earldom back from Ralph de Monthermer, former earl of Gloucester, may have brought him into contact with the minor Duncan, earl of Fife, a ward of Edward I since 1296 and who had been married to Ralph's daughter (Mary, Edward II's niece) at the English king's request about November 1307.[101] It would thus have been natural, too, for Earl David to have thoughts of the Scottish kingship for himself or his line (prompted, too, by his marriage to the daughter of John Comyn of Badenoch). These were certainly ambitions that would be inherited by his son, Earl David VI of Atholl (d.1335), who in the 1330s (as full heir to the Comyns) would rise to be Edward III's most influential Lieutenant of Scotland amongst the lords ultimately disinherited by Robert I. Earl David was touted as a successor vassal king once the aging, childless Edward Balliol died and thus was a hugely disruptive figure. The earl intrigued in the fate of Fife with the then (de Clare) earl of Gloucester and set Bruce loyalists against each other when he, like his father before him, briefly defected in 1335 to the cause of Robert I's son, David II (tempted by no less than a grant of Lochaber from the then royal Lieutenant John Randolph, earl of Moray, Thomas's second son).[102]

All this lay in the future and Robert I, of course, may besides have had plans to deny these contingencies or at least to shuffle the pack after 1313, perhaps even favouring the third option of yet another half-nephew, Thomas Randolph, who made a meteoric rise to be lord of Nithsdale and Annandale and then earl of Moray. Yet, in truth, the king could really do nothing official until he had exhausted all possible means to secure the release of his queen, daughter, sisters and nephew Mar from imprisonment. In the meantime, he may have been obliged not to neglect some stop-gap recognition of alternatives, or at least to allay these concerns with further patronage, in response to pressure from ambitious figures such as Edward Bruce, David of Atholl and Moray.

It is thus in this context of tentatively shaping the succession – and the likely perception of a majority in parliament at Dundee in October 1313 that, barring a miraculous turnaround in fortune, Robert would probably die without a son of his own – that three extant charters of 21–24 October style Edward Bruce as 'earl of Carrick' for the first time: that, and not simply a recognition of Edward's regional and military responsibilities.[103] This was akin to Edward II's grant of the earldom of Norfolk of December 1312, just after the birth of his son, to his teenage half-brother and heir presumptive, Thomas.[104] In addition, however, it may have been about this time that the Bruce brothers followed their grandfather's familiar pattern of tying up concurrent strands of dynastic ambition by seeking a marriage for Edward Bruce, now in his early thirties, with his cousin, Earl David's sister, Isabel Strathbogie of Atholl.

It is once again Archdeacon Barbour or his lost early fourteenth-century sources that provide the infamous tale that Edward Bruce would impregnate Isabel then refuse to marry her, thus provoking Earl David to rejoin the English, attacking the Bruce baggage train on the second day of the battle of Bannockburn.[105] However, in light of the foregoing this seems like a later attempt to pin all blame on a man dead by October 1318 (Edward Bruce) and to mask real disagreements between the king and David of Atholl over far more important matters. Instead, it is likely that at some point between autumn 1312 and, say, February 1314 the betrothal of Edward and Isabel was agreed and took place with the expectation of a retrospective papal marriage dispensation (a common practice). Edward Bruce may have had his head turned by a better offer (and in June 1317 the Papacy would grant him a dispensation to marry Isabel, daughter of William, earl of Ross).[106] Yet it is more probable that it was Edward II's much improved relations with both Philip IV and, crucially, Pope Clement V in 1312–13 (discussed below) which impeded the Scots' quick attainment of this dispensation.[107] Not only, however, did Edward Bruce apparently not take another wife before his death in battle in Ireland in 1318, but Robert I recognised Isabel as countess of Atholl, despite her brother's re-defection, while her son as the king's nephew – given the undeniably royal name of Alexander Bruce – would receive significant patronage after 1314, including his uncle's/father's earldom of Carrick, almost as if he was expected to be legitimised and receive a place in the Bruce succession.[108]

Hope of a Bruce–Atholl heir (and perhaps even Alexander Bruce's birth before Bannockburn) may have been enough to smooth over tensions for the moment. Yet this was surely overshadowed by collective expectations of what would become of the main decision of the October 1313 Dundee parliament: the issue of an ultimatum to Robert I's remaining opponents with Scottish lands that they must enter his peace through homage and fealty to him as king within a year or face final forfeiture. Given the Scottish parliamentary record later in 1314, the date set by the king for this submission may have been 2 November – All Souls' Day, the day of the dead.[109]

It was this deadline that would ultimately set the date and scene for the confrontation of royal hosts at midsummer 1314; not – as according to Barbour's later distortion – Edward Bruce's foolish grant of a whole year's truce to the besieged English garrison in Stirling castle.[110] In late October–November 1313 word of Robert's declaration, spread through mercat (market) cross and pulpit, was surely brought to the English king by Patrick, earl of Dunbar, and Sir Adam Gordon of Huntly (Lothian) as envoys of 'the people of Scotland' in the English king's peace, along with heartfelt complaints about the plundering of corn, livestock and tenants for ransom by the very garrisons of Roxburgh and Berwick meant to protect Edward's Scottish subjects; these Anglophile Scots also claimed to have already (in just three years of raiding) paid Bruce £20,000 for successive truce tributes. In response, although he detained Gordon, on 28 November Edward vowed 'to lead an army to their relief at the following midsummer'.[111]

That Edward II was in a sufficiently recovered position to do so must have given Robert I and his counsel pause for thought, and perhaps widened any cracks between the king and men like Atholl. Edward's trip to France with his queen had worn down his Ordainer opponents, and pardons and a parliamentary settlement were finally agreed by 14 October 1313. As it had when first proposed at Westminster in December 1312, this compromise package, which really favoured the Crown, included a promise from the parliamentary barons to consider subsidy for a Scottish campaign. This was duly granted in November 1313 for collection by 24 June 1314. Crucially, it was to be supplemented by personal loans to Edward II from Pope Clement and access to crusading tenths (including those from southern Scotland) mortgaged against Aquitaine revenues and thus approved by Philip IV in a further meeting with Edward at Boulogne on 12 December; the French may also have been persuaded by Edward's statute of February 1313 relocating the English wool staple at St Omer by the end of the year, depriving the Flemish who continued to supply the Scots.[112] On 23 December 1313 the English parliament approved a feudal levy for the host and three days later Edward summoned eight earls and eighty-seven barons to muster their retinues at Berwick by 10 June 1314.[113]

Word of Edward's commitment must have reached the Bruce Scots by early 1314. It would be stretching the available evidence too far to argue that it had been Robert's plan since October 1313 to bring the English king to battle. Yet in the spring of 1314 guts, luck, opportunity and the will to risk all would converge to forge a Scottish strategy designed to do just that on Robert's terms. Robert and his war captains now deliberately intensified their efforts to destroy key garrison castles within the window of time remaining to them, so as to stretch the English supply line to the upper reaches of the river Forth.[114] Some of this vital work had been attained as early as August 1313 when locals had overrun and razed the tower at Linlithgow, captained by Scot Sir Alexander Livingston, opening a victualling gap of over 30 miles between Stirling and Edinburgh.[115] Then on the night of 17–18 February, Sir James Douglas, perhaps motivated by grants of lands in the Marches from his king, scaled the massive outer walls of Roxburgh with ladders, storming the castle keep two days later, and then razed it to the ground. A month later, on 14 March, Randolph's troops scaled the castle crags of Edinburgh and surprised the garrison. Barbour, perhaps drawing on earlier accounts, would assert that this had been prophesied by St Margaret, 'the gud haly quene', who had had the deed depicted on the wall of her chapel in the castle (a church Robert I later had repaired).[116] The destruction of that stronghold created a 95-mile gap of at

least four or five days' hard march from Berwick to Stirling (and the same
to Bothwell in Lanarkshire), with only Earl Patrick's castle at Dunbar (or
lesser baronial towers at Luffness, Yester or Dirleton) as midway relief.[117]
This double success in the south-east was enough to provoke at least one
substantial local lord to leave English pay in Roxburghshire and submit to
King Robert, namely Alexander Stewart of Bonkle; others may have
followed.[118]

Simultaneously, the Scots sustained pressure on Edward II's subjects in
the Marches. This in itself is surely proof that war, combined with a poor
summer and dismal harvest yield, had left the northern counties' communities struggling to pay the Scots their contracted tribute (although they may
have been encouraged to risk defiance by word of Edward's coming). Just
after Easter (7 April), Edward Bruce appeared in force in Cumberland,
burning the manors of the bishopric of Carlisle and even threatening the city.
He must then have returned north with his plunder of cattle to take over the
siege of Stirling castle that had probably begun in mid-March.[119] The earl of
Carrick did so because King Robert was perhaps ill once more. On 16
February the king was back at the hospital of St Thomas at Scotlandwell,
issuing a grant to Inchaffray Priory in company that included Chancellor
Bernard of Arbroath, Robert of Crail the new abbot of Dunfermline,
Malcolm, earl of Lennox, John Menteith, Gilbert Hay, Robert Keith the
Marischal and, interestingly, Sir Hugh of Airth (a barony with tower house
just 8 miles downstream from Stirling on the Forth).[120]

However, Edward Bruce surely acted in concert with his brother when
about mid-May 1314 he granted Stirling's constable, Scot Sir Philip
Mowbray, just a month's respite (terms that had also been offered to the
Dundee garrison in 1312): if not relieved by the expected English force
advancing to within three leagues by 24 June, the castle was to surrender.[121]
Edward II was at Newminster in Northumberland, heading north to the
Berwick muster, when he heard this news by messenger on about 26–27
May. He adjusted his plans, summoning his magnates a few days earlier to
gather at Newcastle by 1 June and levying more Yorkshire foot to cope with
what Mowbray reported as terrain 'where horses will find it difficult to
enter'.[122] Crucially, the Bruce brothers had now determined the time and
stage of engagement if a battle was to be fought.

## Battle for a Queen, 23–24 June 1314

Since 1307 both Robert I and Edward II had had ample cause to seek or
thank the intercession of saints. Yet in describing the events of 1314 and

Bannockburn, contemporary English and later Scottish commentators, all writing with knowledge of the outcome of the battle and that God chose to favour the Scots, understandably present an image of greater piety in preparation on the part of Bruce.

As he marched north Edward stopped at St Albans and the shrine of a third-century martyr (feast day 20 June) to which he presented a gold reliquary cross. However, a disrespectful halt at Ely Cathedral, a rival for St Alban's relics, upset the clergy (and later chroniclers). Thereafter, there is no evidence that the English king collected the banners of St John of Beverley (whose relics had been translated in 1307) or of St Cuthbert – despite halts at both York and Durham – as his father had done in advance of his Falkirk campaign in 1298. Nor are any English royal household relics reported as captured or returned by the victorious Scots in late 1314–early 1315.[123] Instead, Edward II's spiritual response to the 1314 campaign focused upon thanks given for his survival in defeat, with the king fulfilling a vow to found a college of twenty-four Carmelite friars at Oxford.[124]

Conversely, although no Scottish royal acts (or alms accounts) survive for the four months before the Stirling campaign, it is likely that Robert I spent some time venerating several important cults in Scotland, gathering their symbols as totems for his host. This may have included clergy who brought relics and/or banners of St Andrew, St Kentigern (from Glasgow), St Thomas (from Arbroath), St Columba of Iona (also held by lay *mormaers* at Arbroath as well as at Dunkeld and Inchcolm, feast day 9 June), St Fillan (feast day 20 June), St Serf (from Culross, feast day 1 July), St Margaret (perhaps one of her pieces of the True Cross from Dunfermline Abbey, 20 miles from Stirling, where her Translation would have been celebrated on 19 June) and St Ninian (of Whithorn, feast day 26 August).[125]

Prayer, too, would have marked the hours before battle. For Edward this may have been intensified by the opportunity to affirm his political recovery, although this was tainted by the absence of key magnates from his host, especially the earls of Lancaster and Warwick.[126] However, for Robert and his close supporters this had become not merely a chance to secure God's blessing for their lordship over all Scots, and perhaps more in terms of the status of the realm in Plantagenet eyes; but more immediately it was a gamble to effect the recovery of both Robert's twenty-four-year-old queen and teenage daughter, to ensure a direct Bruce succession. The unfolding course of the battle of Bannockburn over two days would mean that survival and perhaps victory on the field but, either way, culminating in the capture of the enemy king or at least one of his greatest subjects *must* be the Scots' objective.

To fulfil this end Robert took great care in his choice of captains, terrain and tactics. Barbour's description of the Scots' four battles cannot be trusted, marred as it is by the fabrication of a fourth schiltrom of spearmen led by Walter Steward and James Douglas (and their retinue knights) whose descendants the poet sought to honour in the 1370s.[127] Three units seems more likely, with battles for the earls of Carrick and Moray (Edward Bruce and Thomas Randolph) pivoting around a rearguard led by the king himself. The majority of modern studies favour a modest Scottish force with each of the three divisions numbering 2,000–3,000 men or slightly more, with perhaps a roving force of cavalry of about 500 men, nominally attached to Robert's force but led by Sir Robert Keith as Marischal.[128] However, a strong case has been made for the presence of a larger number of Scottish spearmen on foot around Stirling, perhaps allowing the Scottish host to approach 15,000 or even 20,000 men (as in 1298).[129] Barbour also reports the king's division as being made up of men of Carrick, Argyll (led by the Campbells of Lochawe?), the Isles (MacDonalds and MacRuaridhs), and probably the followings of the bishop of St Andrews and the earldoms of Fife and Strathearn (with Malise the younger already intruded into his father's title). However, Carrick was now his brother's fief and Robert may instead (for this and later campaigns) have pooled men from the young Walter's Stewartry alongside the Campbells and Sir John Menteith.[130] There were, besides, men under William, earl of Ross, and Malcolm, earl of Lennox, to deploy with Lennox and Douglas perhaps serving under Edward Bruce, and Ross with Moray (who was lieutenant of the north and lord of Lochaber).[131]

One point is clear, however, that even before battle lines were drawn, David, earl of Atholl, had broken away. He may have been angered by Sir Gilbert Hay's fulfilment of the role of Constable of the host, despite Atholl's restoration to that heritable office in 1312: similar tensions would also weaken cooperation between Gilbert de Clare, the young earl of Gloucester who claimed Edward II's vanguard from his Welsh Marches rival, Humphrey de Bohun, earl of Hereford, England's hereditary Constable. But in truth, Atholl may already have been alienated by the collapse/illegitimacy (despite male issue) of the Bruce–Atholl marriage, deprivation of the Comyns' inheritance or plain fear of defeat by a superior English royal host (which included his Comyn brother-in-law while his wife and son remained in England): Atholl's attack on Robert's supplies at Cambuskenneth Abbey and on a 'Sir William [surely Sir Hugh?] of Airth', as reported by Barbour, suggests an assault from outside the Scottish host.[132]

Thus Robert's divisions saw some shuffling to secure the men he trusted most. However, his choice of ground and strategy was inspired. Edward II's army – some 2,000 to 3,000 cavalry and between 15,000 and 20,000 infantry (including about 4,000 archers) – was obliged to approach along the raised road-line from Falkirk, skirted by high ground and the managed tree-line of the royal hunting park to the north and west, and to the east a mixture of cultivated farmland of raised fields and meadow intersected by causeways, irrigation/drainage ditches and marsh (farmed for peat) between the farm toun of Bannock, its mills and the meandering tidal reaches of the Forth estuary.[133] To this picture we should add the growing evidence for climatic deterioration in this decade that would culminate in Europe-wide harvest failures from 1315 to 1318.[134] A series of very wet summers had raised the already loaded water table of Stirling's clay- and peat-based carse around Bannock, turning this region's characteristic network of 'polles', slow-flowing streams that fed into the Forth, into much deeper water, sometimes fast-moving in places – like the Bannock burn itself, which could approach a torrent even at the height of summer.[135]

Barbour's assertion that Robert further narrowed this front by secreting horse-trap holes astride the approach road from the Tor Wood is believable (Bruce and Comyn as Guardians had already made use of this area while besieging Stirling in 1299).[136] Yet the Scots were also to benefit from the poor leadership and disharmony of the English host, strung out over several miles. It was the impetuous vanguard under the earl of Gloucester that clashed first with the spearmen of Robert's and Edward Bruce's divisions at the edge of the New Park. The *Vita Edwardi Secundi* confirms a dramatic moment of personal inspiration and single combat by Robert when he felled Sir Henry de Bohun's charge with a fatal blow of his battleaxe, a moment of high honour that Barbour would further embellish. Far more damage was done by Randolph's schiltrom when it routed a flanking horse troop led by bannerets Robert Clifford and Henry Beaumont on ground to the west of a chapel dedicated to St Ninian (appropriated to Cambuskenneth Abbey).[137]

After the best of the first day and with Stirling's garrison technically relieved, Robert might have withdrawn. Sir Thomas Gray, whose father was captured during the loss of Clifford's force, suggests that Bruce considered retreat to the Lennox. The Scots king was perhaps wary of an enemy force from the west as that of his father-in-law, Richard of Ulster (who was also Gloucester's father-in-law), had been levied by King Edward for this purpose.[138] However, Gray asserts that as both hosts regrouped during the short hours of midsummer's night, Scot Sir Alexander Seton of Seton left Edward and crossed to Bruce reporting English discouragement and thus convinced the Scots to attack on Monday 24 June, St John the Baptist's day.[139] Seton had supported Robert in 1306, then submitted to England but tried at least once (1309) to rejoin Bruce ranks; however, his Lothian lands had dictated his pragmatic ambivalence.[140] We should, though, take his mid-battle intelligence further: for Seton, who would be very generously rewarded by Robert in the Lothians from 1315, surely brought word of Edward's decision to attempt to flank the Scots by crossing some of the polles and carse by night and then advancing west to open, drier ground (probably covering farmland and its wastes between Bannock, Balquhidderock and Broomridge) so as to best deploy his archers and cavalry.[141] In response, the Scottish schiltroms also shifted position and emerged the following morning from the tree-line and sloping ground of Balquhidderock Wood (according to Gray in 'three divisions') to take the exhausted and advancing English in their right flank.

It is at this moment that verse attributed to Abbot Bernard asserts that Robert delivered a speech to his troops (and perhaps paused to knight some of his young men-at-arms). Emphasising the hardships and losses of Scotland's nobles and Church in search of 'freedom . . . for our right to the kingdom, for honour and liberty', the king proclaimed:

[St John,] St Andrew and Thomas who shed his blood
along with the saints of the Scottish fatherland will fight today
for the honour of the people, with Christ the Lord in the van.[142]

Scottish tradition maintains that Abbot Maurice of Inchaffray – who had helped officiate at Robert's 'coronation' in 1306 – then blessed the Scottish host and also 'put forward a short and effective statement on freedom and the defence of their right'.[143] In truth, even though some of these sentiments may not actually have been expressed on 24 June, they would soon become a fundamental part of Scottish memory of their most famous, God-given victory.

Shriven, the Scots attacked and caught the English unprepared in that 'narrow place'. Unable to bring up their archers (pinned back by a Scots cavalry charge under Keith) or to win enough ground to deploy heavy horse, 'the troops in the English rear fell back upon the ditch of Bannockburn, tumbling one over the other'. The steep ravines (dropping over 4 metres in some places) and swollen waters of the burn would perhaps kill as many as were slain by the Scots' spears and the awful crush of men and horses.[144] It was at this point that Robert's troops may have set themselves to secure a target agreed upon only decisively after hearing Seton's advice the night before – capturing the English king. The intensity of the Scots' pursuit of

Edward's person reported by both the *Vita* and later Gray suggests as much. The king, led from the field by the earl of Pembroke, found his reins seized and at least one horse speared under him by his pursuers. He escaped to the gates of Stirling castle only after a furious rearguard action in which such a celebrated flower of chivalry and veteran as Sir Giles d'Argentein sacrificed himself and the king's household steward, Sir Edmund Mauley, was killed.[145] Edward lost his shield, privy seal (and its keeper), plate, tents and baggage train; several of his clerks together with the muster rolls of the campaign may also have been taken along with the Carmelite court poet Robert Baston (whose work instead for Robert I was later reproduced in Abbot Bower's chronicle). The earl of Gloucester, Robert Clifford of Appleby, as many as forty or fifty other knights and doubtless thousands of English infantry had lost their lives.[146]

It is tempting to suggest that Sir Philip Mowbray's refusal to allow Edward refuge within Stirling's walls was designed to leave him for the Scots to seize.[147] However, although Mowbray would be allowed to surrender the castle on terms and enter Robert's peace, he would receive little or no reward in the years that followed. This would be in stark contrast to the largesse bestowed by Robert upon the Scot Walter Fitz Gilbert (progenitor of the Hamiltons), keeper for the English of the Murray castle at Bothwell (25 miles to the south-west), who admitted the fleeing earl of Hereford and other knights to his keep and then duly surrendered to the Scots.[148] By doing so, it would emerge only after the war-torn air had cooled that, at the last gasp, Gilbert had secured what Robert so badly needed – elite prisoners. For by then Edward II and his remaining retinue had ridden hard to Dunbar, chased all the way by Sir James Douglas who was surely advised of the local terrain by defectors Seton and Stewart of Bonkle. Earl Patrick of Dunbar saw Edward's escape party off to Berwick by ship and then surrendered himself and his castle; like Mowbray, he would find minimal new reward in Robert I's realm.[149]

Auditing the spoils and prisoners, Robert could survey a rich haul. The English baggage train may have yielded enough to feed a hungry army and compensate Stirling locals for their trampled (stunted and sodden) crops as well as to fill the Scottish exchequer for years to come. This was over and above the wealth in arms, armour and even horses scoured from the battle-field and pursuit. Amongst those captured were several key Scottish opponents including Robert, earl of Angus, and his brother, Sir Ingram d'Umfraville; as an undeniable omen of God's blessing (and justification for the murderous act of 10 February 1306), John Comyn of Badenoch (the younger) and his cousin, Walter Comyn of Kilbride, lay among the dead.

Robert now also had the means to oblige further Scottish holdouts to come to terms. In addition to the earl of Hereford, he also held English magnates such as Ralph de Monthermer (Edward II's brother-in-law and the earl of Fife's father-in-law), Anthony de Lucy, John de Segrave, Marmaduke Tweng, John de Eure and John de Clavering for exchange.[150]

Yet anxious questions remained. Would Robert I's captures prove sufficient to trade for what he had really come to Stirling to obtain? Even minor hostages might be redeemed for surprisingly large sums of money, but these were more typically private (rather than 'state') transactions in which prisoners could be released without political repercussions: for example, in 1320, minor Scots knights John Murray and William Barde would be exchanged at a value of 4,000 merks as part of a larger package to secure the freedom from Scotland of Andrew Harcla, sheriff-keeper of Carlisle.[151] In 1314, though, what would happen in regard to Bruce's captive family was clearly dependent upon what happened when Edward II got back to London. Would his political opponents punish Edward's defeat? Might there even be peace? Or how long would it take before men began to mutter 'Robert Bruce defeated the English at Stirling ... but then nothing happened'?

## Part Two

# AFTER BANNOCKBURN

*'Kingship is the best form of sovereignty.'*
Giles of Rome, *De Regimen Principum*, c.1277–79

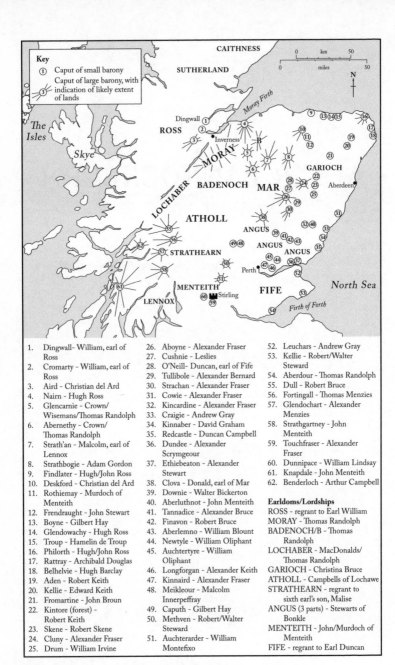

1. Dingwall– William, earl of Ross
2. Cromarty – William, earl of Ross
3. Aird – Christian del Ard
4. Nairn – Hugh Ross
5. Glencarnie – Crown/ Wisemans/Thomas Randolph
6. Abernethy – Crown/ Thomas Randolph
7. Strath'an – Malcolm, earl of Lennox
8. Strathbogie – Adam Gordon
9. Findlater – Hugh/John Ross
10. Deskford – Christian del Ard
11. Rothiemay – Murdoch of Menteith
12. Frendraught – John Stewart
13. Boyne – Gilbert Hay
14. Glendowachy – Hugh Ross
15. Troup – Hamelin de Troup
16. Philorth – Hugh/John Ross
17. Rattray – Archibald Douglas
18. Belhelvie – Hugh Barclay
19. Aden – Robert Keith
20. Kellie – Edward Keith
21. Fromartine – John Broun
22. Kintore (forest) – Robert Keith
23. Skene – Robert Skene
24. Cluny – Alexander Fraser
25. Drum – William Irvine

26. Aboyne – Alexander Fraser
27. Cushnie – Leslies
28. O'Neill– Duncan, earl of Fife
29. Tullibole – Alexander Bernard
30. Strachan – Alexander Fraser
31. Cowie – Alexander Fraser
32. Kincardine – Alexander Fraser
33. Craigie – Andrew Gray
34. Kinnaber – David Graham
35. Redcastle – Duncan Campbell
36. Dundee – Alexander Scrymgeour
37. Ethiebeaton – Alexander Stewart
38. Clova – Donald, earl of Mar
39. Downie – Walter Bickerton
40. Aberluthnot – John Menteith
41. Tannadice – Alexander Bruce
42. Finavon – Robert Bruce
43. Aberlemno – William Blount
44. Newtyle – William Oliphant
45. Auchtertyre – William Oliphant
46. Longforgan – Alexander Keith
47. Kinnaird – Alexander Fraser
48. Meikleour – Malcolm Innerpeffray
49. Caputh – Gilbert Hay
50. Methven – Robert/Walter Steward
51. Auchterarder – William Montefixo

52. Leuchars – Andrew Gray
53. Kellie – Robert/Walter Steward
54. Aberdour – Thomas Randolph
55. Dull – Robert Bruce
56. Fortingall – Thomas Menzies
57. Glendochart – Alexander Menzies
58. Strathgartney – John Menteith
59. Touchfraser – Alexander Fraser
60. Dunnipace – William Lindsay
61. Knapdale – John Menteith
62. Benderloch – Arthur Campbell

**Earldoms/Lordships**
ROSS - regrant to Earl William
MORAY - Thomas Randolph
BADENOCH/B – Thomas Randolph
LOCHABER - MacDonalds/ Thomas Randolph
GARIOCH - Christina Bruce
ATHOLL - Campbells of Lochawe
STRATHEARN - regrant to sixth earl's son, Malise
ANGUS (3 parts) - Stewarts of Bonkle
MENTEITH - John/Murdoch of Menteith
FIFE - regrant to Earl Duncan

2. Robert I's resettlement: Scotland, north of Forth

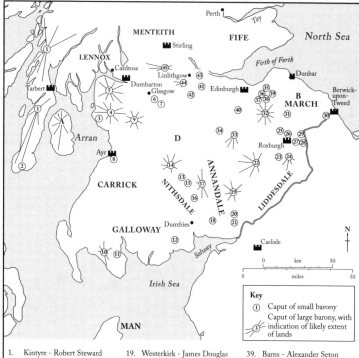

Perth

MENTEITH
Tay

FIFE

North Sea

Stirling

LENNOX

Cardross

Firth of Forth

Linlithgow ● 43
45

Dunbar

Tarbert

Dumbarton
44
41

Edinburgh

Berwick-
upon-
Tweed

● Glasgow
6
7
42

5

35
36 39
37 38

B
MARCH

1

3

4

9

40

32

31

30

Arran

34

33

25 26 29
27 28

Ayr
8

D

Roxburgh

14

22

23 24

2

CARRICK

13
15

NITHSDALE
17

ANNANDALE

19
LIDDESDALE

16

N

GALLOWAY

Dumfries ●

18

20
21

Carlisle

12

0        km        50

0        miles        50

Irish Sea

Solway

MAN

**Key**

① Caput of small barony

③ Caput of large barony, with
indication of likely extent
of lands

| | | |
|---|---|---|
| 1. Kintyre - Robert Steward | 19. Westerkirk - James Douglas | 39. Barns - Alexander Seton |
| 2. Glenbreakerie - John Menteith | 20. Staplegordon - James Douglas | 40. Dalkeith - Robert Lauder |
| 3. Ardrossan - Fergus of Ardrossan | 21. Kirkandrews - Archibald Douglas | 41. Ratho - Walter Steward/Marjorie Bruce |
| 4. Cunningham - Walter/Robert Steward | 22. Hawick - James Douglas | 42. Kingscavil- James Douglas of Lothian |
| 5. Renfrew - Walter/Robert Steward | 23. Bedrule - James Douglas | 43. Barnbougle - Murdoch of Menteith |
| 6. Cadzow - Walter Fitz Gilbert | 24. Jedburgh - James Douglas | 44. Bathgate - Walter Steward/ Marjorie Bruce |
| 7. Machan - Walter Fitz Gilbert | 25. Longnewton/Maxton - Robert Steward | 45. Kirkintilloch - Malcolm Fleming |
| 8. Dalrymple - Robert Boyd | 26. Nisbet - Robert Steward | |
| 9. Kilmarnock - Robert Boyd | 27. Eckford - Robert Steward | **Earldoms/Lordships** |
| 10. Mochrum - Alexander Bruce | 28. Caverton - Robert Steward | A - Arran [John Menteith] |
| 11. Carnesmole - Alexander Bruce | 29. Sprouston - Robert Bruce | CARRICK - Edward/David/Alexander Bruce |
| 12. Buittle - James Douglas | 30. Mordington - Thomas Randolph | D - Douglasdale |
| 13. Morton - Thomas Randolph | 31. Langton - William de Vipont | GALLOWAY - Edward Bruce |
| 14. Durrisdeer (Enoch) - Alexander Menzies/James Stewart | 32. Lauderdale - James Douglas | NITHSDALE - Thomas Randolph |
| 15. Barburgh - Thomas Kirkpatrick | 33. Manor - Adam Marshall | ANNANDALE - Thomas Randolph |
| 16. Dalswinton - Robert Boyd/Walter Steward | 34. Skirling - John de Monfode | MAN - Thomas Randolph |
| 17. Kirkmichael - James Douglas | 35. Seton - Alexander Seton | LIDDESDALE - Robert Bruce |
| 18. Torthorwald - Humphrey Kirkpatrick | 36. Tranent - Alexander Seton | MARCH - regrant to Earl Patrick |
| | 37. Elphinstone - Alexander Seton | B - Bonkle [Alexander Stewart] |
| | 38. Pencaitland - Henry Sinclair/Robert Lauder | |

3. Robert I's resettlement: Scotland, south of Forth

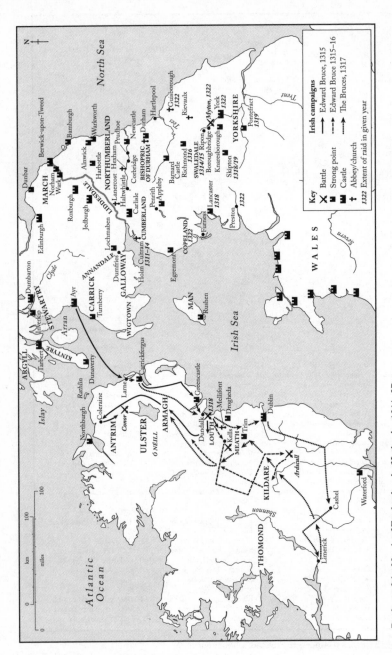

4. Raiding of the North of England and of Ireland, c.1311–27

CHAPTER SIX

# The Desperate Hours
## War and Famine, 1314–17

*By certain other portents the hand of God appears to be raised against us. For in the past year [1314] there was such plentiful rain that men could scarcely harvest the wheat or store it safely in the barn. In the present year [1315] worse has happened. For the floods of rain have rotted almost all the seed . . . and in many places the hay lay so long under water that it could neither be mown nor gathered. Sheep commonly died and other animals were killed by a sudden pestilence. It is greatly to be feared that if the Lord finds us incorrigible after these scourges, he will destroy at once both men and beasts . . .*

*Vita Edwardi Secundi*[1]

### Cambuskenneth and its Consequences, July–December 1314

Many Scots were undoubtedly won over by Bruce's spectacular triumph at Bannockburn and joined him in days and weeks of celebration. We should not underestimate the potency of bonds formed between men, families and a wider community that have come through a long war together and achieved a singular victory against the odds, especially when their shared experience could be framed by Church and faith.[2] Bannockburn recalled the spirit of Stirling Bridge and avenged Falkirk. Yet there survives little or no trace of the banqueting, masses and alms, tournaments and hunts, further knightings, formal patronage, gift-giving and other ritual or pageantry with which Robert, his captains and prelatical councillors must have marked their victory. There exist only faint echoes in verse commissioned by the king and his court to immortalise events and their protagonists; and traces of patronage to the saints' cults that had so blessed Robert's test of arms.[3] With a number of important feasts to be observed throughout the following summer months, these red-letter days of worship may have formed the basis of what would emerge as Robert I's annual liturgy.[4] It may have been in this blood-rush and confirmed faith of victory that Robert commissioned a Latin chronicle history of Scotland and his reign, a work now lost but which both Sir Thomas Gray (fl.1358–63) and the Flemish chronicler Jean le Bel of Liège (fl.1327–60) would read.[5]

The date of 11 July 1314 would have seen the king turn forty. If there nonetheless remained midlife nerves about just what this battle triumph would yield from England, it is to Robert's credit that he continued to press from a position of armed strength and did not trade his bargaining chips cheaply. Late July to early August 1314 witnessed a further step-change in Scottish border raiding.[6] Intelligence of a Bruce descent on Carlisle with ladders and siege engines around 14 July proved false.[7] However, the Lanercost chronicler of the day reports a Scottish force under Edward Bruce, James Douglas and 'John Soules', which crossed the border not through Jedburgh forest but from Berwickshire, between Wark and Norham on Tweed, pushing on through Northumberland and Durham estates to within sight of Richmond, just 50 miles from Edward II at York. It then wheeled back north-west to cut a swathe through Swaledale and Cumberland to Liddesdale.[8]

This assault came before the official end of the pre-Bannockburn truces agreed with individual counties (due to expire at Michaelmas, but which the Bruce Scots surely regarded as breached by Edward II's campaign): fresh tribute was extracted from Durham, the Honour of Penrith and Copeland for respite until January–February 1315.[9] However, the priorities of this campaign were otherwise to destabilise further a northern English regime (now stripped of its active captains) by the depth and wider damage of the chevauchée, and to threaten Newcastle, Durham and Carlisle, destroying several smaller tower houses and burning, trampling and slaughtering what could not be driven ('a huge booty of cattle' or prisoners) or carried away.[10] Present with his forces in the Selkirk–Jedburgh forest, Robert punctuated this lucrative terror raid on 5 September 1314 by issuing letters to Edward II (perhaps a repeat of privy seal credences first sent immediately after Bannockburn) offering talks for a full peace: Gilbert Hay, Robert Keith, Neil Campbell (hinting that Mary Bruce remained a prisoner) and Roger Kirkpatrick were named as Robert's procurators for the exchange talks (at Dumfries).[11] These papers reached the English king in time for a parliament at York, at which the English political community, led by the earl of Lancaster, demanded full implementation of the Ordinances: on 18 September, Edward, under the guidance of a council that his opponents had begun to purge, agreed to talks at Durham on 20 October which would consider a 'perpetual peace', where his embassy would be headed by

Sir John de Boutetort.[12] On 2 October, Elizabeth de Burgh, Marjorie Bruce, 'the sister of Robert Bruce' (it does not specify Christina, Mary or Maud), Donald, earl of Mar, and Bishop Wishart of Glasgow had been sent to Carlisle in anticipation of their release.[13] In the same month, apparently at the request of Philip IV, a general truce was agreed.[14]

It is possible, however, that these Anglo-Scottish peace negotiations, if they took place at all, quickly stalled. Given the commitment of the 'Lancastrian' regime to reinvigorate the northern English defences, on land and at sea, any demands on the part of Robert's envoys that he be recognised as king of an independent realm with its 1286 territory restored would have met an immediate impasse.[15] There may have been early agreement in principle about the need for an elite prisoner exchange. Yet even on this issue Robert may have felt the need to be seen to be magnanimous to get what he really wanted. He liberated Ralph de Monthermer, Marmaduke Tweng, Roger Northburgh and the latter's charge of the English privy seal without a ransom by November 1314; Edward II's shield was also returned as were the bodies of the earl of Gloucester and Sir Robert Clifford.[16]

Thus unlike the Flemings' infantry victory at Courtrai (11 July 1302) over a cavalry army of the French who had then sued for peace with Edward I (25 November 1302), Bannockburn had provoked no swift or substantive English concessions. If Robert and his close counsel were therefore worried about the prospects of recovering Queen Elizabeth and Marjorie Bruce, this may have had some effect on the mood and proceedings of the parliament called for Cambuskenneth Abbey on about 6 November 1314. With only the shortest of records extant, it is difficult to recreate the atmosphere of this assembly. Yet even in triumph – with Edward II's banners perhaps on display behind the high altar of the abbey – this may not have been an easy forum for Robert and his ministers.

The main business of this parliament, and usually its only agenda item discussed by modern historians, was to follow up Robert's ultimatum of circa October 1313. Hence,

> it was finally agreed, adjudged and decreed by the counsel and assent of the bishops and other prelates, earls, barons and other nobles of the kingdom of Scotland, and also all the community of the aforesaid kingdom, that all who died outside the faith and peace of the said lord king in the war or otherwise, or who had not come to his peace and faith on the said day [1 or 2 November 1314?], although they had been often summoned and lawfully expected, should be disinherited

perpetually of lands and tenements and all other title within the kingdom of Scotland.[17]

This wording, though, at least seems to hint ('it was *finally* agreed') at some debate or impatience about this issue, perhaps relating to specific prominent individuals who may not yet have agreed personal terms of submission to Robert since Bannockburn ('although they had been often summoned and lawfully expected'). For example, Duncan, earl of Fife, may have acted around July–August 1314 on his own authority to try to follow Stewart of Bonkle, Gordon, Seton, Fitz Gilbert, the Soules brothers and, most relevant of all, Earl Patrick of Dunbar, into Robert's peace.[18] However, the available evidence suggests that in fact Duncan would conclude (and perhaps actually only open) these discussions as late as spring/summer 1315. Thus kin and tenants of Duncan in Fife, Strathord and Strath Braan (Perthshire) and North Berwick (East Lothian), or the earl himself if he did actually come on parole to Cambuskenneth, may have sought exceptions or delays to the final forfeiture of enemies.[19]

Here, the seventeenth-century antiquarian transcripts that survive as evidence of who sealed this general forfeiture provide little help. Only the seals of Walter Steward and William, earl of Ross, remain on record for the greater magnates, although it is known from charters issued at Cambuskenneth in the days that followed that Edward Bruce of Carrick/Galloway and Randolph of Moray were present.[20] Patrick of Dunbar, however, would only appear as a definite charter witness at Robert's next parliament, on 26 April 1315, and may have remained a prisoner with Robert free to use his seal to help compile a 'ragman' show of unanimity at Cambuskenneth; Fife's seal may have been similarly exploited.[21]

Such exploitation certainly seems to have been the fate of a number of the episcopal seals appended at Cambuskenneth as recorded in the aforementioned antiquarian transcript.[22] Old and blind, Wishart of Glasgow had not yet come home (nor was Bishop Lamberton a completely free agent);[23] and the bishops of the Isles and Caithness – like many of the realm's abbots – more often remained aloof from political events. A similar royal demand for 'ragman' seals may thus also explain the perhaps odd assortment of lesser baronial and freeholder names otherwise recorded in the later transcript of this general forfeiture.[24] As at St Andrews in March 1309, therefore, Robert and his close advisors perhaps worked very hard to stage-manage the decision they wanted in the name of the estates. This may have made for a short parliament with Robert travelling east to Dunfermline Abbey by 16 November, the main feast of St Margaret: here he issued letters directing the bishop of St Andrews, William Lamberton, to confirm his earlier grant of churches to Dunfermline which, significantly, indicated that this patronage was to support the provision of the king's own mausoleum in the abbey next to 'our royal predecessors'.[25]

Conversely, we should not perhaps take the fragmentary evidence too far in one direction. In truth, both the ecclesiastical and lay seals attached to the Cambuskenneth forfeiture may indeed represent men (or institutions and communities) in attendance (and not all under duress), anxious now to lobby their victorious king for both rewards and justice. Loyalists close to the king since 1306–7 may now have sought substantial estates and offices, often from enemy neighbours and in confirmation of what they had acted to occupy anyway since c.1308–9 (or even c.1296); many of these men may reasonably be found amongst those recorded as royal charter witnesses over the coming months. Yet at the same time, men from regions and affinities where the traditional lord was now to be forfeited – Comyn Buchan and Badenoch, Strathbogie Atholl/Strath'an, Menteith (claimed by Murdoch of Menteith, in wardship in England), Umfraville Angus, Balliol and Macdowall Galloway, Macdougall Argyll and Lorn, and a large number of English lords' baronies in Scotland (Ferrers, Zouche, de Guines), including the Moreville-de Quinci inheritance in south-west Scotland shared with Balliol – may have sought Crown assurances about their tenure and liberties.[26] This would have been especially necessary if family charter chests or monastic or burghal cartularies had been lost or if temporary forfeitures or (for churches and their temporalities) prolonged vacancies had been imposed in earlier periods (1286–92, 1292–96, 1296–97, 1304–6). Many local officials or rivals undoubtedly exploited the confusion of war by physical violence or opportunistic legal predation (a reality that would be recognised by parliament in December 1318).

A wide range of subjects may thus have come to petition their king at Cambuskenneth. Robert, still in search of support, would have been happy to accept these appeals to his lordship and to issue assurances at parliament. Although a number of the Crown charters now extant only as seventeenth-century transcript notes may also date from the Cambuskenneth assembly, the evidence nevertheless suggests that the immediate post-battle and post-forfeiture periods were not marked by a sudden outpouring of partisan patronage. Nonetheless, this assembly did surely see further transfer of regional lordship to key Bruce supporters. Only two full charters survive from the Cambuskenneth meeting. The first, a restoration of the office of Constable for Sir Gilbert Hay (12 November), confirmed the betrayal by David, earl of Atholl.[27] It may thus also have been during this parliament

that Robert recognised his brother-in-law, the veteran Neil Campbell of
Lochawe, as custodian of all of Atholl's former lands, thus elevating this
loyalist (and, if born, his young son, John) to comital rank.[28] Hence it is
possible that the Cambuskenneth assembly also saw the king grant the
Umfraville earldom of Angus and its scattered lands to another veteran, Sir
Alexander Stewart of Bonkle (taken in care for the future for his son, John,
approaching adulthood and whose elder sister [?] had by now married
Thomas Randolph).[29] This second promotion is suggested by the Crown's
further grant to Sir Alexander on 4 October 1316 of the forfeited lands of
Sir David de Betoigne of Ethiebeaton (now Monifeith), which lay within
the Tayside portion of the Angus earldom.[30] In the wake of Bannockburn it
is likely that the king intruded a number of loyalists into Forfarshire; by the
close of the reign this regional affinity would include grants of royal demesne
and forfeited lands to such baronial families as the Frasers, Oliphants,
Ramsays, Ogilvies, Barclays, Blounts, Dischingtons, Foullartons, Grahams
and Scrymgeours, as well as lands in this quarter for close royal kin.[31]

The second extant charter from Cambuskenneth saw a grant of Kinross
parish church (dedicated to St Serf) and a chapel at Orwell (on the
northern shores of Lochleven) given in free alms for the souls of the king
and his predecessors to Dunfermline Abbey.[32] However, a royal brieve
ordering an inquisition into the extent and partibility of the Comyns'
earldom of Buchan should also probably be dated to this parliament. This
must only be one of several such inquiries ordered at this time by Robert's
chancery, exchequer, justiciars and sheriffs into lordships and offices set for
forfeiture.[33] Indeed, late 1314 to early 1315 would be characterised by an
intense period of Crown inquiry into landholding and dues.[34] This promised the prospect of new Crown patronage (or confirmations), but only
once due process had been performed and the rights of humbled enemies,
lesser tenants and patrons' ecclesiastical foundations in theory were safeguarded. The facility to petition for a pleadable royal brieve and thus to use
the Crown and seigneurial courts to protect and perhaps recover lands,
offices, annuities or goods called into question by allegiance since 1306,
thus provided an enabling act for Scots still outside Robert's peace
(including the earl of Fife) to begin the process of rehabilitation even after
6 November 1314.[35]

In many ways this mirrored Edward I's attempt to use the courts to
oblige Scottish magnates to recover their lands after their submission in
1304. But this effort by Robert's government to review extant records, the
testimony of local communities and, if need be, to perambulate (physically
inspect the bounds of) territories and resources that were the focus of

dispute or forfeiture (and then draw up new records), formed part of a more general Crown commitment to begin to codify Scots law. Here a number of actors and motivations may have been at work. As well as a need to clear the backlog of disputes aggravated by political upheaval and war since 1296 (really 1286), there was the broader loss of Crown records (including written laws) inflicted by Edward I's invasion, a lacuna doubtless matched by grave wartime losses of charters of lay families, churches and burghs. Lieutenants such as Thomas Randolph, earl of Moray, the northern justiciar Robert Keith and their deputies north of Forth, and whoever Robert selected to re-establish Crown offices in the south-west and Lothians, would need a reliable body of procedure and legal precedent to ease substantial workloads. There may also have been a conscious desire across the Scottish estates in parliament to resume the codification of laws begun by the Crown in the thirteenth century, asserting the written royal writ and courts in particular over regional custom as a means of imposing order and raising revenues.[36] For Robert and a number of his prelates and magnates, however, this may have been shaped by their experience of beginning a further review and codification of 'the laws of King David', and thus eliminating archaic custom (such as the 'laws of the Scots and the Brets'), as part of Edward I's Ordinance for Scottish government of 1304–5.[37]

As a result, it must have been the Cambuskenneth parliament and subsequent meetings of council and parliament in 1315, 1316 and 1317 (for which only fragmentary proceedings survive) that initiated a number of working parties to undertake clarification of Scottish civil (feudal) and criminal law. In this exercise, the expertise of Scottish prelates and their clerks loyal to Robert would be crucial, headed by Chancellor Bernard and Chamberlain William Lindsay. Their work would result in numerous territorial inquests over the next few months and years and, in the medium term, contribute to a substantial body of formularies and statutes approved in a parliament at Scone in December 1318 that upheld freeholders' rights to due process and inheritance notably in cases of 'right', 'mortancestor' or malicious accusation.[38] Beyond this, such work must also have contributed to the compilation and dissemination in the years after 1318 of bodies of written law now known as *Regiam Majestatem* and the *Assisa Regis David*.[39] Given the shared origins of English and Scottish 'common law', these treatises drew heavily upon English compilations as well as evolving Scottish custom and canonical practice. Even though both these collations, and particularly *Regiam Majestatem*'s closing sections of more distinctly Scottish law and precedent, seem to have been rushed in their final stages (perhaps for reasons discussed below), their production clearly points to an inherited awareness within Robert I's regime of the central importance of territorial and legal jurisdiction as a definition of sovereign royal authority and subjects' collective identity.

Therefore this first parliament after the battle for Stirling must be acknowledged as a responsive, reconciliatory body that identified a heavy workload for the years ahead: it reflected not merely the agenda of the king and his close supporters but of key elements of the wider community. However, the practical work of Robert I's settlement would continue to be interrupted by war. The stuttering negotiations with Edward's envoys at Durham in October 1314 must also have been discussed at Cambuskenneth, perhaps alongside Scotland's deteriorating socio-economic conditions after a poor harvest. So, too, crucially, there might have been discussions about approaches from Gaelic elements in Ireland, greatly enthused by the victory at Bannockburn, seeking Bruce intervention in that occupied land.

All this formed a backdrop to the launch of a fresh raid into Tynedale led by Robert himself in November 1314, despite ongoing talks over prisoner exchanges, followed by another incursion into Northumberland in December.[40] That the Scots intended these short chevauchées to maintain pressure upon the English is suggested by Robert's grant at this time of Wark in Tynedale, interestingly to a knight who until recently had been one of his opponents, William Soules, who would soon be restored to his family's border lordship of Liddesdale (adjacent to Annandale), presumably after a Crown inquest.[41] What may thus have been a ploy to bait both Edward and the Scots still in his pay, and which would result in men of Cumberland and Westmorland attacking Soules's new lands, would be exaggerated by the Lanercost chronicler: his narrative asserts that all of Tynedale (which kings of Scots had held of England before 1286 and where positive memories of their less exacting lordship may have persisted) now entered Robert's allegiance.[42]

This tactic may have reflected a general Scots policy of taking homages from northern English inhabitants where they could.[43] In the first instance, this was enough to bring English envoys back to talks at Dumfries, though probably only about prisoner exchange.[44] Robert himself was in that burgh on 10 December (confirming the Knights Hospitaller in their Scottish lands, perhaps in thanks for their mediation over hostages).[45] It is possible that the king then travelled west to Whithorn, on pilgrimage to the shrine of St Ninian, famed for his succour to captives (and thus depicted with broken chains).[46] At the close of the year York officials begged Edward to excuse northern magnates from attending parliament for fear of another Scottish attack.[47]

## Ayr, Heir and Ireland, 1315

But now prominent deaths intruded, which complicated matters. About 25 November 1314, John Balliol passed away aged sixty-four in Picardy; four days later, Philip IV himself succumbed to illness aged only forty-six. News of these deaths came at a time when the Papacy remained vacant following the demise of Clement V in April 1314 (and he would not be succeeded until John XXII's election in August 1316).[48] There is no record of Scottish reaction to these deaths. Both laymen were succeeded by their sons, Edward Balliol (b.1283) and Louis of Navarre (b.1285) respectively, and it was rather the regime of Edward II and the Ordainers that sought to turn the position of these heirs to their advantage in the conflict with Bruce. While an assembly of northern prelates and magnates met at York in early January 1315 to appoint new captains and levy funds for a defensive force, Edward II at Westminster wrote to Louis X of France to request that Edward Balliol be allowed to remain in England (in the household of the king's brother) and send a proxy to do homage for his father's Picardy lands. About the same time, Sir John de Botetourt, Bruce's colleague in Edward I's service in 1302–04, was appointed as admiral of a fleet of east coast ships with orders to sink Scottish privateers and blockade Flemish supply to the Scots, aiding Louis X (until his early death in June 1316) in his inherited conflict with the Count of Flanders.[49]

That England's king and council envisaged a role for the thirty-three-year-old Edward Balliol as a figurehead (perhaps even as a vassal king) to lead disinherited lords, both Scots and English, in returning with force to Scotland, probably through his family patrimony of the south-west and the vulnerable approaches of the Irish Sea, is further suggested by the emerging shape of the war in early spring 1315.[50] By 15 February, John Macdougall of Argyll, backed by fresh resources out of Dublin and kindreds like the Bissets of Antrim, had succeeded in retaking the Isle of Man. This exposed the Solway coast of Balliol's former lordship of Galloway.[51] Into March–April, Macdougall would also be empowered to command a fleet of sixty ships to transport a force of 10,000 men to invest the Western Isles and take its inhabitants into Edward II's peace, including a 'Donald of Islay' (who had presumably submitted), possibly the MacDonald who had attended Robert I's parliament of 1309.[52] Moreover, by 15 March 1315, Edward II's council would have ordered notary Andrew Tange to collate (and possibly edit advantageously once again) a copy of the Scottish succession hearings of 1291–92 and evidence of the Balliol claim, probably for consultation in dealings with Avignon and Paris.[53]

Robert's response to the loss of the Isle of Man and the threat of invasion in the west was decisive and may have brought into focus plans first discussed in the preceding months. He may also have been prompted by the failure of further peace talks in February–March 1315 together with any rumours of Balliol's potential role. In one sense Robert could now afford to be bold. For probably by mid-February (and certainly by Easter, 23 March), Queen Elizabeth, Marjorie Bruce, her aunts, Bishop Wishart, Sir Thomas Morham, Sir Andrew Murray of Avoch and Bothwell and a number of other Scottish prisoners had finally been exchanged for the earl of Hereford and the remaining English captives. Lindsay brother-knights, Simon and Philip of Wauchope and Staplegordon (Dumfriesshire), loyal to England since 1306, may also have been exchanged after their capture at Bannockburn but would enter Robert's peace soon after along with their younger brother, cleric John: this was a pattern of adherence probably matched about this time by a number of Balliol men, including Ingram d'Umfraville and William Soules of Liddesdale.[54] Within his close circle, Robert's grant from Arbroath on 10 February 1315 of Lochawe and other Argyll lands to Sir Colin Campbell further rewarded the kin of the king's brother-in-law, Sir Neil (Colin's father).[55] However, that this grant was given in return for the service of a ship of forty oars was the more important matter, as being the first detectable sign of the Bruce regime's preparations for the seaborne invasion of Ireland, just 30 miles from the Carrick coast.

After installing his restored family at St Andrews or Arbroath, Robert remained at the latter abbey to oversee the outcome of inquests into the Buchan earldom and other lands.[56] He also paused to commemorate Bishop Wishart's release by confirming the assignment of Rutherglen and Cadzow burgh fermes (annual rents) to pay for lights in Glasgow Cathedral.[57] He would leave his Chancellor and Chamberlain to continue to audit and act on such inquiries, but by 25 February Robert, travelling via Perth, was at Dumbarton where he probably remained for much of March to oversee outfitting of the galley fleet necessary for a landing on the north-east Irish coast. On 3 March the king was publicly rewarding the man who had secured the invaluable earl of Hereford as a prisoner, Walter Fitz Gilbert, who was knighted and given the Lanarkshire barony of Cadzow and adjacent lands in return for a rental, 22 chalders of corn and 6 chalders of meal annually. This was a symbolic gift in a time of famine witnessed by Edward Bruce, Randolph, Abbot Bernard, Walter Steward, John Menteith, James Douglas and James Lindsay of Barnweill; other magnates vital to war or western lordship were also in attendance at Dumbarton, including Keith as Marischal, Hay as Constable, Alexander Fraser and Sir Malcolm

Fleming of Biggar (whose family was also rewarded c.1306–15 with the substantial west-central lordship of Kirkintilloch).[58]

Then on 18 March, Robert confirmed and expanded (to a distance of 3 miles in every direction) the privilege of sanctuary of Luss, on the western shores of Loch Lomond, a church dedicated to St Kessog (feast day 10 March), a sixth-century Irish evangelist and reputed son of an Irish sub-king of Cashel (Munster): this power (to be overseen by the earls of Lennox) was surely given as much in the hope of encouraging further defections throughout this saint's *parochia* of that lordship, western Stirlingshire and southern Perthshire, as it was in preparation for landings in Ireland.[59] But it was these war plans that Robert intended to place before a parliament now summoned for Ayr parish church (dedicated to St John the Baptist) at the end of April.[60] In addition, it has been suggested that the king made a journey to Tarbert in northern Kintyre about the end of March to oversee repair and provisioning of the tower there. If he did so, as in 1306, Robert may have found it necessary to intervene not only against Macdougall incursion in the west but in intercine MacDonald rivalry.[61]

Early April 1315 perhaps saw the king visit his queen and family at St Andrews.[62] Robert may have had the difficult personal task of renewing relations in the strong hope of a male heir with a wife he had not seen for over eight years and whose father remained a vassal of Edward II, an enemy about to be the target of a new Bruce military surge. Yet it must be acknowledged that a mixture of duty and sentiment after such a long time in English confinement had made Elizabeth willing to return to her husband and king (unlike Donald, earl of Mar, who chose to remain in Edward II's household until 1327). Moreover, Robert's visit to St Andrews would have afforded a further opportunity to take counsel and formulate contingencies for the royal succession. It was this, and the ramifications of the imminent armada to Ireland, that formed the main focus of the Ayr assembly.

As such, as in 1309, 1312 and November 1314, this parliament was probably not without controversy and saw the king and his ministers act once more to control proceedings. We should, though, question whether they always succeeded. Apart from a single 'statute' and nine extant datable royal grants, we have little with which to assess the political mood in Scotland at this time.[63] The ten months after Bannockburn are in fact a period about which later medieval Scottish annalists say nothing, other than to reproduce one of the Ayr parliament's statutes, a tailzie – a written order or act of succession – and then, following Barbour, move on to Edward Bruce's war in Ireland.[64] Yet, as in previous assemblies, despite select summons by Robert, a number of overlapping issues may have made for a difficult time.

The Ayr meeting of 'the bishops, abbots, priors, deans, archdeacons and other prelates of the church, earls, barons, knights and others of the community of the kingdom of Scotland, both clerics and laymen' consented to seal a document, an act that asserted the right of Edward Bruce and any legitimate male heirs he might have as heirs presumptive to Robert's throne, ahead of Marjorie Bruce and her heirs (both male or female). This sought to avoid the spectre of a living female's royal succession and a repeat of the crisis of 1286–90, but not to exclude it entirely. This was consistent with the historic Bruce position on nearness of (male) degree and also echoed the rhetorical acclamation of recognised 'worth' as well as legal right necessary for an heir to be named as king, first asserted in the declarations of the clergy in 1309–10 about Robert himself but here directed at Edward Bruce: 'a vigorous man and tested on many occasions in acts of war for the defence of the right and liberty of the kingdom of Scotland'.[65]

Nevertheless, this offsetting of succession through a daughter in favour of alternative male heirs was a pragmatic Bruce policy that may have alarmed a number of magnates present, especially those who had recently submitted. Not least, the negotiations with Duncan, earl of Fife, which would culminate at Crichton (East Lothian) on 23 August 1315, also sought to impose an entail of inheritance designed to displace female succession of that ancient title (whose incumbent played a key role in the ceremony of enthronement). It might be argued that fears about similar interference had worsened Edward Bruce's alienation from Isabel Strathbogie (sister of the earl of Atholl), their son Alexander Bruce, and her supporters in northern Scotland (including Henry Cheyne, bishop of Aberdeen, who was denied his diocesenal teinds/tithes by the Crown c.1315).[66]

However, in truth, few people could have expected less from Robert's regime now that his wife had returned (and was perhaps pregnant by summer) and Edward Bruce's expedition to Ireland was imminent. The act did not, in fact, rule out female succession completely – how could it, given the Bruces' own claim of 1286–92?[67] It did not preclude reconciliation with David Strathbogie of Atholl at some later date or retrospective legitimisation of Alexander Bruce (just as the door was left open for Donald of Mar, and Atholl's son would be able to defect in 1335). Nor could those present at (or excluded from) Ayr in April–May 1315 have been surprised by Robert's desire to secure a good marriage for his daughter Marjorie and further possible male heirs. The act of succession indeed referred to the need to see that 'the said Marjory is joined in marriage by the consent of the said lord king, failing whom, which God forbid, by the consent of *the greater part* [my italics] of the community of the kingdom'. It was therefore most likely at this same assembly that the betrothal of Marjorie to Walter the heritable Steward was debated and agreed (but not perhaps unanimously), a reflection of the considerable influence upon Robert I of Walter's father, James Steward (and both families' de Burgh ties). The young couple would receive the valuable Lothian baronies of Bathgate and Ratho on their nuptials shortly there-after.[68] By the same token, few Scots could have been surprised if Robert also considered marriages for his unmarried or widowed sisters whose future sons might also find a place in the succession: Neil Campbell was already married to Mary Bruce with a son, John; but Maud Bruce may have been betrothed to Hugh, son of William, earl of Ross, about this time (their son, William, would be born c.1315–16).[69] These cognate heirs were not referred to in the Ayr act but their consideration may have been implied in the remote contin-gency provided for in the event of Robert, Edward and Marjorie Bruce all dying without heirs of the body, at which point Thomas Randolph, earl of Moray, the king's half-nephew 'shall have the custody of the kingdom until the prelates, earls, barons and other of the community of the kingdom are able to assemble conveniently for ordaining and discussing upon the legiti-mate succession and the governing of the kingdom'.

No, what perhaps angered some of those present at the Ayr parliament or who were subsequently confronted with its decisions was again the use of such a declaration to test men's loyalties at a time when the resettlement of territory, offices and resources undertaken by Robert's government was really just beginning to take shape. The Ayr assembly – and perhaps a concurrent exchequer audit under Chamberlain William Lindsay (who was rector of Ayr church) – presumably reviewed the partitions and grants resulting from a number of the inquests initiated since November 1314, and approved of more to come.[70] Significantly, among the royal charters issued during the parliament there were grants of forfeited Balliol, Ferrers and Zouche lands in Ayrshire to Sir Alan Stewart (for the service of two archers), and several generous estates in free barony in the same shire for Sir Robert Boyd of Noddsdale (for the service of a knight) also now forfeited from John Balliol, Godfrey de Ros and William More.[71] On 28 April the king regranted the barony of Manor in Peeblesshire to the archer Adam Marshall, a grant he had originally made in parliament in March 1309, as its original occupant Sir Alexander Baddeby had now submitted to the king's peace and was to be restored to half his newly stated bounds (again suggesting a review by local inquest).[72] It may have been at about this time, too, that following an inquest into Balliol and Hastings' lands in Garioch, the whole of that north-eastern lordship (including the Bruce portion) was granted to the king's widowed eldest living sister, Christina Bruce (who was perhaps already intended to marry a fellow captive in England, Sir Andrew Murray of Avoch and Bothwell).[73] Early May would also see the king redirect an annual due by one knight he had recently favoured to another Ayrshire retainer, Sir Reginald Crawford (for one archer's service). Robert also confirmed mills at Longforgan in Perthshire and land at Tarbert in Argyll to Sir Robert Keith's brother, Alexander Keith 'dilecto et fideli nostro', after they had been resigned by a former opponent, Gilbert of Glencarnie; again, these are cases that suggest recent inquests.[74]

Robert's need thus to reward his supporters since 1306–7 and now to muster forces against two fronts, Ireland and the Anglo-Scottish border, meant that he had growing cause to worry about the activities of a number of former enemies who had entered his peace since June 1314. This must have been all the more true if some of Robert's ostensible subjects had begun to question his regime's apparent failure as yet to extract any real political gains from Edward II, despite the victory at Bannockburn.[75] By spring 1315 critics could also point to the loss of the Isle of Man and, perhaps, rumours of English plans for Edward Balliol. In that context, indeed, it could be argued that the 1315 act of succession almost directly anticipated its subsequent revision in a parliament at Scone in December 1318. By that time Edward Bruce was dead, Robert still had no son and, as we shall see, there were rumours and a very real threat of a conspiracy amongst magnates within Scotland to restore the Balliol line and its territorial and political support. Thus in 1315 Robert's fear of a continuing threat of internal division in Scotland – on the eve of an incredibly dangerous adventure on enemy soil – saw him use the Ayr succession act to oblige past opponents to seal an oath to 'obey and faithfully defend in all ways the magnificent prince and lord, their liege lord Robert by the grace of God illustrious king of Scots and his heirs male to be legitimately begotten of his body, as their king and liege lord against all mortals'.[76]

Although a number of Robert's acts issued at or just after the Ayr assembly granted or confirmed Church possessions, the seals of the bishops of Argyll, Caithness, Aberdeen and the Western Isles should be questioned in their attachment to the succession act, along with those of a number of abbots.[77] More obviously, while Robert's chancery may in practice have expected all laymen over a certain level of wealth to seal this oath, it is striking that the seventeenth-century transcript of then extant seals details a predominance of minor figures and past opponents. Earl Patrick of Dunbar's seal appears for the first time since the events of the previous summer. While he had thus seemingly been constrained, Patrick may have been troubled by Thomas Randolph's apparent favour to his former Lothian ally, Sir Adam Gordon, who would be confirmed by Robert I in the lands of Stichill in Roxburghshire on 28 June (and was perhaps already favoured with a grant of the forfeited northern Strathbogie lordship for the service of five knights).[78] Yet most suspect of all is the seal of Duncan of Fife and several of his shire knights – members of the Wemyss, Barclay, Balfour and Ramsay kindreds, some of whom would be implicated in the aforementioned Balliol plot against Robert I of 1318–20 – well over three months before the earl's formal submission to Robert under potentially costly terms.

Finally, the enormity of what the Bruce brothers were actually proposing to undertake in Ireland may also have caused ambition and opposition to rear their heads in equal measure at Ayr. The complete loss of Robert's exchequer rolls before 1327 denies us evidence of how much of a drain on the Crown's resources the 1315 invasion and allied expeditions into Argyll and Cumberland actually were and thus whether or not the Ayr parliament had to resort to purveyance and subsidy. Given the spoils of battle and raiding, this may seem unlikely. However, at the end of March, Sir John Botetourt had been ordered to sea to intercept more than a dozen ships loaded by the Scots with arms and foodstuffs sailing from Sluys.[79] Moreover, the allocation of plundered materials to support (and pay?) a Scottish force of probably between 4,000 and 6,000 men set for Ireland (who could not be raised by the common levy of forty days' service per annum) came at a time when a poor 1314 harvest, compounded by another hard winter, boded ill for victual into the second half of the year and through winter 1315–16. Recent English efforts to counter the Scots' raids may already have begun to have a drastic effect. The contemporary *Vita Edwardi Secundi* asserts that Botetourt's blockade of Flemish supplies resulted 'in a short space of time in the Scots being so short of grain that a quarter of wheat was sold for a hundred shillings', presumably in the wake of the widespread failure of the 1315 harvest.[80] Commitment of scarce Scottish resources and a large body of men to the invasion of Ireland might therefore easily have provoked criticism of this endeavour and its captains at a time when much of Scotland's economic heartland in the south-east, including large regions of monastic pasture and arable, remained under English control. By May 1315, Robert had certainly issued relatively few (now extant) charters or brieves relating to lands south of Edinburgh or east of Dumfries.[81]

Competing pressures may be further reflected in a brieve from Robert I of 19 August 1315 in which he ordered his sheriff of Stirling (Sir Hugh of Airth?) to pay Cambuskenneth Abbey an £8 annual and 6 chalders of wheat in exchange for a teind (a tenth or tithe of the income) of the king's demesnes of Stirling (an order that had to be repeated on 17 September 1317).[82] However, the environmental and socio-economic conditions of 1315–16 should also alert us to the possibility that one of the Bruces' secondary reasons for invading Ireland was a growing need to access resources of Irish grain and livestock so as to feed Scotland, as well as to deny victual, revenues and men to the strategically vital English walled towns of Carlisle, Newcastle and Berwick. Modern historians of Ireland have, however, identified a number of additional motives within a British Isles context for a Bruce descent on Ireland.[83]

For Robert I the political risk is undoubtedly explained by the search for a military gain or regional destabilisation that would compel Edward II or his council to recognise his kingship and conclude peace terms with a sovereign Scotland. Over the next three years, Robert would alternate continued Anglo-Scottish border raids and sieges with campaigning in Ireland to this end.[84] Nevertheless, the grave physical dangers that Robert himself would face in 1317, alongside his heir presumptive and the nominated Guardian of the realm in the event of both their deaths, Thomas Randolph, speaks to wider personal ambition and obligation. Edward Bruce's headstrong desire for a throne of his own would be exaggerated by Barbour, who inherited poetic and chronicle attempts to blacken the younger brother's name (and by extension that of his son, Alexander).[85] In reality Robert must have felt a strong debt to the war efforts of his sole surviving brother. As we have seen, both men may also have sought to fulfil obligations incurred when they sought refuge in the Irish Sea and Western Isles in 1306–7. The latter of course built upon their childhood fosterage links to Gaelic kindreds of this zone, perhaps in particular to the Ó Néills of Tyrone in Ulster whose chief, Domnall, had reportedly extended an invitation to Robert to assume the High Kingship of Ireland after Bannockburn.[86] Such a call might also have been urged by native Irish clergy angered by English clerical superiority. Edwardian complaints to the Papacy about the anti-English preaching and practices of houses of Irish Franciscans in particular would be a recurrent feature of the next decade.[87] A strong shared cultural and spiritual heritage – intensified by the *familia* and geographical *parochia* of saints' cults and over a decade of fighting Plantagenet rule – may also have given the Bruce brothers a genuine sense of the potential for a pan-Celtic alliance, encompassing Scotland, Gaelic Ireland and, less than a day's sailing east of Dublin, northern Wales in joint revolt against England.[88] The landing of May 1315 might logically have been preceded and accompanied by more of the propaganda, prophecy and preaching to attract Gaelic Irish support that had marked Bruce appeals for help in 1306–7.[89] Yet neither Robert nor

Edward was surely so quixotic as to believe that they could unite completely the intercine rivals of several Irish counties or overpower the Marcher families of Wales. As a reader and patron of chronicle histories Robert may have been aware of previous native Irish attempts to appeal to foreign leadership (such as Håkon IV of Norway in 1263) or papal intervention (as in 1213 versus King John) so as to throw off English rule.[90] Thus the Bruce campaigns in support of particular Gaelic allies in Ulster, Leinster and Thomond (who were not always trustworthy in a search for local advantage) speak to specific debts incurred through individual lords of Scottish galloglass.[91]

In this context, it is possible that some of the undated charters of Robert I extant only as seventeenth-century notes also belong to the Ayr parliament of April–May 1315 and represent further grants to lords set to participate in Edward Bruce's expedition: these would include (at various times) Randolph, MacDonald and MacRuaridh chiefs (who cannot be firmly identified), Sir John Soules, Sir Philip Mowbray, Sir John Stewart of Jedburgh (brother of Walter the Steward), Sir John Menteith, Sir Robert Boyd, Sir Alexander Seton, Sir Walter Murray and a Fergus of Ardrossan, as well as a number of lesser nobles from Carrick, the Stewartry, Lennox and Argyll (including Campbell scions).[92] Their participation in and influence on Bruce lordship arguably extends the Scots' motivation to include the recovery of past patrimony in Ireland itself, something shared with Edward Bruce now as earl of Carrick (claiming the barony of Upper Glenarm and other lands), Randolph who looked to recover the Isle of Man, and Robert himself, whose wife was the eldest daughter of Richard, earl of Ulster (just as Walter Steward was that lord's nephew and a claimant to Antrim lands).[93] The influence of Queen Elizabeth, indeed, should not be overlooked: after the earl of Ulster arranged her marriage to Bruce, Elizabeth's increasingly indebted and troubled father seems to have done little to secure her release from English captivity from 1306.[94] Finally, given the latter, revenge may also have been a factor, taking the war into the Irish Sea in pursuit, too, of the Macdougalls, Macdowalls and those Anglo-Norman Irish lords who had fought in Edward I's expeditions to Scotland.[95]

### Bruce Wars, 1315–16

Robert I, his queen, daughter and brother remained in Ayr probably through the completion of an exchequer audit by Whitsunday, followed by Trinity (18 May 1315) and Corpus Christi (22 May) feasts, and then the Scots launched their two-pronged assault. Taking ship from Ayr, Edward Bruce's force landed at Glendun in Antrim on 26 May, routing tenants of the absent earl of Ulster and laying siege to Carrickfergus castle throughout June.[96] Simultaneously, Robert, perhaps aided by Edward's returning galleys, dragged ships across the Tarbert peninsula, according to Barbour in fulfilment of an ancient prophecy about the conquest of the Western Isles. As well as reversing recent Macdougall gains in the Isles, the king perhaps also took homages from rival MacDonald lords, including Angus Og, whilst that kindred's dominant chief fought in Ireland.[97] Refurbishment of Tarbert castle as a future royal sheriff's base may be dated to this expedition.[98] Barbour's naming of Walter Steward at the king's side on this campaign may also speak to an emerging preference to utilise the agency of Stewart, Campbell and Menteith lordship more widely in this quarter.[99]

Then at midsummer, a year since Bannockburn, Robert led a force to invest Northumberland once more, according to the Lanercost chronicle sending James Douglas to smash Hartlepool's support of Botetourt's ships while the king plundered Durham's manors of cattle before agreeing a further truce tribute with the bishopric worth 1,600 merks for two years.[100] Within three weeks, however, Robert had recrossed the border with war engines in another attack coordinated with his brother, to lead a siege of Carlisle, the main depot for Irish supplies, from 22 July to 1 August, while Douglas devastated the surrounding countryside. The siege failed (with the Scots' engines sinking into rain-soaked mud) and Robert withdrew.[101] Although his agents surely returned to collect tribute from Durham and other regions (perhaps accepting payment in kind), this brought an end to Scottish incursions into northern England in the second half of 1315. By late autumn it may have become apparent that this was a misjudgement on the part of the Scots as further heavy rainfall devastated crops and led to a murrain of sheep. Although the full effects of famine would not be felt across England, and surely Scotland too, until 1316 (when the harvest would fail again), there was a dire shortage of victual and soaring prices by late 1315.[102] At one level this worked to Robert's advantage with the Berwick garrison especially weakened, with reports to Edward II by October of the necessity for supplies or evacuation.[103] The Scots themselves, with a smaller, less densely packed population (of roughly 750,000 to 1 million people) and a preference for growing hardier oats, may have been able to weather the dearth slightly better than their enemy.[104] Nonetheless, Thomas Randolph's return from Ulster about mid-September with five ships 'full of the goods of the earth of Ireland' (one of which sank), to be disembarked and then for the ships to ferry back 500 reinforcements, speaks to Scottish shortages on both sides of the Irish Sea.[105]

The extant record evidence now also suggests a drop in energy on Robert's part, but this may have been a lull of expectation on a number of fronts. Although his brother had scored several notable victories and been inaugurated as High King of Ireland on 6 June 1315, Carrickfergus – like Berwick – refused to fall; there were recurrent rumours amongst the English in Ireland that the Scots had been 'scattered' and Edward Bruce slain.[106] After the loss of his siege engines to Sir Andrew Harcla's defenders and the earl of Pembroke's relief army at Carlisle, Robert can be found at Crichton south of Edinburgh on 23 August where he accepted the submission of Earl Duncan of Fife (who had perhaps finally ventured north from Newcastle or Durham). The earl resigned his lands and received them back at Robert's grace but with the vital provision that if he did not have (male) issue (and at that time his Monthermer wife, Edward II's cousin, remained in England), then his earldom and its 'honours' (in ceremonially making Scotland's monarch) were to be tailzied via the Crown to 'the assignees lawfully born to the king', and thus to be kept separate from inheritance of the throne. Therefore, as well as denying claims to Fife by an English ward, Murdoch of Menteith (by another written tailzie, of 1309), Robert, with his own queen perhaps pregnant, may already have had the confidence to consider a future transfer of Fife to the issue of Walter Steward and Marjorie Bruce (also pregnant, and who would give birth to a son, Robert, circa February–March 1316), or even to a younger, legitimate son of his own, should he be so blessed.[107]

The remainder of the year's surviving (and datable) royal acts suggest Robert's – or rather his Chancellor's – continued oversight of land and resource inquests, as well as acts of conspicuous piety. Two dated to Inverkeithing (20 September, 10 October) may hint at the queen's lying-in at Dunfermline Abbey, if she was indeed pregnant with a first daughter or stillborn child; the royal couple may thus have sought the intercessionary care of St Margaret whose 'birthing serk', or shirt, was worn by a number of Scottish queens in labour (with Robert's first daughter by Elizabeth probably christened Margaret).[108] One of the Inverkeithing acts, moreover, saw the king assign an annual from the baillies of Kinghorn of 4 merks to pay for lights about 'the tomb' of King William I in Arbroath Abbey.[109] It has been suggested that Robert – or Chancellor Bernard – commissioned an effigy of Frosterley limestone from a Durham workshop during a period of border truce that granted the Scots access to St Cuthbert's lands; the role of Robert's first cousin, the Durham official Robert Fitzmarmaduke, in negotiating truces c.1311–15 may have facilitated such a purpose. If this is the case, Robert and/or Abbot Bernard may have commissioned a full-length royal effigy atop a crouching lion, with attendant figures of mailed earls and royal daughters drawn from the iconography of royal

inauguration. However, in truth, while Robert undoubtedly craved association with a predecessor king who had also defied England and venerated
St Thomas, he most likely commissioned such a monument only after May
1323 when a longer truce prevailed. Thus the lights paid for from October
1315 may simply have marked William's original tomb slab as founder
before Arbroath's high altar while rebuilding work resumed about it to
repair fire damage of 1272.[110]

On 1 November 1315 the king was back at Ayr for further news of
Edward Bruce's campaign after a victory over the earl of Ulster at Conor in
early September.[111] While there the king granted a clutch of lands in barony
in Kincardineshire to Sir Alexander Fraser. The gift in particular of the
substantial holding of Strachan, adjacent to the large royal thanage of
Aboyne (which Fraser had already been given in lease by the king), surely
signalled this loyal knight's elevation in central and north-eastern Scotland
as a leading agent of the Crown. Robert may already have decided to fill the
void left by the death earlier that year of Sir Neil Campbell by offering Sir
Alexander the hand of his widowed sister, Mary Bruce, and looking to him
to oversee the Campbells' Atholl holdings until John Campbell, the king's
nephew, came of age (with the exception of the dowager lands in Atholl
held by Countess Isabel and the king's other nephew, Alexander Bruce); by
late 1319 Fraser would also be Chamberlain, with further generous royal
grants to come.[112] This may also explain the presence as a witness to Fraser's
grant at Ayr of Sir Alexander Menzies who, if not already raised in such a
capacity as a trusted Bruce supporter in central Scotland, was probably
about this time granted control of the sweeping lordships of Fortingall and
Glendochart, contiguous with the western bounds of the Perthshire earldoms of Atholl and Strathearn.[113]

Thomas Randolph of Moray had also been a witness to Fraser's grant
and must not yet have returned with troops to Ireland. Once Moray did
cross back, he helped Edward Bruce launch a chevauchée south from
13 November into Meath (in support of a cadet branch of the de Lacys),
resulting in another victory, at Kells on about 6 December; the English
administration now feared a Scoto-Irish landing in Angelsey, setting parts
of Wales to revolt.[114] In the meantime, two acts dated 5 and 7 December (at
Bernard's Arbroath) saw Robert adding to his royal officers in the north
with a remit to contain MacDonald self-interest: Sir Hugh Ross, Robert's
other brother-in-law, son and heir of William, earl of Ross, was granted the
sheriffdom and burgh of Cromarty by grants that confirmed the forfeiture
of the exiled Mowats.[115] Robert may then have spent a frugal Christmas
with his family at Dunfermline while he planned his next bold stroke.

The Lanercost chronicler is our only source for a possible stealth attack on Berwick on the night of 14 January 1316, allegedly led by Robert I and James Douglas, deploying ladders and small boats against the town's incomplete walls: the chronicle claims the Scots were soundly repulsed (according to other contemporary English narratives, after their plans were betrayed by the Gascon defector and former keeper of Edinburgh castle, Piers Libaud, whom Robert now executed).[116] It is, though, difficult to believe that Robert, about to be a grandfather, might have chanced such a risk out of season, despite the echoes of what Barbour reported as his night attack on Berwick of December 1312. Yet that the king sent a force captained by Douglas at this time is believable given the reported condition of the Berwick garrison by February–March 1316: reduced to scouring the Marches for food (a raid in which they were mauled by a force led by Douglas, William Soules and Henry Balliol) with many killed and scores deserting, while only 50 of their 300 mounted force had full kit and health.[117] Nonetheless, truce generally prevailed on the border until 30 May 1316 while both kings prepared for an English muster.[118] Meanwhile, Edward Bruce's troops had humiliated a fractious Anglo-Irish force led by Edward II's justiciar at Skerries (Ardscull) in Kildare (26 January 1316), but proved too weary and poorly supplied to press home an opportunity to attack Dublin, withdrawing to Ulster where the High King emulated the lordship of his brother in beginning to govern through courts, land conveyancing and perhaps a parliament.[119] Thereafter, Edward II's council – headed for the moment by the earl of Lancaster after a parliament at Lincoln in January–February 1316 – would make a much better fist of organising a coordinated Anglo-Irish land and naval response.[120] English nerves, indeed, must have been considerably calmed by their efficient suppression of the revolt of Llywelyn Bren in Glamorgan, Wales (28 January to 18 March), although this had drawn valuable captains and their followings away from Ireland for a time.[121]

It was a Scottish parliament that brought Robert I to Edinburgh about Lent 1316, an assembly that Edward Bruce and Thomas Randolph may have returned to attend and which, significantly – given mounting pressure on Berwick – saw the king grant several charters of land in the Lothians, Peeblesshire, Selkirkshire and Roxburghshire.[122] Indeed, a number of Robert's 'lost' undated acts noted in seventeenth-century transcripts concerning lands in the Lothians and east and middle Marches may date to this gathering and down to July.[123] During this meeting Robert may in addition have acknowledged a personal debt (relating to his submission to Edward I in 1301–02) through an almonry grant of 10 merks annually from the mills of Carluke in Lanarkshire to pay for eight perpetual lights of one pound each at the 'tomb' of St Machutus in Lesmahagow Priory.[124]

No further proceedings of this parliament survive. Yet it is possible that the prelates and barons had gathered to renew their oaths to the act of succession passed in the previous year following the birth about this time of the king's grandson, Robert Stewart, as well as to plan how to counter an expected English military effort.[125] A Scottish muster seems to have been set for Melrose in May or early June. The king spent the intervening weeks travelling to Strathord, a Perthshire lordship of Duncan of Fife, perhaps as part of a legal review of the earl's rights (with half an eye to their future transfer to the Stewarts).[126] Easter (11 April) was probably then spent at Perth where the next day the king made another gift of alms, this time for the far larger annual sum of 40 merks of Dundee and Perth customs to the Blackfriars of Perth (as 'St John's town'), and granted Sir Henry Sinclair of Roslin more Lothian lands for fractional knight service: the Crown's witnesses included the usual tight-knit core of established allies, namely Abbot Bernard, Moray, Hay, Fraser and Keith.[127]

The general expectation of renewed border war may have been interrupted briefly by the prospect of diplomatic talks. On 28 April 1316 the earls of Lancaster and Pembroke and other council officials were authorised to issue safe conducts for passage to Leicester for 'Robert de Brus' himself or his appointed envoys to discuss 'a truce or even peace'. It is unclear which side had made the first approach, but given the Lincoln parliament's definite grant of March 1316 of two subsidies for war against Scotland and orders for muster at Newcastle on 8 July, this exchange of credences most likely resulted from a 'standard' offer of talks by Robert following the Scots' assaults of January–February and in anticipation of the end of truce tributes at midsummer. Yet if any such talks took place at all (and those scheduled at Durham in October 1314 may similarly not have happened), Robert certainly did not attend in person and negotiations proved abortive.[128]

Instead, while Chancellor Bernard continued to review inquests, Robert travelled south granting further forfeited Peeblesshire lands for knight service and former Balliol lands in Berwickshire in return for two archers. By 8 June the king was at Melrose Abbey (which he would issue with letters of protection later that month, guarding against debt and land claims), from where he dispatched forces on about 24 June through Northumberland and Durham as far as Richmond in Yorkshire and, for the first time, Furness in Lancashire. English authorities had expected him to strike at Berwick or York and offered little defence.[129] Indeed, that Robert chose to plunder and extract tribute once more, rather than persecute a painfully weakened Berwick, perhaps hints as much at the Scots' response to rising prices and another imminent harvest failure as it does to their recent loss of war engines (at Carlisle) and a desire to avoid a prolonged siege. While his captains undertook raids Robert nonetheless lingered at Park of Duns, just 15 miles from Berwick, which the Scots continued to harass. From here on 16 July Robert granted Kimmerghame, less than 3 miles to the south-east, in barony to Sir Alexander Stewart of Bonkle, for one knight, an act witnessed by several local men following the 'resignation' of these lands by a recent defector, Thomas Morham.[130] On his journey home, Robert paused at Dryburgh Abbey (18 July), from where English clerics would be removed about this time, and confirmed some of Melrose Abbey's Ayrshire lands.[131]

## Robert I in Ireland, 1316–17

Although the Scots had failed to make any further gains in the Anglo-Scottish Marches, in the spring and summer of 1316 Edward Bruce's forces had taken coastal strongholds at Greencastle and Northburgh in Ireland, but Carrickfergus still held out. Annals written at Dublin throughout the period assert that it was about late July or early August that Robert Bruce joined his brother in prosecuting the siege there: Carrickfergus surrendered on terms by September. However, although Robert's extant itinerary contains a sufficient gap of time for such an appearance, we have no corroborative English reports of this visit, which may in truth be a confusion with Edward Bruce's own return to Scotland by the end of September at the latest.[132]

On 30 September at the castle-burgh of Cupar in Fife (not far from Earl Duncan's caput at Falkland), during a council of 'prelates, earls and barons', Edward Bruce was present to witness as 'King of Ireland' Robert's confirmation of the earldom of Moray and the Isle of Man to Thomas Randolph. This grant may have been necessary to clear the air between all three men as Edward may have had expectation of the Man 'kingdom' as High King of Ireland, earl of Carrick, lord of Galloway and Robert I's heir presumptive in Scotland.[133] His price for now acknowledging its earlier alienation to Randolph (1312–13) may have included promises from Robert and Moray of more men and resources, and their own presence, in the Irish campaign. Proceedings at Cupar also probably included further inquiries into the lands and rights of the earl of Fife, part of the wider ongoing business of Crown and chancery after Bannockburn. A number of royal charters issued in the next three months hint at this process, including further grants of lands in the south-east.[134] Finally, the Cupar council may have drawn up letters and discussed envoys and traditional gifts for dispatch to Paris and Avignon to congratulate both the new king of France, Philip V, and the new Pope, John XXII, the latter elected after a two-year papal vacancy. If delayed until after late November 1316, these greetings were combined with approaches to the curia to elevate chapter electee Dean Stephen de Donydouer to the vacant bishopric of Glasgow.[135]

All of this would overlap with the engagement once more of King Robert and Randolph in nervy talks about talks with envoys of Edward II, now at York, a repeat of the abortive negotiations of April 1316 that need not have prevented Robert and his council at Cupar from agreeing a muster date for service in Ireland. Indeed, the initiation of these negotiations for a truce on the Marches probably came this time from the English as their planned Newcastle muster of 8 July was twice postponed (to 10 August and then 6 October) because men and materials proved difficult to gather. From 9 October the breach between the earl of Lancaster and Edward II's council was further strained by the vacancy of the bishopric of Durham: in this context the campaign to Scotland was cancelled.[136] It was now that false rumours first began to circulate about Bruce collusion with Lancaster (who was replaced as Pembroke's partner as warden of the March by the earl of Arundel).[137]

On 6 October William de Fogo, abbot of Melrose, received a safe conduct to England, which probably brought English envoys in turn to Jedburgh by 21 November, on which date Robert I was at Melrose from where he issued a brieve to Sir James Douglas and his baillies of Jedburgh to inquire into Melrose Abbey's rights in Roxburghshire lands. On 24 November, English envoys were empowered to make a truce with the Scots; the earl of Moray and Sir John Menteith were also issued passports to York at this time.[138] However, that these exchanges were once again directed towards only a border truce probably confirmed for Robert and his captains the need for decisive action on their second, western front. Following the funeral at Glasgow of his mentor Bishop Wishart around 26 November, Robert would spend Christmas at Coupar-Angus Abbey.[139] Here he may have worshipped at an altar dedicated to Malachy, the saintly twelfth-century bishop of Armagh, whose cult the Bruces of Annandale had offended in the past: the king may have been further minded to pay his respects to this Irish cult before sailing west and after viewing the tomb of Alexander II (1214–49) while at Melrose the month before, a king said to have died of illness contracted after attacking the lands of St Brigit of Larne/Kilbride during a campaign to the Western Isles.[140] Robert and

Moray might also have visited Arbroath, only 30 miles away, for the feast of St Thomas (29 December), before departing for Ireland with a galloglass force in the first week of January 1317 (according to Barbour, via Loch Ryan in Galloway while Sir James Douglas and Walter Steward were to serve as Guardians in Scotland).[141]

Edward Bruce had suffered some recent losses of men but he, his brother and their chief Irish allies, headed by the Ó Néills, were encouraged by spontaneous rebellions against English authority by native kindreds in Leinster, Desmond and Thomond throughout the second half of 1316, fuelled in part by the preaching of anti-English Franciscans; the Scots' dominance in the western seas also seemed to be confirmed by the retirement of a sick, exhausted John of Argyll.[142] Indeed, after a council at Carrickfergus the Bruce force embarked upon a march designed to display Edward's banner in east-central and southern Ireland and to rally a force large enough for a decisive siege of Dublin or battle with Sir Edmund Butler's Anglo-Irish host. As in 1315–16, this may have had a speculative Welsh dimension with Edward Bruce allegedly in contact with the steward of Cardiganshire, Sir Gruffudd Llwyd, and other Welsh lords. Correspondence seized by the English included an open letter from Edward Bruce urging the Welsh people to 'expel from the borders of your land with all force the unnatural and barbaric servitude imposed by the English' and to consider Bruce's elevation, as in Ireland, to 'the chief lordship of your people'. In language surely drawn by a Scottish clerk in Edward Bruce's household, the letter also guaranteed all Welsh customs and hereditary rights.[143] The marauding presence in the Irish Sea of the Scots privateer Thomas Dun facilitated such communication via the hands of Irish and Welsh clerics with strong common ground against English superiority.[144] Yet, without any real Scottish presence in Wales, these approaches (which only survive in later medieval transcripts) proved of no avail other than in provoking reinforcement of Edward II's northern Welsh castles and ships while Llwyd was imprisoned from December 1316 until c.1318.[145]

Marching south from Ulster in early February, Edward Bruce, the king of Scots, Randolph, Domnall Ó Néill and their galloglass pushed past Dundalk to lay waste to Slane in Meath, 7 miles west of the Cistercian abbey of Mellifont founded by St Malachy.[146] By 23 February they were in sight of Dublin where defenders set fire to buildings outside the walls. Panicked, the authorities even arrested the sheltering Ulster earl, Robert's father-in-law.[147] However, as at Berwick, the Scots were not prepared for a long siege (or to imperil Scottish prisoners in Dublin) and veered south-west into Leinster and Munster. Here their potential allies in Thomond, the O'Briens, let them down and the Scots became bitterly entangled in native rivalries, tracked by a force led by Justiciar Butler. The significant tipping point came in early April when a force under the newly appointed Lieutenant of Ireland, Roger Mortimer, landed on the south coast. The Bruces retreated to Ulster, skirmishing with Butler en route. Yet this was a costly, brutalising campaign without any significant encounter. Both sides may have claimed it as a positive demonstration of lordship, but by late May Robert I had returned to Scotland with nothing to show for his stay.[148]

We can only imagine that by this stage, almost three years since the heady days of Bannockburn, Robert I and his chief supporters were on the whole increasingly discouraged by their inability to force a decisive breakthrough. In many ways, the brothers' Irish campaign of January–May typified their efforts of 1314–17: a long, hard, ill-supplied slog over sodden ground, with enemies on all sides, cheered by small victories that enhanced the reputations of Robert, Edward and their captains, and a sustained income of plunder and tribute, but with no landmark gains. Admittedly, there may have been a strong sense of relief simply to have survived the last three years. No irreversible loss had been suffered on the Marches or in the quagmire of Anglo-Irish politics. Moreover, the Scottish realm had weathered the famines of 1315–17 marginally better than much of the British Isles, although the harvest failure of 1316 had inflicted a mortality rate of about 10 per cent or more from hunger and disease across most of north-western Europe.[149]

Nevertheless, during Lent and Easter (3 April) of their Irish jaunt the king of Scots, his adult heir presumptive and their nephew and nominated minority Guardian Thomas Randolph had all come far too close to death by violence or starvation. The Irish annalists lamented the Bruce invasion itself and the English armed response as the actual cause of famine, for 'between them they left neither wood nor lea, nor corn nor crop nor stead nor barn nor church, but fired and burnt them all'.[150] Fordun's near contemporary annalist also asserted that 'in this march, many died of hunger and the rest lived on horse flesh'.[151] Had Robert, Edward and Earl Thomas indeed perished or been captured or killed, then they would have left Scotland without an explicitly designated leader (although Douglas served as interim Guardian). The throne would have passed to a child barely a year old, Robert Stewart, under the influence of his young mother (Marjorie, who would die c.1317) and the Dowager Queen Elizabeth de Burgh of Ulster, or any regime of renewed Guardianship that the likes of Bishop Lamberton and Chancellor Bernard, Walter Steward, Robert Keith and James Douglas might have been able to propose to the community of the realm: but the carefully engineered parliamentary act of succession of April 1315 would have been of little or no help at all.

With the adult alternative of Edward Balliol and the disinherited waiting in the wings, backed by an English king who had recovered considerable domestic authority, the Bruce(-Stewart) kingship would undoubtedly have been challenged at such a moment of crisis; all the more so as Robert I's resettlement of lands and offices since Bannockburn had progressed but by no means reached out to alter the balance of power and allegiance decisively in all quarters of his realm. This was especially the case in the north-east, Fife, the south-east and south-west. In sum, as he returned to Carrick in May 1317, his intermittently poor health further racked by a gruelling Irish campaign, Robert I must have been all too aware of the precarious nature of all that he had set in motion. Not least, he may now have been convinced of the insurmountable nature of the internecine politics of Gaelic Ireland (and Scotland) and the harsh truth that his brother's dynastic cause was a dangerous front too far. What can be rationalised in hindsight to present a picture of Bruce 'military hegemony' over a majority of the British Isles c.1314–17 may thus mask a highly strained reality and unsustainable strands of policy for Robert I and his relatively small government and military circle by 1317.[152] Furthermore, back in Scotland, Robert may now have received word of his fresh excommunication by the Papacy along with that of his brother, issued from Avignon on 28 March. Eleven days before that the Pope had named two envoys to arbitrate an Anglo-Scottish peace; then on 1 May, further encouraged by an Edwardian embassy headed by the earl of Pembroke, John XXII would proclaim a papal truce over the Anglo-Scottish Marches and Ireland.[153]

In practice, such censures meant little to the kind of war and political settlement which Robert was pursuing. However, given Pope John's desire to forward his plans for crusade by favouring France and England respectively in their dealings with 'rebellions' in Flanders and Scotland, while urging all these Christian parties to make peace, this interference did have the potential to disrupt valuable continental supply lines to Scotland as well as Robert's provisions to important Church benefices.[154] More immediately, a second excommunication may have stung the king, coming so soon after the death of the prelate Robert Wishart, who had helped lift the first spiritual penalties imposed upon him.[155] King Robert, of course, would block pronouncement of this punishment in 1317–19 through Scottish pulpits, but this in itself may have been motivated by a fear that Scottish subjects might begin to forget Bannockburn and to connect the long, ongoing war and, worse, the last two years of brutal famine with the ill-will of God inflicted upon the supporters of a sinful king and his equally questionable brother. All this may have added to a growing sense on Robert's part that he had made little real progress at all since midsummer 1314 and thus to a conscious choice, over the next eighteen months, to reduce his support for his heir presumptive and instead to focus resources upon the Anglo-Scottish March. As we shall see, Bruce would at last achieve his breakthrough, and on this front, but it would come with near fatal consequences.

# CHAPTER SEVEN

# Dark Victory
## The Price for Berwick, 1317–19

*And there was a rumour that if he [Edward Bruce] achieved his wish there [in Ireland], he would at once cross to Wales, and raise the Welsh likewise against our king. For these two races are easily roused to rebellion; they bear hardly the yoke of slavery, and curse the lordship of the English.*

*Vita Edwardi Secundi*[1]

### Remonstrance and War, 1317–18

The embassy that Edward II dispatched to Avignon in January 1317 cost over £4,000 and was headed by Aymer de Valence, earl of Pembroke, and the bishops of Norwich and Ely – the latter now John de Hothum, the English council's administrative agent in Ireland in 1315–16. The delegation's purpose was to postpone Edward's commitment to crusade, renegotiate his papal debts, secure provision of English archbishops in Ireland at Cashel and Dublin, and solicit papal condemnation of Irish clergy preaching rebellion in support of Edward Bruce.[2] In these tasks it succeeded. In addition, although it failed to gain John XXII's absolution of Edward II's oaths to uphold the Ordinances, solicitation of censures upon Robert Bruce and the intervention of two Cardinals in truce and peace talks also became a priority. Once secured, these were developments which the Bruce brothers could not simply ignore.[3] Not least, the new Pope's attitude impeded the confirmation and consecration of Stephen de Donydouer as bishop of Glasgow: in June he would be turned away from Avignon and die before he was able to return.[4] The Scots were now to be confronted with a situation similar to that which had been turned upon Edward I by the Scottish Guardians in 1299–1301. Thus, if Edward Bruce and Domnall Ó Néill did hold an assembly at Carrickfergus before King Robert's return to his realm from Ireland circa 22 May 1317 (as Barbour asserts), this body may have begun the preparation of arguments for a letter of protest to the Papacy later known as the 'Remonstrance of the Irish Princes'.[5]

However, it is more likely this response would be drawn up in the summer and autumn of 1317, once Cardinals Fieschi and d'Eauze arrived in England. By that juncture English forces on the Anglo-Scottish border surely welcomed the envoys' presence and the prospect of respite (without expensive tribute) following two costly reverses at Scottish hands. According to Sir Thomas Gray (and later elaborated into a chivalric triumph by Barbour), on about 23 April a substantial force under the new March warden, the earl of Arundel, set out for Lothian but was routed by Sir James Douglas's following at Lintalee in Jedburgh forest.[6] A few weeks later, circa 13 May–11 June, a plunder raid from English ships that came ashore near Dunfermline in Fife was also beaten back. According to Barbour, the Scottish defence had to be led by the inspiring figure of Bishop Sinclair of Dunkeld after a force commanded by Duncan, earl of Fife, and 'the sheriff of Fife' (either still Sir Michael Balfour or Sir David Wemyss) had withdrawn in fear.[7] This explanation is perhaps a later gloss over Fife's equivocal loyalties: for Arundel's two-pronged campaign, on land and sea, had seen participation by such disinherited lords as the Strathbogie earl of Atholl and Sir Henry Beaumont, men who would both be involved in Edward Balliol's successful landing in Bruce Scotland in 1332, again tellingly in Fife (at Inverkeithing), prompting Earl Duncan's defection. Failure in spring 1317, though, saw further plans for an English border muster at Newcastle slip from 8 July to 11 August.[8]

Upon his return from Ireland, Robert I would not be able to capitalise on this English distress to weaken Berwick's defence further. The time remaining of regional tribute truces and then the efforts of the Pope's envoys may have been enough to hamper Robert's plans seriously for at least several months. But some of this lull must have been due to the need for recuperation while a drier early summer brought first fruits and the prospect of better crops. We can relocate the king on 1 June 1317 at Scone in company with Thomas Randolph (styled earl of Moray and lord of Annandale and Man), Steward, Douglas and several knights.[9] The king was again at Scone through 12–14 June to attend what was probably a council or parliament for which no record of formal proceedings survives.[10] This assembly did review the findings of inquests into the exemption from royal exactions of the Cistercian abbey of Balmerino (northern Fife) and the rights of the bishopric of Dunkeld within the Perthshire earldoms of Atholl and Strathearn: an extant charter of the teinds of justice to the bishop's cathedral was witnessed by William

Lamberton, bishop of St Andrews, Nicholas Balmyle, bishop of Dunblane, Chancellor Bernard, Randolph, Malise, earl of Strathearn, Hay, Keith, Roger Mowbray and David Barclay. It has been suggested that in this instance Thomas Randolph was no longer styled 'of Annandale' probably because representations had been made on behalf of an absent Edward Bruce objecting to such renewed regional favour for Thomas while the Isle of Man remained in English hands.[11] In truth, there is no firm corroborating evidence for such tension on this issue. However, a papal dispensation for Edward Bruce to marry Isabel, daughter of Earl William of Ross, granted on 1 June 1317, may represent something of a rapprochement between Edward and Earl Thomas, whose second son, John Randolph (perhaps born c.1316–17), would go on to be betrothed to Robert and Edward's niece, Euphemia Ross, Earl William's granddaughter.[12] What besides surely dominated this assembly's agenda, and perhaps some heated discussion, was how to respond to the papal envoys and expected bulls of truce and censure.

It is more believable, however, that Robert reached a firm decision on what tack to take with England and Avignon in discussions with closer counsel when at Arbroath from 24 June, perhaps up until the Translation feast of St Thomas (7 July).[13] By 24 July he had moved south to Melrose Abbey in company with the bishops of St Andrews and Dunblane, Randolph, Patrick Dunbar, earl of March, Steward, Douglas and Keith to await the messengers of the papal envoys and to put his strategy into effect.[14] This amounted to a consistent refusal to take receipt of papal bulls and other letters that failed to address him as king (just as had the summons to the Vienne Church Council of 1309–10), and to stall and delay the process by which he delivered his response to this effect, avoiding an extended truce and leaving his forces free to strike against the tottering Berwick garrison and continue their Irish action.

Indeed, it is likely that during the summer of 1317 Scottish raiding into the northern counties and sapping of Berwick's walls (and loyalties) continued on a low-key scale. About 8 July Edward II would receive reports of a Scottish incursion into Northumbria as the cause of English abandonment of March defences.[15] In that sense, despite the papal truce, Robert's behaviour was no different from that of his opponents who also continued to prepare for a northern campaign. But what undoubtedly encouraged Robert and his counsel in maintaining their war-footing was regular news of political division in England: deepening tensions between Edward II and the earl of Lancaster, with the latter failing to attend a parliament in July without guarantees relating to the Ordinances and his personal safety from the king's household (headed by the Despensers). This stand-off saw

the Newcastle muster further delayed until 15 September. Although the
earl of Lancaster was an increasingly isolated figure, the very real danger of
an English civil war provided the perfect atmosphere for Robert and
Lancaster finally to begin to collude.[16]

A report on 7 September by messengers of the papal envoys paints a
fragmentary but convincing picture of Robert's calculation.[17] After apparently keeping these messengers waiting for several weeks, the king finally
granted an audience in late August at which he insisted that whilst
committed to Christian peace he would have to take the advice of his
'council' on whether or not to accept letters so improperly addressed and
only then consider their contents: he would thus return with a written reply
at Michaelmas. As the envoys' representatives reported, '[Robert] said all
this to the messengers with a cheerful face and amiable countenance', all
the while aware of the bulls' contents through his own sources at Avignon
(perhaps John Lindsay, rector of [Stewart] Ratho, by August 1317 bishop-
elect to the vacant see of Glasgow).[18] The king's mood must have been
cheered by word of the collapse of attempts by an embassy (including
Pembroke, Hereford and the Archbishop of Canterbury) to negotiate a kiss
of peace between Edward II and Lancaster at Pontefract circa 18–30
August: the earl and his adherents now began to attack Edward II's
supporters in northern England and to blockade the king himself in York.[19]

The papal visitors had also understood that even 'if the lord Robert is
willing to speak to us without our writing to him in another way [styled as
king] or even if he shows himself willing, the [Scottish] barons and council
would refuse', believing that the English were to blame for their king's
improper address.[20] Robert sent the messengers back south in early
September to brief their masters. But they found the envoys in shock, after
having been robbed on the road to Durham in company with the Beaumonts
(one of whom, Louis, was now that see's bishop-elect) by a rebellious
Northumbrian noble, Gilbert Middleton, and a number of Lancastrian
adherents, alleged by some chroniclers (and, according to at least one
English source, by the Cardinals themselves) to be in Bruce pay. Lancaster
would be obliged to make amends to Durham and the Cardinals, escorting
the latter to Edward II's presence at York by 8 September.[21] Yet, by contrast,
Robert can only have been further convinced of the short-term benefits to
his cause of such harassment and dissimulation.

Nonetheless, the interference of papal envoys at Edward's behest (and
English opposition to John Lindsay's confirmation as bishop of Glasgow)
did provoke Robert into a fuller diplomatic response that encompassed his
policies in both northern England and Ireland. A council or parliament was

1. All Souls church in the lordship of Writtle, Essex: a possible birthplace of Robert Bruce.

Alexander Rey
Scotor

Lewellin
princeps
Wallie

2. Edward I presides over his parliament in 1278 with Alexander III in attendance to do homage
for his English lands, from a fifteenth-century manuscript.

3. The ruins of Turnberry castle in the Bruce earldom of Carrick, South Ayrshire, facing west to Ireland.

4. A recreation of Portencross castle, North Ayrshire, illustrating the sea-castle and 'birling' or war galley power projected by Turnberry.

5. Ernest William Tristram's recreation (1927) of the lost Edward I wall-painting of Judas Maccabeus from the Painted Chamber of Westminster Palace.

6. Winchester Great Hall and Edward I's Round Table of c.1290. Robert Bruce and his father may have attended the king here as part of the younger Bruce's service in the English royal household.

7. King John (Balliol) of Scotland (1292–96) does homage to Edward I, for Scotland.

8. Coronation of a King, from an Ordo including the ceremony for Edward II of 1308.

9. Plaque commemorating the site of the Greyfriars in Dumfries where Bruce killed his rival John Comyn of Badenoch on 10 February 1306.

10. The seal of Scone Abbey, illustrating the ceremony of inauguration. Did Robert Bruce attempt a ritual closer to actual coronation on 25 March 1306?

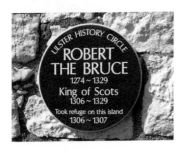

11. Plaque commemorating the tradition of Bruce's exile to the Isle of Rathlin off northern Ireland over the winter of 1306–7.

12. Cults and relics venerated by Robert I.

a) The Breccbennach of St Columba, held by relic-keepers at Arbroath Abbey.

b) The crozier of St Fillan who aided Bruce in both 1306 and 1314.

c) A pilgrim badge depicting the shrine of St Thomas Becket at Canterbury.

13. a) The abbey of Arbroath, Angus, dedicated to St Thomas. Robert I established his chancery here and paid for a tomb effigy for its founder, King William I (r.1165–1214). Below: b) abbey seal.

14. Robert I slays Henry de Bohun at the battle of Bannockburn, 23 June 1314, before Stirling. From a fifteenth-century manuscript of Abbot Walter Bower of Inchcolm's *Scotichronicon*. Note the steep banks of the burn rendered at the foot of the folio.

15. The castle of Bothwell, Lanarkshire, surrendered to Robert I by Walter Fitz Gilbert in the wake of Bannockburn.

16. Images from Robert I's second great seal.
*Left*: a) The king dispensing justice and patronage.
*Right*: b) The king in war.

17. The abbey of Cambuskenneth towards Stirling castle, from John Slezer's *Theatrum Scotiae* (1693). Robert I held a decisive parliament here in November 1314 to forfeit his remaining Scottish opponents.

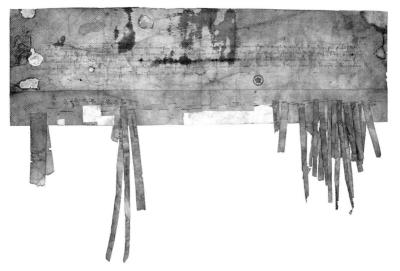

18. *Above*: The Cambuskenneth forfeiture of Robert I's opponents, 6 November 1314.

19. The Bute Mazer, an early fourteenth-century ceremonial bowl decorated with the arms of the Stewarts and Walter Fitz Gilbert.

20. The Savernake horn, its early fourteenth-century baldric decorated with the arms of the Randolph earls of Moray.

21. Images from the *Luttrell Psalter*, c.1320–c.1340, of Sir Geoffrey Luttrell of Irnham, Lincolnshire.

a) Hard winters and wet summers devastated arable and pastoral agriculture across Europe and the British Isles resulting in famine c.1315–18 and cattle plague c.1318–24.

b) A wild man, often taken for a Scottish raider of the assaults with which the Scots sapped northern England of money and victuals c.1315–23.

c) The execution of Bruce's ally, rebel earl Thomas of Lancaster, 1323.

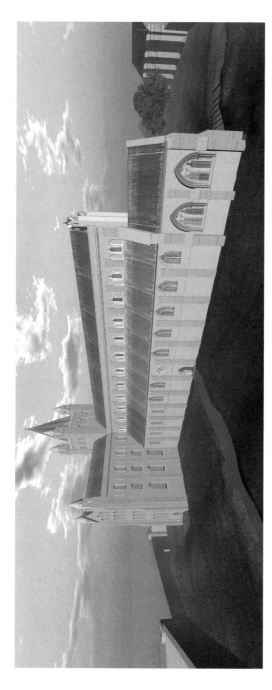

22. St Andrews Cathedral, Fife. Scene of Edward I's conquest parliament in Lent 1304 and Robert I's first recorded parliament of Lent 1309. The Scots king would also oversee a great consecration ceremony here on 5 July 1318.

23. The ruins of Tarbert castle, the Kintyre peninsula, Argyll, above the port and burgh. Robert I first ventured here in force c.1315 and reinforced the castle from c.1325.

24. Mains of Cardross farm, Dumbartonshire, with canal works off River Leven believed to be part of the manor house erected by Robert I c.1325–7 as his main residence until death.

25. Edward III receives Robert Bruce's defiance and declaration of war February 1327. A fifteenth-century manuscript of Jean Froissart's *Chroniques*.

26. Remains of the feretory of St Margaret at Dunfermline Abbey, Fife, where it lay alongside the tombs of six Scottish kings in the choir, including (St) David I (r.1124–53); Robert I's body would be interred here in 1329, probably in the north aisle, beneath a white marble tomb and effigy atop a black Frosterley marble plinth.

27. a) Fragments of Italian white marble from Robert I's tomb of 1329, smashed at the Reformation, 1560.

b) The casket and reliquary used to reinter Robert Bruce's heart at Melrose Abbey in 1996.

held at Edinburgh circa 16–17 September for which, once more, no proceedings survive.[22] It was this brief gathering that authorised the drafting and 'ragman' sealing of a letter in the name of the Scottish earls and barons, to be accompanied by a letter under Robert's own seal, both addressed to Pope John XXII, supporting their king's refusal to recognise bulls that did not style him as such. These Scottish letters are no longer extant but may have anticipated a number of the points that would be made in writing to the same Pope in similar circumstances in April 1320 (via the 'Declaration of Arbroath' and other missives).[23]

Robert might naturally have come under pressure from a number of his close supporters to take such a line and continue to prosecute the war in the south-east: knights such as Keith, Hay, Seton, Stewart of Bonkle, Gordon and even Patrick, earl of March, must have viewed the recovery of Berwickshire as absolutely essential to the restoration of their own lordship in this region (as would Lamberton, bishop of St Andrews). Ambitious men surely also sought further opportunities to enhance their military renown, with James Douglas deliberately targeting English Marcher lords and castles throughout 1317–19.[24] Yet any notion that in 1317 Robert's 'council' or parliament came anywhere near the power actually to dictate to the king in matters of war and diplomacy was surely (just as it would also be claimed in 1320) a carefully controlled political strategy for external consumption.

Moreover, the Scots' letters of autumn 1317 surely had much in common with the so-called 'Remonstrance of the Irish Princes' also drawn up at about this time and which would reach Avignon in January 1318 (again via Cardinals Fieschi and d'Eauze). In its appeal to ancient origins and papal jurisdiction over Ireland against English tyranny, the Remonstrance followed the precedent of Baldred Bisset's reasoned reply to the letters to the Pope of Edward I and his baronage of 1301; it also anticipated the 'Declaration of Arbroath' sent to the Papacy in 1320.[25] Yet these connections might be taken further. The Remonstrance survives only as a text in various manuscript recensions of the Scottish chronicles of John of Fordun and his continuators, particularly Abbot Bower of Inchcolm (fl.1440–49): it is often found within an eclectic dossier of copied materials including the succession hearings of 1291–92; the Papacy's sanction of English lordship over Ireland of c.1155 (the bull *Laudabiliter*); various ancient prophecies; and even the poetry about Bannockburn of the captive Carmelite court poet Robert Baston.[26] This suggests an overlap of purpose and personnel in compiling such declarations between about 1314 and 1320.[27]

In the name of Domnall Ó Néill and various Irish lords (unnamed), who sent 'devout kisses of his blessed feet' (as would the Scots in 1320), the

Remonstrance warned the Pope against English slanders and detailed the descent of Irish forebears from a son of Brutus arriving via Spain to establish a line of 197 native kings in 'Greater Scotia' (Ireland) until the imposition of English tyranny in 1170 (sic); there then followed generations of atrocity inflicted on the Irish Church and people 'for want of a head' of their own. Given such default of English lordship, the princes invited Edward Bruce, brother of 'the Lord Robert by the grace of God the most illustrious king of Scots ("Lesser Scotia"), and sprung from our noblest ancestors', to be 'our king and lord'. We may find further evidence of a contribution to the Remonstrance by Robert I's chancery at Arbroath in its emphasis on the wicked actions of Henry II of England 'by whom St Thomas of Canterbury suffered death': the Irish protest even misdates *Laudabiliter* to 1170, the year of Becket's martyrdom, for greater effect.[28]

Therefore both the Remonstrance and the now lost letters of the Scottish barons and their king of 1317 were designed to justify the Bruces' continued prosecution of war on two fronts in the face of a papally imposed truce.[29] And this is exactly what Robert I did. By 17 September the king was already at Haddington in East Lothian en route to oversee a renewed siege of Berwick town and castle with forces probably led by Sir Alexander Seton and Earl Patrick of Dunbar.[30] It is likely that a mobile Scottish force under Moray and Douglas also resumed raids into Northumberland (plundering the improved harvest). Robert's grant of north Tynedale lands to Sir Philip Mowbray (whose family had held the lordship of Bolton in Yorkshire before 1296) may belong to this period, along with further lost acts concerning Marches territory and the Scots' alleged resetting (abetting) of the outlaw Middleton and his retinue.[31] Edward II and Lancaster had been brought close to reconciliation through the mediation of the Cardinals and the earl of Pembroke. But the final cancellation of the postponed English muster at Newcastle on 24 September gave further impetus to this Scottish campaign. So, too, might word that while returning to London, Edward had almost come to open blows with his aggrieved earl at Pontefract on 29 September.[32]

At the very least, if Berwick finally fell, Robert would recover the last of the occupied territory of Alexander III's realm and secure a vital bargaining chip if he had to relent and participate in peace talks chaired by the Pope's Cardinals. However, still accessible by sea, Berwick held out, reinforced by ships, men and supplies from Yorkshire despite open conflict there between the earls of Lancaster and Surrey. With winter closing in, and despite the increase in victuals, the siege of Berwick seems to have halted in late November, perhaps after agreement of a local truce.[33] By circa mid-October, Robert had finally given his formal reply to the papal envoys' messengers, predictably reiterating the recent letter of his barons (as 'council') refusing to recognise letters that did not address him as king.[34] But he remained in the south-west, gathering men and engines for a fresh assault on Berwick.[35]

Now fully convinced of Robert's evasion of papal jurisdiction, the envoys – at English urging – dispatched a Franciscan friar of their own to confront 'Robert, governor of the realm of Scotland' with the now officially declared (27 November) papal truce. Reaching Robert by 16 December at Aldcambus (a possession of Durham through its daughter house of Coldingham Priory), some 10 miles north along the coast from Berwick, the friar found his access to Robert and the Scottish bishops barred by their retainers who shouted him down as he defiantly narrated aloud the terms of truce. To emphasise the need for Robert's full title, they turned the friar home without safe conduct, whereupon he was robbed of his baggage and letters, with the latter surely acquired for Robert.[36]

The friar's papers must have encouraged Robert to persist with pressure upon Berwick. Nevertheless, it is a testament both to the Scots' exhaustion and their continued hesitancy in prolonged sieges, as well as to the improved English defence works at Berwick, that it would take another six months for the town and castle to fall to Bruce. Robert spent Christmas at Newbattle Abbey, a daughter house of Melrose, and around the Lothians granting baronies in Angus and Ayrshire to loyal knights.[37] But late January 1318 perhaps found him at his chancery in Arbroath where amongst several acts he confirmed Nicholas Scrymgeour in his father Alexander's role as castle-keeper at Dundee (as royal standard-bearer).[38] However, on 26 February the king was at Clackmannan, perhaps heading south once more: his business there, granting the patronage of the church of Killin (in Glendochart) to Inchaffray Abbey (in thanks for succour in 1306), may, though, have been interrupted by couriered news of an offer of defection and betrayal from within the starving town of Berwick, or more likely offers of talks with envoys of Edward II's council.[39]

The contemporary *Vita Edwardi Secundi* certainly laments that, while Edward II's council delayed parliament once more (on 3 March, postponing to 19 June) and devoted its energies (successfully) to arbitration with Lancaster over the Ordinances and royal household (terms formalised in an assembly at Leicester from 12 April), the burgesses of Berwick none-theless 'handed it over to the enemy'.[40] The Lanercost chronicler blames the 'Englishman' Peter de Spalding, bribed by the Scots with 'a great sum of money received from them and by the promise of land', who let the enemy scale the section of wall he was guarding. On 1 May 1319 Robert would indeed grant lands and the keeping of the Angus forest of Kilgarie to Peter de Spalding in exchange for all his tenements in Berwick and the service of a knight.[41]

It is likely that the actual military action – with the town overrun in the six days after the fourth Sunday in Lent (2–8 April) – was overseen by Keith, Seton and Dunbar, who then laid siege to the castle.[42] The earl of Moray and (perhaps until the town was cleared) Douglas seem to have raided south once more both to detect and deflect English attempts to relieve Berwick. About 21 May the Northumbrian castles of Wark, Harbottle and Mitford would also fall to the Scots on terms as by then unrelieved (the latter having been held by Gilbert Middleton until January, when English royal forces had seized it and taken him to London for execution).[43] This allowed one Scottish force to raid as far south as Ripon, burning and stealing cattle and extracting yet more tribute (1,000 marks), while a second force laid waste to Northallerton and Boroughbridge (28 May) before merging with the first to plunder Knaresborough, level with York, perhaps in tentative collusion with Lancastrian rebels. On 8 June Edward II ordered 'the magnates and lieges of Yorkshire to muster the whole force of the county to repel the Scots who he hears have entered it and are doing great damage'.[44] Sometime in June, County Durham also took its by now customary truce tribute from the Scots for 600 marks: however, the coastal town of Hartlepool, property of Robert I's English kin, would bemoan their exclusion from this ceasefire as Bruce had promised to destroy it for seizing a shipload of his armour and victuals.[45] Robert had arrived in Berwick by 12 April at the latest, when he reissued his recent charter to Inchaffray Abbey.[46] Yet although the king was able to celebrate Holy Week in his restored royal patrimony, this punctuated what was still to be a long, brutal action of attrition.

According to Sir Thomas Gray, Berwick castle 'held out for eleven weeks afterwards [until c.18 June] and then surrendered to the Scots for want of relief, as it was not provisioned'.[47] This is borne out in part by Robert's extant charters. On 20 May he was at Colquhoun, between Glasgow and Dumbarton, perhaps en route to receive word from Ireland or supplies: his charter there (of the office of sergeant in Dumbartonshire) was witnessed by Malcolm, earl of Lennox, Sir John Menteith, Douglas, Keith and Hay, suggesting the earl of Moray's command of the ongoing Berwick castle siege.[48] However, it is possible that this visit to Dumbarton related instead to the dispatch of galleys in support of a landing on the Isle of Man: this would also explain Moray's absence as a recorded charter witness and fit with the Scots' retaking of the island sometime after October 1317.[49] But by 5 June 1318 the king was back at Berwick where the garrison's capitulation was judged imminent. That the delay in completely winning Berwick was a source of frustration for Robert and his counsel is suggested by the grossly rewritten account inherited by Barbour. According to this vernacular verse, 'Sym' Spalding's offer to betray the town was made through Keith as Marischal, who was ordered by his king not to inform Moray and Douglas, rivals in chivalric honour, after their companies met up with Robert's at Duns Park; once the town fell, '[Men flocked to Berwick]... vittaill [victuals] they fand in gret foysoun [profusion]', and the castle surrendered after a mere six days.[50]

## Triumph and Defeat, June–October 1318

As physically drained as he and his companions surely were once Berwick castle fell, Robert I had clearly resolved to capitalise on his success with a series of public ceremonies designed to fly in the face of papal censures. A bull not merely expelling Robert himself from the Church but prohibiting all church services and absolving Scottish subjects of their loyalty to Bruce would be issued as early as 28 June 1318 (prompted by the fall of Berwick town): it would be publicised in English churches from 3 September.[51] Shock and anticipation of this repeated excommunication and now kingdom-wide interdict (denying the laity divine office, the sacraments and Christian burial) may explain in part why so few Scottish royal charters are extant from the second half of 1318. But some of Robert's itinerary and pre-emptive response can otherwise be cautiously recreated.[52]

It is likely that after Berwick's English garrison was permitted to leave, Robert took up brief residence in its castle at midsummer. Instead of razing the castle and town walls to the ground, the king, surrounded by his captains, close counsel and household officers, announced his intention to retain and defend the burgh, perhaps installing, as Barbour asserts, his son-in-law Walter Steward as its keeper as well as naming a sheriff for Berwickshire (Alexander Seton or Robert Lauder?). The king could have marked the renewal of his right to the burgh's valuable wool customs levied on the exports of border abbeys through appointing baillies and inspecting the market with its cross and weigh-beam; he could also have used the minting facilities installed by the English administration to produce his own Scottish silver pennies.[53] But most immediately, he must have begun the process of inquests into burgh property and the restoration of Berwick's tenements to Scots whilst continuing (and expanding) the 'murage' levy on burgesses for the upkeep of the burgh's walls, a levy initiated by Edward I in 1296.[54]

Next, we can only speculate that in the intervening ten days Robert may have visited Bannockburn on 23–24 June 1318 then headed east, via the shrine of St Serf (feast day 1 July) at Culross Abbey or his dedicative priory on Lochleven, or even via Dunfermline Abbey (about 29 June, the feast of Apostles Paul and Peter, Rome's first bishop and Pope), moving on to reach St Andrews by at least Wednesday 5 July; alternatively, the king may have taken a ship there directly from Berwick. Regardless of his route, according to the later narrative of Abbot Bower (who clearly had access to the now lost cartulary of St Andrews), on the latter date Robert, 'acting in the presence of seven bishops, fifteen abbots, and nearly all the nobles of the kingdom, both earls and barons', attended a dedication ceremony for St Andrews Cathedral.[55]

This national church had in fact been under construction since the late twelfth century but fully functional only since the last quarter of the thirteenth century, and plans for its dedication may have been in train for some time.[56] Now, however, Robert took the opportunity to link its completion to his force's recovery of the last remaining royal Scottish castle-burgh in English hands, Berwick, as well as to his most famous victory in 1314. It is possible, too, that Bishop Lamberton – with the full extent of his diocese now restored as far as Berwick – counselled his king on the value of such ritual. The indulgences extended to those attending the dedicatory masses would have represented a heady communal experience.

Bower describes the king's gift on 5 July 1318 of an annual sum of 100 merks from the royal exchequer 'in commemoration of the signal victory given to the Scots at Bannockburn by the blessed Andrew, protector of the kingdom', a grant converted by Lamberton into the patronage of the church of Fordoun in the Mearns – some 25 miles north of Arbroath and dedicated, strikingly, to St Palladius (d.c.457–61), the first Christian bishop of Ireland, feast day 7 July. This is an act for which an incompletely dated royal charter does survive.[57] Bower asserts that further grants of churches to the cathedral by Lamberton and Duncan, earl of Fife, the realm's leading prelate and baron, also marked the day.[58] Crucially, though, Robert could have followed this solemn dedication by commemoration the following day of the Translation feast of the saint of his realm's next senior diocese, St Kentigern of Glasgow (6 July, apt given both Lamberton's early career at Glasgow and English provision by 17 July of their own candidate in opposition to John Lindsay as successor to Bishop Wishart).[59] Then, the next day, Robert and his court might even have made a swift journey north, across the Tay to Arbroath Abbey, for the Translation feast of his other personal intercessor, Thomas Becket (whose feast day of 7 July was shared with Palladius). The date of 8 July was the anniversary of the death of Alexander II (buried at Melrose Abbey).[60] Finally, 11 July 1318 was the king's own (forty-fourth) birthday.

These three weeks of military, political and intense spiritual activity converged as a powerful statement of Robert I's kingship, sacrality and support. Together with Berwick's capture they may have had an effect on some of Robert's wavering subjects as profound as that of Bannockburn: for example, Sir David de Brechin, who appears to have defected back to Edward II's allegiance in August 1317 as the Bruces' campaigns seemed in danger of inertia, probably now returned to Robert's peace, as may have the final members of the Soules kindred.[61] Moreover, these religious feasts were an effective riposte to the papal censures which would soon follow and make nonsense of the accusations of the *Vita Edwardi Secundi* that 'when one day Robert Bruce asked for Mass to be celebrated for himself, the chaplain sought to be excused by reason of the interdict; but the tyrant's order prevailed . . . [But] a dove coming down from above clearly appeared to all, and in the sight of everyone carried off the Host, plucked from the priest's hand.'[62]

Robert's venerations may also have served for self-presentation to papal authority as far more devout and selfless than Edward II's expression to a doubting John XXII, circa June 1318, of his desire to undergo a second coronation, this time with the 'holy oil of Thomas Becket'. This alleged gift from the Blessed Virgin to the martyred archbishop was prophesied to have the power to allow the fifth king after Henry II, thus Edward II, to champion the Church and recover the Holy Land; Edward had thought better of its application during his coronation in 1308 but now, amidst the crisis of talks with the intransigent Lancaster, this relic seemed to offer affirmation of royal authority.[63]

However, it is surely the case that Robert also marked his progress by further royal grants, probably to those knights most prominent in Berwick's recovery and allied raids – Moray, Douglas, Keith, Dunbar, Seton, Soules, Mowbray – as well as by turning the chancery's inquests to deal with outstanding legal, ecclesiastical and freeholder issues from the wider Lothians, Berwickshire and Roxburghshire (although swathes of this territory had been depopulated by war).[64] The occasion for some of these royal acts would logically have been a council or parliament in late July or August in Scone, Edinburgh or even back in Berwick itself (where a council would be held in December 1319). Such an assembly would have considered the pressing need to match the achievements on the Anglo-Scottish Marches with long-delayed reinforcements to Ireland.

The Irish annals and Dublin's records are almost totally silent about Edward Bruce's activities in Ireland between May 1317 and October 1318.[65] On 2 July 1317, while the English March reportedly lay 'defenceless' against Scottish attack, privateer Thomas Dun's ships and person were at last captured by English galleys commanded by John d'Athy, English keeper of the Isle of Man.[66] This put an end to Dun's infestation 'of the sea towards the west with a crew of Scots, doing great damage to trade coming to England', and weakened the Scots' lines of supply and intelligence. Before his execution Dun also claimed that Thomas Randolph was about to launch an expedition to recover the Isle of Man and then 'attempt Anglesey by aid of some English traitors', a plan which would surely have engaged Edward Bruce's forces.[67] About August 1317 the bishop of Ferns (Wexford) was disciplined for advising Edward Bruce 'and his brother' on the 'state of the country'.[68] Yet in October 1317 the English still held the Isle of Man and Edward Bruce does not seem to have ventured out of Ulster to aid his de Lacy allies against the host of Roger Mortimer of Wigmore.

It is likely, instead, that Edward's galloglass and their native allies chose to wait for replacement ships, victuals and Scottish troops led by the earl of Moray or King Robert. Yet it is clear in hindsight that Robert's commitment to achieving a breakthrough on the eastern March (and Moray's determination to recover his lordship of the Isle of Man after its charter grant in 1316) had meant a long delay in Edward Bruce's territorial and political campaign, eighteen months in which the English authorities could improve their response and reduce his native support (with the papal truce and threat of excommunication applied similarly on this front).[69]

It might have been Robert I's intention, as in 1314, to follow up Berwick's seizure in 1318 with offers of full peace talks to Edward II. Yet if such approaches were made they have left no trace. Rather, what stands out – as followed the defeat at Stirling Bridge in 1297 – is the ironically calming effect upon England's political crisis of another humiliating Scottish success. Just as with the triumph on Scottish soil at Bannockburn, the recovery of a single walled border town – in this case a former Scottish possession and thus not as damaging to the English as would have been the real 'conquest' of Carlisle or Dublin – was not going to force Edward II to recognise Scottish sovereignty or Bruce's title.

On 7 August Edward and the earl of Lancaster exchanged a kiss of peace before John XXII's Cardinals and England's magnates, pledging their commitment to look to the defence of the north after an October parliament. Their preliminary accord – the treaty of Leake (9 August) – coincided with Edward's authorisation of payment to Andrew de Tange for his notarised instrument of proofs (first begun in 1316) that in 1291 Robert Bruce V of Annandale and the other competitors for the throne of Scotland had recognised the superiority of Edward I.[70] It was clearly the intention of Edward II and his newly formed council to use such evidence to add yet more weight (via the legates) to the Papacy's support for English policing of their Scottish 'land' (and English provisions to Scottish benefices).

With Robert probably focused upon these developments, though perhaps still hopeful of peace talks, the delay of Scottish troops' passage to Ireland increased and Edward Bruce's patience ran out. It may have been the recall of Roger Mortimer from Dublin to England in May 1318 that prompted Edward Bruce to plan a foray south finally to aid the de Lacys in the recovery of Meath from their local rivals, the de Verdons.[71] However, with Scottish troops expected – and perhaps, given the lacunae in his extant charters, with Robert I himself, or Moray, en route to cross the Irish Sea – Edward's chevauchée may also have been designed to reconnoitre and reduce opposition in the direction of Dublin, which the Bruces were now resolved to attempt as a devastating sequel to Berwick and a tipping point towards peace; or to protect the flank of a delayed Scottish assault on the Isle of Man.[72]

Yet despite their long rest and improved sustenance (with the 1318 harvest a much healthier crop), and then a fair choice of familiar ground from which to attack above Dundalk (a town they had burned in 1316), Edward Bruce and his supporters were separated and wiped out in a close, bloody battle at Faughart on 14 October. With Robert's brother fell knights John Soules, John Stewart of Jedburgh and two of his kinsmen, and Sir Colin Campbell of Lochawe and Ardscotnish, as well as likely chiefs of the MacDonalds (perhaps Donald of Islay or 'Alexander Og') and MacRuaridhs (probably Alexander).[73] Some of the galloglass forces may have survived to fight on alongside their Ó Néill and Ó Conor allies: they included at least one more MacDonald lord, but he was apparently slain at Derry later in 1318 alongside Seoan, son and heir of Domnall Ó Néill.[74]

Edward Bruce's body was decapitated, eviscerated and divided in four. As an excommunicate he could have no Christian burial but he was also to be displayed like a rebel. His severed heart, hand and a quarter of his corpse were mounted on Dublin's walls while his head was delivered to Edward II during his parliament at York: the king would reward its bearer, the English commander John de Bermingham, with the earldom of Louth in Ireland (May 1319).[75] News of the English victory and the elimination of the Bruce threat in Ireland undoubtedly further smoothed proceedings in which the concerns of both King Edward and the earl of Lancaster were satisfied by compromise. Although the parliament was not asked to grant a full subsidy to support, at last, a much delayed expedition to Scotland, such finance was initiated in Wales and within the English Church. Not only were the English king and political community reunited in their enthusiasm to meet the Scots in the open field once more but, behind the scenes, Edward Bruce's demise was surely the catalyst for a simultaneous plot to kill and depose Robert, the only remaining Bruce brother.[76]

## Damage Control, October–December 1318

The defeat at Faughart, the loss of perhaps as many as 4,000 men, and the death of his last surviving brother and adult heir presumptive was a heavy triple blow to King Robert. Withdrawal from Ireland for the Scots as a standing force was now unavoidable if Berwick was to be defended. Robert must have called for a parliament at Scone on the instant of hearing of Edward Bruce's death, with the summons possibly ordered by the king while he was actually in Ireland, having arrived there too late.[77] Such an emergency assembly was necessary in the first instance to re-address a freshly exposed vulnerability which Robert, his subjects and enemies all now perceived might be exploited: the royal succession.

That Robert and his close counsel sensed a very real threat in that regard is immediately confirmed by the language of the likely pre-drafted act of succession which this meeting of 'the prelates, earls, barons and others of the community of his kingdom, by the common consent of all and singular of the aforesaid people' agreed to seal on 3 December 1318.[78] The 1315 act of succession had been passed in testing circumstances, but this new tailzie was nothing less than a demand of loyalty to Robert and his infant heir, his grandson Robert Stewart. Its presentation for statutory agreement, widespread sealing, dissemination through chancery copies and then public proclamation through sheriffs, burghs and churches was surely designed to guard against Scots wavering in the face of expected English challenges and continued papal censures:

> in person all and singular people, both clerics and laymen, will obey the aforesaid lord king and his heirs as their king and liege lord in every way, each according to his estate and condition . . . if anyone henceforth, which God forbid, shall be a violator of this ordinance, as a result he shall be considered as a traitor to the kingdom and guilty of the crime of lesé-majesty in perpetuity.

Those present in parliament were required to swear a 'great oath' to uphold this act and the Bruce–Stewart regime on the 'gospels and relics of the saints' of Scone Abbey, just as the act invoked that house's potent dedications to 'the sacred and indivisible Trinity, the Father, Son and Holy Ghost'.

In many ways, the death of Marjorie Bruce circa 1317 had eased some potential worries about the succession, with Robert Stewart isolated as the nearest living male heir after Edward Bruce without the difficulty of an intervening living female. But in late 1318, given Stewart's infancy, Robert I's own recurrent ill-health, and his failure as yet to father a son by Queen Elizabeth (although since 1315 at least one daughter, Margaret, may have been born at Dunfermline and other pregnancies failed), the loss of Edward Bruce now compelled some attempt to outline further contingencies.[79] Thus, the act continued, in the event of a royal minority, first (as by the 1315 act) Thomas Randolph would be Guardian, but failing him Sir James Douglas was also now named to follow in this office. Yet in the event of Robert Stewart's demise without another male heir of Robert I's bodily line, then the right of succession of a daughter or sister of Robert I must be upheld. This last proviso required a strained statement of principle that gives some hint of the degree to which the Bruce regime was now forced to improvise:

> ... since, on some occasions in the past, it had been called into doubt by some, though not with sufficient force, by what law the succession in the kingdom of Scotland, if perhaps it was not clear, should be decided and made lasting, in the same parliament it was determined by the clergy and people that following the custom in inferior fees and heritages then observed in the kingdom, whereas in the succession to the kingdom such a custom had not hitherto been introduced, the said succession should in no way be terminated for the future, but that the nearest male in direct line of descent at the time of the death of the king, or failing a male heir, the nearest female from the same line, or if that line fails completely, the nearest male from a collateral line, attention being paid to the right of consanguinity whereby the right of succession pertained to the said deceased king, ought to succeed the king whose succession is a matter for debate. And this is perfectly consistent with imperial law.

The guiding Roman laws of royal inheritance, as per the Bruce claim of 1291–92, were thus relatively clear, but the unpredictability of future deaths and births – with more male and female heirs likely to be born to Robert I's sisters as well as hopes for his own marriage bed – meant that no further order of cognate transmission for the succession by name(s) could otherwise be stated. No order of seniority was delineated through any Mar or

Campbell/Fraser or Ross nephews/cousins, say, until Robert I's first daughter by Queen Elizabeth, Margaret (who may have been born as late as 1322), could have issue of her own (and here Robert must have given thanks that his other sister, Isabel, had had no sons by Erik II of Norway before his death).[80] Similarly, Robert Stewart's enhanced status could not be recognised with, say, a grant of the Bruce earldom of Carrick (with hope yet for a son born to Robert Bruce); but Stewart may have been granted the adjacent lordship of Cunningham at this time (with tailzie to his father, Walter).[81]

Clearly there was scope for controversy, with the community asked to accept the growing prospect of succession by a minor of the Stewart or another baronial line. Moreover, the current dynastic variables and political context did not allow or tempt Robert and his regime to contemplate the prohibition of female succession that had been adopted in France in February 1317, just a month after the accession of Philip V, following the infant death of a posthumous son born to the widowed queen of Philip's elder brother, Louis X.[82] However, it should be acknowledged that in part the Scots' revised parliamentary tailzie and its retention of female rights may have bowed to pressure from, or sought to offer reassurance to, some key domestic parties, not least the major nobility who might now be assured of female succession of an 'inferior fee' (i.e. non-royal lands): this may have been designed to calm the fears of houses like Fife and Menteith and reflected a softening of Robert I's treatment of these lineages in 1314–15. Indeed, reassurance, as well as a further attempt to draw a firm political line, may have characterised much of the substantial statutory material passed by this Scone parliament, almost thirty enactments in all in Robert's name: 'for the repair of his land, protection of his people and for maintenance and affirmation of the peace of his land'.[83]

In truth, a number of these statutes represent the results of inquests, legal review and resumed codification initiated by earlier assemblies between about 1314 and 1317 for which proceedings are now lost. This fits within the context of the regime's use of definition and deployment of the law and courts as a means of asserting royal authority and territorial jurisdiction over Robert's subjects while managing the process of resettlement of land, resources and offices. However, the timing, profusion and language of the majority of the 1318 statutes suggest that even if these acts were Bruce initiatives, nonetheless petitions and protests by subjects had also contributed much to their formulation. Just as victory in battle created popular clamour for justice and reward, so defeat at Faughart may also have intensified some subjects' complaints (a reality to which Edward II could testify). The death of Edward Bruce, indeed, and the collapse of an expensive overseas campaign that had drained resources and distracted the king, his justiciar of Scotia (Randolph), and often the rest of his government from much of Scottish domestic affairs for over three years, surely encouraged petitions to the Crown about the progress of Robert's resettlement and the conduct of his officers, which the king and his counsel feared might now be linked to support for dynastic change. The recovery of Berwick and its hinterland unleashed a torrent of fresh inquests and disputes over landed holdings, offices, resources, revenues and church provisions now reclaimed from English control for the first time since 1296. As we have seen, between 1305 and 1307 such communities as the burgesses of Berwick and Perth, 'the men of Galloway', the 'king's husbandmen in Scotland' and a large number of southern Scottish monastic houses had certainly learned the value of petitioning royal authority to secure their rights and relief during Edwardian occupation, as had individuals of all estates – just as the Scottish bishops from 1309 to 1312 had forwarded complaints to the Papacy about lay interference.[84]

In 1318 some of these petitions and calls for redress understandably stemmed from the widespread socio-economic distress from which the realm was only just beginning to emerge. Thus the statutes enacted by the December parliament may all have responded to grievances likely to be shared by titled nobility, freeholders, burghs, cathedral churches and monastic estates: statutes to defend the Church and protect its granges from burdensome hospitality; to prevent the clergy and other travellers from exporting badly needed goods; to ensure the royal host paid for its prise victuals while its mustering (and foraging) members were prosecuted should they commit a crime; to manage fishing rights in tidal rivers; and to regulate the treatment of livestock in cases of debt.[85]

These and other statutes may also reflect wider concerns about rising levels of rural brigandage or aggressive seigneurial self-interest inevitably heightened by the hardship of the last few years, and thus an experience Scotland shared with most European realms in this decade.[86] Further appeals about tackling such symptomatic disorder may indeed have been brought to a receptive king and parliament in December 1318, hence:

> *It was ordained and assented by way of statute by the lord king* [my italics] that, if anyone in the past, from this hour on, of whatever status they shall be, shall have been convicted or attainted of homicide, rape, theft or other offences touching life and limbs, that common justice be done on this account without redemption, saving royal power and saving the liberties specially granted by the kings of Scotland ancestors of the lord king

who now is, and by him, to the church and ecclesiastical persons and to
other lords.[87]

Although the closing caveats of this act preserved the franchisal exemption
of regalities and baronies from the interference of royal officers, allied to
this was the telling and very specific ordination that 'no-one should disturb
a tracking dog or the men coming with it for pursuing thieves or seizing
malefactors, and also not trouble men without a tracking dog pursuing
thieves with their goods'.[88]

Moreover, several statutes detailing procedures for the courts' processing
of brieves of 'novel dissasine', 'right' and 'mortancestry' (actions for the
recovery of heritable property) surely spoke in part to rising levels of
disquiet in various localities about the abuse of the courts and legal processes by men and institutions determined to dispossess local rivals, debtors
and, above all, former enemies of the king; or to deny these elements in
turn as claimants. As a result these statutes stipulated that claimants must
henceforth detail in writing the dates, individuals and property brought
into question (to avoid blanket speculation?), and that defendants had a
right to answer only such specified charges but must now pay immediate
damages (in addition to a fine to the Crown) to any vindicated claimants
or injured third parties who had come into possession of lands or goods
following a claimant's dispossession.[89] Background tensions seem to be
confirmed by the simultaneous need to pass statutes insisting that common
justice be done 'as much to paupers as to wealthy people', prohibiting
Crown officers' support of claims on property in return for a share of gains
('champetry'), as well as a general ban on manipulative, 'malicious' instances
of 'essonzie' (being excused from attendance at a day of court).[90] These
provisions also hint at pressure from the middling and lesser sort of tenant
for access to more affordable common-law justice. Similarly, just as Crown
officers and their performance were open to criticism, so there were statutes designed to prevent claimants seizing goods for debt (poinding and
distraint) or accepting payment to ignore theft (redemption) where they
did not have the legal authority of a Crown officer, a clear suggestion that
some men had exploited the upheaval of war to pursue local agendas and
that not all of Robert's officers had been able to assert their jurisdiction.[91]

These statutory statements of due process, good practice and the rights
of plantiffs/defendants made sound legal sense. Their enforcement as royal
law would have been a valuable enhancement of Robert I's legitimacy and
regal authority (and, potentially, his revenue) as well as of community cohesion under one system of courts. As such, they also represent some of the

fruits of the aforementioned legal review and codification that would inform and culminate in the treatises known as *Regiam Majestatem* ('The Royal Majesty', four books of some sixty 'chapters' of civil and criminal law, including those of the December 1318 parliament) and the *Assise Regis David* ('Assizes of King David', about forty-four 'chapters', adapting laws from the twelfth- and thirteenth-century kings, extant in over a dozen manuscripts but to be found in its earliest form in a fourteenth-century text followed by the twenty-nine statutes of the December 1318 parliament). These collections would be completed sometime after this Scone assembly and certainly by the early to mid-1320s.[92] The *Assise* collation in particular reveals a conscious effort by the Bruce regime to legitimise Robert's rule through association with a king, David I (r.1124–53), increasingly regarded as a founding father of Scottish kingship, churches, government and law. This may have been allied to tentative efforts by Robert and his regime to develop a further cult of monarchy around David, one faintly echoed in the later references of Abbot Bower to this king as a saint.[93]

These law treatises, as with Robert's statutes, were also marked by the consistent invocation of the consent of the 'community of the realm'.[94] Such consensus is further reflected in the substantial body of evidence for increased chancery activity and formularies (templates) for royal brieves extant from about 1318–19 onwards.[95] However, the need to respond to subjects' petitions and complaints that intensified in 1318 may explain both this parliament's innovative expansion of the original remit of such brieves as that for dissaine, first established under Alexander II circa 1230, to now allow a case to be brought against one's own lord or near kin (changes then adopted in the *Assise Regis David*), as well as the apparently rushed appendage of entries of distinctly Scottish laws and practices to the closing sections of the earliest *Regiam Majestatem* source text.[96] Such changes also underline the value of this lawyerly and parliamentary process as Bruce propaganda in response to specific circumstances circa 1318, the work of a government which undoubtedly understood the utility in adapting English common law for a separate Scottish kingdom to ensure that, as the preamble to *Regiam Majestatem* asserts, 'the royal majesty should not only be adorned with strength against rebels and those rising against him and the realm, but also with laws to rule over his peaceful subjects and people'.[97]

That the legal guarantees of December 1318 were a direct response to the past thirty years and more of political upheaval and war is further confirmed by the statutory extension of the 'brieve of recognition' to reach back to the holdings of grandparents, as well as by two quite singular acts of universal remit.[98] The first was a general promise that no-one be ejected from his free holding in which he claims he is vest and seised as of fee without the king's pleadable brieve or such a kind of brieve as is similar, and unless the party is reasonably forewarned for a certain day and place concerning his free holding.[99]

The second was a blanket insistence that

because disagreements and grievances arose between certain magnates and nobles of the kingdom after the death of the lord Alexander [III] king of Scotland of good memory, the lord king, for the nourishing of good love between the nobles of the kingdom and for maintaining his firm peace between them and between his people mutually, has commanded and forbidden that henceforth any person cause damage, burden or harm to another, or to any of his men, or procure [it] to be done secretly or openly. But if anyone shall wish to complain concerning another person, he shall have his suit according to the laws of the land.[100]

This last act especially may reflect an attempt to quell current feuds in specific localities where the lordship of former enemies had been displaced, most obviously Buchan, Badenoch, Atholl, Angus, Fife, Galloway and the south-west (now faced with a Bruce power vacuum following the death of Edward as earl of Carrick), as well as the Lothians and the newly liberated south-east.[101] The liberation of Berwick, besides, must have unleashed quite specific accusations not only against burgesses who had worked with the English regime but also against a number of prominent Scottish knights who had served in Edward II's Berwick, Roxburgh and Selkirk garrisons before entering Robert's peace: Patrick, earl of Dunbar, Alexander Seton, David de Brechin, Philip Mowbray, Ingram d'Umfraville and others.

However, this last act also highlights the historic limitations of the common law and the jurisdictional reach and utility of royal brieves and officers in Scotland. Thus, as with the strictures of Birgham (1290), much of the 1318 reforms and legislation might also be said to uphold the status quo of the legal and socio-economic dominance and autonomy of ecclesi-astical and baronial liberties with their own courts. For while Crown tenants-in-chief could initiate actions by brieve to protect their own inter-ests (acting against their neighbours and rivals) or appeal to the Crown for a general 'pleadable brieve' to order a local inquiry into the truth of a legal claim raised, Crown officers remained otherwise unable to intrude upon the liberties of prelates, earls and barons with regality or barony status, jurisdictions that covered by far the majority of the realm. This was a fact acknowledged by the fifth 1318 statute's specific caveat 'saving the liberties specially granted by the kings of Scotland, ancestors of the lord king who now is, and by him, to the church and ecclesiastical persons and to other lords'. Moreover, while the 1318 legislation also extended the brieve of 'right' – as with that of dissasine – to allow sub-tenants to pursue a case against a lord other than the Crown, most less wealthy subjects could still not afford the potential financial cost to risk initiating such actions against their social superiors (although they could use royal brieves to pursue their equals).[102] Thus even though a large amount of land had certainly passed through the Crown's hands as a result of Robert's wars, culminating in the Cambuskenneth forfeitures of November 1314, some two-thirds of the realm, almost half of its parishes, would remain – once confirmed by the king – outside the royal demesne and its sheriffships (a stark contrast to England where the royal writ was excluded by only a handful of liberties).[103] Statutory enhancement of brieves and their procedures may thus have provided a timely and useful supplement to the Scottish courts, but the evidence seems to make it clear that the lion's share of legal disputes over lands and goods would continue to be resolved by privately negotiated compromise or subjects' franchise courts, local inquests and perambulations overseen by regional elites, with the resulting outcome simply reported back to the Crown. These customary structures and practices, which the Scots had acted in community to preserve since circa 1290 (Birgham), provided vital links between the royal household and court and the localities.[104]

In sum, these statutes speak not perhaps to a king 'at the height of his powers ... finally able to govern like a normal king, rather than simply a war leader engaged in a fight for survival'.[105] Nor do they suggest a regime simply imposing its authoritarian will, top-down. Rather these are the acts of a kingship and government that still faced real problems and opposition, as we might expect, striving hard to improve their powers, support and revenues, but also working with established structures and customary interests. The veneer of close Bruce control of assemblies in 1309, 1314 and 1315 had undeniably cracked or was no longer desirable for 'good government'. The recovery of Berwick and the Isle of Man must have further encouraged such a raft of legal renewals and innovations. But too many of these statutes suggest pressures of give and take; criticism of, and some hostility to, the lordship of Robert and his supporters who still wielded only patchy regional control. This is a distinct reminder that the political community – which had acted to fill the void of monarchy after 1286 – could not simply be dictated to and that meetings of the Scottish estates involved an increasingly challenging dynamic.

The need to reach all sensitive localities with an image of impartial government and justice was revealed in the opening assertion of the parliamentary record that all the acts of December 1318 should be

> read and proclaimed publicly at our courts to be held in your bailiaries and in other places where people often assemble, and to be observed inviolably by all as much in the courts of prelates, earls and barons and all others who hold courts as in our own courts; [and] we wish that these people should be given a copy of the statutes by you in order that they do not hold themselves to be excused by ignorance of the same.[106]

The few surviving charters from this parliament also arguably reflect an attempt to balance reform and reconciliation. On the third day of the assembly, 5 December 1318, Robert issued letters of remission to Bishop Henry Cheyne of Aberdeen, restoring him to his temporalities: this was surely designed to bring to an end tension between Crown and prelate over the treatment of the Atholl-Strathbogie inheritance and Edward Bruce's spurned bride, Isabel of Atholl, and their illegitimate son, Alexander Bruce, who as things now stood was excluded from succession to the Crown.[107] Indeed, it may have been in the months before or after the Scone parliament (rather than in late 1314) that Robert finally began to break up the Atholl patrimony, awarding the earldom itself to his young nephew, John Campbell (a potential heir presumptive), son of the late Neil of Lochawe and Mary Bruce (now married to Chamberlain Alexander Fraser), and the northern Strathbogie lordship to a former opponent, Sir Adam Gordon.[108] Similarly, acts survive demonstrating Robert's even-handed lordship to members of the other estates: on 5 December 1318 he inspected Alexander II's confirmation of a grant to Culross Abbey by the grandfather of Duncan, earl of Fife (an act witnessed by nobles including Duncan and Earl Malise of Strathearn and thus enabling the reconstruction of charters reportedly lost during the wars); a day later Robert confirmed the constabulary town of Haddington in all its burghal privileges.[109] It is likely that a number of Robert's now undated acts also belong to this assembly, including the issue of several brieves to aid individuals and institutions in the recovery of land.[110]

However, that the predominant atmosphere of this parliament remained a heightened sense of insecurity and potential division is underlined by the enactment of a statute whereby

> the lord king [Robert I] decreed and forbad that anyone should be a conspirator or an inventor of tales or rumours by which a source of discord

shall be able to arise between the lord king and his people. And if anyone such shall be found and attainted he should be immediately arrested and sent to the king's prison and be kept there securely until the lord king shall command his will concerning him.[111]

Such an act may have sought to dampen general criticism of the Bruce regime and its policies. But, inevitably, its timing suggests that Robert I and his close counsel were already aware of collusion against his rule by former Scottish opponents who had entered the Bruce peace circa 1312–15.

In this context, historians' suspicion has all too easily fallen immediately upon Sir William Soules of Liddesdale whose seal is really the only one belonging to a former lay enemy of the Bruce camp extant on the early-modern transcript of the December 1318 act of succession, seemingly alone amidst what was a tight-knit loyalist gathering.[112] Soules was the grandson of a minor competitor for the throne of 1291–92 and nephew of the Guardian of 1301–4, a Balliol adherent until about the time of Bannockburn who had re-entered Robert I's peace with his brother, John, who had been killed at Faughart.[113] Yet, as the ringleader of the eponymous plot to kill and depose Robert, which would be exposed and smashed in summer 1320, William Soules was not in fact suspected until very late on and would be in receipt of significant patronage and responsibilities from Bruce during the eighteen months following the reconciliation parliament of December 1318.[114]

However, among the witnesses to Bishop Cheyne's pardon recorded as issued during the Scone assembly had been three earls: Duncan of Fife and Malise of Strathearn again, but also, significantly, 'Mordaco ... de Meneteth' – Murdoch of Menteith. As we have seen, Robert I's regime was not above the appropriation of absent or coerced nobles' seals as a means of fabricating community consent in parliament. Yet in this instance, Murdoch's appearance with this title on the surviving copy of Cheyne's pardon most likely arises from the fact that the original December 1318 remission had, for some reason, to be reissued (or backdated), probably about August 1323 (during another parliament at Scone), the first known occasion on which Murdoch does appear as a charter witness with the Menteith title.[115] According to Sir Thomas Gray (and at least one other English near contemporary chronicler), Murdoch, brother of the late Alan, earl of Menteith (d.1309), had spent most of his life in England, but 'came to the Scottish court to reveal this [Soules'] plot, and became Earl of Menteith by quittance of his niece [Mary], the daughter of his elder brother'.[116] This suggests that Murdoch did not reappear in Scotland until the spring or summer of 1320, just as the 'Soules conspiracy' was exposed.

Nevertheless, Murdoch's seal as earl on the 1323 pardon reissue may have served as retrospective rehabilitation, engineered by Chancellor Bernard, just as did Bishop Cheyne's repeated pardon: but both men may have been present in December 1318. That said, Murdoch's seal on the pardon letters of 1323 may have replaced that on the original of his uncle and predecessor, Sir John Menteith of Arran and Knapdale, who would still be styled as 'guardian' of the earldom of Menteith on the barons' letter to the Pope of April 1320 (just as in 1323 the seal of Maurice, bishop of Dunblane, by 1322, may have replaced that of Nicholas Balmyle, bishop of that see in 1318).[117] It is thus possible that Murdoch was admitted to Robert's peace in December 1318 and rewarded, although neither his name nor his seal would appear on the barons' address to John XXII.[118] Moreover, Murdoch's eventual receipt of the Menteith title for life suggests again that Robert had indeed had cause to soften his earlier hard-line interference in the tailzies of that earldom and the interconnected earldom of Fife (which Alan of Menteith's kin – and the Stewarts generally – might claim).[119]

Murdoch may have been encouraged to return to Scotland by Robert I's recovery of Berwick and the Isle of Man (before word of Edward Bruce's destruction). If he did cast suspicion on any noble's loyalty to Bruce, it was perhaps, firstly, that of Sir Gilbert Malherbe, a Stirlingshire baron: he had been a patriot for Balliol before 1306 but loyal to Edwards I and II thereafter, laying claim in 1309–10 to the wardship of Menteith, the keeping of Jedburgh castle and – once he had submitted to Bruce circa 1314 – the wardship of the important regional lord, John Logie of Strathgartney, the substantial barony that bordered upon western Menteith, a man who would be convicted of complicity in the plot in 1320.[120] Significantly, Malherbe had been denied in regard to Logie/Strathgartney by Malise, seventh earl of Strathearn, whose mother, the Dowager Countess Agnes, would also be condemned for her role in the 1320 conspiracy. Therefore, as we shall see, Murdoch may have informed Robert about men such as Malherbe initiating contact with Edward Balliol and other disinherited lords, including Sir John Hastings, nephew of the earl of Pembroke and son of Sir Edmund, who had married the widowed Isabella, daughter of Walter Comyn, earl of Menteith (d.1258), been granted the Menteith earldom by Edward I, and then fallen at Bannockburn.[121] Alternatively, Murdoch may have cast doubt upon the motives of his own uncle Sir John Menteith of Arran and Knapdale, who had also been loyal to Edward I from 1300–6 (surrendering William Wallace in the process and lobbying for control of the earldom of Lennox) but had backed Robert I by circa 1308–9 in return for guardianship of the Menteith earldom.[122] About 1318–20, however, the veteran John (or his namesake son and heir) was at odds with the king and Malcolm, earl of Lennox, over the sheriffship and castle of Dumbarton, a stronghold now all the more strategically vital following the defeat at Faughart, the loss of Carrickfergus to John d'Athy and his ships by December 1318, and the likely emergence of Angus Og as an increasingly independent chief of the MacDonalds.[123] Sometime after October 1318 Sir John would also lose the royal household office of hereditary Butler to none other than Sir William Soules.[124]

Murdoch's possible defection and intrusion into Menteith circa December 1318, though, may not have been the only significant attempt by Robert to redress the balance of magnate loyalties in the wake of his brother's death. The seventeenth-century antiquarian transcript that is our source for the 1318 royal tailzie lists the seal of another long-term absentee amongst those attached: that of Donald, earl of Mar, Robert's nephew by his eldest sister. Donald had refused to return from England during the elite hostage exchange of 1315, remaining a 'valet' in Edward II's household (and perhaps taking a Balliol mistress who would give him a son, Thomas).[125] Again, Robert I was certainly not above making free use of Donald's seal (just as he seems to have done by attaching those of the bishops of Glasgow, Whithorn, Argyll and Sodor/the Isles to the 1318 tailzie).[126] Yet given Donald's strong claim as a royal heir presumptive to Robert I's line, it is possible there had been contact between the two men in 1318. On 20 July 1319 Donald would be granted a safe conduct to come to Scotland; this may not have been his first and he could have attended the Scone parliament in late 1318 in order to protect his interests in Mar adjacent to Garioch (gifted to Robert I's sister Christina in 1315) and the royal succession itself.[127]

At a time of dynastic weakness these tentative defections (with Donald perhaps returning to England) were undoubtedly welcome gains for Robert. Nevertheless, they spoke at once both to the strength and weakness of his position as king. His regime could use parliament and statute to offer assurances and test loyalty as it had at Scone, but it was Robert's patronage, and the actions of his officers and chief supporters, that would be the deciding factors in determining men's allegiance. Over the next eighteen months, Robert, still without a son of his own, would at times struggle to satisfy the seigneurial expectations of a number of nobles, their kindreds and allies. In fact he would often worsen relations through his intervention on behalf of and favour to others (just as had Edward I in trying to conquer Scotland). As a result, the potential conspiracy against his kingship may have grown to a dangerous extent.

These challenges of loyalty and the balance of lordship facing Robert were, moreover, intensified not only by his commitment to retain and revive

Berwick as a Scottish royal port and economic hub, but by the expectation that with Ireland safe Edward II would now be able to launch a substantial military counter-strike into Scotland. The closing statutes of the December 1318 parliament make it clear that this was understood, with detailed provision for the armour and weaponry obligation of all laymen with holdings worth £10 or more (who were to maintain a lance or sword), as well as lesser tenants worth only a cow or more (who were to maintain a lance or bow with twenty-four arrows), all to be readied for a sheriffs' '*wappinschaw*' inspection set for 15 April 1319 (after the octave, or eight days, of Easter). Significantly, that this act stipulated the king's sheriffs were to have power alongside the traditional rights of 'lords of places' (i.e. earls, barons, knights and prelates) to enforce the provision of common army service (imposing heavy fines of half a defaulter's lands and goods) surely reflects two issues: both the disruption of the wars and the inevitable overlap of seigneurial/Crown roles in the localities in an attempt to spread obligations and costs evenly across the realm (rather than purely a blunt Bruce attempt to increase royal authority).[128]

### Defending Berwick, December 1318–October 1319

By 25 November 1318 the orders of the English parliament at York in the previous month had been confirmed and over 23,000 men were called to muster at Newcastle by 19 June 1319 for a Scottish campaign.[129] However, although there is no incontrovertible proof extant that the English king had perhaps been persuaded about the same time to pursue another option, a covert plot against Robert Bruce, such a strategy is at least strongly suggested by his writ of 10 November 1318 – less than a month after the death of Edward Bruce. This ordered the substantial payment of £200 to Edward II's half-brother Thomas, earl of Norfolk, 'out of the money of the tenth in the diocese of Durham, in part payment of £500 that the king promised to give him for the stay of Edward Balliol in his company'.[130] This may have been in part to cover expenses actually incurred around 1311–13 (and for ongoing costs circa 1316–18) by Thomas, who was now expected to contribute his own person and retinue to the forthcoming Scottish campaign (before which he would be knighted).[131] Yet that this much delayed payment was finally released at this time is surely indicative of a significant change in the attitude of Edward II and his council towards Balliol, now about thirty-six years old, who seems to have otherwise drifted since 1315 between his father's debt-ridden estates in Picardy and Norfolk's own household. Besides, Edward II's payments for Balliol continued and increased, with a further 100 merks authorised against £600 by then owed on 17 November 1319; Balliol also seems to have turned up to serve in Norfolk's household in that year's campaign.[132] True, King Edward made no moves to restore Balliol to his father's English lands (despite requests to that effect from the son), not even a prospective grant of Galloway to motivate his potential Scottish supporters. Yet this in itself may have reflected a desire not to draw premature Scottish attention to the organisation of a Balliol fifth column aimed at Bruce.

Just like recent papal entanglements, the prospect of undermining Robert I by sponsorship of an attempt to foment fresh revolt within Scotland may have been highly attractive. The opportunity to advance such a conspiracy – building upon or repairing what beginnings Murdoch of Menteith may have betrayed to Robert I by December 1318 – may have come through a Scottish embassy possibly dispatched to England in early 1319 'pur les busoignes touchantes le dit sire Robert' ('for matters touching the said lord Robert'). Sometime in December 1318 letters were sent to Edward II seeking safe conduct to the king's presence for a substantial Scottish party listed as knights William Soules, Robert Keith, Roger Kirkpatrick, Alexander Seton and William Mowat, with four clerics and three valets.[133] The inclusion of Soules (and, as we shall see, Mowat) in this delegation, if it did travel, points to a moment in time to which his later Bruce accusers might date his complicity and greed for his own royal cause, thus trivialising him and denying what was the reality of a revived Balliol threat. But the connection and Soules's guilt may have been real. Although it is again only circumstantial evidence, on 27 November 1318 Edward II had ordered his escheator north of Trent not to interfere with the tenure of Stanfordham in Northumberland of the widow of one Thomas Soules, William's younger brother – was this a result of William Soules's recent covert indication of a willingness to work in Scotland on Balliol's behalf?[134]

While some initiative may thus have come from Soules, Edward II may have been further encouraged in this strategy as his planned campaign was hindered by bubbling tensions between his council and the earl of Lancaster. Although England's chancery, exchequer and royal household were moved north from Westminster to York, on 22 May 1319 the muster was pushed back to 22 July and in the end suffered further delay. Yet Edward's finances were relatively healthy with about £60,000 raised by subsidy, scutage (payment in lieu of service) and loans.[135] Some funds might thus easily have been directed into facilitating further contact between disinherited Scots in English exile (pensioners Strathbogie of Atholl, Umfraville of Angus, Alan Macdougall of Argyll, Duncan of Frendraught, Dougal Macdowell and Gilbert of Glencarnie, a kinsman of the earls of Strathearn)[136] and English lords with Scottish inheritance claims (Percy, Hastings, Talbot, Beaumont, Ferrers, Wake and Zouche) on the one hand with their potential allies in Scotland on the other.[137]

As well as the aforementioned safe conduct issued to Donald, earl of Mar (20 July 1319), there is some evidence of payments to Sir David de Brechin (in both 1318 and 1319), seemingly travelling back and forth to Scotland: this was contact maintained after his brief return to Edward II's peace through Andrew de Harcla, sheriff of Carlisle, on 7 August 1317.[138] Brechin's mother was a Comyn and he had been a firm Balliol patriot after Dunbar (1296) before serving Edward II against Bruce as a warden of Berwick (1308–12) and in garrisons at Dundee and Ayr (1306, 1312), fighting alongside men like Ingram d'Umfraville and William Soules (and claiming the English lands of his father-in-law Alexander Stewart of Bonkle): captured at Bannockburn, Brechin had received no favour from Robert I despite his status as a prominent Angus baron and a great-grandson of Earl David of Huntingdon. As a crusader of some renown, however, his travel and a facility to talk to both sides may have been toler-ated.[139] In sum, he was just the kind of disappointed, ambitious knight whom any conspirators might ask to join or act for them.

A similar story might be told of Sir William Somerville of Linton (near Kelso) who would be granted a safe conduct from Edward II to visit Scotland to negotiate the release of his daughter on 24 October 1319. Somerville's father, Thomas, had held Roxburgh castle for the English in 1313 along with William Soules and Stewart of Bonkle. But Somerville had only been able to watch from exile as Robert I granted his family's wealthy baronies of Bathgate and Ratho in West Lothian to Sir Walter Steward and his wife, Marjorie Bruce, in 1315 (while Linton presumably was laid waste).[140] Somerville's hopes of recovering his inheritance under a vassal Balliol king are all too understandable.

To this might be added the growing hopes or doubts and secret written appeals to England of a number of other former Balliol Scots. As late as 17 November 1320, Edward II would write to David Strathbogie, the exiled earl of Atholl, that '[the king] understands that some of the Scots who are against the king [Edward II] in war desire to come to his peace, because their conscience is hurt by the sentence of excommunication in which they are involved by papal authority and other causes'. He empowered the earl to receive such men but, tellingly, even then, 'to treat with them as secretly as possible concerning the conditions required . . . he is to come to the king in person so that the king, being fully certified thereof, may do his will in this matter'.[141] The Papacy's excommunication of Bruce and the interdict upon

Scotland also allowed Edward II's government to propose English clerics to almost eighty benefices throughout the dioceses of St Andrews and Glasgow on 19–20 July 1319. Although these men can only have expected to take up their posts once the autumn campaign had succeeded, several of the parishes named fell directly within the interests of the disinherited or of men who had recently submitted to Robert, for example Dunbar, Soules's Westerkirk or Somerville's Liston and Bathgate/Ratho.[142] Finally, that Balliol himself perhaps expected to take up his father's throne is again suggested by the *Vita Edwardi Secundi*'s assertion that in advance of his campaign Edward II 'sent envoys to Scotland to claim the kingdom, offer peace and allow safety in life and limb to Robert Bruce'. If this meant that Edward was now prepared to accept Robert if he would do homage for Scotland, then in truth the English king can only have expected one answer – rejection. But this might also mean he was planning to install another as vassal following a successful, reinvigorating campaign – Balliol.[143]

The movement of ambivalent men between the two realms may have been eased throughout the first half of 1319 by what seems to have been a period of unofficial truce. Robert probably spent Christmas 1318 at Arbroath or Berwick. According to fragmentary English reports it was from the latter that the king sent or led a chevauchée to attack the earl of Lancaster's building project of Dunstanburgh castle in Northumberland, about 8 January 1319. In the meantime, the earl of Moray (and perhaps also Douglas) had led out forces to extract tribute from several regions. About 25 January, Moray, as 'warden of Annandale, Eskdale and Nithsdale' (although Robert would reward Douglas with control of the second of these lordships), had appeared at Lochmaben to conclude a truce for 600 merks with the men of Cumberland and Westmorland.[144] If regional ceasefires were agreed, these perhaps extended to Michaelmas, allowing the Scots to prepare defences for the approach of Edward II's host.

The same badly damaged English administrative reports also assert that circa 20 January the Scots had held 'their parliament' – more probably a smaller council – at which Moray was appointed as 'warden' or 'lieutenant' south of the Forth with custodian roles for William Soules (Hermitage castle in Liddesdale?), Philip Mowbray (perhaps at Selkirk or in Tynedale?), Douglas (Berwick castle) and Alexander Seton (Berwick town walls?).[145] If so this assembly also took place at Berwick from where Robert I issued a charter on 29 January; his previous extant charter had been a grant of Polmoody in Dumfriesshire to Berwick's incoming castle-keeper, 'James, lord of Douglas', in return for twelve arrows annually, a firm sign that Douglas had taken on leadership of the men of the March forests after the death at Faughart of John Stewart of Jedburgh.[146] It is possible that Moray's appointment reflected an intention for the king, still without a son, to take a safely remote position – at Edinburgh or Stirling – once the English host had advanced.

Throughout the spring of 1319, however, Robert remained in the southeast, undoubtedly attending to Berwick's defence by land and sea. About 8 February he granted Coupar-Angus Abbey lands in Perthshire to pay for lights for vespers, matins and conventual masses as well as a perpetual lamp at the altar of St Malachy of Armagh, perhaps as part of obsequies for Edward Bruce. Interestingly, that the witnesses to this grant included knights David de Brechin and William Oliphant (junior) – both former Balliol-Comyn/Edward II men – speaks either to the Bruce regime's lack of information, or fear, about the extent of the potential plot (or, far less believable, a very bold strategy of keeping enemies close), just as had border castle appointments for Soules and Mowbray in January.[147] Then 25–26 March found Robert at Berwick once more in company with William Lamberton, bishop of St Andrews, Duncan, earl of Fife, Thomas Randolph, 'earl of Moray and lord of Annandale and Man', Walter Steward, James Douglas, John Menteith, Robert Keith and Alexander Seton. On that occasion, the anniversary of his enthronement (and a feast of the Virgin), Robert gave a firm indication that it was the man who had defected at the crucial moment in 1314 – Seton – whom the Crown would now look to as its leading agent in the Lothians and south-east: Sir Alexander was confirmed in Barns (East Lothian) and the east mill of Haddington 'for his service in Ireland and Scotland'. A number of Robert's now lost, undated acts (noted in early modern indices) may also belong to this meeting, including grants to Seton of Tranent near Haddington (formerly held by William de Ferrers and Alan le Zouche) and Elphinstone, Gogar and Dundas near Edinburgh.[148]

Robert probably remained at Berwick through Easter (8 April) into early May. On the first day of that month he rewarded Peter de Spalding, the Englishman who had betrayed Berwick to the Scots in 1318, with forest lands in Angus for part of the service of a knight. However, that these lands were exchanged for all Spalding's tenements in Berwick perhaps indicates a shrewd decision on the king's part to remove an unpredictable element from the burgh walls, a timely contrast with Robert's reported execution by circa March 1316 of Gascon castle-betrayer, Piers Libaud: he had surrendered Edinburgh in 1313 but, according to Sir Thomas Gray, '[Bruce] doubted him because he was too open; he believed that he had always been English at heart, and was waiting for his best chance to harm him.'[149] By 24 May 1319 Robert had also turned to inspect his west March

defences, stopping at his family seat of Lochmaben to grant knights
Thomas and Simon Kirkpatrick (the sons of one of his companions in the
Greyfriars in 1306) forfeited lands in Dumfriesshire for the service of at
least two archers.[150]

By the time Edward II's host entered Scotland on 7 September 1319 it
is clear that not only had the king of Scots done more than enough to
prepare and motivate his men but he had already decided upon his strategy
of response. The English army was perhaps some 10,000 strong, well below
the muster expected but still powerful with the retinues of the royal household, six earls (including Pembroke, Hereford, Surrey and Lancaster) and
many experienced barons. The decision to attempt Berwick seems logical
and symbolic, but in fact may only have been agreed late on, as a means to
establish an English base before an advance towards Edinburgh: the
English elite seem to have been relaxed enough initially to hold jousts
before Berwick's walls.[151] Nevertheless, Edward's early assault on the town
on 7–8 September, before his siege engines arrived, was beaten off by a
stout Scottish defence led by several captains including Alexander Seton,
Earl Patrick of Dunbar, Robert Keith, Adam Gordon and Walter Steward
(although Barbour would focus upon the heroism of the latter as *his* king's
father). Vital naval and engineering support also seems to have been
provided by the Scots' Flemish mercenary ally, John Crabbe (who in 1333
would take pay from Edward III and help recover Berwick to the English):
this foiled an attack by Edward II's substantial fleet of ships.[152]

In the meantime, however, Robert – avoiding an encounter between
hosts in the field – had sent Moray and Douglas across the border with a
large, mounted force (while the king himself perhaps remained at
Lochmaben or in the forest). According to a number of English chronicles
the Scots' intention was to approach York by stealth – perhaps led by a
defector, Sir Edmund Darel – and to seize Queen Isabella and Edward's
royal government so as to hold them for ransom to secure peace on Bruce's
terms.[153] If true (and the queen seems to have been spirited out of York to
Nottingham castle), this may have been Robert's own underhand response
to the rumoured Balliol conspiracy in his realm and an attempt to repeat
the elite prisoner (and last-minute) success of 1314. However, the Lanercost
scribe does, rather, narrate a classic Moray-Douglas raid in which their
men 'invaded England with an army, burning the country and taking
captives and booty of cattle, and so pressed as far as Boroughbridge'.[154]

The approach of such a large force was certainly discovered and a
Yorkshire militia led by Archbishop Melton and Bishop Hothum of Ely
confronted the Scots on 12 September. News of the slaughter of the

English that ensued – the infamous 'chapter of Myton' where scores of clergy fell or were captured, including notary Andrew de Tange – reached Edward II's army two days later.[155] It had a critical effect upon the second assault on Berwick's walls that had begun a day earlier. Both contemporary English chronicles and later Barbour describe the outbreak of disagreements between Edward and Lancaster or the southern and northern lords present.[156] A contingent of over 1,000 men (hobelars and archers) had already been diverted back towards Carlisle under Sir Andrew Harcla (the hero of the siege of 1315) to trap the Scots' returning force.[157] But a proposal to split the English host further and continue the siege proved fatal. This saved a nearly exhausted Berwick defence that had destroyed one custom-built English engine, 'the sow', but might not have withstood another without a breach of the burgh's walls. By 16–17 September the English army began to break up and straggle home. Edward II was again humiliated and politically compromised. The Scots raiders, the *Vita Edwardi Secundi* alleged, were able to regain their realm in safety by passing through the lines of their confederate, the earl of Lancaster, whom Bruce is said to have paid £40,000. There was thus paranoia and suspicion aplenty on both sides of the conflict.[158]

# CHAPTER EIGHT

# Dark Passage

## In Search of Respite, 1319–22

*No one will question the art, the vigour and the skill with which the king has employed the force of arms in time of war in withstanding the malicious conspiracy of his enemies.*

*Regiam Majestatem*, c.1318[1]

### The 'Declarations' of Arbroath, October 1319–April 1320

Archdeacon Barbour, inheriting sources commissioned by Robert I and his court, would dedicate an entire book of his vernacular verse to the defence of Berwick and the rout at Myton. The repulse of Edward II's host, beginning on the nativity of the Virgin (8 September) and resumed about the feast of the exaltation of the True Cross (14 September), could indeed be presented as a reaffirmation of God's faith in Robert's cause; so, too, could the destruction of the Archbishop of York's militia, presumably bearing banners and relics of northern saints such as John of Beverley. If necessary, these achievements also allowed Robert and his captains to distance themselves from the defeat at Faughart a year past. Barbour, certainly, would feel free to reorder events completely so as to place an impatient Edward Bruce's final campaign *after* the Berwick and Myton deeds and thus condemn his sortie before Robert's promised reinforcements could arrive.[2]

As in 1314 and 1318, Robert followed up his triumph with raids into northern England. According to Lanercost's scribe at All Saints' (1 November), the earl of Moray and Douglas reappeared

when the crop had been stored in barns, and burnt the whole of Gilsland, both the corn upon which the people depended for sustenance during that year and the houses wherein they had been able to take refuge; also, they carried off with them both men and cattle ... and then returned through Westmorland ... [and] fared through part of Cumberland, which they burnt on their march, and returned to Scotland with a very large spoil of men and cattle.[3]

Even before this blow, Edward II had recognised his inability to defend the north and agreed, on 24 October 1319, to a meeting of envoys at Newcastle.[4] Once full talks were underway, Robert seems to have held a council at Berwick that probably kept in close contact with his representatives: knights William Soules, Robert Keith, Roger Kirkpatrick, Alexander Seton and William Mowat, plus clerics James Ben (then a canon of Moray in Bishop David's retinue) and Walter de Twynham, canon of Glasgow.[5] Significantly, as with the English delegation – headed by the earl of Pembroke, the bishop of Ely and Hugh Despenser the Younger (Edward II's Chancellor) – these envoys were empowered to discuss terms for a full peace if the opportunity arose.[6] In the weeks before these talks, Robert's acts had included letters patent to Constable Sir Gilbert Hay (8 November, while at Dunblane) and letters of confirmation, following Moray's justiciar court inquest earlier in 1319, of justice teinds held by Scone Abbey (22 November, while at Scone itself).[7] Robert's acts issued at Berwick confirmed privileges and market rights of Aberdeen burgh and locate a tight core of loyal prelates and knights in attendance: the bishops of St Andrews and Dunkeld, Chancellor Bernard, Moray, Patrick of Dunbar, Steward, Douglas, Keith, Hay, Sir David Lindsay of the Byres and Sir David Barclay.[8] Sir Alexander Fraser, the king's brother-in-law, also makes his first (extant) appearance as royal Chamberlain. In addition, the king confirmed Sir John Graham's grant of Dumfriesshire lands (Westerker) to William Soules, part of the late John Soules's legacy and a further apparent sign of royal trust in (or a need to placate) Sir William.[9]

However, although the truce concluded by 21 December and confirmed by Robert's letters the next day was to endure for two years beginning on Becket's feast day, 29 December (the day after the two-year papal truce was set to expire), the terms of the ceasefire styled him still only as 'sire Robert de Brus' of 'la terre Descoce'.[10] The conditions were otherwise favourable with mutual guarantees that neither side would build new castles in their March counties (and that Robert would hand back Harbottle castle within eight days for the English to dismantle);[11] that 'subjects, allies and supporters of the English king should not hold communication with Sir Robert or his allies during the truce, without special leave from the English king or his guardian(s) of the truce' (Pembroke, with Moray appointed to this role for the Scots); and even that Berwick would be restored to its fishing rights on the Tweed.[12] It is likely that Robert and his council accepted these terms, while still pressing for further talks about a full peace and political recognition, because of a number of critical emerging circumstances.[13]

From a domestic perspective, Robert may have welcomed an opportunity to focus more closely upon his resettlement of lands, offices and resources both to reward his supporters further and to defuse tensions that had been apparent at the time of the December 1318 parliament. He may also have desired time to face down, isolate or win over former opponents in his peace who might have been tempted to consider conspiracy or open rebellion since the defeat at Faughart. The successful defence of Berwick strengthened the king's mandate to undertake all of this. But perhaps more fundamentally, the Scots – like the English – could not have been anything but war-weary. A significant number of lords had undeniably made a name and extended lordship for themselves and their retinues by the professionalisation of border warfare since circa 1311, not least James Douglas. Yet the natural desires of a generation of barons, clergy, husbandmen, burgesses, craftsmen and their tenants to return to some level of normality must have been an impetus that overwhelmed the threat of a minority of political enemies.

True, the harvests of 1318 and 1319 had seen vastly improved conditions and yields as well as lower prices. However, just as the English failure to recover Berwick underlined Robert's success in restoring Scotland to its original territorial, and potentially its economic, extent, another calamity occurred to remind the peoples of both realms of their vulnerability. A lethal viral disease among cattle – identified by modern historians as probably rinderpest – had now reached the British Isles as it spread west throughout northern Europe. With a mortality rate of on average over 50 per cent of bulls and oxen and 80 per cent of cows amongst infected herds, this outbreak – which would linger in England and Wales until about 1321–22 and scourge Ireland for a number of years more – must have had a devastating effect upon already beleaguered agricultural communities and elite lay and monastic estates and households as well as upon burgh markets and industry, probably all the more so in Scotland where there was a greater reliance on pastoral agriculture.[14]

According to one contemporary English source (the same John, vicar of Tynemouth, who wrote of Murdoch of Menteith's defection to the Scots), 'an unheard of pestilence of animals quickly killed all the oxen led to the siege' of Berwick in August–September 1319, transmitting the epidemic to the north.[15] And, of course, the Scots' raids of late 1319 brought scores of diseased beasts back to their realm. Fordun's contemporary annalist would assert that the worst of this panzootic would be felt in Scotland in 1321, by which time 'nearly all the animals were extinguished'. Yet it is likely its effects were quickly apparent in 1319–20 and intensified as the weather deteriorated with heavier rainfall once more into summer and autumn, which again stunted and rotted both grain crops and animal meadow.[16] The resulting loss of draft power would have drained men (a ratio of about 10 men per ox) and horses away from war and other pursuits to ploughing and everyday carriage of goods to market or households.[17] This would not have prevented a serious reduction of cultivation, manure, meat protein and – above all – dairy nutrition. There would also have been a parallel rise in the price (and thefts) of sheep and horse stock, grain, dairy produce, fish and butchered meat (venison, mutton/lamb, rabbit and fowl) while cattle prices became polarised with the cost of healthy beasts soaring.[18] In sum, this bovine plague must quite swiftly have represented a major socio-economic crisis, causing the food shortages, price fluctuations, local unrest and mortality (about 10–15 per cent) of 1315–17 to flare up again, and which no king or lord could ignore. All this may have had considerable bearing on the decision of both sides to agree to a two-year truce instead of six or nine months (although the restocking of herds often took over a decade to yield results).

Nevertheless, just as political problems also undoubtedly drove Edward II's envoys to seek a longer ceasefire, so for Robert and his govern-ment economic concerns may have been secondary for the moment to the ongoing diplomatic pressures applied by England through the Papacy.[19] With the collapse of his military expedition and accord with the earl of Lancaster, Edward II resumed his spiritual attack. His overtures to John XXII secured fresh papal threats of excommunication of Bruce for breach of the 1318 papal truce, issued on 17 November 1319. A day later bulls were dispatched summoning Robert and three of his bishops (William Lamberton of St Andrews, William Sinclair of Dunkeld and David de Moravia of Moray, with a fourth, Henry Cheyne of Aberdeen, later added) to appear at Avignon by 1 May 1320 on matters 'touching the realm of Scotland': namely that 'the said Robert [Bruce] who has otherwise treated the pope's mission with contempt [insulting legates and refusing to accept curial letters] . . . [has] resisted for more than a year ecclesiastical sentences against him'. More worryingly, this was followed by 6 January 1320 by bulls not only renewing Robert's earlier excommunication for the 'killing of John and Robert Comyn, knights', but instructing Cardinals and English prelates now to 'absolve all subjects of the said Robert from their allegiance to him'.[20] That the latter was designed to enable and encourage Scots to defect to English allegiance, paving the way to the alternative of Edward Balliol as a vassal king, is suggested by the Bruce regime's calculated and carefully considered response.

Probably aware of his personal summons to the curia by late January–early February 1320 at the latest, Robert summoned a 'full council', a body that must have had the authority of a parliament, to the Cistercian abbey of Newbattle in Lothian for the middle of March, with its business divided around Easter Week (30 March).[21] Five acts survive from this assembly. The first (14 March) saw cleric John Lindsay resign to the king his family barony of Staplegordon, which lay in the east March of Dumfriesshire between Bruce/Randolph's Annandale and Soules's Liddesdale (following the death sometime in 1317–20 of John's elder brother, the former Edwardian adherent Sir Philip Lindsay).[22] This resignation surely indicated the king's full confidence in John as bishop-elect of Glasgow, acting in that capacity despite obstacles at Avignon. Moreover, this act and royal intentions for this diocese were allied to plans to build up Sir James Douglas as a Crown agent in the south-west and the west and middle Marches.[23] On 1 April, by which time the king had ridden the 50 miles back to Berwick with his household, Robert granted a sweeping charter of Douglas's family holdings, perhaps given in preparation of their elevation as a full regality for James.[24] The latter had been a witness to Lindsay's resignation along with Bishop Lamberton, Moray, Steward, John Menteith and Soules; the bishop, Earl Duncan of Fife and Andrew Murray of Avoch were among the witnesses to Douglas's grant.

In addition, on 31 March, either while still in council at Newbattle or from Berwick while an exchequer audit continued at the abbey, Robert had also overseen an emphatic assertion of Scottish royal jurisdiction through a charter of the monopolies, market days, bounds, mills, fishings and tolls of the burgesses of Berwick, given in return for an annual sum (in feu-ferme) to the exchequer of 500 merks.[25] This may have replaced a charter of burgh rights given by Edward I, allegedly 'carried off by Robert de Brus in his hand' during a raid.[26] This was accompanied by the Crown's offer of burgage plots and building funds to encourage fresh settlement in Berwick and an agreement with royal authorisation to levy a contribution from the estates to pay for the repair of Berwick's 10-foot walls.[27] This may thus have been the first instance of an extraordinary tax in the Scottish realm justified by 'necessity' and the common good for defence of the realm.[28] However, the witnesses to the Berwick charter had included the very four bishops now summoned to Avignon (St Andrews, Dunkeld, Moray and Aberdeen), alongside Chancellor Bernard, the earls of Moray, Fife and Dunbar, Steward, Douglas, Hay, Fraser and Keith. Their presence surely confirms that the main business of this gathering was for representatives of each estate to begin the process of attaching seals to another round of letters addressed to the Pope, one each in the name of the clergy and the barons, both to be accompanied by a third from the king.

Only a draft chancery copy of the barons' missive has survived relatively intact – celebrated since the early nineteenth century as the 'Declaration of Arbroath'.[29] But this group of three letters thus falls within the established European tradition of such appeals to the curia from royalty and their subjects (exemplified by the letters of Edward I and his barons in 1301) and within a succession of such Scottish documents, the most recent now lost letters in the name of Robert and his subjects in parliament sent to Pope John about September 1317.[30] In fact, since the first formal declaration of Robert's (second) excommunication (July 1318) and the papal truce (September 1318), the king's government may already have sent a number of written protests while maintaining a permanent diplomatic presence at Avignon. In January 1319 an English report from the border noted the Scottish bishops' discussion of an 'appeal' in parliament; in the same month Edward II wrote to John XXII to ask him to detain a Scottish clerical embassy (whose papers he had intercepted), and the Pope seems to have obliged by March that year.[31] This drew on objections of the *Ecclesia Scoticana* to English meddling in the election to the see of Glasgow, to which the vacancy in Dunblane see was added by January 1320, following the death of Nicholas de Balmyle and Edward II's nomination of an English candidate.[32] It was thus all of these issues of papal intervention that Robert and his advisors sought to address in early 1320, as well as what they perceived as an allied political threat.

Robert I's own cover letter (its contents broadly known from a papal summary and John XXII's replies to the king and Scottish barons of 16 and 28 August 1320 respectively) repeated his complaints of circa 1317–19 about failure to use his royal title and the obstruction of Lindsay's elevation to the Glasgow see, as well as declaring his support in general of the Church and clergy in Scotland and asking for relaxation of excommunication censures.[33] In this letter, though, Robert was also probably at pains to echo the statements of his clerics and barons that it was the greed and arrogant aggression of the English that prevented a peace and Christian crusade; he even seems to have insisted to Pope John 'that a certain day has been appointed for the making of final peace between him and the said king of

England'.[34] It has been suggested that Robert may have sent a letter to Edward II about this time (April–May 1320) offering full peace talks.[35] Along with any communications at this time with Philip V (who had held a series of gatherings throughout the winter of 1319–20 to rouse interest in his crusade), such a letter to Edward would also probably have been included in the diplomatic bag to Avignon. It might thus have contributed to an agreement about Anglo-Scottish talks in July–August 1320.[36]

The Scottish clergy's letter to John XXII must have reiterated a number of these points as well as pledged their general support for Robert as king (much as per the clerical declarations of 1309–10). However, given the length of time the Scottish prelates had had to consider their words – and the parallel authorship of the barons' letter by a cleric in Abbot Bernard's chancery or Bishop Lamberton's employ, probably Alexander de Kinninmonth, confirmed as parson of Kinkell church in the Garioch by September 1320 – it is surely the case that they drew on and condensed the best of their archive of governmental, ecclesiastical and chronicle material forged in opposition to England since 1291. This surely allowed them to draft something just as dynamic and eloquent, and armed with biblical and curial precedents, as the letter that survives in the name of the baronial estate.[37]

That now famous barons' document followed at its core the 'Remonstrance of the Irish Princes' but was far more concise and compelling. Its preamble address lists some eight earls and thirty-one barons (probably those present at Newbattle), and refers to the sweeping consent of 'the other barons and freeholders and the whole community of the realm of Scotland'. When compared, say, to the thirty-seven names of nobles of the Scottish realm listed by Henry III in his letters of intervention in Alexander III's minority in 1255, the marked degree to which the wars and Robert I's patronage had altered regional family power and central political participation is plain.[38]

1255: Malcolm earl of Fife, Patrick earl of Dunbar, Nigel earl of Carrick, Malise earl of Strathearn, Walter Comyn earl of Menteith, Alexander Comyn earl of Buchan, William earl of Mar, Alexander Steward, John Comyn [of Badenoch], Robert Bruce [of Annandale], Alan Durward, John Balliol, Walter Murray, David Lindsay, William of Brechin, Hugh Giffard, Roger Mowbray, Gilbert Hay, Robert Menzies, William Douglas, Robert de Ros, Aymer Maxwell, Nicholas Soules, Thomas de Normanville [official of Tynedale],[39] Alexander Uivet, John de Dundemor, David Graham, John Blount, Thomas [Fitz]Randolph, Hugh Gourlie, David Lochore, John Wishart, William of Cadzow.

1320: Duncan earl of Fife, Thomas Randolph earl of Moray/lord of Man and Annandale, Patrick Dunbar earl of March, Malise earl of Strathearn, Malcolm earl of Lennox, William earl of Ross, Magnus earl of Caithness and Orkney, William earl of Sutherland, Walter Steward, William Soules, James lord of Douglas, Roger Mowbray, David lord of Brechin, David Graham, Ingram d'Umfraville, John Menteith guardian of the earldom of Menteith, Alexander Fraser, Gilbert Hay Constable, Robert Keith Marischal, Henry Sinclair, John Graham, David Lindsay, William Oliphant, Patrick Graham, John Fenton, William Abernethy, David Wemyss, William Muschet, Alan Murray, Donald Campbell, John Cameron, Reginald Cheyne, Alexander Seton, Andrew Seton, Andrew Leslie, Alexander Straiton [plus the following names on seal tags: Alexander Lamberton, Edward Keith, John Inchmartin, Thomas Menzies, John Durant, Thomas Morham].

The 1320 letter then traces the Scots' origins out of 'Greater Scythia' and their 'one hundred and thirteen kings of their own royal stock, the line unbroken by a single foreigner'. This was surely the key point of the declaration: to guard against the immediate threat of Edward II trying once more to reassert English (foreign) rule, or to impose the unnamed Edward Balliol as a vassal king. It was thus in Balliol's direction as a potential usurper backed by England that what has been cast as the letter's famous warning of 'contractual-kingship' was in fact aimed:

> Yet if he should give up what he has begun, and agree to make us or our kingdom subject to the King of England or the English, we should exert ourselves at once to drive him out as our enemy and a subverter of his rights and ours, and make some other man who was well able to defend us our king; for as long as but a hundred of us remain alive, never will we on any conditions be brought under English rule. It is in truth not for glory, nor riches, nor honours that we are fighting, but for freedom – for that alone, which no honest man gives up but with life itself.[40]

As a scholarly exercise this passage in curial Latin echoed historic 'charters of liberties' such as Magna Carta (1215) by glossing the Roman historian Sallust's *De Catilinae coniuratione* ('The Catiline Conspiracy'; an attempt to overthrow the Roman Republic in 63 BC).[41] This was in addition to the repeated – if now condensed – deployment, from Baldred Bisset's materials of 1301, of Innocent IV's charges against Emperor Frederick II in 1245, presented as the crimes of Edward I: perjury of oath, sacrilegious sacking of churches, slaughter of clerics and contempt for papal jurisdiction, censures and officials (although this may have read at the time, as it does in hindsight, as more telling of the record of the excommunicate Robert Bruce since 1306).[42] The letter also arguably reflects a similar attitude of expectation and allegiance by subjects towards the office, rather than the person, of the king: as expressed in Edward II's coronation oath of 1308, a legacy of 1215 and 1258–67 in England, echoed in 1290 (Birgham), 1295 (Balliol's council of twelve) and 1301 for the Scots. However, overall, not only did this seek to justify Robert's usurpation of the throne (denying the unnamed John Balliol) but it warned against those Scots who might support Edward II or Edward Balliol, placing them on the wrong side of a kingship and community now well able to express its collective identity and sovereignty as a struggle for political independence and natural justice, calling for the Papacy's general pastoral intervention as 'Christ's vicar' on earth. After fourteen years of its own war the Bruce regime was also able to transcend the patriotic effort of 1296–1304.

Similar language may have been borrowed from Irish protests to appeal for the safeguard from foreign occupation of the Glasgow see – the original 'special daughter' of the Papacy.[43] The barons' letter further reflected this familiar rhetoric. Like the 'people of Israel', brought to the faith by Christ's first Apostle, Andrew 'the Blessed Peter's brother', the Scots remained under papal protection until, 'when our kingdom had no head', Edward I 'came in the guise of a friend and ally to harass them as an enemy'. It took 'our tireless Prince, King and Lord, the Lord Robert' to deliver the Scots from these 'countless evils'. Then, perhaps in an attempt to empathise with the hardship of the decade, Robert is described as having 'met toil and fatigue, hunger and peril, like another Maccabaeus or Joshua' (worthies to whom Edward I was often compared). However, this section closes with a shrewdly ambivalent justification of Robert's right to the throne:

> Him, too, divine providence, his right of succession according to our laws and customs which we shall maintain to the death, and the due consent and assent of us all have made our Prince and King. To him, as to the man by whom salvation has been wrought unto our people, we are bound both by law and by his merits that our freedom may be still maintained, and by him, come what may, we mean to stand.

Given the Papacy's dissolution of Scottish subjects' allegiance to Bruce in 1318–19, this statement was a direct rebuff to such an external threat. Penned by a member of a clerical estate that had defied the strictures of its own supreme head on earth since 1318 (really 1306), the letter then goes even further: it closes with a warning that if John XXII 'puts too much faith in the tales of the English', the resulting failure to bring Christendom in the British Isles to peace for the purposes of crusade, leaving an ongoing 'slaughter of bodies, the perdition of souls, and all other misfortunes that will follow, inflicted by them on us and by us on them, will, we believe, be surely laid by the Most High to your charge'.

All three letters were surely to be delivered by Scottish emissaries (chosen by the Newbattle council?), who were to emphasise the need for excommunication and other penalties to end. With this in view, it is possible that Robert and his council also decided to write (perhaps again through letters from each estate, as in 1309) to Philip V of France. At that time he was awaiting Edward II's much delayed visit to Amiens to perform homage for Aquitaine and Ponthieu and might have been amenable to placing further pressure on his brother-in-law by favouring the Scots' cause with John XXII.[44] That in the spring of 1320 Edward II's council discussed both the need to issue safe conducts to Bruce and his bishops to let them cross the Channel to Avignon, and the likely assistance extended to the Scots at the curia by Philip's envoy, Sire Odard de Maubuisson, suggests that the French were receptive to Robert's approaches. Edward II responded by having his envoys to Paris in May insist that the excommunication of Bruce should be formally proclaimed throughout both France and Flanders.[45]

The external context for the Arbroath Declaration(s) can thus be explained. However, the insistence once more that the barons and prelates attach their seals to such bold statements of support surely speaks to their domestic, Scottish political intent. As a result of the revised statutory act of succession of December 1318 (tabled at a moment when Robert had perhaps first heard of a plot against his regime), the estates of Scotland were indeed 'bound by law' to their king and his heirs, as the barons' letter asserts. Thus, just as in 1309–10, 1315, and by the oaths on the Gospels and relics of 1318, Robert and his council clearly intended these declarations in spring 1320 as an affirmation of loyalty within Scotland at a critical juncture. The assertion that if necessary Bruce could be replaced at the behest of a community that would thus make 'some other man who was well able to defend us our king' was a further echo of the statutory demand of the acts of succession that, failing the Bruce line, Randolph should gather the estates together and do just that.[46]

That the barons' letter is dated 6 April from Arbroath Abbey may indicate an adjournment from Newbattle of a number of weeks in which Robert's chancery took the respective estates' letters on tour for sealing.[47] It may also have been desirable to issue these communications to the curia from a church dedicated to St Thomas in what was a jubilee year for the Becket cult and its Translation feast of 7 July.[48] There would have been a short window for such activity given the need for this collective reply to reach Avignon by about 1 May in lieu of the king and his summonsed prelates: in the end it would arrive late, about 29 July. Nonetheless, there may have been far more pressure applied to the 'ragman' sealing of these missives in Scotland than on previous occasions. This may have gone well beyond the predictable attachment of as many bishops' and abbots' seals as possible to the clergy's letter, even those of the recalcitrant prelates of Whithorn, Argyll and Sodor/the Isles (as in 1309–10, 1315 and 1318).[49] This may also explain why the early sixteenth-century chronicles of Hector Boece (1465–1536, of Aberdeen University) and Adam Abell (c.1480–c.1540, a monk of Inchaffray and Kelso Abbeys) both alluded to a demand by Robert I in parliament in 1320 that his nobles display proof of their holdings, a command that provoked armed confrontation and a plot to remove him. This was most likely a distortion of the regime's heavy-handed demand of seals to attach to the barons' letter, perhaps adding fuel to the 'Soules conspiracy'.[50]

## The Black Parliament, April–August 1320

It is certainly credible that, given events since December 1318, Robert acted after the defence of Berwick to isolate his opponents in Scotland deliberately, forcing them finally to accept his lordship or show their true colours. Even the choice of envoys to Avignon, probably one high-profile lord from each estate of earls, barons and prelates, may have been a test of allegiance. From a fragmentary contemporary English report it is known that Earl Patrick of Dunbar and Sir Adam Gordon, who had both entered Bruce's peace in 1314, were assigned these roles. Upon reaching France, however, Dunbar apparently turned back to Scotland in haste with news that caused Robert to summon parliament to Scone.[51]

This intelligence was word of a plot involving the French connections of lords such as Soules and Ingram d'Umfraville with the Picardy lands of Edward Balliol. But Dunbar's discovery – perhaps rewarded with a marriage to Thomas Randolph's eldest daughter – may have sprung from the presence in France from 19 June to 22 July of Edward II himself with his queen and retinue (with his homage for Aquitaine performed on 30 June); or, as during a truce the declarations' embassy might also pass to the continent via Dover, Earl Patrick perhaps only took ship home with this dramatic report once he was clear of England.[52] The Scots estates' letters were taken on to Avignon by Gordon and perhaps a cleric like Bishop Henry of Aberdeen, recently pardoned by King Robert, or John Lindsay himself; but it may have fallen to the cleric Alexander de Kinninmonth (Bishop Henry's successor by 1329), a lawyer skilled in papal *cursus* and the probable author of the estates' letters, to speak to their content before the Pope.[53]

It is likely that after the envoys' departure the political atmosphere in Scotland was one of rising tension. On 1 April, while still at Berwick, Robert granted the Lindsays' resigned barony of Staplegordon to Sir James Douglas along with the castle, forest and associated Roxburghshire lands of Jedburgh forest (the latter in return for the service of a knight). Then on 11 April the king can be located at Liston to the west of Edinburgh where he and Bishop Lamberton were present at a resignation of lands to Newbattle Abbey.[54] These were acts seemingly confirmed afresh by great seal charters subsequently issued on 6 May from Arbroath Abbey. The recorded witnesses to these grants – along with royal gifts of the patronage of the church of Dumbarton for Kilwinning Abbey (4 May) and the lands/ church of Masterton (Midlothian) to Newbattle Abbey (20 May) – may indeed point to chancery activity (with Arbroath Abbey also in receipt of royal letters of protection on 17 April), which included the collection and attachment of subjects' seals to the papal letters there awaiting dispatch: they included those of the bishops of St Andrews, Dunkeld and Brechin, the earls of Fife, Moray, Dunbar and Strathearn, Steward, Douglas, Hay, Keith, Robert Boyd of Noddsdale and William Soules, styled for the first time as royal 'Butler'.[55]

The household appointment may have been viewed as compensation for Sir William Soules while Douglas's star rose in the Marches. Sir James's grant of Roxburghshire lands was surely a prelude to his appointment as lieutenant or 'warden' of the west and middle March and sheriff of Roxburghshire. The latter was a post with effective control over much of Teviotdale and the forest held in the 1280s by William Soules's grandfather, another William of Liddesdale who had also been justiciar of Lothian.[56] Robert's grant of Staplegordon, indeed, had stipulated that this land directly to the north of Soules's own holding of Westerker in Dumfriesshire (confirmed by the king in November 1319) was to be held in barony and free-forest of the sheriffdom of Roxburgh. This intrusion may have been compounded for Sir William if the Crown had also inter- vened in his inheritance of Kirkandrews (directly to the south of Staplegordon) and Torthorwald (between Annandale and Nithsdale), lands held by his brother, Sir John Soules, killed at Faughart. Moreover, that one of Douglas's supporters in control of the Marches was intended to be none other than the king's own natural son, Robert Bruce, was confirmed sometime between March and July 1320 when that young man (probably born c.1293–99) received a grant of the eastern Roxburghshire barony of Sprouston (former Mowbray lands adjacent to Maxwell, Ednam and Yetholm, in turn forfeited Maxwell, Loval and cadet Balliol lands respectively). Young Robert now formed part of an impressive affinity of Ayrshire (Cunningham-Carrick), Lanarkshire and Marcher lords associated with Walter Steward and James Douglas.[57]

These grants acted unavoidably as a further catalyst to conspiracy by Soules and his associates in Scotland. That a serious crisis did erupt at this time is certainly suggested by the lengthy gap in Robert I's extant charters, until 18 November 1320.[58] Crucially, that this involved an English effort to use Edward Balliol and his support to subvert Bruce's power is suggested by Balliol's presence at Westminster on 6 July 1320.[59] As a result, that this was a dynastic challenge which Robert and his close supporters sought to crush swiftly and then play down is further suggested by the absence or failure of survival of the parliamentary record of August 1320 when treason trials were held at Scone, and by the subsequent whitewash applied to the plot in sources inherited by Archdeacon Barbour, Fordun's annalist, Sir Thomas Gray and Abbot Bower.

Nevertheless, what can be gleaned from these accounts reveals a plot of greater scope than hitherto apparent, which had the potential to raise a substantial portion of the nobility against the king. It is telling that in acting to seize the conspirators Robert's regime arrested and tried a number of innocent men. The decisive spark may indeed have been provided by Earl Patrick's sudden return or news resulting from the defection of Murdoch of Menteith (who might also have been approached afresh by the plotters if he was already in Scotland).[60] But Barbour – perhaps following the Bruce party line – would assert that the conspirators 'ilkane discoveryt war/Throu a lady as I hard say'. It is Barbour's poem that provides us with the most comprehensive list of suspects, a list largely reproduced by Fordun's source and its continuators.[61] Thus Sir William Soules and Agnes, dowager countess of Strathearn, emerge as ringleaders, found guilty of treason by the Scone parliament of August 1320 and sentenced to perpetual imprisonment: according to Barbour, Soules had 'grantyt thar/The deid into plane parleament', confessing all. Agnes may thus be the female informant, motivated by the fact that her husband Malise, sixth earl of Strathearn, had lost his title to his son under pressure from Bruce who had observed the father's loyalty to Edward II until about 1313.[62] One alternative candidate may have been Isabel of Atholl, betraying her exiled brother to secure royal favour for herself and her natural son, Alexander Bruce. However, Countess Agnes was also a niece of John Comyn, earl of Buchan (d.1308); two of that lord's four sisters were the wives of Earl Patrick of Dunbar and Robert d'Umfraville, earl of Angus (brother of Sir Ingram), while two others were mothers to William Soules and David de Brechin.[63]

This provides an obvious connection to the first of the other lords named by the Scottish chroniclers as guilty of treachery: for 'the lords David de Brechin, Gilbert of Malherb, John of Logie, knights, and Richard Broun, esquire, having been convicted of the aforesaid conspiracy, were first drawn by horses and, in the end, underwent capital punishment [including public beheading]'.[64] As we have seen, Brechin had been a regular in English garrisons before 1314 and was now deprived of the lordship of the Comyns and Umfravilles of Angus. Logie of Strathgartney had been a ward of the sixth earl of Strathearn and must have objected to John and Murdoch of Menteith interfering in his locality.[65] While loyal to Edwards I and II, Malherbe (or Morham) and his kin had also coveted Menteith, the wardship of Strathgartney and the keepership of Jedburgh castle, thus finding clear cause by 1320 with Soules against Douglas's recent gains.[66] Finally, Broun, of an Ayrshire landowning kin, had aided Edward I against Bruce in Galloway in 1307 and served in Stirling castle in 1312. On 1 April 1321 his sons 'Thomas, Alexander and William Broun' would be admitted into Edward II's peace accompanied by a Fergus Kennedy (perhaps of Ardrossan, a subscriber to the barons' letter at Arbroath in 1320) and William of Caerlaverock, clearly south-western supporters of Balliol/Soules: in August 1321 Robert I would also write to the baillies of the king of Norway to inquire whether Alexander Broun, 'a Scottish traitor', had sought refuge there.[67]

Richard Broun's service in the Stirling garrison provides a clear link shared with many Balliol-Comyn Scots to Sir Philip Mowbray, the keeper of that castle when it surrendered after Bannockburn. Undoubtedly, the most macabre act of the tableau reported by Barbour and the Scottish annalists was the condemnation in parliament in August 1320 of the body of Sir Philip's brother, Roger Mowbray of Barnbougle and Dalmeny in the Lothians. A Balliol patriot who had served Edward II in Dundee, Perth and Stirling, Roger had acted as a justiciar for Robert I in Kinrossshire in April 1319 but seems to have received no further favour.[68] He may have been in contact with exiled members of his extended kindred about a Balliol revival: on 6 February 1319 a John Mowbray was empowered by Edward II to receive Scots into England's peace.[69] Moreover, by 18 February

1321, Roger's son, Alexander, and a substantial following 'of people who had come with him' had fled Scotland 'poor', seeking refuge in England: this included a William Comyn, William de Caerlaverock, Malcolm de Kinninmonth, Thomas and Patrick Thorinborne, William Haresfield, John Ferrour, Hugh de Crawford and at least a dozen other named servants (many of whom can be located in English garrisons in Scotland before 1314).[70]

The later fourteenth-century Scottish accounts also name a group of lords tried 'but not found guilty in any way' of conspiracy against Robert: 'Eustace of Maxwell, Walter of Barclay, sheriff of Aberdeen, and Patrick of Graham, knights, Hamelin of Troupe and Eustace of Rattray, esquires'.[71] Although cleared, the careers of these individuals illustrate just how this plot cast a wide net of suspicion. Sir Eustace Maxwell, an adherent of the Balliol lords of Galloway, had held Caerlaverock castle in Dumfriesshire, to the south of Dumfries burgh, for Edward II until 1313 before submitting to Bruce. Maxwell would go so far as to slight this stronghold in return for a pension from King Robert in 1324, but like a number of disenchanted regional lords – including the earls of Fife and Strathearn – he would return to his original allegiance when Edward Balliol did invade Scotland with English backing in 1332–33.[72] There is more than one Patrick Graham who might be the suspected rebel of 1320, from a family that held extensive lands at Montrose, Kincardine (Angus), Dundaff (St Ninians, Stirlingshire) and in Fife, Carrick, Dunbar, Strathearn, Lennox and northern England, serving Balliol and then England circa 1296 to 1306.[73] A younger Patrick had briefly supported Bruce until in 1308 he joined his new father-in-law, no less a person than John Macdougall of Argyll, remaining in English service until 1314 with his cousin, David Graham (who had attacked Malcolm Wallace as a Carrick adherent in 1299).[74] This Patrick may have renewed his association with his brother-in-law, Alan of Argyll, who on 20 June 1320 renegotiated his wages with Edward II 'till the king recovers his lands in Scotland, which God grant'.[75] As we have seen, a John Graham (perhaps the lord of Dundaff/Strathcarron, a younger brother of David) had granted Dumfriesshire lands to William Soules: this may explain the apparent order of seniority in the Graham family by 1320, for first David (listed between David de Brechin and Ingram d'Umfraville), then John (between Henry Sinclair and David Lindsay), and lastly the uncertain Patrick (between the namesake heir of the keeper of Stirling for Balliol in 1304, William Oliphant, and a John Fenton) had had their names attached to the Arbroath barons' letter of April 1320.[76] By contrast, Eustace Rattray is easily identified: a Gowrie landowner who had also joined Bruce in 1306 – perhaps in the retinue of John Strathbogie, earl of Atholl (d.1306) – but can be found in the Perth garrison in 1311 after the defection of his lord's son (Earl David).[77]

The two remaining men put on trial in 1320 seem to have had fairly clear pro-Bruce records, but they may have appeared sufficiently ambivalent and open to approach (or slight) by the plotters as their local interests declined. Sir Walter Barclay and much of his kin had sided with the Comyns of Buchan and Badenoch until 1305, but he joined Bruce in 1306 aiding in the conquest of the north (although in 1307 Walter's junior kinsman, David Barclay of Cairny, was briefly granted the Murrays' lordship of Avoch by Edward I before its transfer to Hugh Ross): Walter would remain sheriff of Aberdeen until 1323 but it is possible that around 1319–20 he felt his regional position threatened by Robert's preference for his brother-in-law Alexander Fraser, his future brother-in-law Andrew Murray of Avoch, and even the restored Cheynes of Inverugie and Duffus.[78] Hamelin de Troup had certainly appealed in 1305 to Edward I's parliament against the predation in Banffshire of Duncan Frendraught and Reginald Cheyne, both then Comyn adherents, but his posting as Bruce's sheriff of that shire (still active in 1328) may have left him feeling alienated in turn by royal favour to William, earl of Ross, and his sons Hugh (Robert I's other brother-in-law) and John in former Buchan/Badenoch territory: Ross loyalty to the Bruces after 1332 perhaps ensured that Hamelin died in the service of Edward III around 1338.[79]

To those named by chroniclers as guilty or acquitted we can add other lords with similar records of allegiance and disappointed lordship. A late fifteenth-century collection of treatises (now preserved in the British Library, London) also includes a note of Murdoch of Menteith's betrayal of the 'Soulis conspiracy' as involving Alexander and Philip Mowbray, Patrick Graham and 'David de Weymss [sic]'.[80] This is our only hint that Roger Mowbray's brother, Philip, former keeper of Stirling castle in 1314, may have survived Bruce service in Ireland but rebelled with his kin, perhaps perishing in the process.[81] The Fifeshire lord of Wemyss and his father, Sir Michael (died c.1317), had joined Bruce in 1306 but quickly submitted, serving in the English Dundee garrison of 1312: this family's loyalty to Bruce clearly depended very much on the fortunes of Duncan, earl of Fife, and thus Sir David Wemyss, whose name is also amongst those on the barons' letter to the Pope of 1320, may have been among those charged but acquitted in that year.[82]

A number of other men, like the Brouns and Mowbrays and their substantial followings, seem to have fled into exile in England in the months after the conspiracy collapsed. For example, Sir William Mowat of Cromarty – another subscriber to the barons' letter of 1320 – had served in Edward II's garrison at Dundee in 1312 and thereafter been bluntly displaced by King Robert as sheriff of Cromarty by William, earl of Ross. Although Mowat had entered Robert's peace circa 1314, he had returned to English allegiance by 20 May 1321 and was stripped by Robert of his Stirlingshire lands: Sir Thomas Gray reports Mowat being killed defending Norham against the Scots in 1327.[83] Also forfeited by King Robert by 8 September 1321 was 'rebel' Sir Simon Lindsay of Wauchopdale in Dumfriesshire and Langriggs in Annandale, a brother of John Lindsay, bishop-elect of Glasgow. Sir Simon had served as keeper of Soules's castle of Liddesdale for England in 1307 and (after refusing to return with his brothers to Scotland after Bannockburn) in the 1316 garrison in Carlisle. However, it had been as a 'knight of Ingram d'Umfraville' that Sir Simon had entered English service, accepting payment in London in 1310–11 on behalf of the exiled brother of the Angus earl.[84]

Therefore it should come as no surprise to find that Sir Ingram – who had displaced Robert Bruce as Guardian for the patriot Scots in 1300 – had played a leading role in this Balliol plot. After serving as warden of the west March for Edward II in 1308 against Edward Bruce and Douglas, and then as keeper of Caerlaverock castle, Ingram had been captured at Bannockburn and obliged to ransom himself.[85] His brother, Robert d'Umfraville (d.1325), continued in English pay as warden of Northumbria in 1319 but Ingram seems to have been adrift in Scottish society (like Brechin), excluded from court, government and patronage by Robert I, who may already have indicated his preference for the Stewarts of Bonkle as future earls of Angus (or even issued a now lost charter of this title to them c.1314–20). That Ingram could indeed have been in touch with Balliol and other disinherited lords is confirmed by his receipt from Edward II on 2 April 1320 of a safe conduct to pass through England on business overseas; his name, though, was included on the barons' letter from Arbroath.[86]

Yet Barbour, seemingly following a lost narrative of Ingram's life, asserts that this chivalrous knight was not actually involved in Soules's conspiracy but was rather so disgusted by Robert's trial and execution ('sa vekanys a ded') of the virtuous crusader Sir David de Brechin in August 1320 – for knowledge of the plot but not informing his king – that he sought leave to sell his lands and depart for England, a request that Bruce magnanimously granted. In truth this is just one of several obfuscations sown by Robert's regime in Barbour's narrative. In fact, on 26 January 1321 Edward II ordered border warden Anthony de Lucy to render to Ingram d'Umfraville the services due for English lands held in the past by that lord, 'who was a prisoner in Scotland, has escaped, and shewn that he never left his [Edward's] allegiance'.[87]

This plot, then, had been no minor blip in Robert I's otherwise unstoppable assertion of royal authority over Scotland, as Barbour and many modern histories would have it.[88] After bubbling for almost two years, the conspiracy *was* decisively pre-empted and its perpetrators brought to justice or put to flight. The wisdom of the political and judicial guarantees put in place by Robert's parliament in December 1318 and promises of fair lordship for loyalty had clearly played a decisive role in this police action: not least, Murdoch of Menteith, Patrick of Dunbar and perhaps Isabel of Atholl had divulged plans for *lèse-majesté* in the hope of reward. But there had been fighting, as the probable death by violence of the Mowbray brothers suggests. Barbour also asserts that William Soules came in arms to Berwick with 360 liveried men before being confronted and arrested: his men, all 'sary and wa', were released by the king.[89] The defections of several retinues into England well into 1321 also hint at the hunting down of guilty or suspected parties and their associates for some months after the Scone parliament and the clearance of a number of localities. In all, almost a quarter of the nobles whose names or seals are attached to the barons' letter from Arbroath can be tied to the conspiracy, with almost as many more implicated from contemporary record sources.

The lands, histories and connections of lordship of these men clearly show that such a confederacy had the potential to destabilise the control of Robert and his regime over many regions of the realm, especially the northeast, the ancient central earldoms, Galloway and the Marches: once unleashed, such a reformed coalition might also have activated resentment towards Bruce in Fife and the south-east. These were all arguably areas in which – even six years after Bannockburn – Robert I's resettlement had only just begun to have an impact. The blame attached to Soules's ambition for the throne in Barbour and later chronicles may reflect a conscious decision as early as August 1320 on the part of Robert and his council to avoid all reference to Edward Balliol and his kingship claim. Instead, the Bruce government's charges and rhetoric surely focused upon the 'in-bringing' of the English which the scheme had threatened (as per the barons' letter to Avignon). By the same token, the brutal theatre of the 'Roman' execution of Sir David de Brechin and company, whose limbs were pulled apart by horses, and the senatorial judgment of treason and forfeiture pronounced in parliament over Roger Mowbray's corpse underscored the defence of the Scottish kingdom's republic (again, as per the barons' letter) by their chosen prince.[90] If Soules had sought to murder Robert and take his throne for himself he would surely have been executed, not gaoled. It is moreover possible that in the months following the Scone parliament, Soules – like Umfraville – was helped to escape by sympathetic parties (perhaps by someone in John or Murdoch of Menteith's retinue around Dumbarton castle). Barbour and his followers assert that Soules was gaoled in Dumbarton 'and deit thar in a tour off stane'.[91] Yet a contemporary English chronicle reports that on 16 March 1322 a 'lord William de Soules' was amongst those who fell alongside Humphrey de Bohun, earl of Hereford and Essex, at the end of his rebellion with Lancaster against Edward II, at the battle of Boroughbridge.[92] Thus Soules's escape but early death provided the Bruce regime with a convenient scapegoat.

## War or Peace, August 1320–December 1321

Over the next few years a majority share of the forfeited lands of the 1320 conspirators would be awarded to Robert I's family, close supporters and favoured churches, including Robert Stewart, Robert Bruce the bastard, James Douglas and his brother Archibald (a future Guardian for David II, 1332–33), William Lindsay the former Chamberlain, and Melrose and Dunfermline Abbeys: Murdoch and John of Menteith would also be rewarded while the Stewarts of Bonkle and Arbroath Abbey benefited from the removal of Sir David de Brechin's lordship in Angus.[93] The pre-emptive destruction of this Balliol coup acted both as an effective deterrent for the remainder of Robert's reign and a further motive for action by the enemies of the Bruce dynasty. According to Abbot Bower's fifteenth-century chronicle, in 1330 a former Balliol adherent, 'Twynham Lourison', seized a royal official in Ayr only to be chased by Sir James Douglas into exile where he sought out Edward Balliol: 'Have you not heard of the destruction of the nobility at the Black Parliament? Their families will stand by you; the King of England will provide a powerful force of armed men to help you. Hurry and get started; be of good heart, consult your friends, and take up arms.'[94] However, it does not seem that King Robert indulged in a sudden outpouring of patronage to his close supporters after what must have been a cruel few months of suspicion, arrest and pursuit: this occurred against the ominous backdrop of another wet summer and poor harvest amidst the fear and hardship caused by spreading cattle plague.[95]

Instead, Robert and his government seem to have focused upon defusing any lingering threat from Balliol, the disinherited and England by exploring the possibilities for full peace talks. In this regard, it must be acknowledged that the king's and estates' letters of April 1320, and the simultaneous approach to Philip V, had been fruitful in small but important ways. John XXII did not, of course, style Bruce as king or consider lifting the excommunication and interdict, although he would delay their full implementation (until 1 April 1321).[96] But by late July 1320 he had written to Edward II urging him again to make efforts towards peace with Robert as 'regent of the Scottish kingdom'; and, as always, John XXII remained open to allowing both sides to establish the proofs of their respective claims to independence or superiority.[97] It was the latter diplomatic dispute – which the Scottish envoys must have pressed home – that led in part to the dispatch of another papal envoy (the Archbishop of Vienne) to help negotiate Anglo-Scottish peace, an appointment matched by two arbitrators (and later more) sent on behalf of King Philip. On 28 August Pope John also replied to the Scottish barons' letter, indicating that he had written to Edward and his councillors exhorting them to 'incline his mind to this peace' with the said 'illustrious man Robert, who assumes the title and position of king of Scotland'.[98]

Although French and papal intervention was driven by intertwined agendas, this in itself was a further step towards official recognition by sovereign powers of Bruce's kingship. But would it prove just another hole in the water for Robert? Talks were set to begin as early as August 1320 at Carlisle, but Edward II, significantly, seems to have been anxious to delay the envoys' engagement on the border. This must have sprung from fears that Philip's and John's newly arrived representatives would report back on Edward's rapidly deteriorating relations with the earl of Lancaster (perhaps even endangering the Pope's likely absolution in April–May 1320 of Edward's oath to uphold the Ordinances). But Edward's unexplained request to the Scots for a delay on 14 August – repeated in exchanges at Carlisle throughout the autumn and into winter – may also in part have related to his embarrassing culpability in the Balliol plot (to kill Robert), which was collapsing in Scotland at that time.

Yet despite the flight of conspirators and their allies into England, the truce held and the door to peace talks remained ajar. And this was a door Robert was certainly willing to walk through if he was recognised as king of a sovereign realm. A short, quite submissive letter, from Robert to Edward II, previously assigned to spring 1320 (or October 1310), surely in fact belongs to this period of Edwardian evasion.[99] Sent from Kildrum (Cumbernauld) in the (deanery of) Lennox, this offered personal talks to prevent the shedding of Christian blood and asserted that the Scots were willing to secure peace by everything which we and our people will be able to do by bodily service, or to bear by giving freely of our goods, for the redemption of good peace and for the perpetually flourishing grace of your [Edward II's] good will, we are prepared and shall be prepared to accomplish in a suitable and honest way, with a pure heart.

As the letter was written in papal *cursus*, with the same flair for Latin rhetoric as the Arbroath letters, Alexander de Kinninmonth or his immediate colleagues seem likely authors at Robert's behest, with the message intended more for the consumption of the new papal legate, the Archbishop of Vienne, than for Edward II.[100] As we shall see, some form of Anglo-Scottish alliance and a war indemnity paid by the Scots would certainly be key planks of the peace proposals pushed by Robert I from 1322–23.

The firm contemporary record of Robert's kingship resumes at Scone on 18 November 1320 when he inspected Alexander II's charter to Melrose Abbey (including its exemptions from exactions), a highly suggestive resumption of Marches business that had been interrupted in the spring.[101] The location of Robert and his court for Christmas is unknown, but 14 January 1321 found him at the Premonstratensian abbey of St Congall or Holywood, just north of Dumfries where he granted the Cumbrian Cistercian abbey of Holm Cultram an annual sum of £10 due from the lords of Buittle (the former Balliol barony which would be transferred to James Douglas in 1325).[102] The king's motives for doing so seem obvious at a time when his envoys were still at Carlisle haggling about peace talks. Holm Cultram was a daughter house of Melrose Abbey and a foundation of David I of Scotland (r.1124–53) and his son Prince Henry (d.1152) at a time when the Scottish Crown held the county of Cumberland from England's kings.[103] Holywood was a foundation of the ancient lords of Galloway which Edward Bruce had appropriated after the forfeiture of the Balliols.[104] So, along with the Buittle revenues due to Holm Cultram, Robert provided a timely demonstration of the historic lordship of Scotland's kings over northern England and his complete displacement of Balliol (and hinted at his recent letter's promise to give 'freely of our goods' to secure an end to hostilities). Yet Robert's reasons may also have been personal, penitential, for the Scots' raid of late 1319 may have sacked Holm Cultram where Bruce's own father, Robert VI, was buried.[105]

Five days later, on 19 January 1321, Edward II finally appointed a full delegation, to be led by the earl of Pembroke and the Archbishop of York and chaired by the French and papal envoys, to discuss peace or a prolonged truce with the Scots at Newcastle.[106] This explains Robert's residence at

Berwick once more from January to late April. Tensions must have been heightened by the English arrest at York in December of Scots, and their Flemish and German shipmates from a recent wreck, bearing letters patent from Robert.[107] The negotiations themselves would be delayed again by the English (due to Pembroke's absence in France) until 26 March.[108] In the meantime, Robert resumed the steady pace of patronage of 1319, much of this again resulting from the due process of court inquests, but with a notable increase in geographical scope, to touch on north-eastern and south-western lands. On 31 January he confirmed an inquest's findings into the royal liberties and franchises of his natural son's Roxburghshire barony of Sprouston: a number of the witnesses to this and subsequent acts – Moray, Steward, Douglas, John Menteith, Hay, Keith, Seton, David Lindsay of the Byres/Crawford, Henry Sinclair of Roslin and Robert Lauder of the Bass ('justiciar of Lothian') – point to an intensified settlement of the south-east and may also have been Robert's envoys to Newcastle.[109] It must have been about this time (and certainly by late 1322) that Robert Bruce junior was granted the forfeited Soules's border lordship of Liddesdale with its caput of Hermitage Castle, confirming his importance within the Crown's Marcher affinity.[110]

The weeks spent at Berwick in early 1321 witnessed several further royal grants in return for military services, often of lands and resources forfeited from enemies and recent plotters. The late Sir John Logie's peats were assigned to the Perth Blackfriars (2 February); Sir John Bonville received Collieston and Ardendraught in Buchan (4 February); Edmund Marshall was given Roger Mowbray's Roxburghshire lands of Cessford (30 March); Sir James Cunningham received the Hassendean barony next to Hawick in the same shire (30 March, for half a knight); and Sir James Douglas was gifted half of the forfeited Soules barony of Westerker in Dumfriesshire (20 April), while the patronage of its church (in the Esk deanery of Glasgow diocese) was appropriated to Melrose Abbey (10 April).[111] The latter grant may have represented Robert's thanks at the beginning of Holy Week (with Easter Sunday on 19 March) for spiritual support and good fortune in the Marches and other quarters through the summer of 1320 against Soules and his allies. So, too, perhaps did grants (12 April) of provision to, and income from, Clydeside churches to Kelso Abbey (Roxburghshire), and a gift in free alms for the souls of Robert, his ancestors and successors to the Carmelite chapel of St Mary in the burgh of Banff on the Moray coast (21 April).[112] However, the king's gift to Melrose also allowed Robert to affirm publicly his confidence in John Lindsay as his bishop of the Glasgow see (ordering him to confirm

Westerker's transfer), a nonetheless still disputed election that must have been discussed at Newcastle.

Moreover, the greatest royal favour bestowed at Berwick was directed to Sir Alexander Seton, who received at least five further charters of Lothian lands and privileges: to the forfeited Ferrers'/Zouches' lands of Tranent as well as Barns, Dundas, Craigie, Gogar and his own Seton in free burgh, warren and forest (with a remittance of wool custom), perhaps as a way to offset a sudden loss of livestock and the generally shattered state of this region.[113] As with the king's favour to Douglas, this extension of Seton lordship was a reward to a knight who had acted first in support of Robert as the means of recovering his own family lands but had grown to assume a role of wider regional military and political responsibility for the Bruce cause. It would also have been logical for the Crown to have rewarded esquire Robert Lauder, his justiciar of Lothian, at this time.[114]

Indeed, several more of Robert I's undated or lost acts may also belong to this period. A charter for no fewer than five adjacent baronies in Roxburghshire (just south of the royal burgh and castle) largely shares a witness list with the king's 30 March grant of Hassendean: these baronies were granted to the king's current heir, Robert Stewart (with tailzie to his father, Walter), for one knight's service, and punctuated a determined royal policy of intruding loyal knights into a region in which Soules's influence had recently posed such a threat.[115] There were also perhaps grants to Murdoch of Menteith of the barony of Rothiemay in Banffshire (just north of Adam Gordon's recently acquired Strathbogie lordship), and to John Menteith of wardenship of the extensive ex-Logie lordship of Strathgartney between Menteith and Lennox.[116] Former Chamberlain William Lindsay, a canon of Glasgow, may have received Roger Mowbray's forfeited Dumbartonshire barony of Kirkmichael, also within the Lennox.[117]

All told, these acts point to a far more confident king and close counsel, mandated by the decisive destruction of a Balliol insurgency as well as perhaps by a sense that French and papal sympathies could be turned. This may explain the apparently inflexible stance adopted by the Scottish envoys once talks finally got underway at Bamburgh following the arrival of the substitute lead English delegate, one-time Lieutenant of Scotland (1305–6) John of Brittany, earl of Richmond, armed with Andrew de Tange's dossier pertaining to English superiority. Yet whilst by this stage the English monarch was apparently willing to talk peace, according to a report of his envoys of 8 April, the Scots 'after they had caused great delays . . . would only agree to a long truce, for example of twenty-six years, to which we and your other envoys would not agree without informing you [Edward II]'.[118]

Robert's representatives probably included experienced clerics in Bishop Lamberton's employ such as William, archdeacon of Lothian (a past colleague of Baldred Bisset at the curia), and Alexander de Kinninmonth. Their advice and legal resources surely saw the Scots rehearse their tested arguments of 1299–1301 and, most especially, 1309–10 and 1317–20. They once again refuted the Welsh chronicler Geoffrey of Monmouth's Trojan claims via Brutus to all the kingdoms of the British Isles. Instead they traced a line of '113 native' Scottish kings succeeded by a community fighting for freedom like the Maccabees and now under their chosen worthy prince, Robert 'Dei gratia nunc regi'.[119] In that sense, despite the diplomatic exchanges of 1320 and the presence of Philip V's and John XXII's envoys, little had changed since 1309–10 or 1317–18. Without recognition of his title as king of an independent realm, Robert and the Scots were not willing to compromise; nor did the Scots mention papal jurisdiction over its 'special daughter', Scotland.[120] However, it should be acknowledged that the generation-long truce suggested by the Scots perhaps spoke not only to Robert's wish to focus on rebuilding and consolidating his realm and rule, but also to an obligation of legacy, in search of the conditions of stability under which his successor might prosper and later negotiate a full peace as the English king's equal. Indeed, the Scots' reported proposal of an extended truce of 'twenty-six years' may have been calculated to sustain the ceasefire through the pregnancy and full legal minority (to twenty-five years old) of a child now expected by Queen Elizabeth.[121] As we shall see, Robert's health and longevity may once again have been an issue. But the Scots' proposal may also have been a bluff of bravado on the orders of their nevertheless now expectant-father king, given in the certain knowledge that it would be unacceptable to Edward II (though pleasing to French and papal emissaries seeking a long ceasefire for a crusade). In reality, the Scots were fully prepared to wait and see whether political events in England might lead to further advantageous change.

The date chosen for further talks, 1 September 1321, may have been just beyond Queen Elizabeth's predicted pregnancy term, at which point the Scots would have known whether their dynasty had a direct male blood heir.[122] That the queen was with child is suggested by Robert's grant that summer (8 July) to Dunfermline Abbey of Roger Mowbray's forfeited lands at Inverkeithing and at the 'Queensferry' for pilgrims on the south side of the Forth estuary, along with the Crown's great customs of the abbey's burghs of Dunfermline, Kirkcaldy and Musselburgh. All this was to pay for a perpetual candle in the choir of the royal mausoleum in honour of the Virgin and before the feretory shrine of St Margaret for the souls of Robert's ancestors and successors.[123] The intercessionary powers of Margaret – queen, wife and mother – were well known to help women in labour, and Queen Elizabeth could wear her predecessor's venerated relic of a 'birthing serk'.[124] A month later, 4–5 August 1321, Robert is to be found making his first identifiable trip to the far north in almost four years to Cullen in Banff, seat of a church of the Virgin to which Queen Elizabeth developed a particular attachment, perhaps as a shrine that also had personal meaning for her during her several pregnancies.[125] Moreover, association with Scotland's royal saint had also played a part in the recent Bamburgh talks, during which the Scottish envoys reportedly declared Edward II's Plantagenet line illegitimate: as descendants of William the Conqueror they were usurpers of the Saxon-Wessex line which now hailed through Malcolm III and Queen/St Margaret to their rightful heir, Robert I![126]

With the collapse of peace talks Robert resumed his domestic resettlement. His last act at Berwick had restored the liberties of Lübeck merchants in its wool market.[127] Then a parliament at Scone about 8–10 July – held at the same time as a Scottish Church Council in nearby Perth – must have discussed the recent failed negotiations as well as perhaps patronage and the royal succession (with hope of a royal son underlined by Robert's payment there for Dunfermline lights).[128] Again, the extant records confirm the commitment of Robert and his government to the due process of brieve and inquest in settling land conveyance and disputes: a fairly minor sale of lands in Garioch (since c.1314–15 the lordship of the king's sister, Christina) was confirmed both by the king and Church Council (with a penalty of £1,000 towards the fabrics of St Andrews and Aberdeen Cathedrals if challenged).[129] During this parliament Robert also granted Soules's forfeited Torthorwald (Dumfriesshire) in barony and warren to Sir Humphrey Kirkpatrick for an archer's service; confirmed Dunfermline Abbey's cocket seal in the wool staple of Bruges; awarded John de Kinninmonth, bishop of Brechin, and his chapter a weekly burgh market; and extended Alexander Seton's Lothian presence further east with the barony and (ex-Comyn) superiority of Elphinstone.[130]

At this assembly the king also probably confirmed the loyalist Malcolm, earl of Lennox, in his earldom and the sheriffship of Dumbarton.[131] This act suggests that John Menteith (or David Graham senior, who had lands at Cardross) continued to defy the royal will around Dumbarton.[132] As already noted, 4–5 August found the king at Cullen in Banff, with a retinue of northern knights and officers, Henry Sinclair 'baillie of Caithness', Gilbert Hay, William Oliphant, William Montefichet, Nicholas Hay and Edward

Keith.[133] Robert was asserting royal authority in the region, pursuing the traitor Alexander Broun, but also in a redemptive, conciliatory mood: in a restated grant of the thanages of Dingwall and Ferincoskry to William, earl of Ross, the king required his brother-in-law's father to direct £20 from these lands as an annuity to pay for six chaplains to say masses in the chapel of a saintly bishop of Ross, Duthac, at Tain (feast day 8 March) for the souls of Alexander III and John Strathbogie, earl of Atholl (d.1306).[134]

Further grants followed. About 8 September 1321, John Lindsay was granted Wauchopedale in Dumfriesshire and Langriggs in Annandale, forfeited by his rebellious father, Sir Simon.[135] It may have been about this time, too, that the king confirmed the 11 June 1320 charter of Patrick, earl of Dunbar, of Hassington in Berwickshire to Alexander Seton, and restored to Duncan, earl of Fife, his grant of the substantial Banffshire barony of Strath'an that bounded on Badenoch, Abernethy, Mar and Strathbogie (and had been held of the earls of Atholl but apparently forfeited and granted to Malcolm, earl of Lennox, before Fife's submission in 1315).[136] A council held at Edinburgh about 22 September (of which only a brieve summoning attendance by parties concerned in a Lanarkshire tenement dispute is extant) may have been the occasion for these grants.[137]

A week later, however, the king was at Jedburgh (30 September 1321) en route for Berwick and consultation with his March officials (with the end of the two-year truce looming on 29 December).[138] Acts survive for 13 October (Perth), 16 October (Arbroath) and 20 October (Forfar), but these represent the itinerary of Chancellor Bernard finalising earlier royal charters including a grant (given its weighty witness list probably issued in one of the July or September assemblies) to Arbroath Abbey of the church of St Kentigern in Kirkmahoe (a parish in Dalswinton in Dumfriesshire, ex-Roger Mowbray land).[139] As a gift in honour of God, the Virgin and Robert's personal saint, St Thomas, the latter favour to Arbroath may have been associated with the birth of a second daughter, Matilda, about this time; or in memory of a stillborn child, perhaps interred at the Augustinian priory of Restenneth (as would be another of Robert's issue in 1326).[140] A further grant on 1 April 1322 (ten days before Easter Sunday) of an annuity of 5 merks from Inverkeithing to pay for two chaplains saying masses in the chapel of St James at the northern Queensferry terminal on the Forth, within Dunfermline Abbey's cult of St Margaret, may also speak to a lost child.[141] As such, the king may indeed have travelled to Angus, but certainly from late October 1321 he was focused once more on Anglo-Scottish negotiations, though this time not with Edward II but with that king's sworn enemy – Thomas of Lancaster.

# CHAPTER NINE

# To Have and Have Not
## King of Scotland, 1322–26

*The King of England hardly troubled himself any more about Scotland, since through apathy, he had lost as much as his father had gained ...*

Sir Thomas Gray's *Scalacronica*[1]

### War and Peace, January 1322–May 1323

In truth, as had been the case with the Scots' earlier rumoured dealings with the earl of Lancaster, the secret negotiations between Moray and Douglas on behalf of Robert I, and John Mowbray and Robert Clifford for the increasingly desperate Earl Thomas (coded by his clerk as 'Roi Arthur'), which can be dated from 6 December 1321 to 16 February 1322, were designed to aggravate the civil war that had erupted in England. As the Lanercost chronicler reported of Bruce's dealings with Lancaster, 'how will a man who cannot keep faith with his own lord keep faith with me?'[2]

In the first half of August 1321 Edward II had indeed faced the 'gravest crisis of his reign to date' when an uneasy coalition of the majority of his magnates presented him with an ultimatum in parliament in London: exile the Despensers or face deposition. Edward had had no choice but to comply. Yet by September he had regrouped, determining through the autumn–winter of 1321–22 to restore his friends, turn back waverers like Pembroke and revenge himself upon Lancaster, Hereford and their allies. By early October the violence had begun. For the Scots, Hereford's conflict with the Despensers in southern England and in the Welsh Marches would hopefully bleed into a Crown–Lancaster confrontation in Yorkshire and the exhausted winner would have to give Robert I what he wanted.[3]

To drive this point home and as part of his initial understanding with Lancaster and Hereford, on 6 January 1322 Robert, who was probably laid low by illness, unleashed Moray, Douglas and, it seems, Walter Steward on a two-week raid through Durham diocese, Hartlepool, Cleveland and Richmond.[4] This roused Edward II to action just as the rebel earls' forces threatened to link up: on 9 February he ordered Andrew Harcla, keeper of Carlisle, to negotiate with Bruce about a truce or peace.[5] Robert's extant dated acts resume after a gap since 20 October 1321 and place him on 22 February 1322 once more at Berwick where, in response to a further letter from Earl Thomas, he was preparing to meet Lancaster's envoys.[6] Robert's grants over the next month indeed suggest a man waiting upon events: half of the barony of Stewarton in Ayrshire to Sir William Moray for half a knight (26 February, Ayr); confirmation of the findings of an inquest into Jedburgh's rights in Restenneth Priory's holdings (1 March, Dundee, probably during an exchequer audit); and letters ordering Inverkeithing's officers to raise the aforementioned chaplaincy annual for Dunfermline Abbey (1 April, while still at Dundee).[7]

However, it was Harcla who shattered the Scots' hopes by choosing to muster his hobelars and fight rather than talk. On 16 March at Boroughbridge (while some Scottish raiders may still have been across the border) Harcla's forces routed the English rebel earls' army, killing Hereford and capturing Lancaster: Earl Thomas was executed a few days later and interred in what soon developed as a saintly martyr's grave despite King Edward's publication about 1 March of his captured correspondence with the Scots.[8] Over the following weeks the position of Edward and his close counsel, headed by Hugh Despenser the Younger (raised to be earl of Winchester), would be strengthened and a number of his remaining critics purged (although, unlike Robert in 1320, he did not use parliament as his first bench to condemn treason).[9] Edward also sought an immediate commitment to action against Bruce, whose written promises to aid the rebels in person in England, Wales and Ireland as required in return for support for an Anglo-Scottish peace had been found on Hereford's corpse: this indenture had stipulated that if Robert was ill, then Moray as his Lieutenant would still serve with Douglas and Steward.[10] Provoked by this alliance, as early as 25 March Edward II ordered a wildly ambitious muster of over 50,000 men for 13 June, to include over 7,000 Irish infantry and hobelars and over twenty support ships.[11]

In response, Robert's regime arguably seemed to pause, uncertain of how to recover its lost momentum. Only a handful of minor royal grants survive for the period to mid-May.[12] But on 18 May Robert can be located at Berwick again and with no truce/peace talks in the offing his purpose was surely the familiar tactic of pre-emptive border war. A striking six-month gap now interrupts his datable acts.[13] Subsequent events suggest much of the spring was spent supervising the defence of Berwick anew and the clearing of tenants, livestock, portable foodstuffs and chattels to south-eastern church sanctuary or, more likely, to safer ground in the great forest or north and east of Edinburgh. The same York parliament that revoked the Ordinances (2 May 1322) also postponed Edward's muster at Newcastle until 24 July.[14] This allowed the Scots to launch their natural response. According to the Lanercost scribe, about 17 June Bruce himself led a force into Cumberland, harrying the lands of the prelate with whom the Scots had recently talked peace, the bishop of Carlisle, and, tellingly, venting their frustrations over recent events by plundering the abbey which Robert had tried to win over in January 1321, Holm Cultram.[15] Pushing south he laid waste to Copeland, forcing the Cistercian abbey at Furness (which wielded considerable influence over the Isle of Man) to pay tribute and provide hospitality.[16] He then burned Lancaster town. The Scots' purpose there may have been to seize the late earl's cattle, no doubt to restock their own disease-ravaged herds, although the region's far larger sheep flocks may have been a more immediate target to replace lost milk and meat supplies.[17] Lanercost's account emphasises the large numbers of beasts that Robert's men drove off after linking up with forces under Moray and Douglas to push on to Preston, some 80 miles into England:

> and then all returned with many prisoners and cattle and much booty; so that on the vigil of St Margaret [of Antioch] Virgin [12 July] they came to Carlisle, and lay there in their tents around the town for five days, trampling and destroying as much of the crops as they could by themselves and their beasts.[18]

What historians often treated as a joke at Edward II's expense now reflects a far grimmer reality of this conflict and the harsh socio-economic background of the cattle plague. For having advanced north on 10 August 1322, Edward II's army – avoiding Berwick but perhaps intending to clear southeast Scotland and thus weaken that symbolic port's supply lines – reached the hinterland of the ruined castle at Edinburgh nine days later, completely unchallenged but poorly supplied. Robert had stripped the region of its harvest and withdrawn his host to Culross in Fife, leaving no defence for institutions like Holyrood Abbey which was reportedly sacked by Edward's troops.[19] Yet Barbour would later repeat the jibe that only one lame bull remained to be seized in Sir Alexander Seton's cornfields at Tranent, at which the earl of Surrey scoffed: 'Certis I dar say/This is the derrest best that I/Saw ever yeit, for sekyrly/It cost a thousand pound and mar.'[20]

Edward's army was by no means the massive host he had first summoned, but with ten earls (including the disinherited Atholl and Angus), 20,000 infantry, 1,250 heavy cavalry and 2,100 hobelars it was an even more formidable body than that of the Bannockburn campaign.[21] Robert thus reverted for the most part to his tactics of 1310 and only allowed his captains to attack as Edward withdrew in early September, his ranks starving. As English troops attempted to burn Melrose Abbey (killing the prior and vandalising the altar), its protector Douglas routed them and then the separate Scottish forces of King Robert, Moray and Douglas shadowed the enemy as they crossed south into Northumberland.[22] By 12 October the Scots' reading of the situation had encouraged them in an attempt to repeat their goal of 1314 and 1319, the capture of English royalty, this time either Edward II or his queen. In this they came very close indeed, with Moray and Douglas defeating Pembroke's contingent at Old Byland on 14 October (where the earl of Richmond and the visiting Butler of France, Sir Henry Sully, were captured) while Robert hovered at Northallerton.[23] Edward was forced to abandon his household goods once more and flee to York, leaving Queen Isabella to escape the encircling Scots by sea from Tynemouth (where her husband had just buried his illegitimate teenage son, Adam, who had perished on the Scottish campaign).[24] This was a third Scottish triumph over an English royal host that Robert's court could commemorate and which Barbour would insert into his narrative *before* his short account of Soules's dishonourable conspiracy.[25]

The Scots remained to plunder the East Riding of Yorkshire and then withdrew by Carlisle, pinning down Harcla's hobelars and reaching Scotland by All Souls' (2 November) 1322.[26] With Edward's escape, Robert surely did not expect English compromise or capitulation. This was confirmed as early as 2 December when a parliament at York agreed to a fresh muster (at York, not the exposed Newcastle) for 2 February 1323.[27] The chronology of subsequent events, however, suggests that Robert quickly dispatched envoys to Harcla at Carlisle while he resumed domestic affairs. The king seems to have used his return via the west March to visit troublesome Galloway and his own earldom of Carrick (perhaps receiving news from Ireland). On 24 November he was at the burgh of Innermessan in Wigtownshire, where he granted justice teinds during an anticipated episcopal vacancy in the bishopric of Galloway – where the incumbent, Thomas Dalton, remained an adherent of York – to the Premonstratensian cathedral priory at Whithorn, dedicated to St Martin (feast 11 November) and home to the body shrine of St Ninian.[28] The king had surely visited the priory en route, perhaps as an act of penitential pilgrimage: it may have been about this time that he granted Gilbert, archdeacon of Galloway (a man hitherto loyal to Bishop Thomas and York), the patronage of the Wigtownshire church of Kells (in the Glenken deanery) 'because of the damage, injury and oppression of the church of Whithorn, and especially to its archdeaconry, by his past wars, and because of the devotion he has to St Ninian'.[29] But this visit also allowed Robert to reaffirm his late brother's lordship in the Balliols' former heartland.

Given the tense situation on the Marches and his overtures to Harcla, it is indeed likely that Robert remained in the south, probably returning east from Galloway to Lochmaben.[30] Nevertheless, great seal inspections issued at Forfar on 1 December of founder King William I's great charters to Arbroath Abbey may represent a brief state visit to that church between the 'regressio de exilio' feast of Becket (2 December) and Christmas or Becket's main feast (25/29 December), during which a new tomb with an effigy for William (d.4 December 1214) made of Frosterley limestone from County Durham (perhaps acquired during the recent truce or raids) may have been dedicated.[31] However, this ceremony must have been concluded quickly. By 3 January 1323 Robert, acting through Moray, was able to conclude a mutual if conditional indenture with Andrew Harcla, now earl of Carlisle, sealed at Lochmaben 'to promote peace' between the separate realms of Scotland and England.[32]

Harcla's motives for risking an initiative 'on behalf of all those in England who wish to be spared and saved from war with Robert Bruce and all his followers', and which he promised to persuade King Edward to accept within a year, surely lie in the provisions that guarded against a repeat of the recent Scottish alliance with English rebels against Edward: this had resulted in attacks on those remaining loyal to the English king, with sustained assaults especially on Harcla's charge of Cumberland. Thus neither party to the indenture was to make any agreement with a third party to that effect. More generally, if Edward could not protect the northern counties from repeated Scottish attack, then the leaders of that region (sorely depleted by the events of 1322) must act alone.[33] The treaty ruled out the future annexation of territory in either realm but said nothing about the restoration of already occupied land: this was surely Robert's way of retaining control of the Isle of Man (at a time when Robert was also pressing for the appointment of his own candidate, Gilbert, as bishop of Sodor or the Western Isles). In addition, the treaty included a practical innovation in laying down a shared court system to settle March disputes overseen by twelve 'arbiters', six border lords chosen by each side. After over a decade of economic and material devastation at the hands of the Scots it is little wonder that Harcla felt this would be acceptable to other northern barons and communities.[34]

However, the indenture also betrayed Bruce concerns. For its terms stipulated that neither king, if peace followed, would be obliged to restore the lands and lordship of anyone in their realm who had fought against them. As we shall see, this would prove a highly controversial issue for Robert and the Scots in final peace negotiations with England in 1327–28. The apparently decisive line taken in 1323 surely reflected the Bruce Scots' recent experience in 1318–20 of the grave threat posed by Edward Balliol and the disinherited as well as the degree to which Robert's territorial resettlement had advanced since the foiling of that plot: but it did not rule out the restoration of cross-border landholding on a case-by-case basis, leaving hope for Scottish churches and individual noble houses in Robert's peace seeking to recover their English lands. The reported fury of Sir Henry Beaumont, denied his claim by marriage to the title and a share of the Comyn earldom of Buchan when Edward II did conclude a long truce with Bruce later in 1323, suggests that this point in January's draft peace originated as a Scottish demand.[35]

In that context, Robert saw the need to include some further induce-ments to persuade Edward to accept a Bruce dynasty in a sovereign Scotland as a partner in this peace (which Harcla may have begun to negotiate with the approval of the York parliament of November 1322).[36] The first, a promised payment of 40,000 merks (£26,667) over ten years, would be included (though reduced) in the eventual peace terms of 1328 and was intended as reparation for border raiding. It may not, though, have impressed Edward II whose coffers were remarkably full by 1323, holding over £90,000 as a result of the unused war subsidy granted in the previous year.[37] However, Robert's second promise, to allow the English king to determine the marriage of his 'heir male', was surely an even greater sign of the Bruce's pressing desire for closure. True, marriage was a conventional method of cementing peace and William I had offered his daughters' marriages in accords with England in 1209 and 1213.[38] Yet often sick as Robert I was and still without a son of his own, this clause in 1323 would have been applied to his grandson, the young Robert Stewart, but at this point it came with no written stipulation that this should lead to a royal match. By 1328, in the face of very different political circumstances in England, this term would have been sharpened into a Scottish demand that Robert's infant son and heir should marry an English princess.

The third carrot, that Robert would found a monastic house in Scotland worth 500 merks a year, would be dropped entirely from the 1328 peace talks (perhaps for fiscal reasons). Yet in 1323 such an offer may have represented a sincere gesture of penance on Robert's behalf, not just a means to retain the support of papal representatives or the hearts and minds of war-weary northern English lords.[39] We can only speculate, though, as to where and to which saint such a memorial would have been dedicated: presumably somewhere accessible on the Marches, perhaps to one or more of saints Thomas, Cuthbert, Ninian, John of Beverley or John the Baptist. One alternative possibility was a dedication to the unifying spiritual figure of St Kentigern, seventh-century evangelist of Strathclyde and Cumbria, following an apparent Anglo-Scottish compromise over the disputed election to the see of Glasgow arbitrated by the Papacy.[40] By 15 March 1323 it would be agreed that Edward II's candidate would be installed instead as bishop of Conor in Ireland and that John Lindsay, a cleric known to the English king before 1314 but Robert's man since then, would finally be confirmed as Kentigern's and Wishart's successor.[41]

Robert was not so naive as to believe that the package he had assembled with Harcla would actually turn Edward II to relinquish his father's claim to superiority over Scotland and give up hopes of revenge for his personal humiliations of 1314, 1319 and 1322. That Robert was, though, prepared to channel such offers to Edward through Harcla may also betray his awareness that Edward was finally close to shutting down a vital artery of wartime supply and mercenary naval support to the Scots, namely from Flanders. Indeed, the truce concluded on 5 April between Edward and a new Count of Flanders, Louis (grandson of Count Robert who had been so defiant in his support of the Scots), was as potentially damaging to Scottish trade and secret supply as had been Philip IV's threat to sever this economic lifeline to King John and the Scots in 1294–95.[42] Without a long truce or full peace treaty of his own with England, Robert would soon find it increasingly difficult to rely only on smuggling from Flanders and the Baltic realms, especially at a time when he hoped to reboot the economic fortunes of Berwick and Scotland's wool trade (a vital source of customs, the majority of Scottish royal income, indeed, which would likely have been assigned to pay the 40,000 merks of war damages and found a new monastery). This harsh reality surely goes a long way to explaining why, within a matter of weeks of his deal with Harcla, Robert was willing to settle for apparently a lot less.

It is possible, indeed, that Robert had also approached Edward II for an extended truce, drawing on the terms of the two-year ceasefire of 1319 and employing the captive French Grand Butler, Sir Henry Sully, as a go-between in an attempt to involve Charles IV of France who had acceded in February 1322 following the death of his brother, Philip V. These offers may thus pre-date Harcla's brutal fate, an outcome that must have shocked even King Robert. Arrested on 25 February, the earl of Carlisle was condemned for treason and executed on 1 March, with his head and limbs displayed in northern towns.[43] In the meantime, Robert had remained in the south-east of his realm.[44] On 1 February 1323 he was to be found at Berwick, where he was still in residence three weeks later to reply in writing to Sully.[45] The contents of this letter in French make it clear that Sully had already made trips back and forth between the kings and a short truce had been provisionally agreed (to last from 21 March until 22 May), to allow time for further talks. Robert insisted that 'we desired and desire always to negotiate peace with the king of England'. Yet he remained highly sensitive to his lack of royal title, complaining that 'there is no more reference made to us [as king] than to the meanest of our realm'. However, Robert's threat to refuse the truce without such a vital courtesy was just consistent posturing: his initial envoys – the knights Alexander Seton and William de Montefichet with Walter, archdeacon of Teviotdale – were ready to depart for Newcastle.[46]

It would require further short periods of provisional truce, 28 April–5 June, before an accord could be reached.[47] It is surely the case that during that time, the Scottish embassy – which grew to include Bishop Lamberton, Moray, Sir John Menteith and Sir Robert Lauder – did press, on Robert's instruction from Berwick, for discussion and acceptance of the drafted King Robert–Harcla peace or a variation of its terms.[48] But in the end it was Edward II's party, headed by Pembroke and the younger Hugh Despenser, who had the better of the negotiations. As such, these talks expose the fundamental weakness of Robert's position. Scotland and the northern English counties remained too far from Edward's political, economic and spiritual heartlands; as in Ireland, the Scots remained really incapable of capturing and holding a major English walled town or castle like Durham or Carlisle. Royal solvency and the fate of Lancaster and Hereford besides ensured that Edward II remained, for the moment, in the ascendant politically, of which an important part was his commitment to recover his father's conquest of the land, not kingdom, of Scotland.

Thus, England's peace with Flanders having already been concluded, on 30 May it was another Anglo-Scottish truce that was agreed at Bishopthorpe in Yorkshire, although this time to last for thirteen years, until 12 June 1336, and to survive the death of either King Edward or, tellingly, 'Robert de Brus'.[49] That this duration would see Edward II's eldest son and heir, Edward (b.1312), reach his full majority does seem to place the initiative with the English by contrast with the Scots' suggestions of early 1321.[50] Similarly, English copies of the truce also show that it was agreed Robert and his adherents might seek absolution from papal excommunication (hinting at why Robert's early proposals through Sully suggested papal confirmation), but only for the period of the truce if full peace were not subsequently concluded: Edward thus retained the ability to deny this pardon to the Scots.[51]

Robert also seems to have conceded that although neither side was to aid parties making war on the other, this would not apply to the Anglo-French treaty of 1303: although here he may have reasoned with good cause that Charles IV was more likely to fall out with his brother-in-law, Edward II, than help him in a war against Scotland. Otherwise, the truce terms agreed were predictable and familiar: occupied territory was to be restored (and this was perhaps intended to include the Isle of Man as an appurtenance of Edward's title as 'King of England and Ireland'); no castles were to be built on either side of the Marches, where noble guardians were to resolve disputes and control communication; and the rights of merchants and their cargoes were mutually guaranteed. It may have been accepted that 'because making peace will take time', such a long ceasefire was necessary to allow thorny issues to be broached at future summits. Nevertheless, there must have been an inescapable sense for Robert and the Scots that their years of military dominance, and Edward II's ability to create troubles of his own, had in the long run amounted to really very little at the bargaining table.

## The Birth of an Heir, May 1323–October 1324

That there was some understandable disappointment about aspects of the 30 May truce terms agreed with Edward II in 1323 may be reflected in the simple separation of their confirmation from Scottish domestic affairs. On 7 June at Berwick, Robert's letters patent recorded the outcome of the Bishopthorpe talks; three days later he was at Peebles on the road to Edinburgh, en route to Scone for a parliament summoned for the end of July.[52] However, no formal ratification of the truce is extant from this assembly; rather its focus seems to have been a resumption of Robert's landed resettlement and judicial oversight.[53]

Indeed, this gathering may have marked something of a watershed review of the progress of royal patronage thus far. This may have been undertaken both as an audit of loyalty and royal income from all quarters of the realm but also with a view now to committing resources to major rebuilding projects within a prolonged period of truce. The latter had arguably been anticipated when on 1 May, while still at Berwick, Robert had assigned the justice teinds from Galloway and Wigtownshire (between the rivers Cree and Nith) to Holyrood Abbey to assist its reconstruction following Edward II's assault in 1322.[54] However, this act may mask Robert's actual need to compensate Simon de Wedale, abbot of Holyrood, for delay in his advancement to be bishop of Galloway. Certainly, by 10 April 1323 officials in the archbishopric of York believed that Simon had been elected to this see against their right: but in truth Robert would have to wait for the death of the incumbent Thomas de Dalton (d.1326).[55] Such an allocation of royal income, though, linked the efficient administration of a region of traditional Balliol adherence to the well-being of a monastic house outside Edinburgh, the royal heartlands. In the extant Chamberlain's and sheriffs' accounts for 1327–28, we can find credible echoes of the structures and revenue streams largely in place by mid-1323.[56] Over the next few months Robert and his close counsel would turn to assert the royal writ in such parts of the realm necessarily neglected since 1318, particularly the west, south-west and north-east. The next four years, all told, would see the majority of Robert I's extant patronage issued.

That said, the surviving evidence suggests continued Crown caution, allowing local inquests to clarify matters of dispute. The surviving business of the July–August Scone parliament includes confirmation, after inquiry, that Dunfermline Abbey had recovered Perthshire lands originally granted to the house by an earl of Fife but subsequently leased to the Strathbogies as earls of Atholl, all of whose holdings had been forfeited to the Crown in November 1314. Significantly, however, this confirmation allowed Mary Bruce, the king's sister, to conclude a contract with Dunfermline Abbey to take up these lands in the name of her son, John Campbell.[57] This is our best evidence yet that the king had favoured this young nephew (and potential heir presumptive) to replace the Strathbogie Atholl earl, with Campbell kin and Mary's new husband, Chamberlain Sir Alexander Fraser, acting as guardians of Atholl lands in the meantime.[58]

This Campbell business was conducted in a parliament that gave considerable thought to the stability of the western approaches. From 26 July comes Robert's only extant confirmation of an act by his late brother, Edward, as 'king of Ireland', of Ayrshire lands to one of his knightly retinue.[59] On 28 July the king further rewarded (with West Lothian and Stirlingshire lands) Sir Walter Fitz Gilbert, the crucial defecting captain of

Bothwell in 1314, who had probably taken up a valuable castellan role in Clydeside in the following of Steward or Malcolm of Lennox, perhaps at Dumbarton.[60] The same day saw the king inspect Alexander II's charter of the burgh of Glasgow to its bishop and 'St Mungo' (Kentigern). That this original 1225 grant was recorded (in error) as being issued from 'Cardross' (rather than Cadzow) may indicate that Robert had already identified this riverbank land – probably originally a manor of the Crown or Glasgow see – as a suitable site for a royal residence with a defensive posture down the Clyde estuary to the west. To obtain Cardross for this purpose Robert would have to make an exchange with Sir David Graham.[61] However, most significant of all was Robert's grant of 1 August to Sir John Menteith of Arran and Knapdale, former sheriff of Dumbarton (or, more likely now, his namesake son and heir), of the lands of Glen Breackerie at the southern tip of Kintyre around Dunaverty castle (18 sea miles south, 9 miles off Ayr) and the Isle of Ailsa, all in return for the service of a twenty-six oared ship: this was an act witnessed by, among others, Murdoch of Menteith, appearing in the record for the first time as 'earl of Menteith'.[62] It may also have been about this time that John Menteith was granted the vast forfeited lordship of Strathgartney, north of Menteith and Lennox.[63]

Given what was to follow, this is a firm indication that the Bruces' former allies, the MacDonalds of Islay (who probably suffered their own disputed succession from 1318) and MacRuaridhs of Garmoran, were now viewed as a problem to be contained with naval power and not merely by way of enforcing the Anglo-Scottish truce across the Irish Sea.[64] This Scone parliament may also have authorised further building work at the isthmus castle of Tarbert in northern Kintyre (funded by a transfer of Buchan revenues) and allowed the king to extend favour further north along the Argyll coast to the wider Campbell family.[65] The extant account of the constable of Tarbert, John de Lany, for the period 1325–26, records provision of building materials and funds by Dugall Campbell (a son of Sir Neil of Lochawe's first marriage) as 'sheriff of Argyll' and 'baillie of Atholl'.[66] It may have been in 1321 (when two parliaments had been held) that the Crown had first moved to establish a separate sheriffship of Argyll with two regional constabularies, Dunoon and Dunstaffnage, and a sheriff's court and seat at Tarbert (abandoning Alexander III's and John I's plans to create three smaller jurisdictions in Kintyre, Lorn and Skye).[67] However, the evidence suggests that much of the consolidation of this shire really belonged to 1323–24, after the truce and when Robert was not distracted by war and diplomacy in the south. It may thus have been at the Scone parliament of summer 1323 that Sir Arthur Campbell was appointed constable of Dunstaffnage and granted further castles and lands at Benderloch (on the coast some 70 miles north of Tarbert), Ardstaffnage, Inverawe and elsewhere in Lorn, bluntly overturning Robert's earlier grants (c.1308–10) of Macdougall lands to Ruari MacRuaridh.[68] The late Neil Campbell's brother, Donald, was also perhaps in receipt of lands in Benderloch at this time: if so, this may have been a grant designed to allow him, his nephews and Sir Arthur and his sons to act on behalf of the king's grandson, Robert Stewart, who was probably granted the lordship of Kintyre at this turning point, thus further challenging MacDonald expansion.[69]

Such royal grants undoubtedly served to endorse aggressive local ambitions of lordship (and even internecine Campbell rivalries) already established since around 1318 by an extensive maritime network of Stewart–Menteith–Campbell kin and their allies, one that would be further encouraged in its expansion into former Macdougall and current MacRuaridh and MacDonald holdings on the west coast into 1324–25.[70] At this time, either as part of parliamentary proceedings or as simultaneous business, a pacifying concord was reached (3 August) between Dugall Campbell, sheriff of Argyll, and his namesake and cousin over income and church patronage in Kilmartin: a similar 'appointment' concluded between Walter Steward (on behalf of his son) and the 'barons of Argyll' may also belong to the time of this assembly or its aftermath.[71]

The remaining business of the 1323 Scone parliament may also have seen agreement that ambassadors be sent to Flanders, Paris and Avignon with briefs regarding trade access and the lifting of papal censures. Edward II certainly received a request from Robert about this time for safe conduct through England for forty knights and retinue, surely for Thomas Randolph, earl of Moray, who would be at Avignon by mid-January 1324.[72] Moreover, on 10 August, Robert I's letters would confirm the privileges of the merchants trading in Scotland on behalf of William, count of Hainault, Edward II's uneasy ally.[73] The Scots king and estates may also have authorised further justiciars' inquiries, for example into the lost, removed and damaged charters of Scone Abbey.[74] Moreover, this assembly may have seen a reissue of the December 1318 pardon extended to Bishop Henry Cheyne of Aberdeen, an act of assurance perhaps necessitated by the further dispersal of Atholl territory: the witnesses to this repeated remission (and further acts in August 1323) included Murdoch as earl of Menteith and Maurice, the former abbot of Bruce's favoured house of Inchaffray, but, since his consecration at Avignon in March 1322, now bishop of Dunblane.[75] Robert's domestic confidence is neatly illustrated by his recorded reply to the aforementioned appeal of Sir Alexander Baddeby, upset that the Marshalls had been granted half of his lands of Manor in Peeblesshire: 'he was still to hold himself content in the choice of the said Sir Alexander concerning the same grace and ordinance, or give sasine back to our said lord king of the said half granted to him, and our lord king will make full justice to him concerning his petition'.[76] Thus told to put up or shut up, Baddeby rested content. However, while all this spoke to a constructive beginning to what at least on paper promised to be a decade of rule uninterrupted by war, there may have been another reason for royal poise: Queen Elizabeth was again pregnant.

A very early sign that this was known may be the king's grant of 1 August 1323, while still at Scone, of lands to furnish bread, wine and wax for services for his soul and those of his ancestors and successors at a new chapel to the Virgin founded for the Carmelite Order in Banff, a region in which the queen had already shown a spiritual interest.[77] Normal business resumed with the king travelling to Kinross where he granted the royal thanage of Belhelvie, east of Garioch (worth £40 a year), to Sir Hugh Barclay (14 September) and the Kincardineshire lands of Auchincarnie to Chamberlain Sir Alexander Fraser (22 September).[78] Three royal grants survive from nearby Lochleven (23–25 September) with its priory dedicated to St Serf, including a grant of the burgh of Cromarty to the king's brother-in-law, 'Hugh of Ross', and relief for Aberdeen's burgesses from customs of ale and fish once Sir Walter Barclay stepped down as sheriff.[79] Robert's court then moved south via Kinross – granting afresh the lands in the forest of Drum in Aberdeenshire to Sir William Irvine on 4 October – most probably to take up a long, restful residence for the king and his pregnant queen at Dunfermline Abbey.[80] Royal nerves would have been quite understandable a few months into any term with child, but Robert's may have been especially strained if it was apparent that Elizabeth, at age thirty-five, was carrying more than one child.

As Robert had favoured the abbey and royal mausoleum very generously with forfeited lands and the right of a cocket seal in 1321–22, it is likely that Dunfermline had already begun the refurbishment of its refectory guest quarters: English complaints as early as May 1318 that the Scots were attempting to annex Coldingham Priory in Berwickshire to Dunfermline may also reflect royal attempts to aid the abbey's recovery further.[81] This would have allowed the royal couple to stay at Dunfermline in anticipation of another birth and thus to allow Elizabeth once more to wear St Margaret's 'birthing serk' relic. During their stay Robert would surely have had the opportunity to conduct the 'private arbitration' apparently required between Dunfermline Abbey and Maurice, bishop of Dunblane, over obedience due to the bishop for teind lands in Stirlingshire.[82] It may also have been about this time that Robert gave further serious thought to his own (and his wife's) funerary monument at Dunfermline (first announced in November 1314) as well as, perhaps, taking advantage of the truce to refresh the tombs of Alexander III and his ancestors with new uniform stones of Frosterley limestone from County Durham.[83] The court was present at Dunfermline over the feast of St Margaret (16 November), through Christmas and still there on 16 January 1324, when the king granted Sir Alexander Seton's home burgh a customs exemption and weekly market; and on 20 January when he awarded lands and a merchant guild to Ayr burgh to support royal household visits.[84]

However, the expectant father was taken north to Aberdeen between mid to late February and at least 8 April.[85] This journey must have been necessitated by some specific problem in the former Comyn-dominated north-east, perhaps provoked by attempts by the king's brother-in-law Sir Hugh Ross (who had succeeded his father, William, as earl of Ross after 28 January 1323) or Sir Adam Gordon to assert their new lordship in Buchan and Strathbogie respectively, or by unfinished business relating to Bishop Cheyne's reissued pardon.[86] While at Aberdeen, on 29 February the king granted the Aberdeenshire coastal barony of Crimond-Rattray and adjacent lands to Archibald Douglas, the brother of the good Sir James: that the recorded witnesses for this great seal act included Thomas Randolph, earl of the regality of Moray – who was then undeniably absent at Avignon – underlines the apparent need for an assertion of legitimate lordship and royal agency in this zone.[87] The slight possibility that this royal itinerary involved some display of force is also suggested by Robert's next-generation grant on 12 March of the office of royal standard-bearer and some of Roger Mowbray's forfeited lands at Inverkeithing in Fife to Nicholas Scrymgeour.[88] Then on 28 March the king granted an annual sum from Kincardineshire lands forfeited by John Comyn, earl of Buchan, and now resigned by Hugh, earl of Ross, to the exchequer clerk Thomas Charteris of Kinfauns (a possession of Scone Abbey), who would be charged with purchasing foreign luxuries for a royal wedding in 1328 and materials for Robert I's tomb in 1329, rising to be Chancellor for David II.[89] A last extant act on 8 April rounded out Robert's stay in the northern burgh with a grant of lands in Aberdeen itself for the prominent royalist Sir Alexander Seton.[90] But other key Crown men may have received further patronage in this region at this time: for example, Chamberlain Alexander Fraser, already installed in the royal thanage of Aboyne east of the earldom of Mar, may now have received the neighbouring western barony of Cluny (adjacent to the Leslie's barony of Cushnie).[91]

It must have been something of import or even danger that kept Robert in the north-east away from his queen at Dunfermline and still there when news reached him that must have been greeted with an overwhelming sense of relief, joy and God's blessing: the birth, at last, on Monday 5 March 1324, and in a leap year, not just of a single son and male heir, but of twin boys – an heir and a spare.[92]

History has lost sight of the child who was probably the elder of the two princes, christened John, as he would die an infant in 1326, and it has focused instead on the future boy king, David II.[93] He was surely named after a mixture of Dunfermline Abbey's saintly founder David I (who had held the northern English counties), his grandson (and William I's brother) Earl David of Huntingdon, through whom the Bruces claimed the throne, and the biblical King David (feast day 1 March). But much of the later reign of Robert's surviving son and successor, David, makes greater sense if John Bruce was indeed the older twin. The choice of 'John', which was not a Bruce family name, may represent a confluence of motives: celebration of the cult of St John the Baptist, on whose feast day (24 June) Robert I had enjoyed his greatest battle triumph; or homage to the current Pope, John XXII, before whom Moray was then engaged in overtures to secure an end to Robert's excommunication and mistitling (as well as, perhaps, to gain the full royal rite of unction and coronation). Yet in reality a preference for 'John' may have been expressed since even before Bannockburn as a means of further obliterating the kingship (1292–96) of John Balliol: for John Bruce would surely have reigned as 'John I'. An awareness of this priority may have encouraged noble kindreds close to the king – some of them also present on the battlefield in 1314 – to name their sons John, too: Randolph's second son, Hugh of Ross's second son by Maud Bruce, John Campbell of Atholl, Chamberlain Alexander Fraser's eldest son by Mary Bruce, even John MacDonald (the first 'Lord of the Isles' by 1336) and, further down the line, John Stewart of Kyle, Robert Stewart's eldest boy.[94] A ceremony of baptism at Dunfermline – a rite for an innocent permitted by the Papacy during interdict – provided another communal moment.[95]

The weeks after the birth of these royal heirs must have been characterised by an even greater dose of the anxiety that naturally accompanied the early life of any infant in the Middle Ages. However, the Easter venerations of Robert's court (15 April) may have been punctuated by a brief council called at Scone or even Berwick once more.[96] This might logically have received news of Moray's embassy to Avignon, sent while the earl lingered in France from where he could also convey intelligence about the rapid deterioration of Anglo-French relations. The latter followed the French Crown's claim to lordship over the Benedictine priory of St Sardos in Aquitaine and the violence of English officials' reply in October 1323.[97] Moray's approaches to John XXII in person had proven only partly successful (even though he had impressed the Pope by seeking an indult to visit the Holy Sepulchre in Jerusalem).[98] On 13 January 1324 the Pope had written to Edward II advising him that he would now style Bruce 'king of Scots' to ease the peace process, without prejudice to either realm: but although he had refused English petitions of 1322 for the spiritual censures upon the Scots to be increased, he showed no signs of absolving the excommunication.[99]

However, on 22 May 1324 a papal nuncio in London wrote to Avignon warning:

> he who acts as king of Scotland has held his solemn council in a certain castle called Berwick. Although what was discussed is not known, it is generally believed that if there should be war [between England and France], which God avert, Bruce will come to Charles IV's aid by every means in his power.[100]

Robert may have been happy to stoke this English fear of a two-front attack to see what peace concessions from Edward it might shake loose: he was in touch with Charles IV through Sir Henry Sully and other French captives from Old Byland whose release he had arranged without ransom.[101] But overall the Scots' commitment to truce, further diplomatic entreaties to Avignon and the prospect of peace talks with England held fast throughout 1324, surely now affirmed as the correct course after the birth of twin boys had given the Bruce dynasty promise of longevity. Indeed, all four of Robert's children by Elizabeth de Burgh held out possibilities to contract a range of strategic marriage alliances across the British Isles and Europe.

On 15 July Edward II granted safe conducts for Bishop Lamberton and Moray (with the latter to come from France) to attend peace talks in England.[102] However, once Edward's own emergency embassy to Paris proved unsuccessful and actual war broke out in Aquitaine in August, Anglo-Scottish negotiations would be postponed. Edward had already attempted to bring Edward Balliol back to England once more from Picardy before hostilities erupted; on 23 September a second (and now joint) passport for Lamberton and Moray (back in Scotland by late July) would be issued.[103] In the meantime, Robert can be located at the episcopal burgh of Glasgow around 10–12 June, probably for an exchequer audit. Most of the surviving royal grants issued about this time relate to this process, a number in particular touching on the temporality resources and diocesenal churches of the Glasgow see.[104] However, of greater moment was a royal act of 13 June granting to the 'captains and men of Galloway' the right under the laws of that county to judgment by a 'good and faithful assize' of their neighbours and thus exemption from the summary exactions of royal officers – namely *surdit de sergeaunt*, presumably the seizure of goods and chattels to cover obligations and debts alongside 'other burdens, aids, prises, tallages and contributions'.[105] This is surely a sign of a strong negative reaction on the ground to enforcement of justice and collection of revenues in this former Balliol lordship by Sir James Douglas and other officers but, crucially, one that did see the community of that region appeal for redress directly to Robert as king (just as it had appealed to Edward I's Westminster parliament in 1305); Robert responded sympathetically.[106]

Robert can be found at Stirling by 27 August 1324 and, perhaps, Arbroath by 6 September. On the latter date, his confirmation of Alexander II's grant of the church of Kilbride in Lorn (dedicated to St Brigit of Larne) to the diocese of Argyll may represent an attempt to win over Andrew, bishop of that see since 1300, hitherto in English allegiance but now named as present at Arbroath as grantee.[107] This undoubtedly sought to complement the extension of royal lordship into Argyll and the inner Hebrides through the Campbells and their allies. More generally, it was important that Robert win over the support of a rapidly aging Scottish episcopal bench (half of whom would die within what remained of the king's own lifetime down to June 1329), gaining control of important episcopal and allied benefice provisions from a Papacy that still regarded him as excommunicate and listened to English advice on Scotland's church vacancies and contributions to St Peter's Pence.[108] This goes some way to explaining why during the next round of Anglo-Scottish peace negotiations the Scots placed renewed emphasis on papal approval.

### Demanding Peace, November 1324–February 1325

Further safe conducts to York were granted to Bishop Lamberton and the earl of Moray on 3 November 1324 for talks a fortnight later.[109] Just as in 1321, the importance of these proceedings for Robert and his regime was reflected in his holding a simultaneous council at Berwick.[110] This began about 1 November and was marked, arguably, by intensive dispensation of patronage and justice, much of it apparently confirming in writing changes to, and the recovery of, landed lordship since circa 1318. From just the first week of residence at Berwick there survive grants of an annual sum to fund the rebuilding of the Carmelite friary in Aberdeen; to confirm Sir Robert Keith's hereditary office and numerous lands as Marischal with a tailzie to his grandson, Robert, and brother, Edward; and assignment of the customs of Inverness burgh to Thomas Randolph as earl of the regality of Moray.[111] However, the king's most substantial favour was directed on this occasion to Sir James Douglas in what must have been a moment of deliberate lordly theatre. On 8 November the king granted Douglas effective regality control of justice and freedom from Crown exactions throughout his lands in Douglasdale, the Selkirk and Jedburgh forests, Dumfriesshire and the constabulary of Lauder. This was a gift given in part as stated compensation for the loss of 4,400 merks (£2,933) estimated as the ransom of three additional French captives from Old Byland whom the king preferred to release unburdened: in return Douglas was to furnish the king with the token of a pair of spurs each year (in addition to the six knights' service he otherwise owed), but at the same time 'from our hand we personally invest the hand of James with a ring ... an emerald in token of the sasine to James and the heirs of his name'.[112] This generous display of favour may have marked an agreement between Douglas and his king over control and direction of revenues in the south to the further rebuilding of Berwick, now with its walls restored and perhaps functioning as a royal mint, as well as of Melrose Abbey and other southern monastic houses.[113]

Thus the atmosphere of this council seems to have been one of royal and communal self-assurance, buoyed by survival thus far of both the king's baby boys as well as by Edward II's predicament in France where his troops had had the worst of the six-week War of St Sardos and been forced to accept a six-month truce (to 14 April 1325).[114] These factors – along with a desire to overturn the bitter taste of the Scots' failed efforts to press home their diplomatic goals in talks with Edward's envoys in May 1323 – coalesced in a package of forceful Bruce demands when talks opened at York about 18 November 1324. Our only source for the substance of these exchanges is the contemporary *Vita Edwardi Secundi*. This chronicler's account of the Scots' conditions for peace and Edward's reported response should thus be treated with caution: most obviously, contrary to this narrative, Edward II was certainly not present at talks in northern England in person, remaining instead in the south to receive papal envoys sent to arbitrate over the tensions in Aquitaine.[115] However, this scribe (who stopped writing in 1325–26) may well have had access to these Anglo-Scottish exchanges and his report suggests that the Scottish delegation drew, as ever, on their archive of legal and historical material.

According to the *Vita*, Robert's offer of peace was prefaced by the warning that if only a truce prevailed then those of his subjects who had accepted the ceasefire 'reluctantly' would prefer to resume war, lest they become 'old', 'unmanly' and 'unwarlike', a hawkish enthusiasm for 'the fury of a violent throng', indeed, which seems best to fit the man just invested with his 'Emerald charter', James Douglas.[116] This was a ploy that later Scottish monarchs – from Robert II (r.1371–90) to James IV (r.1488–1513) – would use to excuse the aggression of their border lords (often in conjunction with alliance with France).[117] However, the *Vita* continues with what appears to be the Scots' actual list of points as presented by their envoys at York:

> The Scots demanded that Scotland should be for ever exempt and free from every exaction of the English kingdom; they demanded by right of conquest and lordship the whole land that they had traversed as far as the gates of York. There was also a certain barony in Essex which Robert Bruce had long ago forfeited on account of his rebellion; Robert demanded that this should be restored to him, with the profits, moreover, that the king had received from it in the meantime. The Scots also demanded that the royal stone should be returned to them, which the elder King Edward had long ago taken from Scotland and placed at Westminster by the tomb of St Edward ... To improve the treaty and strengthen the peace, Robert Bruce proposed that his daughter should be joined in marriage with the king's son. Finally, the Scots wished that, with all those concerned being present before the lord pope, the nobles' wishes should be confirmed by the king of France, so that the treaty of peace then agreed and strengthened by such authority, should never be broken.[118]

This was surely not all the Scots sought: for example, there is no mention of ending English obstruction of the lifting of papal censures or of recognising 'Robert I'; or of a principle tabled in 1323, that neither king be obliged to restore the lands of anyone who had fought against them. However, the insistence upon the return of the former Bruce patrimony at Writtle and Hatfield (those lordships closest to the shrine of St Thomas at Canterbury rather than the family's more valuable holdings in Yorkshire) did point to a willingness to seek selective restoration of cross-border land-holding.[119] The insistence upon the return of the Stone of Scone and the suggestion, this time, of an explicitly *royal* marriage between Robert's daughter and Edward II's son were also consistent developments of the terms of 1323 and anticipated those of 1328, just as the need for Scotland to be free from every English exaction, i.e. 'free and quit', as a sovereign realm was always Robert's priority.

Moreover, if truthfully reported, through these talks the Scots clearly attempted to exploit current Anglo-French tensions to exact a good price for their neutrality. The insistence upon ratifying any peace in the presence of the French king (and then the Pope, or his representatives then in Westminster and Paris) was a term that would place a Scottish settlement under the oversight of Edward II's superior for Gascony, Ponthieu and the Agenais. It was offered in the same month in which the English king and his council were trying amidst increasing anxiety to prolong the recent six-month truce in those French holdings and to assure Charles IV of a commitment to do homage for these lands (by 1 November 1325 at the latest). In this context, the Scots' stipulation that Robert's daughter (Margaret) should marry Prince Edward of Chester may have sought to stir up these bubbling tensions by tabling an alternative to Edward II's offer of September 1324 to James II of Aragon to make an alliance (directed against Charles IV) based upon the marriage of his son to a daughter of Aragon. Both Edward and Charles had certainly set in train large-scale musters for war for the following spring.[120]

It is, though, the aggressive demand for annexation by 'right of conquest' of all northern English lands 'traversed as far as the gates of York' that has stretched modern historians' acceptance of these terms. Such a demand to annex what might have amounted to Northumberland, County Durham, Cumberland, Westmorland, the Yorkshire Ridings and the Duchy of Lancaster was surely designed by the Scots to provoke rejection, justifying a resumption of war.[121] However, given the contemporary context, this may be the Scots' attempt to mirror Charles IV's insistence that he should continue to hold territory occupied (the Agenais) during the brief conflict of 1324. Alternatively, this term as reported might be a deliberate distortion by the *Vita* (which was consistently critical of Edward II) of the aggressive opening stance of Robert's envoys on an issue that in fact had more to do with ecclesiastical jurisdiction. For the reference to 'the gates of York' may point to the desire of Robert and his ministers finally to refute the archbishopric of York's hold over the dioceses of Wigtown/Galloway and the Isles/Sodor (while he also retained lordship of the latter's diocesenal centre of the Isle of Man) as well as to overturn English opposition to Scottish petitions in general at the curia.

That this was central to Robert's strategy is suggested by five further royal grants issued during his parallel council at Berwick in late 1324. The first three, of 12 December, were inspections of royal charters to the border abbey of Jedburgh by David I, his son Earl Henry of Northumbria, and Alexander II, and make mention of that house's rights in northern English lands from periods of Anglo-Scottish amity, cross-border landholding and royal intermarriage.[122] The fourth, on 20 December, saw the king grant the lordship of the Isle of Man afresh to Thomas Randolph.[123] Significantly, amongst the witnesses recorded for all these acts was, for the first time under Robert I, 'Gilbert [MacLelan] bishop of [the Isles/]Sodor [and Man]'. A Galloway man, but now apparently loyal to Robert, Gilbert had been confirmed in the see sometime after the death of his predecessor, the Durham adherent Alan of Galloway, in February 1322.[124] This provision and others, discussed below, may reflect John XXII's growing willingness, expressed to Edward II in 1323–24 after the conclusion of the long Bishopthorpe truce, to accept the election of Scottish rather than English clerics to Scottish benefices so as to ensure genuine care for Scottish souls, all the while encouraging a full Anglo-Scottish peace.[125] Thus, in December 1324, just two months after the first extant record of Andrew, bishop of Argyll, appearing at Robert's court, the bishop of the Isles/Sodor also recognised the legitimacy of Bruce kingship over the Anglo-Scottish Marches, south-west Scotland and the Western Isles: tellingly, both Bishops Alan and Gilbert (d.1327) would be buried not at Peel Cathedral on the Isle of Man but in St Mary's church on Rothesay, a Stewart lordship, just as the Argyll diocese saw a probable shift of its administrative centre to the Stewart caput of Dunoon.[126]

Finally, a fifth act, held over for processing by Chancellor Bernard until 20 May 1325 at Arbroath but bearing a very similar witness list to those issued during the late 1324 council at Berwick (including the bishop of Sodor), saw Robert confirm Whithorn Cathedral Priory in all its lands and resources, with particular emphasis on its gifts from Edward Bruce as late lord of Galloway and Randolph as lord of Annandale.[127] By this point, Thomas de Dalton, the aged original Bruce placeman as bishop of Galloway of 1293–94, was probably incapable of office or still in exile in the see of York: as we have seen, in November 1322 Robert had already begun to arrange for the disposition of Galloway's temporalities during an antici-pated vacancy.[128] Therefore, in late 1324 all three dioceses, Argyll, Sodor and Galloway, the latter two hitherto controlled by Edward II through York, had been targeted by Robert I. This rounded out a period of consid-erable success since 1322 for the Bruce regime in securing the election of its candidates to Scottish dioceses (Dunblane, Sodor, Glasgow and Galloway). In this we can surely detect the guiding hands of Bishop Lamberton and Chancellor Bernard (who would himself become bishop of

Sodor in 1328). Little wonder that in 1322 the English delegation to the Papacy had complained that 'it is the prelates of Scotland who encourage the nobility, gentry and people in their evil acts'.[129]

Whatever the Scottish envoys intended at York the sticking point, as ever, remained Edward II's refusal to compromise over what he maintained as the historical superiority of his Crown. According to the *Vita*, the English king felt that 'the Scots have come not to draw us towards a peace but to seek opportunities for further discord and for unprovoked breaches of the truce'. Although he was reportedly willing to return the inauguration stone from Westminster and at least 'at present' could not agree to the marriage suggested, he refused point blank to concede restoration of Bruce lands forfeited by Edward I or the Scots' claim to have won the Anglo-Scottish March 'by perambulation'.[130] His rejection of the Scots' terms saw an end to the talks in December without apparent agreement on a continuation at a later date: but the truce would be observed.[131]

For the moment, Robert may have been content with this predictable answer. He had set out his stall to the English king far more forcefully than in 1323 and remained prepared to wait upon events. No formal record of the proceedings of the Berwick council of November–December 1324 survives. But the witnesses to Robert's charters there were arguably the strongest and most widely representative of his reign to date. In addition to the aforementioned acts, on 20 December he had also confirmed by way of 'renewal' Randolph's regality of Moray, delineating its bounds from Badenoch, Buchan, Glencarnie and Kincardine, north and west to Ross and down the Great Glen to enclose Lochaber.[132] The inclusion of the latter lordship, of course, confirmed Robert's disregard or annulment of his grant of Lochaber, perhaps as early as the battle of Ben Cruachan (1308), to the MacDonalds of Islay. The witnesses to this 1324 grant of the largest physical lordship of Robert's reign were recorded as the bishops of St Andrews, Dunkeld, Aberdeen, Moray and Sodor; the earls of Fife, Dunbar (now married to Thomas Randolph's daughter Agnes), Strathearn and Ross; Walter Steward, James Douglas and Gilbert Hay.[133] Additional witnesses to Berwick acts included royalist knights Malcolm, earl of Lennox, Alexander Seton, Alexander Menzies of Fortingall, Henry Sinclair and Justiciar Robert Lauder. Then on 26 December the king also reissued Robert Keith's charter and tailzie of his hereditary office as Marischal, naming his grandson, Robert, then brother, Edward, and entailing lands in East Lothian, Lanarkshire and Aberdeenshire.[134]

Drawing strength from this assembly in his rebuilt principal market burgh, Robert may have remained at Berwick until early March in the knowledge that a parliament had been called (with council business continued) to Scone for the end of that month.[135] Significantly, on 24 February he granted James, lord Douglas, the former Balliol caput lordship of Buittle in Kirkudbrightshire (Galloway) with further exemption from exactions and as a quasi-regality (excluding only 'the pleas of the crown' – murder, treason, rape, arson and serious robbery).[136] Together, Robert's favour at Berwick to Randolph, Douglas and Keith represented a designation of office to men expected to play a crucial role in raising the king's sons: i.e. Randolph then Douglas as future Guardians, and Robert Keith (in the end, the grandson) as royal tutor in arms.[137]

That mortality, succession and family were on Robert I's mind at this time is certainly suggested by his grant of 20 November 1324 to the head of his hereditary family of Gaelic doctors, 'Gille Pàdraig' Beaton, 'chief physician of the king', of lands in Forfarshire, Carrick and Wigtown.[138] The loss of Robert's exchequer rolls before 1327 may mask the dispensing throughout this period of medicines for Robert's chronic and recurrent condition as well as long periods of convalescence: this may point to a far greater role in determining policy for Thomas Randolph and other magnates from around 1324–25 (or even earlier).[139] Robert's grant to Pàdraig had also stipulated the provision to the royal household of a surgeon-physician. Moreover, on 31 December the king granted an annual sum to support masses for the soul of his late brother-in-law, the English knight Sir Christopher Seton (d.1307), at the chapel of the Holy Cross founded in his honour by his widow, Christina Bruce.[140] Finally, about 10–12 January 1325, in his last extant act from this stay in Berwick, Robert granted Thomas Randolph the forfeited barony of Aberdour in Fife; the king's nephew would assign the revenues of this land to Dunfermline Abbey to pay for lights around his own planned tomb in the abbey choir on three great festivals each year: Christmas, Candlemas (2 February) and the Assumption of the Virgin (15 August).[141]

### 'Gifts and transfers', 1325

No record of formal proceedings survives for the Scone parliament in the last week in March 1325, but this assembly continued the Berwick council's mood of royal assertiveness. Probably beginning the day after the Annunciation feast of the Virgin, the anniversary of Robert's elevation to the throne, the estates may have discussed a wide range of weighty issues, including Anglo-Scottish and Franco-Scottish relations, what to do in the wake of the stalled peace talks, law and order, and royal finance. Only two dated royal grants survive from this occasion. The first, on 26 March, witnessed the king's assignment of £2,000 worth of Roxburghshire feudal casualties – to be collected and accounted for by his chief agent in the Marches, James, lord Douglas – for the fabric 'being constructed anew' of Melrose Abbey, the house where Robert would request the interment of his heart at death in search of indulgences and prayers for his soul and those of his ancestors and successors.[142]

However, together with other recent alienations of royal income to support burghal and ecclesiastical rebuilding projects, as well as patronage of the nobility, this grant may also have prompted initial discussions about the possible necessity in the near future of an extraordinary subsidy levied on the realm to support the king's household and government. This potentially controversial innovation would result in a grant of tax in a parliament just over a year later.[143] Increased customs rates on particular commodities such as wool and hides might also have been authorised in March 1325 in this context.[144] But such fiscal pressures may already have determined the advance gathering of a Scottish Church Council at Scone circa 21–22 March 1325, chaired by Bishop Sinclair of Dunkeld as 'Conservator'. The fragments of known business of this assembly included something of a test-case precedent, a formal acknowledgement from John Lindsay, now bishop of Glasgow, that the Crown had the right to collect and dispense the temporalities of his (and thus any Scottish) see right up to the moment at which a vacancy was filled (i.e. while an incoming prelate remained an unconsecrated 'bishop-elect'). This was undoubtedly linked to growing pressure from the king and his clerical advisors to be able to determine the choice of new prelates and their chapter officers in the face of English opposition at the curia, as well as to maximise vacancy revenues.[145]

All these points can be related to the financial support of the estates, which may also have been required to underwrite the decision to send a substantial embassy to Paris to seek an alliance with Charles IV, a treaty that would also be ratified just before the parliament of July–August 1326.[146] It is probable that the detail of what would be sought from the French was determined in subsequent close counsel between the king and his nearest advisors: certainly Robert's letters of procuration for Thomas Randolph, Robert Keith and a trio of experienced clerical envoys from Lamberton's diocese – James Ben, archdeacon of St Andrews, Adam de Moravia, rector of Kilmany (Fife) and Walter de Twynham, canon of Glasgow – were issued three weeks later, on 20 April, through the chancery at Dundee.[147] By that juncture it must certainly have been known to the Scots that by around 20 March Edward II had followed the advice of papal arbitrators and his own council, to send his queen, Isabella, to negotiate peace with her brother, Charles IV.[148] Nevertheless, demands for a swift agreement on Edward II's homage and French retention of occupied Gascon lands seemed to make renewed conflict unavoidable. On 9 April, just five days before the Gascon truce was set to end, officials in Bordeaux reported back to England that in the event of war 'they say the Scots would come upon the English, if they saw their advantage'.[149] Events in early 1327 would confirm that the Scots would be willing to break their long truce with England when circumstances were advantageous, and this would surely also have applied in 1325. But by offering an alliance to Charles IV at a time when that king might quite soon need support against a league between England, Aragon/Castile and Flanders, the Scots might at least in turn create an opportunity to force Edward II to buy them off with a full peace settlement, even if in the end papal arbitration prevailed on the continent.

A Scottish presence in Paris at the same time as Isabella's visit served to keep the Scots informed. It is likely that the envoys' brief was soon expanded to include travel on to Avignon to confirm a Scottish election to the bishopric of Ross (after the death of the aged Thomas de Dundee by 17 April 1325) and to resume efforts to lift Robert's excommunication and the general interdict upon the realm.[150] It was also at this time that efforts led since circa 1313 by David de Moravia, bishop of Moray, culminated in an endowment to support a handful of Scottish students within the 'English-German nation' at the University of Paris, the seed of a later Scots college.[151] However, although provision of another St Andrews cleric, Roger de Ballinbreich, had been made to the Ross vacancy by 19 May, John XXII's attitude seems to have cooled (with Edward's agents playing up the Scots' recent provocative terms for peace), and the excommunication of Robert and the interdict upon Scotland would be officially confirmed before the arrival of Randolph and company at the curia.[152]

Yet before these diplomatic developments unfolded, Robert's Lenten Scone parliament had also dealt with difficult matters of lordship. On 27 March the king granted the Banffshire barony of Deskford (adjacent to land already awarded to Murdoch of Menteith, at Rothiemay, and Hugh, earl of Ross, at Findlater), to Sir Christian del Ard/of the Aird, the lordship between Urquhart and Cromarty on the Moray Firth.[153] That the recorded witnesses to this act included the earls of Moray (absent) and Ross underlines its relevance of northern personnel to the only other identifiable item of business conducted by king and estates at Scone, the forfeiture of Ranald ('Roderick') MacRuaridh of his lands of Garmoran in Argyll.[154]

This penalty most likely followed Christina MacRuaridh of the Western Isles's undated grant (c.1321/24) of Moidart, Arisaig, Morar, Eig, Rum, Eilean Tioram and other castle-islands to Sir Arthur Campbell's son and heir, also Arthur. It consequently disinherited her nephew, Ranald, of a substantial part of the inheritance that Robert I had perhaps arranged and certainly confirmed and strengthened around 1308–10 for her brother, Ranald's father, Ruaridh.[155] It was surely Ranald's armed reaction to this Campbell acquisition that justified his forfeiture in 1325. That this was a change of lordship largely endorsed by the Crown is suggested, first, by the witness list to Christina's grant of these lands in return, it should be noted, for the service of a twenty-oar ship for the royal host: namely, Sir John Menteith, Donald and Duncan Campbell, Alexander McNaughton and Neil and Donald MacLean. The network of Stewart–Menteith–Campbell maritime and military power throughout Argyll had grown rapidly since around 1321. This was thus an assertion of lordship and Crown agency underpinned on the ground by the services of men such as McNaughton, who would receive a grant of Western Isles lands from David II, and the MacLeans, who would maintain Tarbert and other strongholds in northern Argyll.[156]

However, at some point in 1325 this parliamentary forfeiture and Campbell presence would be reinforced by a visit to Tarbert by the king himself (recorded without date by castle-keeper John de Lany), accompanied by Sir James Douglas and the bishop of St Andrews.[157] This journey was surely launched by royal galley from Cardross in Dumbartonshire where the king seems now to have begun in earnest the building of a new manor house. Edward II's critics often attacked his unkingly 'idling and applying himself to making ditches and digging and other improper occupations', such as rowing a boat.[158] Yet at Cardross, too, Robert I indulged himself in commissioning a personal project that required the digging of ditches, substantial building works and the employment of a large household staff. The extant chamberlain's accounts for 1328 detail a structure at Cardross with king's and queen's chambers and glazed windows, a chapel, kitchens, bake- and brew-houses, falcon aviary, (medicinal) garden, gatehouse, protective moat and a hunting park. There was also a jetty and beaching area for the 'king's coble' (for fishing) alongside the 'king's great ship' (as well as Sir Thomas Randolph's 'ships') which would also be re-rigged at Tarbert in 1328–29.[159] As well as adding to the extensive sea-castle and galley power arrayed around the Clyde and Western Isles by the Crown's adherents, these vessels and ports may have provided access to her Irish homeland for Queen Elizabeth, for example, on the death of her father, Earl Richard, in 1326.[160] Moreover, while most of the mainland's major royal castles had remained in their razed state since around 1313–14, Cardross manor was perhaps a modest residence sympathetic to Scottish subjects' privations through a long war, repeated famines and livestock pandemics.[161] Until Cardross was habitable in 1327, Robert's main residence was at Scone Abbey.[162]

Robert would make an official exchange of the lands at Cardross for those of Old Montrose in Angus with Sir David Graham in March 1326. But his extant charters place him at Cardross on three occasions in 1325 – 12 May, 18 June and 11 July: this suggests a passage to Tarbert in the first half of the summer.[163] Robert presumably felt it best to settle Argyll with his presence at this time rather than linger in the south-east for further diplomatic news, as by the end of May it appeared that an Anglo-French war had been averted with Edward II agreeing to do homage for Gascony (by 15 August), pay a war indemnity and allow Charles to retain occupied lands.[164] If so, this was to be Robert's first visit to the west beyond the Clyde since 1315 and may have sent a definitive signal, too, to Angus Og MacDonald and his heir, John, that the Crown and its Gaelic-speaking Stewart, Campbell and Ross in-laws were determined to redraw the map of lordship in that quarter. There is no evidence extant of violence in the north-west or Argyll during the remainder of Robert's reign. The MacDonald's caput of Islay in fact supplied Tarbert with horses and victuals during this period, and Dougal Campbell was able to intromit (through Tarbert) some £56 13s 4d as sheriff of Argyll in 1326.[165] However, as we shall see, the native kindred of these regions resisted royal exactions down to 1328–29 and beyond. In that context, some of the tensions that would lead to John MacDonald assuming the title of *Rí Innse Gall*, 'Lord of the Isles', by 1336 and then forging an alliance with Edward III and Edward Balliol, must lie in the Crown's policies of the 1320s. In the longer term this was a rift that would necessitate the Bruce regime's acceptance of restoration of, first, Ranald MacRuaridh (until his murder by William, earl of Ross, in 1346), and then, remarkably, in the 1350s, the Macdougalls of Argyll.[166] Often presented as part of a violent 'resurgence' of Gaelic lordship in the north and west (akin to tensions in Ireland and Wales at this time), these developments are rather to be seen as the consequences of the western lordship rivalries and power vacuums of circa 1296–1310, played out on a larger stage.[167]

The Scone parliament of March 1325 thus set in train a number of policy initiatives against the background of Robert's established administration. During his time in the west, the king's extant grants included a

5-merk annuity from the Crown's mills of Libberton (West Lothian) for the Blackfriars of Edinburgh ('for the souls of the king and his predecessors'); a charter of the lands of Cairnie in Aberdeenshire for Chamberlain Fraser; and lands in Thornton, Angus, for barber Richard Young for the service of an archer.[168] In Robert's absence, Chancellor Bernard also processed a further grant of the Angus demesne lands, this time of the thanage of Aberlemno to Sir William Blount, for two archers' service; the aforementioned confirmation of Whithorn Priory's holdings; a charter of the barony of Cessford, Roxburghshire, to Sir William Sinclair of Herdmanstoun for four archers' service; an inquest into the market liberties of the burgesses of Dundee (conducted by a convention of the royal burghs held at Dundee circa 22–25 June before the Chancellor and Chamberlain); and an inquest into the royal park at Fyvie (Aberdeenshire) with the rights of Arbroath Abbey and the bishop of Moray's burgh of Fyvie therein.[169]

Given that William Blount's grant also concerned landed bounds carefully identified by inquest, it is tempting to date to this period much of the Crown's further redistribution of lands in and around the forfeited Umfraville earldom of Angus in Forfarshire (at a time when John Stewart of Bonkle, who would certainly be earl of Angus by 1328, perhaps remained a legal minor). Blount was of a landed/mercantile/clerkly family in Angus, the brother (or son) of the 'Sir Stephen Blount' who had served Edward II in Dundee to 1312, escorted the 'Lady de Bruys' (Elizabeth de Burgh) north in 1314–15, then become deputy-chamberlain for the English regime in Scotland (1315), supported by his presentation to a Berwickshire benefice (1317), but reduced to the role of storekeeper at Newcastle by 1318–19; William may only have entered Robert's peace after the treaty with Harcla in 1323.[170] Thus Blount's recovery of his lands in 1325 may have been accompanied by further (now undated) royal grants in Forfarshire to Isabel of Atholl and 'nepoti nostro', Alexander Bruce (in Tannadice), as well as to the king's natural son Robert Bruce (Fothnevin) and a number of other lesser barons of that shire.[171] Sir John Menteith junior (sheriff of Kincardine) also seems to have had his holdings in Angus and neighbouring Kincardineshire enhanced, including lands in the baronies of Cortachy (resigned by Malise, earl of Strathearn, and which lay between the main detached portions of the Angus earldom) and Arbuthnot: the latter, tellingly, were granted by the king 'by [exchange] of some lands in Argyll'.[172] An undated grant to Sir Donald Campbell (the late Sir Neil's brother) of half of the coastal Forfarshire barony of Red Castle, forfeited by the Umfravilles and Sir Henry Percy, may also date to this period.[173]

Robert's extant acts resume on 12 October 1325 at Scone, where he confirmed Ayrshire lands to Sir William Oliphant of Dupplin and Aberdalgie, cousin of the Balliol keeper of Stirling in 1304 (who had died c.1313), and to whom the king had already awarded the Angus barony of Newtyle and Kinpurney in 1317.[174] Along with further grants including one of March 1326 of Newtyle lands (Auchtertyre), forfeited by 'John Comyn of Bretherton', and Sir William's appointment by 1329 as a 'king's escheator', this confirmed the Oliphants' rehabilitation under the Bruce regime.[175] However, Robert's residence at Scone at this time may have reflected estates' business carried forward from March. On 20 October the king confirmed lands in Dundee, resigned by Chamberlain Alexander Fraser, as a plot for the burgh to build a new tollbooth and prison, facilities that were no doubt expected to serve for royal exchequer audits prompted by the growing complexity of royal finance and talk of the need for a subsidy.[176] Word must also have been received by autumn of the progress of the embassy of Moray and Keith, present in Paris in June and Avignon by 1 October. Further instructions may have been dispatched in regard to the terms under consideration for alliance with Charles IV and efforts to lift papal excommunication. But some slowing of this diplomacy may have been unavoidable as much of north-western Europe hung fire while Edward II stalled and then sen is son to do homage at Vincennes as duke of Aquitaine (on 24 September), yet became increasingly frantic when thereafter Queen Isabella refused to return to England with the prince and heir.[177]

With these matters pending (and perhaps carried forward once more to March 1326), Robert travelled south to Melrose Abbey by 1 November.[178] This may have been part of a wider circuit of the south-east at this time, inspecting defences in case an Anglo-French war resumed and the Scots had to fight once more to press for a full peace settlement. In January 1326 Edward II's government in southern England succumbed to its usual worries about being 'troubled by the Scots', although northern lords reported that 'the Scots are peaceful, and wish to preserve the truce, as most people say'.[179] Yet even without a threat of conflict, it is possible that – ignoring acts that reflected the itinerary of Chancellor Bernard – King Robert remained at the great border abbey and Scottish Cistercian mother house through Christmas, from where he authorised what may have been a highly personal as well as political act of spiritual patronage. For on 10 January 1326 the chancery would issue the king's charter of a very generous annuity of £100 from the fermes or 'new custom' of Berwick (and 'if necessary' Edinburgh and Haddington, suggesting, indeed, a raising of tariffs on foreign merchants' exports of Scottish wool, woolfells and hides in the estates' assemblies of March or October 1325).[180] This grant was to pay for a daily 'king's dish' of 'rice in almond or pea-water' for all of Melrose's fifty or so monks, or as paupers' pittances if unconsumed; the house was also to clothe and shoe fifteen paupers each year.[181]

This charitable gift, linking one of Scotland's wealthiest monastic houses, most recently recovered from English control, to its counterpart burgh and economic hub, Berwick, might simply be interpreted as a statement of lord-ship.[182] It reaffirmed the full recovery of an independent Scottish kingship and socio-economic ties exemplified by the importance of both Melrose and Berwick to Scotland's wool trade (and thus to the Crown's income from customs). Moreover, this grant may also have commemorated Robert's decision – for these same territorial and political as well as personal reasons – to bequeath his heart for separate burial at Melrose.[183] Although prohibited by a bull of Boniface VIII of 1299, the division of the body with separate burials of corpse, heart and entrails with different churches and orders remained a popular strategy for elite patrons throughout medieval Europe to multiply the votive masses that would speed their soul through Purgatory to Heaven.[184]

However, the specificity of an expensive pottage of rice in almond milk (suitable for fast days as an alternative to meat and dairy products) may also have had a medicinal motive. Generally accepted as an excellent stomach-settler for intestinal complaints, this alms meal may reflect medical treatment provided to the king at Melrose at this time, necessitated by his ongoing and debilitating health complaints. Rice was an expensive import, usually through northern Italy (just as the ledgers of contemporary wool merchants from that region testify to the importance of Melrose's sheep herds and wool stocks).[185] Thus this treatment may also represent Robert's first contact with the medical and dietary advice of a newly graduated doctor of medicine of Paris University, Maino de Maineri (c.1295–1368), a Milanese (i.e. from the region held to be the first cultivator of rice in Europe). Sometime after April 1326, Maineri left Paris to take up residence in Scotland as surgeon-physician to the king.[186] His introduction to the ailing monarch may, though, have come through collegiate contact with the large body of Scottish students (and staff) at the University of Paris, or through the Moray/Keith embassy to Paris of 1325, and begun with consultation and suggested treatments by correspondence.[187] The extant exchequer rolls for 1327–29, as well as attesting to the presence of Maineri as a guest in the house of the Perth burgess John Aylebot, also record regular payments for the import of large quantities of rice and almonds, although both were also delicacies of court and feast.[188] It should be noted, though, that medical treatment and regimen advice may also have been sought in early 1326 for John Bruce, Robert's eldest son, or perhaps Queen Elizabeth or even Walter Steward, all of whom would pass away within the next eighteen months. Nevertheless, some community awareness that Robert I, too, was terminally ill and that his reign was drawing to a close may now have been inescapable.

# CHAPTER TEN

# Dead Reckoning

## Peace and Piety, 1326–28

*This year [1327] also there was fertility and plenty everywhere in the abundance of all products of the earth and foodstuffs, more so than in the memory of those then alive.*

Abbot Walter Bower's *Scotichronicon*[1]

### A Seminal Year, 1326

A prolonged stay at Melrose Abbey for an ailing king is a compelling vignette, but the royal court in fact may have spent much of the winter and into spring of 1325–26 at Scone. Robert's dated acts of 14 and 29 December 1325 both sprang from an inquest to reconstitute the lost charters and rights of Scone Abbey.[2] The king was certainly there by 16 January 1326 when he appropriated the Dumbartonshire church of Kilmarnock to Cambuskenneth Abbey (perhaps in compensation for his decision to bury his heart, instead, at Melrose Abbey).[3] A larger court certainly gathered between 1 and 5 March (around his twin sons' birthday), during which the king's extant acts included an inspection of Malcolm IV's charter of 1163–64 to Scone Abbey of all its possessions and the conclusion of Robert's dealings with Sir David Graham over Cardross: the bishops of Dunkeld and Dunblane, the abbots of Coupar-Angus and Dunfermline, the earls of Fife, Strathearn, Dunbar and Ross, knights Henry Sinclair, William Oliphant, David Barclay and the king's natural son, Robert, can be added to the otherwise regular household witnesses.[4] Just as the king favoured Coupar-Angus Abbey with its new fishings while at Scone, he may also have granted some of these men further favour.[5] For example, Sinclair had already been well rewarded between 1316 and 1321 with Lothian lands and offices as baillie of Caithness and keeper of royal forests north of the Forth, to which the king added Invernessshire lands sometime before granting this knight a 40-merk pension in December 1328 (in lieu of further lands);[6] on 20 March, Oliphant received Auchtertyre in Angus for three archers' service;[7] Barclay, sheriff of Fife, had received lands in Glenesk, Perthshire, forfeited by David de Brechin, and would soon become steward of the royal princes' household;[8] Robert Bruce (the son) may have received Sir Alexander Abernethy's forfeited Perthshire lands and a hostillage in Scone about this time, and by 1327–28 would be in receipt of a very generous (and perhaps controversial) royal pension of £500 each year.[9] Finally, the attendance at court in Scone of Robert de Crail, abbot of Dunfermline, may have seen the agenda and tactics prepared for a general chapter meeting of the Benedictine Order in Scotland, which would be held at Dunfermline Abbey in October.

That this Lenten Scone gathering perhaps amounted to another brief assembly of the estates hitherto unnoticed by historians is suggested not only by the location and witnesses but, as in autumn 1326, by the business pending: negotiations with France and royal finance as well as chancery inquests and patronage.[10] By now, a further twist had been added to the international situation through Queen Isabella's association with the Despensers' sworn enemy, the exiled Roger Mortimer of Wigmore, and the couple's steady gathering of support from disaffected English nobles and prelates, including the earls of Kent and Richmond and the future ring-leader of the 'Disinherited' of Scotland, Sir Henry Beaumont. Charles IV had also proposed that Prince Edward of Aquitaine, still in France with his mother Isabella, should marry Philippa, the daughter of Count William of Hainault (Beaumont's kinsman). However, while the French king in truth wished to finalise peace and see his sister Isabella return to her husband Edward II, a defensive alliance with Scotland at this moment might help guarantee her safety in Edward's realm.[11]

A final discussion of terms to be sought by Thomas Randolph and company may thus have occupied the Scottish estates at Scone.[12] The Franco-Scottish treaty itself was concluded at Corbeil on 26 April 1326 and was, like the 1295 agreement between representatives of King John and Philip IV, one of mutual defence that on paper favoured the French.[13] Once again, if war broke out between England and France, the king of Scots and his successors and subjects were to make war on England, with any truce or peace between Scotland and England automatically nullified; but if war were to break out between Scotland and England, the French were only to provide 'help and advice' as required. Therefore this alliance was agreed while Isabella, Mortimer and Prince Edward remained in

France, before their move to Hainault in June–July where Count William was readying a fleet and troops for their cause. But it was again enough to prompt Edward II and his council to look to their northern border: orders were issued to improve defences at Carlisle (12 April), and Norham, Alnwick, Dunstanburgh and Wark (29 April), after reported Scottish stealth attacks.[14] However, although Robert I had thus shown he was willing to break the Anglo-Scottish truce after just three years if a wider war erupted, like Charles IV he surely viewed this treaty as a means of obliging Edward II to offer satisfactory peace terms: it was not an alliance sought in the face of imminent attack.

Robert's court would reassemble at Stirling by 12 July to ratify their treaty formally with France, in advance of a parliament at Cambuskenneth Abbey which must have been summoned in early June. However, although there remained ongoing business to discuss, this assembly and one of its most important agenda items may have been prompted by news that had a profound dampening effect on the mood of the estates: the death of the infant prince, John Bruce, just over two years old. That the, likely elder, twin is known to have been buried in the Augustinian priory of Restenneth, dedicated to St Peter, might suggest a date of death for this child about the feast day of this universal cult, 29 May, or simply the presence of the royal court in and around Arbroath, Coupar-Angus and Scone in early 1326.[15] But the loss of one of the blessed twins of 1324 prompted an immediate move by Robert's administration to define the royal succession yet further.

This was by no means, though, a crisis akin to that caused by Edward Bruce's death at Faughart. Indeed, the presentation and sealing of a revised statute of succession in this Cambuskenneth parliament on 15 July 1326 may have provided a ceremony in which the expanded, unchallenged extent of the estates' acceptance of Bruce kingship since 1320 (and certainly March 1324) could be demonstrated convincingly. Oaths on the Gospels and relics were once more required of those present but need not have been a 'ragman' test of loyalty subject to the same manipulation of attendance and seals by Robert's chancery as had been the tailzies of 1315 and 1318. Nevertheless, no antiquarian transcript of the 1326 statute has survived.[16] Taking its lead from the relative stability of Robert's regime by this stage, this act may in fact have gone further than the terms it is usually accepted to have contained.[17] It did generally sharpen the details of 1318: the naming of, first, David Bruce then Robert Stewart as royal heirs, under a Randolph or Douglas Guardianship during a minority, failing whom an unspecified heir was to be determined by nearness of (male) degree or, only if all male lines failed, through female succession. Admittedly, it would have remained

highly problematic to sift through the sons of Robert I's sisters to designate
a provisional heir: Donald, earl of Mar, surely the eldest nephew, remained
in England, although John Campbell, now earl of Atholl, was arguably the
next clear choice after the king's grandson (and had the right name). Yet it
would nonetheless have been prudent for the ailing Robert, aged fifty-two,
to have considered naming acceptable guardians beyond Randolph and
Douglas, both also now middle-aged. Indeed, it is suggestive that amongst
the charters issued just after this parliament, on 22 July at the tower-house
home of the king's natural son at Clackmannan, was a grant of the valuable
lordship of Garioch to the royal Pantler (provider of bread to the royal
household), Sir Andrew Murray of Bothwell and Avoch (a widower with
two sons, John and Thomas), and his new wife, Christina Bruce (a match
from which there could be no issue given her age): Robert I's new brother-
in-law, the posthumous son of William Wallace's companion of 1297,
would serve as Guardian for David II in a crucial time of war, in 1332 and
1335–38.[18]

Furthermore, in July 1326 the succession statute could be sealed in the
presence of the infant heir, Prince David, and of Robert's grandson, Robert
Stewart (now ten), visible proof of dynastic succession. According to the
anonymous contemporary annals preserved by Fordun and Bower, this act
to recognise David and Robert was accompanied by swearing of 'fealty and
homage' by 'the whole of the clergy, the earls and barons and all the nobles
of Scotland with all the people gathered there . . .'.[19] Archdeacon Barbour,
however, takes the description of any such ceremonies much further, motivated by a desire to assert the retrospective reality of Bruce kingship *before*
the invasion and rival coronation of Edward Balliol at Scone in 1332, as
well as to affirm the legitimacy of his own royal Stewart patrons. According
to Barbour's verse narrative, such an act of succession was indeed sworn to
and sealed by Robert's subjects, but during a parliament that also crowned
David within his own father's lifetime, reportedly as Robert had intended,
along with David's new child-bride, Joan of England (thus dating Barbour's
events to 1328, *after* the peace treaty with Edward III).[20] Barbour's telescoped and distorted account hints at some higher order of ceremony in the
actual parliament of July 1326. David was certainly from now on styled
'earl of Carrick' with his own household.[21] Some form of quasi-installation
of the boy king-elect in 1326 may also in part explain why the Scots
under Randolph as Guardian would wait over two years after Robert I's
death in June 1329 to crown David II properly, significantly in another
parliament on 24 November 1331 (at Scone, thus the Scottish realm's first
'coronation parliament').[22] The possible use of royal relics in such an earlier

parliamentary ceremony is at least suggested by the king's visit to Dunfermline Abbey by 22 July 1326.[23] Overall, any such attempt to further enhance and proclaim the legitimacy and sacrality of a Bruce dynasty was in keeping with the evolving propaganda, ceremony and liturgy of Robert's reign.

The extant evidence pertaining to the succession discussions in 1326 is thus far from satisfactory. Fortunately, a good deal more survives of the Cambuskenneth parliament's grant on the same day, 15 July, of a lifetime subsidy for King Robert of a tenth of all the realm's fermes and rents:[24]

it was proposed by the same lord king that the lands and rents which were accustomed of old to pertain to his crown had become so diminished by various gifts and transfers made because of the war that he did not have appropriate support for his position without intolerable charges and inconveniences to his people. Wherefore he asked of them urgently that because, both in his own person and in his property, he had sustained many adversities, in order to recover and resume the liberty of all, it should please them, out of the gratitude they owed him, to find a manner and way whereby he could be sustained in accordance with what is proper to his position, without any greater burden on his people ensuing ... considering and acknowledging the aforegoing motives of the lord king to be true and, what is more, how many other benefits had accrued to them in his times through him, and his petition to be reasonable as well as just, having had common and diligent discussion upon the foregoing, unanimously, with joy and in a spirit of goodwill granted and gave to their abovesaid lord king, annually, at the terms of Martinmas [11 November] and Whitsun [seven weeks after Easter] in proportion, for the entire time of the life of the said king, a tenth penny of all money from their fermes and rents, both from their lands, demesnes and wards and from whatsoever their other lands, within or outwith liberties, both within and outwith burghs, according to the old extent of lands and rents in the time of the lord Alexander [III] by the grace of God illustrious king of Scots of good memory who died most recently.

Robert's potentially straitened circumstances were not an exaggeration. Since Bannockburn in 1314 he had indeed alienated royal demesne and income at a steady rate, with the pace quickening from 1318, and again from late 1320 and early 1324. In recent years, feudal casualties, justice teinds and even customs had been assigned as annuities in support of major burghal and ecclesiastical rebuilding projects; nobles, too, had often been granted exemption from royal exactions to offset damage to recovered or newly acquired lands. The fragmentary extant exchequer rolls of 1327–29 also reveal a number of individuals in receipt of substantial pensions, from the comital income pension of the king's natural son, to the nursemaids of the king's infant children on just a few pounds of bounty.[25]

Nor had the king retained many of the lands forfeited by political opponents in November 1314, or by the conspirators of 1320. At the same time a survey of former royal thanages in Scotland north of the Forth reveals a consistent royal policy of alienating these lands (often with royal forest) and their regular incomes to nobles in search of their support and local governance in regions adjacent to areas of former Comyn, Strathbogie, Mar and Umfraville lordship. Thus the wealth of royal demesne from Forfar to Inverness that had characterised the kingships of Alexander II and Alexander III (but which both those kings had admittedly started to use for patronage annuities or to farm out to secure a fixed income) was sorely diminished by the end of Robert's reign.[26] In addition, echoing the experience of magnates and their tenants elsewhere in the early fourteenth century (e.g. in Richard de Burgh's Ulster), Robert may have found it necessary to grant many holdings in return for specified military services not simply because he needed men in the field (providing more affordable, deadly archers or spearmen instead of expensive knights) but because it was not otherwise possible to exact an annual fiscal rent due to repeated harvest failures, war damage and depopulation. Such military obligation would supplement the common annual (or 'forinsec') service which otherwise remained the backbone of the Scottish host.[27]

A partial Chamberlain's account for 1264 reveals a royal income for Alexander III of circa £5,413, with £2,896 of that total raised from Crown lands.[28] Similarly, a fourteenth-century collection of materials datable to circa 1292–1344 – and which may be related to preparations by Edward I's regime for its Ordinance of Scotland of 1304–5 – records the estimated 'true value' of twenty-five listed Scottish shires (including demesne rents, judicial fines etc.) as £8,099 14s 10d.[29] By contrast, in June 1328, as we shall see, Robert I's new Chamberlain Robert Peebles could only then return total receipts of £3,793, with just £465 raised from burgh fermes (despite the royal policy of leasing these to the most important burghs for a fixed ferme): a similar sum was intromitted from customs and the remainder from the sheriffs' collection of demesne rents, justice teinds and feudal casualties.[30] Moreover, in the same 1327–28 account, the Chamberlain would only be able to record total receipts of the king's 'decimum denarium' as £1,714. Therefore, two years into the parliamentary grant of his tenth of fermes and rents for life, Robert's income – although undoubtedly rising – was still barely half of that collected for his recognised predecessor as king two generations earlier. Nevertheless, Robert's explanation of poverty in parliament in 1326 may not have reflected the reality of his reserves of wealth. As it will appear, when a second annual teind was authorised by the estates from 1328 to pay off a £20,000 war indemnity promised to the English as part of the final peace treaty, then it is surely the case that parliament's consent to first one, then a second, tenth, was – even if fully paid by all subjects throughout the realm – always expected to be supplemented by royal reserves of cash and material resources (or else the costly route of seeking bankers' loans).[31] The obvious source of such funds would have been plunder and tribute from raids into northern England circa 1311–19 and 1321–23. Robert I's son and successor, David II, would also retain a notorious 'king's deposit' of ready cash in Edinburgh castle: this seems to be a practice inherited from his father who in 1329 is recorded as having a 'king's deposit' at Lochleven of unknown size and in receipt of a further payment of £199 6s 8d.[32]

Understandably, despite improved harvests since 1322 and the steady truce-time restoration of the realm's southern economy, not everyone can have consented to this tax 'with joy'.[33] Prices remained high throughout the 1320s while erratic weather and the continuing spectre of war must have made for a climate of uncertainty.[34] It is moreover telling of the evolving nature of Crown–magnate relations through parliament that the Crown did not on this occasion in its 'necessity' simply seek to exact, without consultation, a common aid (*auxilia* or, as in England – and guarded against by the Scots in the treaty of Birgham [1290] – a 'tallage') in cash or kind-for-sale from all royal demesne tenants who did not otherwise have a written charter clause of exemption (as apparently William I had done around 1189 to secure funds to purchase the Canterbury quitclaim of English superiority for £10,000, and Alexander II had done to finance war against England in 1216).[35] Instead, Robert and his ministers now sought to establish the custom of securing the consent of the estates in parliament to a subsidy but one that, significantly, would now be applied across *all* subjects, on *all* lands and moveable goods, but which would at least have to be cursorily assessed for war damages (despite the act's stated intention that the levy would be levied using *antiquo taxio* papal valuations of circa 1249–65).[36]

In this context, it would have been logical for a Church Council and a 'Convention' of royal burghs both to have met at Stirling in 1326 in advance of this parliament (surely at royal urging), to intercommune and take forward the consent to subsidy of these estates in response to Crown procurators. It may have been the prelates, many of whom had been involved in collecting English occupation levies circa 1291–1318 (at higher rates and across a wider tax base), who were able to press upon the Crown the necessity of otherwise returning to the pre-war *antiquo taxio*.[37] Moreover, it is clear that in the Cambuskenneth parliament of July 1326 – and in his itinerant court over the next few months – Robert and his Chancellor/Chamberlain were subject to numerous appeals from religious communities, burgesses, rural freeholders and individual nobles for exemptions to be re-applied to such annual exactions. Indeed, the majority of Robert's extant letters and grants issued in the second half of 1326 speak to such appeals and the need for further inquests and Crown officer intervention to enforce debt collection, fair payments and legitimate exemptions.[38] Further caveats attached to the subsidy also reflected reservations or rights expressed by the estates that the king had been obliged to accept (and vice versa). Firstly, lands that could be shown to have been damaged by war and that were still suffering might expect a reduction of a tenth penny on their *antiquo taxio* rate (after a sheriff's inquest to validate their distress). Secondly, once collected this tenth should only be for the 'king's own use' without alienation or remission to others, or the whole grant would be void. Thirdly, although all subjects were obliged to pay, those with liberties (regalities and baronies) were to undertake to collect their share themselves and to hand this over 'in full to the king's servants': only if they refused or failed to do so could sheriffs then act to enter these lands and force tenants to yield up the correct contribution. In return, the royal household had to promise to take and pay prompt market price 'on the nail' for prise and carriages of goods only in the immediate vicinity of the king (and this would stop after any future war damage). Last, and by no means least, this subsidy would only continue for the remainder of King Robert's life, a consideration that must have been a very conscious factor for the estates – and the king – given his obvious ill health. As such, this give-and-take grant 'of necessity' drew the Scottish Crown and estates into the dynamic of tax and redress-of-grievance long experienced by the English political community. In negotiating their rights and seeking to supervise royal finance, the magnates holding franchisal liberties and the local communities that made up the estates further defined and intensified their own political participation but also the reach of the Crown.[39]

It fell to Chancellor Bernard and Chamberlain Fraser and their staffs to deal with these practical issues. Robert's attention was distracted by dramatic events in England. Just as Edward and his council were on alert for a French landing from Normandy, the Franco-Scottish alliance created inevitable tension on the Anglo-Scottish Marches and the king, earl of Moray (as sworn Guardian of the truce) and Douglas probably spent much of the summer and autumn ranging between Lochmaben, Hermitage and Berwick. They attended to their defences; acted to prevent breaches of the truce by colluding bands of Scots and Cumbrians/Northumbrians; and lobbied for English conservators to attend to the cases of Scots assaulted while travelling over land under English safe conduct or Scottish merchants/ mariners arrested when they put in to English ports, were shipwrecked, boarded by pirates or worse (as in the case of over thirty Scottish merchants, pilgrims and women robbed of £2,000 worth of cargo then killed by English pirates off Whitby, Yorkshire, in September).[40] At the end of August 1326, Edward II responded to communications from Robert about border transgressions (without specifying the guilty side) by appointing further 'conservators' under Sir Anthony de Lucy to work alongside the Scots on days of March arbitration.[41]

These strained exchanges were also surely enough to distract Robert from paying close attention to the Benedictine general chapter that met at Dunfermline Abbey about 26 October: but amongst its items for discussion seems to have been a further attempt to deprive Durham Cathedral of control of its Benedictine daughter house of Coldingham Priory (10 miles north of Berwick) and to annex it to Dunfermline itself (a transfer that may have further aided the abbey's building projects).[42] After a long gap in his extant acts from 16 August (a charter enforcing Robert's annuity from Berwick customs to Melrose Abbey), the king can be relocated at Berwick on 14 November.[43] By then matters had taken a very different turn. King Edward had ordered the arrest of all Frenchmen in England and the muster of a fleet: in early September he dispatched a pre-emptive landing against Normandy, with little effect.[44] These actions were a prelude to war with Charles IV which, under the terms of the treaty of Corbeil, Robert must have assumed would dictate his immediate resumption of hostilities against England barely two months after his ratification of the alliance. However, the perceived threat from France proved to be Edward's fatal mistake.

On 24 September 1326, Queen Isabella and Mortimer (with Prince Edward in their care) landed in Suffolk. The resulting collapse of Edward's and the Despensers' regime was remarkably swift but still took over six weeks, time aplenty for it to be recognised that Robert must have taken a decision to wait upon events (as did Charles IV). Significantly, Isabella was joined by a number of English prelates, Henry (brother of Thomas) of Lancaster and further disinherited lords and Edward Balliol associates,

including the English king's half-brother the earl of Norfolk, Thomas
Wake and Alan le Zouche.[45] This party pursued Edward as he fled a riotous
London into Wales and then took ship.[46] The Lanercost chronicler reported
that,

> alarmed at the coming to England of the French and some English with
> the queen, the king had been so ill-advised as to write to the Scots, freely
> giving up to them the land and realm of Scotland, to be held independ-
> ently of any King of England, and (which was still worse) bestowed upon
> them with Scotland great part of the northern lands of England lying
> next to them, on condition that they should assist him against the queen,
> her son, and their confederates.[47]

There is no extant evidence of such an offer from Edward II or a reaction
from Robert I. Overtures might have been delivered by Donald, earl of
Mar, Robert's nephew and a loyal knight in Edward's household defence at
Bristol in November 1326, who would escape or be allowed to return to
Scotland in 1327.[48] Robert would surely have preferred to reach accord
with England's legitimate monarch with whom he already had a truce and
with whom the Papacy and Charles IV still sympathised.[49] However,
although Edward was cornered and seized by his enemies as early as 16
November – with the Despensers and others tried and executed within a
matter of days – there had been sufficient time for the Scots, poised on the
border since August, to act in Edward's defence or even simply their own
interests.[50] Rather it seems that Robert, who more than anyone knew the
possibilities of rebellion against English royal authority, did not underestimate the chances of Isabella's rebellion and was prepared still to wait.

## A Last Campaign, January–December 1327

While resident at Scone, Robert I would have been brought up to date with
the tumultuous developments in England by refugees from Edward II's
household, Donald, earl of Mar, and his cousin Rhys ap Gruffudd and their
retinues.[51] The contacts of these men surely also allowed the Scottish king
and his council to be informed within a matter of days about subsequent
events at Westminster and Edward II's imprisonment at Kenilworth in
Warwickshire, and to time their opportunity to best effect. What was
reported to them was the public face of a forceful, stage-managed transfer
of English royal power, legitimated by community assent and egged on by
the London mob, a process which Robert I could read only too well.[52]

On 13 January 1327 'articles' declared Edward II's 'inadequacy' as king – citing his evil counsel, his loss of Scotland and lands in Ireland and Gascony as well as his breaches of coronation oath – and justified pledges of support from a powerful minority for his son, Edward of Aquitaine, to take up his inheritance as king in the name of 'the prelates, earls, barons and the whole community of the realm'. By 21 January a delegation of these prelates and magnates sent to Edward's prison at Kenilworth had forced the humiliated king to abdicate. The fifteen-year-old Edward III would be guided by a regime headed by his mother Isabella (with whom he resided until March), the otherwise unnamed Mortimer, Henry, earl of Lancaster (as Steward), and a council of twelve prelates, earls and barons. At Westminster Abbey on 1 February Edward's coronation was preceded by knighting and popular acclamation, and included the contractual oath introduced in 1308.[53]

On the very same day, reports the Lanercost chronicle, 'the Scots, having already heard thereof, came in great force with ladders to Norham Castle'.[54] Robert had thus ordered the truce to be broken finally not when Edward II had sent ships to attack Normandy (September 1326) – thus fulfilling Scotland's obligation to France – but right at that moment when legitimate authority in England was most in doubt. He attacked a regime which Charles IV in fact could only recognise given his sister's leading role and the imminent marriage of the new king, Edward III, to Philippa, the daughter of France's ally, the Count of Hainault. Indeed, Anglo-French peace terms were agreed at Paris by 31 March, although these saw Charles extract control of much of western Gascony and over 70,000 marks in war damages.[55] In that sense, the treaty of Corbeil had served King Charles's purpose. But in this rapidly evolving context, we would be wise not to rush to 1328 and the final Anglo-Scottish peace. Rather, in early 1327, the Scots' incursion was perhaps once again a more modest resumption of independent tactics (not dictated by their alliance with France) that had served them well before 1323. At best, the siege of Norham and subsequent raids were undertaken with a view to provoking further instability in England, from which acceptable peace terms *might* emerge. These attacks may also have had a more basic material and corporate motive.

However, as the Lanercost scribe reports the captains of this season's Scottish forces to be Moray, Douglas and Donald, earl of Mar, there remains the possibility that during the next seven months the ailing Robert's renewal of 'the disease of war' was pursued ostensibly in support of Edward II's restoration as rightful king. If ever there had been a moment when the beleaguered English monarch had reached out for potential

Scottish assistance, it had been the winter of 1326–27, and Mar, indeed, may have brought word that '[Edward] had yielded to them [the Scots] their country free, together with a large part of the English march'.[56] Yet if Isabella and Mortimer, preferring to focus upon Westminster affairs, had offered similar peace terms at the first sign of Scottish aggression, Robert would surely have recognised their authority to act for Edward III: in that sense Mar was but a tool.

The return of Earl Donald to Scotland, though, must have caused controversy. Just months after declaring his royal demesne sorely depleted and requesting subsidy, Robert I restored his nephew to his earldom, thus depriving the Crown of further valuable income (and most likely Sir Andrew Murray of Garioch of the keeping of the Edwardian-built Kildrummy castle in Mar).[57] As the king's oldest full nephew, Donald was entitled to his place in the royal succession, perhaps giving pause for thought to Sir Walter Steward on behalf of his son, Robert, as well as to John Campbell, earl of Atholl, Hugh, earl of Ross, and perhaps even Alexander Bruce. For the king's grandson, there might now also have been a further question of rank, for the main branch of the Stewart kindred were not yet earls. Therefore, it may have been in this period that the ambition of the hereditary royal Steward's line to possess the ancient title of Fife as closest conjuncts of the Bruce dynasty first came into focus (alongside an awareness of their right to their cadet kindred's title of Menteith). As per the terms of Earl Duncan of Fife's tailzie submission in 1315, Robert as Steward, as an assignee 'lawfully born to the king' via his daughter Marjorie Bruce, might receive this earldom as Duncan had failed as yet to father a son (and probably would not have his only child, a daughter, Isabella, by his Monthermer wife until c.1327–32). This Steward expectation of the Fife title and lands would lead to serious tension between David II and Robert Steward/d from 1341.[58] In this context, it is very tempting to construe the undated note of a striking grant by Robert I to Earl Duncan (the only gift he seems to have received from the king apart from his original 1315 submission) of the baronies of O'Neill (Aberdeenshire), Kinoull (eastern Perthshire) and Calder (Lothian, adjacent to both of Steward's Bathgate and Ratho), as timely compensation for his lineage's anticipated loss of comital lordship; by the same token, another of Robert I's lost acts, a grant of Roger Mowbray's forfeited Perthshire barony of Methven (just half a dozen miles to the west of Scone) to the king's grandson may date to this period, anticipating a future enthronement role for the Stewarts as earls of Fife.[59]

Other men and their affinities might also now have had cause to worry about how their status would be affected by Earl Donald of Mar's return. For example, James, mere *lord* of Douglas, over his role as a future Guardian; Andrew Murray likewise, as well as in regard to his regional lordship in the north-east (Garioch) alongside Malcolm of Lennox (in Strath'an), Adam Gordon (Strathbogie), Alexander Fraser (Aboyne and Cluny) and even the earl of Moray (Badenoch). The Stewart–Menteith–Campbell bloc in the west might also now fear the restoration of patrimony tied to a pre–1296 Mar–MacRuaridh marriage.[60] The king (or these noble houses) may have sought to offset these rivalries by arranging further strategic marriages in central Scotland. For example, John Campbell (born c.1306 or c.1314–16), earl of Atholl, would marry Joanna Menteith, sister of Sir John Menteith (and already a widow of Malise, seventh earl of Strathearn).[61] About the same time, Donald of Mar seems to have married Isabel, sister of John Stewart of Bonkle, by now surely earl of Angus (and already brother-in-law to Thomas Randolph).[62] Nevertheless, a number of these magnate tensions would surface in the summer of 1332 when Mar was actually chosen as Guardian for David II by a parliament, but only after 'a great deal of wrangling and sundry disputes'. There were clearly doubts about Mar's associations with England and Edward Balliol – enough to cause the illegitimate Robert Bruce of Clackmannan/Liddesdale to accuse Mar of treachery: but both Bruce junior and Mar (and the new Stewart Angus earl) would be killed fighting off the disinherited in 1332 (with John Campbell, earl of Atholl, similarly slain in 1333).[63] Moreover, in 1327, the origins of these tensions might easily have led to muttering about the possibility of other exiled/disinherited lords abandoning England and returning to the north (Strathbogie of Atholl, Macdougall of Argyll, Umfraville of Angus, Macdowall): this prospect would cause grave unease within the Scottish community during the peace process of 1328.[64]

These were lordship concerns which King Robert must have had to work hard to allay alongside apprehension about further royal alienations of demesne and the lifetime tenth which his Chamberlain had now begun to collect. The king's extant acts for the first half of 1327 (indeed, for all of that year) suggest a conscious attempt at parsimony. Robert himself was surely too unwell to engage in war: this may thus mark the beginnings of an increased leadership role for Thomas Randolph. From 1 February to about Easter (12 April) the king probably kept residence at Stirling (in the Blackfriars). Here his grants included an annual sum for the Constable, Sir Gilbert Hay, minor lands to knights in Lanarkshire and Forfarshire (for archer service), parkland in Kincardineshire for Chamberlain Fraser (and his young son, John, yet another nephew by a sister of the king), and remittances from dues for Coupar-Angus Abbey and St Andrews Priory.[65] Then on 31 March the king was attended by the earl of Moray, Douglas, Walter

Steward, Andrew Murray, Hay and Robert Keith, a decidedly royalist core, at the beginning of a formal council that must have discussed such live issues as the situation in England, the Scots' military strategy, Mar's return and tax collection. Again, no record of the proceedings survives.[66]

Matters were interrupted and the royal household depleted, though, on 9 April when Robert's son-in-law, Walter Steward, passed away. This was a sudden death noted by Barbour and later chronicles (under Stewart kings), prompting a court funeral held at Paisley Abbey; Robert Steward may now have entered the royal household alongside Prince David and his sister and a number of other magnates' children.[67] Resuming business, by 23 May the king had moved south to Berwick.[68] This suggests that after the failure of their surprise attack on Norham (and then Alnwick), the Scots had perhaps raided until the north-eastern English communities bought individual truces once more, whereupon Robert, true to form, offered full peace talks: this may be what the contemporary visitor, eyewitness and subsequent chronicler (of events from 1290–1360), cleric Jean le Bel of Liège described as Robert's message of defiance about Easter 1327, threatening to 'burn and lay waste as far as he'd done after the disastrous defeat at Stirling'.[69] Thereafter the Scots withdrew to await the response of Edward III's new government.

Isabella and Mortimer had at first imposed a strict adherence to the truce, declaring its general continuity on 6 March 1327 and appointing conservators to serve until 31 May.[70] A large embassy – including the abbot of the Yorkshire Cistercian house of Rievaulx (mother to Melrose Abbey), the Archbishop of York, Henry Percy and Henry Beaumont – was commissioned in late April–early May to open talks for peace with 'Robert de Brus'.[71] Then on 10 June an open passport for 100 Scots 'of any rank and their attendants' was issued for talks on the Marches.[72] However, the passport was valid for only fifteen days; the appointment of their English counterparts was cancelled and from mid-April troops were mustered while Edward III had moved to York by late May.[73] Just as in 1310 and 1322, the English Crown and its council sensed an opportunity for political capital in a victory over the Scots at a moment of crisis in England.[74] A large measure of this motivation continued to stem from the support for Isabella provided by English lords who had inherited forfeited Scottish titles, most notably Henry Beaumont (the earldom of Buchan, the Isle of Man, Roxburgh castle, the sheriffship of Wigtown and associated lands, and the Crail barony in Fife), and northern lords Henry Percy of Alnwick (a truce conservator, Urr in Galloway and Redcastle in Forfarshire), William de la Zouche of Ashby (a portion of the Galloway-de Quinci inheritance, claims he would soon sign over to Ralph de Stafford) and Thomas Wake of Liddel (the Liddesdale lordship and Kirkandrews barony in Dumfriesshire, both of which would be claimed by Percy after 1329).[75] Robert's response was equally pre-emptive and two- (really three-) handed.

About 15 June Scottish forces under Moray, Douglas and Mar (with Barbour adding James Stewart of Durisdeer, the late Walter's brother, and Archibald Douglas, Lord James's brother, to his heroic narrative) crossed the border, laid waste to Weardale and reached Appleby by early July, just as English forces mustered to enter the Scottish eastern March.[76] At the same time, Mar's contingent broke off to ride hard for the Welsh Marches, where he was reported to be rousing support for Edward II and opposition to Roger Mortimer by 26 June and on through the summer.[77] But most troubling of all for the English must have been word that Robert himself – now well enough to travel again – had crossed to Glendun in Ulster.[78]

Here Robert's objective was not to renew his late brother's war (although a Scottish force had recently attempted Rathlin) but to intrude himself into the minority lordship of his teenage nephew, William de Burgh, earl of Ulster, and to turn the uncertain loyalties of both Gaels and Anglo-Normans in this region, to whom the kingship of Edward III was only declared on 13 May, against the English minority government. There is evidence to suggest that in the weeks before his passage to Ulster, Robert had had contact with both Sir John Darcy (Edward II's former Justiciar of Ireland) and the de Lacys and other enemies of Roger Mortimer within the lordship. Robert may have been deflected from any direct role in rousing concerted Anglo-Irish opposition to the new English royal regime, thanks to intervention by his wife's brother-in-law, the earl of Kildare. Yet on 12 July the Scots king did conclude a tribute-truce with Henry de Mandeville, the steward of Ulster, to last until 1 August 1328 and in which 'the native Irish adhering to the king are [to be] included'.[79] Robert thus deliberately redirected his policy of 1315–18 away from purely native insurgence to associate himself with the leading family loyal to the English Crown. Significantly, too, his price for withholding his forces was not cash but victuals – an annum of 100 chalders of wheat and barley.[80] As well as supplementing Scottish needs if the Anglo-Scottish borders once more became a war zone, this tariff might also weaken Carlisle, which the Scots were reportedly threatening to attack. A successful attempt to impose Bruce lordship over north-eastern Ireland (perhaps by sponsoring Alexander Bruce in the future?) as well as the Isle of Man might also tip the balance of power in favour of Robert's adherents throughout the Western Isles and Argyll. As the Irish lordship (and Munster in particular) slipped towards violent chaos in late summer–autumn 1327, the mere threat of Robert's interference may thus have proved decisive.[81]

In all of this, there is undeniably a growing sense of Bruce impatience not to be denied this time and to effect a lasting settlement with England. The added pressure here was surely Robert's own deteriorating health as well as his generally aging Scottish war generation: a pressing need to secure favourable peace terms before the minority of David II began and that of Edward III ended. It was reported back to York that while in Ulster Robert 'was so feeble and so weak that he will not last much longer from this time, with the help of God, because he cannot move anything except his tongue'.[82] The angry Lanercost scribe certainly asserted that Bruce 'who had become leprous, did not invade England on this occasion'. Many years later Le Bel, too, recalled Robert as then having 'grown very old and was suffering, it was said, from the unclean sickness (*la grosse maladie*)'.[83] However, this English taunt and news of Robert's decline cannot have arrived in time to serve as solace for the young Edward III's host.

Striking out from York on 10 July 1327, the English army (for which no records of service survive) of several thousand infantry and heavy cavalry (including 500 Hainaulters) would spend the next few weeks chasing the Scots' smaller mounted contingents (travelling light and living off the land and simple oat cakes, according to Le Bel's now famous description) all across Weardale, but they failed to bring them to battle.[84] The rain-sodden fells and valleys, the poor temper of Edward's forces (with Le Bel reporting that their hosts hated the Hainaulters more than the Scots) and the Scots' tactics made this yet another triumph for Bruce's court of chivalry to celebrate at length in verse inherited and amplified by Barbour.[85] According, too, to Lanercost's scribe, Sir Thomas Gray and Le Bel, Douglas did indeed lead a surprise attack on the first night of a three-week stand-off between the opposing forces across Stanhope Park (just over 20 miles from Durham): the Scots (to cries of 'Douglas! Douglas!') cut the ropes of Edward III's tents and otherwise terrorised their enemy with fires, horns and howls throughout the short nights.[86] But by 6–7 August the Scots had slipped away, back to their own realm, judging that they had done enough to exhaust the English and prevent their advance into south-eastern Scotland, where they would surely have done serious damage to the rebuilt Berwick, Roxburgh, Lothians and Edinburgh. A reserve contingent of 5,000 Scots, under Patrick, earl of Dunbar, and John Stewart (of Bonkle), earl of Angus (reported by Gray), had probably been positioned in the Marches to guard against this threat; Robert I himself, returned from Ireland, formed part of its rearguard.[87] As a sign of the economic frailties that still underlay the war, all the English found in the Scots' abandoned encampment was 'five hundred big, fine, fat cattle newly killed: the Scots had slaughtered them because they'd have been too slow to follow them and they didn't want to leave them alive for the English.' No wonder Edward III wept.[88]

As the English host withdrew the Scots pressed home their advantage, with Robert I himself present in Northumberland. Gray reports the king's fresh siege of Norham (held by Gray senior) in which the exiled conspirator Sir William Mowat was killed, as well as an assault by Moray and Douglas on Percy's castles at Alnwick and Warkworth (which ended through mutual agreement marked by 'grand jousts'): Douglas is also said to have frustrated a Percy raid on Teviotdale.[89] With much of Northumberland in flames, the Durham see, Cumberland, Westmorland and the communities of Cleveland and Richmond all saw the sense in purchasing a further six months' truce 'for a large sum of money', until 22 May 1328. That Robert now sensed a genuine opportunity to pile irresistible pressure upon Isabella and Mortimer's regime is suggested by his grant of 4 September (from an unrecorded location) of Belford in Northumberland to his own standard-bearer, Sir Nicholas Scrymgeour, for whom he had recently bought an expensive new horse.[90]

This was surely not Robert's only such grant at this time.[91] His efforts certainly contributed to a perfect storm of problems that now forced an Edwardian parliament at Lincoln in mid-September to seek peace terms. The disastrous Weardale campaign had exhausted the regime's financial reserves. Although a tax was granted for the defence of the north, Northumberland, Cumberland and Westmorland had all been so heavily damaged by the Scots' renewed attacks that they would seek exemption from this levy.[92] Mounting criticism of the English Crown's capitulation to Charles IV's expensive demands was magnified by this failure in the north. But, worst of all, the threat of revolt in Ireland and Wales had panicked Mortimer into moving 'Edward, the king's father' around in secret and then ordering his slaughter at Berkeley castle (Gloucestershire) on 21 September.[93] Now accusations against the Queen Mother's highly partisan administration mushroomed. In that context, the English council empowered Henry Percy and William Denholme to open peace talks with the 'nobles of Scotland' on 9 October.[94]

## A Difficult Peace, October 1327–August 1328

Along with the 'Declaration of Arbroath' and the military adventures celebrated by Barbour, the peace demands which Robert I now presented and the eventual Anglo-Scottish treaty of Edinburgh-Northampton concluded in March–May 1328, are the most familiar elements of the Bruce reign after Bannockburn. However, what has been underestimated is the level of disquiet that some of the conditions of peace unleashed within the Scottish political community, issues which might indeed have provoked a strong backlash against Robert's government had he and his ministers not worked hard to adjust, offset and evade these terms. These tensions might also be said to form part of wider potential problems for his rule – centred around royal finance and Crown–magnate relations – which must have resulted in a number of serious political confrontations had he lived longer (and which would be unavoidable for his son and his minority regime).[95]

On 18 October 1327, from Berwick, Robert's letters put forward six conditions for peace, which were a clear refinement of those tabled at York in November 1324 (and perhaps already indicated to the English in early 1327).[96] (1) The Scottish realm was to be 'free, quit and entire', without any obligations to the kings of England; (2) a marriage was to be arranged, this time stipulated as between Robert's son, David, and a sister of Edward III (although no dowry was mentioned); (3) 'nobody who is in the allegiance of the king of England, or of his adherents, can demand land or tenement within the realm of Scotland, or its appurtenances, nor can any man of Scotland, nor of the adherents of Robert, demand land or tenement within the realm of England'; (4) a mutual alliance should be formed between Scotland and England (saving the alliance already made between Robert I and France); (5) an indemnity of £20,000 would be paid by the Scots over three years; and, finally, (6) the king of England 'shall furnish help and counsel and support, [tellingly] without dissimulation' in securing the repeal of papal censures upon Robert and his followers.

By 30 October, Edward III, advised by his council, had already agreed to talks at Newcastle and indicated a willingness to accept peace generally as well as terms (2) and (5), extending assurances as to the likelihood of term (1) being met 'in good faith' and a promise to 'beseech our Holy Father the pope by letter' for the repeal of the excommunication (6). However, terms (3) and (4) were to be subject to negotiations led for the English by Sir Henry Percy. On 23 November a full English embassy under the Archbishop of York was appointed for talks now relocated to York (where Edward III was married in January and held a parliament from 7 February) and an interim truce was agreed until 13 March 1328.[97]

Despite Robert's stated demands of 1324 and 1327 that no former enemy should recover lost lands, the fact that the king may have been willing to contemplate some return to the pre-1296 cross-border landholding by Scottish and English nobility and churches (and the Scottish Crown itself) is at least indicated by three factors: the demand for Bruce family lands in Essex (1324); Robert's recent dispensation of charters of Northumbrian lands; and, from Newbattle Abbey on 26 December 1327, a grant of five stags annually from the Selkirk forest to Durham Cathedral Priory, to be caught on the feast of the Assumption of the Virgin (15 August) and delivered through its daughter house of Coldingham Priory in time for the Translation feast of St Cuthbert 'on account of the devotion which [Robert] has towards' that saint.[98] The symbolism of the latter grant as heralding, along with the proposed royal marriage, a return to the elite relations of the eleventh, twelfth and thirteenth centuries, must have been apparent to contemporaries; all the more so, as Louis de Beaumont, bishop of Durham, was brother of the envoy Sir Henry, one of the leading English disinherited lords, and a little over a year earlier, in October 1326, Robert's regime had attempted to annex Coldingham to Dunfermline Abbey.[99] Veneration of the shrine of St Cuthbert and its associated relics and churches in northern England represented a vibrant inherited tradition for many Scottish families and churches alongside the exaltation of MacMalcolm kings throughout the twelfth and thirteenth centuries.[100] Robert, indeed, may also have faced considerable lobbying by a number of elements within Scotland for a return to just such a relationship: abbeys such as Melrose, Jedburgh, Newbattle, Kelso, Arbroath, Sweetheart, Dundrennan and Dunfermline seeking the recovery of valuable Scottish border, English (and even Irish) estates alongside magnates like Earl Patrick of Dunbar, Donald of Mar, Duncan of Fife (also anxious to stabilise relations with his de Monthermer wife) and even the Douglases.[101]

Beneath these landed connections, moreover, lay important ties of family, cult and patronage, often manifested in confraternity agreements between churches or between churches and their lay benefactors.[102] On 16 March 1328, four days before St Cuthbert's main feast day and one day before a Scottish parliament would ratify the peace treaty's various elements, Robert would inspect past charters by two kings of Scots, Edgar I (r.1097–1107) and David I, as well as by Patrick (I), earl of Dunbar (d.1232), all of them given to Coldingham Priory which was now confirmed as a daughter house of Durham.[103] James Douglas would also recover his family's past holdings in Essex and Northumberland in 1329–30, just as would Arbroath Abbey (Haltwhistle church, Northumberland), Jedburgh Abbey (Arthuret church, Cumberland) and some lesser Roxburghshire nobles such as the Bissets of Upsetlington and Prendergasts of Akeld/Kirknewton.[104]

However, the most compelling force that brought King Robert round to compromise on his apparently principled objection to the restoration of the disinherited must have been the insistence of Isabella and Mortimer's envoys – including Sir Henry Percy – that exclusion of their rights would be a deal-breaker from an English point of view.[105] This group represented a quite vocal lobby determined that their interests should not be ignored (as they had been in 1323).[106] The eventual peace treaty constituted a series of indentures, notarial instruments and letters patent from both kings, Robert I and Edward III.[107] As Anglo-Scottish relations began to break down once more through 1330–31, in the run-up to the outbreak of war in 1332–33, Edward would write insistently to Thomas Randolph as Guardian for David II, demanding the restoration of English Church and noble lands in Scotland 'in accordance with the treaty'.[108] Thus at the very least the 1328 peace must have contained some assurances to individual disinherited lords and their English heirs. According to King Edward's letters of December 1330, Robert had issued letters patent to this effect to such influential individuals as Henry Percy, Henry Beaumont and Thomas Wake, underwriting their right to claim back lands through the due process of Scottish courts.[109] Sir Thomas Gray – perhaps following a Scottish source he consulted in Edinburgh in the 1350s – would also assert that in the parliament at York in July/August 1328, which saw the English community ratify the peace, Edward III had agreed that 'all his adherents should lose their inheritance in Scotland, except for lords de Wake, Percy, Beaumont and la Zouche. Nothing was settled about their situation, and great evil arose from this later [after 1332].'[110] A charter from Robert dated at Glasgow on 28 July 1328 is certainly extant restoring Sir Henry Percy to the lands and possessions held in Scotland by his father 'not withstanding any forfeiture of war'; again, this may be only one of several such grants by Robert but the only one to have survived from this period.[111]

English demands on this issue during the talks of November 1327–February 1328 may have been facilitated by two further pressure points for the Bruce regime. First, the inevitable march of time and Robert's need for closure within his own lifetime. This reality must have been brought home all too bitterly to the king and his close associates when on 26 October 1327 Queen Elizabeth died, aged thirty-eight, probably at Cullen (of causes now unknown). Obsequies at Dunfermline, Cullen and Cardross (where the king can be located on 15 February) must have interrupted Robert's residence close to the border and the York talks throughout the winter.[112] By the time of the parliament at Holyrood Abbey in March 1328, which ratified the peace treaty, Robert was reportedly once again too ill to participate.[113]

However, by then the worrying practical ramifications of a second issue, Scottish royal finances, had also made themselves apparent. They may have already done so, indeed, in 1327, but the survival of partial exchequer accounts intromitted at Dumbarton between 4 January and 26 February 1328 at last allows for the analysis of Robert's royal income and expenditure in some detail. Accounts returned by the provosts and custamars of burghs suggest a very patchy and low-level yield of the teinds owed by the estates as per the 'decimum denarium', or king's tenth, granted in parliament in July 1326. Only the officials of Perth, Edinburgh, Lanark, Rutherglen, Haddington, Peebles and Roxburgh returned monies for this purpose (totalling just over £40), with accounts from officials in the north (Inverness, Cullen, Banff, Aberdeen), Angus and the Mearns (Dundee, Forfar), Fife (Cupar, Inverkeithing, Crail), the south-west (Ayr, Wigtown, Dumfries), and the two symbolic centres of Stirling and Berwick making no reference to this exaction.[114] To ensure sufficient revenue to cover the additional three-yearly payments of war indemnity now promised under the peace treaty would necessitate both a parliamentary grant of another tenth (probably eased by a quiet dropping of the king's personal tenth) and far more forceful collection of dues from regions of past Balliol/Comyn sympathy and/or still recovering from the effects of war, famine and disease. In this context, the English envoys may have shrewdly applied further pressure to Robert's position by setting the default indemnity at £100,000 to be owed by the Scots if Prince David did *not* promptly marry Edward III's sister, Joan of the Tower, an amount due in 1338 (when King Edward would be twenty-five years old).[115] As it was, the agreed dower to be provided to Joan by the Scottish Crown was the sum of £2,000 worth of lands a year, immediately adding further pressure to Robert I's strained resources. That there was to be no reciprocal dowry from Edward III perhaps ensured that the actual reparations figure of hard cash to be paid by the Scots in three years remained as low (and manageable) as it did.[116]

Therefore, despite Scottish military success in 1327 and the difficult situation facing Isabella and Mortimer, as in the truce talks of 1323 the smaller, poorer kingdom still had to make a number of compromises during the final peace negotiations to secure an agreement and, in this instance, its all-important recognition of sovereignty. Nevertheless, the formal ratification was still an occasion of great legitimisation and pomp for Robert I. The king had summoned a parliament to Holyrood Abbey for 28 February 1328, which began by preparing the ground for the treaty's war indemnity by reviewing the estates' grant of 1326 of a tenth of teinds and rents to support Robert's household. In this context, a simultaneous Church

Council and Convention of Burghs may once more have been held in Edinburgh to allow the estates' consent to these fiscal measures to be presented to parliament.[117] However, introducing an innovation to match the occasion, Robert, his Chancellor Bernard and Chamberlain Peebles may have bypassed the need to send procurators to these subsidiary assemblies by instead summoning prelates with their seals as well as six procurators with 'special authority' from the community of the royal burghs (ordered to bring their common seals) to attend the parliament. Such representative but select attendance might have enabled the king and his officers to ensure consensus, even on the more unpopular terms of the peace, and to impress upon the burghal procurators the need for fulsome payment of first and future tenths.[118] Parliament may then also have examined the results of the promised inquest (June 1325) into the liberties of the burgh of Dundee, with the king issuing a fresh charter to that burgh based upon the privileges now enjoyed by Berwick. Amongst the witnesses to this act was Robert's new bishop of Moray, John de Pilmuir, following the death of David de Moravia in January 1326.[119] A number of charters also punctuate the first weeks of March 1328 while the king and court waited in Edinburgh for the arrival of the English ambassadors, the bishops of Lincoln and Norwich, Henry Percy, William de la Zouche and Henry Scrope.[120] They had probably arrived by 16 March when Robert inspected the aforementioned charters of Durham Cathedral Priory.[121]

The first order of business, on St Patrick's Day, 17 March 1328, was formal ratification of the several documents of the peace indenture including inspection of Edward III's formal letters of quittance of 1 March.[122] These recognised, as desired, Robert's right as 'illustrious king of Scots', and the rights of his heirs and successors, to hold Scotland 'free, and quit, and without any subjection, servitude, claim, or demand' from the kings of England, given 'on behalf of ourselves, our heirs, and all our successors, with the common counsel, assent, and consent, of the prelates, magnates, earls, barons and communities of our realm assembled in our [Edward's] parliament.' Whatever the uncertain price of disinherited restoration, this concession under Edward III's seal made it all worthwhile for King Robert. The separate terms in regard to David's marriage, Joan's dower, agreement not to aid each other's enemies in Ireland and the Isle of Man, English assistance to lift the papal excommunication, the war indemnity (and its steep default) and procedures for March Days, all flowed from this quittance for the Scottish estates' approval.[123] So, too, did Scotland's continued alliance with France, although there may have been some private doubts around this point following the death without direct male heir of Charles IV on 1

February 1328. Robert and his government may have heard with rueful relief by May of the conversion of the brief 'regency' of Charles's cousin, Philip of Valois (a grandson of Philip III, d.1285), into his kingship as Philip VI, after the late French king's widow gave birth to a posthumous daughter (thus not another Capetian king). The French, fearful of the intentions of Isabella, the English Queen Mother, on behalf of her son, Edward III (grandson of Philip IV, d.1314), preferred a similar contingency of adult male succession as that legislated for by Robert I in Scotland in 1315, 1318 and 1326. The Scots surely anticipated further English distraction over Gascony and now the wider Capetian inheritance, an assumption seemingly confirmed when Isabella protested the Valois succession before Philip VI's coronation, a move the new French king responded to by pressing for Edward III's prompt homage in person for his Duchy lands: this was a ceremony that would take place in Amiens on 6 June 1329, the day before Robert I himself died.[124]

Whatever the possible outcome of these tensions, the Anglo-Scottish peace went ahead. In March 1328 Holyrood Abbey may have been chosen for its geographic convenience for the English embassy, Scottish subjects from all quarters, and an ailing king and his chancery. But it may also have had some symbolic role to play in a period that would see the anniversary of Robert I's 'coronation' (25 March, the Virgin's Annunciation feast) and then Easter (3 April), all in a leap year in calendar alignment with Robert's momentous opening 'anno regni primo' of 1306. For it was at this stage of proceedings that English promises to restore Scottish relics removed in war were confirmed, including the inauguration stone of Scone and St Margaret's piece(s?) of the Holy Cross, the Black Rood. Yet these were to be accompanied, too, by the return of Scottish Crown records and – a demand again noted by both the Lanercost chronicler and Sir Thomas Gray – surrender of the 'Ragman' rolls of Scottish submission of 1296, a document that included recognition of Edward I's superiority by Robert as earl of Carrick, as well as the names and seals of many a Scot now in his royal government and peace.[125] Once proceedings were completed, there would have been feasting, possibly even a joust.[126]

Robert I had therefore been able to stand fast on his most important conditions for peace. Nevertheless, even before its clauses were ratified he must have known that some elements that would have a direct impact upon his domestic rule would require subtle management, and that one in particular, the partial restoration of the disinherited, was, in truth, unpalatable, perhaps unworkable. It may have been the king's plan even before the final ratification to stall and obfuscate on this issue, going through the motions of restoring some key northern English lords and churches, until he had secured those elements of the peace he regarded as indispensable: the quittance of sovereignty, his son's marriage and papal absolution. Yet beyond that Robert may have had no real intention of restoring lords such as Henry Percy to significant Scottish holdings.

If so, this was a risky bluff. Yet it may, admittedly, have been one in which Robert felt reasonably confident that for their part Isabella and Mortimer, too, would allow certain matters to slip – the disinherited, Joan's marriage or dower – as long as their northern border was secure and their coffers were recovered. It may also have been of fundamental importance to Robert's subjects that *Scottish* disinherited lords – Macdougall and the child earls of Atholl and Angus, and the Macdowall heir (and certainly Edward Balliol) – did seem to be excluded from any discussion of restoration throughout the talks of 1327–28.

The English parliament ratified the treaty (by 'a majority') on 4 May 1328.[127] In the meantime, some of Robert's extant acts in the days and weeks immediately after the treaty ratification give the distinct impression of a start to conciliatory, compensatory moves. Some went to obvious losers by the peace, like a grant of yet more royal demesne in Angus (worth £20) to the disappointed Donald, earl of Mar.[128] Favour was perhaps also shown to men now willing to accept the reality of Bruce power: for example, a grant of 3 July of the lands of Glassmount in Fife in barony to Sir David Wemyss, a knight who, though possibly among those acquitted of treason in 1320, would still follow Duncan, earl of Fife, into Edward Balliol's camp in 1332 along with a large affinity of Fifeshire men.[129] Other grants perhaps spoke already to individual and institutional concerns about the burden of two tenths now due to the Crown: for example, a gift of the patronage of Rathen church to Aberdeen Cathedral, a chapter from which an additional teind was already traditionally assigned to the justiciar of Scotia.[130]

However, most important of all, in spring 1328 the king also offered material assurances to nobles worried about how their kindred's regional power might be affected by the restoration of any disinherited. For example, on 17 March – the very date of the treaty's ratification – a substantial royal pension of 128 merks owed to Holyrood Abbey (which had been assigned Galloway justiciary income) was redirected to the king's grandson, Robert Steward, though reduced to reflect the decline in value of the source lands since 1286 and with exemption from prise and other burdens.[131] This may have been prompted by the king's letters patent ostensibly restoring Henry de Beaumont and Thomas Wake, alongside Percy, to their border lands. Percy's restoration might be slowly permitted, at most displacing Robert's grants to Sir Donald Campbell and Randolph of half of the baronies of Redcastle (Angus) and Urr (Galloway) respectively.[132] But Beaumont laid claim to the earldom of Buchan, the Constableship of Scotland, the sheriffdom of Wigtownshire (and its barony caput of Cruggleton), and Roxburghshire lands at Sprouston and Hawick, a direct challenge to King Robert's alienation of these titles and offices to several of his leading supporters: Randolph, the house of Ross, Sir Gilbert Hay, Sir Robert Keith, James Douglas and his brother Archibald, Robert Steward, Holyrood Abbey, Melrose Abbey, Whithorn Priory and the king's natural son, Robert Bruce. The same might be concluded of the remarkable 500-merk annuity first recorded as paid to the latter, in an account submitted in June 1328, perhaps in compensation for his anticipated loss of the west March lordship of Liddesdale to Thomas Wake: the latter also claimed Kirkandrews and Barlocco in Dumfriesshire, held again after 1318 by the good Sir James's brother, Archibald (future Guardian 1332–33).[133]

All told, although the paucity of sources must render any firm conclusions tentative, the impression nonetheless persists that the peace reached with England in March 1328 quickly became something of an anticlimax, a settlement surrounded by anxiety and doubts as to whether it would hold. Over and above worries about its implications within Scotland, the Scots must have become aware of the refusal of a number of English nobles – headed by Henry, earl of Lancaster – to ratify the peace (and other Isabella–Mortimer policies and appointments).[134] But the concerns of the Scottish community of the realm must have been magnified, still, by Robert's poor health and life expectancy (as well as the infancy of his son). No payments are extant to physicians or apothecaries at this time, but the English envoys' report of Robert's incapacity during the Holyrood assembly rings true.[135] Certainly, on 16 May 1328 Thomas Randolph, earl of Moray and future Guardian, gifted £24 annually to Elgin Cathedral in Moray for five chantry masses 'with music' dedicated to 'St Thomas Becket, martyr', and in memory of King Robert, with additional masses for feasts of the Virgin, the dead (All Souls') and St John the Baptist (24 June, Bannockburn day).[136] One further sign that the community was now waiting nervously for their king's end was that there would be no council or parliament held in autumn 1328 or Lent 1329.

Scottish nerves and Crown–subject relations may have been tested, too, by preparations for Prince David's wedding to Princess Joan at Berwick in the summer, and an exchequer audit of 5 to 27 June that reveals much of the state of royal finances (although clerk Thomas Charteris, empowered to purchase luxuries in Bruges for the nuptials, was to be exempt from audit).[137]

The death in office on 20 May 1328 of Bishop William Lamberton of St Andrews and the loss of his considerable experience in mediating with the English and across the Scottish polity must have been a further blow at this sensitive stage.[138] It came a little over a month after Abbot Bernard of Arbroath had demitted office as royal Chancellor, in anticipation of his consecration in the bishopric of Sodor/the Isles (which was completed by November).[139] At least these changes brought the Crown valuable temporalities from St Andrews (potentially over £2,000 per annum) to offset its growing obligations. This income was immediately assigned to the household of David Bruce, earl of Carrick, and the cost of his nuptials, although James Ben, archdeacon of St Andrews, would be consecrated in the realm's chief see by August that year (a promotion secured at Avignon in defiance of the split chapter choice in June of none other than Alexander de Kinninmonth as the bishop-elect).[140] In addition, a sizable portion of the fee income of the royal chancery (£56 in 1329) would also no longer be siphoned off (legally) to support Arbroath Abbey, as Ben's ambassadorial colleague of 1324–25, Master Walter de Twynham, canon of Glasgow, had now taken over as Chancellor.[141] However, even with this shuffle and welcome windfalls, and before the wedding expenditure (over £2,400) was factored in, the royal Chamberlain, now the professional clerk Robert de Peebles, was obliged to record a deficit in June 1328, with an over-expenditure of more than £1,776 against a Crown income of just £3,793.[142]

This was the reality despite what appears in the extant record to be a quite efficient and fully manned bureaucracy of burgh provosts and custamars alongside sheriffs and their baillies.[143] A few more burghs were able to contribute teind for the king's household tenth and to the 'contribution for peace' in 1328–29, including Cullen, Banff, Aberdeen, Dundee, Montrose and Forfar, but these remained at a modest, often quite erratic level, and no such contribution was or could be provided through other markets such as Inverness, Dumbarton, Ayr, Dumfries, Roxburgh or Berwick.[144] Moreover, in 1328–29, the burghs would challenge their obligation to contribute to this exaction from their fermes and customs.[145] The return of rental and ferme teinds from the sheriffdoms was admittedly far stronger, with the officers of the shires of Banff (£43), Aberdeen (£221), Forfar (16s 8d, strikingly low after all Robert's alienations of demesne there), Stirling (£80), Fife (with Crail, £7), Edinburgh (including Haddington and Lintlithgow, £205), Selkirk (£14), Roxburgh (£169) and Berwick (£115) all making returns in June 1328; but, again, these ranged in value quite widely.

It is uncertain whether these variable returns reflected simple administrative delays (quite probable in the case of the large shire of Perth), lingering war damage to the populace and economy or more recent payment resistance and/or disruption to a locality. However, it is striking that no king's tenth or peace contributions were returned in this fiscal year by the sheriffs of Cromarty, Dingwall, Inverness, Nairn/Forres (Moray), Perth, Kincardine, Clackmannan, Dumbarton, Argyll, Ayr, Lanark, Wigtown, Dumfries or Peebles. It is certainly credible that what the source gaps hide are territorial disputes, tax resistance and variable levels of disorder in these northern, central, western and south-western regions of former Balliol/ Comyn sympathies or of lordship displaced in 1307–10, 1314 or 1320. Some such regional disruption may have been ongoing in some quarters since before 1300 or 1306, and certainly since the parliament of December 1318 had forbade nobles to prosecute disputes 'arising from the war'.[146] For example, in the far north, by the 1330s–1340s, the house of Ross can certainly be found embroiled in a number of disputes with neighbouring kindreds such as the Mackenzies of Kintail: as Guardian, Thomas Randolph would have to intervene in the north-west in 1331 to hang over fifty outlaws from the walls of Eilean Donan castle.[147] Tensions in this locality must have bled, too, into ongoing Stewart–Menteith–Campbell clashes with the MacDonalds and MacRuaridhs and their allied kin in Clydeside, Kintyre, mainland Argyll and Lochaber.[148] The peace treaty itself had made provision for prohibiting English aid to Robert's enemies in the event of a revolt 'in the Isles of Man or in the other Isles of Scotland'.[149] That the west and south-west also remained a troubled zone is suggested by the pilgrimage-come-recruitment drive that the king himself would make from Cardross to Whithorn in 1329 (discussed below), apparently with good effect as far as the teind returns of that region were concerned by summer 1329. Still, Randolph as Guardian would be targeted by a gang of assassins from Galloway just before much of this region came out in armed support of Edward Balliol in 1332.[150]

We should not, though, over-exaggerate the threat that these predictable areas of resistance to Bruce rule represented. Following Prince David's marriage, Robert's government would clearly work very hard to improve teind/peace collection: here it must be acknowledged that the moral weight of requiring contributions to a peace indemnity for the 'common good' may have helped. An account intromitted in August 1329 at Scone by Alexander de Ber, abbot of Dunfermline (from circa spring 1328), as 'receiver' of the peace funds would include income for the previous year from the sheriffs of Kincardine (£27), Clackmannan (£7), Lanark (£102, perhaps for two years), Wigtown (£44), Dumfries (£180, perhaps for two years), Peebles (£44) and Perth (£273, almost certainly for two years), in addition to a second round of tenths from all the sheriffs who had intromitted a peace contribution in 1328.[151] The abbot also returned what may have been delayed peace contributions from the dioceses of Ross (£71), Caithness (£64), Moray (£196), Aberdeen (£144), Brechin (£380), Dunkeld (£120), Dunblane (£112) and St Andrews (£992), as well as a number of monastic houses.[152] In the same fiscal year to August 1329, the exchequer would also record one-off peace contribution payments (though not 1326 king's tenths) from the earldom of Carrick (£100) and the Isle of Man (£150), and further clerical contributions, including arrears from the diocese of Glasgow (for which the figure is lost) and £36 from its neighbouring see in Whithorn/Galloway. All this amounted by summer 1329 – when the first war indemnity payment of 10,000 merks was due to be transferred to England through agents in Bruges – to well over £7,000 in teinds collected.[153] However, given that, as we shall see, at least £2,000 seems to have been assigned to vital expenditures at the Papacy at that time, this does seem to confirm that Robert's regime would still need to be able to rely not only on sustaining (really, raising) this level of exaction over the next two years but also on calling upon some cash reserves to cover any shortfall owed to England or required for the domestic household and government.[154] Indeed, the Chamberlain's extant account of August 1329 records an impressive £12,131 in total income but set against an expenditure of £13,466.[155] It is understandable that in this context the Scots requested – and were permitted by the English on 13 May 1328 – to split their first year's indemnity payment, handing over half at midsummer 1329, half at Martinmas (11 November). At the close of his reign, therefore, Robert remained firmly in the red, and even if three years of shared fiscal pain could be weathered, the Crown would not necessarily emerge in sustainable financial health.[156]

Such worries for the immediate future may explain the exchequer's apparent accountancy trick of holding over the £2,000 and more of expenditures in Paris, Flanders and Scotland by Robert's agents for food, spices, wine and cloth for the celebration of David's wedding to Joan at Berwick on 17 July.[157] However, what should again have been another moment of great triumph and closure for the Bruce Scots was also drawn into question by the absence of both kings. Edward III reportedly refused to endorse this match arising from the 'shameful peace', withholding a dowry and staying away as Robert was apparently ill.[158] The latter could easily have been the case, or perhaps Robert, too, absented himself. Nevertheless, he charged Moray, Douglas and other officials as his agents to act both as hosts for their wedding guests – with Joan accompanied by her mother – and to deal with issues pending from the peace treaty. It was on this occasion that Robert surely sought to balance minimal satisfaction for the disinherited English lords against further pressure upon Isabella and Mortimer's regime (at that time faced with mounting criticism of their maintenance of law and order within England). On this occasion, Isabella had certainly been charged by her son's council to treat with the king of Scots 'of the lands which Scots used to have in our land of England, and to grant them to them in our name according to what she perceives to be to our honour and profit, inasmuch as the said king of Scotland does similarly towards our Englishmen regarding their lands in Scotland'.[159] Some further tentative agreement over the restoration of selected disinherited lands was evidently reached. On 16 July, the day before the nuptials of Prince David and Joan, the king's great seal was used to confirm a further Durham/Coldingham grant; then, on 28 July, perhaps through a chancery clerk at Glasgow while Robert resided at Cardross, the king issued his aforementioned charter to Sir Henry Percy, empowering him to seek restoration to any of his father's lands and possessions in Scotland to which he had or felt he could prove a legal right in court – but, crucially, naming no specific estates.[160]

Moray and Douglas were both present as witnesses to the latter act, having accompanied David and Joan from Berwick to Cardross. While the young couple now set out for David's separate Carrick household at Turnberry, King Robert and Moray prepared to press home the second advantage gained at Berwick through dealings with Isabella.[161] This had been afforded by the presence at the wedding of Robert's young nephew, William de Burgh, earl of Ulster. Isabella's desire to secure Ulster's support and control of Carrickfergus castle may have allowed Robert to reach an understanding or, more likely, act to exploit Isabella and Mortimer's fears of further unrest in Ireland. For, by 13 August, Robert – transferred by litter to his great ship at Dumbarton – had crossed once more to Larne in County Antrim with his nephew, where he oversaw William's installation as earl and secured his physical control of Carrickfergus castle, despite (or perhaps via) letters of commission from Isabella.[162] This was an agreeable family intervention by Robert, one that like his visit of 1327 might help to consolidate his lordship over the western approaches and Isles of Scotland. But by appearing as the influential patron of the leading Anglo-Norman kindred in Ireland, Robert perhaps also made it plain to Isabella what might arise if he also became superior and patron to leading northern English lords such as Percy, Wake and Beaumont, should he restore them their Scottish lands (just as Rhys ap Gruffudd's sympathies gave Robert a potential anti-Mortimer foothold in Wales). According to Irish annals, Robert may even have attempted to organise a meeting at Greencastle with the council of the acting English justiciar, Roger Outlaw.[163]

Robert's continued influence in Ireland was therefore – along with the promised indemnity to the bankrupt English regime – key to forcing Isabella and Mortimer to drop active support for the restoration of the disinherited in Scotland. It perhaps explains why, although the king seems to have pressed in 1328 for the restoration of lands in County Meath to the Cistercian abbey of Dundrennan in Dumfriesshire (aided by the sympathies of the English peace envoy, the abbot of Rievaulx, Dundrennan's mother house), he did not forward the claims of the earldoms of Carrick or Atholl or the Stewarts to their lost Irish lands at the same time.[164] Such a threat carried far more leverage than grievances expressed about Isabella's inability to return the stone of Scone (and probably other important relics, including St Margaret's original 'Black Rude') at Berwick, as she had been empowered to do, following vociferous protests by the community and tenants of Westminster Abbey (supported by Edward III).[165] However, in the medium term, this would also provoke a majority of the disinherited lords in the southern realm, both Englishmen and Scots, to abandon the Queen Mother and the offensive Mortimer, now aspiring to control of Ireland, and instead to support the rebellion of Henry, earl of Lancaster, from October 1328 to January 1329. The allegiances and outcome of this bloodless, failed revolt (which cost Lancaster his head) justified the wisdom of Robert's evasive policy towards the disinherited and hint at collusion with Isabella.[166] For, while Sir Henry Percy remained loyal to Isabella as Lieutenant in the north, Beaumont and his new son-in-law, David Strathbogie, earl of Atholl, Wake and other lords with a claim to Scottish lands, such as Ralph Stafford and Henry Ferrers (who both claimed Zouche's inheritance of the thirteenth-century Moreville/de Quinci holdings), had all backed the losing side and were forfeited and exiled.[167] However, typically, this proved only temporary, and after October 1330 an independent, angry Edward III would favour their cause and Edward Balliol anew.[168]

# CHAPTER ELEVEN

# Beat the Devil

## Preparing for the End, 1328–29

*This agreement [peace with Scotland, 1328] was wholly unacceptable to Edward III, but because of his young age, the queen and Mortimer arranged it all, which was one of the causes of their downfall afterwards.*

Sir Thomas Gray, *Scalacronica*[1]

### The Final Ayres, August 1328–June 1329

Robert I was now indulging in a short-term strategy because he knew he had little time left. On 5 November 1328, Pope John XXII would grant him permission to receive plenary remission of sins from his unnamed personal confessor at the hour of death, a rite he must have requested that summer (permitted by canon law in spite of the interdict).[2] Robert's extant datable acts resume, after his August trip to Ulster, on 16 October 1328 with the king in reflective mood, visiting Kinkell, the head church of his sister Christina's lordship of Garioch (and a parsonage held by Alexander de Kinninmonth).[3] The Bruce siblings probably acted together in a royal grant of Aberdeenshire lands to the hospital of Turriff, originally founded by the Comyn earl of Buchan in 1272, to support a chaplain saying mass for the soul of their younger brother, Neil Bruce (d.1306). This formed part of a last royal ayre to the north-east, which included a stay at Cullen: here the king finalised his foundation of a chaplainry, praying for the soul of his late queen over the interment of her viscera in the Lady Chapel of that burgh.[4]

Robert was also to combine his spirituality with a final demonstration of royal authority, one directed to that unresolved, humbling frontier of his realm, the Gaelic west and south-west. Early November found him back at his manor house at Cardross while an exchequer audit was underway in

Glasgow, approving the settlement of debts incurred for his son's wedding and inspecting the rights of the merchants of the bishopric of Glasgow to trade in Argyll.[5] But sometime in the second half of November, Robert – probably accompanied by the earl of Moray, Bernard, the new bishop of the (Western) Isles, Murdoch, earl of Menteith, Sir John Menteith junior, and Stewart and Campbell knights – boarded his 'great ship' and sailed one last time for Tarbert castle.[6] He resided there for over a month, enforcing royal and surely diocesenal power as best possible in this porous, troubled zone. A charter of 6 February 1329, granting Sir Duncan Campbell his father's lands of Benderloch (on Loch Etive) in return for the continued service of a twenty-six-oared galley, recorded that these lands had recently been resigned to the king in the presence of 'the barons of Argyll'.[7] Clearly, in the last few months of Robert's life the settlement of the west was on his mind, and the king's continuing strategy of reliance upon several kindreds with strong mainland ties was also surely informed by his recent visit to Ulster.

His last Christmas found the king at the hall of Glenkill on Sir John Menteith's island of Arran, en route to see his son Prince David at Turnberry in Carrick. It is likely that at this point the king fell ill once more, slowing his itinerary and postponing any plans that might have been in train for a council or parliament: his son and daughter-in-law Joan thus seem to have come to him for Yule.[8] Robert did reach his boyhood home, however, and 6 February 1329 found the king still at Turnberry's sea-castle. This was the beginning indeed of a 'long drawn-out and surely painful pilgrimage' through Carrick and Wigtownshire to the shrine of St Ninian at Whithorn.[9] In venerating Ninian, Robert acted on his own genuine personal belief in that saint's powers, but this also allowed him to embrace a cult swelling in regional and indeed national popularity with Scottish subjects.[10] Yet as with his recent voyage to Tarbert, this was also a journey broken at several stops, which saw Robert extend further patronage both to family members, close supporters and, in return for specific military services, to tenants throughout the south-west, Argyll and the Isles.[11] Indeed, in total, Robert's final ayre secured to the Crown the services of at least two galleys, four archers and five spearmen. Of the twenty-five or so royal acts that can be dated to this period (down to April), a dozen related to lands in Dumfriesshire and Galloway and four to lands in Argyll.[12] Moreover, Robert was visited by a number of magnates and representatives of clerical and burghal communities, aware that their king was drawing close to death, who would not otherwise have ventured into the south-west: these people moved in and out of a household otherwise supplied by the sheriffdom of Wigtown, Crossraugel Abbey and Whithorn Cathedral Priory.[13]

This creeping court began at Turnberry with a grant of Wigtownshire lands to John, son of Neil of Carrick. Then at Girvan (6 February), still within Carrick, Robert granted all Aberdeen burgesses willing to serve in war exemption from prise, other burdens and judicial authority (as with some of his lay patronage, a recognition that this war-damaged community could not sustain a cash rent or heavy taxes at this time); and he granted an annuity of £20 from the fermes of Ayr to the Dominicans of that burgh (who supplied tutors for his son).[14] By the close of the same day Robert had moved south 7 miles to Carleton (from where the Bruces of Carrick drew lairdly servants), where his aforementioned charter of Benderloch in Argyll to Sir Duncan Campbell was issued.[15] It may have been during this stop that the king and his officials heard word that no revenues had been returned from the Western Isles by the sheriff of Argyll (Duncan's nephew, Dugall) or through the bishopric of the Isles/Sodor.[16] This did not prevent the king from donating £4 for construction of the tomb of the late Gilbert Maclelan, bishop of Sodor, possibly at the behest of his former Chancellor (and Gilbert's successor), Bernard.[17] The witnesses to Sir Duncan's and most subsequent acts of this royal tour included the Chancellor, the earl of Moray, Douglas, Hay, Keith and a number of familiar knights, many of them drawn from Prince David's Carrick household such as Alexander Seton, Adam More, Robert Boyd of Kilmarnock/Noddsdale and Malcolm Fleming of Biggar/Kirkintilloch (who would be confirmed by David II as earl of Wigtown in 1341).[18]

Almost a fortnight later, 18 February, Robert can be located only another 20 miles south at Inchmichael (east of present-day Stranraer). Here his illness took hold and the company paused for at least six weeks: temporary shelter was built and supplies brought in (including barley, some of which the king dispatched by ship to Tarbert).[19] It is logical to infer that from hereon, although Robert was able to fulfil some aspects of his kingship, Thomas Randolph, earl of Moray, assumed much of effective royal power. This halt certainly allowed Moray to make excursions to attend to business in his lordships of Annandale and the Isle of Man, from which £150 in peace contribution was intromitted at this time (but problems in collecting further revenue from this Isle were noted).[20] The king's grants while resting at Inchmichael included Kirkcudbrightshire lands for a local retainer, Martin MacGech; milling privileges for the Dominicans of Ayr; a repeat of Aberdeen burgh's recent rights; and Perthshire lands for John de Dunfermline as clerk of the liverance.[21] But there was also favour paid to

Prince David's two immediate heirs presumptive: Robert Steward (as lord of Kintyre, he might well have accompanied the king to Tarbert), who now received the Lanarkshire barony of Renfrew (21 March); and Donald, earl of Mar, who received a charter of Saline in Clackmannanshire (now west Fife) and Mountblairy in Banffshire, but with the condition that they be retained for the duration of her life by Isabel of Atholl, his cousin.[22] This allows us to include in the records of this Lenten period three undated, summarised royal grants to Alexander Bruce, Isabel's son by Edward Bruce, earl of Carrick and lord of Galloway: this youth, whom Guardian Randolph would ensure became earl of Carrick, too, after Robert's death and David II's accession, now received the baronies of Dun in Forfarshire (north of Arbroath) and Carnesmole and Mochrum in Wigtownshire.[23] These latter lordships bordered the estates of the cathedral priory of Whithorn, suggesting Alexander's presence during the king's pilgrimage to this church in 1329 and pointing strongly to a Crown intention to promote his nearly adult nephew (born c.1312–15) to his father's full patrimony as lord of Galloway. For Robert Steward, by the 1330s, this would have raised real concerns about Alexander's possible rehabilitated place within the royal succession.[24]

Recovering somewhat by 29 March, Robert moved on to another house of Galloway foundation, Glenluce Abbey, Dundrennan's daughter house: here he repeated his favour to Donald of Mar and Isabel of Atholl.[25] Two days later the king had reached Monreith, 7 miles from Whithorn.[26] By 1 April, three weeks before Easter, he had finally reached the shrine of St Ninian at Whithorn (which also held lands in Kintyre and the Isle of Man). Robert's extant acts here include several grants to lesser local nobles and further lands to Sir Arthur Campbell in northern Argyllshire in return for the service of a 'birling' of twenty oars.[27] Aside from a gift of wood to the bishop of Galloway (for the repair of church fabric, thus probably earning the king an indulgence), no evidence of alms or other firmly datable acts of veneration of St Ninian are extant. But it is likely that Robert, frail as he was, remained at Whithorn, penitent throughout Holy Week.[28]

By early May at the latest the king had been transported back to his manor house at Cardross, which he would never leave again. His acts continued to mix government business with spiritual lights. On 3 May he sent letters to Edward III requesting restoration of stated Northumbrian holdings for his favoured abbey of Arbroath, in veneration of 'St Thomas of Canterbury', including Haltwhistle church, the Bruce family's gift of the late twelfth century.[29] This was arguably a further reflection of Robert's preparedness to make exceptions to his unspoken rule of preventing full mutual restoration of the disinherited. Robert's letters stressed his own part in 'daily restoring benefices to English churchmen', a claim at least partly substantiated by his favour in 1328–29 to Coldingham/Durham (and which may also be extended to permitting monks of 'English' birth expelled from houses from Jedburgh to Dunfermline now to return to their brethren). However, this request may have been designed to ease the way for other more pressing appeals to Edward III's regime. Not least, on 13 May 1329, letters of the English king would agree to the Scots' staggering of their first year of indemnity payment.[30] Moreover, the day before this postponement was conceded, Sir James Douglas had been restored to his family manor of Faudon in Northumberland and other lesser lands (including holdings in Essex).[31] There remained, though, further practical issues arising from the peace over which compromise could not be reached. Also on 12 May, separate letters by Robert protested the English innova-tion of a levy of three pence in the pound on Scottish merchants' goods imported to, or exported from, England.[32] Proof that the Scottish burghs had had an opportunity to petition their dying king on this issue directly, in the absence of a council or parliament, may survive from 28 May when a charter converted the rents of Edinburgh and Leith to a fixed feu-ferme (an arrangement already struck with a number of burghs, including Scotland's key wool port, Berwick) of 52 merks per annum.[33] Yet appar-ently unsatisfied on this issue by the English, Robert and his ministers (or Randolph's first assembly as Guardian) responded by raising customs on foreign merchants' goods entering and exiting Scotland to a pointed four pence in the pound.[34]

As well as the gathering of materials for his monument, and considera-tion of its design, Robert now turned finally to testify to his desire that his heart should be removed from his body (once more in defiance of papal mandates) and taken on armed pilgrimage to the Holy Land.[35] On 11 May he issued letters of protection to Melrose Abbey, where his heart was to be interred upon its return from the Holy Land, and also requested that his son and successors maintain and increase the annuity of Berwick burgh fermes and other royal revenues assigned to that house for the repair of its fabric and support of the monks' daily 'king's dish'.[36] That some of these requests were expressed by the king through a spoken (and perhaps written) personal testament, delivered to his attendant son and chief subjects, has long been an accepted tradition of Robert I's last days. As Barbour later had it:

Tharfor his lettrys sone send he
For the lordis off his cuntre
And thai come as thai biddyng had.
His testament than has he maid
Befor bath lordis and prelatis . . .[37]

Jean le Bel, too, wrote of Robert's deathbed explanation to his subjects of his vow to go to the Holy Land once his throne was secure.[38] Some proof that his arrangements with Melrose Abbey at this time were accompanied by his request to Sir James Douglas to lead a retinue charged with the king's bodily relic may lie in the extant royal grant of Eshiels in Peeblesshire to William Douglas of Lothian, esquire, one of several retainers who might be expected to follow his cousin, Sir James, on his crusade.[39]

The choice of Melrose Abbey was perhaps not as important as the heart's pilgrimage itself, a bold statement to Robert's own subjects and Christian Europe that would reward his soul with a posthumous plenary indulgence, evading Purgatory at a time when his envoys were still lobbying at the curia for the lifting of his excommunication and Scotland's inter-dict.[40] His heart's journey may also have served as a response to Edward I's reputation as a crusader.[41] Melrose itself, however, stood as one of the realm's wealthiest houses, a Cistercian mother house that would multiply votive prayers for Robert across the kingdom as well as eternalise his name in a church that also housed the tomb of Alexander II (d.1249), perhaps the king of Scots perceived by Robert and his subjects as the most defiant and independent of Plantagenet England before 1286.[42] Both Alexander and Robert had suffered excommunication in the course of war against England and may also have chosen Melrose for part of their obsequies as that house had an exemption from any papal interdict placed upon the wider realm. Indeed, in 1217 Alexander had undergone a penitential ritual of pardon for his excommunication at Berwick (imposed after he had waged war on England and taken the homage of Northumbrian knights at Melrose).[43] Some part of Robert I's selection of Melrose Abbey for his heart's interment may thus have sought to ensure its presence there for a posthumous ceremonial aspersion and pardon reconciling him officially to the Church should he not live long enough to see the excommunication and interdict lifted (as indeed transpired).[44] More obviously, alongside its burghal counterpart at Berwick, the abbey of Melrose represented Robert's full recovery of the territorial and spiritual lordship of his kingdom. The king's preparations for his heart were also accompanied by bequests for the interment of his viscera in the chapel of St Serf near Cardross and for perpetual soul masses to be funded there and at Ayr and Berwick Blackfriars, as well as at Dunfermline.[45] We lack evidence of the specific feast days ('collects') requested by Robert for these perpetual masses, but they would surely have reflected his lifelong veneration of such saints as the Virgin, Andrew, Margaret, Thomas, Kentigern, Ninian, Cuthbert, Fillan, Serf, Machutus and Malachy, as well as the anniversary of Bannockburn, St John the Baptist's Day, 24 June.[46]

The end, when it came, did so quietly. Robert's final extant acts of 28 and 31 May 1329 concern the gift of an annual sum of 20 merks to the Greyfriars of Dundee and an inspection of a wedding gift by a Peeblesshire freeholder for his daughter, records that suggest Robert remained approach-able in person by his subjects until the last.[47] The recorded witnesses to these acts remained, as throughout his last few months, the Chancellor, Thomas, earl of Moray, James Douglas, Gilbert Hay, Robert Keith and Adam More, a group thus dominated by a core of his surviving military captains. It is possible that in his last hours Bernard, bishop of Sodor, the king's long-serving former Chancellor and abbot of Arbroath, acted as his confessor: 'On 7 June 1329, died Robert Bruce, of pious memory, the illus-trious king of Scots, at Cardross, in the twenty-fourth year of his reign. He was, beyond all living men of his day, a valiant knight.'[48]

## What Killed the King?

Just what caused the death of Robert I a month before his fifty-fifth birthday has remained an unsolvable, 'interminable debate'.[49] An objective assessment might conclude that we simply cannot state what had ailed Robert since around 1308, just as historians are unable to identify what illness claimed the life of Edward I.[50] Contemporary accusations that Robert suffered from leprosy, the 'unclean sickness' – the present-day, treat-able Hansen's disease – derived, as we have seen, from English and Hainault chroniclers.[51] Their bias rings far more loudly as false propaganda than the vague descriptions of Robert's infirmity by later Scottish verse and chron-icle sources. To Robert's enemies, too, such condemnation, with the king suffering Purgatory-on-earth, was a fitting punishment for an excommu-nicate, sacrilegious murderer, usurper, traitor and slaughterer of women, children and clerics.[52]

However, even when primed for the slanders of those whom Robert defied, it also remains very difficult to accept the notion of a functioning king serving in war, performing face-to-face acts of lordship, holding parliament and court, travelling widely and fathering several children, all while displaying the infectious symptoms of a leper. The same might be said, however, of the symptoms of extra-pulmonary tuberculosis (though these may slumber asymptomatically for years), which might manifest most obviously as a chronic cough, bloody spit, fever, weight loss (hence 'consumption') and scrofula – lymphadenopathy in the form of growing masses around the neck.[53] Moreover, accusations of scrofula offered a direct challenge to Robert's claim to be a true king. For his counterparts as anointed monarchs of England and France were able to use the ceremonial 'royal touch' to cure scrofula, or the 'king's evil', in their subjects, who in fact probably suffered from a wide range of afflictions.[54] Edward I 'touched' thousands of his scrofulous subjects, including over nine hundred who sought him out from November 1304 during his final Scottish residency.[55] Edward II continued this tradition and distribution of a penny in alms to each subject touched (though in smaller numbers); he also regularised a second English royal 'miracle' of distributing rings, made from silver and gold coins blessed on the altar of the Holy Cross each Good Friday, as a cure for epilepsy and other muscular conditions.[56] By contrast, with the exception of the pious William I in old age, attributed with a single cure of scrofula performed at York in 1206, no king of Scots seems to have attempted to 'touch' away their subjects' sufferings.[57]

Nevertheless, Robert's veneration of such saints' cults as those of Becket, Ninian, Kentigern and even (Queen) Margaret hint at a search for a cure from leprosy or a similar affliction.[58] Even his manor house at Cardross lay just over a dozen miles from a celebrated curative centre at Inchinnan in Renfrewshire where a seventh-century evangelist from Ireland, St Convall (feast day 28 September), chief disciple of Glasgow's Kentigern, was said to have been buried, leaving behind a miraculous stone that cured sick men and beasts: from 1327 onwards, Robert's exchequer supported 'lights' in St Convall's church from the burgh fermes of Rutherglen.[59] Moreover, Barbour's descriptions of Robert suffering 'sik a sekness' as benumbed his limbs and sapped his strength and appetite (1308) or left him paralysed (1328–29) does fit with symptoms of leprosy or scrofula.[60] About 5 per cent of the human population have no immunity to the bacteria that cause leprosy and which if not effectively treated can manifest variously as skin lesions (penetrating to bone and bodily tissues), paralysis, alopecia, eye complaints, respiratory (and thus speech) problems, sterility, impotence, and a dangerously reduced immunity to other ailments.

However, although better diet and shelter may have allowed an elite medieval figure to live with such a serious illness for a number of years, in an age of limited medical knowledge, heavily structured by Vulgate Scripture, '*lepra*', like 'fever' (and 'scrofula'), was a label applied by an uneducated laity to a multitude of conditions, particularly those resulting in skin lesions such as venereal infections or cancers (and even trauma). Not least, it has in recent studies of medieval medicine morphed into an early form of trepenomal disease or pre-1492 (New World) syphilis, the 'pox' thereafter or (as it was known by 1632) 'venereal leprosy'.[61] Bruce, who had several illegitimate children by different women before 1300 and then while separated from his second wife, may have contracted such a sexually transmitted condition.[62] A number of Scottish trepenomal cases have recently been identified from excavated medieval skeletons, including one possible example at Whithorn.[63] Infected individuals would also suffer from skin lesions penetrating to the bone (especially on the skull), as well as cartilage loss, darkened teeth enamel and eroded joints. All this might easily present to an uneducated onlooker or enemy as symptoms associated with *facies leprosa*. Yet it would not necessarily cause a contemporary medical practitioner to make a misdiagnosis.[64]

By the same token, however, the modern reader is confronted with fragmentary or generalised records from Robert I's exchequer circa 1327–29 for purchases of herbs, spices, minerals, liquids and other materials, often in bulk, which could have been used to create purgatives to purify a patient's humours of black bile or for baths and salves for tortured skin: yet these might also have been applied by medieval physicians to treat *lepra* or a *pox* (or were intended innocently for the kitchen).[65] In his last months Edward I also received herbal and mineral treatments including baths, ointment and special breeches for his legs and, suggestively, a 'plaster' for his neck.[66]

Conversely, we should not dismiss completely Barbour's inherited explanation of Robert's infirmity as being due to hard campaigning in bad weather. Throughout 1306–9, and again during the Irish campaigns of 1315 and 1317, Robert and his followers suffered extreme privation of diet and shelter, a fact reflected in the rhetoric of the 'Declaration of Arbroath'.[67] Even such elite figures may thus have found their health compromised by the grain famine of 1315–17 and the cattle/dairy pandemic of 1319–21.[68] A resulting severe intestinal and digestive complaint affecting the king's whole constitution, worsened by cold and wet weather, and later rich court food, may also have been a contributory factor in Robert's death. His Milanese physician circa 1326–29, Maino de Maineri, did criticise the king's eating of eels as dangerous to his health in advancing years.[69]

## Funeral and Sepulchre

In 1818, workmen clearing the rubble of the ruined abbey choir at Dunfermline to make way for a new Protestant church found a stone grave containing a skeleton shrouded in lead directly to the west of the position of the high altar. Given its location and an incision in the sternum of the corpse to allow removal of the heart, it was (and remains) generally accepted that these were the bones of Robert I.[70] Late twentieth-century facial reconstructions, based upon plaster casts of the skull of this skeleton taken in 1819 before it was re-interred in a coffin brimmed with pitch, seemed to confirm the likelihood of Robert's leprous condition. This archaeology has produced the image of an impressive, thickset man but with facial lesions to the bone, scarred by both disease and war (with a healed blade blow to the jaw).[71] However, all of this is moot if the remains examined and cast in 1819 were not those of Robert I. After the destruction of all the royal tombs at Dunfermline during the Reformation (1560) and their ruins' subsequent exposure to the elements for over three centuries, only ambivalent circumstantial evidence remains to point to the grave and skeleton found in 1818 as being indeed those of the Bruce king.[72] Most royals and aristocrats indulged in separate heart burial well into the fourteenth century.[73] Moreover, as with chroniclers' frustratingly vague descriptions of the location of royal tombs, so the symptoms attributed to Robert, if treponematous, might just as easily be ascribed to a number of earlier kings, along with any battle wounds, such as Malcolm III, Alexander I, David I or even Alexander III, all of whom fought wars or jousted, lived past middle age, and were buried in Dunfermline.[74]

Robert I did begin the preparation of his tomb at Dunfermline during his own lifetime. But would he have chosen to place it alone directly before the high altar?[75] Given the nature of the monument commissioned, discussed below, this would have been a bold gesture, in keeping with a man prepared to kill to seize the throne, attempt a coronation ritual, push the Papacy for this full rite, and generally propagandise his legitimacy throughout his reign, aided by the *Ecclesia Scoticana*. Fordun's contemporary clerical source (from St Andrews), followed by Abbot Bower, both of whom would have visited Dunfermline regularly, assert that Robert was indeed buried 'in the middle of the choir'.[76] However, Bower also stated earlier in his narrative that when Queen Elizabeth died in 1327, she was 'buried in the choir at Dunfermline next to her husband King Robert'.[77] This abbot of Inchcolm (less than 10 miles away) was of course reporting what he could see in his own day, but this does rather suggest that the royal couple were buried side by side. The logical place for such a close pair of tombs would have been in the north aisle of the choir, within ambulatory space leading to St Margaret's feretory shrine at the east end of the church: the style of Robert's tomb indeed suggested by the evidence of the extant exchequer rolls (and contemporary royal tombs elsewhere) also favours a canopied box-tomb with effigy, placed within or helping delineate aisle space. This would also have placed Robert's and Elizabeth's tombs at the entrance to the substantial Lady Chapel in Dunfermline, an extension probably completed later in the fourteenth century and in which, by circa 1357, many of Robert's relatives and key supporters were interred: his sisters Christina, Mary and Maud, his daughter Margaret (who married the earl of Sutherland in the 1340s), and Guardians Thomas Randolph and Andrew Murray.[78] Above all, the fragments of white marble attributed to Robert's tomb and collected by Georgian antiquarians from the rubble-strewn floor of the ruined, roofless choir, could have come from anywhere in that space.[79]

In this context, it would be far more logical that the grave and skeleton unearthed and inspected in 1818–19 belonged not to Robert I but in fact to the king who had raised this house to abbatial status and built the choir, David I (r.1124–53): according to Bower's earlier sources, he was 'buried before the high altar under the paved part of the middle of the choir'.[80] Such a prestigious royal burial for the founder – originally under a deco-rated slab, not a monument with effigy – may also explain why in 1818 when the grave was opened no vestments, crown, sceptre or seal ring were found with the bones. These were the muniments of kingship that adorned the body of Edward I interred in Westminster Abbey in 1307 (as inspected in 1774) and which we might expect Robert's burial in 1329 would have emulated.[81] Instead, only fragments of a shroud of cloth of gold and, report-edly, a simple (lead?) coronet (which disintegrated on contact with air or was spirited away by locals) were found in 'King Robert's' grave.[82]

However, regardless of where Robert's tomb was situated, the nature of the memorial and his funeral ceremony that can be partly reconstructed undoubtedly point to an impressive and expensive assertion of Bruce monarchy. There may have been a delay between Robert's passing and his funeral, although because this did not, as it turned out, precede a prompt coronation service for David II, this period may have been extended. It may have allowed enough time for word to reach Scotland of the Papacy's lifting of its ecclesiastical censures on Robert and his kingdom; along with a bull granting his heirs and successors as kings the full rite of coronation and unction (dated 13 June 1329).[83] As with the Papacy's support for John Balliol's releases in 1299 and 1301, Avignon now really recognised Scottish sovereignty and granted these rites because the Pope was obliged to satisfy the demands of the French monarchy (from both Isabella as Queen Mother of Edward III and from Philip VI).

Jean Froissart (who may have visited Dunfermline Abbey with David II in 1365 and who otherwise drew on Jean le Bel's probable contact with James Douglas's party when it arrived in Bruges in 1330 with the king's heart) states that Robert was not buried until '7 November 1327' (sic): however, this may simply be a confusion for the date of death, 7 June, or a funeral on, say, 7 July (the Translation feast of St Thomas) in 1329.[84] In fact, Robert may have been buried within just two or three weeks of his demise, perhaps even on 24 June, the anniversary of Bannockburn.[85] After removal of the heart and viscera, the king's body was embalmed and carried east by a carriage decked in black lawn, with stops recorded at Dunipace and Cambuskenneth Abbey (after passing Bannockburn?), but also perhaps at Culross Abbey to provide a suitable church, dedicated to St Serf, for a night vigil before a final 7-mile procession to Dunfermline.[86] A file of mourners on foot including Robert Steward and a number of knights dressed in new black gowns (perhaps bearing symbolic gifts of gold-leaf cloth) accompanied the funeral party into the abbey, where the scene and assembled community would have been lit by hundreds of lights (with over 8,000 lb of wax purchased), many of them attached to a canopy chapel or 'hearse' of imported Baltic ('Eastland') wood probably decorated with heraldic arms.[87] Robert's body in a wooden coffin was then interred within a stone vault beneath the floor, underneath a box tomb of white Italian marble purchased in Paris after June 1328.[88]

This monument was surely decorated with the lion rampant arms of the king of Scots as well as those of the Bruces of Carrick and Annandale.[89] Incised 'kinship' figures with arms on the tomb's panels would also have commemorated Robert I's links to the houses of Plantagenet England, de Burgh Ulster, Norway, Steward, Mar, Randolph, Murray, Campbell, Ross and Fraser.[90] A plinth of black fossilferous limestone from Frosterley probably topped this structure – linking this royal interment to the tombs of its predecessors in Dunfermline (back to St Margaret and Malcolm III in their feretory shrine) and at Arbroath and Melrose.[91] Atop this plinth a white marble effigy of Robert, painted and gilded, linked the whole tomb in style to the ranks of black-and-white marble monuments of the kings and queens of France and their chief subjects, represented at the Benedictine Abbey of St Denis in the late thirteenth century (and which Thomas Randolph had surely seen in 1323–24 or 1325–26).[92] This was thus a conscious continuation of a spiritual, political and artistic tradition that drew from the land and monarchy of Scotland's ally, France, but may also have contained elements shared with the alabaster kinship tomb, effigy and Gothic canopy erected for Edward II at Gloucester Cathedral.[93]

The whole of Robert's tomb – to which a more permanent canopy may later have been added – was soon surrounded by an iron rail, suggesting that it stood indeed within a processional space.[94] Robert had bequeathed sufficient funds to pay for thousands of obituary masses in the abbey and elsewhere, on a scale similar to that of his French and English counterparts.[95] His tomb would thus be the site of daily votive prayers, more throughout the first year after Robert's death and on subsequent anniversaries. Moreover, as part of the liturgy of the funeral, Bishop Bernard of Sodor may have concluded his task of compiling a verse history of the reign by composing an epitaph for his late king, inscribed around the top of the tomb (and later preserved in the margins of a manuscript of Bower's *Scotichronicon*). It was a fitting summary of all that Robert I and his closest supporters surely hoped to convey and assert by his last public act:

Here lies the invincible blessed King Robert. Whoever reads about his feats will repeat the many battles he fought. By his integrity he guided to liberty the kingdom of the Scots. May he now live in Heaven.[96]

# Conclusion
## Bruce Kingship and the Legacy of Scotland's Wars, c.1286–c.1329

*Robert Bruce [the symbol of] the integrity of his country lies in the earth,*
*the prince of delight, upright, bold, dependable in all respects;*
*he was considered to be like Paris in appearance, like Hector in warfare;*
*the king was the rose of chivalry, as fluent a speaker as Socrates, Cato and*
*Maro.*
*He was born of Priam, he was like Achilles the leader of the Greeks,*
*as praiseworthy as Ajax, and as Ulysses the man of wiles,*
*as well-loved as the Macedonian, and like Arthur the jewel among men,*
*he was another intelligent Maccabee, the leader of peoples.*
*He was as conscientious as Aeneas, his strength was as extensive as that of*
*Pompey;*
*he was as gentle as Andrew, his strength as wonderful as Jonathan's;*
*this Saturn adorns the shores of Crete;*
*the rainstorm which crossed the Aegean goes away, summer has come into*
*bloom.*
*He was a Julius Caesar; in the hope he aroused he was an allegory of Simeon.*
*He was a distinguished King Charles, with the understanding of Solomon.*
*He was a law maker like Gaius, and a leader in thrall to Dido.*
*A Jason at heart, an upright Sejus, a bold spring of Helicon.*
*He had the strength of Samson, the blood of Bartholomew,*
*the steadfast faith of Simon, and a censer of Sabean.*
*He was seemly in his giving, and of royal pedigree,*
*a very bright daystar under Juno's Jupiter.*

Anonymous, Contemporary Epitaph[1]

There is much that is conventional in this rhetorical eulogy, presumably composed shortly after Robert's death.[2] It draws upon the 'mirrors of princes'

of the day, advice books for rulers informed by biblical and classical scholarship. These included the rediscovered *Politics* of Aristotle, and were works
based, really, upon the experience and ideals of Italian city states but magnified by the *Unam Sanctum* clash between Philip IV and Boniface VIII circa
1302–3. When applied throughout north-western Europe, such works were
more effective in defining and strengthening royal authority than in limiting
it. They were undoubtedly familiar to Scottish churchmen and literate laity
through Oxford and Cambridge and the continental universities and the
much copied works of such scholars as John of Salisbury (*Policraticus*, 1159),
Gerald of Wales (*Liber de Principis Instructione*, c.1193), Vincent of Beauvais
(*De Eruditione Filiorum Nobilium*, c.1250, a work heavily cited by Abbot
Bower), Thomas Aquinas (*De Regimine Principum*, c.1260), John of Paris
(d.1306, *De Potestate Regi et Papali*) and Giles of Rome (*De Regimine
Principum*, c.1277–79); and perhaps even through the more recent, contro-
versial treatises of Dante Alighieri (*Monarchia*, c.1308–21) or Marsilius of
Padua (*Defensor Pacis*, c.1324) aiding Emperor Louis IV against John XXII's
papal monarchy.[3]

At the same time this epitaph betrays the perspective of Scots looking
back wistfully upon the achievements of Robert's reign after the resumption
of war against England, Edward Balliol and the Disinherited in 1332–33
(punctuated by two costly defeats in battle for the Scots). As a result, this
verse, too, gives pre-eminence to Robert's military success. He was understandably to be best remembered as a leader of his people in war before he
was recalled as a paragon of other expected kingly virtues such as diplomacy,
justice, wisdom, erudition and piety. The latter, it might seem, were qualities
more readily found and praised in such contemporary monarchs as Edward I
(r.1272–1307), Philip IV (r.1285–1314) and, above all, the 'negotiatory',
learned rule of Robert of Naples (r.1309–43).[4] Yet martial prowess and guile
(a different kind of wisdom) in the cause of freeing his people and kingdom
were also the kingly characteristics which Robert himself and his close
followers chose to emphasise, chiefly through verse and chronicle that would
be inherited by Archdeacon Barbour and then Fordun and his continuators.[5]
This chivalric image is certainly intensified by Abbot Bower's recitation in
the 1440s of a vignette about a herald at the court of Edward III who spoke
out to insist that the 'noble Robert king of Scotland' had been a greater
fighter than Henry VII of Luxembourg (d.1313) – who, raised at the court
of his powerful overlord, Philip IV of France, had defied that monarch
and the Papacy as he fought his way to be crowned king of Italy and Holy
Roman Emperor in 1308–9 – and even a better commander than the famed
knight Giles d'Argentent (killed at Bannockburn): Bruce was thus first of the

'three Roberts who are the best warriors in the world . . . [ahead of] the king of Sicily [Robert of Naples, who had in turn defied claims of Imperial superiority by seeking papal lordship] and [the] Count Morain'.[6] By the same token, contemporaries and their near descendants may have gone so far as to rank Robert alongside the pantheon of the Nine Worthies of Chivalry, to several of whom indeed (Hector, Alexander the Great, Julius Caesar, King Arthur, Charlemagne and Judas Maccabeus) Robert I was compared by the epitaph above and by Barbour.[7]

Nevertheless, the development of the Bruce martial image – both for contemporaries and later generations – served to obscure from history the belief of important individuals and institutions amongst his subjects that a number of different aspects of his character and domestic rule after Bannockburn were equally vital and praiseworthy.[8] In that sense, the poetic memorial above assessed Robert as king of Scots in his own time and, although laced with mourning hyperbole, was largely free as yet of the domineering shadow of 'Robert the Bruce', the hero king, a national icon invoked, idealised and recast by successive generations of Scots to serve contemporary agendas.[9] As such, we should not ignore what this contemporary eulogy has to say about Robert I and his reign's attention to patronage, justice and law, counsel, piety and communal identity. These factors, symbolised in part by the armed knight and enthroned majesty on either side of Robert I's great seal (drawn from French models), should be given equal scrutiny in explaining his hard-fought survival and eventual success as king of Scots, particularly after Bannockburn, just as have been his undoubted personal grit, perseverance, charisma and military skills.[10]

## Patronage

Was Robert I 'seemly in his giving'? Previous studies have remarked generally upon: the hesitancy of Robert's patronage before November 1314; his extensive reward of the core of his noble supporters headed by Edward Bruce, Randolph, Douglas and Stewart, especially after the Cambuskenneth forfeiture of November 1314; his nonetheless seemingly 'conservative' treatment of former enemies and the established conditions of the wider noble class (for example, only forfeiting three of the Scottish kingdom's thirteen earldoms by 1329 – Buchan, Atholl and Angus – and creating only one new comity in Moray); but, overall, the cumulative effect, in his search for support and regional agents, is of alienations of royal demesne and forfeited estates, often as free baronies or full regalities granted beyond the everyday intervention of royal officers, and thus to the detriment of the royal income and authority left to his son, David II, and his guardians.[11] Many aspects of these broad observations hold true. However, the detailed survey of Robert's reign attempted here also reveals the complexity and evolving nature of royal patronage over fifteen long, difficult years of mature rule.

There was indeed a conscious attempt by Robert to balance immediate and necessary reward to his supporters and valuable defectors (surely actively expected and solicited of their new king by individual lords) with the opportunity for enemies to enter his peace and recover their lordship (even after 1314). Nevertheless, despite his apparent caution, by 1318–19 what Robert had overseen had already amounted to a radical realignment of provincial secular lordship throughout medieval Scotland: this would have been the case even if the Balliols, Comyns, Macdougalls and Umfravilles had been the only casualties. This provoked a plot, the 'Soules conspiracy', under the banner of Bruce deposition/destruction and Balliol restoration, to restore the fortunes of a significant network of noble families that had been prominent in the Scottish resistance of 1295–1304. This challenge had the very real potential to undermine and turn the allegiance of a significant proportion of the political community in the wake of the catastrophic defeat of a Scottish army in Ireland in October 1318 and the death of Robert's adult heir presumptive, his brother Edward.

Yet, in hindsight, it was the very betrayal of this intrigue by aristocrats anxious or encouraged to secure some of Robert's increasingly convincing lordship, and the energetic destruction of the conspirators by supporters anticipating further reward, that really confirmed Robert's commitment to focus his patronage upon a *familiares regis*, a core of regional lords and their kin networks closely allied to him through blood, marriage and personal lordship, alongside wider ties of service and hereditary/regional office. Robert's apparently most confident and expansive periods of largesse, indeed, belong to 1320–21 and the period after the birth, at last, of his twin sons John and David in 1324. Nevertheless, even at what emerged as the close of his reign, the king and his closest advisors could still be troubled, even divided, by uncertainty in regard to royal patronage and lordship: witness the ambiguity that surrounded Robert's promises in the course of the peace of 1328 to allow certain disinherited lords (or their English heirs) to recover their Scottish holdings, and the clear unease amongst Robert's noble supporters about the regional and political impact of the return from England of Donald, earl of Mar.

By the same token, it is really too simple to criticise Robert's alienation of earldoms, lordships, baronies and thanages, and his particular favour to families such as the Douglases, Stewarts or Rosses, as weakening the Crown, propelling it towards poverty and 'bastard feudalism' (e.g. the buying of loyalty through pensions); or as storing up inevitable clashes for his son, David II, with several such lords who viewed themselves as 'self-made men' entitled to regional dominance (although this was, admittedly, a far smaller group of magnates than might have put pressure on the Bruce regime after 1329, following the heavy casualties at the battles of Dupplin Moor, 1332, Halidon Hill, 1333, and Neville's Cross, 1346).[12] But in the context of the late 1310s and 1320s, Robert I's grants of lands with privileged jurisdiction (barony or regality) or, latterly, annuity income, as well as his appointments to office, clearly provided an opportunity to reflect, establish and – through ritual at 'court' or on ayre – publicise strong relationships of personal lordship with a deepening pool of regional lords and lesser nobility, as well as rural freeholders and burgesses.[13] Such connections are exemplified at either end of Robert's reign by the ceremonial pardon and grant of northern and north-eastern lands to William, earl of Ross, and his sons in 1308 and Bruce's 'Emerald' regality charter of March lands to James Lord Douglas in 1324.[14] Similar potentially binding and persuasive Crown–subject or lord–man relations may lie behind many more of Robert's more straightforward extant royal charters or letters, even those that did not detail specific military services in return for a grant of land. Barbour's epic, too, enshrines vignettes of personal lordship, usually involving the king rewarding martial prowess, between Robert and a number of nobles whose descendants' loyalty to the Bruce dynasty was vital to its survival after 1332.

The circumstances of the wars, of course, meant that a good many of Robert's grants had to seek to modify and clearly define military obligation to the Crown beyond common 'Scottish' or 'forinsec' service: Robert's reign was thus marked by a resurgence of grants in return for knight, spearman, archer and galley service.[15] Such acts of lordship, however, should not be presented only as (an attempt to achieve) the intensification of central (or 'feudal') authority under Robert as king.[16] For at the same time, such grants and possessions were also solicited by and/or responsive to the concerns, ambitions and economic realities of regional lords, many of them expanding and asserting their own lordship over new lands in the shifting vacuum of war after 1296 and 1306. Thus such royal patronage bound men to the Bruce kingship but also enabled magnate kindreds like the Randolphs, Douglases, Stewarts, Rosses, Setons, Frasers, Stewarts of Bonkle, Keiths, Hays, Murrays, Oliphants, Menteiths, Campbells, Ogilvies, Gordons, Lindsays, Menzies, Boyds, Barclays, Sinclairs, Grahams, Flemings and even natural Bruce sons – many of them of only minor provincial families before 1296 and several of them former enemies of Robert circa 1306–14 – to establish their lordship and develop affinities in new and/or enlarged territories.

Engaging with this dynamic of lordship, Robert did inevitably make what later emerged as unsustainable short-term grants and missteps. Not least, his early largesse to the MacDonalds and MacRuaridhs – so vital for the survival of his cause circa 1306–8 – had to be reversed after the failure of the Irish campaign and sacrificed to royal mainland security and the ambitions of allied and competing Stewart, Campbell and Menteith kin. The mishandling of David Strathbogie, earl of Atholl, circa 1312–14 was arguably very nearly repeated by apparent Bruce distrust and containment of the earls of Fife, Menteith, Strathearn and even Dunbar and Mar. This in itself had perhaps been conditioned not only by Robert's own experiences as earl of Carrick before 1306 but compounded by the failure of his efforts to accommodate former opponent lords such as Soules of Liddesdale, Ingram d'Umfraville, the Mowbrays, Mowats and Brouns after Bannockburn, with potentially fatal results. Finally, it remained highly uncertain at Robert's death whether his young (illegitimate?) nephew, Alexander Bruce, held out prospects of real royal control of the former Balliol–Comyn south-west of Scotland, something never even really established by Edward Bruce. Alexander's anticipated lordship in Carrick and Galloway may have been set to mesh into a southern nexus of Brucean support alongside Stewart in Cunningham and Durisdeer, Boyd in Noddsdale, Randolph in Nithsdale, Annandale and the Isle of Man, Robert Bruce the bastard in Liddesdale and Douglas throughout the west and middle Marches. Yet for the last two years of Robert's reign (and presumably throughout the decade and more before that) no Bruce-appointed justiciar of Galloway (a former Comyn office) can be identified.[17] Similar alarm bells may also have begun to sound by the late 1320s about the reliability of such lords as the Rosses and their emergent role in the north and former Comyn north-east (where they would clash with David II over that region's justiciarship).

Nevertheless, it was in many ways in the face of such adversity and in guarding against such weak spots on his borders that Robert ultimately found real strength and effective kingship. Until the personal rule of James IV (1488–1513) no king surely knew the full geographical extent of what he claimed as his realm, with all its diverse territorial, linguistic and political regions, as well as Robert.[18] His personal ayres, landed patronage, office appointments and military strategies brought regions considered before 1286 to be peripheral or unknown to royal control into direct and (periodically) sustained contact with the king himself or his agents. Robert's efforts to change the balance of political lordship and allegiance in these regions – the north-east, Argyll, the western approaches and Wigtown/ Galloway especially – played a crucial part in determining the assertion of his authority throughout Scotland and the sovereign independence of his realm from Edwardian control (as did his interventions in Ireland in 1315–18 and 1327–28). Moreover, between late October 1320 and May 1323 (thus surely spurred by the Soules plot) Robert and his close supporters' declared shift in peace talks to an intolerance of the restoration of the disinherited and traditional cross-border landholding – and the Scots' strategic dissimulation on this point during the peace process of 1327–28 – coincided with the king's most emphatic patronage to his core of loyal noble kindred affinities, local communities and institutions. As Robert himself had experienced as earl of Carrick in 1292–94, 1300–2 and 1304–5, consensus, legitimacy and real authority could require motivation by the deliberate exclusion of opponents, a partisan community. By giving full vent to his patronage, and the ambitions, of his key supporters from, really, late 1320 (through a decade in which he would also fill a loyal bench of bishops), Robert put in place the key individuals and families who would fight to preserve their elevated status, lands, goods and offices within a Bruce kingdom of Scotland from 1332.[19]

## Justice

In important ways, the long timescale of Robert's evolving patronage circa 1309–29, the fact that it was not introduced wholesale overnight in November 1314, and even passed through generations in the case of some key kindreds (for example, Ross, Strathearn, Menteith, Steward, Stewart of Bonkle, Campbell, MacDonald, Keith, Lindsay and Murray), gave it and his regime greater credibility and resilience.[20] So, too, did a striking commitment after Bannockburn to allow subjects to use law and the courts – through baronial, ecclesiastical, burghal, sheriff and justiciary inquests, perambulations and, ultimately, appeal by royal brieve or to parliament – to recover disputed lands and customary rights, and to reconstitute lost charters.

These were processes that really shine through Robert's extant acts and even his fragmentary parliamentary rolls. Admittedly, as reflected in the Scone parliament of December 1318, these legal mechanisms could be subject to manipulation and abuse by the Crown as well as its agents and private individuals in the localities, and thus the focus of complaint by subjects.[21] But here, once again, Robert's own experiences as a magnate before 1306 (undergoing King John's inquest on Carrick in 1293, being forfeited twice by a Balliol-Comyn guardianship in 1296 and 1302, nevertheless acting as co-Guardian 1298–1300, helping to appoint Edwardian officers in central Scotland around 1303, facing an English inquest on Annandale's liberties in 1304, and serving himself as sheriff of Ayr and Lanark circa 1304–05) seem to have ensured that as king he and his ministers were sympathetic and responsive to the concerns of local society and government. The maintenance (and indeed expansion) of long-established and 'loose-limbed but resilient' structures of royal and local justice, finance and defence was one of the key strengths of Scottish guardianship in the decade after the death of Alexander III.[22] It formed a vital component of the separate and historic institutions and customs which the Scots worked hard – and with genuine success – to protect and liberate from Edward I's predation, enabling Scottish leaders to oversee the relatively swift restoration of royal and regional officers and bureaucracy on more than one occasion once war broke out (for example, c.1297–1302 and c.1307–13, and again c.1338–46). This prevented much, if not all, of the kind of governmental collapse, irrevocable aristocratic atomisation and destructive civil conflict that affected other European polities faced with a succession crisis and/or foreign invasion in this period, for example Sicily (and to a lesser extent the rival principalities of Poland).[23]

However, not only did Robert I and his regime oversee the restoration of Scottish governance, but his victory at Bannockburn was used as a mandate to reform and codify the laws that underpinned the Scottish polity. Yet the raft of legislation extant from the emergency parliament of December 1318, and the subsequent bodies of law known as *Regiam Majestatem* and *Assise Regis David*, were, again, not simply tools of Crown control crafted to the dynastic and political crisis of that period (although some important elements were drawn up with that purpose). Rather, this saw Robert's government and estates advance a codification project first initiated by the Crown and subjects in the mid to late thirteenth century – as in England and other European realms.[24] In doing so, they responded not only to the disruption of war and political upheaval induced by a contested succession but also to deeper, wider fluctuations in socio-economic (and climatic) conditions, all of which had had an impact on the expectations of different classes and localities of subjects of the king of Scots. The nature and scale of this legislation, and the scope of Robert's extant chancery formularies (which survived in large numbers from circa

1318), necessitated input and had uptake from all types of subject: lay magnates and lesser rural freeholders, burgh leaders and craftsmen, secular and regular church leaders and their communities and professional clerical jurists, as well as the king and his officers, the latter a group drawn naturally from the prelatical, comital and baronial estates.[25] Thus, after Bannockburn, the deployment of the law by Robert and his ministers and officers responded not merely to immediate (and quite partisan) political concerns but to the problems and expectations of the majority of elements of the political community. In the extensive rebuilding projects which Robert and his government initiated, particularly after 1318, this interconnectedness is most apparent with the extension of credit and land offered to defend and restore the economic hub of Berwick (and perhaps other burghs such as Aberdeen), linked in turn to the funding of major monastic restoration in central-southern Scotland (Scone, Dunfermline, Holyrood, Melrose) through assigned feu-ferme customs and teinds from provincial justice ayres. It was this commitment to law and access to justice that surely earned Robert his epitaph's comparison to 'Gaius the lawmaker' and Solomon.

Above all, such collective activity underlines Robert's passage from the uncertain, often painfully isolated and at times quite petty figure of ambitious noble heir before 1306 – deprived of the open support of even his father and siblings until he was thirty – to a leader able to assume the full authority and apparatus of the office of an established kingship. In doing so, without denying his undoubted personal drive, magnetism and political and military abilities, arguably the strongest theme to emerge from a detailed survey of all of Robert's reign is the degree to which he was surrounded and shaped by an impressive circle of community leaders committed to the full restoration of the independent kingdom and its liberties and customs. Indeed, there emerges an inescapable sense that without such interventionist support and direction Robert would certainly not have been capable of all that he achieved. This did not mean, however, that consensus was always easy to secure.

## Parliament and Community

A modern audience will readily recognise the maxim that war can 'make the state'.[26] If the kings of Scots, and thus Robert I, had a natural ally in the task of developing and asserting royal authority and government, it lay of course in the clerical estate. The role of prelates and personal faith in first persuading Robert to uphold the kingdom's cause circa 1297–98, exploiting his sacrilegious slaughter of Comyn of Badenoch to set the parameters of his rule through his enthronement oath in 1306, restoring and manning his government from circa 1308 (including a resumption of law codification), and shaping and voicing his relations with other sovereign monarchs and the Papacy down to 1329, all testify to one thing: the seemingly strong personal and 'civic' relationships which Robert formed with such clerics as Robert Wishart of Glasgow, William Lamberton of St Andrews, Bernard of Arbroath/Sodor and Alexander Kinninmonth (latterly bishop of Aberdeen).

Relevant here, however, as integral to the development of Scottish law, were strong continuities in the Crown–Church relationship in Scotland from before 1286, not least in the *Ecclesia Scoticana*'s historic resistance of English ecclesiastical superiority. At the same time, the clergy – also members of elite regional or kindred networks – were subject to strong conflicting currents of political development and allegiance that would be echoed in the wider community experience of the late thirteenth and early fourteenth centuries, magnified by the Scottish succession crisis and the resulting war as well as by the position of successive popes vis-à-vis a fragmenting Holy Roman Empire, the kings of France, England and other rulers circa 1286–1329. Evolving ideas about clerical representation had set many national churches and their leaders down the path to conciliar challenge of centralised papal monarchy, patronage and taxation. Yet at the same time, these *ecclesias* also sought to shape and often limit the power of their own secular rulers (and metropolitan clerics) to interfere in these concerns.[27]

The domestic forums in which prelates sought to define, defend and develop their estate's rights were of course the emerging representative assemblies of the European realms. By 1284–86 Scottish councils and parliaments were already an increasingly regular feature of consultative royal government: the succession crisis meant that almost annual assemblies of the estates provided legitimacy and consensus for the lordship and actions of the chosen Guardians and then the inexperienced King John's rule.[28] Robert Bruce VII's own experience of such meetings may, understandably, have been dominated by the impression that his family's political opponents carefully controlled the agenda, attendance and decisions of such occasions to their advantage. Equally, as we have seen, Carrick cannot have failed to be struck by Edward I's exploitation of conquering royal power's prerogative to dictate the location, timing, personnel and agenda of meetings of the subjugated Scottish estates (such as at St Andrews in March 1304), and the contribution of their select representatives at English parliaments. It seems logical that Robert's contact with such assemblies before 1306 had a profound influence on the efforts of his own royal regime to control the attendance, agenda and resulting 'community' decisions and statements of the estates, especially in the first few challenging years of his rule (1309–13), when his meetings often served as swift 'war councils', but also at moments of subsequent political crisis (1318–20, 1326).

However, the experience of representative assembly before 1306 of both Robert and many of those who emerged as his closest advisors was, crucially, far more varied and often positive. The Bruce family itself had been able to voice and sustain political opposition in several Scottish Guardianship assemblies, had witnessed telling appeals against King John's authority in 1293–94, and strong demands for change in royal policy and personnel coupled to wider redress of grievances in Edwardian parliaments between 1297 and 1302. Parliament's chosen representatives, the Guardians, had also acted to protect the Scottish kingdom's liberties and customs in negotiations with Edward I circa 1289–92, efforts which make it clear that the lessons of Magna Carta and the Barons' Wars had not been lost on the less-governed northern realm. Carrick's representation of the Scottish estates at Westminster in Lent 1305 had also given him first-hand knowledge of the methods and value of Crown responsiveness to subjects' individual and communal petitions, as a means of securing consensus, enhancing royal authority, offsetting less popular royal (especially fiscal) policies and, in general, of 'good governance': such petitions and redress were a burgeoning custom which Edward II neglected at his peril.[29]

The evidence for councils and parliaments during Robert's reign remains fragmentary (as it does for 1286–1306). Nevertheless, it has been argued above that Robert I, his ministers and close circle of lay supporters may have been faced with criticisms, petitions and calls for discussion of a number of issues even in some of his earliest, smaller assemblies (such as circa 1309–13), those his government worked hardest to choreograph and which often saw the deliberate appropriation of secular and clerical seals to fabricate an impression of community support. Crucially, however, the response of Robert and his ministers does not seem to have been simply to shout down, intimidate or ignore such voices of appeal or dissent (as Edward II too often did), but, in addition to strategic coercion, to try to work with them through the mechanism of legal courts, council, parliament or daily counsel.

As such, Robert I's kingship and engagement of his estates in assembly might be said to have been marked by an astute mixture of authoritarian action (as in 1309, 1313, 1314 or 1320) with timely assurances, concessions and genuine governmental consultation (as at Scone in December 1318 or at Stirling in July–August 1326). In this regard, Edward I had clearly been a valuable teacher to the younger Robert. But from around 1307–8 Robert must also have listened carefully to the advice of experienced Scottish prelates and nobles. Indeed, the difficult factional and violent personal origins of Robert's kingship, and his greater need of legitimacy as both a former baron and excommunicate usurper in the eyes of Scottish subjects well into the 1320s, arguably meant that council and parliament had to serve as a far more conciliatory body than in Edward I's England: a venue for significant, binding patronage (including the aforementioned grants to Ross and Douglas and to Edward Bruce, Randolph, Stewart, Keith, Hay and others) and a regular social and cultural 'court', as well as the home of routine local and 'greater' state business, of genuine oral as well as written exchange. We might also argue that under Robert parliament, and less so council, became an anticipated public event (and economic opportunity) for many lesser subjects, one held in restored royal burghs and churches, often coinciding with a major religious festival, thus increasingly surrounded by crowds, ordinary petitioners, popular discussion and (later) literary digest of the issues of the day (powerful forces reflected in the vernacular verse inherited and reworked by Barbour and Prior Wyntoun).[30] The stipulation of the parliament of December 1318 that all of the king's and the community of the realm's statutes be 'read and proclaimed publicly at our courts to be held in [all] bailiaries and in other places where people often assemble' must have further spread this sense of inclusion.[31]

The detailed survey above suggests that, beyond the 'war council' years of circa 1306–13, the estates were consulted at least once, often twice, each year: a total of over thirty assemblies, indeed, can be identified and must have contributed much to a growing sense of community cohesion and shared political and diplomatic goals.[32] An analysis of the only apparently full legislative record of one of Robert's parliaments that has survived, for December 1318, suggests that as much as the king and his advisors continued to seek to use meetings of the estates to test loyalty and direct a united front, both to internal and external power centres, the Bruce regime was also prepared to listen to subjects' concerns. Even the infamous 'Black Parliament' of August 1320 tried and forfeited political opponents before the community of the realm (as had the general forfeiture issued at Cambuskenneth in November 1314) rather than depending on Edward II's preferred method of dealing with treason, namely royal proclamation. It is surely fair to speculate that a number of Robert's assemblies for which no records survive, particularly those after 1321, involved consultation, often perhaps quite fractious, on such relevant issues as royal patronage, law and order, land value re-assessment, customs tariffs and coinage regulation (themes that can be shown to be the staples of assemblies of the estates in the later fourteenth and fifteenth centuries).

Over and above the chaos and disruption to lordship caused by war and political upheaval after 1296, such consultative rule was in many ways necessitated by the intense climatic and socio-economic crises of the period: through repeated famines in the 1290s and 1310s (with a loss of population of between 10 and 20 per cent), the economic ruin and depopulation of mutual border raiding from around 1311, and the devastating cattle plague of circa 1319–22 and other livestock pandemics. The evidence for petitions and complaints by Robert's subjects admittedly remains slight.[33] At the same time, it does not seem as if Robert's Scotland was subject to the kind of concerted political alliances of opposition in representative assemblies or popular communal protests as manifested themselves, say, in a search of charters of subjects' liberties against French royal taxation in 1314–15, in large-scale rural uprisings against central exactions in Flanders circa 1323–28 or, of course, in pursuit of the Ordinances to reform Edwardian rule in England.[34] Moreover, the influence and scope of the Scottish estates in council and parliament developed from 1286 not, as in contemporary England, as a counter-balance to royal demands for war subsidy and then against the perceived tyranny of the Crown and its favourites (as well as general magnate abuses in the provinces), but in the wake of a succession crisis that threatened internal conflict and external interference.[35] Yet in Scotland, too, parliament had to be a forum that responded to the real grievances of subjects, particularly at a local level.

In that regard Scotland's experience and political evolution between 1286 and 1329 seem at first glance to have more in common in its ongoing 'Europeanisation' with events in contemporary Sweden (1290–1302), Castile (1295), Naples (1295–1309), the Low Countries (1297, 1300–4, 1312), Sicily (1302, 1314), Denmark (1320), Mallorca (1324) and even distant Poland (1295–1300, 1320), Hungary (1301, 1309–21) or Bohemia (1306–11).[36] In these realms in the late thirteenth and early fourteenth centuries, failed lineages, disputed inheritance and minorities broadly saw an expansion in the power of representative bodies of lay and clerical magnates and, increasingly, urban leaders, often in defiance of internal rivalries or intervention and exactions by stronger neighbouring rulers and the Papacy. The struggle for legitimacy of the dynasts who emerged as rulers in these kingdoms, through both civil and national conflicts, contributed in most realms (though in Holland/Zealand/Hainault, Sicily and Poland not until the second half of the fourteenth century) to the seemingly 'irresistible development' of a growing dialogue between count/

prince/king and subjects.[37] In all of these polities this interaction was heightened in this period by major socio-economic crises.

Certainly, in the early wartime years of Robert's reign, the concern of community leaders and past Guardians, particularly prelates, to ensure that the new king worked to preserve the independence, institutions and customs of the Scottish kingdom provided subjects with their most direct line through which to negotiate with and manage royal power. This was quickly coupled, as we have seen, not only to their efforts to advance, protect and recover individual and local lordships, but to serious doubts (until as late as March 1324) about Robert's legitimacy as king and the stability of his house (with a captive queen and daughter and no prospect of a lawful son until 1315, and an unmarried, sometimes erratic adult brother down to 1318). The parliamentary acts of succession of April 1315 and December 1318 may have been issued, indeed, as much in response to pressure from subjects for discussion, parliamentary input and clarification on this issue – beginning as early as 1312 – as from a Crown desire to compel recognition of Bruce legitimacy. That this formed part of a wider evolving consultative dynamic, more akin to that better documented for the contemporary kingdom of England, is suggested by the extant evidence for the Stirling parliament of July–August 1326. A third act of tailzie was then recognised by the estates without any apparent need to repeat earlier parliaments' falsification of attendance and sealing, thus enshrining the community of the realm's right to supervise a future infant monarch through guardianship or to determine collectively a vacant royal succession.[38] In the same assembly, burgess representatives were also present to add their approval of a new treaty with France and, along with a Council of the Scottish Church, confirm their consent and commitment with the nobility to furnish their king with an annual tenth of rents and fermes for the rest of his life, further enhancing the intrusive powers of the royal exchequer and its officers.[39] The efforts of Robert and his government – perhaps beginning with a royal speech delivered by proxy in parliament – to explain and justify to all of his estates the need (*necessitas*) for such a subsidy after he had 'diminished' the royal demesne in pursuit of the common good of the kingdom's recovery and restoration (rather than simply commanding a common 'aid'), was allied to other factors: a willingness to promise his barons, clerics and burgesses that he would (as the agreement at Birgham in 1290 had tried to impose upon Edward I) otherwise 'live of his own', and to limit future prise and purveyance (and where necessary reassess the taxable worth of his subjects after decades of war, famine and disease). Thus although this would reflect an intensification of royal government in this period through chancery, exchequer, brieve and sheriff, it was at the same time the case that these officers and the Crown became more accessible to subjects and communities, fostering a broadening of political participation. In the months following this grant of subsidy, Robert showed himself sensitive and open to his subjects' economic difficulties by granting a number of exemptions or reductions to, and (with the estates' consent) redirections of, this and other royal exactions. Moreover, when a second tenth was necessitated by the peace treaty of 1328 (both decisions confirmed by a parliament at Holyrood, again attended by burgh procurators and coincident with a Scottish Church Council), the evidence suggests that Robert's regime may have quietly dropped much of the collection of his earlier personal tenth and pressed efforts to ensure even contributions to the war indemnity from across the realm.[40]

That the dynamic of council and parliament had been cemented into a central role in Bruce Scotland is confirmed by developments after Robert's death. Not only were the estates' tailzies of succession and guardianship upheld, but, in the spirit suggested by the 'Declaration of Arbroath' of 1320, distinction of the office of kingship from the person of the king, and thus the subjects' right (through parliament) to supervise the monarchy, could be extended to threats by the then Guardian and royal heir presumptive Robert Stewart, in a parliament in February 1352, to depose the captive David II for his offer to admit one of Edward III's sons to the Scottish succession (and perhaps also allow the restoration of some of the pre-1329 disinherited) in return for the cancellation of a hefty ransom.[41] In the 1370s Barbour would inherit and elaborate on memories of an idealised Scottish parliament to close Robert's reign (conflating those of 1326 and 1328), in which the Bruce-Stewart succession was settled and the newly married David Bruce crowned (and the French treaty sealed).[42] This naturally leads us back to speculate about the exact content and intent of the mutual oaths given by a minor king and his subjects at what was, significantly, a much delayed coronation *parliament* for David only in November 1331. Just as on 25 March 1306, did the momentum of political development since the thirteenth century and the immediate challenging circumstances of political rivalry and renewed war against intensely governed royal England coalesce to sharpen the reciprocal expectations and obligations of the Scottish king and subjects?

In this sense, from the status quo defended in the treaty of Birgham in 1290, via magnates' apparent supervision of King John, on through 1306 to 1331, Scotland might be said to have experienced its own version of shifts in political power played out in England: these had been reflected in the

English coronation oaths of 1308 and 1327, via the supervisory demands of the Ordinances which had themselves invoked principles tabled during the Barons' Wars of the 1260s and through 'Remonstrance' to Edward I for Magna Carta (1215), the common law and other rights to be upheld circa 1297–1303.[43] Emulating that astute English king, Robert I, aided by his ministers, certainly had to develop skills of political and parliamentary management to add to the traditional, more federal lordship and personal rule of the Scottish Crown.

As such, at no time did the level of control exercised over council and parliament by Robert and his oligarchy of ministers loosen to the point suggested in an English-authored guidebook to the Scottish royal household and government of circa 1292–96. This was a quite radical text, actually giving vent to ideals of supervisory government in England, and which asserted that the king of Scots' daily council or annual parliament of local representatives should choose all his officers, from Chancellor and Chamberlain/Treasurer to the thirty or so sheriffs and ensure that the royal accounts were regularly audited.[44] Yet at the same time nor was Robert's evolving attitude to meetings of his estates as rigidly authoritarian as the view expressed around 1320 in another idealistic English treatise, the *Modus Tenendi Parliamentum* ('The Mode of Holding Parliament'). Although this later work exaggerated the emerging influence of the Commons in England (knights of the shire, burgesses and lesser clergy), it opened by admitting that 'the king is the head, the beginning and the end of parliament'.[45] The extant parliamentary record of Robert's reign is consistent throughout in recording 'the lord king's statute[s]' ordained as 'the lord king decreed and forbad' or as 'the king wishes and commands' or 'proposed by the said lord king'.[46] But after 1314 Robert's personal style and cautious acceptance of and sensitivity to counsel, petition and dialogue contributed greatly to the emergence of council and parliament within a far more comfortable working relationship for the northern realm during his lifetime: this engagement with the community was thus surely not sustained merely as a 'veneer' of legitimising rhetoric.[47]

## Piety and Martial Identity

While the art of effective management of parliament thus emerged as an important extension of government for Robert and his ministers, his extended epitaph dwelt far more on his kingly role as pious exemplar: as 'gentle as Andrew … sacred food for the soul … [placing] his hope in Christ for the guarding of his right'. Royal faith and its patronage were of course natural preoccupations of the Church, its clerks and chroniclers; the projection of a convincing image of piety was also vital to a usurper and excommunicate. Again, spiritual counsel including ceremonial and diplomatic direction from leading Scottish ecclesiastics who also sought to secure papal support for the provision of Scottish chapter clergy to vacant benefices and, from 1318, the removal of the interdict upon Scotland, proved crucial. However, Robert's evolving and genuine, carefully considered piety remains the most neglected strand of his kingship and its innovative search for legitimacy.

It is perhaps stretching the extant evidence too far to suggest that Robert I's piety amounted to a completely convincing association of his kingship with the *beata stirps*, the hereditary sacrality and sanctity of his royal ancestors, and that this had an overwhelming, decisive effect in winning over the hearts and minds of many of his subjects. Nevertheless, Robert's veneration of St Margaret with lights and alms did culminate, as he had begun to plan as early as November 1314, in his own burial at Dunfermline Abbey amidst his predecessor kings, including now St Malcolm (III) and St David (I), and his intention to inter his heart at Melrose Abbey (shrine of another 'royal' saint, Waltheof) after its penitential pilgrimage to the Holy land. Robert's extended family and war allies would also join him in rest at Dunfermline. Such worship and display were surely far more than mere cynical emulation of the contemporary dynastic spirituality developed by the Capetians, Plantagenets, Angevins and Hungarian Árpáds in conjunction with their respective 'national' Churches and saints' cults in France (Charlemagne, Clovis, St Louis IX), England (St Edward the Confessor), Naples (St Louis of Anjou) and Hungary (St Stephen et al.).[48] Robert and his prelates, after all, succeeded in wresting from the Papacy a prize which the Scottish monarchy and *Ecclesia* had sought for centuries, the full rite of royal coronation and unction, achieving this through reconciliation with the Roman Church after over a decade of interdict. Long before the award of this rite by a papal bull in 1329, Robert and his clergy had restored and developed a meaningful royal liturgy and overseen several conscious public demonstrations of his legitimacy and God-given authority as king of a sovereign Scotland (replacing a number of lost muniments in doing so). This included such innovative ceremonies as his 'coronation' in 1306; his parliaments at St Andrews in Lent 1309 and at Berwick in Easter 1319; the births (and baptisms?) of his children (including twin boys) at Dunfermline; parliamentary acts of succession sworn on holy relics in 1315, 1318 and 1326; and the consecration of St Andrews Cathedral by king and community in July 1318 following the recovery of Berwick to that diocese and the realm. All this blended tradition with immediate needs.

An examination of Robert's identifiable religious interactions before his seizure of the throne similarly reveals elements of his heritage and development, often relating to moments of failure and contrition. Yet, as we have seen, after 1306, Robert's engagement with the relics and *parochia* of Margaret in battle, childbirth and burial was but one facet of his invocation of a wide range of saints, feasts, relics, individual churches and religious orders that had provincial, Scottish and often anti-English significance. His worship of such cults as those of Fillan (1306, 1314), Thomas Becket (1297, 1314), Andrew (1314, 1318), Serf (1314, 1329) and Ninian (1329), was on numerous occasions integrated with the muster-in-arms, military success, royal patronage and political consultation of his subjects to powerful effect. This established a firm Bruce connection with several major royal churches founded by his predecessor kings, including St Andrews, Dunfermline, Scone, Holyrood, Arbroath, Melrose and Whithorn.

Such spirituality could thus be bound up with the restoration of Scotland's landed society, government, judiciary, churches and economy as well as the general well-being of the king's subjects. It was directly relevant to nobles, clerics, farmers, burgesses, craftsmen, serfs, all men and women, indeed, in local communities within the allegiance of the king of Scots. God's favour for the Bruce (and thus Scottish) cause after 1307 was also sustained through further natural crises, not least famine circa 1315–18 and cattle plague around 1319–22. Robert's piety, therefore, was in many ways a far more universal, tangible and (given cartulary survivals) measurable reflection of the communal identity which his rule sought to forge and project than the allied if arguably narrower, more abstract notions of (chivalric) patriotism.

There is, though, no doubting the universal impact that repeated military success in major engagements, all against the odds, must have had on Scottish subjects: this was an irrefutable sign of God's blessing of Robert's reign. Commemoration of this battle record could be tied to liturgy, shepherded by a clergy who, as we have seen, preached a just war against England in the manner of a crusade.[49] Royal secular patronage could also be linked explicitly to service in particular campaigns. But it was as a bonding, shared experience that such a martial record surely had its real value to Robert, and not merely Bannockburn, but also the recovery and defence of Berwick in 1318–19 (avenging 1296) and the humiliation of Edward II's forces in 1322 and those of his son in 1327: these campaigns expunged the defeat at Faughart in 1318 and, crucially, allowed former enemies and post-Bannockburn defectors such as Alexander Seton, Adam Gordon, Patrick, earl of Dunbar, Murdoch of Menteith and even Donald, earl of Mar, to reclaim a place in the patriotic war narratives of 'the Lion', now under the Bruce banner. Barbour's collated vernacular narratives – adaptable as song and verse for both courtly and common firesides, as tournament theatre or as sermon material – relate Robert's struggles as a hunted fugitive king circa 1306–7, his early victories over his Scottish opponents (1308–10) and then his and his lieutenants' great run of triumphs (1312–28) from Perth, Roxburgh and Edinburgh through Bannockburn (and Robert's combat triumph over Bohun), on to Berwick, Myton and Weardale. This surely reflects a highly popular, compelling collective identity nurtured by the king and his ministers. As his tomb inscription declared, 'whoever reads about his feats will repeat the many battles he fought'. This was a corporate ethos that even 'my bishop', the fighting William Sinclair of Dunkeld, could embrace.[50]

The two years of Robert's exchequer rolls that survive at least suggest that he followed Edward I and his contemporaries by badging this martial identity with heraldic livery (just as Bower's preservation of Robert's commissioned verse in 1314 from the captive cleric, Robert Baston, testifies to royal literary commemoration).[51] The lost years of Bruce royal expenditure (1306–26) may also hide from view ceremonial knightings, jousting and further liturgy designed to celebrate these important victories. This must have done much to further obscure memory of Robert's questionable record of allegiance before 1306, especially in 1296–97 and 1303–4. Finally, a large measure of the strategic political motivation for rejecting (rather fudging) a return to cross-border landholding from 1328 must have been fuelled by the hardening identity of a self-made war generation and its acculturated offspring who, although they could still understand English lords and knights as aristocratic equals, also saw them increasingly as ethnic and seigneurial 'others', arrogant and tailed invaders to resist and challenge. These were sentiments and a conviction in recent history that must have been confirmed by the 'betrayal' of Edward III, Edward Balliol and the Disinherited in 1332–33.[52] It would fall to the next generation of Scots down to the 1370s and 1380s to fully garb itself in a Brucean patriotic mantle.

* * *

It is possible, then, to penetrate the rhetoric of Bruce propaganda and Barbour's mythology in search of a more realistic assessment of the aristocratic upbringing and early career, personal rule, politics and problems of

Robert I, especially during the fifteen years of his reign after Bannockburn. What emerges is not radically different from the picture formed by earlier studies that focused upon events to midsummer 1314. Yet in its nuance and detail it reveals the fundamental links between the inability of Robert and his brother, war-lieutenants and ministers to make a decisive impact upon even such a beleaguered king as Edward II, and Robert's own continuing problems of legitimacy, regional control and factional opposition, well on into the 1320s.

Not least, this drew the Scots to overreach themselves in war on two fronts by circa 1315–18, recovering Berwick but sacrificing Edward Bruce and his host in Ireland. This was a loss that incurred further papal censure and provoked a major plot to depose Robert in Scotland by those deprived or dissatisfied by his territorial resettlement. The king survived this conspiracy and was strengthened by its destruction. But it was really not until the birth of twin sons in 1324 that wider baronial uncertainty about his direct succession and thus the stability of the political realignment he offered were turned to the point of willing majority consensus. Indeed, Robert's late provision of a male heir should in many ways be held up as *the* vital watershed moment of his reign, one that legitimated all that had gone before it. Yet it should still be acknowledged that a significant portion of Robert's support of the 1320s would fragment once more in 1332–33 during what was, after all, a Bruce minority.

A chronological survey also reveals Robert's considerable skill as king in deploying his growing mandate of support and a well-tried albeit limited formula of military tactics to persevere and exploit the final crisis of Edward II's reign. In hindsight, this would provide only temporary closure with an illegal regime. But within the context of Robert's own failing health and the immediate prospects of his child male heirs it was an impressive solution significantly underpinned by binding relations of lordship with an array of now solely 'Scottish' noble kindreds, a solid bench of loyalist prelates, and a treaty with a newly Valois France already sensitised to English aggression.[53]

All told, these were miraculous, heroic achievements given the repeated failure of Bruce dynastic ambitions between 1286 and 1302, the frequent isolation of Robert himself before 1306, and the seemingly certain doom of the vulnerable new king, his kin and close supporters in 1306–7. Even when we expose his propaganda, political manipulation, mistakes and weaknesses, Robert still convinces, through the crisis of 1318–20 and certainly the remainder of the last decade of his reign, as a fully rounded monarch in terms of his military leadership, his balanced reward of support, his ruthlessness tempered by grace towards enemies, his piety and his commitment to justice and controlled, consultative government with his subjects. Indeed, it was the king's willingness to embrace and reward the counsel and service of his subjects as well as to lead them – to develop a necessary 'art' of royal politics as well as make short-term concessions – that arguably proved his greatest strength.

Robert's son and successor, David II, would struggle to emulate this model of rule, sometimes succeeding, sometimes failing. But it was a style in turn that the first Stewart kings, Robert II (Bruce's grandson, r.1371–90) and Robert III (r.1390–1406), would celebrate (and even emulate through acts of succession in 1371 and 1373) yet quickly retreat from, avoiding parliaments and taxation in the face of their own legacy of baronial opposition against the Crown (during David II's reign) and of the resurgent interests of provincial magnates.[54] As a result, it was really only through the Stewart monarchies of the fifteenth century, James I to IV, that Robert I's successors began to cultivate the seeds of personal monarchy, service nobility and increasingly intensive royal government which he and his ministers had sown.[55] Within what might at first appear a largely 'statist' framework, the first Bruce king therefore remains fully deserving of his glowing contemporary epitaphs written by men close to his person and rule, elevating him as a benchmark for all later kings of Scots. But Robert's was also a reign to which numerous baronial families and community interests – parliament, the Church and burghs in particular – would date their recovery from a foreign invasion and their real arrival on the national political stage of the Scottish realm.

In the end, have we come any closer to knowing the character of this great king? Professor Barrow's classic if spare assessment of Robert seems to hold true: 'one of the best of medieval kings, prudent, conscientious, vigorous and patriotic'.[56] But there is more to say. Before the turn of the fourteenth century, as he entered into political life, what is most striking is Robert's frustration and uncertainty, his search as much for a meaningful role and inspiring lordship as for an opportunity to forward his own dynastic ambition. Bishop Wishart, James Steward and, ironically, Edward I did much to teach him patience, persistence and compromise. Yet Robert was prone to lash out at obstruction. The clash with Comyn of Badenoch at Peebles in August 1299 signalled the end for their co-Guardianship and marginalisation for Bruce as earl of Carrick. It also foreshadowed their fatal confrontation at Dumfries in February 1306. In the intervening years Robert arguably did remarkably well to steer a course through treacherous political and military waters and to preserve some level of independence for his cause. The slaughter of Comyn nearly brought complete disaster to Robert's person and party, but it can surely be understood that at thirty-three he must have felt it was now or never if he was to press any serious bid for the throne.

Amidst the shock and grave personal loss of 1306–7 (with three brothers slain and his womenfolk captured) and rising from his refuge in the Gaelic west, a true leader emerged, one able to exploit the vacuum of Edward Longshanks' death. In the years following his return from exile Robert's personal bravery and tactical and political skills cannot be denied: but nor should his ruthlessness and calculation in war, against noble opponents, churches, farmers and towns. These were necessary tools of terror that Barbour's later poetic epic would shroud in a cult of chivalry and honourable martial service. Yet once brutal deeds were done, the mature Robert had a true politician's capacity to stand back, both to make examples of, or reach accommodation with, influential enemies. He could listen to counsel and was accessible to appeal, could crush and reward. He displayed a facility for the daily grind of bureaucracy and had real skills in diplomacy, law and administrative and ecclesiastical appointment by meritocracy (which must have required a good measure of men). In many ways, from around 1309–10, he was indeed the most complete king the independent realm of Scotland would ever see.

In that regard it is of great importance that Robert was as equally effective and resident as a westward monarch of Scotland as he was an east coast, Lowland king. Robert's likely Gaelic upbringing, together with his family's Scottish and English lordships and his service as a bachelor in Edward I's household (circa 1292, an apprenticeship mirrored by that of Edward Bruce), crucially heightened what might be described as his four-realms perspective. This was a vision he shared with the old English king. The resources of the Scottish kingdom would prove too limited to effect lasting political change beyond its own borders. In attempting to force such change Robert almost perished. But the Scots' sustained actions in northern England and their three-year foray into Ireland (followed by Robert's later avuncular yet intimidating visits in 1327–28), and even their king's hesitant interventions in Wales, all underline his awareness of the crucial connections of lordship, culture and identity between these realms. Ultimately, this understanding saved the Scottish kingship and helped establish the Bruce dynasty.

However, it is in his moments of personal violence at Peebles, Dumfries, and on the first day of Bannockburn (facing Bohun alone in the New Park), in his periods of fatigue, hunger and cold, in his long wait for a son, and in his own prolonged illness and death, that we find the most human facets of Robert Bruce. Much of this coalesced in his personal piety and public spirituality. Religion was a key component in legitimising Robert's rule and relations with Europe's Crowns and the Papacy (to strong effect by 1329): in this, the counsel and service of his bishops and Chancellor Bernard clearly sharpened his eye for symbolic ritual. Nevertheless, Robert's obsequies for family and friends and his veneration of such cults as those of St Margaret at Dunfermline, under whose care his sons were born, St Malachy of Armagh (and Coupar-Angus), St Fillan (Inchaffray), St Ninian (Whithorn) and, of course, St Thomas (Arbroath), provide tangible glimpses of his moments of uncertainty, regret, penance, grief, physical pain, hope and gratitude as both earl then king. Ultimately, Robert's consistent return to these private and civic acts of worship reveals his struggle to secure the throne and thrive as king to have been a test of faith.

# Appendix
## Councils and Parliaments of Robert I, 1306–29

Italicised assemblies = suggested from evidence of *RRS*, v, and chronicles, but not listed in *RPS*.

1308: 31 October, Auldearn, 'Unidentified Assembly'
1309: 16 March, St Andrews, parliament
*1310: 7 April, Inchture, council?*
*1310: 12 April, Dundee, parliament* (Scottish Church Council, Dundee)
*1312: circa spring, Ayr, parliament?*
*1313: 1 March, Scotlandwell, council?*
*1313: 21 October, Dundee, council/parliament?*
1314: 6 November, Cambuskenneth, parliament
1315: 26 April, Ayr, 'Unidentified Assembly'
*1316: circa Lent, Edinburgh, council/parliament?*
*1316: 30 September, Cupar, council?*
*1317: February/March, Carrickfergus, Irish council?*
*1317: 12–14 June, Scone, parliament?*
*1317: 16–17 September, Edinburgh, parliament?*
*1318: July/August, Scone/Edinburgh/Berwick? council?*
1318: 3 December, Scone, parliament
*1319: 20 January, Berwick, council?*
1319: 10 December, Berwick, 'Unidentified Assembly'
1320: 14 March, Newbattle, council
1320: 6 April, 'Arbroath', 'Unidentified Assembly'
1320: early August, Scone, parliament
*1320: 18 November, Scone, parliament?*
1321: 9 July, Perth/Scone, parliament (Scottish Church Council, Perth)
1321: 22 September, Edinburgh, council
1323: 7 June, Berwick
1323: 25 July, Scone, parliament
*1324: April/May, Berwick, council?*
1324: 7 November, Berwick, council
1325: 26 March, Scone, parliament (21–25 March, Scottish Church Council, Scone)
*1326: March, Scone, council/parliament?*
1326: 15 July, Cambuskenneth, parliament (Scottish Church Council/Burgh Convention, Cambuskenneth)
1327: 8 March, Holyrood, parliament
1327: 4 April, Stirling, council
1328: 28 February, Holyrood, parliament (Scottish Church Council, Holyrood)

## Council/Parliament Sites

Scone 8; Berwick 5; Edinburgh/Holyrood 5; Ayr 2; Cambuskenneth 2; Arbroath, Auldearn, Cupar, Dundee, Inchture, Newbattle, Scotlandwell, Stirling – 1; unknown 2.

## Main Royal Act Issue Sites (*RRS*, v, 785–6)

Berwick 68, Arbroath 66, Scone 39, Edinburgh 31, Dundee 15, Cardross 14, Ayr 13, Glasgow 12, Perth 11, Forfar 9, Scotlandwell 9, Cambuskenneth 8, Stirling 8, Aberdeen 7, Inchmichael 6, Clackmannan 5, Dunfermline 5, Melrose 5, Dumbarton 4, Newbattle 4, Girvan 3, Kilwinning 3, Lochmaben 3, St Andrews 3, Whithorn 3.

# Abbreviations

| | |
|---|---|
| Abulafia, ed., *NCMH*, v | Abulafia, D., ed., *The New Cambridge Medieval History, v: c.1198–c.1300* (Cambridge, 1999) |
| AN | Archives Nationales, Paris |
| *Anglo-Scottish Relations* | E. L. G. Stones, ed., *Anglo-Scottish Relations, 1174–1328: Some Selected Documents* (London, 1965) |
| *APS* | *The Acts of the Parliaments of Scotland*, ed. T. Thomson and C. Innes (12 vols, Edinburgh, 1814–75) |
| *Barbour's Bruce* | *Barbour's Bruce*, ed. M. P. McDiarmid and J. A. C. Stevenson (Scottish Text Society, 3 vols, Edinburgh, 1986) |
| Barrow, *Robert Bruce* | G. W. S. Barrow, *Robert the Bruce and the Community of the Realm of Scotland* (4th edn, Edinburgh, 2005) |
| Beam, *Balliol Dynasty* | A. Beam, *The Balliol Dynasty, 1210–1364* (Edinburgh, 2008) |
| *BIHR* | *Bulletin of the Institute of Historical Research* |
| BL | British Library, London |
| Blakely, *Brus Family* | R. Blakely, *The Brus Family in England and Scotland, 1100–1295* (Woodbridge, 2005) |
| BN | Bibliothèque Nationale, Paris |
| *The Bruce* | *John Barbour – The Bruce*, ed. A. A. M. Duncan (Edinburgh, 1997) |
| CCA | Canterbury Cathedral Archives |
| *CCR* | *Calendar of Close Rolls* (1892–) |
| *CDS* | *Calendar of Documents Relating to Scotland*, ed. J. Bain (5 vols, Edinburgh, 1881–88) |
| *CFR* | *Calendar of Fine Rolls* (1911–) |
| *Chron. Bower* | Walter Bower, *Scotichronicon*, ed. D. E. R. Watt et al. (9 vols, Aberdeen, 1987–99) |
| *Chron. Fordun* | Johannis de Fordun, *Chronica Gentis Scotorum*, ed. W. F. Skene (2 vols, Edinburgh, 1871–72): i. Latin, ii. English translation |
| *Chron. Guisborough* | *Chronicle of Walter of Guisborough*, ed. H. Rothwell (Camden Society, Third Series, lxxxix, London, 1989) |

| | |
|---|---|
| *Chron. Lanercost* | *The Chronicle of Lanercost, 1272–1346*, ed. H. Maxwell (Glasgow, 1913) |
| *Chron. Langtoft* | *Chronicle of Pierre de Langtoft*, ed. T. Wright (Rolls Series, London, 1886) |
| *Chron. Rishanger* | *William of Rishanger, Chronica et Annales*, ed. H. T. Riley (Rolls Series, London, 1865) |
| *Chron. Scalacronica* | *Sir Thomas Gray: Scalacronica (1272–1363)*, ed. A. King (Surtees Society, 209, 2005) |
| *Chron. Wyntoun* | Andrew of Wyntoun, *The Original Chronicle of Andrew of Wyntoun*, ed. A. Amours (Scottish Text Society, 6 vols, Edinburgh, 1903–14) |
| *CIM* | *Calendar of Inquisitions, Miscellaneous* (1916–) |
| *CIPM* | *Calendar of Inquisitions, Post Mortem* (1898–) |
| *CPL* | *Calendar of Entries in the Papal Registers relating to Great Britain and Ireland: Papal Letters*, ed. W. H. Bliss et al. (16 vols, London, 1893) |
| *CPR* | *Calendar of Patent Rolls* (1891–) |
| DCM | Durham Cathedral Muniments |
| Duncan, *Kingship* | A. A. M. Duncan, *The Kingship of the Scots, 842–1292: Succession and Independence* (Edinburgh, 2002) |
| *Edward I and the Throne of Scotland* | E. L. G. Stones and G. G. Simpson, eds, *Edward I and the Throne of Scotland: An Edition of the Record Sources for the Great Cause* (2 vols, Glasgow, 1978) |
| *EHR* | *English Historical Review* |
| *ER* | *The Exchequer Rolls of Scotland*, ed. J. Stuart et al. (23 vols, Edinburgh, 1878–1908) |
| *ESSH* | *Early Sources of Scottish History, AD 500 to 1286*, ed. A. O. Anderson (2 vols, Stamford, 1990) |
| *Fasti* | D. E. R. Watt and A. L. Murray, eds, *Fasti Ecclesiae Scoticanae Medii Aevi Ad Annum 1638* (Edinburgh, 2003) |
| *FCE* | *Fourteenth-Century England* (Woodbridge, 2000–) |
| *Foedera* | *Foedera, Conventiones, Litterae et Cuiuscunque Generis Acta Publica*, ed. T. Rymer (20 vols, London, 1704–35) |
| *Handlist* (Scoular) | *Handlist of the Acts of Alexander II, 1214–1249*, ed. J. M. Scoular (Edinburgh, 1959) |
| *Handlist* (Simpson) | *Handlist of the Acts of Alexander III, the Guardians and John, 1249–1296*, ed. G. G. Simpson (Edinburgh, 1960) |
| *HMC* | *Historical Manuscripts Commission* |
| *HR* | *Historical Research* |
| *IR* | *Innes Review* |
| *JMH* | *Journal of Medieval History* |
| Jones, ed., *NCMH*, vi | M. Jones, ed., *The New Cambridge Medieval History, vi: c.1300–c.1415* (Cambridge, 2000) |
| McNamee, *Wars of the Bruces* | C. McNamee, *Wars of the Bruces: Scotland, England and Ireland, 1306–28* (East Linton, 1997) |

| | |
|---|---|
| *MRH: Scotland* | I. B. Cowan and D. E. Easson, *Medieval Religious Houses: Scotland* (2nd edn, London, 1976) |
| *NH* | *Northern History* |
| NLS | National Library of Scotland, Edinburgh |
| NRS | National Records of Scotland, Edinburgh |
| *ODNB* | *Oxford Dictionary of National Biography* |
| *ODS* | *Oxford Dictionary of Saints*, ed. D. H. Farmer (Oxford, 1978) |
| Ormrod, *Edward III* | W. M. Ormrod, *Edward III* (London, 2012) |
| Palgrave, *Documents* | *Documents and Records illustrating the History of Scotland*, ed. F. Palgrave (London, 1837) |
| Penman, *David II* | M. Penman, *The Bruce Dynasty in Scotland: David II, 1329–71* (East Linton, 2004) |
| Phillips, *Edward II* | J. R. S. Phillips, *Edward II* (London, 2010) |
| Prestwich, *Edward I* | M. Prestwich, *Edward I* (London, 1988) |
| *PROME* | *The Parliament Rolls of Medieval England*, ed. C. Given-Wilson et al. (CD-ROM, London, 2005) |
| *PSAS* | *Proceedings of the Society of Antiquaries of Scotland* |
| *RMS* | *Registrum Magni Sigilii Regum Scotorum*, ed. J. M. Thomson and J. B. Paul (11 vols, Edinburgh, 1882–1914) |
| *Rot. Scot.* | *Rotuli Scotiae in Turri Londinensi et in Domo Capitulari Westmonasteriensi Asservati*, ed. D. Macpherson (2 vols, London, 1814–19) |
| *RPS* | *The Records of the Parliaments of Scotland to 1707*, ed. K. M. Brown et al. (St Andrews, 2008–), http://www.rps.ac.uk |
| *RRS* | *Regesta Regum Scottorum, v: The Acts of Robert I, 1306–29,* ed. A. A. M. Duncan (Edinburgh, 1986) |
| *Scottish Formularies* | A. A. M. Duncan, ed., *Scottish Formularies* (The Stair Society, Edinburgh, 2011) |
| *SHR* | *Scottish Historical Review* |
| *SP* | J. B. Paul, *The Scots Peerage* (9 vols, Edinburgh, 1904–14) |
| Stevenson, *Documents* | *Documents Illustrative of the History of Scotland, 1286–1306*, ed. J. Stevenson (2 vols, Edinburgh, 1870) |
| *TCE* | *Thirteenth-Century England* (Woodbridge, 1986–) |
| *TDGNHAS* | *Transactions of the Dumfriesshire and Galloway Natural History and Antiquarian Society* |
| TNA | The National Archives (Kew) |
| *TRHS* | *Transactions of the Royal Historical Society* |
| *Vetera* | *Vetera Monumenta Hibernorum et Scotorum Historiam Illustrantia*, ed. A. Theiner (Rome, 1864) |
| *Vita* | *Vita Edwardi Secundi*, ed. W. R. Childs (Oxford, 2005) |
| Watson, *Under the Hammer* | F. Watson, *Under the Hammer: Edward I and Scotland, c.1286–1307* (East Linton, 1998) |
| Watt, *Scottish Graduates* | D. E. R. Watt, *A Biographical Dictionary of Scottish Graduates to A.D. 1410* (Oxford, 1977) |

# Notes

### A Note about Distances, Money and Bibliography

1. R. D. Connor and A. D. C. Simpson, *Weights and Measures in Scotland: A European Perspective*, ed. A. D. Morrison-Low (East Linton, 2004), 94.
2. J. M. Gilbert, 'The Usual Money of Scotland and Exchange Rates against Foreign Coin', in D. M. Metcalf, ed., *Coinage in Medieval Scotland, 1100–1600* (Oxford, 1977), 131–51; A. Grant, *Independence and Nationhood: Scotland, 1306–1469* (Edinburgh, 1984), 240.

### Introduction: Re-opening the 'Book on Bruce'

1. *Chron. Wyntoun*, v, 354.
2. *RRS*, v, nos 41–4; *RPS*, 1314/1.
3. *Chron. Scalacronica*, 73–7.
4. TNA E39/4/6A; Palgrave, *Documents*, 323–4; *CDS*, ii, no. 1917.
5. *RRS*, v, no. 41; *RPS*, 1314/1.
6. Including the earldoms of Fife, Atholl, Menteith, Buchan, Angus, Mar and perhaps Dunbar; and such lordships as Galloway, Badenoch, Strathbogie, Garioch, Lochaber and Lorn.
7. A. A. M. Duncan, 'The War of the Scots, 1306–23', *TRHS*, 6th series, ii (1992), 125–51, at 149.
8. *Rot. Scot.*, i, 131–4; *CDS*, iii, nos 371–2, 393; *CPR, Edward II, 1313–17*, 18.
9. Of the 569 acts identified by A. A. M. Duncan in *RRS*, v, only nos 1–39 are extant from before Bannockburn, c.1306–14, plus a further twenty or so undated acts which may belong to this period (nos 384–90, 400–2, 417–23).
10. *RRS*, v, nos 40, 424; *Chron. Lanercost*, 22.
11. *RRS*, v, no. 42.
12. *RMS*, i, App. ii, no. 639.
13. *RRS*, v, no. 43; S. Boardman, 'Dunfermline as a Royal Mausoleum', in R. Fawcett, ed., *Royal Dunfermline* (Edinburgh, 2005), 139–54, at 154.
14. M. Penman, '"Sacred Food for the Soul": In Search of the Devotions to Saints of Robert Bruce, King of Scotland, 1306–1329', *Speculum*, 88, 4 (2013), 1–28.
15. In 1290 the Papacy had granted one year and forty days of plenary indulgence for all those visiting the shrine of St Margaret during her own and other key feasts (*CPR*, i, 520).
16. *RRS*, v, no. 44.
17. *The Bruce*, 518–19.
18. *Barbour's Bruce*, i, 39–45; *The Bruce*, 14–31. And see S. Boardman and S. Foran, eds, *Barbour's Bruce and Its Cultural Contexts: Politics, Chivalry and Literature in Late Medieval Scotland* (Woodbridge, 2015).
19. *The Bruce*, 55, ll. 168–71; M. Penman, '"A fell coniuracioun agayn Robert the douchty king": The Soules Conspiracy of 1318–20', *IR*, 50 (1999), 25–57.
20. *The Bruce*, 749.
21. Barrow, *Robert Bruce*, chs 13–14. This has been the structure adopted by popular histories: for example, R. M. Scot, *Robert the Bruce, King of Scots* (Edinburgh, 1982); C. Bingham, *Robert*

*the Bruce* (London, 1998). Colm McNamee redresses this balance, covering c.1274–1314 in seven of twelve chapters in *Robert Bruce: Our Most Valiant Prince, King and Lord* (Edinburgh, 2006). Michael Brown's studies provide scholarly synthesis, a long-take and British Isles' context for Robert I's reign: *The Wars of Scotland, 1214–1371* (Edinburgh, 2004); *Bannockburn: The Scottish War and the British Isles, 1307–1323* (Edinburgh, 2008); *Disunited Kingdoms: Peoples and Politics in the British Isles, 1280–1460* (London, 2013).

22. For excellent discussions of the historiography of change across the late medieval period see: S. Kelly, *The New Solomon: Robert of Naples (1309–1343) and Fourteenth-Century Kingship* (Leiden, 2003), ch. 7; J. Watts, *The Making of Polities: Europe, 1300–1500* (Cambridge, 2009), chs 1–2; S. Bagge, *From Viking Stronghold to Christian Kingdom: State Formation in Norway, c.900–1300* (Copenhagen, 2010), Introduction.

23. See the 'national' chapters in Jones, ed., *NCMH*, vi; J. V. A. Fine jr., *The Late Medieval Balkans* (Ann Arbor, MI, 1987), chs 4–5; D. Nicholas, *Medieval Flanders* (London, 1992), ch. 8; C. R. Backman, *The Decline and Fall of Medieval Sicily: Politics, Religion and Economy in the Reign of Frederick III, 1296–1337* (Cambridge, 1995), ch. 1.

24. W. C. Jordan, 'The Capetians from the Death of Philip II to Philip IV', in Abulafia, ed., *NCMH*, v, 279–313; P. Herde, 'From Adolf of Nassau to Lewis of Bavaria, 1292–1347', and A. Forey, 'The Crown of Aragon', in Jones, ed., *NCMH*, vi, 515–50 and 595–618 (at 595–7); Kelly, *The New Solomon*, 5–8, 109–10.

25. M. Prestwich, 'Parliament and the Community of the Realm in Fourteenth-Century England', in A. Cosgrove and J. I. McGuire, eds, *Parliament and Community* (Historical Studies XIV, 1983), 5–24.

26. Barrow, *Robert Bruce*, 20–6, 380–404; N. Reid, 'The Kingless Kingdom: The Scottish Guardianship of 1286–1306', *SHR*, lxi (1982), 105–29.

27. D. E. R. Watt, 'Scottish University Men of the Thirteenth and Fourteenth Centuries', in T. C. Smout, ed., *Scotland and Europe, 1200–1850* (Edinburgh, 1986), 1–18.

28. A more critical, factional take on Robert I's reign was offered by Duncan's review of Barrow's first edition (1965), in A. A. M. Duncan, 'The Community of the Realm of Scotland and Robert Bruce', *SHR*, xlv (1966), 184–201; by R. Nicholson in *Scotland: The Later Middle Ages* (Edinburgh, 1974), chs 4–5; and by A. Grant, *Independence and Nationhood: Scotland, 1306–1469* (Edinburgh, 1984), ch. 1.

29. *RPS*. Contrast R. J. Tanner, 'Cowing the Community? Coercion and Falsification in Robert Bruce's Parliaments, 1309–1318', in K. M. Brown and R. J. Tanner, eds, *Parliament and Politics in Scotland, 1235–1560* (Edinburgh, 2004), 50–73, with the quite friction-less, consensual parliaments in N. H. Reid, 'Crown and Community under Robert I', in A. Grant and K. J. Stringer, eds, *Medieval Scotland: Crown, Lordship and Community: Essays presented to G. W. S. Barrow* (Edinburgh, 2003), 203–22.

30. A. Taylor, 'Leges Scocie and the Lawcodes of David I, William the Lion and Alexander II', *SHR*, lxxxviii (2009), 207–88; *Scottish Formularies*.

31. *Chron. Bower*, ix, 234–364; S. Boardman, 'Chronicle Propaganda in Fourteenth-Century Scotland: Robert the Steward, Fordun and the "Anonymous Chronicle"', *SHR*, lxxvi (1997), 23–43; D. Broun, 'A New Look at *Gesta Annalia* Attributed to John of Fordun', in B. E. Crawford, ed., *Church, Chronicle and Learning in Medieval and Early Renaissance Scotland* (Edinburgh, 1999), 9–30; J. Fraser, 'A Swan from a Raven: William Wallace, Brucean Propaganda and *Gesta Annalia II*', *SHR*, lxxxi (2002), 1–22.

32. A. Gransden, *Historical Writing in England, from c.550 to the Early Sixteenth Century* (2 vols, 2nd edn, London, 1997), *ad indecim*; C. Given-Wilson, *Chronicles: The Writing of History in Medieval England* (London, 2004), chs 1–3.

33. P. Contamine, 'Froissart and Scotland', in G. G. Simpson, ed., *Scotland and the Low Countries, 1124–1994* (East Linton, 1996), 43–58. French chronicles otherwise contain a spare, white-washed (anti-Balliol) account of the Scottish wars, influenced by the exiled Bruce court in France, 1334–41, under Robert I's son, David II (Penman, *David II*, 52).

34. *RMS*, i, App. ii; *RRS*, v, 215–30 (discussion of extant rolls), 231–48 (lost rolls), 705–30 (table of lost acts duplicated in other sources). Many medieval Scottish rolls were lost (at sea) when seized by England in the seventeenth century: D. Stevenson, 'The English and the Public Records of Scotland', *Stair Society Miscellany 1* (Edinburgh, 1971), 156–70.

35. *RRS*, v, 135–58 ('Itinerary').

36. *ER*, i, *passim*; *RRS*, v, 172–7.

37. A strong theme in English history: M. Prestwich, 'The Piety of Edward I', in W. M. Ormrod, ed., *England in the Thirteenth Century* (Grantham, 1985), 120–8; J. R. S. Phillips, 'Edward II and the Prophets', in W. M. Ormrod, ed., *England in the Fourteenth Century: Proceedings of the 1985 Harlaxton Symposium* (Woodbridge, 1986), 189–201; *idem, Edward III*, 63–72. Barrow, *Robert Bruce*, 412–15, notes Bruce's religion as 'conventional'.

38. R. E. Lerner, *The Age of Adversity: The Fourteenth Century* (Ithaca, NY, 1968), *passim*; J. R. Strayer, *The Medieval Origins of the Modern State* (Princeton, NJ, 1970), 89.

## Chapter 1 *Body and Soul:* Formative Years, 1274–92

1. *Chron. Bower*, vi, 31.

2. M. Hammond, 'Ethnicity and the Writing of Medieval Scottish History', *SHR*, lxxxv (2006), 1–27.

3. Barrow, *Robert Bruce*, 35 (and his *ODNB* entry for Robert I). Not even such Homeric poems as Patrick Gordon's *Famous Historie of the Renown'd and Valiant Prince Robert sirnamed the Bruce* (1613) or John Harvey's *The Life of Robert Bruce* (Edinburgh, 1727) assigned a firm birthplace; nor did early nineteenth-century historians Lord Hailes, Patrick Tytler, Walter Scott or Robert Kerr, or novelist Jane Porter in her popular novel, *The Scottish Chiefs* (1800). Rather the Turnberry attribution entered popular memory by the later Victorian period: see A. F. Murison, *King Robert the Bruce* (Edinburgh, 1899), 18.

4. *Chronicon Galfridi le Baker de Swynebroke*, ed. E. M. Thompson (Oxford, 1889), 38, 178; A. H. Dunbar, *Scottish Kings: A Revised Chronology of Scottish History 1005–1625* (Edinburgh, 1899), 127; *SP*, i, 7.

5. Blakely, *Brus Family*, Appendix 3 (Brus charters), nos 184–96. The National Archives, Kew, accepts Robert I's birth in Writtle (TNA C241/18/59).

6. Writtle would be the only English land demanded by Robert for restoration in peace talks in November 1324 (*Vita*, 223–5).

7. *Chron. Bower*, v, 385.

8. R. Frame, *The Political Development of the British Isles, 1100–1400* (Oxford, 1990), ch. 3 ('The Aristocratic Nexus'); R. R. Davies, *Lords and Lordship in the British Isles in the Late Middle Ages*, ed. B. Smith (Oxford, 2009), ch. 1 ('The Higher Aristocracy: Identity and Memory').

9. *CDS*, i, nos 1429, 1431, 1503; Blakely, *Brus Family*, ch. 5 and Appendices 2 (Chester/Huntingdon inheritance) and 3 (Brus charters). Earl David's son, John, earl of Huntingdon and Chester, died in 1237.

10. Blakely, *Brus Family*, 76–83, 116–17; *CDS*, ii, nos 312, 1073–4, 1540.

11. *Chron. Fordun*, i, 302–3, ii, 299–300; R. D. Oram, *The Lordship of Galloway* (Edinburgh, 2000), chs 4–7.

12. A. Macquarrie, *Scotland and the Crusades, 1095–1560* (Edinburgh, 1985), 56–65. Adam, earl of Carrick, and David Strathbogie, earl of Atholl, also died on crusade c.1271–72.

13. Blakely, *Brus Family*, 115; M. F. Moore, *The Lands of the Scottish Kings in England* (London, 1915), ch. 5; K. J. Stringer, *Earl David of Huntingdon, 1152–1219: A Study in Anglo-Scottish History* (Edinburgh, 1985), chs 4–7, esp. p. 111. A Scottish knight's fee in this period is estimated at about £20 (*CDS*, iii, nos 1617, 1737).

14. P. Corser, 'The Brus Lordship of Annandale, 1124–1296', in R. D. Oram and G. Stell, eds, *Lordship and Architecture in Medieval and Renaissance Scotland* (Edinburgh, 2005), 45–60; *CPR, Edward I, 1281–92*, 227, 277, 292, 315, 352, 394, 494.

15. R. Greeves, 'The Galloway Lands in Ulster', *TDGNHAS*, xxxvi (1959), 115–22; A. A. M. Duncan, 'The Bruces of Annandale, 1100–1304', *TDGNHAS*, lxix (1994), 89–102; S. Duffy, 'The Lords of Galloway, Earls of Carrick, and the Bissets of the Glens: Scottish Settlement in Thirteenth-Century Ulster', in D. Edwards, ed., *Regions and Rulers in Ireland, 1100–1650: Essays for Kenneth Nicholls* (Dublin, 2004), 37–50; Blakely, *Brus Family*, chs 4–6.

16. Beam, *Balliol Dynasty*, ch. 2.

17. *Regesta Regum Scottorum*, iv, pt i: *The Acts of Alexander III, 1249–86*, eds, C. J. Neville and G. G. Simpson (Edinburgh, 2012), no. 22; *CPR, Edward I, 1281–92*, 186; *Anglo-Scottish Relations*, no. 10. See also the 65+ transactions listed for Robert V by *The People of Northern England, 1216–1286* database (http://www.poms.ac.uk/record/person/1938, accessed on 20/8/13).

18. *CDS*, ii, nos 236, 237; *Calendar of the Charter Rolls Preserved in the Public Record Office, 1226–1516* (6 vols, London, 1903–27), iii, p. 183; F. M. Powicke, *King Henry III and the Lord Edward: The Community of the Realm in the Thirteenth Century* (2 vols, Oxford, 1947), ii, 466n.

19. *Regesta Regum Scottorum*, iv, pt i, 87, 117, 193; Dunbar, *Scottish Kings*, 117–18.

20. *RRS*, iv, pt 1, no. 73; H. L. MacQueen, 'Linguistic Communities in Medieval Scots Law', in C. W. Brooks and M. Lobban, eds, *Communities and Courts in Britain, 1150–1900* (London, 1997), 13–24.

21. R. Ingham, 'The Persistence of Anglo-Norman, 1230–1362: A Linguistic Perspective', in J. Wogan-Browne, ed., *Language and Culture in Medieval Britain: The French of England, c.1100–c.1500* (York, 2009), 44–54.

22. *Registrum de Dunfermelyn* (Bannatyne Club, Edinburgh, 1842), no. 321; *Anglo-Scottish Relations*, no. 12; Duncan, *Kingship*, 160–4.

23. J. Watts, *The Making of Polities: Europe, 1300–1500* (Cambridge, 2009), 122–31; P. Strohm, *Hochon's Arrow: The Social Imagination of Fourteenth-Century Texts* (Princeton, NJ, 1992), 3–10.

24. *The Bruce*, 122, 132; M. A. H. Newth, ed. and trans., *Fierabras and Floripas: A French Epic Allegory* (New York, 2010).

25. *Chron. Bower*, vi, 367–7; *Barbour's Bruce*, i, 38–45; *The Bruce*, 14–31.

26. N. Bryant, trans., *The True Chronicles of Jean le Bel, 1290–1360* (Woodbridge, 2011), 62; *Chron. Scalacronica*, cxlvi–cxlvii, 57.

27. *ER*, i, 297, 431.

28. A. A. M. Duncan, 'A Question about the Succession, 1364', *Scottish History Society Miscellany*, xii (Edinburgh, 1994), 1–57, at 25.

29. *Chron. Bower*, vii, 45–51.

30. Blakely, *Brus Family*, Appendix 3 (charters to Guisborough, Rievaulx, Durham, Holm Cultram, Melrose and Finchale); DCM Misc. Chs nos 801–6, bishops of Whithorns' grants of 40 days indulgence for pilgrimage to St Cuthbert's tomb, Durham, 1248–1302.

31. Blakely, *Brus Family*, Appendix 3, nos 160–1 (Lindores), 167–71 (Huntingdon), 172 (Writtle church of All Saints); *Chartulary of Lindores Abbey, 1195–1479* (Scottish History Society, Edinburgh, 1903), pp. xxv, xxx–xxxii, and nos 41, 116.

32. *Chron. Lanercost*, 111–14; R. C. Reid, 'Caput of Annandale or the Curse of Malachy', *TDGNHAS*, xliv (1955), 155–66.

33. CCA, Register E, f.127a, nos 2 and 3 (a 1220 Bruce/Stewart gift to Canterbury witnessed by 'Thomas, nephew of St Thomas'), f.143; R. Foreville, *Le Jubilé de Saint Thomas Becket du XIIIe au XVe siècle (1220–1470): Étude et documents* (Paris, 1958), ch. 1; M. Penman, 'The Bruce Dynasty, Becket and Scottish Pilgrimage to Canterbury, c.1178–c.1404', *JMH*, 32 (2006), 346–70, at 350–1.

34. It may have been Robert (VI) Bruce who asked for two rings to be placed on St Thomas's altar at Canterbury (CCA, Register E, f.127a, no. 1, f.143r and DCc Eastry Correspondence, EC III/3).

35. R. D. Oram, *Domination and Lordship: Scotland 1070–1230* (Edinburgh, 2011), chs 3–4.

36. *Liber S. Thome de Aberbrothoc* (2 vols, Bannatyne Club, Edinburgh, 1848–56), i, no. 37; K. J. Stringer, 'Arbroath Abbey in Context, 1178–1320', in G. Barrow, ed., *The Declaration of Arbroath: History, Setting, Significance* (Edinburgh, 2003), 116–42.

37. N. Orme, *From Childhood to Chivalry: The Education of English Kings and Aristocracy, 1066–1530* (London, 1984); Prestwich, *Edward I*, ch. 1; Phillips, *Edward II*, 33–76.

38. Macquarrie, *Scotland and the Crusades*, 58–9, details Robert V's charter at Clairvaux in 1273 witnessed by Sir Adam de Torthorwald (steward of Annandale), Sir Robert de Herries, Sir William de Saint Michael and Sir William de Duncorry. Sir Roger Kirkpatrick would be with Bruce when John Comyn of Badenoch was killed at Dumfries in 1306; his son, Sir Humphrey, would be granted Torthorwald in Annandale in 1321 (*RRS*, v, no. 189) and may have tutored David II (*ER*, i, 52, 123, 183).

39. *The Bruce*, 104–10, 448–52. Robert would be appointed as a forest-keeper in Moray by Edward I c.1304–5 (*CDS*, ii, nos 1709, 1736).

40. *ER*, i, 127, 130.

41. *CDS*, ii, no. 1540.

42. Barrow, *Robert Bruce*, 34, 431 n26; S. Duffy, 'The Bruce Brothers and the Irish Sea World, 1306–29', in *idem*, ed., *Robert the Bruce's Irish Wars: The Invasions of Ireland 1306–1329* (Stroud, 2002), 45–71, at 60.

43. *ER*, i, 114, 144–8, 208, 210, 278, 458; *HMC*, v, 197; Blakely, *Brus Family*, ch. 7 and Appendix 3, nos 174–5, 183.

44. *The Bruce*, 247.

45. Stevenson, *Illustrations*, 2–10, at 3.
46. Barrow, *Robert Bruce*, 431 n26; Duffy, 'The Bruce Brothers', 60. Duffy offers a more cautious assessment of Bruce fosterage in 'The Gaelic Account of the Bruce Invasion *Cath Fochairte Brighite*: Medieval Romance or Modern Forgery?', *Seanchas Ard Mhacha*, xiii, pt 1 (1988), 59–121, at 76–7.
47. *ER*, i, 126, 127, 136; W. S. Reid, 'Sea Power and the Anglo-Scottish War, 1296–1328', *Mariner's Mirror*, xlvi (1960), 7–23.
48. R. R. Davies, 'The Peoples of Britain and Ireland, 1100–1400, i. Identities' and 'ii. Names, Boundaries and Regnal Solidarities', *TRHS*, 6th series, iv (1994), 1–20, and v (1995), 1–20.
49. R. A. MacDonald, *The Kingdom of the Isles: Scotland's Western Seaboard, c.1100–c.1336* (East Linton, 1997), ch. 6; S. Boardman, *The Campbells, 1250–1513* (Edinburgh, 2006), ch. 2.
50. *Registrum Monasterii de Passelet* (Maitland Club, Glasgow, 1832), 128–9.
51. J. A. Claffey, 'Richard de Burgh, Earl of Ulster (c.1260–1326)', unpublished PhD, University College of Galway (1970), 42–72, 103–13.
52. *Chron. Scalacronica*, 35.
53. TNA E101/351/25 m.1 and /26 m.1; B. F. and C. R. Byerly, eds, *Records of the Wardrobe and Household, 1285–1286* (London, 1977), nos 357, 1024, 1044, 1177, 1247, 1294, 1677, 1679, 1753, 1794, 2125, 2156; *idem*, eds, *Records of the Wardrobe and Household, 1286–1289* (London, 1986), nos 2558, 2564; *CDS*, ii, nos 309, 312. For Robert VI: *Cal. Chancery Rolls, 1277–1326*, 365, 372; *CCR, Edward I, 1302–7*, 368.
54. See the Wardrobe book gaps for Edward I's years eighteen, nineteen and twenty through TNA E101/352 and /353. Rolls of robes payments are extant, though, for 1289 and 1290–1.
55. TNA C241/31/103.
56. Edward I stayed at Winchester (or nearby) c.10–17 February 1292, 14–23 August 1293 and 23 September 1294, *Itinerary of Edward I, part II: 1291–1307* (List and Index Society, no. 132, London, 1976), 19, 44, 61.
57. *The Royal Charter Witness Lists of Edward I (1272–1307)*, 73–4; M. Morris, 'Edward I and the Knights of the Round Table', in P. Brand and S. Cunningham, eds, *Foundations of Medieval Scholarship: Records Edited in Honour of David Crook* (York, 2008), 57–76.
58. *CDS*, ii, no. 1516.
59. The Bruces' lands in Bury, Huntingdon, perhaps brought contact with a Margaret relic held at a leper hospital dedicated to her cult (Blakely, *Brus Family*, Appendix 3, no. 168).
60. *Chron. Fordun*, i, 307–8, ii, 301–2. Edward I had lost three sons and five daughters by August 1284 (Prestwich, *Edward I*, 125–32).
61. By contrast, in Norway in 1273 an act of succession had listed the order of heirs through twelve possible living male successors (Duncan, *Kingship*, 169).
62. *APS*, i, 424; *Foedera*, I, ii, 638; Duncan, *Kingship*, 171.
63. *Chron. Wyntoun*, v, 164–9, 180–3, 185–209; *Chron. Bower*, vi, 9–11; *Liber Pluscardensis*, ed. F. J. H. Skene (Edinburgh, 1877), 121–3. These chronicles draw on a contemporary St Andrews source while Fordun's annalist simply states that the nobles often discussed the succession amongst themselves (i, 312; ii, 306).
64. *Regesta Regum Scottorum*, iv, pt i, no. 132; *APS*, i, 421–4; *Foedera*, I, ii, 595–6; *CDS*, ii, no. 197.
65. *Regesta Regum Scottorum*, iv, pt i, no. 133; *Edward I and the Throne of Scotland*, ii, 188–90.
66. Duncan, *Kingship*, 165–71.
67. *Chron. Fordun*, i, 320, ii, 314; *CIPM*, ii, no. 771.
68. *Chron. Bower*, vi, 9. Duncan translates this as a 'bitter pleading' and notes its omission by Barrow's *Robert Bruce*, in *SHR*, lxv (1966), 184–201, at 185; *idem*, 'The Early Parliaments of Scotland', *SHR*, xlv (1966), 35–57, at 37–8.
69. N. H. Reid, 'The Kingless Kingdom: The Scottish Guardianship of 1286–1306', *SHR*, lxi (1982), 10–29; A. Young, *Robert the Bruce's Rivals: The Comyns, 1212–1314* (East Linton, 1997), 90–104; Duncan, *Kingship*, 175–80; A. A. B. McQueen, 'Parliament, the Guardians and John Balliol, 1284–1296', in K. M. Brown and R. J. Tanner, eds, *Parliament and Politics in Scotland, 1235–1560* (Edinburgh, 2004), 29–50.
70. Palgrave, *Documents*, 42; *Chron. Bower*, vi, 8.
71. *ER*, i, 36–41.
72. Duncan, *Kingship*, 70–1. The third claimant of Robert V's generation, Henry Hastings, a son of the third daughter of Earl David, had died in 1269.
73. *Chron. Bower*, vi, 9.

74. Byerly, eds, *Records of the Wardrobe and Household, 1286–1289*, nos 719, 2146–7. Bickerton is in North Yorkshire. The Ragman Rolls of 1296 list John Bickerton in Linlithgowshire, Eustace Bickerton rector of Auchtermuchty, Fife, and Walter Bickerton baron of Craigie, Fife (*CDS*, ii, no. 857 and pp. 205, 209); Robert I would grant the Angus thanage of Downie to Walter on 20 March 1309 for a knight's service (*RRS*, v, no. 6).

75. Stevenson, *Documents*, i, no. 12; W. Fraser, ed., *The Red Book of Menteith* (2 vols, Edinburgh, 1880), ii, 219–20.

76. Claffey, 'Richard de Burgh, Earl of Ulster (c.1260–1326)', 42–72, 103–13; Duffy, 'The Bruce Brothers', 54–63, and *idem*, 'The Turnberry Band', in S. Duffy, ed., *Princes, Prelates and Poets in Medieval Ireland: Essays in Honour of Katharine Simms* (Dublin, 2013), 124–38. The Band coincided with a 'great hosting' in 1286 by Earl Richard against enemies in Ulster/Connacht. Carrick contact with Ireland is confirmed by safe conducts issued to Earl Robert to travel there to buy 'corn, wine and other victuals' (*CPR, Edward I, 1281–92*, 24, 442; *CPR, Edward I, 1292–1301*, 69).

77. E. Hamilton, *Mighty Subjects: The Dunbar Earls in Scotland, c.1072–1289* (Edinburgh, 2010), chs 15–18; Macquarrie, *Scotland and the Crusades*, 47–8, 60–1.

78. *Chron. Bower*, vi, 11, states that the Guardians gathered at Clackmannan about 25 November 1286 to await the birth of Yolande's child, a respectful distance from Dunfermline Abbey where the queen could wear the 'birthing serk' of St Margaret while in labour.

79. Young, *Robert the Bruce's Rivals*, 39.

80. *RPS*, 1293/2/16–18; W. D. H. Sellar, 'Hebridean Sea Kings: The Successors of Somerled, 1164–1316', in E. J. Cowan and R. A. MacDonald, eds, *Alba: Celtic Scotland in the Medieval Era* (East Linton, 2000), 187–218, at 211–12.

81. The Turnberry Band's inclusion of Earl Patrick may have neutralised a claim to the throne through a Dunbar marriage to another illegitimate daughter of William I; Patrick was said to have married Christina, a daughter of Robert V (*Edward I and the Throne of Scotland*, i, 116, and ii, 134, 189–90).

82. Stevenson, *Documents*, no. lxxx.

83. M. Brown, 'Aristocratic Politics and the Crisis of Scottish Kingship, 1286–96', *SHR*, xc (2011), 1–26, at 10–11; A. Ross, 'Men for All Seasons? The Strathbogie Earls of Atholl and the Wars of Independence, c.1290–c.1335. Part I: Earl John and Earl David III', *Northern Scotland*, xx (2000), 1–30.

84. *Chron. Bower*, vi, 33 and 206n.

85. *SP*, v, 577–83.

86. *RRS*, v, 416n and 648n.

87. Duncan, *Kingship*, 179. However, *Chron. Bower*, vi, 9 and 33, asserts that Fife was replaced first with the bishop of Dunkeld and then by Sir Andrew Murray of Avoch who arrested Hugh Abernethy. For the 1288–90 sheriffdoms, see *ER*, i, 35–51, with Ayr (James Steward) and Lanark (Hugh Dalyell) at 39, 45.

88. Stevenson, *Documents*, i, no. lxxv; *Foedera*, I, ii, 719–20; *RPS*, 1290/3/1; Duncan, *Kingship*, 177–83.

89. *CDS*, ii, no. 386. Robert VI Bruce also received £100 from the English royal Wardrobe on 2 November 1288 (TNA E101/352/12 2r).

90. *Anglo-Scottish Relations*, no. 13; *Regesta Regum Scottorum*, iv, pt i, no. 146. By 1288–89, illustrated genealogical rolls had been produced in England hinting at this marriage (N. H. Monroe, 'Two Genealogical Roll Chronicles', *Bodleian Library Record*, x (1981), 215–21).

91. *CDS*, ii, no. 675.

92. Stevenson, *Documents*, nos lxxv, xcii, ciii, cxxi; *RPS*, 1290/3/2.

93. Stevenson, *Documents*, no. cviii; *RPS*, 1290/7/1.

94. W. Stevenson, 'The Treaty of Northampton (1290): A Scottish Charter of Liberties', *SHR*, lxxxvi (2007), 1–15.

95. Watt, *Scottish Graduates*, 23–4, 107–9, 203–4, 585–6; I. J. Sanders, ed., *Documents of the Baronial Movement of Reform and Rebellion, 1258–1267* (Oxford, 1973), nos 3, 5, 9, 11–12, 40, 44. Echoes of Montfortian ideas circulating in Scotland may be found in the *Opusculum* [little work] *de Simone* about the Barons' Wars appended c.14 April 1286–c.May 1291 to the closing sections of the chronicle of the Cistercian border abbey of Melrose: this account hedged its bets by praising all parties, including Bruce; see D. Broun and J. Harrison, eds, *The Chronicle of Melrose: A Stratigraphic Edition* (Scottish History Society, 2007), 8–9, 168–9.

96. K. J. Stringer, 'States, Liberties and Communities in Medieval Britain and Ireland (c.1100–1400)', and A. Grant, 'Franchises North of the Border: Baronies and Regalities in Medieval Scotland', both in M. Prestwich, ed., *Liberties and Identities in the Medieval British Isles* (Woodbridge, 2008), 5–36 (at 13, 15–19) and 155–99 (at 160–1, 164, 171); K. J. Stringer, 'The Scottish "Political Community" in the Reign of Alexander II (1214–49)', and D. Carpenter, 'Scottish Royal Government in the Thirteenth Century from an English Perspective', both in M. Hammond, ed., *New Perspectives on Medieval Scotland, 1093–1286* (Woodbridge, 2013), 53–84 and 117–59.

97. Prestwich, *Edward I*, 360–2; M. Morris, *A Great and Terrible King: Edward I and the Forging of Britain* (London, 2008), 227–8.

98. *Foedera*, II, i, 741; *CDS*, ii, no. 459; *Edward I and the Throne of Scotland*, ii, 3.

99. Duncan, *Kingship*, 197–202.

100. *Anglo-Scottish Relations*, no. 14; Brown, 'Aristocratic Politics', 10–14. See also TNA DL 25/82, an 'undertaking' by William, earl of Sutherland, to assist Annandale in obtaining his right to the throne c.1291/95.

101. *Edward I and the Throne of Scotland*, ii, 5–6.

102. *Chron. Bower*, vi, 159, 177.

103. Stevenson, *Documents*, nos lxxxvi, cii, cxxv.

104. Duncan, *Kingship*, 198.

105. Ibid., 203–5.

106. Powicke, *King Henry III and the Lord Edward*, ii, 732–3.

107. Beam, *Balliol Dynasty*, 193. On 16 August 1291 Edward I gifted ten harts to Robert Bruce from Engelwode (*CCR, Edward I, 1288–96*, 167).

108. TNA E101/352/16 and /18; TNA E101/357/27 (167 masses in 1300, including ten for 'St Thomas'); J. Alexander and P. Binski, *The Age of Chivalry: Art in Plantagenet England, 1200–1400* (London, 1987), 361–6.

109. Prestwich, *Edward I*, chs 7–13; Morris, *Great and Terrible King*, chs 6–8.

110. P. A. Brand, 'Edward I and the Judges: The "State Trials" of 1289–93', in *TCE*, i, ed. P. R. Coss and S. D. Lloyd (Woodbridge, 1986), 31–40.

111. Prestwich, *Edward I*, 147–57.

112. Barrow, *Robert Bruce*, 41–70; Prestwich, *Edward I*, ch. 14; Duncan, *Kingship*, 205–315.

113. *Edward I and the Throne of Scotland*, i, ch. 6 and ii, Appendix A.

114. Prestwich, *Edward I*, 148, 150, 152, 355. Edward brought 140 horses for his household to Norham/Berwick, with 1,000 horses all told for his embassy.

115. A. A. M. Duncan, 'The Process of Norham, 1291', in P. R. Coss and S. D. Lloyd, eds, *TCE*, v (Woodbridge, 1995), 207–30; *idem, Kingship*, chs 10–11; *idem*, 'Revisiting Norham, May–June 1291', in C. Given-Wilson, A. Kettle and L. Scales, eds, *War, Government and Aristocracy in the British Isles, c.1150–c.1500* (Woodbridge, 2008), 69–83.

116. *Chron. Guisborough*, 232–5; *Anglo-Scottish Relations*, no. 15.

117. *Anglo-Scottish Relations*, no. 16; *Edward I and the Throne of Scotland*, ii, 20–1; P. A. Linehan, 'A Fourteenth-Century History of Anglo-Scottish Relations in a Spanish Manuscript', *BIHR*, xlviii (1975), 106–22, at 120.

118. Duncan, *Kingship*, 154–64, 216–17.

119. Ibid., 237–9; *Edward I and the Throne of Scotland*, ii, 38–9 (Bruce's submission, backdated by English notary John de Caen to 2 June).

120. Duncan, *Kingship*, 238–9; Beam, *Balliol Dynasty*, 103–4.

121. *Chron. Lanercost*, 81; Duncan, *Kingship*, 250–4.

122. Duncan, *Kingship*, ch. 11 passim. For Edward I's fealty tour: *Itinerary of Edward I, part II*, 10–11; Barrow, *Robert Bruce*, 50–1; P. G. B. McNeill and H. L. MacQueen, eds, *Atlas of Scottish History to 1707* (Edinburgh, 1996), 86.

123. P. Herde, 'From Adolf of Nassau to Lewis of Bavaria, 1292–1347', in Jones, ed., *NCMH*, vi, 515–16.

124. Barrow, *Robert Bruce*, 54–5; Duncan, *Kingship*, 257–61.

125. *Edward I and the Throne of Scotland*, ii, 80–5.

126. Robert's later royal government may have fabricated a chronicle record of a law of c.1005 upholding 'Imperial' royal succession by nearness of degree, first passed by Cinaed II, king of Scots (Duncan, *Kingship*, 27–8).

127. Barrow, *Robert Bruce*, 57–65; Duncan, *Kingship*, 265–8. Balliol also detailed the 'rebellious conduct' of Annandale and Carrick from 1286 to 1290 (*CDS*, ii, no. 608).

128. *Itinerary of Edward I, part II*, 12–24; Prestwich, *Edward I*, 118–19.
129. *Rot. Scot.*, i, 1–15; Young, *Robert the Bruce's Rivals*, 115–17.
130. *ER*, i, 35–51. However, these 1288–90 accounts may omit some office-holders as they survive only in a seventeenth-century abridgement (*ER*, i, xxxv).
131. A.A.M. Duncan, 'Brus, Robert (V) de', http://www.oxforddnb.com/view/article/3752, accessed 10/6/13.
132. Duncan, *Kingship*, 299–306; *CPR, Edward I, 1281–92*, 508.
133. *Edward I and the Throne of Scotland*, ii, 185–6; Duncan, *Kingship*, 122–6.
134. *Edward I and the Throne of Scotland*, ii, 196, 358–65, 401; Duncan, *Kingship*, 311–15; *Chron. Bower*, vi, 13 (Paris opinions) and vi, 11–27 (dossier of 'Great Cause'); *Chron. Wyntoun*, v, 185–209 (Paris opinions).
135. Beam, *Balliol Dynasty*, 111–13.
136. *Chron. Fordun*, i, 310–21, ii, 306–15; *Chron. Wyntoun*, v, 210–17; *Chron. Bower*, vi, 9–11, 27–33.
137. *Chron. Bower*, vi, 31–3; *The Bruce*, 53–5.
138. Barrow, *Robert Bruce*, 65; Prestwich, *Edward I*, 368–9.
139. *Edward I and the Throne of Scotland*, ii, 222–8. '[Annandale] said to his son . . . "You take our Scottish lands, if you'll agree, for we will never be his [John's] men"' (*Chron. Scalacronica*, 35).
140. A. Grant, 'The Death of John Comyn: What Was Going On?', *SHR*, lxxxvi (2007), 176–224, at 199–207.

## Chapter 2 *Conflict*: Earl of Carrick, 1293–99

1. *Chron. Fordun*, i, 326, ii, 319; *Chron. Bower*, vi, 75.
2. *Anglo-Scottish Relations*, no. 20; *CDS*, ii, nos 657–8.
3. *RPS*, 1293/2/1–4, 8, 12, 13, 14, 15, 16–19; *Scottish Formularies*, nos E46, E67; Beam, *Balliol Dynasty*, 132–42, 298–313.
4. *RPS*, 1293/2/20 and 1293/8/5–6; *CDS*, ii, nos 357–8, 468.
5. *RPS*, 1293/8/8; *Scottish Formularies*, nos E31, E39–41, E68. For the unusual 'handbook' describing Scottish royal household government drawn up for the inexperienced King John, see M. Bateson, ed., 'The Scottish King's Household and Other Fragments', *Scottish History Society Miscellany*, ii (Edinburgh, 1904), pp. 1–43, at 7–8. However, this guide may speak more to the ideals of an English clerk seeking to expand checks upon Edwardian monarchy (D. A. Carpenter, ' "The Scottish King's Household" and English Ideas of Constitutional Reform', http://www.breakingofbritain.ac.uk/blogs/feature-of-the-month/october–2011–the–scottish–kings–household/, accessed on 12/6/2013).
6. *RRS*, v, nos 416, 648.
7. *CDS*, ii, no. 675; *CPR, Edward I, 1281–92*, 508.
8. *CDS*, ii, nos 681, 685–6; Barrow, *Robert Bruce*, 75–81; Beam, *Balliol Dynasty*, ch. 4.
9. *CCR, Edward I, 1288–96*, 295, 349, 367.
10. On 27 July 1293 Robert VI was issued a safe conduct to Norway (*CPR, Edward I, 1292–1301*, 33).
11. *Chron. Bower*, vi, 41.
12. *APS*, i, 102–3; *Scottish Formularies*, A67, E16, E78, B74, B74bis (and notes); *Chron. Lanercost*, 108, reports hundreds of ships claimed by that year's storms (ibid., 109).
13. *Chron. Lanercost*, 102.
14. 'A continuous drenching downpour of rain, so that very little or none of the new crop could be harvested before Michaelmas', in A. Gransden, ed., *The Chronicle of Bury St Edmunds, 1212–1301* (London, 1964), 123.
15. R. Britnell, *Britain and Ireland, 1050–1530: Economy and Society* (Oxford, 2004), chs 9 and 14; B. M. S. Campbell, 'Benchmarking Medieval Economic Development: England, Wales, Scotland and Ireland, c.1290', *Economic History Review*, 61, 4 (2008), 896–945.
16. J. Donnelly, 'Skinned to the Bone: Durham Evidence for Taxations of the Church in Scotland, 1254–1366', *IR*, 50 (1999), 1–24, at 11, 19. With pressure to convert parish teind income in kind to cash, a higher proportion of crops (and thus seed) may thus have been 'taxed', approximately 15–23 per cent (ibid., 19).
17. Ibid., 3, 16–17. In the 1290s the exemption from crusade levies of Cistercian and Premonstratensian houses in Scotland was also suspended.

18. *Diocesis Karliolensis: Registrum Johannis de Halton* (2 vols, Canterbury and York Society, 1906), i, 16–21, 35–6, 41–6.

19. *CPR, Edward I, 1292–1301*, 69; *CCR, Edward I, 1288–96*, 295, 367. That crusading tenths affected nobles directly is underlined by Donald, earl of Mar's 'contumacious' withholding of arrears from the Aberdeen diocese in 1293 (Donnelly, 'Skinned to the Bone', 9).

20. *Chron. Lanercost*, 103; *Register of John le Romeyn, Lord Archbishop of York, 1286–1296, Part II, and of Henry of Newark, Lord Archbishop of York, 1296–1299* (Surtees Society, 1913–17), 114–33; R. J. Brentano, 'The Whithorn Vacancy of 1293–94', *IR*, iv (1953), 71–8.

21. *CDS*, ii, no. 695; Prestwich, *Edward I*, 376–81.

22. *Chron. Guisborough*, 270.

23. Prestwich, *Edward I*, 219–32; M. Morris, *A Great and Terrible King: Edward I and the Forging of Britain* (London, 2008), 275–80.

24. *Chron. Lanercost*, 114–15; *Chron. Langtoft*, 223; *Chron. Rishanger*, 371; H. R. Luard, ed., *Flores Historiarum* (3 vols, Rolls Series, London, 1890), iii, 281; Barrow, *Robert Bruce*, 83–5.

25. F. Watson, 'The Demonisation of King John', in E. J. Cowan and R. J. Finlay, eds, *Scottish History: The Power of the Past* (Edinburgh, 2000), 29–45, at 32–3; Beam, *Balliol Dynasty*, 148–54.

26. *RPS*, A1296/2/1; *Chron. Bower*, vi, 45–51; *CDS*, ii, nos 719–20; A. Stevenson, 'The Flemish Dimension of the Auld Alliance', in G. G. Simpson, ed., *Scotland and the Low Countries, 1124–1994* (East Linton, 1996), 28–42.

27. J. Watts, *The Making of Polities: Europe, 1300–1500* (Cambridge, 2009), 56–7; P. Herde, 'From Adolf of Nassau to Lewis of Bavaria, 1292–1347', in Jones, ed., *NCMH*, vi, 515–50, 518–19.

28. *Chron. Rishanger*, 371; Beam, *Balliol Dynasty*, 148–9.

29. *Chron. Fordun*, i, 327–8, ii, 321; *Chron. Bower*, vi, 81.

30. It might also have been expected that an odd number of councillors would have been appointed, to prevent split decisions, as with the fifteen (1258) or nine (1264) elected to oversee the English council (S. Ambler, 'Simon de Montfort and King Henry III: The First Revolution in English History, 1258–65', *History Compass*, 11/12 (2013), 1076–87).

31. R. Nicholson, 'The Franco-Scottish and Franco-Norwegian Treaties of 1295', *SHR*, xxxviii (1959), 114–32.

32. *Chron. Guisborough*, 259; *Chron. Lanercost*, 111–12; *CDS*, ii, nos 711–12.

33. *CPR, Edward I, 1292–1301*, 147; *CDS*, ii, nos 236–7, 716.

34. *CDS*, ii, nos 718, 736 (pp. 171–5, list per English county of Scots arrested/lands seized by April 1296).

35. *Anglo-Scottish Relations*, no. 22; *Chron. Guisborough*, 283–4; 'Voyage of Kynge Edwarde', in P. Hume Brown, ed., *Early Travellers in Scotland* (Edinburgh, 1891), 1–6, at 2.

36. Barrow, *Robert Bruce*, 90–2; *Chron. Guisborough*, 270–1; *Chron. Lanercost*, 115.

37. *Chron. Fordun*, i, 325, ii, 318; *Chron. Wyntoun*, v, 286; *Chron. Bower*, vi, 61; G. W. S. Barrow, 'The Scottish Clergy in the War of Independence', *SHR*, xli (1962), 1–22, at 5, 6 n2.

38. *CDS*, ii, no. 732; *Chron. Guisborough*, 272–4; *Chron. Lanercost*, 135–7; *Chron. Scalacronica*, 37.

39. 'Voyage of Kynge Edwarde', 3; *Chron. Fordun*, i, 323–5, ii, 317–19.

40. *Chron. Bower*, ix, 79–81 (*Liber Extravagans*).

41. *CPR, Edward I, 1292–1301*, 204; D. S. Bachrach, 'The *Ecclesia Anglicana* Goes to War: Prayers, Propaganda and Conquest during the Reign of Edward I of England, 1272–1307', *Albion*, 36, 3 (2004), 393–406; D. Simpkin, *The English Aristocracy at War: From the Welsh Wars of Edward I to the Battle of Bannockburn* (Woodbridge, 2008), 60, 93, 127.

42. *Itinerary of Edward I, part II*, 132 (List and Index Society, London, 1976), ii, 86–94; P. G. B. McNeill and H. L. MacQueen, eds, *Atlas of Scottish History to 1707* (Edinburgh, 1996), 87.

43. *Anglo-Scottish Relations*, no. 23 (presented to Edward at Berwick on 5 April); M. Strickland, 'A Law of Arms or a Law of Treason? Conduct in War in Edward I's Campaigns in Scotland, 1296–1307', in R. W. Kaeuper, ed., *Violence in Medieval Society* (Woodbridge, 2000), 39–77, at 41–4, 48–9, 61–3.

44. *Chron. Lanercost*, 129–30, 136–8, 168; *Chron. Guisborough*, 274–5; *Chron. Scalacronica*, 37; *Chron. Fordun*, i, 324, ii, 318; *Chron. Bower*, vi, 57–9.

45. *CDS*, ii, no. 742.

46. Ibid., no. 736.

47. *Chron. Fordun*, i, 326, ii, 319; *Chron. Bower*, vi, 75.

48. *Chron. Scalacronica*, 39, 218 n16. Sir Thomas Gray's father entered Surrey's service in Scotland in June 1297.

49. *Chron. Langtoft*, ii, 234–64, including nine anti-Scottish poems c.1296–c.1306; T. Wright, ed., *Political Songs of the English Nation* (Camden Society, 1839), 305–7; A. King, 'Englishmen, Scots and Marchers: National and Local Identities in Thomas Gray's *Scalacronica*', *NH*, xxxvi (2000), 217–31; M. Brown, 'War, Allegiance and Community in the Anglo-Scottish Marches: Teviotdale in the Fourteenth Century', *NH*, xli (2004), 219–38; D. Matthews, *Writing to the King: Nation, Kingship and Literature in England, 1250–1350* (Cambridge, 2009), ch. 2.

50. D. B. Tyson, 'A Royal Itinerary: Edward I's Journey to Scotland in 1296', *Nottingham Medieval Studies*, xlv (2001), 127–44.

51. *Chron. Scalacronica*, 39; *CDS*, ii, no. 823, pp. 193–215; *RPS*, A1296/8/1; B. A. McAndrew, 'The Sigillography of the Ragman Roll', *PSAS*, 129 (1999), 663–752.

52. 'Voyage of Kynge Edwarde', 4–6. *Chron. Lanercost*, 145, notes 8 July 1296 as the anniversary of the death of Alexander II of Scotland.

53. *Chron. Wyntoun*, v, 292–5; *Chron. Bower*, v, 385. Arbroath petitioned Edward's parliament of Lent 1305 regarding damages done by Balliol on abbey lands in 1296 (*PROME*, Lent 1305, Roll 12, nos 379–83).

54. T. Walsingham, *Historia Anglicana*, ed. T. H. Riley (Rolls Series, London, 1863), i, 78; *Chron. Rishanger*, 191.

55. *Chron. Lanercost*, 145, 179. King John knew the value of Becket in defying England: he sent Henry, abbot of Arbroath, to deliver his withdrawal of homage to Edward I (*Chron. Fordun*, i, 322, ii, 315–16). The contemporary 'Voyage of Kynge Edwarde', 5, added that when the king stopped at Arbroath, 'it was said that the abbot of that place made the people [of Scotland] believe that there was but women and no men in Englande'; Henry was removed from office in 1296.

56. *CDS*, ii, nos 835, 840, 1027; *Regesta Regum Scottorum*, iv, pt i: *The Acts of Alexander III, 1249–86*, eds, C. J. Neville and G. G. Simpson (Edinburgh, 2012), 37–9 ('The Inventory of 29 September 1282'); TNA E101/370/3; DCM MS B.II.35, 'An Inventory of Relics', 1383 (ff. 192r–198v, at f. 1r–v). A number of Scottish prelates venerated Margaret's rood at Durham after 1296, including the bishops of St Andrews, Argyll and Ross (DCM Miscellaneous Charters, nos 809–13, 825, 830).

57. *CDS*, v, no. 494; Stevenson, *Documents*, ii, 142–6; Duncan, *Kingship*, 137–8; R. Welander, D. J. Breeze and T. O. Clancy, eds, *The Stone of Destiny: Artefact and Icon* (Edinburgh, 2003), chs 4.1, 4.2 and 4.3.

58. *CDS*, ii, no. 823; A. Grant, 'Thanes and Thanages, from the Eleventh to the Fourteenth Centuries', in Grant and Stringer, eds, *Medieval Scotland*, 39–81, at 65.

59. *Registrum Johannis de Halton*, i, 73–5, including £1,305 from St Andrews, £2,200 from Glasgow (in arrears), £798 from Aberdeen, £750 from Moray/Ross/Caithness, £250 from the Isles and £264 from Argyll. Halton used Scottish abbots as collectors, e.g. of Holyrood, Newbattle, Dunfermline and Coupar-Angus in St Andrews' diocese.

60. *RPS*, A1296/8/1; H. G. Richardson and G. O. Sayles, 'The Scottish Parliaments of Edward I', *SHR*, xxv (1928), 300–17, at 307–8.

61. *Rot. Scot.*, i, 27–9; Watson, *Under the Hammer*, 30–4.

62. *Rot. Scot.*, i, 34; *CDS*, ii, no. 853, with Percy given control of Wigtown, Cruggleton and Buittle castles while James Steward was to hold Dumbarton.

63. *CDS*, ii, no. 852.

64. Ibid., no. 823, with the Bruces, March and Angus at p. 197.

65. *Chron. Lanercost*, 259–61; *Chron. Scalacronica*, 101; *Anglo-Scottish Relations*, no. 38.

66. *CDS*, ii, nos 884–98.

67. *Chron. Guisborough*, 295

68. Watt, *Scottish Graduates*, 203–6; *CDS*, ii, 264; *Chron. Fordun*, i, 329, ii, 322–3.

69. *Registrum Episcopatus Glasguensis* (2 vols, Bannatyne Club, Edinburgh, 1843), i, no. 72; Blakely, *Brus Family*, 175, 220.

70. Watt, *Scottish Graduates*, 585–90; M. Ash, 'The Administration of the Diocese of St Andrews, 1202–1328', unpublished PhD, University of Newcastle-upon-Tyne (1972), chs 5–6; Barrow, *Robert Bruce*, 124–5.

71. Watt, *Scottish Graduates*, 66–7; *Fasti*, 198; Barrow, *Robert Bruce*, 186, 218–19.

72. A. H. Dunbar, *Scottish Kings: A Revised Chronology of Scottish History, 1005–1625* (Edinburgh, 1899), 141. St Kentigern's *Vita* surely resonated with Robert: for example, Kentigern's

resistance of Anglian kings and his blessing of the barren queen of 'King Redered', which helped conceive a son and heir, namely (St) Constantine I, see *Lives of S Ninian and S Kentigern*, ed. A. P. Forbes (Edinburgh, 1874), xciii, 95; H. Birkett, *The Saints' Lives of Jocelin of Furness: Hagiography, Patronage and Ecclesiastical Politics* (York, 2010), 184–90; A. A. M. Duncan, 'St Kentigern at Glasgow Cathedral in the Twelfth Century', in R. Fawcett, ed., *Medieval Art and Architecture in the Diocese of Glasgow* (London, 1998), 9–24.

73. E.g. *Registrum Episcopatus Glasguensis*, ii, no. 548; *RRS*, v, nos 50, 52–3, 203, 209.

74. *Chron. Bower*, vi, 29.

75. D. Broun, 'The Church and the Origins of Scottish Independence in the Twelfth Century', *Records of the Scottish Church History Society*, xxxi (2002), 1–35; D. E. R. Watt, *Medieval Church Councils in Scotland* (Edinburgh, 2000), chs 3–4; Duncan, *Kingship*, ch. 6; D. Broun, *Scottish Independence and the Idea of Britain: From the Picts to Alexander III* (Edinburgh, 2007), ch. 5.

76. D. Broun, 'Contemporary Perspectives on Alexander II's Succession: The Evidence of King-Lists', in R. D Oram, ed., *The Reign of Alexander II, 1214–49* (Leiden, 2005), 79–98; D. Broun, *Scottish Independence and the Idea of Britain*, ch. 9; *The Chronicle of Melrose: A Stratigraphic Edition*, ed. D. Broun and J. Harrison (Scottish History Society, Woodbridge, 2007), 4.

77. *Chron. Fordun*, i, 15, ii, 14; *Chron. Bower*, i, 43; K. J. Stringer, 'Kingship, Conflict and State-Making in the Reign of Alexander II: The War of 1215–17 and its Context', in Oram, ed., *The Reign of Alexander II*, 99–156.

78. *Chron. Bower*, ix, 13.

79. *CDS*, ii, no. 1017 (1306, William Comyn, provost of St Mary's of the Rock, St Andrews, claims he was elected Fraser's successor, but he was superseded by Lamberton); M. Ash, 'William Lamberton, Bishop of St Andrews, 1297–1328', in G. W. S. Barrow, ed., *The Scottish Tradition: Essays in Honour of Ronald Gordon Cant* (Edinburgh, 1974), 44–55, at 45; Watt, *Scottish Graduates*, 318–25.

80. *Anglo-Scottish Relations*, no. 2.

81. G. W. S. Barrow and A. Royan, 'James Fifth Stewart of Scotland, 1260(?)–1309', in K. J. Stringer, ed., *Essays on the Nobility of Medieval Scotland* (Edinburgh, 1985), 166–94.

82. *CDS*, ii, nos 737, 740, 847, 853.

83. *Scottish Formularies*, no. E113; Watson, *Under the Hammer*, 34–5. Alexander's brother was Sir John Menteith of Arran and Knapdale.

84. E. M. Barron, *The Scottish War of Independence: A Critical Study* (2nd edn, Inverness, 1934), chs 3–6; Barrow, *Robert Bruce*, 103–9; Watson, *Under the Hammer*, 30–47.

85. *Chron. Guisborough*, 294, 297.

86. TNA E405/1/11; Watson, *Under the Hammer*, 37–8.

87. *Rot. Scot.*, i, 40; *CDS*, ii, nos 733, 930, 961; *Chron. Scalacronica*, 39.

88. G. W. S. Barrow, 'The Highlands in the Lifetime of Robert the Bruce', in *idem, The Kingdom of the Scots* (2nd edn, Edinburgh, 2003), 332–49; R. A. MacDonald, *The Kingdom of the Isles: Scotland's Western Seaboard, c.1100–c.1336* (East Linton, 1997), 153–65; W. D. H. Sellar, 'Hebridean Sea Kings: The Successors of Somerled, 1164–1316', in E. J. Cowan and R. A. MacDonald, eds, *Alba: Celtic Scotland in the Medieval Era* (East Linton, 2000), 212–13.

89. Barron, *Scottish War of Independence*, chs 4–5. Hence *Chron. Lanercost*, 195: '. . . but all those who were with the English were merely feigning, either because it was the stronger party, or in order to save the lands they possessed in England; for their hearts were always with their own people, although their persons might not be so.'

90. *Chron. Lanercost*, 163–4.

91. Barrow, *Robert Bruce*, 102–10; A. Fisher, *William Wallace* (Edinburgh, 1986), ch. 3.

92. *Chron. Guisborough*, 295; J. R. Davies, 'New Light on William Wallace's Position as National Leader in 1297', http://www.breakingofbritain.ac.uk/blogs/feature-of-the-month/september 2011 the guardians in 1286 and wallaces uprising in 1297, accessed on 12/6/13.

93. *Chron. Guisborough*, 295–7.

94. A. A. M. Duncan, 'The Community of the Realm of Scotland and Robert Bruce', *SHR*, xlv (1966), 184–201.

95. A. Grant, 'The Death of John Comyn: What Was Going On?', *SHR*, lxxxvi (2007), 213–24.

96. Stevenson, *Documents*, ii, 206–9; *CDS*, ii, no. 917.

97. *Chron. Guisborough*, 296.

98. M. Brown, *Disunited Kingdoms: Peoples and Politics in the British Isles, 1280–1460* (Harlow, 2013), 115. Barrow's translation of this chronicle entry (*ex qua procreatus sum*) as 'in which I was born' (which would be *in quibus natus sum*) seems to over-sharpen an ambivalent phrase (*Robert Bruce*, 110).

99. TNA E39/99/13; *CDS*, ii, no. 907; Stevenson, *Documents*, ii, 198–200.

100. M. Prestwich, ed., *Documents Illustrating the Crisis of 1297–98 in England* (Camden Society, 1980), no. 98.

101. *Chron. Guisborough*, 297–8; *Chron. Scalacronica*, 41.

102. TNA C47/22/12/41 and E39/99/13; *CDS*, ii, nos 907–9, 918, 919.

103. *CDS*, ii, nos 933, 961; *CFR, Edward I, 1272–1307*, 392.

104. TNA E39/4/6G; *CDS*, ii, no. 910.

105. *CDS*, ii, nos 957, 960, 1054–5.

106. Ibid., p. 196; D. E. R. Watt and N. F. Shead, eds, *The Heads of Religious Houses in Scotland from the Twelfth to Sixteenth Centuries* (Edinburgh, 2001), 5, 127; *RRS*, v, 198–203. Bernard was also a charter witness for James the Steward in this period (Barrow and Royan, 'James Fifth Stewart of Scotland, 1260(?)–1309', 188–90).

107. Penman, '"Sacred Food for the Soul" in search of the devotions to saints of Robert Bruce, king of Scotland, 1306–29', *Speculum*, 88, 4 (2013), 12–15, 17–18. For example, the king's request about 1312 to Bishop Wishart that he appropriate to Kilwinning Abbey the church of Kilmarnock, dedicated to St Winnin (feast day 21 January), for 'our soul' (*RRS*, v, no. 422).

108. *Chron. Guisborough*, 298–303; *Chron. Lanercost*, 165–6; *Chron. Scalacronica*, 41; Barrow, *Robert Bruce*, 111–16; Prestwich, *Edward I*, 421–7, 477–9.

109. *Chron. Guisborough*, 303–8; *Chron. Bower*, vi, 83–93; J. Stevenson, ed., *Documents Illustrative of Sir William Wallace, his Life and Times* (Maitland Club, Aberdeen, 1841), no. xv; *Anglo-Scottish Relations*, no. 26; C. McNamee, 'William Wallace's Invasion of Northern England, 1297', *NH*, xxvi (1990), 40–58.

110. *Chron. Bower*, vi, 87, 238n.

111. TNA E159/70; Stevenson, *Documents*, ii, no. 455.

112. *Chron. Rishanger*, 384; Barrow, *Robert Bruce*, 447 n38.

113. *Chron. Fordun*, i, 328–9, ii, 322–3; Barrow, *Robert Bruce*, 127–8.

114. And in Wallace's efforts to force and train men to muster and fight, e.g. threatening the burgesses of Dundee, Robert would find a model for raising his own force c.1306–9; see R. Nicholson, *Scotland: The Later Middle Ages* (Edinburgh, 1974), 56.

115. Barrow, *Robert Bruce*, ch. 7; R. J. Goldstein, 'The Scottish Mission to Boniface VIII in 1301: A Reconsideration of the Context of the *Instructiones* and *Processus*', *SHR*, lxx (1991), 1–15.

116. D. Caldwell, 'Scottish Spearmen, 1298–1314: An Answer to Cavalry', *War in History*, 19 (2012), 267–89, at 271–6, 283; *Chron. Guisborough*, 323–8; *Chron. Lanercost*, 166–9; *Chron. Scalacronica*, 43; *Chron. Fordun*, i, 329, ii, 323; *Chron. Wyntoun*, v, 312–21; *Chron. Bower*, vi, 93–7.

117. *Chron. Guisborough*, 308–16; Prestwich, *Edward I*, 425–35.

118. *CDS*, ii, nos 995, 1049; B. A. McAndrew, *Scotland's Historic Heraldry* (Woodbridge, 2006), 120; G. J. Brault, *Rolls of Arms of Edward I, 1272–1307* (2 vols, Woodbridge, 2008), ii, 79–80.

119. *Chron. Fordun*, i, 329, ii, 323. Some of Bower's fifteenth-century manuscripts preserved material of c.1304–7, which sought to blacken Bruce's name and support the Balliol–Comyn party (*Chron. Bower*, ix, 67–89; Grant, 'Death of John Comyn', 192–217). Bek's division of over thirty bannerets at Falkirk included the earls of Angus and Dunbar (who had submitted with the Bruces at Berwick in 1296) but not Carrick (*Chron. Scalacronica*, 43, 219 n28).

120. *Chron. Bower*, vi, 95–7 and notes.

121. M. Penman, 'Reputations in Scottish History: King Robert the Bruce (1274–1329)', *Études Écossaises*, 10 (2005), 25–40.

122. *Chron. Guisborough*, 328–9.

123. Barrow, *Robert Bruce*, 136–8; Prestwich, *Edward I*, 481–4; Watson, *Under the Hammer*, 65–78.

124. *CCR, Edward I, 1296–1302*, 460 (Edward Balliol in Wallingford castle, 2 August 1301).

125. A. A. B. McQueen, 'Parliament, the Guardians and John Balliol, 1284–1296', in K. M. Brown and R. J. Tanner, eds, *Parliament and Politics in Scotland, 1235–1560* (Edinburgh, 2004), 49.

126. As Barrow, *Robert Bruce*, 138, 449n notes, Sir Walter Logan, sheriff of Lanark for the Scots in 1301 would follow Bruce into rebellion in 1306, in *Liber Sancte Marie de Calchou* (2 vols, Bannatyne Club, Edinburgh, 1846), i, no. 193; *CDS*, iv, 387–8.

127. NAS GD137 Scrymgeour of Wedderburn Muniments, Box 40, bundle 1, no. 311; NRS RH1/2/78; *Highland Papers*, ed. J. R. N. MacPhail (Scottish History Society, 4 vols, Edinburgh 1914–34), ii, 129–32, nos iv and v. For further evidence for the two as Guardians see: *Liber S. Thome de Aberbrothoc* (2 vols, Bannatyne Club, Edinburgh, 1848–56), i, no. 231 (Buchan as justiciar North of Forth, Aberdeen, February 1300); *HMC*, 5th Report, Appendix, no. 612; Barrow, *Robert Bruce*, 137–9.

128. *CDS*, ii, 535–6, no. 3.

129. *Chron. Rishanger*, 184.

130. In late 1298, Adam Crokedak, steward of Robert VI's lands in England, undertook an inquest of the Northumbrian abbey of Hexham, 'burned by the Scots', in *CCR, Edward I, 1296–1302*, 466; *Calendar of the Charter Rolls Preserved in the Public Record Office, 1226–1516* (6 vols, London, 1903–27), ii, 474.

131. TNA C47/22/8; *CDS*, ii, no. 1978; Barrow, *Robert Bruce*, 140–2.

132. *CDS*, ii, nos 1072, 1079–80; *Anglo-Scottish Relations*, no. 28; Barrow, *Robert Bruce*, 151–3. About the same time the Pope consecrated a new Scottish bishop, David de Moravia of Moray (Watt, *Scottish Graduates*, 411–13).

133. *Chron. Bower*, vi, 101–9.

134. Ibid., ll. 63–76.

135. Ibid., ll. 76–7.

136. Ibid., vi, 309, ll. 79–85.

137. Prestwich, *Edward I*, 495; Goldstein, 'The Scottish Mission to Boniface VIII in 1301', *SHR*, lxx (1991), 1–13.

138. *Chron. Scalacronica*, 43.

139. AN (Paris) J632/32, cited in Beam, *Balliol Dynasty*, 173–4.

140. *Chron. Walsingham*, i, 78; *Chron. Rishanger*, 191; Beam, *Balliol Dynasty*, 169, 316, no. 76. Edward married Margaret of France on 9 September 1299; their first child, a son, was christened Thomas (*Chron. Lanercost*, 169).

141. *Annales Londoniensis*, in *Chronicles of the Reigns of Edward I and Edward II*, ed. W. Stubbs (3 vols, Rolls Series, London, 1882), i, 105–8; *Chron. Lanercost*, 171; Fisher, *William Wallace*, 96–8.

142. A second brother, John Wallace, would be captured fighting in support of Bruce in 1307 and executed in London (*Chron. Lanercost*, 182). For the Wallace family, see F. Watson, 'Sir William Wallace: What We Do – and Don't – Know', and A. A. M. Duncan, 'William, Son of Alan Wallace: The Documents', in E. J. Cowan, ed., *The Wallace Book* (Edinburgh, 2007), 26–41, 42–63.

143. G. O. Sayles, 'The Guardians of Scotland and a Parliament at Rutherglen in 1300', *SHR*, xxiv (1927), 245–50.

144. Watson, *Under the Hammer*, 85–6.

## Chapter 3 *Dead End*: Vacillation, 1300–6

1. A. Gransden, ed., *The Chronicle of Bury St Edmunds, 1212–1301* (London, 1964), 133.

2. *CDS*, ii, 283–4.

3. *CDS*, ii, nos 1108–9; *Handlist* (Simpson), no. 416.

4. G. O. Sayles, 'The Guardians of Scotland and a Parliament at Rutherglen in 1300', *SHR*, xxiv (1927), 245–50.

5. A. A. M. Duncan, 'The Community of the Realm of Scotland and Robert Bruce', *SHR*, xlv (1966), 195.

6. *Chron. Lanercost*, 177; *CDS*, ii, nos 728–9; Barrow, *Robert Bruce*, 145.

7. G. Dickson, 'The Crowd at the Feet of Pope Boniface VIII: Pilgrimage, Crusade and the First Roman Jubilee (1300)', *JMH*, 25 (1999), 279–307; J. Watt, 'Spiritual and Temporal Powers', in J. H. Burns, ed., *The Cambridge History of Medieval Political Thought, c.350–c.1450* (Cambridge, 1988), 399–410.

8. Stevenson, *Documents*, ii, 12–13; *CDS*, ii, nos 853, 1657.

9. *CDS*, v, no. 243; *Itinerary of Edward I, part II*, 158.

10. D. Simpkin, 'The Galloway Roll (1300): Its Content, Composition and Value to Military History', *HR*, 82 (2008), 1–27. Edward I gave 7s in alms in honour of St Thomas on 12 July, after the castle had fallen (*Liber Quotidianus Contratotulatoris Garderobiae, 1299–1300*, ed. J. Topham et al. [London, 1787], 41).

11. J. A. Claffey, 'Richard de Burgh, Earl of Ulster (c.1260–1326)', unpublished PhD, University College of Galway (1970), 148, 171.

12. *Chron. Guisborough*, 334; *Foedera*, I, iii, 924; *CDS*, ii, nos 1147–8, 1159, 1163–4.

13. *CPL*, i, 590; *Chron. Fordun*, i, 331–2, ii, 324–5; Watt, *Scottish Graduates*, 23–5, 49–51, 176–7, 206–7. Soules would be provided with a new French-made seal for King John by November 1302 (Stevenson, *Documents*, ii, 449).

14. Barrow, *Robert Bruce*, 147–51.

15. Stevenson, *Documents*, ii, 611; *CDS*, ii, no. 1307.

16. *CDS*, nos 1194, 1198; *Anglo-Scottish Relations*, no. 29; Watson, *Under the Hammer*, 114–18.

17. *Chron. Bower*, vi, 133–89 (Bisset's texts); Barrow, *Robert Bruce*, 152–7; R. J. Goldstein, 'The Scottish Mission to Boniface VIII in 1301: A Reconsideration of the Context of the *Instructiones* and *Processus*', *SHR*, lxx (1991), 1–15. Beam, *Balliol Dynasty*, 179–86.

18. E. L. G. Stones, 'The Submission of Robert I to Edward I, c.1301–2', *SHR*, xxxiv (1955), 122–34, at 125n.

19. *Handlist* (Simpson), no. 418; NRS GD137, Box 40, bundle 1, no. 311.

20. *Chron. Bower*, vi, 159, 177.

21. Ibid., 111–33; *Anglo-Scottish Relations*, nos 29–31.

22. J. Watt, 'The Papacy', in Abulafia, ed., *NCMH*, v, 167–71; P. Herde, 'From Adolf of Nassau to Lewis of Bavaria, 1292–1347', in Jones, ed., *NCMH*, vi, 518–24.

23. *Chron. Bower*, vi, 135, 167–9; S. Tebbit, 'Papal Pronouncements on Legitimate Lordship and the Formulation of Nationhood in Early Fourteenth-Century Scottish writings', *JMH*, 40, 1 (2014), 44–62.

24. *Chron. Bower*, vi, 139–41, 171. Alexander III's support of Henry III against Montfort as an act of goodwill rather than obligation was offered (as in 1299) by Bisset as further proof of Scotland's sovereignty (ibid., 103, 159, 175).

25. D. Broun, 'The Declaration of Arbroath: Pedigree of a Nation', in G. Barrow, ed., *The Declaration of Arbroath: History, Setting, Significance* (Edinburgh, 2003), 1–12. Thus when the Bruce crown's 'Declaration of Arbroath' of 1320 asserted the native rule of '113 Scottish kings', the count perhaps inadvertently included John Balliol.

26. Prestwich, *Edward I*, 496–7.

27. NAS GD439/142.

28. *CDS*, v, pt II, no. 259; *Chron. Lanercost*, 172; Stones, 'The Submission of Robert Bruce', 130.

29. *CDS*, ii, no. 1301, pp. 535–6, no. 3.

30. Ibid., nos 1291, 1301–3.

31. T. Hog, ed., *Nicholai Triveti Annales Sex Regum Angliae* (London, 1845), 397 n7; Barrow, *Robert Bruce*, 454 n87; TNA E101/8/27/37–9, E101/9/1, E101/9/16; *CCR, Edward I, 1296–1302*, 421, 540. John de St John was a witness to Edward's charters at Dunipace on 15 October 1301, Linlithgow on 2 December 1301, Edinburgh on 12 February 1302, and Roxburgh on 16–17 February 1302 (R. Huscroft, *The Royal Charter Witness Lists of Edward I (1272–1307)* [List and Index Society, Vol. 279], 148–50).

32. *CDS*, ii, nos 1121, 1220; Stevenson, *Documents*, ii, 431–3; Watson, *Under the Hammer*, 123–38.

33. *MRH: Scotland*, 69; H. L. MacQueen, 'Girth: Society and the Law of Sanctuary in Scotland', in J. W. Cairns and O. F. Robinson, eds, *Critical Studies in Ancient Law, Comparative Law and Legal History* (London, 2001), 333–52.

34. *ODS*, 254, 259; J. M. Mackinlay, *Ancient Church Dedications in Scotland* (2 vols, Edinburgh, 1914), ii, Non-Scriptural Dedications, 203–8.

35. TNA E101/361/21, reproduced in M. Vale, *The Princely Court: Medieval Courts and Culture in North-West Europe, 1270–1380* (Oxford, 2001); *Itinerary of Edward I, part II*, 177–8, 318 (Table 14); *Itinerary of Edward I, part II*, 177–8.

36. *RRS*, v, nos 85, 401; *RMS*, i, App. ii, no. 189; A. P. Forbes, ed., *Kalendars of Scottish Saints* (Edinburgh, 1872), 382. The (English) Translation feast of Machutus was 11 July, Bruce's birthday.

37. *CDS*, ii, no. 1282; Barrow, *Robert Bruce*, 159–62.

38. Stones, 'Submission of Robert Bruce', 132–4; *Anglo-Scottish Relations*, no. 32. It is likely that (as in 1296) following Bruce's defection a parliament under the Guardians held at Scone in February 1302 forfeited Carrick, Annandale and his other lands (*APS*, i, 454).

39. *CDS*, ii, nos 1108, 1125, 1286, 1299, 1771; W. Fraser, ed., *The Red Book of Menteith* (2 vols, Edinburgh, 1880), i, 52–8. By 1302 John Hastings held Berwick (and Edmund held Inchmahome in Menteith); in 1306 John would be granted the earldom of Menteith following Bruce's rebellion.

40. A petition from Robert VI to Edward I for recovery of Annandale 'as he had been held out of them for four years' may date to 1302 (TNA SC8/313/E82).

41. Watson, *Under the Hammer*, 129–34, 147–52.

42. *CDS*, ii, nos 1257, 1260, 1264, 1277; TNA E101/9/part 24 m. 3; TNA E101/10/18/part 2 m. 170; TNA E101/353/10 m. 9v.

43. Along with his whereabouts in 1298, Bruce's defection by 1302 proved controversial with eighteenth-, nineteenth- and early twentieth-century historians assessing his 'patriotism'. See H. Maxwell, *Robert the Bruce and the Struggle for Independence* (Glasgow, 1899); A. McMillan, *Mainly About Robert Bruce: In Vindication of Scotland's Hero King* (London, 1901); A. M. Mackenzie, *Robert Bruce, King of Scots* (London, 1935), and her novel *Apprentice Majesty* (London, 1944); M. Penman, 'Reputations in Scottish History: King Robert the Bruce (1274–1329)', *Études Écossaises*, 10 (2005), 31–3.

44. *Anglo-Scottish Relations*, no. 29, p. 90 (Canterbury legal advice regarding Edward's *Scimus Fili* reply). For past papal 'depositions' (the Holy Roman Empire 1245/1301, Castile 1245, Nassau 1298) and 'awards' of royal or ducal titles (Hungary 1290/1301, Flanders 1298), see J. Watts, *The Making of Polities: Europe, 1300–1500* (Cambridge, 2009), 49–59.

45. TNA E101/11/5; *CDS*, ii, nos 903, 1395, 1403, 1462, 1694; R. A. MacDonald, *The Kingdom of the Isles: Scotland's Western Seaboard, c.1100–c.1336* (East Linton, 1997), 163–6.

46. Beam, *Balliol Dynasty*, 348 (Appendix E, Edward Balliol's English Payments).

47. Prestwich, *Edward I*, 494; Watson, *Under the Hammer*, 109–34.

48. Claffey, 'Richard de Burgh, Earl of Ulster', 171–8; J. Lydon, 'Edward I, Ireland and the War in Scotland, 1303–1304', in *idem*, ed., *England and Ireland in the Later Middle Ages: Essays in Honour of Jocelyn Otway-Ruthven* (Dublin, 1981), 43–61.

49. *CDS*, ii, no. 1295.

50. TNA E101/9/16 m2, TNA E101/9/30/16, /10/15 and TNA E101/52/10/18/84–6; *CDS*, ii, no. 1337.

51. Ibid., nos 1246, 1287, 1297.

52. *CCR, Edward I, 1288–96*, 167.

53. James Steward overrode Melrose's exemption in 1286–87 against the then Bruce uprising (*Liber Sancte Marie de Melros* [Bannatyne Club, 2 vols, Edinburgh, 1837], i, nos 351, 396).

54. J. R. Strayer, *The Reign of Philip the Fair* (Princeton, NJ, 1980), 270–2; Watt, 'Spiritual and Temporal Powers', 399–402.

55. Barrow, *Robert Bruce*, 162–5; Beam, *Balliol Dynasty*, 186–7.

56. Watt, 'Spiritual and Temporal Powers', 399–402; W. C. Jordan, *Unceasing Strife, Unending Fear: Jacques de Thérines and the Freedom of the Church in the Age of the Last Capetians* (Princeton, NJ, 2005), 1–17.

57. E. L. G. Stones, 'An Undelivered Letter from Paris to Scotland [1303]?', *EHR*, lxxx (1965), 86–8.

58. *CDS*, ii, no. 1431; TNA SC1/21/166, trans. Barrow, *Robert Bruce*, 155.

59. Palgrave, *Documents*, 333; Barrow, *Robert Bruce*, 165–7, 454n, suggests the Scots took Edinburgh castle in June 1302.

60. M. Haskell, 'Breaking the Stalemate: The Scottish Campaign of Edward I, 1303–4', in M. Prestwich, R. Britnell and R. Frame, eds, *TCE*, vii (Woodbridge, 1999), 223–41; D. S. Bachrach, 'Military Logistics during the Reign of Edward I of England, 1272–1307', *War in History*, 13 (2006), 423–40; S. Rose, 'The Provision of Ships for Edward I's Campaigns in Scotland, 1300–06', in *idem*, ed., *The Naval Miscellany VII* (Aldershot, 2008), 1–56; M. Prestwich, 'Edward I's Armies', *JMH*, 37 (2011), 233–44.

61. *Chron. Fordun*, i, 333, ii, 325–6; A. Grant, 'The Death of John Comyn: What Was Going On?', *SHR*, lxxxvi (2007), 219–20.

62. *CDS*, ii, no. 1334.

63. *Chron. Langtoft*, ii, 336–7; Watt, *Scottish Graduates*, 66.

64. CCA, Register E, fol. 127a, no. 1, fol. 143r and DCc (Prior Henry) Eastry Correspondence, EC III/3.

65. *CDS*, ii, no 1356; Stevenson, *Documents*, ii, no. 438.

66. *CDS*, ii, no. 1516.

67. *Itinerary of Edward I, part II*, 209–17; P. G. B. McNeill and H. L. MacQueen, eds, *Atlas of Scottish History to 1707* (Edinburgh, 1996), 89–90; Watson, *Under the Hammer*, 178–80.

68. Barrow, *Robert Bruce*, 165–6; Watson, *Under the Hammer*, 176–7.

69. *CDS*, ii, no. 1385; Lydon, 'Edward I, Ireland and the War in Scotland, 1303–1304', 44–59; Watson, *Under the Hammer*, 180–1.

70. *CDS*, ii, nos 1420, 1437. A collection of materials c.1292–1344, held by Corpus Christi College, Cambridge, includes a valuation roll of twenty-five Scottish shires, probably compiled for the 1305 Edwardian settlement of Scottish government: this valued the sheriffships of Ayr and Lanark at £291 and £494 respectively; see M. Bateson, ed., 'The Scottish King's Household and Other Fragments', *Scottish History Society Miscellany* (Edinburgh, 1904), ii, 24–5.

71. *CDS*, ii, nos 1658, 1709; J. M. Gilbert, *Hunting and Hunting Reserves in Medieval Scotland* (Edinburgh, 1979), 29–31, 360; *Atlas of Scottish History to 1707*, 221–2.

72. *CDS*, ii, no. 1392–3.

73. *Itinerary of Edward I, part II*, 217–23; Huscroft, *The Royal Charter Witness Lists of Edward I (1272–1307)*, 161–5.

74. TNA SC 8/98/4879.

75. *CDS*, ii, nos 1404–1465 *passim*, includes business with Sir Robert Keith, William, earl of Ross, and his countess, the countess of Lennox, the bishop of Brechin, Patrick, earl of Dunbar, and the abbot of Jedburgh. In addition, see: TNA E39/99/42 (list of attendees at court at Dunfermline, printed as Palgrave, *Documents*, 262); E101/10/20/7 (privy seal letter issued at Dunfermline); E101/364/24 appeals at Dunfermline.

76. BL Add MS 8835, fols 121r, 122v; *CDS*, iv, nos 486–7; TNA E101/370/3, l.2. My thanks to Dr David Simpkin for these jewellery references. Tradition alleges that English troops burned the abbey at this time. This seems an exaggeration, although while resident Edward did order ditches and timber structures built and may have desired these dismantled; in 1304–5 he also granted the abbey a market day and compensated it for roof lead stripped for the siege of Stirling (*CDS*, ii, nos 1408, 1624, 1646, 1653, 1687). However, Geoffrey de York, a Dunfermline monk, appealed to Edward II c.1307 that he had been expelled from his abbey 'by the Scots because he was born in England, and especially because he uncovered certain Scottish plots against the late king', which may date to the 1303–4 residency (TNA SC 8/46/2255). *Flores Historiarum*, ed. H. R. Luard (3 vols, Rolls Series, London, 1890), iii, 311–12, provides a description of the pillaging of the abbey circa 1303–4.

77. *CDS*, ii, nos 1413, 1407; Phillips, *Edward II*, 91–5.

78. Palgrave, *Documents*, 262–6; *CDS*, ii, nos 1445, 1447–9, 1451 (talks with Comyn, facilitated by Richard, earl of Ulster); *Chron. Scalacronica*, 47.

79. *CDS*, ii, no. 1433.

80. Ibid., no. 1465.

81. Ibid., no. 1516, pp. 393–4.

82. Barrow, *Robert Bruce*, 188; A. Young, *Robert the Bruce's Rivals: The Comyns, 1212–1314* (East Linton, 1997), 161–91.

83. *RPS*, 1302/1 (an assembly at Scone, 23 February 1302) and 1302/9/1 (a 'parliament' at Aberdeen c.8 September 1302, reported to Edward I); G. O. Sayles, 'Ancient Correspondence', *SHR*, xxiv (1927), 325–6, at 325. These are the eighth and ninth known assemblies of the Guardianship after 1296.

84. Palgrave, *Documents*, 279–88.

85. *CDS*, ii, nos 1444, 1452, 1574, 1695, 1713 and pp. 424–5; ibid., iv, pp. 482–3; *Foedera*, I, ii, 949; Palgrave, *Documents*, 276, 286–8, 345–9; F. Watson, 'Settling the Stalemate: Edward I's Peace in Scotland, 1303–1305', in M. Prestwich, R. Britnell and R. Frame, eds, *TCE*, vi (Woodbridge, 1997), 127–43.

86. Prestwich, *Edward I*, 535–7; A. Spencer, 'Royal Patronage and the Earls in the Reign of Edward I', *History*, 93 (2008), 20–46, at 35–9; *idem*, 'A Warlike People? Gentry Enthusiasm for Edward I's Scottish Campaigns, 1296–1307', in A. R. Bell et al., eds, *The Soldier Experience in the Fourteenth Century* (Woodbridge, 2011), 95–108.

87. Prestwich, *Edward I*, 500–3; Watson, *Under the Hammer*, 189–92.

88. Barrow, *Robert Bruce*, 186–7.

89. *RPS*, A1304/1; Hog, ed., *Nicholai Triveti Annales Sex Regum Angliae*, 402 n2; H. G. Richardson and G. O. Sayles, 'The Scottish Parliaments of Edward I', *SHR*, xxv (1928), 310–11. Bruce received a further English Wardrobe imprest for £20 on 14 March and another for £10 on 14 June (TNA E101/353/10 m. 11v and m.13r).

90. Stevenson, *Documents*, ii, 465, 478, 481–3; *CDS*, ii, nos 1433, 1493, 1495, 1510 (which notes that Carrick had kept back the 'rod of the great engine'), 1540, 1546–8, 1588, 1720; *CIM, Edward I, iv* (1913), nos 220, 280; *CFR*, Edward I, 1272–1307, 495.

91. *CDS*, ii, no. 1495.

92. Blakely, *Brus Family*, 115–17; M. Bailey, 'Per impetum maris: Natural Disaster and Economic Decline in Eastern England, 1275–1350', in B. M. S. Campbell, ed., *Before the Black Death: Studies in the 'Crisis' of the Early Fourteenth Century* (Manchester, 1991), 184–208; B. M. S. Campbell and K. Bartley, *England on the Eve of the Black Death: An Atlas of Lay Lordship, Land and Wealth, 1300–49* (Manchester, 2006), *passim*, esp. ch. 18.

93. *CDS*, ii, no. 1548.

94. TNA SC 8/94/4653; *CDS*, ii, no. 1657. At the same time Robert petitioned for his expenses in fortifying Ayr castle (TNA E101/10/20).

95. *CDS*, ii, no. 1588. Further inquests would be overseen in Fife, Lanark, Roxburgh, Peebles, Dumfries and Stirling throughout 1303–4 (Watson, *Under the Hammer*, 200–1). About 20 November 1304, Edward's escheator south of Forth would account for two years' worth of income including receipts from the shires of Lanark (£325), Ayr (£92, with 25 merks from Robert of Carrick for the fermes of Ayr burgh), Dumfries (£16) and Annandale (£194, before Robert's re–entry) (*CDS*, ii, no. 1608, pp. 423–9).

96. Ibid., no. 1604; Watson, *Under the Hammer*, 206–7.

97. *PROME*, Edward I, Roll 12, no. 430.

98. Just as he kept Edward Balliol in his household (TNA E101/367/16 m37 [June 1305]).

99. James Steward, John Soules and Ingram d'Umfraville were similarly charged (Palgrave, *Documents*, 276).

100. TNA E39/4/6A; Palgrave, *Documents*, 323–4; *CDS*, ii, no. 1917.

101. Grant, 'Death of John Comyn', 200–12.

102. Strayer, *Reign of Philip the Fair*, 278–81; Watt, 'The Papacy', 162–3.

103. Grant, 'Death of John Comyn', 203–4; A. Broadie, 'John Duns Scotus and the Idea of Independence', in E. J. Cowan, ed., *The Wallace Book* (Edinburgh, 2007), 80–5; Watt, *Scottish Graduates*, 318–19.

104. Watt, 'Spiritual and Temporal Powers', 397–423; W. J. Courtenay, *Parisian Scholars in the Early Fourteenth Century: A Social Portrait* (Cambridge, 1999), 107; Watts, *Making of Polities*, 49–59.

105. Watson, *Under the Hammer*, 198–9.

106. *Calendar of the Charter Rolls Preserved in the Public Record Office, 1226–1516* (6 vols, London, 1903–27), iii, 67; Watt, *Scottish Graduates*, 66.

107. *CDS*, ii, no. 1606; *Cal. Charter Rolls*, iii, 93, 115.

108. *CDS*, ii, nos 1651, 1652; *PROME*, Edward I, Roll 12, no. 14.

109. Prestwich, *Edward I*, 450, 463, 503, 537; J. R. Maddicott, *The Origins of the English Parliament, 924–1327* (Oxford, 2010), 924–1327, 325–7.

110. P. Binski, *The Painted Chamber at Westminster* (London, 1986), 71–104; *idem, Westminster Abbey and the Plantagenets: Kingship and the Representation of Power 1200–1400* (London, 1995), 98–9, 112–14.

111. *PROME*, Edward I, Introduction, Lent 1305; P. Bradford, 'A Silent Presence: The English King in Parliament in the Fourteenth Century', *HR*, 84 (2011), 189–211, at 191.

112. Prestwich, *Edward I*, 515, 556–7.

113. *PROME*, Edward I, Roll 12, nos 280–475, although much of the 'Scottish' business was brought by English burgesses and officials in occupied Berwick, Roxburgh and elsewhere; G. Dodd, *Justice and Grace: Private Petitioning and the English Parliament in the Late Middle Ages* (Oxford, 2007), 42–54.

114. E.g. *PROME*, Edward I, Roll 12, nos 6, 7, 56, 91, 485; C. Burt, *Edward I and the Governance of England, 1272–1307* (Oxford, 2013), 206–11.

115. *CDS*, ii, nos 1651–2, saw Wishart and Carrick also witness Edward I's grant to Coldingham Priory, 20–24 March 1305.

116. *PROME*, Edward I, Roll 12, nos 289 (Scone), 292–4, 296, 297–9 (Priory of St Andrews), 313, 315–19 (Melrose), 323 (Kelso), 334, 343, 353 (bishop of St Andrews), 364, 373 (Coupar-Angus), 379–83 (Arbroath), 390, 396, 406 (Coldingham), 409, 414, 448 (Jedburgh), 428, 436–7, 442–3 (bishop of Glasgow), 449, 465–6 (bishop of Aberdeen). In October 1305 Carrick would be ordered to release timber from the northern forests in his care to a canon of Moray and the Comyn, earl of Buchan, who was also to receive ten hinds as a gift (*CDS*, ii, no. 1709; *CCR, Edward I, 1302–7*, 297).

117. *PROME*, Edward I, Roll 12, nos 287, 288, 351, 410–12, 430.

118. Ibid., nos 280, 300, 308, 310–11, 321, 329–30, 345, 371, 391, 415–18, 423–4, 427, 440, 450–3, 455, 457, 461, 467, 474, 479.

119. Ibid., no. 14.

120. *RPS*, A1305/1; *Anglo-Scottish Relations*, no. 33; Richardson and Sayles, 'Scottish Parliaments of Edward I', 312. It is not clear whether the English regime also required consent from a simultaneous Scottish Church Council and royal burgh convention, a pattern which Robert I's government would adopt.

121. *APS*, i, 113–17 (a 1291 Edinburgh castle inventory of royal records by English clerks including two rolls of the 'laws and assizes of the kingdom of Scotland'); H. L. MacQueen, 'Canon Law, Custom and Legislation in the Reign of Alexander II', in R. D. Oram, ed., *The Reign of Alexander II, 1214–49* (Leiden, 2005), 221–51; *idem*, 'The Berne Manuscript – Introduction', http://www.stairsociety.org/bernems.htm, accessed on 5/9/13; A. Taylor, '*Leges Scocie* and the Lawcodes of David I, William the Lion and Alexander II', *SHR*, lxxxviii (2009), 207–88.

122. *Anglo-Scottish Relations*, no. 33, p. 123; Watson, *Under the Hammer*, 215–16.

123. *Chron. Lanercost*, 176; Watson, *Under the Hammer*, 211–12. By the fifteenth century, the Scottish political community's expectations of patriotism were such that Bruce could be presented as weeping before the dismembered corpse of Wallace, thus inspired to the cause; see A. McKim, ed., *Blind Harry, The Wallace* (Edinburgh, 2003), 377–87.

124. *CDS*, ii, nos 1255, 1474, 1695, 1719, 1730, 1785; TNA E101/353/10 m. 15r, an imprest for £10 on 22 September 1305 for Menteith.

125. *CDS*, ii, p. 443; *Liber Sancte Marie de Calchou* (2 vols, Bannatyne Club, Edinburgh, 1846), i, no. 193.

126. Young, *Robert the Bruce's Rivals*, 193–5.

127. Palgrave, *Documents*, 293. Also listed were the bishop of Ross and abbots of Melrose, Coupar, Jedburgh and Dunfermline.

128. *PROME*, Edward I, Roll 12, no. 14; *CDS*, ii, no. 1691, p. 459; *Anglo-Scottish Relations*, no. 33, p. 127.

129. *CDS*, ii, nos 1303, 1462, 1472, 1694 (Abernethy); 1592, 1633, 1669 (Atholl); 1564, 1691, 1785 (Bisset); 1691, 1734, 1736 (Cheyne, accused of attacking Troup's lands but also appealing to Edward I for enforcement of his right to timber from Bruce's northern forests in 1304); 1734–5 (Frendraught/Troup); 1691 (Leslie); 910, 1444–5, 1447 (Lindsay). A. Ross, 'The Lords and Lordship of Glencarnie', in S. Boardman and A. Ross, eds, *The Exercise of Power in Medieval Scotland, c.1200–1500* (Edinburgh, 2003) 159–74. Lindsay would come out for Bruce in 1306.

130. *CDS*, ii, no. 1745; M. Morris, *A Great and Terrible King: Edward I and the Forging of Britain* (London, 2008), 352–3.

131. *HMC*, xiv, Appendix, 177; Barrow, *Robert Bruce*, 189, 459 n1.

132. *CPR, Edward I, 1301–07*, 415. Brittany was further delayed until 17 February 1306.

133. *CDS*, ii, nos 950, 1004, 1025–6, 1067, 1088, 1171, 1307, 1356, 1418; Young, *Robert the Bruce's Rivals*, 141, 158, 162, 186, 194. In April 1304 local people of Dumfriesshire complained that the interim sheriff, Sir Matthew Redmayne, extorted 'tallages' and fines for entry to Edward I's peace (*CDS*, ii, no. 1562; Watson, *Under the Hammer*, 210). *Chron. Bower*, vi, 73, recites a tale around events after the battle of Dunbar in April 1296 when Sir Walter Siward, having denounced his brother, Richard, as 'the most perfidious traitor of the kingdom', is stabbed in the back by an English retainer.

134. *Chron. Guisborough*, 366–7.

135. *CDS*, ii, no. 1691. However, an inquest of August 1304 names the justiciars of Lothian (John de Lisle and Scots knight Adam Gordon) to report on Annandale's privileges (ibid., no. 1493).

136. TNA C47/22/8; *CDS*, ii, no. 1978; Barrow, *Robert Bruce*, 140–2.

137. *Flores Historiarum*, iii, 128, 322–3; Grant, 'Death of John Comyn', 183–4.
138. *Chron. Langtoft*, ii, 364–7, 380–1; T. M. Smallwood, 'An Unpublished Early Account of Bruce's Murder of Comyn', *SHR*, liv (1975), 1–10; Grant, 'Death of John Comyn', 184–5.
139. Gray senior would have custody of Robert's sister, Christina Bruce, widow of Christopher Seton, from 1307 (*CDS*, ii, no. 1841, and iii, no. 28; Grant, 'Death of John Comyn', 209).
140. *Chron. Scalacronica*, 51–3.
141. Ibid., xliv–lii, 56–7, in which Gray refers to 'lez croniclis de sez' (Bruce's 'gestis'), which he had read. This may have been a verse chronicle written by Bruce's chancellor, Abbot Bernard of Arbroath, which is frequently cited by Bower; or another Scottish source, used by Barbour but lost by the late fourteenth century (*Chron. Bower*, vi, 361; *Barbour's Bruce*, i, 38–45; *The Bruce*, 14–15).
142. D. Broun, 'A New Look at *Gesta Annalia* Attributed to John of Fordun', in B. E. Crawford, ed., *Church, Chronicle and Learning in Medieval and Early Renaissance Scotland* (Edinburgh, 1999), 14–15, 19; Grant, 'Death of John Comyn', 189–97, 206–7; Penman, *David II*, 56–7.
143. *Chron. Fordun*, i, 337–8, ii, 330–1.
144. Ibid., i, 340. This follows the translation of Skene's volume ii, 333. Grant, 'Death of John Comyn', 196, offers a fresh translation: 'You lie! A lethal wound is inflicted in the church of the friars, and the wounded man is laid behind the altar by the friars.' But this seems to ignore the phrase 'maledicenti' (evil-speaker) of the original, translated as 'slanderer' by the modern editors of *Chron. Bower* (vi, 311).
145. *The Bruce*, 70–5, ll. 507, 512–13, 579–81.
146. Ibid., 79–81, l. 36. For this and the rest of Robert's reign, Prior Andrew de Wyntoun refers his readers to Barbour (*Chron. Wyntoun*, v, 353–73).
147. *Chron. Bower*, vi, 301, ll. 31–2.
148. Ibid., 303–9, l. 30.
149. Ibid., 313–15, ll. 22, 30–1. Bower also worked in a prophecy that fifty years later, the heirs of Sir James Lindsay and Sir Roger Kirkpatrick would fall out and kill each other over their role in the killings (ibid., 311–13); but it was Sir Alexander Lindsay of Barnweill who was likely at Dumfries with Bruce (*CDS*, v, no. 472). Like Fordun's annals, Bower places the betrayal of Wallace *after* Bruce's killing of Comyn (*Chron. Bower*, vi, 313–17).
150. *The Bruce*, 70n.
151. *Liber Sancte Marie de Melros*, ii, no. 349.
152. D. Broun and A. B. Scott, 'Liber Extravagens (Supplementary Book)', in *Chron. Bower*, ix, 54–127, at 79, ll. 259–60.
153. Ibid., 54–63. Part of the annals of William Comyn of St Mary's of the Rock at St Andrews, describing events c.1285 down to the 1320s. Comyn, provost of St Mary's, would run the St Andrews see c.1306–8 for Edward I when Lamberton was gaoled (Watt, *Scottish Graduates*, 109–11). Bower interpolated this poem by inserting lines regarding Bruce taking up the throne in 1306, 'having been discovered to be of the stock of kings . . . [and thus] a warlike heir'.
154. Grant, 'Death of John Comyn', 202–7.
155. *CDS*, ii, nos 1812–18, 1822; Palgrave, *Documents*, 335–6.
156. *Chron. Bower*, vi, 319–21.
157. Marquis of Bute, 'Notice of a Manuscript of the Latter Part of the Fourteenth Century, Entitled *Passio Scotorum Perjuratorum*', *PSAS*, xix (1884–5), 166–92, at 168–70.
158. Grant, 'Death of John Comyn', 223; W. D. H. Sellar, 'Was it Murder? John Comyn of Badenoch and William, Earl of Douglas', in C. J. Kay and M. M. MacKay, eds, *Perspectives on the Older Scottish Tongue: A Celebration of DOST* (Edinburgh, 2005), 132–8, at 132–6.
159. M. A. Penman, ' "Sacred Food for the Soul": In Search of the Devotions to Saints of Robert Bruce, King of Scotland, 1306–1329', *Speculum*, 88, 4 (2013), 12–13, 20–2.
160. Instead, on 31 December 1324, Robert would endorse his sister Christina Bruce's foundation of a chapel dedicated to the Holy Cross in Dumfries in memory of her first husband, Sir Christopher Seton, betrayed to and executed by Edward I in 1306 for his role in Comyn's death (*RRS*, v, no. 262).

Chapter 4 *You Can't Get Away with Murder*: King Robert, 1306–10

1. *Chron. Lanercost*, 176.
2. *Anglo-Scottish Relations*, no. 34.

3.  A Malcolm Macquillan (or le fitz Engleys) had reportedly turned Dunaverty over to Bruce, the same man from whom Edward I had ordered the MacDonalds to seize this castle c.1296–97 (*CDS*, ii, nos 235–6; *CPR, Edward I, 1292–1301*, 52, 200; Barrow, *Robert Bruce*, 191–3).

4.  *The Bruce*, 81–9; *CDS*, ii, nos 1747, 1817–18; *Anglo-Scottish Relations*, no. 35.

5.  Ibid., no. 34, p. 133.

6.  A. A. M. Duncan, 'The War of the Scots, 1306–23', *TRHS*, 6th series, ii (1992),134; A. Grant, 'The Death of John Comyn: What Was Going On?', *SHR*, lxxxvi (2007), 221.

7.  *Anglo-Scottish Relations*, no. 34, p. 131. In theory, absolution for such a crime and excommunication were within the power of a bishop as spiritual superior; see P. D. Clarke, *The Interdict in the Thirteenth Century: A Question of Collective Guilt* (Oxford, 2007), 238.

8.  Duncan, *Kingship*, chs 10–11, esp. pp. 216–18.

9.  *RRS*, v, nos 50, 203; J. Dowden, 'The Inventory of Ornaments, Jewels, Relicks, Vestments, Service Books &c. belonging to the Cathedral Church of Glasgow in 1432 . . .', *PSAS*, 33 (1898–99), 280–329, at 298–9. St Kentigern's *vita* presented him as an ally of St Thomas (H. Birkett, *The Saints' Lives of Jacelin of Furness: Hagiography, Patronage and Ecclesiastical Politics* (York, 2010) , 184–90).

10. *Chron. Bower*, vi, 413; H. Laing, ed., *Descriptive catalogue of impressions from ancient Scottish seals . . . from A.D. 1054 to the commonwealth* (2 vols, Bannatyne Club, Edinburgh, 1850–66), ii, plate vi, no. 2.

11. *CDS*, ii, nos 1786, 1799 (Edward I's claim that Wishart's capture pleased him almost as much as if Carrick himself had been taken), 1817–18, 1827–8.

12. *Anglo-Scottish Relations*, no. 34, pp. 133–4.

13. *CDS*, ii, no. 1828; Palgrave, *Documents*, 348–9.

14. *CDS*, ii, no. 1818, whereby he did Robert 'honour on the day of coronation'.

15. *Chron. Fordun*, i, 340–1, ii, 333–4; *Chron. Bower*, vi, 317. Both these works describe Bruce as being crowned while on the 'royal throne' or 'seat'; thus some substitute for the Stone of Scone was found.

16. *Chron. Guisborough*, 367; *Chron. Scalacronica*, 53, 222n; Barrow, *Robert Bruce*, 196.

17. J. W. M. Bannerman, 'The King's Poet and the Inauguration of Alexander III', *SHR*, lxviii (1989), 120–49; Duncan, *Kingship*, ch. 7; L. Dean, 'Crowns, Processions and Wedding Rings: Continuity and Change in the Representations of Scottish Royal Authority in State Ceremony c.1214–c.1603', unpublished PhD, University of Stirling (2013), ch. 2.

18. Duncan, *Kingship*, 146; D. Broun, *Scottish Independence and the Idea of Britain: From the Picts to Alexander III* (Edinburgh, 2007), ch. 6, esp. 179–83.

19. *Chron. Fordun*, i, 294–5, ii, 289–90; *Chron. Lanercost*, 86; *Flores Historiarum*, ed. H.R. Luard (3 vols, Rolls Series, London, 1890), iii, 85; *CDS*, v, nos 492(xvii); 727; *Edward I and the Throne of Scotland*, ii, 250.

20. H. G. Richardson, 'The Coronation of Edward I', *BIHR* (1937–8), 94–9; P. Binski, *Westminster Abbey and the Plantagenets: Kingship and the Representation of Power 1200–1400* (London, 1995), ch. 4, esp. 122–36; M. Morris, *A Great and Terrible King: Edward I and the Forging of Britain* (London, 2008), 110–15, 128–30.

21. Duncan, *Kingship*, 150–8.

22. A written *ordo* may have been compiled for David II's coronation in 1331, perhaps drawing on earlier materials (*ER*, i, 381; Dean, 'Crowns, Processions and Wedding Rings', 124–6). For emerging evidence of the nature of the Scone Abbey site see http://canmore.rcahms.gov. uk/en/site/28191/details/scone+palace+boot+hill.

23. M. Bloch (trans. J. E. Anderson), *The Royal Touch: Sacred Monarchy and Scrofula in France and England* (London, 1973), 115.

24. S. Bagge, *From Viking Stronghold to Christian Kingdom: State Formation in Norway, c.900–c.1350* (Copenhagen, 2010), 59–60, 89–90, 163, 166–7. Håkon IV's saga records an unnamed Scottish knight at the Norwegian coronation of 1261 in Bergen Cathedral weeping at the site of the full coronation (Broun, *Scottish Independence and the Idea of Britain*, 1).

25. S. Menache, *Clement V* (Cambridge, 1998), 13–22.

26. A. H. Dunbar, *Scottish Kings: A Revised Chronology of Scottish History 1005–1625* (Edinburgh, 1899), 129; *RRS*, v, 127.

27. In 1308 burgesses of Perth complained to Edward II that when he was 'crowned' at Scone, Robert had forced them to hand over £54 of 'king's rents for Whitsunday (22 May 1306) . . . on pain of death' (*CDS*, iii, no. 68).

28. M. Ash, 'The Administration of the Diocese of St Andrews, 1202–1328', unpublished PhD, University of Newcastle-upon-Tyne (1972), 113.

29. David I or Alexanders II/III may have sought to develop Dunfermline as a coronation church; see A. Taylor, 'Historical Writing in Twelfth- and Thirteenth-Century Scotland: The Dunfermline Compilation', *HR*, 83 (2010), 228–52, at 249–50. On 28 June 1309 Wishart re-pledged loyalty to Edward II on a holy cross relic of St Margaret (*CDS*, v, no. 525).

30. M. Strickland, 'Treason, Feud and the Growth of State Violence: Edward I and the "War of the Earl of Carrick", 1306–7', in C. Given-Wilson, A. Kettle and L. Scales, eds, *War, Government and Aristocracy in the British Isles, c.1150–c.1500: Essays in Honour of Michael Prestwich* (Woodbridge, 2009), 84–113. Bruce pretensions to coronation in 1306 may explain why *Flores Historiarum*, iii, 323, would claim that when made king Robert changed his name to David, perhaps associating his title with the biblical King David.

31. TNA SC7/10/32; *CDS*, v, nos 432, 470; P. C. Ferguson, 'Clement V to Scone Abbey: An Unprinted Letter from the Abbey Cartularies', *IR*, 40 (1989), 69–71.

32. Marquis of Bute, 'Notice of a Manuscript of the Latter Part of the Fourteenth Century, Entitled *Passio Scotorum Perjuratorum*', *PSAS*, xix (1884–85), 169.

33. *CDS*, ii, no. 1914, and iii, pp. 396, 415–16. The Durham family of Coigneres/Conyers held lands in Staplegordon, Dumfriesshire (*Regesta Regum Scottorum, ii: The Acts of William I, 1165–1214*, ed. G.W.S. Barrow and W.W. Scott (Edinburgh, 1971), no. 79).

34. Alexander Bruce's office was forfeited and given to Stephen de Segrave, clerk for Edward I; see *CPL*, i, 28. Thus the 1329 bull granting the kings of Scots coronation with unction was perhaps retrospective as were so many other responses to papal supplications (ibid., 291; *Vetera*, 244–5, no. 480, '. . . to be crowned and anointed by the bishop of St Andrews, according to custom, or by the bishop of Glasgow, assisted by a fitting number of bishops').

35. *Anglo-Scottish Relations*, no. 22.

36. Morris, *Great and Terrible King*, 115.

37. *CDS*, ii, no. 1811, 1842; Palgrave, *Documents*, 319; *RRS*, v, no. 1; Barrow, *Robert Bruce*, 195–6, 199–206, 421–6 (Appendix of forfeited Scots, 1306).

38. When captured about 24 July 1306, Randolph was described as recently knighted (*CDS*, ii, no. 1807).

39. *Chron. Scalacronica*, 55; T. Summerfield, 'The Testimony of Writing: Pierre de Langtoft and the Appeals to History, 1291–1306', in R. Purdie and N. Royan, eds, *The Scots and Medieval Arthurian Legend* (Woodbridge, 2005), 25–41, at 39–40.

40. *RRS*, v, 178–86, for discussion of an early (now lost) great seal, a first surviving great seal (c.1313–17) and a second extant great seal, as well as a privy seal known from c.1309.

41. *RMS*, i, App. ii, nos 90, 111–12, 154; *RRS*, v, nos 400, 401, 471, 473. Paisley, the Stewart's Cistercian foundation, was burned c.1307 (*Chron. Bower*, vi, 335).

42. £852 from Coldingham priory, £1,073 from Jedburgh Abbey, £1,123 from Kelso Abbey, £1,305 from St Andrews Cathedral priory, £595 from Coupar-Angus Abbey, £2,076 from Cambuskenneth Abbey, £850 from Kinloss Abbey and £70 from Whithorn Cathedral priory (*Diocesis Karliolensis: Registrum Johannis de Halton* (2 vols, Canterbury and York Society, 1906, ii, 300; my thanks to Alasdair Ross for this reference).

43. Barrow, *Robert Bruce*, 199–206, 421–6; *CDS*, ii, no. 1827.

44. Barrow, *Robert Bruce*, 200–7; E. M. Barron, *The Scottish War of Independence: A Critical Study* (2nd edn, Inverness, 1934), ch. xx.

45. *RMS*, i, App. ii, nos 7, 12, 19, 21, 23, 24, 31, 40, 160–2; *RRS*, v, nos 463, 468, 470, 474.

46. Ibid., nos 2–12, 417–20.

47. Ibid., p. 3; *Flores Historiarum*, iii, 130 (which suggests Robert considered killing Elizabeth but instead exiled her to Ireland); Bute, 'Notice of a Manuscript', 168–9; D. Matthews, *Writing to the King: Nation, Kingship and Literature in England, 1250–1350* (Cambridge, 2009), 85–90.

48. *CDS*, iii, nos 68, 71.

49. Ibid., ii, nos 1782, 1790, 1908.

50. *Anglo-Scottish Relations*, no. 34, although this source also named Simon Fraser and the earl of Atholl as loyal (the latter perhaps in error for [Umfraville] earl of Angus).

51. *CDS*, ii, nos 1826, 1854, 1862; *CIM*, i [1219–1307] (Chancery, 1916), no. 2029; *RRS*, v, nos 1, 417–18; C. J. Neville, 'The Political Allegiance of the Earls of Strathearn during the War of Independence', *SHR*, lxv (1986), 133–53.

52. *CDS*, ii, nos 1780, 1785, 1787, 1790–1, 1803, 1807; J. R. S. Phillips, *Aymer de Valence, Earl of Pembroke, 1307–1324: Baronial Politics in the Reign of Edward II* (Oxford, 1972), 24.

53. *Chron. Scalacronica*, 53–5; *Chron. Bower*, vi, 323, 329; *The Bruce*, 89–105; Barrow, *Robert Bruce*, 199, 461 n51. Oslo Schøyen Collection MS 679 states Fraser was captured c.15 August 1306; see J. R. Davies, 'New Light on William Wallace's Position as National Leader in 1297', part of *The Breaking of Britain: Cross-Border Society and Scottish Independence, 1216–1314* project, http://www.breakingofbritain.ac.uk/blogs/feature-of-the-month/september-2011-the-guardians-in-1286-and-wallaces-uprising-in-1297.

54. R. J. Goldstein, *The Matter of Scotland: Historical Narrative in Medieval Scotland* (Lincoln, NB, 1993), chs 5–7; S. Tolmie, 'Sacrilege, Sacrifice and John Barbour's *Bruce*', *International Review of Scottish Studies*, 32 (2007), 7–32.

55. *Chron. Fordun*, i, 337–43, ii, 330–6.

56. G. Márkus, 'Dewars and Relics in Scotland: Some Clarifications and Questions', *IR*, 60 (2009), 95–114; M. A. Hall, 'Of Holy Men and Heroes: The Cult of Saints in Medieval Perthshire', *IR*, 56 (2005), 61–88.

57. *ODS*, 149; *RMS*, i, App. ii, nos 465, 476–7; D. P. Menzies, ed., *The Red and White Book of Menzies* (Glasgow, 1894), 45–6.

58. S. Taylor, 'The Cult of St Fillan in Scotland', in T. R. Liszka and L. E. M. Walker, eds, *The North Sea World in the Middle Ages: Studies in the Cultural History of North-Western Europe* (Dublin, 2001), 175–210, at 188–90.

59. *RRS*, v, nos 39, 134–5, 138; *ER*, i, 214. Robert granted Inchaffray the church of Killin in Strathfillan. Malise, earl of Strathearn, claimed that Robert and his men attacked his manor at St Fillans in 1306 (*The Bruce*, 89).

60. *Chron. Fordun*, i, 342, ii, 334–5; *The Bruce*, 113–27.

61. *Chron. Fordun*, i, 342, ii, 334–5; *The Bruce*, 127. Robert is unlikely to have made it as far north as Aberdeen before the skirmish at Dail Righ, as Barbour asserts (ibid., 107–13).

62. Ibid., 131–5; *RMS*, i, App. ii, nos 194–6.

63. M. Penman, 'The MacDonald Lordship and the Bruce Dynasty, c.1306–c.1371', in R. D. Oram, ed., *The Lordship of the Isles* (Leiden, 2014), 62–87.

64. *RMS*, i, App. ii, nos 56–8, 653.

65. *The Bruce*, 143–7.

66. *The Acts of the Lords of the Isles, 1336–1493*, ed. J. and R. W. Munro (Scottish History Society, Edinburgh, 1986), xxv–xxvi, lxiv–lxv, lxxiv–lxxvi; *CPL*, iii, 381.

67. Barrow, *Robert Bruce*, 231, 408; *The Bruce*, 148; *CDS*, iv, no. 1822; *Acts of the Lords of the Isles*, 282; *RPS*, 1309/1. C. McNamee, *Robert Bruce: Our Most Valiant Prince, King and Lord* (Edinburgh, 2006), 323 n31, and W. D. Lamont, 'Alexander of Islay, Son of Angus Mór', *SHR*, lx (1981), 160–9, at 168–9, dismiss Donald's existence. In contrast, 'The "Continuation" of Nicholas Trevet: A New Source for the Bruce Invasion', ed. S. Duffy, *Proceedings of the Irish Academy*, xci, 12 (Dublin, 1991), 311–12, followed by D. H. Caldwell, *Islay: The Land of the Lordship* (Edinburgh, 2008), 45, argue that 'Donald' was a cousin of brothers Alexander and Angus; R. A. MacDonald, *The Kingdom of the Isles: Scotland's Western Seaboard, c.1100–c.1336* (East Linton, 1997), 187–8, argues that 'Donald' was perhaps a son of Alexander or Angus, who contested the family succession c.1318/1325.

68. *The Bruce*, 145, ll. 670–1. Does the sixteenth-century history of the MacDonalds protest too much? 'He [Angus Og] was always a follower of King Robert Bruce in all his wars.' See *Highland Papers*, ed. J.R.N. MacPhail (4 vols, Scottish History Society, Edinburgh, 1914–34), i, 1–103, at 17. For further discussion of MacDonald genealogy, see Caldwell, *Islay*, 43–5, which suggests Alexander of Islay died not in 1299, but c.1309, relating the tale that Alexander died after Robert I besieged him in Castle Sween in Argyll then gaoled him in Dundonald castle: this might mean that, as per Barbour, it was Alexander of Islay, not his brother Angus Og, who handed over Dunaverty to Robert I in 1306, and thus that lord (with a Macdougall wife) from whom Bruce feared treason. For a case that Alexander was killed in 1299, see W. D. H. Sellar, 'Hebridean Sea Kings: The Successors of Somerled, 1164–1316', in E. J. Cowan and R. A. MacDonald, eds, *Alba: Celtic Scotland in the Medieval Era* (East Linton, 2000), 212–13.

69. *The Bruce*, 147–9.

70. *CDS*, ii, no. 1829, and v, no. 472; *The Bruce*, 155–67.

71. *Chron. Fordun*, i, 342, ii, 335; *The Bruce*, 153.

72. *CDS*, ii, no 1811; *Chron. Scalacronica*, 55; *Chron. Lanercost*, 178–80. Those executed included knights John of Cambo (Fife), John Somerville, Ralph Herries, Alexander Scrymgeour (royal

standard-bearer), Bernard Mowat, Robert Wishart, Cuthbert de Carrick and Walter Logan of Hartside. The Bruce Scots at first thought Christopher Seton, the king's brother-in-law, had been betrayed by Gilbert de Carrick (though in fact it was Dougal Macdowall): Gilbert received a pardon from Robert c.1308–9 (*RRS*, v, no. 384).

73. *CDS*, ii, no 1851; C. J. Neville, 'Widows of War: Edward I and the Women of Scotland during the War of Independence', in S. S. Walker, ed., *Wife and Widow in Medieval England* (London, 1993), 109–39.

74. *Chronicles of the Reigns of Edward I and Edward II*, ed. W. Stubbs (3 vols, Rolls Series, London, 1882), i, 146–7 (*Annales Londoniensis*); J. R. Maddicott, *The Origins of the English Parliament, 924–1327* (Oxford, 2010), 327–8.

75. *CDS*, ii, nos 1837, 1842; Barrow, *Robert Bruce*, 421–6. Robert's lands north of Forth were requested by Sir Alexander Abernethy.

76. *The History of the Houses of Douglas and Angus, Hume, David, of Godscroft* (3 vols, Edinburgh, 1644), i, 77, and ii, 487 n77 ll. 16–26.

77. *The Bruce*, 121, 125, 132–3; J. B. L. Tolhurst, 'Notes on a Printed Monastic Breviary Used at Arbroath Abbey', *IR*, 5 (1954), 108–13.

78. *Chron. Guisborough*, 369–70, reports Bruce with Irish and Scottish support resident in Kintyre, drawing Carrick rents in Martinmas 1306, c.11 November; *The Bruce*, 167–79.

79. W. D. H. Sellar, 'MacDonald and Macruari Pedigrees in MS 1467', *Western Highlands Notes and Queries*, xxviii (1986), 3–15; J. Lydon, 'The Scottish Soldier Abroad: The Bruce Invasion and the Galloglass', in G. G. Simpson, ed., *The Scottish Soldier Abroad, 1247–1967* (Edinburgh, 1992), 1–15; K. Nicholls, 'Scottish Mercenary Kindreds in Ireland, 1250–1600', in S. Duffy, ed., *The World of the Galloglass: Kings, Warlords and Warriors in Ireland and Scotland, 1200–1600* (Dublin, 2007), 86–105, at 86–9.

80. *RRS*, v, no. 564; *Scottish Formularies*, no. E94; S. Duffy, 'The Bruce Brothers and the Irish Sea World, 1306–29', in *idem*, ed., *Robert the Bruce's Irish Wars: The Invasions of Ireland, 1306–29* (Stroud, 2002), 52; Barrow, *Robert Bruce*, 408, ignores Duffy, placing this letter in 1315.

81. A. A. M. Duncan, 'The Scots' Invasion of Ireland, 1315', in R. R. Davies, ed., *The British Isles, 1100–1500: Comparisons, Contrasts and Connections* (Edinburgh, 1988), 110–15.

82. *Chron. Fordun*, i, 343, ii, 335, emphasises the aid of Christina of the Isles, who would grant Uist lands and a chapel of the Holy Trinity to Inchaffray Abbey (*Charters, bulls and other documents relating to the Abbey of Inchaffray*, ed. W. A. Lindsay, et al. (Edinburgh, 1908) 142–3).

83. *CDS*, ii, nos 1888, 1893, 1895, 1896.

84. Ibid., v, no. 492; *Chron. Lanercost*, 179–80; *The Bruce*, 177–201.

85. *Chron. Scalacronica*, 57; *The Bruce*, 283–309; Barrow, *Robert Bruce*, 221–5. And see D. Caldwell, 'Bannockburn: the Road to Victory', in M. Penman, ed., *Bannockburn, 1314–2014: Battle and Legacy* (Donington, 2016), 15–35, at 23–33, on the importance of Loudon Hill as a testing ground for tactics deployed at Bannockburn.

86. TNA C47/22/5/71; *CDS*, ii, no. 1926.

87. *CFR, Edward I, 1272–1307*, 558–9; *Chron. Guisborough*, 379; *Chron. Lanercost*, 182; *Chron. Fordun*, i, 344, ii, 336 (5 April, *sic*); *Chron. Bower*, vi, 331 ('Translation of St Thomas the Martyr'); *The Bruce*, 160–6.

88. M. Penman, 'The Bruce Dynasty, Becket and Scottish Pilgrimage to Canterbury, c.1178–c.1404', *JMH*, 32 (2006), 346–70.

89. *RRS*, v, no. 4 and pp. 198–9.

90. Ibid., 198; D. E. R. Watt and N. F. Shead, eds, *The Heads of Religious Houses in Scotland from the Twelfth to Sixteenth Centuries* (Edinburgh, 2001), 5.

91. Watt, *Scottish Graduates*, 23–5.

92. *Foedera*, I, ii, 987; *Chron. Lanercost*, 180–1; *Chron. Bower*, vi, 319–31, 430–1n; S. Menache, *Clement V* (Cambridge, 1998), 269–74.

93. *Chron. Bower*, vi, 319–21, 430–1. However, *Chron. Lanercost*, 190, relates a fresh sentence of excommunication pronounced against Robert de Brus in the English parliament at Northampton in 1309.

94. *Chron. Bower*, vi, 363–5.

95. Verse preserved in recensions of Abbot Bower's fifteenth-century *Scotichronicon* links Edward I's death on Becket's feast to the evils of his reign (*Chron. Bower*, vi, 331–5).

96. *Chron. Lanercost*, 183–4. Edward II left Scotland on 31 August 1307 and was in France between 23 January and 2 February 1308 to marry Isabella, sister of Philip IV, with Valence and Clifford among the guests; see *The Itinerary of King Edward II and his Household, 1307–27*, ed. E. M. Hallam (List and Index Society, no. 211, London, 1984), 21–7; Phillips, *Edward II*, 130–5.

97. *The Bruce*, 311–17; *Chron. Bower*, vi, 340–1; P. M. Barnes and G. W. S. Barrow, 'The Movements of Robert Bruce between September 1307 and May 1308', *SHR*, xlix (1970), 46–59; Barrow, *Robert Bruce*, 225–33; P. G. B. McNeill and H. L. MacQueen, eds, *Atlas of Scottish History to 1707* (Edinburgh, 1996), 95–6, 166.

98. *CDS*, iii, no. 80; Sellar, 'Hebridean Sea Kings', 213–15.

99. Barnes and Barrow, 'The Movements of Robert Bruce', 57–9; *CDS*, iii, no. 147.

100. *CDS*, iv, no. 14.

101. Balmyle secured a reduction of half of his provision dues 'on account of the notorious desolation of the whole of Scotland' (Barrow, *Robert Bruce*, 468 n45).

102. *Chron. Fordun*, i, 344–5, ii, 336–7; *The Bruce*, 318–20, where Robert fell ill after making a truce with Sir Gilbert of Glencarnie, retiring to Banff.

103. *Chron. Fordun*, i, 344–5, ii, 337; *The Bruce*, 319–35; *CDS*, iv, no. 1837.

104. *Chron. Bower*, vi, 329–31. Robert may have appointed Sir Robert de Keith keeper of the nearby royal forest of Kintore (*RMS*, i, App. ii, no. 46).

105. *Chron. Bower*, vi, 343; *The Bruce*, 333–5, 360n. The purging of Moray is exemplified by such local legends as 'Randolph's Leap' on the river Findhorn, where Comyn supporters leapt the waters in flight from Bruce men.

106. *Chron. Bower*, vi, 343–5, 444–5n; *The Bruce*, 345–55.

107. *Chron. Fordun*, i, 345, ii, 338; *The Bruce*, 361–7; *Scottish Formularies*, no. E46.

108. *RRS*, v, nos 2–4, 388 (a grant to Kinloss Abbey of all fishings on the river Findhorn, witnessed by Malcolm, earl of Lennox, Alexander Menzies, William Wiseman, Walter Normanvill, James Douglas and Alexander Fraser, dated to Aberdeen, 5 March 1309/24 March 1310, but possibly after the fall of Aberdeen in autumn 1308); *RMS*, i, App. ii, nos 31, 32 (to Hay of forfeited Frendraught lands), 146 (to Menzies, of Durisdeer, Dumfriesshire).

109. *RMS*, i, App. ii, nos 62, 649, 683; Barrow, *Robert Bruce*, 225–8.

110. Barrow, *Robert Bruce*, 235; *RRS*, v, no. 247; *RMS*, i, App. i, nos 23, 27, and App. ii, nos 12, 19, 20, 23, 69.

111. *RPS*, 1308/1; W. Fraser, ed., *The Sutherland Book* (3 vols, Edinburgh, 1892), iii, no. 9; Barrow, *Robert Bruce*, 229–30.

112. *CDS*, ii, no. 1494, and iv, no. 14; Fraser, ed., *Sutherland Book*, i, 22–4.

113. *RRS*, v, no. 196; *ER*, i, 26; *CDS*, ii, no. 1631; A. Grant, A., 'Thanes and Thanages, from the Eleventh to the Fourteenth Centuries', in A. Grant and K. J. Stringer, eds, *Medieval Scotland: Crown, Lordship and Community – Essays Presented to G. W. S. Barrow* (Edinburgh, 1993), 65, 72. Glendowachy thanage in Banffshire may also have been granted to Earl William's son, Hugh, at this time (*RMS*, i, App. i, no. 5). Ross had petitioned Edward I for these thanages in March 1305 to cover £1,000 of expenses in conquering the outer Isles for the occupation regime (*PROME*, Edward I, Roll 12, no. 451).

114. *SP*, vii, 236–7.

115. *RRS*, v, no. 2.

116. Ibid., nos 3, 11; *RMS*, i, App. ii. nos 109–110; *Chron. Bower*, vi, 383–5; Watt, *Scottish Graduates*, 496–7; *Charters of the Abbey of Coupar-Angus* (Scottish History Society, 2 vols, Edinburgh, 1947), i, nos lxxxiii, lxxxvi; NRS RH1/6/27.

117. *RRS*, v, no. 4 and pp. 198–9.

118. *RMS*, i, App. i, nos 29, 30, and App. ii, no. 114. Barbour's coverage of the Buchan herschip, the fall of Forfar and then a jump to the siege of Perth in 1313, is adopted by Fordun, Wyntoun and Bower (*The Bruce*, 333–5; *Chron. Bower*, vi, 341–3 and notes).

119. Grant, 'Thanes and Thanages', 60–5, 76–8; *Atlas of Scottish History to 1707*, 161–3, 188, 199; R. D. Oram, *Alexander II, 1214–49: King of Scots* (Edinburgh, 2012), 27, 85, 160.

120. *RRS*, v, 262–7 ('A Model for Chancery?').

121. *Foedera*, II, i, 63; *Vita*, 1–17; Phillips, *Edward II*, 146–62, 167–8. *Chron. Lanercost*, 184, 189, alleged that Gaveston did not like Aymer de Valence and was behind his replacement as Lieutenant in Scotland with John of Brittany (now earl of Richmond).

122. *Vetera*, no. 184; *CPP, Letters*, ii, 1305–42, 33, 96–7; *Fasti*, 100–1, 125; Menache, *Clement V*, chs 3 and 7; Phillips, *Edward II*, 153–4.

123. *RPS*, A1304/1; Barrow, *Robert Bruce*, 237–41.

124. *RPS*, 1309/3; *APS*, i, 289. *The Bruce*, 345–55, nonetheless credits Edward Bruce with a significant victory in the south-west.

125. *RPS*, 1309/1; *RMS*, i, App. ii, no. 564. Yet the celebrated 1309 parliament is not mentioned by Barbour or Scottish chroniclers.

126. *RPS*, 1309/1, 1309/3. The seals extant include in addition those of Donald and Nigel Campbell ('brothers'), Gilbert Hay, Robert and Edward Keith ('brothers'), Hugh Ross, Thomas Randolph, 'Gillespie MacLacuhlan', William de [Vipont?], Alexander Fraser and a Thomas Campbell.

127. *Foedera*, I, ii, 79; *CPR, Edward II, 1307–13*, 107; A. A. M. Duncan, 'The Declarations of the Clergy, 1309–10', in G. Barrow, ed., *The Declaration of Arbroath: History, Setting, Significance* (Edinburgh, 2003), 32–49, at 39.

128. Beam, *Balliol Dynasty*, 188–90.

129. *RPS*, 1309/3; R. Tanner, 'Cowing the Community? Coercion and Fabrication in Robert Bruce's Parliaments, 1309–18', in K. M. Brown and R. J. Tanner, eds, *Parliament and Politics in Scotland, 1235–1560* (Edinburgh, 2004), 59–61.

130. *RPS*, 1309/2. This letter in its 1309 version survives as two seventeenth-century transcripts (BL MS Harl 4694 ff.5r–6rA and ff.35r–36rB); the version revised by the Scottish Church Council at Dundee in 1310 (NRS SP13/4[c]) survives as an original by the same scribe as royal charter *RRS*, v, no. 9, dated 8 August 1309, at Loch Broom.

131. Duncan, 'Declarations of the Clergy', 34. The bishops of St Andrews, Glasgow and Whithorn were summoned to Vienne (which suggests the Scottish guest list had been determined with English advice); the kings of Ireland and Scotland were excluded.

132. *Chron. Bower*, vi, 101–89; *Anglo-Scottish Relations*, no 30. In 1309 Edward II's government drew up letters in the name of England's barons addressed to Avignon objecting to papal abuses in benefice provisions; these were circulated for sealing (Phillips, *Edward II*, 160 n181).

133. *RPS*, 1309/2; Duncan, 'Declarations of the Clergy', 36–7, translation at 44–5.

134. Menache, *Clement V*, 23–34, 191–245, 284–7.

135. S. Reynolds, *Kingdoms and Communities in Western Europe, 900–1300* (Oxford, 1984), chs 2, 7–8; B. Guenée (trans J. Vale), *States and Rulers in Later Medieval Europe* (Oxford, 1985), chs 5–6; K. Pennington, 'Law, Legislative Authority and Theories of Government, 1150–1300', and J. Quillet, 'Community, Counsel and Representation', in J. H. Burns, ed., *The Cambridge History of Medieval Political Thought, c.350–c.1450* (Cambridge, 1988), 424–53 and 520–72; J. Watts, *The Making of Polities: Europe, 1300–1500* (Cambridge, 2009), ch. 2, esp. pp. 49–59; J. Canning, *Ideas of Power in the Late Middle Ages, 1296–1417* (Cambridge, 2011), chs 1–3.

136. Watt, *Scottish Graduates*, 11–12, 117–18, 308–10, 589–90; *Fasti*, 79; *RRS*, v, no 7.

137. *CDS*, iii, nos 29, 58, 61, 94, 141, 188, 194, 223; Duncan, 'Declarations of the Clergy', 40; Tanner, 'Cowing the Community?', 55–9.

138. D. E. R. Watt, *Medieval Church Councils in Scotland* (Edinburgh, 2000), 103–10.

139. This was complicated by further Scots 'annates' owed to the Papacy, a tenth of vacant benefice income to be paid within three years of 1 February 1306, collected by an English official to finance crusade; its low yield would prompt complaint at Vienne in Aquitaine (ibid., 110–11).

140. *RPS*, 1314/1.

141. *Chron. Scalacronica*, 69, reports that knights Walter Bickerton and Alexander Fraser had struggled to take Cupar castle from Sir Thomas Gray senior, in 1308.

142. *RRS*, v, nos 384, 385, 469, 473. According to *Chron. Bower*, vi, 447–7, Sir John submitted after a failed attempt to trap the king in 1308 (a tale not in Barbour's *The Bruce*) and received a 'remission' and grant of Lennox; however, this is surely in error for wardship of Menteith, the earldom of his nephew Alan (d.1309); it was Edward I who granted Lennox to Sir John in summer 1306 (*RRS*, v, no. 419 and pp. 358–9; *CDS*, ii, nos 961–2, 1786 and p. 225).

143. E.g. *RRS*, v, nos 6, 7, 459, 475 (a brieve of perambulation for Dunfermline Abbey holdings, with Robert I visiting Dunfermline on 20 March 1309).

144. Watt, *Medieval Church Councils in Scotland*, 109–10.

145. *RRS*, v, no. 386 and p. 206; *RMS*, i, App. ii. no. 33; Watt, *Scottish Graduates*, 354–5. William was rector of Ayr and the Lindsays had served as chamberlains and justiciars to Alexander II and in the 1250s (*SP*, iii, 1–110).

146. *RRS*, v, nos 5, 60, 476.

147. Ibid., v, no. 6, 475, witnessed by Chancellor Bernard, William, earl of Ross, James Steward, John Menteith, Gilbert Hay, Robert Keith, Robert Boyd and William Wiseman.

148. Ibid., no. 7, via Arbroath (although this may have been Bernard's stop).

149. Ibid., no. 8 and p. 785.
150. *Chron. Bower*, vi, 345; *RRS*, v, no. 473.
151. *RRS*, v, no. 9.
152. Ibid., nos 10, 386; *CDS*, iii, nos 131–2; *The Bruce*, 366.
153. *RRS*, v, no. 11. This assignment may be explained by the *parochia* of sixth-century bishop St Serf which ran from Clackmannanshire into western-central Fife; a chapel at Cardross in the Lennox was also connected to this cult, perhaps through a hereditary family of relic keepers whom the earl used as sheriff-deputies; see J. M. MacKinlay, *Ancient Church Dedications. Vol. II: Non-Scriptural Dedications* (Edinburgh, 1914), ii, 483–90; S. Taylor and G. Márkus, *The Place-Names of Fife: Vol. 1 – West Fife between Leven and Forth* (Donington, 2006), 283–7, 308–11.
154. *RRS*, v, no. 12; *RMS*, i, App. ii, no 105; *Chartulary of Lindores Abbey, 1195–1479* (Scottish History Society, Edinburgh, 1903), nos 10 and 21 and pp. 474–5, Keith recorded as 'justiciar from the Forth to the mountains of Scotland' in judgment c.19 February 1310 over a dispute between Lindores Abbey and Newburgh burgh about five years of fermes withheld by the burgh: the outcome favoured the abbey.
155. *RMS*, i, App. ii, nos 148–9; *SP*, iii, 1–10; Watt, *Scottish Graduates*, 354–5; J. Gledhill, 'Loyalty and Allegiance: English Lothian, 1296–1318', in A. King and D. Simpkin, eds, *England and Scotland at War, c.1296–c.1513* (Leiden, 2012), 158–82, at 173–6.
156. Duncan, 'War of the Scots', 125.

### Chapter 5 *The Harder they Fall*: Victory in Scotland, 1310–14

1. *Chron. Bower*, vi, 321.
2. M. C. Gaposchkin, 'Boniface VIII, Philip the Fair and the Sanctity of Louis IX', *JMH*, 29 (2003), 1–26; Phillips, *Edward II*, 139–44.
3. Phillips, *Edward II*, 144–6.
4. *Foedera*, II, i, 33, 36; Phillips, *Edward II*, 141–3.
5. Phillips, *Edward II*, 146–51; J. A. Claffey, 'Richard de Burgh, Earl of Ulster (c.1260–1326)', unpublished PhD, University College of Galway (1970), 273–4.
6. *CCR, Edward II, 1307–13*, 70; *Foedera*, II, i, 79; Phillips, *Edward II*, 151–60.
7. *CCR, Edward II, 1307–13*, 224–5; Phillips, *Edward II*, 155–60, 169. Ulster had been appointed to discuss 'peace' with Bruce's envoys, Sir John Menteith and Neil Campbell, in August 1309, just as he would again a year later (*CDS*, iii, nos 100–1).
8. Phillips, *Edward II*, 161–7.
9. *Rot. Scot.*, i, 80; *CDS*, iii, no. 186 (truces for Berwick, Roxburgh and Edinburgh shires c.1307–10); *Chron. Guisborough*, 384–5; *Chron. Lanercost*, 188–90.
10. *RPS*, 1309/2; D. E. R. Watt, *Medieval Church Councils in Scotland* (Edinburgh, 2000), 105; Barrow, *Robert Bruce*, 349–50.
11. *Chartulary of Lindores Abbey, 1195–1479* (Scottish History Society, Edinburgh, 1903), nos 10 and 21 and pp. 474–5; *RRS*, v, nos 400, 459.
12. A. A. M. Duncan, 'The Declarations of the Clergy, 1309–10', in G. Barrow, ed., *The Declaration of Arbroath: History, Setting, Significance* (Edinburgh, 2003), 40–5; Watt, *Medieval Church Councils in Scotland*, 105–11; S. Menache, *Clement V* (Cambridge, 1998), 256–74.
13. *RRS*, v, no. 13.
14. *Rot. Scot.*, i, 80, *CDS*, iii, no. 221; McNamee, *Wars of the Bruces*, 46–9.
15. *Rot. Scot.*, i, 86. On 14 January 1311 Edward II banned his Irish subjects from selling 'provisions, horses, armour, or other supplies' to the Scots (*CDS*, iii, no. 190).
16. *Rot. Scot.*, i, 96.
17. BL Cotton Titus A XIX, fo. 87r, transcribed and translated in D. Broun, 'June 2013 – A New Letter of Robert I to Edward II', http://www.breakingofbritain.ac.uk/blogs/feature-of-the-month/june-2013/, accessed on 9/8/13.
18. *The Itinerary of King Edward II and his Household, 1307–27*, ed. E.M. Hallam (List and Index Society, no. 211, London, 1984), 7. Edward would pass on to Renfrew and then head east to Linlithgow. On 6 October Robert was reported 'with his forces . . . on a moor near Stirling' (*CDS*, iii, no. 166).
19. *RRS*, v, no. 14. Bernard was probably already abbot elect by August 1310 (*Liber S. Thome de Aberbrothoc* (2 vols, Bannatyre Club, Edinburgh, 1848–56), i, nos 332–3).

20. Phillips, *Edward II*, 161, 168–70; D. Simpkin, 'The English Army and the Scottish Campaign of 1310–1311', in A. King and M. Penman, eds, *New Perspectives: England and Scotland in the Fourteenth Century* (Woodbridge, 2007), 14–39.

21. *CDS*, iii, no. 95.

22. Ibid., no. 170; McNamee, *Wars of the Bruces*, 48–51; Phillips, *Edward II*, 170–1.

23. *Chron. Lanercost*, 190; *CDS*, iii, nos 168, 176.

24. *Chron. Lanercost*, 191.

25. *Chron. Guisborough*, 386; *CDS*, ii, no. 201; McNamee, *Wars of the Bruces*, 50–1.

26. *CDS*, iii, no. 202.

27. *Chron. Fordun*, i, 345, ii, 338; *Chron. Bower*, vi, 347.

28. *Chron. Lanercost*, 192; A. King, 'Thomas of Lancaster's First Quarrel with Edward II', in W. M. Ormrod, ed., *FCE*, *iii* (Woodbridge, 2004), 31–26; Phillips, *Edward II*, 174–5.

29. *CDS*, iii, no. 197.

30. *Vita*, 22, 23–7; *Chron. Lanercost*, 188.

31. *CDS*, iii, nos 197, 214.

32. Ibid., no. 197.

33. *RRS*, v, no. 15.

34. TNA E101/374/20 m.10 (1,200 merks to John MacDougall for his personal retinue of three knights, thirty men-at-arms, seventy hobelars, forty balisters and eight hundred footmen); *Rot. Scot.*, i, 86; *CDS*, iii, no. 203. John's father, Alexander, had just died (ibid., no. 191).

35. *Chron. Guisborough*, 386; *CDS*, iii, no. 202; Phillips, *Edward II*, 171.

36. Ibid., 171–5.

37. *Chron. Lanercost*, 194–5.

38. Ibid., 192–3; *Liber S. Thome de Aberbrothoc*, i, nos 332–3; McNamee, *Wars of the Bruces*, 53–5.

39. Ibid., 55–66; *Chron. Lanercost*, 195.

40. Ibid., 195; J. Gledhill, 'Loyalty and Allegiance: English Lothian, 1296–1318', in A. King and D. Simpkin, *England and Scotland at War, c.1296–c.1513* (Leiden, 2012), 173–6. The English also supplied strongholds at Haddington, Luffness, Dirleton, Yester, Dunbar, Selkirk and Cavers.

41. *CDS*, iii, no. 245: e.g. Robert Keith, who had been forced to surrender about Christmas 1309, for the barony of Keith (100 merks, now worth £40), or Thomas Hay, submitted Christmas 1309 (£30, now 180s.).

42. *CDS*, iii, no. 279; Phillips, *Edward II*, 176–80.

43. *RRS*, v, no. 16.

44. Ibid., no. 17, witnessed by the bishops of Aberdeen, Moray and Dunblane, William, earl of Ross, Malcolm, earl of Lennox, Gilbert Hay 'Constable' and Robert Keith 'Marischal'.

45. *CDS*, iii, nos 221, 238, 268 and p. 401; *RRS*, vi, nos 18–20.

46. Other witnesses included the bishops of St Andrews, Aberdeen, Dunblane and Brechin, the earls of Ross and Lennox, and Gilbert Hay. An act of c.1313 survives by Randolph as lord of Annandale granting his nephew, William de Moravia, lands in Dumfriesshire, witnessed by Annandale knights William de Carlisle, Roger Kirkpatrick, Wilfred de Bosco and Walter de Corry (*HMC*, v, p. 197).

47. *RRS*, v, no. 20; E. Ewan, *Townlife in Fourteenth-Century Scotland* (Edinburgh, 1990), 148.

48. Barrow, *Robert Bruce*, ch. 11; A. A. M. Duncan, 'The War of the Scots, 1306–23', *TRHS*, 6th series, ii (1992), 140–50; McNamee, *Wars of the Bruces*, chs 2–3; M. Brown, *Bannockburn: The Scottish War and the British Isles, 1307–1323* (Edinburgh, 2008), ch. 4.

49. *Vita*, 33–9; R. M. Haines, *King Edward II: His Life, His Reign and Its Aftermath, 1284–1330* (London, 2003), 76–81; Phillips, *Edward II*, 182–4.

50. *Vita*, 27, 39–41.

51. *CDS*, iii, nos 239, 274, 279; Phillips, *Edward II*, 184.

52. *CDS*, v, no. 554; G. O. Sayles, 'Ancient Correspondence', *SHR*, xxiv (1927), 325; *Vita*, xxiv–xxv.

53. *Chronicles of the Reigns of Edward I and Edward II*, ed. W. Stubbs (3 vols, Rolls Series, London, 1882), i, 203–4 (*Annales Londoniensis*); Phillips, *Edward II*, 185–6.

54. *Vita*, 41. Robert's queen, Elizabeth de Burgh, was moved to Windsor castle about 6 February (*CDS*, iii, no. 239; *CCR, Edward II, 1307–13*, 394).

55. Mary Bruce had been offered in exchange for Walter Comyn of Kilbride in March 1310: in 1312 Mowbray was ordered that 'if he cannot effect this . . . to get what he can for her'. But

in September 1312 Mary was still a prisoner at Newcastle (*CDS*, iii, nos 131, 244, 248, 340). However, on 2 October 1314 Bishop Wishart, Queen Elizabeth, *one* unnamed sister of Robert I, his daughter and Donald, earl of Mar, were all to be exchanged, suggesting that two sisters, probably the younger Maud and Mary, may have been released c.1312–14 (ibid., no. 393).

56. *Vita*, 42–3. Edward sent embassies to Philip and the Papacy in February and May 1312 (Phillips, *Edward II*, 188–9).

57. *Foedera*, II, i, 163; Phillips, *Edward II*, 187 n350. When Gaveston had had a daughter at York on 20 February, the king's company celebrated with minstrels, including a satirical 'King Robert' (ibid., 183).

58. *CDS*, iii, no. 279.

59. *Vita*, 43–53; *Chron. Lanercost*, 196–8; Haines, *King Edward II*, 87–94; Phillips, *Edward II*, 185–93.

60. *CDS*, iii, no. 279.

61. *Chron. Lanercost*, 198.

62. Ibid., 199–200 (asserting £2,000); *Anglo-Scottish Relations*, no. 37; *RRS*, v, no. 21.

63. *RRS*, vi, nos 22, 23, 474; A. Ross, 'Men for All Seasons? The Strathbogie Earls of Atholl and the War of Independence, Part 1 – Earl John (1266x1270–1306) and Earl David III (c.1290–1326)', *Northern Scotland*, 20 (2000), 10–12.

64. *CDS*, iii, nos 108, 193, 283.

65. TNA E101/374/20 m.2; *CDS*, iii, no. 303.

66. *CDS*, nos 3, 200. The real cost was 10,000 merks but with half paid by Edward II.

67. This is indicated by John of Atholl's pledge to Edward I of eight knights and sixteen men-at-arms from Perthshire to serve in Flanders in 1296–7, including Menzies, Inchmartin, Murray, Ramsay, Hay and Barclay men (*CDS*, ii, p. 241).

68. *CDS*, iii, nos 512, 748, 863; CCA, MS Scrapbooks, MS SB/c 145.

69. *RRS*, v, no. 389; *RMS*, i, App. i, no. 31; *Registrum Episcopatus Moraviensis* (2 vols, Bannatyne Club, Edinburgh, 1837), no. 264. See A. Ross, 'The Province of Moray, c.1000–1230', unpublished PhD, University of Aberdeen (2003), 25–37, for discussion of why certain adjacent lordships and davochs/parishes were excluded from the regality by reason of Crown favour to other magnates (e.g. David, bishop of Moray, who controlled Keith) or retention of demesne (e.g. the earl of Fife's Strath'an and Cromdale or the earl of Mar's Abernethy). The original 1312 charter is lost and we are reliant upon an early fifteenth-century transcription that may contain errors (or reflect intervening changes).

70. *RMS*, i, App. i, no. 31 and App. ii, nos 146, 311. Menzies, first a royal charter witness on 5 October 1308, also sealed the Moray grant of 1312 along with the bishops of St Andrews, Aberdeen and Dunkeld, Chancellor Bernard, Malcolm of Lennox, Hay, Keith and Sir Henry Sinclair (*RRS*, v, nos 3, 389).

71. *RMS*, i, App. ii, nos 56–8, 653; *The Acts of the Lords of the Isles, 1336–1493*, ed. J. and R. W. Munro (Scottish History Society, Edinburgh, 1986), xxx–xxxii. By late 1314, when he had defected back to the English, David of Atholl was also heir to the adjacent Comyn lands including Lochaber (Ross, 'Men for All Seasons? Part 1', 14).

72. *RMS*, i, App. i, nos 11, 108, and App. ii, nos 17, 49, 70, 662; A. Grant, 'Thanes and Thanages, from the Eleventh to the Fourteenth Centuries', in A. Grant and K. J. Stringer, eds, *Medieval Scotland: Crown, Lordship and Community: Essays presented to G. W. S. Barrow* (Edinburgh, 1993), 65–6, 72–4.

73. *RRS*, v, no. 26.

74. Ibid., no. 27.

75. Ibid., nos 24–5; *APS*, i, 461–3.

76. B. Crawford, *The Northern Earldoms: Orkney and Caithness from AD 870 to 1470* (Edinburgh, 2013), 314–16. This strengthened relations with Orkney and Caithness through the Sinclairs of Roslin (who would inherit the Orkney title in 1379): Sir Henry Sinclair, another witness to the Moray earldom charter, was baillie of Caithness (*RRS*, v, no 92 and *ad indecim*; *RMS*, i, App. i, no 31, and App. ii, nos 181, 378). Tradition maintains that a Halcro of Orkney served at Bannockburn with three hundred men, celebrated to this day by midsummer bonfires on Orkney and legendary visions of St Magnus as a mounted knight; see R. W. Saint-Clair, *The Saint Clairs of the Isles* (Wellington, 1898), 85–8. Earl Magnus (V) of Orkney and Caithness would also be listed on the 'Declaration of Arbroath' in 1320. Robert I did grant £5 a year from Aberdeen's customs to Orkney's cathedral of St Magnus (*ER*, i, 60, 90, 261).

77. *Chron. Lanercost*, 200–2.

78. *The Bruce*, 339–43; *Chron. Bower*, vi, 347.

79. *CDS*, iii, nos 247, 259, 264 and pp. 425–7. Barbour claims the earl was captured by his own son, Malise VII, who had broken his parole to Edward II: Malise senior died shortly thereafter; see *The Bruce*, 336, 342; *CDS*, iii, no. 208 and pp. lxii–lxiii, and C. J. Neville, 'The Political Allegiance of the Earls of Strathearn during the War of Independence', *SHR*, lxv (1986), 148–51.

80. *Chron. Scalacronica*, 73; *Chron. Lanercost*, 202; *Chron. Bower*, vi, 347–9; Ross, 'Men for All Seasons? Part 1', 16. Gray senior's lord was Sir Henry Beaumont, father-in-law of Earl David's son, David (IV).

81. *Chron. Lanercost*, 202; *Regesta Regum Scottorum, vi: The Acts of David II, 1329–71*, ed. B. Webster (Edinburgh, 1982), no. 481; *CDS*, iii, nos 436–7.

82. *Chron. Bower*, vi, 349; *CDS*, iii, nos 219, 235, 304, 336.

83. *RMS*, i, App. i, nos 12, 35, 38, 154, and App. ii, nos 116, 117, 126, 191, 223–34; M. Brown, *The Black Douglases: War and Lordship in Late Medieval Scotland, 1300–1455* (East Linton, 1998), 23–6.

84. *MRH: Scotland*, 50, 74, 93.

85. J. M. MacKinlay, *Ancient Church Dedications. Vol. II: Non-Scriptural Dedications* (Edinburgh, 1914), ii, 179, 483–90; S. Taylor with G. Márkus, *The Place Names of Fife. Vol. I: West Fife between Leven and Forth* (Donington, 2006), 283–7, 308–11, 346–9, 352–6.

86. *MRH: Scotland*, 50, 74; *Registrum de Dunfermelyn* (Bannatyne Club, Edinburgh, 1842), 7, 43 and ad indecim; *RRS*, iv, pt 1, nos 102–3.

87. *RRS*, v, nos 43–4.

88. *RRS*, i, App. i, no 25; *RRS*, v, nos 313–14.

89. *RRS*, v, nos 28–34, 390; Phillips, *Edward II*, 214–15. *Chron. Lanercost*, 206, would take this criticism further, condemning Edward's neglect of his father's wartime veneration of 'English saints, Thomas of Canterbury, Edmund, Hugh, William, and Cuthbert'. Yet Edward with his queen visited Thomas's shrine at Canterbury at least sixteen times between 1307 and 1323 (Phillips, *Edward II*, 70–1).

90. *CDS*, iii, no. 337; Watt, *Scottish Graduates*, 323; *RRS*, v, nos 28–34, to which the witnesses include the bishops of St Andrews, Aberdeen, Moray and Brechin, the prior of St Andrews, the abbots of Arbroath and Dunfermline, Edward Bruce (lord of Galloway), David, earl of Atholl (constable), the earls of Ross, Moray, and Lennox, and Robert Keith.

91. *Chronica Regum Manniae et Insularum: Chronicle of Man and the Sudreys (1257–1376)*, ed. P. A. Munch (Douglas, 1924), 39; McNamee, *Wars of the Bruces*, 58.

92. *Chartulary of St Mary's Abbey, Dublin*, ed. J. T. Gilbert (3 vols, Rolls Series, London, 1886), ii, 342; S. Duffy, 'The Bruce Brothers and the Irish Sea World, 1306–29', *Cambridge Medieval Celtic Studies*, xxi (1991), 55–86, repr. in S. Duffy, ed., *Robert the Bruce's Irish Wars: The Invasions of Ireland 1306–1329* (Stroud, 2002), 50–2, 62–3, 68–70.

93. Phillips, *Edward II*, 194–6.

94. *Chron. Lanercost*, 203; *Rot. Scot.*, i, 112–13; *CDS*, iii, no. 337, and v, nos 581, 583; McNamee, *Wars of the Bruces*, 55–7.

95. Phillips, *Edward II*, 212–13.

96. Duncan, 'War of the Scots', 149; *The Bruce*, 376–8, notes for ll. 305–830.

97. *RRS*, v, nos 35–7. These acts were witnessed by the bishops of St Andrews, Aberdeen, Moray and Brechin, the prior of St Andrews and abbot of Dunfermline, Edward Bruce, David of Atholl, Randolph of Moray, Malcolm of Lennox, John Menteith, Robert Keith, Gilbert Hay, Henry Sinclair and Alexander Menzies.

98. A. H. Dunbar, *Scottish Kings: A Revised Chronology of Scottish History 1005–1625* (Edinburgh, 1899), 142; Phillips, *Edward II*, 201, 211. Robert's mistresses are variously held to have included Christina MacRuaridh of the Isles and a Christina of Carrick. Edward Bruce's son, Alexander, may have been born c.1312/14; Thomas and John Randolph were surely born c.1310/16, William Douglas c.1312/16 and Robert Stewart in 1316.

99. *CDS*, iii, no. 302.

100. *RRS*, v, no. 72, with notes pp. 355–9; P. G. B. McNeill and R. Nicholson, eds, *An Historical Atlas of Scotland, c.400–1600* (Edinburgh, 1975), 204; Penman, *David II*, 60, 68, 102.

101. *CPR, Letter, i, 1305–42*, 30, with a papal dispensation granted 'as a confirmation of the peace made between the English and the Scots'.

102. A. Ross, 'Men for All Seasons? The Strathbogie Earls of Atholl and the War of Independence, Part 2 – Earl David IV (1307–35)', *Northern Scotland*, 21 (2001), 1–15; Penman, *David II*, 61, 103–4.

103. *RRS*, v, nos 35–7.

104. Phillips, *Edward II*, 202.

105. *The Bruce*, 12, 504–5.

106. *Vetera*, no. 414. William, earl of Ross's son Hugh would marry the Bruce brothers' sister (*SP*, vii, 236–7). *The Bruce*, 504, asserts that Edward Bruce lamented the death of the Scots knight 'Sir Walter Ross' at Bannockburn as he loved his sister 'paramouris/Luffyt, and held all at rebouris [distaste]/His awne wyff dame Ysabel'.

107. Menache, *Clement V*, 267–74. Edward II paid the expenses of Sir Alexander Abernethy, a past Atholl adherent, 'going on the King's affairs to the court of Rome' between 9 August and 29 November 1312 (TNA E101/374/20, m.2; *CDS*, iii, no. 312). William Sinclair's provision to Dunkeld was only secured when in June 1311 the Pope awarded the archbishopric of Dublin to Thomas de Leek, the canon elected to Dunkeld by Edward II, and William (via his brother Sir Henry Sinclair) made peace with the English king (*Foedera*, ii, 155; *CDS*, iii, no. 301): he was consecrated at Vienne on 8 May 1312 (Watt, *Scottish Graduates*, 496). Edward II blocked Robert Wishart's appeals to the Pope and sought Stephen de Segrave's appointment as bishop of Glasgow in 1311–12, with Wishart even taken to Avignon in 1313 for hearings (*CDS*, iii, nos, 194, 207, 342).

108. *RRS*, v, pp. 416–17 and nos 372–3; *RMS*, i, App. ii, nos 319, 320, 441, 460, 622–4.

109. *RPS*, 1314/11/1; Duncan, 'War of the Scots', 149.

110. *The Bruce*, 376, notes ll.305–830, 405–9. Barrow, *Robert Bruce*, 255, still presents this year-long respite as fact.

111. *CDS*, iii, nos 273, 337, 344; *Rot. Scot.*, i, 113–14; BL Cotton Vespasian cxvi, foiv; A. King, 'Bandits, Robbers and *Schavaldours*: War and Disorder in Northumberland in the Reign of Edward II', in M. Prestwich et al., eds, *TCE*, ix (Woodbridge, 2003), 115–29, at 115–16. On 8 November Edward II had thanked a number of Scots for their continued defence of Roxburgh – Adam Gordon, Edward Letham, Robert Colville, John Landale, Alexander Stewart of Bonkle, William Soules and Thomas Somerville.

112. W. S. Reid, 'The Scots and the Staple Ordinance of 1313', *Speculum*, xxxiv (1959), 598–610; Phillips, *Edward II*, 208–19, 223–7.

113. Phillips, *Edward II*, 227 n210, contra Barrow, *Robert Bruce*, 269.

114. D. Cornell, 'A Kingdom Cleared of Castles: The Role of the Castle in the Campaigns of Robert Bruce', *SHR*, lxxxvii (2008), 233–57; *idem*, *Bannockburn: The Triumph of Robert the Bruce* (London, 2009), ch. 8.

115. *The Bruce*, 371–3.

116. Ibid., 377–99; *Chron. Bower*, vi, 349–51; *ER*, i, 239.

117. *Atlas of Scottish History to 1707*, 97, 99. In 1314 Edward II's route via Lauderdale and Soutra ran about 98 modern miles.

118. *CDS*, iii, no. 357.

119. *Chron. Lanercost*, 205–6; *The Bruce*, 400–2; *CDS*, iii, nos 279, 304.

120. *RRS*, v, no. 39; *CDS*, iii, no. 300.

121. *The Bruce*, 402.

122. *Rot. Scot.*, i, 126; Brown, *Bannockburn*, 108–9.

123. *Vita*, 76–7; Phillips, *Edward II*, 68–9, 228; Cornell, *Bannockburn*, 147–8. Nor did Edward II emulate his father's wearing of a piece of the True Cross around his neck in battle: see M. Prestwich, 'The Piety of Edward I', in W. M. Ormrod, ed., *England in the Thirteenth Century* (Grantham, 1985), 114. *Chron. Bower*, vi, 355, recounts a vision on 23 June 1314 at Glastonbury Abbey of two mounted men-at-arms en route to Bannockburn to 'bring revenge for the unjust deaths of Sir Simon de Montfort earl of Leicester and his followers'.

124. TNA SC8/11/512, cited in Phillips, *Edward II*, 68.

125. A. Fenton, ed., *Angels, Nobles and Unicorns: Art and Patronage in Medieval Scotland* (Edinburgh, 1982), 9–11 (A4, the Monymusk reliquary, and A6–7, St Fillan's bell and crozier), 20–1 (B26–7, the Whithorn crozier and reliquary, the latter engraved with the names of Saints Ninian, Andrew and Margaret), 55–8 (D12–13, St Fillan's *Quigrich* crozier and the Guthrie bell shrine); D. H. Caldwell, 'The Monymusk Reliquary: The *Brecchennach* of St. Columba', *PSAS*, 131 (2000), 262–82. A subsequent grant to Dunfermline of mill rights around Bannock, Skeoch and the New Park, disputed by Cambuskenneth Abbey, may relate to the contribution of its relics on 23–24 June (*Registrum de Dunfermelyn*, no. 215).

126. J. R. Maddicott, *Thomas of Lancaster, 1307–1322* (Oxford, 1970), 157–9; J. R. S. Phillips, *Aymer de Valence, Earl of Pembroke, 1307–1324: Baronial Politics in the Reign of Edward II* (Oxford, 1972), 72–4; *idem, Edward II,* 225–8; Cornell, *Bannockburn,* ch. 9.

127. *The Bruce,* 415–23; S. Cameron, 'Keeping the Customer Satisfied: Barbour's *Bruce* and a Phantom Division at Bannockburn', in E. J. Cowan and D. Gifford, eds, *The Polar Twins* (Edinburgh, 1999), 61–74.

128. Barrow, *Robert Bruce,* 273; McNamee, *Wars of the Bruces,* 62–3; Brown, *Bannockburn,* 109; Cornell, *Bannockburn,* 151–3; Phillips, *Edward II,* 226–7, 229.

129. D. Caldwell, 'Scottish Spearmen, 1298–1314: An Answer to Cavalry', *War in History,* 19 (2012), 283.

130. S. Boardman, 'Highland Scots and Anglo-Scottish Warfare, c.1300–1513', in King and Simpkin, eds, *England and Scotland at War,* 231–53, at 239–42.

131. *Vita,* 90–1, asserts that Douglas was in charge of the Scots' front rank on 24 June. Does this perhaps suggest his command of a separate schiltrom within a division?

132. *The Bruce,* 504–6; *Vita,* 892–3; Phillips, *Edward II,* 230.

133. Barrow, *Robert Bruce,* ch. 12, remains the classic starting point for a study of the battle, to be read with A. A. M Duncan's 'Bannockburn Commentary' in his edition of *The Bruce,* 440–7. See also the military, archaelogoical and environmental reinterpretations of the battle in Penman, ed., *Bannockburn 1314–2014.*

134. For a description of the landscape a few miles to the north, around the lands of Cambuskenneth Abbey, see the record of a dispute of 1224 involving Dunfermline Abbey (*Registrum de Dunfermelyn,* no. 216): my thanks to Alasdair Ross for this reference.

135. I visited the battle zone in June 2012 (a wet summer) and June 2013 (a very dry summer) and the contrast was marked with the Bannock burn running very fast in 2012. Barrow's narrative assumes a dry setting ('the dust flew') and there would have been long daylight hours; a contemporary poem quoted by Abbot Bower also stated that 'the dry ground of Stirling sustains the first conflicts' (*Chron. Bower,* vi, 373). The nature of the water courses must have been very different from the post-drainage landscape of today with the ground level now some 20 feet higher in some areas; see T. C. Smout and M. Stewart, *The Forth: An Environmental History* (Edinburgh, 2012), ch. 7. For the battlefield location debate, see F. Watson, *The Battle of Bannockburn: A study for Stirling Council* (Stirling, 2001).

136. *The Bruce,* 423; *CDS,* ii, nos 1108–9.

137. *Vita,* 89–91; *Chron. Lanercost,* 207; *Chron. Scalacronica,* 73–5; *Chron. Fordun,* i, 346–7, ii, 339–40; *The Bruce,* 431–9, 449–57; *Chron. Bower,* vi, 357–65; *Regesta Regum Scottorum ii: The Acts of William I, 1165–1214,* ed. G.W.S. Barrow and W.W. Scott (Edinburgh, 1971), no. 145.

138. *Chron. Scalacronica,* 75; Claffey, 'Richard de Burgh, Earl of Ulster', 317–18. Ulster had been at Newminster on 27 May but certainly made no westward flanking march.

139. *Chron. Scalacronica,* 75.

140. *CDS,* iii, no. 245; G. Mackenzie, *Lives and Characters* (3 vols, Edinburgh, 1708–22), iii, 210–11 (Seton's band in support of Bruce in 1308 with Hay of Borthwick and Campbell of Lochawe); *SP,* viii, 563–70; Barrow, *Robert Bruce,* 195, 291, 370–1. But Seton is not mentioned in *The Bruce* or in later Scottish chronicle narratives of the battle.

141. High tide on 24 June 1314 was reached at 05:36 a.m. and 17:36 p.m.; my thanks to Dr Richard Tipping (University of Stirling) for this point.

142. *Chron. Bower,* vi, 363–5. Barbour has Bruce ask his 'Lords' whether they should stay and fight a second day (*The Bruce,* 457–65). In December 1314, Oxford University's Chancellor delivered a sermon which asserted that punishment for Becket's martyrdom would be visited upon the fourth generation after his death – i.e. through Bannockburn (Phillips, *Edward II,* 278).

143. *Chron. Bower,* vi, 365; *The Bruce,* 425.

144. *Vita,* 91–5; *Chron. Scalacronica,* 75–7; *Chron. Lanercost,* 208. A contemporary Irish annal refers to the battle site as '*Srub Liath*', meaning a grey spout (steep-sided ravine) or promontory; thanks to Alasdair Ross for this reference; *The Annals of Connacht (AD 1224–1554),* ed. A. M. Freeman (Dublin, 1944), 230–2.

145. *Vita,* 91–3; *Chron. Scalacronica,* 75–7; *The Bruce,* 465–99.

146. *Chronicles of the Reigns of Edward I and Edward II,* i, 231 (*Annales Londoniensis*), listing thirty-six knights killed; *Vita,* 93; *Chron. Bower,* vi, 367–75; Cornell, *Bannockburn,* App. ii.

147. *Vita,* 95; *The Bruce,* 499; *CDS,* iii, no. 242 and p. 402; *RRS,* v, no. 428.

148. *RRS,* v, nos 51, 236, 494; *ER,* i, 125; *HMC,* xi, pt vi, nos 2–4; *The Bruce,* 501. About 21 September 1323 Walter would witness a Stewart charter with Robert Bruce of Liddesdale (the king's natural son), Simon Lockhart of Lee and William Lindsay, the Chamberlain, and some of his kin (*RRS,* v, no. 255).

149. *Vita*, 95; *Chron. Scalacronica*, 77; *RRS*, v, nos 408, 444 (royal confirmations of Dunbar charters only). For an alternative view on Dunbar fortunes see A. MacDonald, '"Kings of the Wild Frontier?"' The Earls of Dunbar or March, c.1070–1435', in S. Boardman and A. Ross, eds, *The Exercise of Power in Medieval Scotland, c.1200–1500* (Dublin, 2003), 139–58.

150. *The Bruce*, 503; Barrow, *Robert Bruce*, 299–303; Phillips, *Edward II*, 233–8. Barbour relates that Marmaduke Tweng, surrendering himself to Robert in person, was chivalrously freed with gifts (*The Bruce*, 507–9).

151. *CDS*, iii, no. 697; A. King, ' "According to the Custom Used in French and Scottish Wars": Prisoners and Casualties on the Scottish Marches in the Fourteenth Century', *JMH*, xxviii (2002), 263–90.

## Chapter 6 *The Desperate Hours*: War and Famine, 1314–17

1. *Vita*, 111–13.

2. J. Huizinga, *The Autumn of the Middle Ages*, trans. R. J. Payton and U. Mammitzch (Chicago, IL, 1996), 82–6, 119–20; R. W. Kaeuper, *Chivalry and Violence in Medieval Europe* (Oxford, 1999), chs 3–4.

3. *RMS*, i, App. ii, nos 235–52, a series of minor grants of lands in and around Stirling, may reward local men for their part in the battle or compensate damage caused by the hosts.

4. *Chron. Bower*, vi, 357–75 (poetry); M. A. Penman, ' "Sacred Food for the Soul": In Search of the Devotions to Saints of Robert Bruce, King of Scotland, 1306–1329', *Speculum*, 88, 4 (2013), 27–8 (Table 1).

5. *Chron. Scalacronica*, xlv–xlvii, 57; *The True Chronicles of Jean le Bel, 1290–1360*, trans. N. Bryant (Woodbridge, 2011), 62; *Chron. Bower*, vi, 359–61.

6. McNamee, *Wars of the Bruces*, ch. 3, esp. 73–6.

7. *CDS*, iii, no. 369.

8. *Chron. Lanercost*, 210–11. It must have been about this time that Sir John Soules was restored to his lands of Torthorwald (Annandale) and Kirkandrews (Dumfriesshire) (*RMS*, i, App. ii, nos 142–3): these lands were claimed from Edward II by Soules's English son-in-law, Richard Lovel (*CDS*, iii, no. 530).

9. *CDS*, v, no. 593; McNamee, *Wars of the Bruces*, 77–8. Moray was at Durham on 17 October (to collect 800 merks tribute) and in early February; see J. Raine, ed., *Historia Dunelmensis Scriptores Tres* (Surtees Society 9, London, 1839), App., xciv, cxiii; McNamee, *Wars of the Bruces*, 77, 116 n28.

10. *Chron. Lanercost*, 211.

11. *RRS*, v, no 40 (citing TNA C47/22/18[28]). On 23 August in Nithsdale, Edward Bruce issued letters of credence for the initial embassy of the same clerk (*RRS*, v, no. 570). A. A. M. Duncan disentangles Robert's itinerary in 1314–29 from that of his Chancellor, Abbot Bernard of Arbroath, from where sixty-six extant royal acts were issued, behind Berwick with sixty-eight (from 1318) and ahead of Scone with thirty-nine (*RRS*, v, nos 135–58, 785–6).

12. *Rot. Scot.*, i, 131; Phillips, *Edward II*, 239.

13. *CDS*, iii, nos 371–2 (Christina and others to York, July 1314), 393 (2 October 1314); *Rot. Scot.*, i, 131–4; *CPR, Edward II, 1313–17*, 183.

14. *Rot. Scot.*, i, 133; McNamee, *Wars of the Bruces*, 77.

15. Phillips, *Edward II*, 239–47.

16. *The Bruce*, 506–8; Barrow, *Robert Bruce*, 301–3.

17. *RPS*, 1314/1; *RRS*, v, no. 41.

18. Patrick of Dunbar may have been granted a confirmation of all his lands about this time (*RMS*, i, App. ii, no. 115).

19. *RRS*, v, no. 72; *Registrum de Dunfermelyn* (Bannatyne Club, Edinburgh, 1842), nos 348–9 (Duncan's homage for lands held of the abbey of Dunfermline, 7 January 1316). According to Barbour in 1306 Edward I had gone so far as to offer 'all Fyfe' to whoever 'ta or sla' Bruce (*The Bruce*, 91).

20. *RPS*, 1314/1; *RRS*, v, nos 41–3. At least one forged charter can be identified dated to this assembly (ibid., p. 331).

21. *RRS*, v, no. 58; *RPS*, 1315/1.

22. R. Tanner, 'Cowing the Community? Coercion and Fabrication in Robert Bruce's Parliaments, 1309–18', in K. M. Brown and R. J. Tanner, eds, *Parliament and Politics in Scotland, 1235–1560* (Edinburgh, 2004), 61–4; Barrow, *Robert Bruce*, 342–51.

23. *CDS*, iii, no. 390; Watt, *Scottish Graduates*, 323–4.

24. *RPS*, 1314/1 – 'Gilbert de la Hay, constable of Scotland, [Robert de Keith, Marischal of Scotland], Hugh de Ross, James de Douglas, John Sinclair, Thomas Ross, Alexander de Seton, Walter de Haliburton, David de Balfour, Duncan de Wallace, Thomas de Dischington, Andrew de Murray, Archibald de Beton, Ranulph de Lyle, Malcolm de Balfour, Norman de Lesley, Nigel de Campbell, Mornus de Muschamp, knights, with many other seals of which the majority are in a broken or mutilated condition'. Antiquarian Sir James Balfour (d.c.1658) overlooked the bishops of Dunkeld and Brechin and added two Balfours (Barrow, *Robert Bruce*, 388–9, 488 n108).

25. *RRS*, v, no. 44.

26. Barrow, *Robert Bruce*, 362–5: Skirling (Peeblesshire), Durisdeer, Staplegordon and Westerkirk (all Dumfriesshire) and Cunningham lands.

27. *RRS*, v, no. 42. On 8 October 1314 Edward II granted Atholl new lands in England equivalent to his former Essex possessions; Atholl invoked the Ordinances to reclaim the latter (*CDS*, iii, nos 396, 424–5).

28. *RMS*, i, App. ii, no. 639. This note of Campbell's grant is followed by Hay's of the Constableship (ibid., no. 640).

29. The death of Sir Alexander by c.25 December 1316/10 November 1319 may have seen the wardship of John and the Angus lands revert to the Crown until John came of age. As late as 28 October 1328 John [Stewart] 'lord of Bonkle' would receive a dispensation to marry Margaret Abernethy. But a 1320 dispensation for Patrick, earl of Dunbar, to marry Thomas Randolph's daughter styled him merely as 'Patrick de Dunbar' and Agnes as 'daughter of Ralph', so papal correspondence does not date Angus's transfer (*Vetera*, 212, 241).

30. *RRS*, v, no. 102 (noted as *RMS*, i, App. ii, no. 13). Betoigne was in English pay up to 1320 (TNA E403/188 m.3 and E403/186 m.5).

31. E.g. from Robert I's undated 'lost rolls': *RMS*, i, App. ii, nos 10 (Patrick Ogilvy, barony of Kettins, also within Angus earldom), 12 (Alexander Fraser, barony of Panbride), 16 (William Ramsay, barony of Auchterhouse), 222 (Robert Stewart, the king's grandson, of Kellie barony between Dundee and Arbroath), 441 and 460 (Alexander Bruce, the king's illegitimate nephew, of the barony of Dun west of Brechin), 442 (Gilbert Hay), 432 and 445 (John Menteith, of Aberluthnot barony), 448 (William Oliphant, Auchtertyre and Newtyle baronies), 451 (Donald Campbell, half of Redcastle barony).

32. *RRS*, v, nos 42–3. Further possible grants to Dunfermline confirmed at Cambuskenneth may survive as ibid., nos 406–7.

33. Ibid., no. 557; *Scottish Formularies*, no. E17. As Constables the earls of Buchan held a hostillage in each royal burgh; so Hay's restoration may have been a factor.

34. *RRS*, v, no. 426; *Scottish Formularies*, nos E18, E36–7.

35. Barrow, *Robert Bruce*, 388–9. Consider the undated *RRS*, v, no, 558, a template brieve of protection for any former enemy of the king and his men (*Scottish Formularies*, no. E43).

36. H. L. MacQueen, *Common Law and Feudal Society in Medieval Scotland* (Edinburgh, 1993), 86–9; A. Taylor, '*Leges Scocie* and the Lawcodes of David I, William the Lion and Alexander II', *SHR*, lxxxviii (2009), 243.

37. *Anglo-Scottish Relations*, no. 33, at p 125; A. Taylor, 'The Assizes of David I, King of Scots, 1124–53', *SHR*, xci (2012), 197–238, at 225–35.

38. *RPS*, 1318/1 to 1318/29; *RRS*, v, no. 139.

39. *APS*, i, 315–25 (*Assisa Regis David*, not included in the new *RPS* edition); Lord Cooper, ed., *Regiam Majestatem & Quoniam Attachiamenta* (Stair Society, Edinburgh, 1947); *Scottish Formularies*, 39–112 (Edinburgh University Library MS 207, MS E); H. L. MacQueen, '*Regiam Majestatem*, Scots Law and National Identity', *SHR*, lxxiv (1995), 3–11; Taylor, 'The Assizes of David I, King of Scots, 1124–53', 198–200. The 'Ayr Miscellany', a fragmentary law compilation of c.1318–29 (NRS PA5/2 fos 2r–7r; *Scottish Formularies*, 3–45), shares a number of items with *Regiam Majestatem* and includes the earliest version (out of thirteen known manuscripts) of the *Assisa Regis David*. Dr Taylor is preparing an edition of these treatises: *The Auld Lawes of Scotland: Law and Legal Culture in Medieval Scotland* (Stair Society, forthcoming).

40. *Chron. Lanercost*, 212; TNA E159/102, m.114d.

41. *RRS*, v, no, 424. Robert would similarly grant past enemy Sir Philip Mowbray lands in North Tynedale during a raid in 1317 (ibid., no. 428).

42. *Chron. Lanercost*, 212; K. J. Stringer, 'States, Liberties and Communities in Medieval Britain and Ireland (c.1100–1400)', in M. Prestwich, ed., *Liberties and Identities in the Medieval British Isles* (Woodbridge, 2008), 14–15, 29–31.

43. *CDS*, iii, no. 476, March 1315 regarding Cumberland tenants who had 'joined the Scots'.

44. Ibid., no, 402, 20 November 1314, Thomas Morham and two Lindsay brothers released from the Tower in exchange for Sir John de Segrave.

45. *RRS*, v, no. 45; I. B. Cowan, P. H. R. Mackay and A. Macquarrie, eds, *The Knights of St John of Jerusalem in Scotland* (Scottish History Society, Edinburgh, 1983), xxx–xxxi, xxxiin, 47–8 no. 5.

46. J. Higgitt, '*Imageis Maid with Mennis Hand*': Saints, Images, Belief and Identity in Later Medieval Scotland – The Ninth Whithorn Lecture, 2000* (Whithorn, 2003), n.p. n49.

47. J. R. Maddicott, *Thomas of Lancaster, 1307–1322* (Oxford, 1970), 167–8.

48. Beam, *Balliol Dynasty*, 202–3; S. Layfield, 'The Pope, the Scots, and their "Self-Styled" King: John XXII's Anglo-Scottish Policy, 1316–1334', in A. King and M. Penman, eds, *New Perspectives: England and Scotland in the Fourteenth Century* (Woodbridge, 2007), 157–171, at 157–9.

49. *Foedera*, II, i, 75, 87; *Rot. Scot.*, i, 143; *CDS*, iii, nos 348, 449; *CPR, Edward II, 1313–17*, 281, 338. Robert I's letters of marque (intercepted by the count of Hainault and sent to Edward II), issued to Scottish ships licensed to prey on English/Hainault shipping, may date to this period (*RRS*, v, no. 425). Louis X refused Balliol the right to make proxy homage; in May 1315 the English council approved Balliol's departure from the earl of Norfolk's household and he returned in September.

50. A. Beam, 'Edward Balliol: A Re-evaluation of his Early Career, c.1282–1332', in King and Penman, eds, *New Perspectives*, 73–93, at 80–2.

51. *CDS*, iii, nos 420–1, 481, 521; McNamee, *Wars of the Bruces*, 78.

52. *CDS*, iii, no. 420; *RPS*, 1309/2.

53. TNA E101/376/7, f.18; Phillips, *Edward II*, 285 n33.

54. *CDS*, iii, nos 371–3, 393, 402–3.

55. *RRS*, v, no. 46. Neil's seal would be attached to the April 1315 act of royal succession, but he had perhaps died just before then (S. Boardman, *The Campbells, 1250–1513* (Edinburgh, 2006), 41–2).

56. *RRS*, v, nos 47–9: a grant of Edmund Hastings's forfeited Perthshire/Angus lands to Sir Andrew Gray; confirmation of war-damaged Buchan earl charters to Deer Abbey; and letters permitting Arbroath Abbey to take Kincardineshire lands 'in default of the earls of Buchan'.

57. Ibid., nos 50, 52–4.

58. Ibid., nos 4, 494; *RMS*, i, App. i, no. 82. A grant to Walter Fleming of Angus lands at Kettins may have followed an inquest into Umfraville lands (ibid., no. 56, 20 March). In 1294 Walter Fitz Gilbert had witnessed a grant by James Steward to Paisley Abbey; in c.1314–16 and 1321 he would receive lands in Bute from Walter Steward (*HMC, XI, part vi, Dukes of Hamilton*, 2–12; NRS RH1/2/86 and 93). On 12 July 1320 Walter founded an altar to St Mary with a full set of vestments in Glasgow Cathedral, and paid for masses there and at a nearby chapel to St Thomas; *Registrum Episcopatus Glasguensis* (2 vols, Bannatyne Club, Edinburgh, 1843), i, no. 267.

59. *RRS*, v, no. 55; J. M. MacKinlay, *Ancient Church Dedications. Vol. II: Non-Scriptural Dedications* (Edinburgh, 1914), 136–8; A. Macquarrie, ed., *Legends of Scottish Saints: Readings, Hymns and Prayers for the Commemorations of Scottish Saints in the Aberdeen Breviary* (Dublin, 2012), 76–8.

60. J. M. MacKinlay, *Ancient Church Dedications. Vol. I: Scriptural Dedications* (Edinburgh, 1914), 319.

61. *RRS*, v, nos 136–7; *The Bruce*, 564n.

62. *RRS*, v, no. 57, a grant of Kingscavil and Calder-Clere (Lothians) to Sir James Douglas of Lothian, witnessed by Edward Bruce, Randolph, Walter Steward, Menteith, and James, lord of Douglas and Robert Keith.

63. *RPS*, 1315/1; *RRS*, v, nos 58–67.

64. *Chron. Fordun*, i, 346–7, ii, 339–40; *Chron. Bower*, vi, 375–81; *The Bruce*, 519–21.

65. *RPS*, 1315/1; *RRS*, v, no 58 (Balfour's transcription, BL Harl. MS 4694 fos 28–31). See J. Watts, *The Making of Polities: Europe, 1300–1500* (Cambridge, 2009), 63–4, for 'elective kingship' and acclamation.

66. *RRS*, v, nos 72, 140 and notes pp. 356–60, 415–17. Echoes of effort in 1315 by the Bruces to persuade their subjects to accept inheritance by a brother before a daughter may be reflected in this principle, outlined by Parisian academics (during the Great Cause of 1291–92), and recounted by Prior Wyntoun of Lochleven c.1410–20 (*Chron. Wyntoun*, v, 185–209).

67. Robert and his prelates may have taken a lead from the French *Parlement* which in 1311, anticipating Philip IV's death leaving only a daughter, had expressed a preference for Philip's brother, Louis, to succeed by nearness of male degree. In 1317, however, the French would move to bar female succession altogether: see C. Taylor, 'The Salic Law and the Valois Succession to the French Crown', *French History*, 15, no. 4 (2001), 358–77.

68. *RRS*, v, no, 391, witnessed by the bishops of St Andrews, Dunkeld and Dunblane, Chancellor Bernard, the earls of Dunbar, Moray, Lennox, James lord Douglas, Hay and Keith.

69. *SP*, i, 434–5 and vii, 235–7. R. W. and J. Munro, 'Ross, William Earl of', http://www.oxforddnb.com/view/article/, accessed on 20/6/13, argues that William was born c.1323. Yet Hugh would seal the 1328 peace treaty on Robert I's behalf and die in battle in 1333, at which time his son, William, is held to have been banished to Norway and unable to inherit until 17 May 1336: this would seem odd if he was only then thirteen; it makes more sense if he was born c.1315–16 and thus at least eighteen in 1336. Maud would die by 24 November 1329, with Hugh marrying Margaret, daughter of David Graham of Old Montrose.

70. *RRS*, v, nos 61–6: including lands for Melrose Abbey and confirmation of all the possessions of the Cistercian abbey at Kinloss (Moray).

71. Ibid., nos 59, 67.

72. Ibid., nos 5, 60, 476. As Barrow, *Robert Bruce*, 362, notes, Baddeby was unhappy and appealed in 1323 (*RMS*, i, App. i, no. 96).

73. *RRS*, v, no. 405. Sir Andrew Murray's was one of the seals listed by Balfour on the 1315 succession act (*RPS*, 1315/1).

74. *RRS*, v, nos 57, 68–9. A number of 'lost' acts may also date to this period: e.g. Robert's grant of the baronies of Durisdeer and Enoch (adjacent to Randolph's Morton) to Sir Alexander Menzies, later diverted to the Stewarts (*RMS*, i, App. ii, nos 142–3, 146, 311, 312).

75. S. Duffy, 'The Bruce Invasion of Ireland: A Revised Itinerary and Chronology', in *idem*, ed., *Robert the Bruce's Irish Wars: The Invasions of Ireland 1306–1329* (Stroud, 2002), 9–44, at 10.

76. As they would in 1318, subjects presumably swore an oath on the Gospels and/or relics (*RRS*, v, no. 301, notes pp. 560–1).

77. *RPS*, 1315/1; *RRS*, v, nos 61–6, 401, 567; Tanner, 'Cowing the Community?', 61–4.

78. *RRS*, v, nos 70, 490. Randolph's original grant (c.24 June 1314/May 1315) was witnessed by Douglas, Keith, and Gordon's former associates in English service, Stewart of Bonkle, Edward Letholm, John Landale, Henry Haliburton and Robert Lauder; see W. Angus, ed., 'Miscellaneous Charters, 1315–1401, from Transcriptions in the Collection of the Late Sir William Fraser', *Scottish History Society Miscellany*, v (Edinburgh, 1933), no. 1.

79. *CCR, Edward II, 1313–18*, 218–19; Phillips, *Edward II*, 260 n139.

80. *Vita*, 111. This was an exaggeration as in this period wheat sold for an average of 5s–6s per quarter with a crisis average high of 20s–40s; see I. Kershaw, 'The Great Famine and Agrarian Crisis in England, 1315–22', *Past and Present*, 59 (1973), 3–50, at 6–8.

81. *RRS*, v, no. 65.

82. Ibid., nos 71, 124. See also no. 473, a quittance of dues from Paisley Abbey in the Lennox in return for five chalders of oatmeal per annum for Dumbarton castle.

83. R. Frame, 'The Bruces in Ireland, 1315–18', *Irish Historical Society*, xix (1974), 3–37; A. A. M. Duncan, 'The Scots' Invasion of Ireland, 1315', in R. R. Davies, *The British Isles, 1100–1500: Comparisons, Contrasts and Connections* (Edinburgh, 1988); S. Duffy, 'The Bruce Brothers and the Irish Sea World, 1306–29', in *idem*, ed., *Robert the Bruce's Irish Wars*; J. Lydon, 'The Bruce Invasion of Ireland', in Duffy, ed., *Robert the Bruce's Irish Wars*, 71–106; McNamee, *Wars of the Bruces*, ch. 5, esp. 166–9, 186–90.

84. McNamee, *Wars of the Bruces*, 169–86.

85. *The Bruce*, 521–2, 595–7 ('Edward Bruce and the Irish kings; his failings'); McNamee, *Wars of the Bruces*, 194–9; Penman, *David II*, 23–4, 40–3.

86. J. R. S. Phillips, 'The Irish Remonstrance of 1317: An International Perspective', *Irish Historical Studies*, xxvii (1990), 112–29, at 126 n57 (Ó Néill's charter to the cathedral of Armagh – associated with St Malachy – dated to year one of 'King Edward' Bruce's reign); Phillips, *Edward II*, 254 n108 (fake nineteenth-century accounts of this invitation) and 260 n139 (a Scots envoy, 'Henry', gaoled in Dublin from 16 February 1315).

87. J. A. Watt, *The Church and Two Nations in Medieval Ireland* (Cambridge, 1970), 184–97; N. Gallagher, 'The Franciscans and the Scottish Wars of Independence: An Irish Perspective', *JMH*, 32 (2006), 3–17; *idem*, 'The Emergence of National Identity among the Religious of Britain in the Thirteenth and Fourteenth Centuries', in S. Duffy and S. Foran, eds, *The English Isles: Cultural Transmission and Political Conflict in Britain and Ireland, 1100–1500* (Dublin, 2013), 103–17.

88. McNamee, *Wars of the Bruces*, 190–4; Duffy, 'The Bruce Brothers', 58–70.

89. *Scottish Formularies*, no. E94; *RRS*, v, no. 564; R. Nicholson, 'A Sequel to Edward Bruce's Invasion of Ireland', *SHR*, xlii (1963), 30–40, at 38–9; 'The "Continuation" of Nicholas Trevet: A New Source for the Bruce Invasion', ed. S. Duffy, *Proceedings of the Irish Academy*, xci, 12 (Dublin, 1991), 311–12.

90. A. A. M. Duncan, ed., 'A Question about the Succession, 1364', *Scottish History Society Miscellany*, xii (Edinburgh, 1994), 57; Duffy, 'The Bruce Brothers', 54–8

91. McNamee, *Wars of the Bruces*, 173–7.

92. *The Bruce*, 520n. The *Laud Annals* add John Campbell, Thomas Randolph junior, a John de Bosco and John Bisset in Edward's following. Barbour highlights deeds of 'Gib the Harper' and the death of a 'Neil Fleming'. A contemporary English Dominican recorded almost thirty names of Irish and Scottish supporters of Edward Bruce, including a 'Donald of the Isles', John Soules, three Stewarts (John, Alan and Walter), a Duncan Campbell, a William of Galloway, a William of Turnberry and a Duncan Carleton (Duffy, 'The Continuation of Nicholas Trevet', 310–12, 314–15). *RRS*, v, no. 68, 4 May 1315, Robert's grant while at Kilwinning Abbey in Ayrshire after the parliament, of a pension in return for the service of an archer to Sir Reginald Crawford, son of the knight captured with Alexander and Thomas Bruce in 1307, may indicate another participant. Ibid., no. 148, March 1319, is a gift of Barnes (East Lothian) to Sir Alexander Seton for service 'in Ireland and Scotland'. Carrick/Ayrshire service in Ireland is known from Robert I's confirmation in 1323 of a grant by Edward as 'king of Ireland' to a John de Carleton of Ayrshire lands (ibid., no. 235).

93. S. Duffy, 'The Lords of Galloway, Earls of Carrick, and the Bissets of the Glens: Scottish Settlement in Thirteenth-Century Ulster', in D. Edwards, ed., *Regions and Rulers in Ireland, 1100–1650: Essays for Kenneth Nicholls* (Dublin, 2004), 37–50.

94. Contra *Flores Historiarum*, ed. H. R. Luard (3 vols, Rolls Series, London, 1890), iii, 130, which states that Robert exiled Elizabeth to live with her father and she was then 'honourably received' by Edward I/II.

95. *CDS*, iii, 421, 447 (John of Argyll awaits a Cinque Ports fleet at Dublin, September 1315), 479 (John as 'Admiral of the Fleet', March 1316, at Dublin with his knights Dougal Macdowall and Duncan MacGoffrey, who had captured the Isle of Man in 1315).

96. Duffy, 'Bruce Invasion of Ireland', 10–13; McNamee, *Wars of the Bruces*, 169–70.

97. *The Bruce*, 560, 564–5; *Rot. Scot.*, i, 121, 139; W. D. Lamont, 'Alexander of Islay, Son of Angus Mór', *SHR*, lx (1981), 165.

98. *RRS*, v, 137; *ER*, i, 52–8; J. G. Dunbar and A. A. M. Duncan, 'Tarbert Castle, a Contribution to the History of Argyll', *SHR*, l (1971), 1–17.

99. *The Bruce*, 564.

100. *Chron. Lanercost*, 212–13; McNamee, *Wars of the Bruces*, 79–80, 160 n50.

101. *Chron. Lanercost*, 213–16; McNamee, *Wars of the Bruces*, 80–1.

102. *Vita*, 107, 111–12; *Chron. Lanercost*, 217; *Chron. Bower*, vi, 411; Kershaw, 'Great Famine', 10–13; W. C. Jordan, *The Great Famine: Northern Europe in the Early Fourteenth Century* (Princeton, NJ, 1996), ch. 1.

103. *CDS*, iii, no. 452. On 30 October, Berwick-bound supply ships had to dump barley overboard to escape Scottish privateers (ibid., no. 455).

104. R. D. Oram, 'Death, Disease and the Hereafter in Medieval Scotland', in E. J. Cowan and L. Henderson, eds, *A History of Everyday Life in Medieval Scotland, 1000 to 1600* (Edinburgh, 2011), 196–25.

105. *Chartulary of St Mary's Abbey, Dublin*, ed. J.T. Gilbert (3 vols, Rolls Series, London, 1886), ii, 346–7; *RRS*, v, no. 101.

106. *Vita*, 107. For a potential (re)re-dating of Edward Bruce's inauguration to 1316 see Duffy's paper in D. Ditchburn, P. Crooks and S. Duffy, eds, *The Irish-Scottish World in the Middle Ages* (Dublin, forthcoming), which contains several new papers reassessing the Bruce invasions including Penman, 'The Bruce Invasion of Ireland: A Scottish Perspective'.

107. *RRS*, v, no. 72 and notes pp. 356–60.

108. Ibid., nos 73–5, brieves and orders to officials to enforce payments due to Holyrood and Arbroath Abbeys; *ER*, v, 447, 512 ('serk').

109. *RRS*, v, no. 74.

110. G. S. Gimson, 'Lion Hunt: A Royal Tomb-Effigy at Arbroath Abbey', *PSAS*, 125 (1995), 901–16; G. Henderson, 'A Royal Effigy at Arbroath', in W. M. Ormrod, ed., *England in the Fourteenth Century* (Woodbridge, 1996), 88–98. Abbot Bernard may have been anxious to mark the centenary of William's death (December 1214) or Arbroath's ritual confirmation by Alexander II c.February 1215 (*Handlist* [Scoular], nos 1–40).

111. Duffy, 'Bruce Invasion of Ireland', 18; *The Bruce*, 545–55.

112. *RRS*, v, no. 76 and p. 206; *RMS*, i, App. ii, nos 12, 425, 427, 431, 437, 483; *Registrum Episcopatus Aberdonensis* (2 vols, Spalding and Maitland Clubs, Edinburgh, 1845), i, 157; *SP*, vii, 425–9; A. Fraser, ed., *The Frasers of Philorth* (3 vols, Edinburgh, 1879), i, 49–76, and ii, 196–9, 309–10. Alexander and Mary would also have a son, John, another royal nephew with a remote place in the succession.

113. *RMS*, i, App. ii, nos 465, 476–7, 652; P. G. B. McNeill and H. L. MacQueen, eds, *Atlas of Scottish History to 1707* (Edinburgh, 1996), 204.

114. *Calendar of Ancient Correspondence Concerning Wales* (Cardiff, 1935), ii, 253–4; Duffy, 'Bruce Invasion of Ireland', 18–19.

115. *RRS*, v, nos 77–8; *RMS*, i, App. i, nos 11, 108, and App. ii, nos 49, 70, 662.

116. *Chron. Lanercost*, 216; *Vita*, 48; *Chron. Scalacronica*, 73, 227–8n; *The Bruce*, 376–8, 398–400; *RRS*, v, p. 137. On 8 March 1316 Robert would grant the late Peter [Lubaud]'s forfeited Lothian lands to Robert Lauder of the Bass (*RRS*, v, no. 84; *RMS*, i, App. ii, no. 178).

117. *CDS*, iii, nos 470, 472, 477.

118. Ibid., 473–4; *Rot. Scot.*, i, 153.

119. Duffy, 'Bruce Invasion of Ireland', 23–6; S. Duffy, ed., *Atlas of Irish History* (Dublin, 1997), 28–9, 42–3; McNamee, *Wars of the Bruces*, 177–9; Phillips, *Edward II*, 256–7.

120. J. R. S. Phillips, 'The Mission of John de Hothum to Ireland, 1315–16', in J. Lydon, ed., *England and Ireland in the Later Middle Ages: Essays in Honour of Jocelyn Otway-Ruthven* (Dublin, 1981), 62–86, at 66–70; *idem, Edward II*, 260–2.

121. Phillips, *Edward II*, 271–3 (150 men-at-arms and 2,000 infantry, including Roger Mortimer of Wigmore).

122. *RRS*, v, 137 and nos 79–88; this assembly is not listed in *RPS*.

123. E.g. *RMS*, i, App. ii, nos 115–25 (Berwickshire), 126–34 (Roxburghshire), 135–9 (Selkirkshire), 169–85 and 253–70 (the Lothians), plus monastic confirmations, e.g. nos 87–9, 139, 184 (Newbattle Abbey).

124. *RRS*, v, no. 85.

125. *Chron. Bower*, vi, 385.

126. *RRS*, v, p. 137–8 and nos 89–9.

127. Ibid., nos 91–2.

128. *CCR, Edward II, 1313–17*, 450–1; Phillips, *Edward II*, 274–5 and n216 (noting omission of these talks in Barrow, *Robert Bruce*).

129. *RRS*, v, nos 93–6; *Chron. Lanercost*, 216–17; *CDS*, iii, no. 440, misdated to 1315.

130. *RRS*, v, no. 99.

131. *CCR, Edward II, 1313–17*, 557; *RRS*, v, no. 100, witnessed by the Chancellor, Moray, 'Patrick Dunbar, Earl of March', Steward, Douglas, Alexander Stewart and Keith.

132. Duffy, 'Bruce Invasion of Ireland', 29–30; *The Bruce*, 555–63.

133. *RRS*, v, nos 101, 427; Duffy, 'The Continuation of Nicholas Trevet', 308, 314; McNamee, *Wars of the Bruces*, 179–81.

134. *RRS*, v, nos 102–7.

135. Wishart was last active about 25 June 1316 with his successor's chapter election on 26 November 1316 (Watt, *Scottish Graduates*, 151, 590).

136. Phillips, *Edward II*, 274–6, 280–2.

137. *Vita*, 130–1.

138. *RRS*, v, no. 108; *CCR, Edward II, 1313–18*, 472. Moray was at Lauder on 6 December (NAS RH6/83, cited in *RRS*, v, p. 84 n13) and reported in the Borders about 28 December 1316 (*CDS*, iii, no. 462) to negotiate a tribute-truce for Lancaster's castle-barony of Bamburgh until Easter 1317 (TNA SC 8/218/10871).

139. *RRS*, v, nos 109–11; Duffy, 'Bruce Invasion of Ireland', 33.

140. *Chron. Lanercost*, 111–14; Barrow, *Robert Bruce*, 33, 413; Blakely, *Brus Family*, App. 3 (Brus charters), no. 163; M. Penman, 'Royal Piety in Thirteenth-Century Scotland: The Religion and Religiosity of Alexander II (1214–49) and Alexander III of Scotland (1249–86)', in J. Burton, P. Schofield and B. Weiler, eds, *TCE*, xii (Woodbridge, 2009), 13–30, at 20–1. On

8 February 1319 Robert would pay for perpetual lights at Malachy's altar in Coupar-Angus (*RRS*, v, no. 145). Close to death, Robert would offer support to a chapel of St Brigit near Sundrum in Ayrshire (*ER*, i, 162, 268, 303).

141. *The Bruce*, 581; Duffy, 'Bruce Invasion of Ireland', 29–31; McNamee, *Wars of the Bruces*, 84, 181–2.

142. *CDS*, iii, nos 636, 912; *The Bruce*, 583–97; Watt, *Church and Two Nations*, 185–6; W. D. H. Sellar, 'Hebridean Sea Kings: The Successors of Somerled, 1164–1316', in E. J. Cowan and R. A. MacDonald, eds, *Alba: Celtic Scotland in the Medieval Era* (East Linton, 2000), 217.

143. *Foedera*, II, i, 318–19; *RRS*, v, no 571; J. B. Smith, 'Gruffudd Llwyd and the Celtic Alliance', *Bulletin of the British Board of Celtic Studies*, xxvi (1976), 463–78 (with Llwyd's reply to Edward at 477–8); McNamee, *Wars of the Bruces*, 191–2.

144. *CDS*, iii, no. 549; W. S. Reid, 'Sea Power and the Anglo-Scottish War, 1296–1328', *Mariner's Mirror*, xlvi (1960), 7–23; McNamee, *Wars of the Bruces*, 173, 174, 176, 180–1, 184, 190–1, 194.

145. McNamee, *Wars of the Bruces*, 204 n138; Phillips, *Edward II*, 271–3. Llwyd had helped Edward II put down the revolt of Llwelyn Bren in 1316 and would serve in Scotland in 1319; but he would link up with the Scots c.1327–8 in opposition to Roger Mortimer.

146. Edward II complained to Cistercian leaders at Citeâux that Mellifont had barred English clerics; the damage done to Mellifont by the Scoto-Irish force in 1317 was inadvertent and repented (Watt, *Church and Two Nations*, 189).

147. *The Bruce*, 582n; Claffey, 'Richard de Burgh, Earl of Ulster', 341–9.

148. Duffy, 'Bruce Invasion of Ireland', 36–8; McNamee, *Wars of the Bruces*, 182–4; R. Frame, 'The Campaign against the Scots in Munster, 1317', in *idem*, ed., *Ireland and Britain, 1170–1450* (London, 1998), 99–112.

149. Kershaw, 'Great Famine', 151.

150. *Annals of Connacht (AD 1224–1554)*, ed. A. M. Freeman (Dublin, 1944), 233; Duffy, 'Bruce Invasion of Ireland', 32; McNamee, *Wars of the Bruces*, 168–9.

151. *Chron. Fordun*, i, 347, ii, 340; *Chron. Bower*, vi, 383–5.

152. J. Scammell, 'Robert I and the North of England', *EHR*, lxxiii (1958), 385–403 (which estimates that a fifth of the English realm paid tribute to Bruce by 1328); McNamee, *Wars of the Bruces*, 254–6.

153. *Foedera*, II, i, 321–2, 327–8; *CPL, ii*, 127, 138; Phillips, *Edward II*, 287 n46.

154. P. N. R. Zutshi, 'The Avignon Papacy', in Jones, ed., *NCMH*, vi, 657–9, 669–70; S. Layfield, 'The Pope, the Scots, and their "Self-Styled" King: John XXII's Anglo-Scottish Policy, 1316–1334', in King and Penman, eds, *New Perspectives*, 159–62.

155. *Chron. Bower*, vi, 319–31, 430–1n.

## Chapter 7 *Dark Victory*: The Price for Berwick, 1317–19

1. *Vita*, 107.

2. J. R. S. Phillips, *Aymer de Valence, Earl of Pembroke, 1307–1324: Baronial Politics in the Reign of Edward II* (Oxford, 1972), 107–13; *idem, Edward II*, 286–7.

3. *Foedera*, II, i, 321–2, 327–8.

4. Watt, *Scottish Graduates*, 151.

5. *The Bruce*, 583, 594, 613–15; S. Duffy, 'The Bruce Invasion of Ireland: A Revised Itinerary and Chronology', in *idem*, ed., *Robert the Bruce's Irish Wars: The Invasions of Ireland 1306–1329* (Stroud, 2002), 38.

6. *Chron. Scalacronica*, 77; *The Bruce*, 567–79, 597–607.

7. BL Soc. Antiq, London MS 120, pp. 56, 102; *The Bruce*, 597–613; *Chron. Bower*, vi, 383; *Rot. Scot.*, i, 166–8.

8. *CDS*, iii, no. 576; McNamee, *Wars of the Bruces*, 84, 149–51; Penman, *David II*, 47–8; Phillips, *Edward II*, 288–97. This was a situation further aggravated by the capture and ransoming of Pembroke during his return from Avignon.

9. *RRS*, v, no. 113, a grant of Skene in Aberdeenshire in barony to Robert Skene. But on 3 June, Robert was recorded at his natural son's tower house at Clackmannan (along the Stirling–Dunfermline road) where he gave Sir Henry Sinclair the wardship/marriage of William Bisset of Merton (ibid., no. 114).

10. Ibid., nos 115–16; again, this is not noted in *RPS*.
11. *RRS*, v, p. 140.
12. *Vetera*, 195, no. 414; *SP*, vi, 295–7, and vii, 236–7. It is possible that Edward and Isabel had married as early as 1314–15 (thus provoking Earl David of Atholl's fury?). In 1355 the widowed Euphemia Ross would become Robert Steward's second wife (and thus queen in 1371), bringing Badenoch as her dowry (*Vetera*, 307, no. 620; *CPL*, iii, 287, 574).
13. *RRS*, v, nos 117–19, 121. This period saw the king visit Restenneth Priory in Angus perhaps as part of obsequies for a royal infant born c.1315–17; on 19 June 1317 he confirmed Perth's monopoly over the unloading of goods along the upper Tay after a ruling at Dundee on the previous day, suggesting an exchequer audit in that burgh. Acts of 24 June at Arbroath (confirmation of the earl of Lennox's private agreement with Arbroath Abbey, the only extant royal act issued on Bannockburn's anniversary), of 12 July at Perth, and 28 July at Aberdeen indicate the location of chancery, not Robert.
14. Ibid., no. 120, after an inquest (ibid., no. 108). The king was also perhaps at Melrose for the funeral of Alexander Stewart of Bonkle (ibid., nos 102, 110; *CPL*, ii, 208).
15. TNA SC 1/49/22; Phillips, *Edward II*, 294.
16. *Chron. Lanercost*, 218–19; J. R. Maddicott, *Thomas of Lancaster, 1307–1322* (Oxford, 1970), 205–7; Phillips, *Edward II*, 290–7.
17. TNA C47/32/1/4; *Foedera*, II, i, 340; *RRS*, v, 141–2; Barrow, *Robert Bruce*, 321–2.
18. Watt, *Scottish Graduates*, 351–3.
19. Phillips, *Edward II*, 297–8.
20. *Foedera*, II, i, 370–1.
21. *Chronica Monasterii de Melsa*, ed. E. A. Bond (3 vols, London, 1868), ii, 33; Maddicott, *Lancaster*, 205–6. Middleton's cousin, Adam de Swinburne, had been arrested after chiding Edward II about neglect of defence of the north (*Chron. Scalacronica*, 79–81).
22. *RRS*, v, 142 and nos 122–4, with John's cousin, William Lindsay, Chamberlain, present as a witness for the first time.
23. Ibid., 140–1.
24. E.g. *The Bruce*, 571–9: 'Neville challenges Douglas; Douglas's reputation'.
25. J. R. S. Phillips, 'The Irish Remonstrance of 1317: An International Perspective', *Irish Historical Studies*, xxvii (1990), 112–29; *idem*, *Edward II*, 262–4.
26. *Chron. Bower*, vi, 385–411 and notes. For example, the Trinity College Dublin MS 498 of *Scotichronicon* (c.1480–1500) has *Laudabiliter*, the Remonstrance, the cardinal's letter c.1308 regarding Bruce's absolution, and King John of England's submission to the Pope of 1213.
27. It is possible the author was a Franciscan, Michael McLochlainn, an unsuccessful Irish nominee as bishop of Armagh in 1303 (Phillips, *Edward II*, 264). A John Maclachlan's gift of lands in Sorbie (Wigtownshire) would be confirmed by Robert I on 20 May 1325 with other gifts to Whithorn Priory, including lands from Edward Bruce to support 'St Ninian's light' (*RRS*, v, no. 275).
28. *Chron. Bower*, vi, 155, 387.
29. In response, John XXII admonished Edward II and his officials who at least made an effort to pay the annual tribute owed to the curia for England and Ireland; see J. A. Watt, *The Church and Two Nations in Medieval Ireland* (Cambridge, 1970), 196–7, and Phillips, *Edward II*, 263.
30. *RRS*, v, 142 and no. 125 (an exemption for Dunfermline Abbey from prise etc. unless 'for the defence of the realm').
31. Ibid., v, no. 430; *CDS*, iii, no. 539. By the 1340s local memory of Middleton's seizure of the Cardinals asserted that Moray and Douglas had participated (ibid., no. 1356).
32. Phillips, *Edward II*, 301.
33. *CDS*, iii, nos 554–5, 575. July–August had seen the English regime take the sons of Berwick burgesses as hostages to enforce their keeping of its defence, and exact a toll from them to pay for these defences despite Edward I's grant of an exemption in this regard.
34. *RRS*, v, no. 430.
35. Ibid., no. 126.
36. *Foedera*, II, i, 351; TNA C47/32/1; *RRS*, v, 143 and no. 431.
37. *RRS*, v, nos 127–8, 499.
38. Ibid., no. 129. Further charters were issued at Arbroath: on 10 February (no. 131) of former Balliol lands in Dundee to Scrymgeour; on 14 February (no. 132) of forest park rights for Arbroath Abbey, with Philip Mowbray present as a witness; and on 18 February (no. 133) to Gilbert Wiseman of lands at Rothes (Moray), for a half a knight's service.

39. Ibid., 143, 284 n22a and no. 134.
40. *Vita*, 147–8.
41. *Chron. Lanercost*, 219–20; *Chron. Scalacronica*, 79; *Chron. Fordun*, i, 348, ii, 340; *The Bruce*, 616, 620, 626; *Chron. Bower*, vi, 413; *RRS*, v, no. 150; J. Stevenson, *Illustrations of Scottish history, from the twelfth to the sixteenth century; selected from unpublished manuscripts in the British Museum, and the Tower of London* (London, 1834), 5.
42. *RRS*, v, 144–5 for what follows of Robert's itinerary; *Liber Sancte Marie de Melros* (2 vols, Bannatyne Club, Edinburgh, 1837), ii, no. 372.
43. Phillips, *Edward II*, 302, 313 n183. The execution of 'Robert (sic) Middleton' is reported by *Chron. Fordun*, i, 347, ii, 340, confusing Gilbert with his brother Richard who built a tower at Houxty, Northumberland, and defected to Bruce c.1318 (Barrow, *Robert Bruce*, 311).
44. *Chron. Lanercost*, 220–1; *CDS*, iii, no. 599; McNamee, *Wars of the Bruces*, 85, 151–2; S. Werronen, 'Ripon and the Scottish Raids, 1318–22', *NH*, xlix (2012), 174–84.
45. TNA SC 8/51/2537; *CDS*, iii, no. 602; *CPR, Edward II, 1317–21*, 354.
46. *RRS*, v, no. 135.
47. *Chron. Scalacronica*, 79; *CDS*, iii, nos 593–4, 596, 597; *The Bruce*, 626n.
48. *RRS*, v, no. 136.
49. *CDS*, iii, nos 562, 618, 636–7; McNamee, *Wars of the Bruces*, 184. When privateer Thomas Dun was captured in July 1317, he claimed Moray was planning an assault on the Isle of Man.
50. *The Bruce*, 617–27.
51. *Foedera*, II, i, 151, 152; *Chronicles of the Reigns of Edward I and Edward II*, ed. W. Stubbs (3 vols, Rolls Series, London, 1882), i, 283 (*Annales Paulini*); *Chron. Lanercost*, 224–5.
52. P. D. Clarke, *The Interdict in the Thirteenth Century: A Question of Collective Guilt* (Oxford, 2007), 59–68, 130. Only one dated royal act is extant before December 1318, *RRS*, v, no. 138, 27 July, from Leitfie in Angus, confirming a charter to Inchaffray Abbey. However, Robert's extant rolls do otherwise suggest a step up in chancery activity about this time with the rolls generally collated c.1317–18 (*Scottish Formularies*, 41–2; *RRS*, v, chs 18–19 and pp. 145–6).
53. *CDS*, iii, 433; M. Allen, *Mints and Money in Medieval England* (Cambridge, 2012), 79.
54. *The Bruce*, 627–9; *APS*, i, 112; *RRS*, v, no. 560; *Scottish Formularies*, no. E60, a brieve to secure inhabitants for a town (Berwick) by offering a burgage or money (within forty days of the brieve), and no. E98, a commission to collectors north of the Forth for a contribution for the keeping 'of a town B'[erwick], to be paid to the keeper at 'the monastery of D'[unfermline]'.
55. *Chron. Bower*, vi, 413–15. And see M. Penman, 'Who is this King of Glory? Robert I of Scotland (1306–29), Holy Week and the Consecration of St Andrews Cathedral', in K. Buchanan, L. Dean and Penman, eds, *Medieval and Early Modern Representations of Authority in Scotland and the British Isles* (Abingdon, 2016), 85–104.
56. *Liber Carta Prioratus Sanctii Andree in Scotia* (Bannatyne Club, Edinburgh 1841), xxvi; D. McRoberts, 'The Glorious House of St Andrew', in *idem*, ed., *The Medieval Church of St Andrews* (Glasgow, 1976), 63–121; M. Ash and D. Broun, 'The Adoption of St Andrews as Patron Saint of Scotland', in J. Higgitt, ed., *Medieval Art and Architecture in the Diocese of St Andrews* (Leeds, 1994), 16–24; I. Campbell, 'Planning for Pilgrims: St Andrews as the Second Rome', *IR*, 64 (2013), 1–22.
57. *RRS*, v, no. 500. The grant of Fordoun, plus Robert's gift in 1324 of Kirkmahoe church in Dumfriesshire to Arbroath, would be confirmed by papal nuncios in late 1329 (*CPL, ii*, 304). Palladius was a papal envoy and apostle to Ireland; a late *vita* has it that in later life he settled in Scotland and perhaps sent St Serf to preach in the Orkneys; see J. M. MacKinlay, *Ancient Church Dedications. Vol. II: Non-Scriptural Dedications* (Edinburgh, 1914), 104.
58. NLS Adv. MSS 15.1.18 no. 13 (Lamberton confirms Pittenweem Priory to St Andrews Priory, 6 July 1318).
59. Watt, *Scottish Graduates*, 352–3.
60. *Chron. Fordun*, i, 294, ii, 288; an obituary noted by *Chron. Lanercost*, 145.
61. *CDS*, iii, nos 530, 550, 552, 569, 609, 614, and pp. 320–1, 374.
62. *Vita*, 155.
63. Phillips, *Edward II*, 324–7. Edward did worship Thomas at Canterbury on 13 June 1318.
64. About July 1318 Earl Patrick of Dunbar and Bishop Lamberton confirmed past grants to Dryburgh Abbey; see *Liber Sancte Marie de Dryburgh* (Bannatyne Club, Edinburgh 1847), nos 285, 293–4. Nevertheless, this house would struggle to recover from the loss of its close

Balliol patronage and to maintain itself throughout the later medieval period; see R. Fawcett and R. D. Oram, *Dryburgh Abbey* (Stroud, 2005), 18–25.

65. Duffy, 'Bruce Invasion of Ireland', 38–43.

66. *CDS*, iii, no 562.

67. Ibid., nos 636–7. *Scottish Formularies*, no. E88, is a summons to the chiefs of Galloway to take part in an expedition to the Isle of Man within forty days 'under pain of death'.

68. *CCR, Edward II, 1313–18*, 561.

69. The cardinals' messengers to Ireland condemned Irish aid to the Scots (*Foedera*, III, i, 620–2).

70. Phillips, *Edward II*, 285 n33, 308–21; *Edward I and the Throne of Scotland*, i, 45–7, 81–2, and ii, 378–80.

71. Duffy, 'Bruce Invasion of Ireland', 39–42.

72. *Chron. Lanercost*, 225, writes of Edward's 'Irish adherents and a great army of Scots which had newly arrived in Ireland to enable him to invade and lay waste that land'.

73. *The Bruce*, 667–79; *Chron. Bower*, vi, 413; 'The "Continuation" of Nicholas Trevet: A New Source for the Bruce Invasion', ed. S. Duffy, *Proceedings of the Irish Academy*, xci, 12 (Dublin, 1991), 309–12, 314–15; McNamee, *Wars of the Bruces*, 185–6, 255; S. Boardman, *The Campbells, 1250–1513* (Edinburgh, 2006), 41–2.

74. *The Annals of Loch Cé*, ed. W. M. Hennessy (2 vols, London, 1871), i, 594–5; R. Frame, *English Lordship in Ireland 1318–61* (Oxford, 1982), 133.

75. *CDS*, iii, nos 640, 644, 645, 971.

76. Phillips, *Edward II*, 328–36.

77. *RRS*, v, 145.

78. *RPS*, 1318/30; *RRS*, v, no. 301.

79. A. H. Dunbar, *Scottish Kings: A Revised Chronology of Scottish History 1005–1625* (Edinburgh, 1899), 141–2, places Matilda as Robert's first daughter; but given her marriage to an unknown esquire and Margaret's name and later marriage to William, earl of Sutherland (and David II's consideration of the offspring of this match, a son John, d.1361, as a potential heir presumptive instead of the Stewarts), Margaret was surely the eldest (Penman, *David II*, 114–16).

80. Isabel (d.1358) had a daughter, Ingeborg, before Eric died in 1299 (*Norsk Biografisk Leksikon*, http://nbl.snl.no/Isabella_Bruce/utdypning, accessed on 17/8/2013).

81. *RRS*, v, no. 409, undated but witnessed by Bishop Lamberton, Patrick of Dunbar, Randolph of Moray/Annandale/Man, John Menteith, Douglas, Keith, David Brechin, Philip Mowbray and Adam Gordon.

82. M. Penman, 'Diffinicione successionis ad regnum Scottorum: Royal Succession in Scotland in the Later Middle Ages', in F. Lachaud and M. Penman, eds, *Making and Breaking the Rules: Succession in Medieval Europe, c.1000–c.1600* (Turnhout, 2008), 43–60, at 50–1.

83. *RRS*, v, 145 and no. 139 (twenty-nine parliamentary statutes used as the basis for *RPS*, 1318/1–29).

84. *PROME*, Edward 1, Roll 12, nos 280–475; D. E. R. Watt, *Medieval Church Councils in Scotland* (Edinburgh, 2000), 109–10.

85. *RPS*, 1318/3, 1318/26, 1318/6–7, 1318/13, 1318/14. This includes the first such extant regulation of fishing practices in medieval Europe, surely a further reflection of difficult economic conditions.

86. A. King, 'Bandits, Robbers and *Schavaldours*: War and Disorder in Northumberland in the Reign of Edward II', *TCE*, ix, ed. M. Prestwich et al. (Woodbridge, 2003), 115–19; W. C. Jordan, *The Great Famine: Northern Europe in the Early Fourteenth Century* (Princeton, NJ, 1996), 112–14, 162–6; N. Jamieson, ' "Sons of Iniquity": The Problem of Unlawfulness and Criminality amongst Professional Soldiers in the Middle Ages', in J. C. Appleby and P. Dalton, eds, *Outlaws in Medieval and Early Modern England: Crime, Government and Society, c.1066–c.1600* (Aldershot, 2009), 91–110. In England, Parliament received complaints in 1315 about abuses by sheriffs often in collusion with magnates and gentry, resulting in the 1316 Statute of Sheriffs; five further complaints about the state of law and order would be lodged down to 1320; see J. R. Maddicott, *The Origins of the English Parliament, 924–1327* (Oxford, 2010), 345–9.

87. *RPS*, 1318/5.

88. Ibid., 1318/19.

89. Ibid., 1318/15–21; A. Taylor, 'The Assizes of David I, King of Scots, 1124–53', *SHR*, xci (2012), 220–1.

90. *RPS*, 1318/4–5, 1318/8, 1318/12. Between 1321 and 1327 the English Parliament also heard Commons' complaints about the need for justice to be done to 'rich and poor' alike, and corrupt royal officers and lords taking bribes for failing to fulfil Crown writs properly in summoning defendants and jurors (Maddicott, *Origins of the English Parliament*, 352–7).

91. *RPS*, 1318/10–11.

92. H. L. MacQueen, '*Regiam Majestatem*, Scots Law and National Identity', *SHR*, lxxiv (1995), 3–11; Taylor, 'The Assizes of David I', 197–201, 231 (but see 236–7 for her revision of the dating of *Regiam*). The sky-high bloodfeud price of 1,000 cows or 3,000 pieces of gold for killing a king listed in *Regiam* may point to a date of c.1320–1 for this treatise, coincident with a plot against Robert and a cattle pandemic, discussed below; see *Regiam Majestatem & Quoniam Attachiamenta*, ed. Lord Cooper (Stair Society, Edinburgh, 1947), bk iv, ch. 36.

93. *Chron. Bower*, iii, 71, and iv, 3, 251; *Chron. Wyntoun*, iv, 408; J. Huntingdon, 'David of Scotland: "Vir tam necessarius mundo"', in S. Boardman, J. R. Davies and E. Williamson, eds, *Saints' Cults in the Celtic World* (Woodbridge, 2009), 130–45.

94. Taylor, 'The Assizes of David I', 229–30, 231–5. The preamble of *Regiam* also claims its contents to be the work of David I; see A. Harding, '*Regiam Majestatem* among Medieval Law-Books', *Juridical Review*, 29 (1984), 97–111, at 110–11.

95. *RRS*, v, 258–72 and nos 557–69; *Scottish Formularies*, nos E17–19, 35–43, 51–71. Although a number of these also reflect the considerable work of the Guardians' assemblies of c.1286–92, 1297–1304 and the reign of King John, 1292–96.

96. Taylor, 'The Assizes of David I', 225–8. That there remained some dissatisfaction in the later fourteenth century with Robert I's legislation is suggested by the further treatises known as *Quoniam Attachiamenta* and the *Laws of Malcolm MacKenneth*; see A. A. M. Duncan, 'The Laws of Malcolm MacKenneth', in A. Grant and K. J. Stringer, eds, *Medieval Scotland: Crown, Lordship and Community – Essays Presented to G. W. S. Barrow* (Edinburgh, 1993), 239–73; S. Reynolds, 'Fiefs and Vassals in Scotland: A View from Outside', *SHR*, lxxxii (2003), 176–93, at 192.

97. Cooper, ed., *Regiam Majestatem & Quoniam Attachiamenta*, 58.

98. *RPS*, 1318/25.

99. Ibid., 1318/27.

100. Ibid., 1318/22.

101. H. L. MacQueen, *Common Law and Feudal Society in Medieval Scotland* (Edinburgh, 1993), 106–7, 146–53.

102. Taylor, 'The Assizes of King David I', 222–3; D. Carpenter, 'Scottish Royal Government in the Thirteenth Century from an English Perspective', in M. Hammond, ed., *New Perspectives on Medieval Scotland, 1093–1286* (Woodbridge, 2013), 138–52. These studies demonstrate that the fine payable to the Crown (amercement) for a failed charge brought under a brieve remained a fixed £10 in Scotland (as against about £1 in England), in addition to the return of any seized lands or chattels plus financial compensation to the defendant (first mentioned in Robert I's 1318 statute, *RPS*, 1318/15): these were costs that most subjects could not afford given the present economy and that a Scottish knight's fee in this period averaged around £20.

103. A. Grant, 'Franchises North of the Border: Baronies and Regalities in Medieval Scotland', in M. Prestwich, ed., *Liberties and Identities in the Medieval British Isles* (Woodbridge, 2008), 160–1, 164. An additional twenty-five regalities were created by royal grant c.1312–1404, of which three were Robert I's creations for Randolph (ibid., 167, 194 [Table 1]).

104. C. J. Neville, *Land, Law and People in Medieval Scotland* (Edinburgh, 2010), chs 1–2; *idem*, 'Neighbours, the Neighbourhood, and the Visnet in Scotland', in Hammond, ed., *New Perspectives on Medieval Scotland*, 161–74. Edward I's inventory of Scottish royal records in 1291 (incorporating a Scottish audit of 1282) included over ninety 'small rolls, schedules and memoranda concerning diverse inquiries, perambulations and extents of land' but also a similar number of rolls recording disputes where parties had reached a private compromise (*APS*, i, 112–14; *RRS*, iv, pt 1, 37–9). Only one of a handful of cases heard in Aberdeen in 1317 for which records survive was resolved by an action brought by a royal 'brieve of right' (*RRS*, v, no. 121). Robert I's income from processing brieves was insignificant, only £56 from 255 royal letters issued (including brieves) in 1328–29; this stands in stark contrast to about 29,000 common-law writs per annum raised by the English chancery in the 1320s (*RRS*, v, 213–14 and nos 230, 269; *RPS*, 1325/1; Carpenter, 'Scottish Royal Government in the Thirteenth Century from an English Perspective', 141–6).

105. R. Tanner, 'Cowing the Community? Coercion and Fabrication in Robert Bruce's Parliaments, 1309–18', in K. M. Brown and R. J. Tanner, eds, *Parliament and Politics in Scotland, 1235–1560* (Edinburgh, 2004), 69.

106. *RPS*, 1318/1.

107. *RRS*, v, no. 140, and pp. 416–17.

108. Ibid., nos 490, 497; *The Records of Aboyne, 1230–1681* (New Spalding Club, Aberdeen, 1894), 353–62.

109. *RRS*, v, nos 141–2. This suggests the Crown's simultaneous review of the twelfth-century *Leges Burgorum* (Laws of the Burghs) in the wake of Berwick's recovery as one of the realm's original four 'head burghs' alongside Edinburgh, Stirling and Roxburgh (which last now lost out to Haddington); see H. L. MacQueen and W. J. Windrum, 'Laws and Courts in the Burghs', in M. Lynch, M. Spearman and G. Stell, eds, *The Scottish Medieval Town* (Edinburgh, 1988), 208–27, at 216–7.

110. *RRS*, v, nos 435, 481–90.

111. *RPS*, 1318/12. That this was as a means of prosecuting enemies for treason (once discovered), rather than dictating subjects' loyalty day to day, is underlined by Edward II's proclamation (so not a parliament statute as in Scotland) on 21 April 1320, as anti-Despenser feeling grew, ordering over seventy nobles not to believe false rumours (Phillips, *Edward II*, 377).

112. *RRS*, v, no. 301, notes pp. 560–1 (BL MS Harl. 4,694 fos 31[v]–34[v]; NLS, MS Adv. 34.3.11, fo.31r–v); Tanner, 'Cowing the Community?', 71.

113. *ER*, i, 45, 47; *SP*, viii, 249–50; M. McMichael, 'The Feudal Family of de Soulis', *TDGNAHS*, xxvi (1956–7), 38–48.

114. M. Penman, '"*A fell coniuracioun agayn Robert the douchty king*": The Soules Conspiracy of 1318–20', *IR*, 50 (1999) 36–8.

115. *RRS*, v, nos 140, 239. Perhaps as part of his penance Bishop Henry founded a chapel at Alyth in Perthshire which he gifted to the nearby abbey of Coupar-Angus, with 6 merks a year due on 24 June (Bannockburn day). According to Hector Boece in the early sixteenth century, Robert I also ordered the choir of St Nicholas church, Aberdeen, to be completed at the bishop's expense; see C. Rogers, ed., *Rental Book of the Cistercian Abbey of Coupar-Angus* (2 vols, Grampian Club, London, 1879), i, 27–31; *Hectoris Boetii Murthlacensium et Aberdonensium Episcoporum Vitae* (New Spalding Club, Aberdeen, 1894), 16–18.

116. *Chron. Scalacronica*, 79; V. H. Galbraith, 'Extracts from the *Historia Aurea* and a French "Brut" (1317–1347)', *EHR*, xliii (1928), 203–17; W. Fraser, ed., *The Red Book of Menteith* (2 vols, Edinburgh, 1880), i, 95–101. Murdoch had served as a valet of Sir William de Ferrers in 1310–11 and as an esquire in Dundee garrison in 1312–13 (*CDS*, iii, no. 193 and p. 429).

117. *RPS*, 1320/4/1; *Fasti*, 101.

118. Murdoch can last be found in English pay in January 1317 (*CDS*, iii, p. xxvii and no. 534): a search of English Wardrobe accounts and other sources does not locate him c.1318–20 whereas other Scots – Atholl, Betoigne, Glencarnie, Macdougall of Argyll, etc. – remain grouped in English receipts (e.g. ibid., no. 701).

119. *RRS*, v, no. 72, notes pp. 356–60.

120. *CDS*, ii, nos 1517, 1949, and iii, no. 410 and p. 433; Barrow, *Robert Bruce*, 138–9, 450n.

121. *CDS*, ii, nos 1771, 1827, and iii, nos 47, 192, 273; Fraser, ed., *Red Book of Menteith*, i, pp. xlii–xliv, 46–59.

122. *CDS*, ii, nos 1474, 1730, 1785, 1786, 1888, 1961, and iii, nos 101, 423; Fraser, ed., *Red Book of Menteith*, i, 73 (which notes the incorporation of the Stewart earls of Menteith's lordship of Knapdale into the new Macdougall sheriffdom of Lorn, 1293), 433–67, and ii, 222–3 (Edward I's grant of all Macdougall lands and custody of Alexander and John of Argyll into the control of Alexander, earl of Menteith in 1296).

123. *RRS*, v, no. 194; *The Acts of the Lords of the Isles, 1336–1493*, eds, J. and R. W. Munro (Scottish History Society, Edinburgh, 1986), 281.

124. *RRS*, v, nos 166–7.

125. *Rot. Scot.*, i, 836, 850; *CDS*, iii, nos 372, 393, 564, 671, 704, 727; *SP*, v, 583.

126. Tanner, 'Cowing the Community?', 71.

127. *Rot. Scot.*, i, 201; *RRS*, v, no. 405.

128. *RPS*, 1318/29; A. Taylor, 'Common Burdens in the *Regnum Scottorum*: The Evidence of Charter Diplomatic', in D. Broun, ed., *The Reality behind Charter Diplomatic in Anglo-Norman Britain* (Glasgow, 2010), 166–234, at 197–219.

129. Phillips, *Edward II*, 337, 342.

130. *CCR, Edward II, 1318–23*, 26.

131. Beam, *Balliol Dynasty*, 203–5. Balliol petitioned to re-enter Thomas's household in 1316–17.

132. TNA E403/189 m.8; *CCR, Edward II, 1318–23*, 140. Balliol was paid £83 and £28 in April 1319 (TNA E403/187 m.1, E403/189 m.8), £84 in January 1320 (ibid., E403/193 m.4), £24 in July 1320 (ibid., E403/191 m.14), and £184 in January 1321 (ibid., E403/194 m.5).

133. *RRS*, v, no. 434, incorrectly dated to 7 January 1320 by *Foedera*, II, i, 412.

134. *CCR, Edward II, 1318–23*, 309. Stanfordham was placed in Edward Balliol's gift in 1335–36 (*CDS*, iii, no. 614).

135. Phillips, *Edward II*, 342–3.

136. *CDS*, iii, no. 701 (English payments to these Scots, 12 October 1319–6 July 1320).

137. Barrow, *Robert Bruce*, 362–5; R. Nicholson, *Edward III and the Scots: The Formative Years of a Military Career, 1327–35* (Oxford, 1965), ch. 5 ('The Disinherited').

138. TNA E403/186 m.5, E403/188 m.3; *CDS*, iii, no. 569. For payments to Mar of £40 in 1320 and 1321, see TNA E403/191 m.13 and E403/196 m.4.

139. *CDS*, ii, nos 883, 1455, 1584, 1876, 1961, and iii, nos 29, 200, 238, 267, 273; *SP*, ii, 218–22.

140. *CDS*, iii, no. 67; *Rot. Scot.*, i, 114, 203; *RRS*, v, nos 102, 391; *RMS*, i, App. ii, nos 13–14, 45, 119, 178, 180, 717.

141. *CCR, Edward II, 1318–23*, 280, orders that were cancelled on 11 December 1320.

142. *CDS*, iii, no. 653; *Foedera*, III, i, 410. The English candidate for the deanery of Glasgow, Robert de Coucy, had a claim on the Berwickshire lands at Lamberton of Bruce's bishop-elect of Glasgow, John Lindsay (Watt, *Scottish Graduates*, 353).

143. *Vita*, 161; *RRS*, v, 147.

144. Ibid., 145–6, citing evidence of fragmentary letters, BL Cotton Charters, ii, 26.

145. Ibid., 146 (§150).

146. Ibid., nos 143–4, witnessed by the chancellor, Moray, Hay, Keith, John Wishart and Fergus Marshall (son of Adam?).

147. Ibid., no. 145, place-dated Arbroath (by the chancellor). Letters of 4 March, issued from Edinburgh, confirmed Haddington Priory's pre-1286 revenues (ibid., no. 146).

148. Ibid., nos 147–9; *RMS*, i, App. ii, nos 170, 255–7, 259, 459, 680; G. Seton, *A History of the Family of Seton* (2 vols, Edinburgh, 1896), i, 81–6.

149. *RRS*, v, nos 84, 150; *Chron. Scalacronica*, 73. Barbour asserts that the angry English garrison at Berwick killed Spalding in 1318 (*The Bruce*, 626).

150. *RRS*, v, nos 152, 404.

151. Ibid., p. 147; Phillips, *Edward II*, 345; B. Wells-Furby, 'The "Boroughbridge Roll of Arms" Reconsidered', *HR*, 86 (2013), 196–206.

152. *Vita*, 163, 167, 175–9; *Chron. Lanercost*, 226–8; *Chron. Scalacronica*, 87, 141; *Anonimalle Chronicle, 1307 to 1334*, ed. W. R. Childs and J. Taylor (Leeds, 1991), 96–9; *The Bruce*, 629–41; *Chron. Fordun*, i, 348, ii, 340–1; *Chron. Bower*, vi, 415; McNamee, *Wars of the Bruces*, 90–4.

153. *Vita*, 163; *Flores Historiarum*, ed. H. R. Luard (3 vols, Rolls Series, London, 1890), iii, 189; Phillips, *Edward II*, 347.

154. *Chron. Lanercost*, 236.

155. *Vita*, 165–7; *Anonimalle Chronicle*, 98–9; *Chronica Monasterii de Melsa*, ii, 337; *The Bruce*, 643–7; Phillips, *Edward II*, 347–9.

156. *Vita*, 167–9; *Flores Historiarum*, iii, 188; *The Bruce*, 647–59; Phillips, *Edward II*, 349–51.

157. *The Bruce*, 631n.

158. *Vita*, 167; Maddicott, *Lancaster*, 249–50; Phillips, *Edward II*, 351.

## Chapter 8 *Dark Passage*: In Search of Respite, 1319–22

1. *Regiam Majestatem & Quoniam Attachiamenta*, ed. Lord Cooper (Stair Society, Edinburgh, 1947), 58.

2. *The Bruce*, 629–65, 667–79.

3. *Chron. Lanercost*, 227–8; McNamee, *Wars of the Bruces*, 95–6.

4. *Foedera*, II, i, 404.

5. *RRS*, v, 148, 203–6 and nos 157–8; *RPS*, 1319/1; Watt, *Scottish Graduates*, 36, 549–50.

6. Phillips, *Edward II*, 352.

7. *RRS*, v, nos 155–6. Robert may have been at Dunblane for the funeral of Bishop Nicholas de Balmyle and to discuss his successor with the chapter (*Fasti*, 101).

8. *RRS*, v, nos 157–8, including Stocket forest, first granted to Aberdeen during the October 1313 Dundee assembly (ibid., no. 37) and now set in feu-ferme, a fixed annual rent to the Crown, for £213.

9. Ibid., no. 160. On the same day Robert granted Symington barony in Lanarkshire to Thomas Fitz Richard, a neighbour and follower of James Douglas.

10. *CDS*, iii, no. 681, and v, no. 657; *RRS*, v, no. 162; Phillips, *Edward II*, 352–3.

11. *CDS*, iii, no. 738, on 25 August 1321 the earl of Hereford was ordered to destroy this castle.

12. Scottish and English merchants were also to enjoy mutual customs exemption in each other's markets/ports (*Scottish Formularies*, no. E70).

13. A safe conduct for the same embassy of twelve Scots was reissued circa 7 January 1320 (*Foedera*, II, i, 412; *CPR, Edward II, 1317–21*, 414) but perhaps not used (*RRS*, v, 149).

14. T. Newfield, 'A Cattle Panzootic in Early Fourteenth-Century Europe', *Agricultural History Review*, 57 (2010), 155–90; P. Slavin, 'The Great Bovine Pestilence and its Economic and Environmental Consequences in England and Wales, 1318–50', *Economic History Review*, 65 (2012), 1239–66. Rinderpest is a close cousin of measles in humans and the two were often concurrent pandemics.

15. V. H. Galbraith, ed., 'Extracts from the *Historia Aurea* and a French "Brut" (1317–1347)', *EHR*, xliii (1928), 210.

16. *Chron. Fordun*, i, 349, ii, 341; Slavin, 'The Great Bovine Pestilence', 1245–6.

17. *Chron. Lanercost*, 228–9.

18. S. DeWitte and P. Slavin, 'Between Famine and Death. England on the Eve of the Black Death: Evidence from Paleoepidemiology and Manorial Accounts', *Journal of Interdisciplinary History*, xliv (2013), 37–60, at 38, 51–4, 59–60; E. Gemmill and N. Mayhew, *Changing Values in Medieval Scotland: A Study of Prices, Money and Weights and Measures, c.1260–1542* (Cambridge, 1995), 251 (Table 30, cow prices), 259 (Table 33, ox prices), 268 (Table 36, sheep prices).

19. R. M. Haines, *King Edward II: His Life, His Reign and Its Aftermath, 1284–1330* (London, 2003), 109–121; Phillips, *Edward II*, 350–4.

20. TNA SC 7/24/18; *Foedera*, II, i, 407–8, 412–13; *Vetera*, nos 427–8.

21. *RPS*, 1320/3/1.

22. BL Add Ch 76,752; TNA E101/8/27/30; *Registrum Honoris de Morton* (2 vols, Bannatyne Club, Edinburgh, 1853), ii, no. 24; *RPS*, 1320/3/1. This act is omitted from *RRS*, v, but Staplegordon's gift to James Douglas at Arbroath on 6 May is included (no. 166).

23. A grant of circa 1320 by Sir William Fraser of Drumelzier (Peeblesshire), of lands to Roger Tweedie, was witnessed by 'John, bishop of Glasgow', Sir John Wishart, dean of Glasgow, James Douglas, Robert Keith, Gilbert Fleming, Patrick Fleming, sheriff of Peebles, and William Mowat; this would be confirmed by Robert I on 12 June 1324 at Glasgow (*HMC*, v, 8–9, nos 5–6; *RRS*, v, no. 255).

24. *RMS*, i, no. 77, and App. i, no. 35.

25. *RRS*, v, no. 163, with Seton likely *custos* of the burgh, as he would render the 1327 account with Reginald More (*ER*, i, 63–4).

26. *Rot. Scot.*, i, 428–9.

27. *Scottish Formularies*, nos E60, E98.

28. *RRS*, v, nos 163, 560, contributions from north of the Forth. But a Melrose Abbey plea of November 1320 for exemption from this and other levies shows it was also levied in the south; exemption for foreign merchants may also be related (ibid., nos 169, 562).

29. *RPS*, 1320/4/1; *Chron. Bower*, vii, 4–10; *The Bruce*, 779–82; G. Barrow, ed., *The Declaration of Arbroath: History, Setting, Significance* (Edinburgh, 2003), xiii–xv.

30. G. G. Simpson, 'The Declaration of Arbroath Revitalised', *SHR*, lvi (1977), 11–33, at 22–4.

31. *RRS*, v, 146; *Foedera*, II, i, 362–3, 370, 384, 388–90; *CPR, Letters, i, 1305–42*, 199.

32. *Fasti*, 101. On 30 January 1320 Edward nominated a Richard de Pontefract. But Maurice, abbot of Inchaffray, would be consecrated as bishop in March 1322.

33. *Foedera*, II, i, 432; *Vetera*, no. 431; *RRS*, v, no. 440.

34. G. Donaldson, 'The Pope's Reply to the Scottish Barons in 1320', *SHR*, xxix (1950), 119–20.

35. *RRS*, v, 149–50 and no. 569, citing *Liber Epistolaris of Richard de Bury*, no. 463.

36. Phillips, *Edward II*, 369–71.

37. *CPL, i, 1305–42*, 208; Barrow, *Robert Bruce*, 400–1; Watt, *Scottish Graduates*, 299–301. Kinninmonth would be Robert's preferred successor at St Andrews in 1328 but would have to settle for the Aberdeen bishopric by 1329 instead.

38. *Anglo-Scottish Relations*, no. 32; K. J. Stringer, 'The Scottish "Political Community" in the Reign of Alexander II (1214–49)', in M. Hammond, ed., *New Perspectives on Medieval Scotland, 1093–1286* (Woodbridge, 2013), 61–4, 66, 78–9.

39. Stevenson, *Documents*, i, 1–2.

40. D. Broun, 'The Declaration of Arbroath: Pedigree of a Nation', in Barrow, ed., *The Declaration of Arbroath*, 1, 8–9 n2.

41. J. R. Philip, 'Sallust and the Declaration of Arbroath', *SHR*, xxvi (1947), 75–8; R. Nicholson, 'Magna Carta and the Declaration of Arbroath', *Edinburgh University Journal*, xxii (1965), 140–4.

42. S. Tebbit, 'Papal Pronouncements on Legitimate Lordship and the Formulation of Nationhood in Early Fourteenth-Century Scottish Writings', *JMH*, 40, 1 (2014), 44–62.

43. *Chron. Bower*, vi, 385–403; D. Broun, *Scottish Independence and the Idea of Britain: From the Picts to Alexander III* (Edinburgh, 2007), ch. 5.

44. Edward II told his York parliament of January 1320 he would visit France after 9 March, but he only reached Amiens on 19 June (Phillips, *Edward II*, 355–6).

45. *Foedera*, II, i, 431–2; *RRS*, v, 150; Phillips, *Edward II*, 371.

46. D. Broun, 'Re-reading the "Deposition Clause" in the Declaration of Arbroath', http://www.breakingofbritain.ac.uk/blogs/feature-of-the-month/july–2012/, accessed on 25/06/13.

47. A. A. M. Duncan, 'The Making of the Declaration of Arbroath', in D. A. Bullogh and R. L. Storey, eds, *The Study of Medieval Records* (Oxford, 1971), 174–88.

48. R. Foreville, *Le Jubilé de Saint Thomas Becket du XIIIe au XIVe siècle (1220–1470): Étude et Documents* (Paris, 1958), 13–14, 40–1.

49. R. Tanner, 'Cowing the Community? Coercion and Fabrication in Robert Bruce's Parliaments, 1309–18', in K. M. Brown and R. J. Tanner, eds, *Parliament and Politics in Scotland, 1235–1560* (Edinburgh, 2004), 72–3.

50. *The Chronicles of Scotland, compiled by Hector Boece, translated by John Bellenden*, ed. E. C. Batho and H. W. Husbands (Scottish Text Society, Edinburgh, 1961), 281–2; S. Thorson, 'Adam Abell's *The Roit or Quheill of Tyme*: An Edition', unpublished PhD, University of St Andrews (1998), 194–5; A. A. M. Duncan, 'The War of the Scots, 1306–23', *TRHS*, 6th series, ii (1992), 128–30; A. Grant, *Independence and Nationhood: Scotland, 1306–1469* (Edinburgh, 1984), 15–16.

51. TNA SC1/49/70, identified by Barrow, cited in Duncan, 'War of the Scots', 129–31.

52. NAS RH2/6/4/6; *CPL, i, 1305–42*, 201; Phillips, *Edward II*, 354–60. Dunbar's marriage dispensation was granted on 18 August 1320 but regranted on 16 January 1324 (*Vetera*, 227).

53. *CPL, i*, 208; Donaldson, 'The Pope's Reply to the Scottish Barons in 1320', 119–20.

54. *RRS*, v, no. 499; *RMS*, i, no. 77, and App. i, no. 35.

55. *RRS*, v, nos 164–8.

56. *ER*, i, 45, 47.

57. *RRS*, v, no. 172 = *RMS*, i, App. ii, no. 291. A number of the king's undated acts concerning Dumfriesshire (ibid., nos 293–326) and Roxburghshire (ibid., nos 278–92) may date to this period, including grants to Robert Boyd, Archibald Douglas, Robert Bruce and members of the Kirkpatrick, Moffat, Edzear, Maxwell and Kinninmonth kindreds, plus a 'William Carlisle' described as spouse of the king's (natural?) sister, 'Margaret'.

58. *RRS*, v, 150–1 and nos 168–9.

59. Balliol was paid 20 merks by the earl of Pembroke in the same account as eight other exiled Scots (*CDS*, iii, no. 701 – 'David de Betoigne, Gilbert Glencairny, Margery Frendroughit, Dougall Macdowall, Alan Argyll...').

60. *Chron. Scalacronica*, 79.

61. *The Bruce*, 699–701; *Chron. Fordun*, i, 348–9, ii, 341; *Chron. Bower*, vii, 3.

62. C. J. Neville, 'The Political Allegiance of the Earls of Strathearn during the War of Independence', *SHR*, lxv (1986), 133–53.

63. A. Young, *Robert the Bruce's Rivals: The Comyns, 1212–1314* (East Linton, 1997), xi.

64. *Chron. Fordun*, i, 348–9, ii, 341.

65. *CDS*, iii, no. 410; *RRS*, v, nos 173, 227, 502; *Chron. Bower*, 163 n13.

66. *CDS*, ii, nos 1517, 1949, and iii, no. 410 and p. 433; Barrow, *Robert Bruce*, 138–9, 450n.

67. *CDS*, iii, nos 15, 731 and pp. 395–6, 400, 409–10; *RRS*, v, no. 195; *Chron. Bower*, vii, 162 n14.

68. *RMS*, i, App. ii, nos 27, 29, 125, 221, 222, 263, 294, 485, 493, 505, 514, 549, 590 (which also included lands in Roxburghshire and near Inverkeithing); *CDS*, iii, nos 192, 220, 392, 769.

69. TNA E101/378/4 m.16, a payment to 'Gilbert of Glencairnie' and 'Thomas Morham' as knights of Sir John Mowbray, 1319–20.

70. *CDS*, iii, nos 723–4, 729; BL Stowe MS 555, fo.57v (Alexander Mowbray serving with the earl of Atholl, 1322–23); BL Add. MS 9,951, fos20v, 21r, 25r, 27r; Galbraith, 'Extracts from the *Historia Aurea* and a French "Brut" (1317–47)', 211–12.

71. *Chron. Fordun*, i, 348–9, ii, 341; *Chron. Bower*, vii, 3.

72. *CDS*, iii, nos 219, 1149 and p. 317; *RMS*, i, App. ii, nos 278, 304, 366; *Chron. Lanercost*, 269.

73. *CDS*, ii, p. 165 and nos 570, 586, 598, 629, 633, 658, 940, 970, 975, 1849, 1967; *ER*, i, 38, 47; *Regesta Regum Scottorum*, iv, pt i: *The Acts of Alexander III, 1249–86*, eds, C. J. Neville and G. G. Simpson (Edinburgh, 2012), 21–2 and nos 19, 119, 132, 162; *SP*, vi, 200–11.

74. *CDS*, iii, nos 43, 62, 65, 193, 303, 311.

75. Ibid., nos 699, 701.

76. *RRS*, v, no. 160; *RPS*, 1320/4/1.

77. *CDS*, iii, 425–6.

78. *CDS*, ii, nos 400, 942, 1691, and iii, no. 1741 and p. 458; *RMS*, i, App. ii, no. 729; *APS*, i, 477; *RRS*, v, no. 247. From August 1320, David Barclay would become lord of Brechin by right of his marriage and rise to be Robert I's sheriff of Fife and steward of Prince David's household (*SP*, ii, 122).

79. *PROME*, Edward I, Roll 12, nos 416–18; *CDS*, ii, nos 1734–6, and iii, no. 1258; *ER*, i, clxxx; *RMS*, i, App. ii, no. 729.

80. BL Add MS 34,193, fo.106.

81. *The Bruce*, 698n.

82. *CDS*, ii, nos 1786–7, and iii, pp. 427–8. According to *Chron. Lanercost*, 272, in 1332 Duncan, earl of Fife, came to Edward Balliol's peace and coronation with 'thirteen knights … to wit, David de Graham, Michael de Wemyss, David de Wemyss, Michael Scott, John de Inchmartin, Alexander de Lamberton, John de Dunmore, John de Bonville, William de Fraser, [William] de Cambo, Roger de [Mortimer], John de Laundel and Walter de Lundy'.

83. *RRS*, v, nos 77, 86; *RMS*, i, App. ii, nos 248(n), 700; *CDS*, iii, 421–2, 430, and no. 735; *Chron. Bower*, vii, 35; *Chron. Scalacronica*, 101.

84. *CDS*, iii, nos 192, 514.

85. BL Add. MS 35,093 fo.4r; *CDS*, iii, nos 43, 95, 121, 219, 235, 302, 373–4; A. Beam, ' "At the Apex of Chivalry": Sir Ingram de Umfraville and the Anglo-Scottish Wars, 1296–1321', in A. King and D. Simpkin, *England and Scotland at War, c.1296–c.1513* (Leiden, 2012), 53–76.

86. *CDS*, iii, no. 694; BL Add. MS 9,951 (Wardrobe Book Edward II 1320–31), fo.20r, which prompted Duncan to suggest Umfraville was to carry the 'declarations' (*The Bruce*, 705n).

87. *The Bruce*, 28–30, 703–7 (704 n119); *CDS*, iii, no. 721.

88. Both R. Nicholson, *Scotland: The Later Middle Ages* (Edinburgh, 1874), 102, and Barrow, *Robert Bruce*, 402–3, accept the plot as an attempt to put Soules on the throne.

89. *The Bruce*, 701.

90. *Chron. Fordun*, i, 348–9, and ii, 341; *Chron. Bower*, vii, 3.

91. *The Bruce*, 701.

92. *Flores Historiarum*, ed. H. R. Luard (3 vols, Rolls Series, London, 1890), iii, 347. Hereford was the uncle of the de Bohun killed by Robert I in 1314; in 1311 Hereford had governed Annandale and surely knew Soules, with Hereford also serving as Constable in 1318–20 for the Berwick campaign (*CDS*, iii, nos 226, 388, 393).

93. *RRS*, v, nos 172, 173, 175(A), 176, 179, 184, 188, 200, 201, 239, 263, 413; *RMS*, i, App. ii, nos 125, 221, 222, 227, 263, 283, 294, 329, 451, 455, 504, 516, 639, 663.

94. *Chron. Bower*, vii, 65–6.

95. *Chron. Lanercost*, 228–9; *Chron. Fordun*, i, 349, ii, 341; *Chron. Bower*, vii, 11.

96. *Vetera*, nos 431–3; Barrow, *Robert Bruce*, 313–14.

97. P. A. Linehan, 'A Fourteenth-Century History of Anglo-Scottish Relations in a Spanish Manuscript', *BIHR*, xlviii (1975), 109, Scots' text at 112–22; *Vetera*, 209; Phillips, *Edward II*, 369–73.

98. Donaldson, 'The Pope's Reply to the Scottish Barons in 1320', 120.

99.  BL Cotton Titus A XIX, fo.87r, translated in D. Broun, 'June 2013 – A New Letter of
     Robert I to Edward II', part of the *Breaking of Britain* project, http://www.breakingofbri-
     tain.ac.uk/blogs/feature-of-the-month/june-2013/. Fifteenth-century scribes at the
     Cistercian abbey of Kirkstall in Yorkshire transcribed this letter into a commonplace book
     and could easily have cropped the dating clause from its original 1 October 1320 ('anno
     regni nostri quinto *decimo*'). Another copy (*Liber Epistolaris of Richard of Bury*, 325–6, no.
     403, translated by Barrow, *Robert Bruce*, 408, and Phillips, *Edward II*, 369) may have been
     archived c.1323–24 (minus any dating clause) along with other papers relating to Anglo-
     Scottish talks held in northern England (e.g. at Bamburgh in May 1321), reused in talks at
     Kirk Yetholm in 1401 (*Anglo-Scottish Relations*, no. 38 and pp. 173–84), or at York in 1327
     overseen by the abbot of the Cistercian mother house in Yorkshire at Rievaulx.
100. *RRS*, v, no. 569 and notes.
101. Ibid., no. 169; *RMS*, i, App. i, no. 17.
102. *RRS*, v, no. 170. Edward Bruce had planned to endow a hospital for eighteen paupers at
     Holywood, work that had to be completed in the later fourteenth century by James
     Douglas's natural son, Archibald, lord of Galloway and third earl of Douglas, 'in honour of
     Robert I, David II, Edward Bruce and James Douglas' (*MRH: Scotland*, 101–2).
103. *The Register and Records of Holm Cultram*, ed. F. Grainger and W. G. Collingwood (Kendal,
     1929), 34–60, 140–3.
104. R. D. Oram, *The Lordship of Galloway* (Edinburgh, 2000), 80, 88, 90, 92, 218, 241–2, 255–6;
     Beam, *Balliol Dynasty*, 24, which also details Edward Balliol's favour to Holm Cultram in
     1336 (*Registrum Episcopatus Glasguensis* (2 vols, Bannatyre Club, Edinburgh, 1843), i, no. 286).
105. *RRS*, v, 150; *Chron. Lanercost*, 237.
106. *Foedera*, II, i, 441; *CPR, Edward II, 1317–21*, 504, 554; *RRS*, v, no. 171. Thomas de Dalton,
     bishop of Galloway, was appointed as a proxy for the Archbishop of York who was absent
     in France with Edward II.
107. *CCR, Edward II, 1318–23*, 284, 297; J. W. Dilley, 'Scottish-German Diplomacy', *SHR*,
     xxxvi (1957), 80–7, at 82–3.
108. *RRS*, v, nos 171–85; Phillips, *Edward II*, 372–3.
109. *RRS*, v, nos 172–85; on 10 April the bishops of St Andrews and Dunkeld are listed as
     witnesses, suggesting the collapse of the talks (*Anglo-Scottish Relations*, no. 38, p. 152).
110. *RMS*, i, App. i, no. 53, and App. ii, nos 283, 355; *RRS*, v, nos 244, 415; M. Brown, 'War,
     Allegiance and Community in the Anglo-Scottish Marches: Teviotdale in the Fourteenth
     Century', *NH*, xli (2004), 221–38.
111. *RRS*, v, nos 173–6, 179, 184; P. G. B. McNeill and H. L. MacQueen, eds, *Atlas of Scottish
     History to 1707* (Edinburgh, 1996), 350–1. Further letters of protection were also issued to
     Arbroath Abbey on 24 February: this may relate to guarantees sought during any peace
     talks for the abbey's hopes of recovering its former northern English churches and lands,
     such as the Bruce gift of Haltwhistle in Northumberland.
112. *RRS*, v, no. 181; *RMS*, i, App. i, nos 13, 91.
113. *RRS*, v, nos 177–8, 182–3, 443.
114. *RMS*, i, nos 55, 62, 68, 89, and App. ii, nos 169, 176, 182, 203, i.e. Pencaitland, between
     Seton, Tranent and Keith in East Lothian; lands in Dalkeith, Midlothian; and Lethberd,
     Stirlingshire, forfeited by Sir Philip Lindsay.
115. *RRS*, v, no. 414: the adjacent Roxburghshire baronies of Eckford, Nisbet, Longnewton,
     Maxton and Caverton (*Atlas of Scottish History to 1707*, 204).
116. *RRS*, v, nos 490, 501–2; *Atlas of Scottish History to 1707*, 203–4. Both Murdoch and John
     would also receive davoch and barony lands respectively in Angus c.1320/29 (*RMS*, i, App.
     ii, nos 359, 372, 445, 452) while Murdoch gained forfeited Mowbray and Soules lands near
     Edinburgh (ibid., no. 516).
117. *RRS*, v, no. 503.
118. *Anglo-Scottish Relations*, no. 38, at p. 152. The Scots envoys questioned the safe conducts
     issued to them by English bishops as they were not sworn 'on Edward II's soul'.
119. Barrow, *Robert Bruce*, 313–15; Phillips, *Edward II*, 172–3.
120. Linehan, 'A Fourteenth-Century History', 112–22.
121. Although adult at twenty-one, kings of Scots would undertake a 'revocation' of grants made
     during their legal minority only at age twenty-five (Lord Cooper, ed., *Regiam Majestatem &
     Quoniam Attachiamenta* (Stair Society, Edinburgh, 1947), 151).
122. *Anglo-Scottish Relations*, no. 38, p. 152.

123. *RRS*, v, no. 188. At the same time Robert may first have decided to award the abbey a cocket seal for trade privileges – a grant made official on 10 September 1321 (ibid., no. 199) – and a forfeited Berwick burgess's tenements (ibid., nos 411, 413). In 1321 Thomas Randolph, earl of Moray, would grant nearby Fife lands at Aberdour and a 40s. annual sum from Scone lands to pay for chaplains to say daily mass for his soul over his intended tomb at Dunfermline 'in the chapel below the conventual church', with a candle at his head and foot during high mass (*Registrum de Dunfermelyn* (Bannatyre Club, Edinburgh, 1842), no. 357).

124. *ER*, v, 447, 512.

125. *RRS*, v, nos 126, 195–6; *ER*, i, xciv, cxxiv, 61, 91, 170, 271, 310, 355, 408, 469, 477, 549. The loss of the *ER* for the years to 1327 may hide other gifts to Dunfermline/Cullen.

126. Linehan, 'A Fourteenth-Century History', 112–22; S. Boardman, 'Late Medieval Scotland and the Matter of Britain', in E. J. Cowan and R. J. Finlay, eds, *Scottish History: The Power of the Past* (Edinburgh, 2002), 47–72.

127. *RRS*, v, no. 185; J. Donnelly, 'An Open Port: The Berwick Export Trade', *SHR*, lxxviii (1999), 145–69, at 151.

128. *RRS*, v, p. 151 and no. 188; *RPS*, A1321/7/1; *RMS*, i, no. 84, and App. i, no. 24; D. E. R. Watt, *Medieval Church Councils in Scotland* (Edinburgh, 2000), 111–12.

129. *RRS*, v, no. 442.

130. Ibid., nos 189–93.

131. Ibid., no. 194.

132. W. Fraser, ed., *The Lennox* (2 vols, Edinburgh, 1874), i, 77–8, 236; C. J. Neville, *Native Lordship in Medieval Scotland: The Earldoms of Strathearn and Lennox, c.1140–1365* (Dublin, 2005), 36–7.

133. *RRS*, v, nos 29, 195–6, 249A.

134. *RRS*, v, no. 196. The earls of Ross were said to wear the shirt of Duthac in battle. There were Duthac altars in the Blackfriars of Ayr and Haddington and in a chapel of St Mary at Arbroath; see J. M. MacKinlay, *Ancient Church Dedications. Vol. II: Non-Scriptural Dedications* (Edinburgh, 1914), 223–8.

135. *RRS*, v, no. 198.

136. Ibid., nos 445, 446–7; *RMS*, i, App. ii, no. 418. Alexander Mowbray had also held lands in Strath'an/Strathavon (ibid., no. 35).

137. *RMS*, i, App. i, no. 74; *RRS*, v, 151. On 10 September Robert ordered his custamars (customs collectors) at Perth to pay new great custom dues owed to Dunfermline Abbey (ibid., no. 199).

138. *RRS*, v, nos 200–1; *CPR, Edward II, 1321–4*, 21 (Edward II's orders for Harbottle to be razed as the truce was about to end).

139. *RRS*, v, nos 200–3, the last witnessed by the bishops of St Andrews, Dunkeld and Brechin; the abbots of Kelso, Melrose, Jedburgh and Paisley; the earls of Moray and Fife, Steward, Douglas, Hay, Keith, Roger Kirkpatrick and Robert Boyd.

140. *RRS*, v, nos 445, 446–7; *RMS*, i, App. ii, no. 29; *Regesta Regum Scottorum, vi: The Acts of David II, 1329–71*, ed. B. Webster (Edinburgh, 1982), nos 52–3.

141. *RRS*, v, no. 206; *Registrum de Dumfermelyn*, no. 367. On 5 July 1321 Edward II's queen gave birth to a daughter, Joan, in the Tower of London, the future wife of David II (Phillips, *Edward II*, 394).

## Chapter 9 *To Have and Have Not*: King of Scotland, 1322–26

1. *Chron. Scalacronica*, 79.

2. *CDS*, iii, no. 746; *Foedera*, II, i, 472–4; *Chron. Lanercost*, ed. J. Stevenson (Maitland Club, Glasgow, 1839), 241–2.

3. J. R. Maddicott, *Thomas of Lancaster, 1307–1322* (Oxford, 1970), 278–303; R. M. Haines, *King Edward II: His Life, His Reign and Its Aftermath, 1284–1330* (London, 2003), 121–35; Phillips, *Edward II*, 381–406.

4. *Chron. Lanercost*, 230–1; *RRS*, v, 151; McNamee, *Wars of the Bruces*, 96–7. Lancaster reportedly refused to use his troops in Yorkshire against Bruce's force. On 20 March the earl of Richmond reported that the 'Earl of Carrick' was at Perth and had taken a truce to Michaelmas – probably for the see of Durham (*CDS*, iii, no. 747).

5. *CDS*, iii, no. 745.

6. *RRS*, v, nos 204, 559; *CDS*, iii, no. 746; *Foedera*, II, i, 474, 479; *Chron. Fordun*, i, 349–50, ii, 341–2.

7. *RRS*, v, nos 204–6; *RMS*, i, App. i, no. 29.

8. *Vita*, 203–15; *Chron. Lanercost*, 231–7; *Chron. Scalacronica*, 87–9; *Chron. Bower*, vii, 11; *Foedera*, II, i, 463, 472, 484; *CDS*, iii, no. 746; *CCR, Edward II, 1318–23*, 525–6; Phillips, *Edward II*, 436–8. *Chron. Fordun*, i, 350, ii, 341, omits Boroughbridge and Lancaster's fate as does Barbour's *The Bruce*.

9. Haines, *King Edward II*, 135–51; Phillips, *Edward II*, 408–16. Clifford, Bedesmere and John Mowbray were among those executed; 117 men were forfeited with £15,000 levied in fines.

10. *Foedera*, II, i, 479; *RRS*, v, 151.

11. *CCR, Edward II, 1318–23*, 532; Phillips, *Edward II*, 424. Indeed, Edward's original plan in late 1321 had been to crush the rebel earls and then take a force on to Scotland.

12. *RRS*, v, nos 207–10.

13. Ibid., 151–2 and no. 211.

14. Phillips, *Edward II*, 424.

15. *Chron. Lanercost*, 237–8; McNamee, *Wars of the Bruces*, 98.

16. Robert I secured a Gilbert McLelan as bishop of the Isles c.1321/22, denying the patronage rights of the abbot of Furness (*Fasti*, 262).

17. *Chron. Lanercost*, 238; Maddicott, *Lancaster*, 29–30. By 27 September 1322, tenants were reportedly fleeing with their 'cattle' from the North Riding into Durham (*Foedera*, II, i, 496).

18. *Chron. Lanercost*, 238.

19. *Chron. Fordun*, i, 350, ii, 342; *Chron. Bower*, vii, 11–13.

20. *The Bruce*, 679–81; *Chron. Fordun*, i, 350, ii, 342; *Chron. Bower*, vii, 11. *Chron. Scalacronica*, 83–5, also describes an undated raid by Sir Adam Gordon on Norham, 'thinking to catch the beasts which were being pastured outside the castle', repulsed by its keeper, Sir Thomas Gray senior.

21. Phillips, *Edward II*, 425–31.

22. *The Bruce*, 681–5; *Chron. Fordun*, i, 350, ii, 342; *Chron. Bower*, vii, 11–13; Barrow, *Robert Bruce*, 316–17; McNamee, *Wars of the Bruces*, 99. In revenge the Scots may have sacked Rievaulx and Byland Abbeys; see *Chronica Monasterii de Melsa*, ed. E. A. Bond (3 vols, London, 1868), ii, 346.

23. *Chron. Lanercost*, 239–40; *Chron. Scalacronica*, 89; *The Bruce*, 683–97.

24. *Chron. Scalacronica*, 89, with Sir Thomas Gray senior in charge of the queen.

25. *The Bruce*, 677–99.

26. *Chron. Lanercost*, 240–1.

27. *CCR, Edward II, 1318–23*, 687, 690; Phillips, *Edward II*, 431–2.

28. *RRS*, v, no. 212; *RMS*, i, App. ii, no. 92 (a grant of Cruggleton, Wigtownshire, forfeited by William Soules). York was aware of Robert's election of Simon de Wedale, abbot of Holyrood, to the Galloway diocese by April 1323 (*Fasti*, 170).

29. *RMS*, i, App. i, no. 22.

30. *RRS*, v, 152.

31. Ibid., nos 213–14. William I's obituary date was 4 December. The witnesses to these acts hint at an important occasion: the bishops of St Andrews, Dunkeld, Aberdeen and Brechin; John, prior of St Andrews, William, abbot of Kelso (Arbroath's mother house); Moray, Fife, Steward, Douglas, Hay, Keith, David Barclay and Andrew Gray.

32. *RRS*, v, no. 215; *CDS*, iii, no. 803; P. Munch, 'Concordia facta inter Anglicos et Scotos, 3rd January 1322–23', *PSAS*, iii (1857–59), 458–61; *Chron. Lanercost*, 241–2; *Anglo-Scottish Relations*, no. 39; Barrow, *Robert Bruce*, 322–6; Phillips, *Edward II*, 431–6.

33. Before the Lancaster/Hereford rebellion, Harcla allegedly appealed to Edward II to aid the people of the north as no one was willing to act 'as a wall' against the Scots (*Vita*, 205).

34. H. Summerson, 'The Early Development of the Laws of the Anglo-Scottish Marches, 1229–1448', in W. M. Gordon and T. D. Fergus, eds, *Legal History in the Making: Proceedings of the Ninth British Legal History Conference* (London, 1991), 29–42; C. J. Neville, *Violence, Custom and Law: The Anglo-Scottish Border Lands in the Later Middle Ages* (Edinburgh, 1997), 18–19.

35. *Foedera*, II, i, 520; Phillips, *Edward II*, 435, 449. Sir Henry's brother, Louis, bishop of Durham, was also in poor odour with Edward II for failing in defence against the Scots.

36. On 8 January 1323 Edward II had ordered Harcla and other Marchers not to make a truce with the Scots without his knowledge (*Foedera*, II, i, 502; *CDS*, iii, nos 800–1).

37. Phillips, *Edward II*, 419–22.

38. A. A. M Duncan, 'John King of England and the Kings of Scots', in S. D. Church, ed., *King John: New Interpretations* (Woodbridge, 1999), 247–71.

39. The variant extant texts of his indenture with Bruce suggest that Harcla was to be allowed to alter the content so as to 'seduce' his king and fellow Englishmen (*RRS*, v, no. 215, notes).

40. There were at least nine Kentigern (or Mungo) dedications in late medieval Cumbria (where Kentigern had been exiled), and Jocelin of Furness (d.1214) had written *vitae* of both Kentigern (as an ally of St Thomas Becket) and St Waltheof of Melrose (d.1160, an abbot stepson of King David I of Scots); J. M. MacKinlay, *Ancient Church Dedications. Vol. II: Non-Scriptural Dedications* (Edinburgh, 1914), 178–87; H. Birkett, *The Saints' Lives of Jocelin of Furness: Hagiography, Patronage and Ecclesiastical Politics* (York, 2010), 184–90.

41. *RRS*, v, nos 504–5; Watt, *Scottish Graduates*, 351–3; *Fasti*, 190. Oslo Schøyen Collection MS 679 states that Lindsay was consecrated on 9 October 1323; see J. R. Davies, 'New Light on William Wallace's Position as National Leader in 1297', part of *The Breaking of Britain: Cross-Border Society and Scottish Independence, 1216–1314* project, http://www.breakingofbritain.ac.uk/blogs/feature-of-the-month/september–2011-the-guardians-in-1286-and-wallaces-uprising-in–1297.

42. *Foedera*, II, i, 511; A. Stevenson, 'The Flemish Dimension of the Auld Alliance', in G. G. Simpson, ed., *Scotland and the Low Countries, 1124–1994* (East Linton, 1996), 37–8; Phillips, *Edward II*, 427, 434.

43. *RRS*, v, no. 449 (TNA C47/22/13); Barrow, *Robert Bruce*, 325; Phillips, *Edward II*, 433–4.

44. *RRS*, v, nos 217–19, 221, the Chancellor at Arbroath (8 January–1 February).

45. Ibid., nos 220, 222.

46. *Foedera*, II, i, 500.

47. Ibid., 508; *RRS*, v, 152; Phillips, *Edward II*, 434.

48. English hostages were surrendered until the earl of Moray's return (*RRS*, v, no. 226, 22 April). Robert I remained at Berwick until at least 7 June (ibid., nos 223–5, 227–31).

49. *Foedera*, II, i, 524; *RRS*, v, no. 232.

50. Robert Stewart would, though, be about twenty-one years old.

51. *RRS*, v, 503n.

52. Ibid., nos 232–3. The Peebles charter (full text *RMS*, i, no. 85) was a grant of Sauchie in Clackmannanshire to Henry of Annan, adjacent to the lands of the king's natural son.

53. *RPS*, 1323/7/1 to 4.

54. *RRS*, v, nos 230, 410.

55. Watt, *Scottish Graduates*, 578–60; *Fasti*, 170.

56. E.g. *ER*, i, 102–8, 111–22.

57. *RPS*, 1323/7/1–2; *RRS*, v, no. 394.

58. *RRS*, v, no. 497, undated, may also belong to this period, a note of a grant to 'John Campbell, earl of Atholl', with tailzie, of a third of the king's annual from Dundee and a third of the adjacent land of Pitkerro.

59. Ibid., no. 235, with Edward Bruce's witnesses listed as Philip Mowbray, Adam More, John Knockdalian, Gilbert Fitz Donald, Richard Edgar and Colin Fitz Duncan (a Campbell?).

60. Ibid., no. 236.

61. Ibid., nos 292, 294, 452A; *RMS*, i, App. ii, no. 204.

62. *RRS*, v, no. 239; *RMS*, i, App. ii, no. 350. Murdoch's interest in Argyll is indicated by his grant to Walter Menteith (son of John) of Coughol in Argyll, which he held of Walter Steward (NAS GD198/38 and 198/216).

63. *RRS*, v, no. 502; W. Fraser, ed., *The Red Book of Menteith* (2 vols, Edinburgh, 1880), ii, 238–9.

64. R. A. MacDonald, *The Kingdom of the Isles: Scotland's Western Seaboard, c.1100–c.1336* (East Linton, 1997), 188–96; M. A. Penman, 'The MacDonald Lordship and the Bruce Dynasty, c.1306–c.1371', in R. D. Oram, ed., *The Lordship of the Isles* (Leiden, 2014), 64–87.

65. *ER*, i, 57, 207; *RRS*, v, no. 393 (c.25 March 1321/24 March 1322, a grant of land in Lorn and Benderloch to Sir Arthur Campbell for a quarter of a knight's service).

66. *ER*, i, 52–8; J. G. Dunbar and A. A. M. Duncan, 'Tarbert Castle, a Contribution to the History of Argyll', *SHR*, l (1971), 1–17.

67. *RRS*, v, 241–2; S. Boardman, *The Campbells, 1250–1513* (Edinburgh, 2006), 44–5.

68. *RRS*, v, 242 and no. 239; *RMS*, i, App. ii, nos 350–3 (on roll vi, folio 2, headed 'Vicecomitatus Ergadie') and 368.

69. *RMS*, i, App. ii, nos 660–1; *The Acts of the Lords of the Isles, 1336–1493*, ed. J. and R. W. Munro (Scottish History Society, Edinburgh, 1986), xxv–xxvii.

70. Boardman, *The Campbells*, 42–9.

71. *RMS*, i, App. ii, nos 692, 695; *RPS*, A1323/7/3.

72. *Foedera*, II, i, 541; *RRS*, v, no. 450.

73. *RRS*, v, no. 243; Phillips, *Edward II*, 440–1, 459–61, 493–4.

74. *RRS*, v, no. 242.

75. Ibid., nos 140, 240. That the allegiance of Bishop Cheyne was again reviewed at this time is suggested by a charter of West Lothian lands to Sir Reginald Cheyne, the younger, on 28 July 1323 (ibid., no. 238).

76. *RRS*, v, nos 5, 60, 476; *RPS*, A1323/7/4; Barrow, *Robert Bruce*, 362.

77. *RRS*, v, no. 240. This act bears the strongest witness list of all the extant Scone acts: the bishops of St Andrews, Dunkeld, Aberdeen and Dunblane; the Chancellor and the earls of Fife, Strathearn and Menteith. The pregnancy must have been conceived circa 5 June 1323.

78. *RMS*, i, App. i, nos 7, 72; *RRS*, v, no. 244.

79. *RRS*, v, nos 245–7.

80. Ibid., nos 220, 223, 248.

81. *CCR, Edward II, 1313–18*, 611–12.

82. *RRS*, v, no. 414.

83. Ibid., no. 44; M. Penman, 'A Programme for Royal Tombs in Scotland? A Review of the Evidence, c.1093–c.1542', in *idem*, ed., *Monuments and Monumentality across Medieval and Early Modern Europe* (Donington, 2013), 239–53, at 242–3.

84. *RRS*, v, nos 249–50, with witnesses including the earls of Fife and Dunbar, Walter Steward, Douglas and Hay.

85. *RMS*, i, App. i, no. 66; *RRS*, v, nos 251–3.

86. *SP*, iv, 510–13, and vii, 235–7.

87. *RMS*, i, App. i, no. 66; P. G. B. McNeill and H. L. MacQueen, eds, *Atlas of Scottish History to 1707* (Edinburgh, 1996), 203.

88. *RRS*, v, nos 251, 506.

89. Ibid., nos 17, 252; *ER*, i, 59, 113, 149, 213, 462, 464.

90. *RRS*, v, no. 253.

91. Ibid., no. 493.

92. *Chron. Bower*, vii, 15, 176–7n, reproduces verses commemorating David's birth, the first (anonymous) celebrating 'a two-fold birth'. *The Bruce*, 744(n)–5, names only David, at the time of his wedding in 1328 (but A. A. M. Duncan as editor identifies John Bruce as his twin).

93. Our only firm evidence for John Bruce is David II's grant of a £20 annual fee of Dundee's customs to the priory of Restenneth on 10 June 1344 for the soul of his brother John (*RMS*, i, App. i, no. 118).

94. *SP*, i, 434–5; v, 37; vi, 33 and 294–5; vii, 236 and 428–9. This also explains David II's preference for alternative royal heirs presumptive instead of Robert Steward from 1341, including his full nephew John Sutherland; his nephew by marriage John of Gaunt; and John Stewart of Kyle; see M. Penman, 'Diffinicione successionis ad regnum Scottorum: Royal Succession in Scotland in the Later Middle Ages', in F. Lachaud and M. Penman, eds, *Making and Breaking the Rules: Succession in Medieval Europe, c.1000–c.1600* (Turnhout, 2008), 53–5. 'John' was a highly popular forename before the Wars, third with 5.6 per cent after Robert (5.8 per cent) and William (9.4 per cent) of 14,642 personal names identified by a recent project; see M. Hammond, 'The Paradox of Medieval Scotland, 1093–1286', in *idem*, ed., *New Perspectives on Medieval Scotland 1093–1286* (Woodbridge, 2013), 1–52, at 30–48.

95. P. D. Clarke, *The Interdict in the Thirteenth Century: A Question of Collective Guilt* (Oxford, 2007), 130, 263.

96. *RRS*, v, 152–3.

97. M. Vale, *The Origins of the Hundred Years War: The Angevin Legacy, 1250–1340* (Oxford, 1990), 227–44; Phillips, *Edward II*, 455–7, 459–66.

98. *Foedera*, II, i, 541; *CPL*, ii, 239.

99. *Foedera*, II, i, 542; Phillips, *Edward II*, 451. Edward II objected to no avail by letter on 1 April 1324.

100. Barrow, *Robert Bruce*, 327, translating Vatican Archives, Instrumenta Miscellanea, 944.

101. *RRS*, v, nos 222, 232, 448.

102. *Foedera*, II, i, 561; Phillips, *Edward II*, 457–9.

103. *Foedera*, II, i, 558 and 567 (Balliol), 570 (Moray/Lamberton); *RRS*, v, 153; Beam, *Balliol Dynasty*, 206–10, 348–50.

104. *RRS*, v, nos 254–6, 504 (an order to the bishop of Glasgow to appropriate the church of Kilmarnock, South Ayrshire, to Cambuskenneth Abbey) and 505 (same as last, of Kirkmahoe church, Dumfriesshire, dedicated to St Kentigern, appropriated to Arbroath Abbey).

105. *RMS*, i, App. i, no. 59; *RRS*, v, no. 275; H. L. MacQueen, 'The Laws of Galloway: A Preliminary Survey', in R. D. Oram and G. Stell, eds, *Galloway: Land and Lordship* (Edinburgh, 1991), 131–43. The men of Galloway, 'preferring to have one lord', had first petitioned the Scottish Crown in 1234, seeking direct royal lordship to offset the death of their lord, Alan, leaving only three legitimate daughters (*ESSH*, ii, 493–4).

106. *PROME*, Edward I, Roll 12, no. 288; *CDS*, ii, no. 1874.

107. *CDS*, ii nos 257–8; *Fasti*, 261–2.

108. G. Donaldson, 'The Rights of the Crown in Episcopal Vacancies', in *idem*, *Scottish Church History* (Edinburgh, 1985), 31–9.

109. *Foedera*, II, i, 577–8; P. Chaplais, ed., *The War of Saint-Sardos (1323–1325): Gascon Correspondence and Diplomatic Documents* (Camden Society, 1954), 76; *RRS*, v, 153.

110. *RRS*, v, nos 259–63; *RPS*, 1324/1.

111. *RMS*, i, App. i, nos 33, 47; *RRS*, v, no. 259; *RPS*, 1324/1.

112. *RMS*, i, App. i, no. 38; M. Brown, *The Black Douglases: War and Lordship in Late Medieval Scotland, 1300–1455* (East Linton, 1998), 25–6, 160, 166. The Douglases would also adopt the Bruce 'blood red' heart for their coat of arms. According to Douglas family history, Bruce also presented Lord James with a sword inscribed with the legend: 'So manie, so good, as of Douglas hes beine/Of one surname, we never in Scotland seine'; see *The History of the Houses of Douglas and Angus, Hume, David, of Godscroft* (3 vols, Edinburgh, 1644), i, 460n; W. Fraser, ed., *The Douglas Book* (4 vols, Edinburgh, 1885), i, 184.

113. J. M. Gilbert, 'The Usual Money of Scotland and Exchange Rates against Foreign Coin', in D. M. Metcalf, ed., *Coinage in Medieval Scotland, 1100–1600* (2nd Oxford Symposium on Coinage and Monetary History, British Archaeological Reports, no. 45, 1977), 131–51.

114. Phillips, *Edward II*, 464–6.

115. *Vita*, 223–9; Phillips, *Edward II*, 467–70. Barrow, *Robert Bruce*, 326–8, omits these talks. It is not known who the English envoys were: the earl of Pembroke died on 23 June 1324; Richmond and Henry Beaumont were involved in exchanges with France.

116. *Vita*, 223.

117. S. Boardman, *The Early Stewart Kings: Robert II and Robert III, 1371–1406* (East Linton, 1996), ch. 4; N. A. T. Macdougall, *James IV* (2nd edn, Edinburgh, 1997), 126–9, 248–64.

118. *Vita*, 223–5.

119. These Essex lands represented a lost income for the Bruce of about £3,060 since 1306 (Blakely, *Brus Family*, chs 5–6).

120. Phillips, *Edward II*, 465–6.

121. Ibid., 458.

122. *RMS*, i, App. i, nos 92–4; *Handlist* (Scoular), nos 133, 384; *RRS*, i, no. 44; G. W. S. Barrow, ed., *The Charters of King David I: The Written Acts of David I King of Scots, 1124–53, and of his Son Henry Earl of Northumberland, 1139–52* (Woodbridge, 1999), nos 167, 174–5.

123. *RMS*, i, App. i, no. 32.

124. *Fasti*, 261–2.

125. *Foedera*, II, i, 542. In July 1325 the Papacy would order the bishop of Glasgow and abbots of Kelso and Melrose to pass judgment on the abbot and canons of Jedburgh who had fled during the war and then been replaced by Scots (*CPL*, ii, 245).

126. *Cronica Regum Mannie et Insularum*, ed. G. Broderick (Douglas, 1979), 51; R. D. Oram, 'Bishops' Tombs in Medieval Scotland', in Penman, ed., *Monuments and Monumentality*, 171–98, at 193–4; I. MacDonald, *Clerics and Clansmen: The Diocese of Argyll between the Twelfth and Sixteenth Centuries* (Leiden, 2013), 7, 46–7, 70.

127. *RRS*, v, no. 275.

128. Ibid., no. 212; *Fasti*, 170.

129. *Foedera*, II, i, 541; Barrow, *Robert Bruce*, 325–6 (incorrectly dated to 1324).

130. *Vita*, 227–9. Edward II told John XXII that the Scots' terms would mean the disinheritance of his throne (*Foedera*, II, i, 595).

131. Phillips, *Edward II*, 458–9.

132. *RMS*, i, App. i, no. 31; *Atlas of Scottish History to 1707*, 202.

133. *RMS*, i, App. i, no. 32; *Vetera*, p. 227, no. 452 – this was 'Black Agnes' Randolph (whose mother was a Stewart of Bonkle), who would be famed for her defiance of an English siege of Dunbar in 1338 (*Chron. Bower*, vii, 127–31).

134. *RRS*, v, no. 261.

135. Ibid., p. 153.

136. Ibid., no. 267.

137. Robert's chancery recognised the political importance of key men by collation of a separate roll (now lost roll no. v in *RMS*, i, App. ii) bringing together royal grants to Moray, Steward and Douglas.

138. *RMS*, i, App. i, no. 75, and App. ii, no. 446.

139. J. Bannerman, *The Beatons: A Medical Kindred in the Classic Gaelic Tradition* (2nd edn, Edinburgh, 1998), 58–60; *ER*, i, 66, 176, 213.

140. *RMS*, i, App. ii, no. 318; *RRS*, v, no. 262; *A History of the Family of Seton during Eight Centuries*, ed. G. Seton (Edinburgh, 1896), i, 76–7.

141. *RRS*, v, no. 263; *Registrum de Dunfermelyn* (Bannatyne Club, Edinburgh, 1842), nos 357–8. Sometime circa March 1324/March 1325 Randolph was granted the Berwickshire barony of Mordington in the far south-east of the realm by Berwick, surely to enhance his standing as border warden (*RRS*, v, no. 451).

142. *RRS*, v, no. 269 or *RPS*, 1325/1. *RRS*, v, no. 271, 1 April 1325, from Cambuskenneth, saw a brieve issued ordering the chamberlain and sheriff of Kinross to stop levying an annual fee on Kinross lands held by Melrose Abbey. For the recovery of Melrose until its decimation in war in 1385, see R. Fawcett and R. D. Oram, *Melrose Abbey* (Stroud, 2004), 36–45.

143. *RRS*, v, no. 335; *RPS*, 1326/1.

144. *ER*, i, xcix; *RRS*, v, no. 289, 10 January 1326, a grant to Melrose Abbey out of Berwick's 'new custom'.

145. *Registrum Episcopatus Glasguensis* (2 vols, Bannatyne Club, Edinburgh, 1843), i, no. 270; *Charters of the Abbey of Coupar-Angus* (2 vols, Scottish History Society, Edinburgh, 1947), i, nos 105–6; D. E. R. Watt, *Medieval Church Councils in Scotland* (Edinburgh, 2000), 112–14. The Papacy's right to fill benefices vacated when a cleric rose to be a bishop – vacating a plurality of valuable lesser churches, prebends and offices – made this a vital tool of patronage. A brieve, *RRS*, v, no. 566, datable only to 1323/25, demanding payment of meal and 200 merks due from the bishopric of Glasgow for two years during its vacancy when it was in the king's hands (*contra* its administrator's claims that this had been remitted) may relate to this Council's business.

146. *RRS*, v, no. 299.

147. Ibid., nos 272–3. Adam de Moravia would be Robert's choice as bishop of Brechin in 1327–28.

148. C. Lord, 'Isabella at the Court of France', in C. Given-Wilson, ed., *FCE* (Woodbridge, 2002), ii, 45–52; P. Doherty, *Isabella and the Strange Death of Edward II* (London, 2004), 80–2.

149. *CDS*, v, no. 699; *The War of Saint-Sardos (1323–1325)*, 264–5.

150. *CPL*, ii, 243, 461, 468; Watt, *Scottish Graduates*, 23, 450–1; *Fasti*, 348.

151. V. M. Montagu, 'The Scottish College in Paris', *SHR*, iv (1906–07), 399–416; W. J. Courtenay, *Parisian Scholars in the Early Fourteenth Century: A Social Portrait* (Cambridge, 1999), 118, 129–217. The extant university *compotus* lists some twenty-nine Scottish students and staff (rectors/regents) enrolled in Paris by 1329–30, including a Donald of Mar, Gilbert Fleming (a future chaplain for David II and the Papacy); William Greenlaw ('of Dunbar', papal collector in Scotland by 1352 and archdeacon of St Andrews c.1366); William Pilmuir (archdeacon of St Andrews by the 1330s); possibly William Landellis (future bishop of St Andrews, 1342–85); John and William Douglas (sons of Archibald, nephews of lord James, with John becoming archdeacon of Lothian c.1334); Richard Pilmuir (bishop of Dunkeld by 1344); and John and Thomas Wedale (kin of Simon, bishop of Galloway). There were seventeen German, fourteen English and eleven Swedish/Danish scholars. Douglas family history asserts that Sir James had been schooled in Glasgow then Paris (*A History of the House of Douglas*, i, 68), while Barbour describes his three years in France as 'rybbaldaill' (*The Bruce*, 61–3).

152. *Foedera*, II, i, 613; Barrow, *Robert Bruce*, 250; Phillips, *Edward II*, 459. Edward II sent a letter of thanks to the Pope.

153. *RRS*, v, no. 270; *RMS*, i, App. ii, no. 502.

154. *RMS*, i, App. ii, no. 699; *RPS*, A1325/2.

155. *RMS*, i, App. i, no. 9; Boardman, *The Campbells*, 45–6.
156. *RRS*, v, 68, 648; *RMS*, i, App. ii, no. 863; *ER*, i, 57, 201, 238; D. McNaughton, *The Clan McNaughton* (Edinburgh, 1977), 18; Boardman, *The Campbells*, 47–8.
157. *ER*, i, 53, 58.
158. J. S. Hamilton, 'The Character of Edward II: The Letters of Edward of Caernarfon', and M. Prestwich, 'The Court of Edward II', both in G. Dodd and A. Musson, eds, *The Reign of Edward II: New Perspectives* (Woodbridge, 2006), 5–21 and 61–75; Phillips, *Edward II*, 277 and n225; Haines, *King Edward II*, 35–48.
159. *ER*, i, 123–30. Excavations of 2008–09 identified the likely site of the Cardross manor house at 'Pillanflatt', Renton, beside the river Leven, opposite Dumbarton and some 4 miles east of the modern town of Cardross; however, historic cultivated land, quarry and canal works at Mains of Cardross may also point to a possible location for Robert's manor (*RMS*, i, no. 117).
160. J. A. Claffey, 'Richard de Burgh, Earl of Ulster (c.1260–1326)', unpublished PhD, University College of Galway (1970), 365.
161. *RMS*, i, App. ii, no. 289 (undated), a grant of the keeping of Roxburgh to a Bernard Hauden need not mean its castle was relatively intact.
162. *ER*, i, 66 (king's larder at Scone), 246 (queen's kitchen at Scone), 123–54. The rebuilding of royal castles would be confined largely to English garrisons of 1333–41, although Robert did pay for development of royal parks at Stirling and Edinburgh: in the latter he also installed a tilting ground and (re)built 'a chapel' to the Virgin erected by St Margaret (ibid., 238, 239).
163. *RMS*, i, App. i, no. 23; *RRS*, v, 153–4 and nos 274–80.
164. Phillips, *Edward II*, 473–5.
165. *ER*, i, 57, 74.
166. *Acts of the Lords of the Isles*, lxii–lxv, lxxiv–lxxv, nos 1–3, 5; Penman, 'The MacDonald Lordship of the Isles and the Bruce Dynasty'. Robert I initiated a perennial fourteenth- and fifteenth-century Crown policy in dealing with the Isles by taking a hostage, holding young kin of his cousin MacRuaridh from 1325 (*ER*, i, 63, 313, 398). It is surely possible that in this context the MacDonalds approached England circa 1325–29.
167. B. Davis, 'Lordship in the British Isles, c.1320–c.1360: The Ebb Tide of the English Empire', in C. Given-Wilson, A. Kettle and L. Scales, eds, *War, Government and Aristocracy in the British Isles, c.1150–c.1500: Essays in Honour of Michael Prestwich* (Woodbridge, 2009), 153–63, at 161–2; M. Brown, *Disunited Kingdoms: Peoples and Politics in the British Isles, 1280–1460* (Harlow, 2013), 165–89.
168. *RMS*, i, App. i, no. 23; *RRS*, v, nos 277, 279.
169. *RMS*, i, App. i, nos 29, 80; *RRS*, v, nos 274–6, 278, 280.
170. *CDS*, iii, nos 403, 438, 536, 606, 660, pp. 318 (William Blount back in Edward III's pay, 1333–35) and 428.
171. *RMS*, i, App. ii, nos 438–61 ('vicecomitatus de forfar'); Blount also received an annual fee from holdings in Atholl (no. 470).
172. Ibid., App. ii, nos 585 (a repeat of 432), 588.
173. Ibid., App. i, no. 457 with undated text at App. i, no. 76, in a run of six charters regarding Forfarshire lands, including a repeat of physician Patrick Beaton's (no. 75, 20 November 1324), Sir Robert Harcarres (no. 77, incorrectly dated to August 1321), Sir William Dishington, Sir Geoffrey Fullerton (24 March 1327) and Sir William Blount (2 May 1325).
174. *RRS*, v, nos 127, 281.
175. *ER*, i, 247–8; *RRS*, v, no. 295; *RMS*, i, App. ii, nos 171, 248, 448, 657, 700. William's son, Walter, also married a natural daughter of Robert I, Elizabeth; see A. H. Dunbar, *Scottish Kings: A Revised Chronology of Scottish History 1005–1625* (Edinburgh, 1899).
176. *RRS*, v, no. 282. Keith could only have been a 'witness' to this act if his seal was attached by the Chancellor in search of a strong list of royal officers alongside himself, Douglas (justiciar of Galloway), Hay (Constable) and Lauder (justiciar of Lothian).
177. Haines, *King Edward II*, 166–73; Phillips, *Edward II*, 474–86.
178. *RRS*, v, no. 283.
179. *CDS*, v, nos 702–3; northern officers promised to send to the Marches for better intelligence.
180. *RRS*, v, nos 288–9; *ER*, i, p. xcix.
181. On the same day the king granted Melrose an exemption from exactions on its Carrick and other Ayrshire lands (*RRS*, v, no. 287).

182. The Bible, Numbers 17, relates how Levi was chosen of all the people of Israel by means of Aaron's rod which bore sweet and bitter almonds on its opposing sides: if the people followed God they would be rewarded with sweet almonds. William I of Scotland used his papal golden rose or 'Aaron's rod' as a sceptre; A. Davidson et al., eds, *Oxford Companion to Food* (2nd edn, Oxford, 2006), 665; Duncan, *Kingship of the Scots*, 137–8.

183. The Cistercians' exemption from teinds would also mean that Melrose would not be obligated by the 1326 lifetime tenth that parliament would grant Robert.

184. E. A. R. Brown, 'Death and the Human Body in the Later Middle Ages: The Legislation of Boniface VIII on the Division of the Corpse', *Viator*, 12 (1981), 221–69.

185. D. Ditchburn, *Scotland and Europe: The Medieval Kingdom and its Contacts with Christendom, 1214–1560* (East Linton, 2000), 164–5, discussion of the wool price-guide of Italian merchant Francesco Pegolotti (c.1275–c.1318–21), including abbey clips from Melrose, Jedburgh, Dundrennan, Glenluce and Coupar-Angus.

186. C. Proctor, 'Physician to The Bruce: Maino de Maineri in Scotland', *SHR*, lxxxvi (2007), 16–26.

187. Courtenay, *Parisian Scholars in the Early Fourteenth Century*, 118, 129–217. Charles IV also recruited a physician from the university, John de Dia, regent master in the faculty of medicine, 1325–32 (ibid., 173).

188. *ER*, i, pp. cxv, 169, 238 (Maineri); for rice e.g. ibid., 75 (100 lb), 119 (600 lb for David Bruce's wedding), 122 (3,097 lb), 233 (2,092 lb); for almonds ibid., 75 (100 lb), 117 (400 lb), 220 (1,020 lb). It is also tempting to link purchases of spices (ginger, galangal, pepper, mace, nutmeg and saffron) and condiments (sugar, salt, verjuice, vinegar and olive oil) to the recipes recommended by Maineri in his *Regimen Sanitatis* (1331); see C. Proctor, 'Perfecting Prevention: The Medical Writings of Main de Maineri (d.c.1368)', unpublished PhD, University of St Andrews (2005), 7, 252, 253, 255.

## Chapter 10 *Dead Reckoning*: Peace and Piety, 1326–28

1. *Chron. Bower*, vii, 35.

2. *RRS*, v, nos 240, 284, 285 and notes. No. 285 extended exemption from prise to all Scone's lands (the only extant royal act dated on the main feast of St Thomas in any year of Robert's reign); on 26 March the king would also reserve Scone Abbey fishings to support the royal household (ibid., no. 297).

3. Ibid., no. 290.

4. Ibid., nos 291–4; *Regesta Regum Scottorum, i: The Acts of Malcolm IV, 1153–65*, ed. G.W.S. Barrow (Edinburgh, 1960), i, nos 243–53.

5. *RRS*, v, no. 298, processed 5 May 1326 at Arbroath.

6. *RMS*, i, App. ii, no. 378; *RRS*, v, no. 360; *ER*, i, 209.

7. *RRS*, v, no. 295.

8. *RMS*, i, App. ii, no. 455; *ER*, i, 102, 118, 137.

9. *RMS*, i, App. ii, nos 356, 462, 485, 548; *ER*, i, 115, 212, 214, 288.

10. *RPS*, A1327/3/1 (misdated); *RRS*, v, no. 296; *RMS*, i, App. ii, no. 700.

11. Phillips, *Edward II*, 486–500. Le Bel asserted that Isabella left France for Hainault with Jean de Beaumont and his brother, the count, offered aid if Prince Edward would marry his daughter; *The True Chronicles of Jean le Bel, 1290–1360*, trans. N. Bryant (Woodbridge, 2011), 26–7.

12. John XXII urged Moray to return to Scotland in February 1326; Keith returned by 5 May 1326 (*CPL*, ii, 461, 468, 471, 476; *RRS*, v, 154 and no. 298).

13. AN, J.677, no. 6; *RRS*, v, no. 299; N. A. T. Macdougall, *An Antidote to the English: The Auld Alliance, 1295–1560* (East Linton, 2001), 25–7.

14. *CDS*, iii, nos 882–3; Phillips, *Edward II*, 495.

15. *Regesta Regum Scottorum, vi: The Acts of David II, 1329–71*, ed. B. Webster (Edinburgh, 1982) vi, nos 52–3.

16. *RRS*, v, no. 301; *APS*, vi, 628a, 664a; *RPS*, 1326/2; NRS PA3/2, fo.84r, and PA3/2/8, fo.155v. Sir James Balfour produced the act in parliament on 25 December 1650 but the original (and any copies) have since been lost.

17. R. Nicholson, *Scotland: The Later Middle Ages* (Edinburgh, 1974), 116; Barrow, *Robert Bruce*, 382–3

18. *RMS*, i, App. i, no. 70; *CPL*, ii, 246 (dispensation for Andrew and Christina, October 1325); *Chron. Bower*, vii, 125; Penman, *David II*, 61–7.

19. *Chron. Fordun*, i, 351, ii, 343; *Chron. Bower*, vii, 35: 'At the same time Andrew de Moray married the Lady Christina, the sister of the king.'

20. *The Bruce*, 749.

21. *ER*, i, 127–54. Hence *RRS*, v, no. 302, 20 July 1326 at Cambuskenneth, a royal confirmation of all previous earls of Carrick grants to Crossraguel Abbey.

22. Coronation within a predecessor's lifetime was a regular French royal practice; see M. Bloch (trans. J. E. Anderson), *The Royal Touch: Sacred Monarchy and Scrofula in England and France* (London, 1973), 128.

23. *RRS*, v, no. 303.

24. Ibid., v, no. 300; *RPS*, 1326/1 and 1328/1.

25. *ER*, i, 115, 179, *ad indecim* by individual; *RRS*, v, *ad indecim* 'pension'.

26. A. Grant, 'Thanes and Thanages, from the Eleventh to the Fourteenth Centuries', in A. Grant and K. J. Stringer, eds, *Medieval Scotland: Crown, Lordship and Community: Essays Presented to G. W. S. Barrow* (Edinburgh, 1993), 65–6; Nicholson, *Scotland: The Later Middle Ages*, 109–13; Barrow, *Robert Bruce*, ch. 14, esp. 351–72.

27. J. A. Claffey, 'Richard de Burgh, Earl of Ulster (c.1260–1326)', unpublished PhD, University College of Galway (1970), 167–8, 282. By contrast, in England, in 1290 the Crown passed the *Quia Emptores* statute prohibiting subinfeudation of lands in return for such services and other obligations (*PROME*, Edward I, Easter 1290, SC9/1, no. 56; A. Grant, 'Service and Tenure in Late Medieval Scotland, 1314–1475', in A. Curry and E. Matthew, eds, *Concepts and Patterns of Service in the Later Middle Ages* (Bristol 2000), 145–79, at 152–4). The increasing poverty of the English nobility obliged the Crown to shift from mixed feudal, paid and voluntary forces to fully contracted/paid armies, the norm under Edward III; see D. Simpkin, *The English Aristocracy at War: From the Welsh Wars of Edward I to the Battle of Bannockburn* (Woodbridge, 2008).

28. *ER*, i, xxxv, 1–34 (accounts 1263–66), at 10–11.

29. 'The Scottish King's Household and Other Fragments', ed. M. Bateson, *Scottish History Society Miscellany*, ii (Edinburgh, 1904), 24–5. This includes no figures for a sheriff of Argyll (or Lorn, Kintyre or Skye).

30. *ER*, i, 111–22.

31. The Frescobaldi then Bardi banking families financed English occupation of Scotland to circa 1314 (*CDS*, iii, nos 159, 192, 728, and v, nos 382, 492, 512, 575, 624). Barrow, *Robert Bruce*, 388–90, asserts papal loans were sought to pay the Scots' war indemnity and curial costs in 1328–29: however, these loans of £1,000 each from two papal nuncios (plus £400 expenses) advanced fees which the Scots were in the process of raising themselves at home and were promptly repaid (*ER*, i, 110–11, 396, 403).

32. *ER*, i, 222, and ii, 220. Royal reserves are suggested by the 1,000 merks intended for masses for Robert I's soul diverted in 1334–35 to ransom Guardian Andrew Murray (ibid., i, 451).

33. I. Kershaw, 'The Great Famine and Agrarian Crisis in England, 1315–22', *Past and Present*, 59 (1973), 15–16. Sheep scab was reported amongst the herds of St Andrews Cathedral in 1329 (*ER*, i, 148).

34. E. Gemmill and N. Mayhew, *Changing Values in Medieval Scotland: A Study of Prices, Money and Weights and Measures, c. 1260–1542* (Cambridge, 1995), 12, 147–325 (price tables for crops, livestock, wool, fish).

35. A. Taylor, 'Common Burdens in the *Regnum Scottorum*: The Evidence of Charter Diplomatic', in D. Broun, ed., *The Reality behind Charter Diplomatic in Anglo-Norman Britain* (2010), 166–234; G. L. Harriss, *King, Parliament and Public Finance in Medieval England to 1369* (Oxford, 1975), 12–16.

36. In 1366 parliament undertook a full re-evaluation of lands and goods, the *verus valor*, revealing a drop in values of a third to a half across the Scottish realm. This process also recorded figures for the *antiquo taxio* often lower than those noted by thirteenth-century sources listing the *antiquo taxio*: this may reflect adjustment following assessment for war damage c.1326, with the dioceses of St Andrews (the Lothians and East March, from approx. £8,000 to approx. £5,400) and Aberdeen (including Buchan, burned in 1308, from approx. £1,600 to approx. £1,490) suffering the greatest decline (*RPS*, 1366/7/18). My thanks to Alasdair Ross for discussion of these points.

37. J. Donnelly, 'Skinned to the Bone: Durham Evidence for Taxations of the Church in Scotland, 1254–1366', *IR*, 50 (1999), 21–4.

38. *RRS*, v, nos 302, 303, 304, 305, 306, 307, 308, 310, 311, 312–14(A), 315–18, 481 and 452 (a brieve of action for debt).

39. J. R. Maddicott, *The Origins of the English Parliament, 924–1327* (Oxford, 2010), 119–25, 218–25, 266–71 and chs 6–7.
40. *RRS*, v, 154; *Foedera*, II, i, 164; CPR, *Edward II, 1323–7*, 85; *CDS*, iii, nos 887–9; C. J. Neville, *Violence, Custom and Law: The Anglo-Scottish Border Lands in the Later Middle Ages* (Edinburgh, 1997), 21–4. Barbour states that Robert I broke the truce in 1327 as he 'saw men wald nocht ma/Redres of schippys that war tane' (*The Bruce*, 711).
41. *RRS*, v, no. 453; *Foedera*, II, i, 639.
42. *Liber S. Thome de Aberbrothoc* (2 vols, Bannatyne Club, Edinburgh, 1848–56), i, no. 356; *RRS*, v, 590. English officials first complained about Scottish attempts to annex Coldingham in May 1318 (*CCR, Edward II, 1313–18*, 611–12).
43. *RRS*, v, nos 308–9; *RMS*, i, App. ii, no. 19.
44. Phillips, *Edward II*, 502.
45. N. Fryde, *The Tyranny and Fall of Edward II, 1321–1326* (Cambridge, 1979), 176–92; R. M. Haines, *King Edward II: His Life, His Reign and Its Aftermath, 1284–1330* (London, 2003), 173–86; Phillips, *Edward II*, 502–4.
46. Ibid., 508–13.
47. *Chron. Lanercost*, 253.
48. Barrow, *Robert Bruce*, 336, 354; Phillips, *Edward II*, 511, 546, 566–7.
49. McNamee, *Wars of the Bruces*, 239.
50. Phillips, *Edward II*, 513–15.
51. *RRS*, v, nos 310–14, and *RMS*, i, App. i, no. 25; *SP*, v, 580.
52. C. Valente, 'The Deposition and Abdication of Edward II', *EHR*, 113 (1998), 852–81; Maddicott, *Origins of the English Parliament*, 359–64; Phillips, *Edward II*, 521–9; Ormrod, *Edward III*, 40–54.
53. Phillips, *Edward II*, 529–39; Ormrod, *Edward III*, 55–7.
54. *Chron. Lanercost*, 256; *Chron. Scalacronica*, 97; *The Bruce*, 711.
55. Ormrod, *Edward III*, 64.
56. *Chron. Lanercost*, 253, 256–7.
57. *CDS*, ii, no. 1691; *ER*, i, 445; *RRS*, v, no. 405. Mar is only extant as a royal charter witness once, on 16 July 1328 at Berwick, during David Bruce's wedding (ibid., no. 352).
58. *CDS*, iii, nos 688, 741, 877, 1221; *RRS*, v, no. 72 (and notes); *SP*, iv, 11–13; Penman, *David II*, 40, 102–4. Sir Thomas Gray, privy to Atholl and Gloucester dealings with Duncan of Fife in the 1330s, would also assert that Duncan's daughter, Isabella '. . . had been destined to be sold in marriage to Robert the Steward of Scotland . . .' (*Chron Scalacronica*, 147–9). The Stewarts would acquire Strathearn (1358), Menteith (1361) and Fife (1362/71).
59. *RMS*, i, App. ii, nos 222, 405, 554. Similarly, Robert Bruce, the king's natural son, was granted a hostillage at Scone, perhaps to facilitate attending parliament (ibid., no. 462).
60. *RMS*, i, App. ii, no. 708; S. Boardman, *The Campbells, 1250–1513* (Edinburgh, 2006), 45–9.
61. *SP*, i, 435.
62. Ibid., v, 583; *RRS*, v, no. 497. Their son, Thomas, earl of Mar, would be seized as a minor by Edward III's invasion in 1334 and raised in England (Penman, *David II*, 8, 51). John Stewart (of Angus) would have a papal dispensation to marry Margaret Abernethy on 28 October 1328 (*CPL*, ii, 283): they would also have a son, Thomas.
63. *Chron. Fordun*, i, 354–6, ii, 346–7; Penman, *David II*, 47–8.
64. *Chron. Scalacronica*, 107. The Atholl and Umfraville heirs were minors at this point (*CDS*, iii, nos 900, 905).
65. *RMS*, i, App. i, nos 41, 79, 65, and App. ii, nos 40, 442, 454, 583, 640; *RRS*, v, nos 315–20; *ER*, i, 67, 86, 160.
66. *RPS*, 1327/4/1; *RMS*, i, App. i, no. 41.
67. *The Bruce*, 709–11; *Chron. Bower*, vii, 35; *ER*, ii, 622, and iii, 222; S. Boardman, 'Robert II (1371–90)', in M. Brown and R. Tanner, eds, *Scottish Kingship, 1306–1542: Essays in Honour of Norman Macdougall* (Edinburgh, 2008), 72–108, at 84, 103–4n.
68. *RRS*, v, no. 321; *RMS*, i, App. i, no. 65.
69. *True Chronicles of Jean le Bel*, 34–5; BN MS Fr. 2,643 f.6.
70. *CDS*, iii, nos 906–9, 914.
71. Ibid., no. 913; ibid., v, nos 1781–4, 1787, 1798.
72. Ibid., v, no. 1799.
73. *Rot. Scot.*, i, 212.
74. *CDS*, v, nos 1779, 1785–6, 3264–3282.

75. R. Nicholson, *Edward III and the Scots: The Formative Years of a Military Career, 1327–35* (Oxford, 1965), ch. v; Beam, *Balliol Dynasty*, 209–34.

76. *Chron. Lanercost*, 256–7; *Chron. Scalacronica*, 97–8; *The Bruce*, 711–13; *Chron. Fordun*, i, 351–2, ii, 344; *Chron. Bower*, vii, 35; Nicholson, *Edward III and the Scots*, 16–17; McNamee, *Wars of the Bruces*, 240–1; Barrow, *Robert Bruce*, 328–9.

77. *CDS*, iii, no. 919; *CPR, Edward III, 1327–30*, 139; *CCR, Edward III, 1327–30*, 157, 212. By September, Rhys ap Gruffudd was reported in south Wales plotting to restore Edward II (Phillips, *Edward II*, 548; Ormrod, *Edward III*, 66–7).

78. *ER*, i, 69, 196; J. O'Donovan, ed., *Annals of the Kingdom of Ireland by the Four Masters* (Dublin, 1848), i, 537; J. R. H. Greeves, 'Robert I and the De Mandevilles of Ulster', *TDGNHAS*, xxxiv (1955–6), 59–73; R. Nicholson, 'A Sequel to Edward Bruce's Invasion of Ireland', *SHR*, xliii (1963), 155, 161.

79. *Foedera*, II, ii, 683, 688–9; McNamee, *Wars of the Bruces*, 242–5; R. Frame, *English Lordship in Ireland, 1318–1361* (Oxford, 1982), 138–40, 174–83. One later Irish source asserts falsely that William de Burgh was captured by Edward Bruce in 1315; see B. MacCarthy, ed., *Annals of Ulster* (3 vols, Dublin, 1893), ii, 433.

80. *RRS*, v, no. 322, but with reduction for recent damages to Rathlin.

81. In 1328–29 Robert extended trade with Ireland buying grain, barley and hides for Cardross (*ER*, i, 132, 134, 135, 186, 189, 201, 214).

82. BL Add. MS, no. 25,459 fo.130, cited in Nicholson, 'A Sequel to Edward Bruce's Invasion of Ireland', 156.

83. *Chron. Lanercost*, 257; *True Chronicles of Jean le Bel*, 34.

84. *True Chronicles of Jean le Bel*, 39–41; *The Bruce*, 775–8. For this campaign see: Nicholson, *Edward III and the Scots*, ch. 3; McNamee, *Wars of the Bruces*, 240–2; Ormrod, *Edward III*, 65–6.

85. *True Chronicles of Jean le Bel*, 36, 42; *The Bruce*, 711–41.

86. *Chron. Lanercost*, 258; *Chron. Scalacronica*, 99; *True Chronicles of Jean le Bel*, 47–8.

87. *Chron. Scalacronica*, 99; *The Bruce*, 729; *RRS*, v, no. 323, 14 August 1327, at Melrose.

88. *True Chronicles of Jean le Bel*, 49; *Chron. Lanercost*, 260; *Chron. Scalacronica*, 99.

89. *Chron. Scalacronica*, 101, 235 n11; *Anonimalle Chronicle, 1307 to 1334*, ed. W. R. Childs and J. Taylor (Leeds, 1991), 138.

90. *RRS*, v, nos 323, 324.

91. The Archbishop of York and other officials reported that Robert conferred lands on his men in Northumberland; see J. Raine, ed., *Historical Papers and Letters from Northern Registers* (Rolls Series, London, 1873), 344–6, 349–50; *Rot. Scot.*, i, 221–2, 230. Barbour would write: 'And till thaim that war with him thar/the landis off Northummyrland/That neyst to Scotland war liand/In fe and heritage gave he' (*The Bruce*, 743).

92. *CDS*, iii, no. 940; Ormrod, *Edward III*, 67–8.

93. *CPR, Edward III, 1327–30*, 180, 191; Phillips, *Edward II*, 533–65; Ormrod, *Edward III*, 67–8.

94. *Rot. Scot.*, i, 222–3; *Chron. Scalacronica*, 101, 235 n12.

95. Penman, *David II*, ch. 1. For an alternative view, see N. H. Reid, 'Crown and Community under Robert I', in Grant and Stringer, eds, *Medieval Scotland*, 203–22.

96. *Anglo-Scottish Relations*, no. 40; *RRS*, v, no. 326.

97. *Foedera*, II, ii, 728; *Rot. Scot.*, i, 223–4; Nicholson, *Edward III and the Scots*, 47–8. Terms 4 and 5 also speak to the 'bodily service' and the 'giving freely of our goods, for the redemption of good peace' proposed by Robert in October 1320.

98. *RRS*, v, nos 329–3.

99. *Liber S. Thome de Aberbrothoc*, i, no. 356; Phillips, *Edward II*, 281–2, 299–300.

100. R. Lomas, 'St Cuthbert and the Border, c.1080–c.1300', in C. D. Liddy and R. H. Britnell, eds, *North-East England in the Later Middle Ages* (Woodbridge, 2005), 13–28.

101. A number of Scottish prelates had continued to visit and grant indulgences for pilgrimage to Durham, including Lamberton of St Andrews (DCM Misc Charters nos 805, 809–10, 812–13, 825, 830). In 1327 Patrick, earl of Dunbar, confirmed his family's past grants to nearby Coldingham (ibid., no. 791). At least eleven churches in St Andrews diocese were dedicated to St Cuthbert (often appropriated to Scottish abbeys) while St Andrews churches appropriated to Durham Cathedral priory itself included: Aldcambus, Lamberton, Holy Trinity Berwick, Edrom (Nisbet), Fishwick, Ayton, Swinton, Lennel and Stitchill; M. Ash, 'The Administration of the Diocese of St Andrews, 1202–1328', unpublished PhD, University of Newcastle-upon-Tyne (1972), appendix 5.

102. I am grateful to a 2013 conference paper by Dr Judith Frost (York), illustrating Nostell Priory's (west Yorkshire) approximately fifty confraternity agreements with other churches, including St Andrews Cathedral Priory and Jedburgh and Kelso Abbeys in Scotland. See also: J. E. Burton, 'Confraternities in the Durham *Liber Vitae*', in D. and L. Rollason, eds, *The Durham Liber Vitae* (3 vols, Woodbridge, 2007), i, 73–5, and ii, 26–32.

103. *RRS*, v, no. 340.

104. *CDS*, iii, no. 984 (Haltwhistle, restored 25 May 1329); ibid., nos 974 and 999 (Arthuret, restored January–February 1329); ibid., nos 1024, 1035–6 (Upsetlington disputed by Durham Cathedral Priory, 1330–31); *Foedera*, II, i, 762, and *CDS*, iii, no. 992 (Sir Henry Prendergast, restored in 1330, a Berwickshire landowner associated with Coldingham Priory); ibid., no. 982 (Douglas lands of Faudon, etc., in Northumberland restored, 12 May 1329).

105. S. Cameron and A. Ross, 'The Treaty of Edinburgh and the Disinherited (1328–1332)', *History*, lxxxiv (1999), 237–56. E. L. G. Stones first noted the likely inclusion of restoration of the disinherited but then changed his mind to assert its exclusion (ibid., 239 n6); E. L. G. Stones, 'An Addition to the *Rotuli Scotiae*', *SHR*, xxix (1950), 51–2; *idem*, 'The Anglo-Scottish Negotiations of 1327', *SHR*, xxx (1951), 49–54, at 53–4; *idem*, 'Historical Revision no. CCX: The Treaty of Northampton, 1328', *History*, xxviii (1953), 57. According to Nicholson, *Edward III and the Scots*, 57, the treaty made 'no mention' of the disinherited. Barrow, *Robert Bruce*, 335–9, argues that no part of the treaty dealt with the 'vexed question' of the disinherited at Robert's insistence, that his absence due to illness from the wedding of David and Joan at Berwick in July 1328 would see his nobles 'imprudently' agree to the partial restoration of Percy, Beaumont and Wake.

106. TNA SC8/269/13425 (a petition by the disinherited c.1328).

107. *RRS*, v, nos 342–5; *Anglo-Scottish Relations*, no. 41.

108. *Foedera*, II, i, 804, 806; *CDS*, iii, nos 1013, 1023–4, 1029, 1035–6.

109. *Foedera*, II, i, 804; *CDS*, iii, no. 1013.

110. *Chron. Scalacronica*, 101. Zouche surrendered his claim to Ralph Stafford, who joined Balliol's invasion in 1332 (Nicholson, *Edward III and the Scots*, 58).

111. *RRS*, v, nos 353, 457; *Anglo-Scottish Relations*, no. 42. On 16 July 1328 the king also confirmed a grant by Durham Cathedral Priory to Coldingham Priory (*RRS*, v, no. 352).

112. *ER*, i, 11; *RRS*, v, nos 333–4.

113. Stones, 'An Addition to the *Rotuli Scotiae*', 48; *idem*, 'The English Mission to Edinburgh in 1328', *SHR*, xxviii (1949), 121–32.

114. *ER*, i, 59–83. Perth returned £17 17s 11d, Edinburgh £7 16s 11d, and the rest less.

115. *RRS*, v, no. 343; *RPS*, A1328/3.

116. By autumn 1313 northern England complained that it had already paid out £20,000 in tribute to the Scots (*CDS*, iii, no. 337); £20,000 was roughly a quarter less than the sum Robert agreed with Harcla in 1323 (ibid., no. 803).

117. *RRS*, v, no. 335; D. E. R. Watt, *Medieval Church Councils in Scotland* (Edinburgh, 2000), 114–15.

118. *RPS*, 1328/1a; *RRS*, v, no. 563 (brieve of summons to the February 1328 parliament); A. A. M. Duncan, 'The Early Parliaments of Scotland', *SHR*, xlv (1966), 53–5.

119. *RRS*, v, no. 336; *CPL*, ii, 250; Watt, *Scottish Graduates*, 450–1.

120. *CDS*, v, no. 716; *Anglo-Scottish Relations*, no. 41(b); *RRS*, v, nos 337–9.

121. *RRS*, v, no. 340.

122. *Anglo-Scottish Relations*, no. 41(a). The importance of this concession was echoed in 1416 when, during (failed) talks about release terms for the captive King James I of Scotland that included demands of English overlordship, the Scots had Edward III's letter of 1328 read out and sealed in full council by clergy and papal notaries (*RPS*, 1416/1).

123. *Anglo-Scottish Relations*, no. 41(c); *RRS*, v, nos 342–5; *RPS*, 1328/3.

124. Ormrod, *Edward III*, 81–2.

125. *CDS*, v, no. 494; *Chron. Lanercost*, 260; *Chron. Scalacronica*, 101; *RRS*, v, no. 342. A Yorkshire source asserts that the Ragman Roll was burnt at a public gathering; *Chronica Monasterii de Melsa*, ed. E. A. Bond (3 vols, London, 1868), ii, 358.

126. *ER*, i, 238, notes a park made for jousting at Edinburgh (August 1329 account).

127. *PROME*, Edward III, 24 April–14 May, Introduction; Ormrod, *Edward III*, 72.

128. *RRS*, v, no. 341, issued during the Holyrood parliament, 16 March. There was also a grant on 18 March of Aberdeenshire lands to Mar's neighbour, Sir Edward Keith, in barony for the service of a knight (ibid., no. 347).

129. Ibid., no. 349; *Chron. Lanercost*, 272.

130. *ER*, i, clxxv–clxxxii; *RRS*, v, no. 348; *RMS*, i, App. ii, no. 712; *Registrum Episcopatus Aberdonensis* (2 vols, Spalding and Maitland Clubs, Edinburgh, 1845), ii, 38–68. Teinds would be the subject of dispute between William, earl of Ross (as justiciar north of Forth), the Aberdeen chapter and David II in the 1330s, 1340s and 1360s (*Regesta Regum Scottorum*, vi, nos 50, 57–8, 235, 426; *RPS*, A1330/1, 1344/6–7, 1360/4/1).

131. *RRS*, v, no. 346.

132. *Foedera*, II, i, 804; *RMS*, i, App. i, no. 76, and App. ii, nos 211, 451. Percy declared himself satisfied on 20 December 1330, when Edward III complained the same had not been done for Beaumont and Wake (*CCR, Edward III, 1327–30*, 174).

133. *ER*, i, 115; *RMS*, i, no. 28, and App. ii, nos 293, 504; Nicholson, *Edward III and the Scots*, 57–74.

134. Nicholson, *Edward III and the Scots*, 55–6; Ormrod, *Edward III*, 72–5.

135. Stones, 'An Addition to the *Rotuli Scotiae*', 48: the ratification took place 'in a chamber within the precincts of the monastery of Holyrood in Edinburgh where the lord king was lying'.

136. *Registrum Episcopatus Moraviensis* (2 vols, Bannatyne Club, Edinburgh, 1837), i, no. 224, which Moray would embellish 'for the soul of the most noble prince, the lord Robert, of good memory, king of Scotland', in October 1331 (ibid., pp. 291–3).

137. *ER*, i, 113, 149.

138. *Chron. Fordun*, i, 353, ii, 345; Watt, *Scottish Graduates*, 325. Lamberton's death may have been unexpected, as in April he was on a visitation to Arbroath Abbey.

139. *Fasti*, 262; *RRS*, v, 205.

140. *Vetera*, 239; *ER*, i, 109–11; Watt, *Scottish Graduates*, 36–8.

141. *RRS*, v, 203–5.

142. *ER*, i, 111–22.

143. Ibid., xxxiii–viii, lxxix–ci.

144. Ibid., 84–100, 102–8. The highest return came from Perth at £7 to £14, then Edinburgh and Dundee at £7; Aberdeen returned only 7s 4d.

145. *ER*, i, cvii–iii; 84–90. The burghs' contribution was set for 1329–30 as a feu of 500 merks.

146. *RPS*, 1318/22.

147. *Chron. Bower*, vii, 57–61; Penman, *David II*, 39–40. Signs of feud may lie in notes summarising an agreement about Invernessshire lands between Sir Andrew Murray and Hugh, earl of Ross, in the presence of the king on 3 July 1328, and further undated 'querela' (*RMS*, i, App. ii, nos 702–5).

148. Boardman, *The Campbells*, 47–8, 56–9; R. A. MacDonald, *The Kingdom of the Isles: Scotland's Western Seaboard, c.1100–c.1336* (East Linton, 1997), 184–96.

149. *Anglo-Scottish Relations*, no. 41(c); Barrow, *Robert Bruce*, 483 n93.

150. *Chron. Bower*, vii, 57–9.

151. *ER*, i, 181–2.

152. There survives a chancery brieve of circa 1328–29 to compel 'an abbot of B and the Master of the hospital to pay the tax granted by the clergy' (*Scottish Formularies*, no. E114): this must be the Cistercian abbey of Balmerino in Fife and the Master of the Hospitallers of St John in Scotland (which had properties worth about 600 merks per annum including tofts in all royal burghs).

153. *ER*, i, 137–202, with Galloway/Man at 151.

154. *Vetera*, 247, no. 485.

155. *ER*, i, 203–35.

156. *CDS*, iii, no. 983. Ormrod, *Edward III*, 72, suggests it 'is doubtful that Bruce paid anything other than a small contribution towards the promised reparations'. In fact, 5,000 merks would be paid on 24 June 1329, another 5,000 merks at Martinmas 1328, 10,000 merks on 24 June 1330, and the final instalment on 24 June 1331 (plus £200 in damages for splitting the first year's payment) (*ER*, i, cx–cxi, 211, 217, 221, 403; *Foedera*, II, ii, 762, 775, 793, 805).

157. *ER*, i, 137–54, 218. For discussion of the lavish display of this wedding, including sculpted desserts decorated with royal coats of arms, see L. Dean, L., 'Crowns, Processions and Wedding Rings: Continuity and Change in the Representations of Scottish Royal Authority in State Ceremony c.1214–c.1603', unpublished PhD, University of Stirling (2014), ch. 3, section 1.

158. Ormrod, *Edward III*, 72–3. Barbour has it that the king lay ill at Cardross but sent Moray and Douglas as his 'devisors' (*The Bruce*, 745–7).

159. TNA C81/155/1972; Cameron and Ross, 'The Treaty of Edinburgh and the Disinherited', 241 n5; Ormrod, *Edward III*, 73–8.

160. *RRS*, v, nos 352–4. The witnesses to these acts were Chancellor Twynham, Moray, Strathearn, Douglas, Keith, Robert Bruce, Alexander Seton, Malcolm Fleming and David Graham (all officers in Prince David's household), a Henry Balliol, Robert Lauder, Robert Menzies, John Forton, William Blount, Hugh Fleming and William Erskine.

161. *CDS*, v, no. 719; *ER*, i, 259; *RRS*, v, 156.

162. Ibid., nos 355, 358; *ER*, i, 199, 200; Nicholson, 'A Sequel to Edward Bruce's Invasion of Ireland', 157–60; McNamee, *Wars of the Bruces*, 252–3.

163. *Chartulary of St Mary's Abbey, Dublin*, ed. J. T. Gilbert (3 vols, Rolls Series, London, 1886), ii, 367; *The Annals of Loch Cé*, ed. W. M. Hennessy (2 vols, London, 1871), i, 607; Frame, *English Lordship in Ireland*, 187–9.

164. *Foedera*, II, ii, 758; *CDS*, iii, nos 1123, and iii, nos 967, 969, 1157; *MRH: Scotland*, 74. Murdoch, earl of Menteith, was also reported to be with Robert I in Ulster, hinting at his Argyll concerns (*ER*, i, 179, 210).

165. *Foedera*, II, ii, 745; *Calendar of Plea and Memoranda Rolls of the City of London, 1324–1457*, ed. A. H. Thomas (London, 1926), 63. On 7 January 1346 the 'Blak Rud' was still in the English Treasury from where it was passed to Edward III's household; see L. Rollason, 'Spoils of War? Durham Cathedral and the Black Rood of Scotland', in D. Rollason and M. Prestwich, eds, *The Battle of Neville's Cross, 1346* (Donington, 1998), 57–65.

166. P. Doherty, *Isabella and the Strange Death of Edward II* (London, 2003), 108; Ormrod, *Edward III*, 76–8. Isabella and Mortimer also procured two half instalments of the Scots' war indemnity, on 17 January and 3 April 1330 (*Foedera*, II, ii, 777, 785).

167. Nicholson, *Edward III and the Scots*, 61–3: a Lancaster confederate confessed to a plot involving Beaumont and Donald, earl of Mar, with Scottish support to restore a still-living Edward II.

168. *CDS*, iii, no. 110; *CPR, Edward III, 1327–30*, 547; Beam, *Balliol Dynasty*, 211–12.

### Chapter 11 *Beat the Devil*: Preparing for the End, 1328–29

1. *Chron. Scalacronica*, 101.

2. *Vetera*, 243, no. 476; P. D. Clarke, *The Interdict in the Thirteenth Century: A Question of Collective Guilt* (Oxford, 2007), 130. Randolph (d.1332) secured the same right in November 1329 (*CPL*, ii, 312).

3. *RRS*, v, no. 356; Watt, *Scottish Graduates*, 299.

4. *HMC*, iii, 404; *ER*, i, xciv, cxxv, 61, 91, 170, 271. Elizabeth left bequests to her servants (ibid., 90, 116, 216) and a frontal for the altar of St Mary at Dunfermline Abbey (ibid., 239).

5. *RRS*, v, 156 and nos 357–9.

6. Ibid., 156; *ER*, i, 123–36, account of 'Adam, son of Alan, constable of Cardross', 17 February 1327, to 30 July 1329. Adam was granted Lanarkshire lands on 12 November 1328 (*RRS*, v, no. 358).

7. *RSS*, v, no. 366.

8. Ibid., v, 156; *ER*, i, 213, where 'natale' means Nativity of Christ, not Robert's birthday or David's birthday as per the published *ER* index. John the apothecary was recorded as being paid £18 in fees, 66s in costs and a gift of £14 in the same section of the Chamberlain's account as Robert's stay at Glenkill (*ER*, i, 213).

9. Barrow, *Robert Bruce*, 414.

10. J. M. MacKinlay, *Ancient Church Dedications. Vol. II: Non-Scriptural Dedications* (Edinburgh, 1914), ii, 22–35; P. Yeoman, *Pilgrimage in Medieval Scotland* (London, 1999), 33–44; R. D. Oram, 'The Medieval Bishops of Whithorn, their Cathedral and their Tombs', in C. Lowe, ed., *'Clothing for the Soul Divine': Burials at the Tomb of St Ninian – Excavations at Whithorn Priory, 1957–67* (Edinburgh, 2009), 131–66.

11. M. Penman, ' "A fell conuiracioun agayn Robert ye douchty king": The Soules Conspiracy of 1318–20', *IR*, 50 (1999), 56–7.

12. *RRS*, v, 156–7 and 362–374(A); *RMS*, i, App. ii, rolls xvi, xvii and xviii cover acts issued during this ayre.

13. *ER*, i, 151–3.

14. *RRS*, v, nos 363–5; *RMS*, i, App. ii, nos 614, 618–19; *ER*, i, 297, 431.

15. *RRS*, v, no 366; *RMS*, i, App. ii, nos 620–1.

16. *ER*, i, 52, 196.

17. Ibid., 151–2; *Fasti*, 262. See also *CPL*, ii, 311, for 1329 papal mandates to confirm the appropriation, by the late Walter Stewart, earl of Menteith (d.1294, Murdoch's grandfather), and Andrew, late bishop of Argyll, of churches in Knapdale to the abbey of Kilwinning, plus Bishop John Lindsay of Glasgow's appropriation of Dumbarton church to Kilwinning.

18. *Regesta Regum Scottorum*, vi: *The Acts of David II, 1329–71*, ed. B. Webster (Edinburgh, 1982), nos 30, 39.

19. *ER*, i, 153.

20. Ibid., 151; W. Fraser, ed., *The Annandale Family Book of the Johnstones, Earls and Marquises of Annandale* (2 vols, Edinburgh, 1894), i, no. 15: Randolph's grant at Lochmaben on 29 March 1329 to John Carlisle of the park of Kinmount, witnessed by Roger Kirkpatrick, three de Boscos, William Carlisle, Adam de Corry and several others of Annandale.

21. *RRS*, v, nos 367–9; *RMS*, i, App. ii, no. 610.

22. *RRS*, v, nos 371–3; *RMS*, i, App. ii, no. 617.

23. *RMS*, i, App ii, nos 319–20, 622–24. A friar, Thomas of Mochrum (Wigtownshire), visited Robert at this time (*ER*, i, 152); Penman, *David II*, 23–4, 27, 39, 40–3.

24. Penman, *David II*, 40–1. Thus when a pretender Alexander Bruce appeared at court in 1344, he was executed at Ayr 'in the presence of Robert Steward, Malcolm Fleming [of Wigtown] and many others' (*Chron. Bower*, vii, 159). Moreover, later pro-Stewart chronicles increasingly smeared Alexander's memory; *Chron. Wyntoun*, v, 426; *Chron. Bower*, vii, 83–5; *Liber Pluscardensis*, ed. F. J. H. Skene (Edinburgh, 1877–80), 200.

25. *RRS*, v, no. 373. The king may also have issued, inspected or confirmed favour to these southwestern houses (*RMS*, i, App. ii, nos 81–6).

26. *RMS*, i, App. i, no. 99, and App. ii, no. 608.

27. *RRS*, v, no. 374; *RMS*, i, App. i, nos 99–102, and App. ii, nos 614–16, 620–1. To these should be added notes of undated minor grants of Dumfriesshire/Galloway lands (ibid., nos 607, 609–10, 612–13). For Whithorn Priory's lands, see *RRS*, v, no. 275; A. M'Kerral, 'The Kintyre Properties of the Whithorn Priory and the Bishopric of Galloway', *TDGNAHS*, xxvii (1948–9), 173–82 and 183–92.

28. *RMS*, i, App. ii, nos 92–95, gathers gifts to Whithorn by the Crown within a roll of monastic grants; see also ibid., nos 140–1, 144–6, 150, 157, 501.

29. *Liber S. Thome de Aberbrothoc* (2 vols, Bannatyne Club, Edinburgh, 1848–56), i, no. 37; *RRS*, v, no. 376.

30. *Foedera*, II, ii, 763.

31. Ibid., 762; *CDS*, iii, no. 982; W. Fraser, ed., *The Douglas Book* (4 vols, Edinburgh, 1885), i, 58.

32. *RRS*, v, no. 377.

33. Ibid., no. 381.

34. *ER*, i, cxxxvi, 314–22, 335, 336, 350, 351, 355, 361, 363, 374, 393 (the 'parva custama').

35. *Vetera*, 520, no. 498 (a papal dispensation of 6 August 1331); S. Cameron, 'Sir James Douglas, Spain, and the Holy Land', in T. Brotherstone and D. Ditchburn, eds, *Freedom and Authority: Scotland c.1050–c.1650: Historical and Historiographical Essays presented to Grant G. Simpson* (East Linton, 2000), 108–17.

36. *RRS*, v, nos 379–80.

37. *The Bruce*, 751; *RRS*, v, no. 458.

38. *The True Chronicles of Jean le Bel, 1290–1360*, trans. N. Bryant (Woodbridge, 2011), 52–3.

39. *RRS*, v, no. 378. The knights named as falling alongside Douglas in Spain on 25 August 1330 were Robert Menzies, William Sinclair, two Logan brothers and Simon Lockhart of Lee; only Sir William Keith survived; *Oeuvres de Froissart publiées avec les variantes des divers manuscrits*, ed. K. de Lettenhove and H. Baron (24 vols, Paris 1870–7), ii, 207–11, and xvii, 29–32; B. K. Heredia, 'Sir James Douglas's Death in Spain, 1330', *SHR*, 187 (1990), 84–95.

40. G. G. Simpson, 'The Heart of King Robert I: Pious Crusade or Marketing Gambit?', in B. E. Crawford, ed., *Church, Chronicle and Learning in Medieval and Early Renaissance Scotland* (Edinburgh, 1999), 173–86; A. L. Bysted, 'Indulgences, Satisfaction and the Heart's Contrition in Twelfth-Century Crusading Theology', in T. M. S. Letitonen et al., eds, *Medieval History Writing and Crusading Ideology* (Tampere, 2005), 85–93.

41. Prestwich, *Edward I*, ch. 3. C. A. Bradford, *Heart Burial* (London, 1933), 102–4, debunks the antiquarian supposition that Edward's heart was also taken to the Holy Land.

42. G. Ewart, D. Gallagher and P. Sherman et al., 'Graveheart: Cult and Burial in a Cistercian Chapter House: Excavations at Melrose, 1921 and 1996', *PSAS*, 139 (2009), 259–304; R. D. Oram, *The Reign of Alexander II, 1214–49* (Leiden, 2005), 221–2.

43. *ESSH*, ii, 425. In 1245 Dunfermline Abbey had been granted a slighter papal exemption from excommunication if it came into contact with excommunicates; *Registrum de Dunfermelyn* (Bannatyne Club, Edinburgh, 1842), no. 599. Stow church and Melrose Abbey were often used as venues for Scottish prelates to meet papal officials (*ESSH*, ii, 425; *RRS*, v, 152).

44. Clarke, *Interdict in the Thirteenth Century*, 235–59, esp. 246–7.

45. *ER*, i, 162, 216, 245, 267, 288, 298, 303, 340.

46. M. A. Penman, ' "Sacred Food for the Soul": In Search of the Devotions to Saints of Robert Bruce, King of Scotland, 1306–1329', *Speculum*, 88, 4 (2013), 27–8.

47. *RRS*, v, nos 382–3.

48. *Chron. Fordun*, i, 353, ii, 345; *Chron. Bower*, vii, 45.

49. C. Rawcliffe, *Leprosy in Medieval England* (Woodbridge, 2006), 53 n37.

50. Prestwich, *Edward I*, 515, 566–7.

51. *Chron. Lanercost*, 264; *Chron. Scalacronica*, 107; *True Chronicles of Jean le Bel*, 40, 52; *Chronica Monasterii de Melsa*, ed. E. A. Bond (3 vols, London, 1868), ii, 357–8.

52. *Chron. Lanercost*, 229.

53. M. Bloch (trans. J. E. Anderson), *The Royal Touch: Sacred Monarchy and Scrofula in England and France* (London, 1973), 11–12. But, like leprosy, this would have been infectious to those at court, with about fifteen people in contact with the king falling ill each year. Robert's Milanese physician, Maino Maineri, noted in his *Regimen Sanitatis* (1331), which must have drawn on his experiences in Scotland circa 1326–29, an earlier treatise he had written on treatment of consumptive ailments; C. Proctor, 'Perfecting Prevention: The Medical Writings of Maino de Maineri (d.c.1368)', unpublished PhD, University of St Andrews (2005), 9–10.

54. Bloch, *Royal Touch*, 12–27, 51–4.

55. Ibid., 55–60.

56. Ibid., 92–101. Good Friday would see the English king prostrated before a fragment of the Holy Cross as part of this rings ceremony.

57. *Chron. Fordun*, i, 279, ii, 274–5. Contemporary chronicles noted David I's shock at seeing his mother, (St) Margaret, and sister, Matilda (wife of Henry I of England), washing the feet of lepers and paupers (*Chron. Bower*, iii, 123–5).

58. Rawcliffe, *Leprosy in Medieval England*, 169 n57, 170–9; J. MacQueen, ed., *St Nynia* (Edinburgh, 1990), 113; R. Bartlett, ed. and trans., *The Miracles of St Aebbe of Coldingham and St Margaret of Scotland* (Oxford, 2003), xxxix, 91 (a cure of paralysis), 116–17 (a boy cured of leprosy by mixing water with dust from Margaret's tomb), 117 (elephantiasis), 129 (tumours), 137 (dropsy); *Lives of S. Ninian and S. Kentigern*, ed. A. P. Forbes (Edinburgh, 1874), 117 ('at his [Kentigern's] tomb sight is restored to the blind . . . cleanness of skin to the lepers').

59. *ER*, i, 70, 87, 163, 270, 300, 357; A.P. Forbes, ed., *Kalendars of Scottish Saints* (Edinburgh, 1872), 277.

60. *The Bruce*, 320–1.

61. G. M. M. Crane-Kramer, 'Was There a Medieval Diagnostic Confusion between Leprosy and Syphilis?', in C. A. Roberts, M. E. Lewis and K. Manchester, eds, *The Past and Present of Leprosy* (Leeds, 2002), 111–18; Rawcliffe, *Leprosy in Medieval England*, 87–9.

62. A. H. Dunbar, *Scottish Kings: A Revised Chronology of Scottish History 1005–1625* (Edinburgh, 1899), 144, lists six natural sons and daughters.

63. P. Hill, ed., *Whithorn and St Ninian: The Excavation of a Monastic Town, 1984–91* (Stroud, 1997), 542, 592; O. Lelong with J. A. Roberts, 'St Trolla's Chapel, Kintradwell, Sutherland: The Occupants of the Medieval Burial Ground and their Patron Saint', *Scottish Archaeological Journal*, 25 (2003), 147–63; R. D. Oram, 'Death, Disease and the Hereafter in Medieval Scotland', in E. J. Cowan and L. Henderson, eds, *A History of Everyday Life in Medieval Scotland, 1000 to 1600* (Edinburgh, 2011), 203–7, 213–14.

64. Barrow, *Robert Bruce*, 418–19, largely accepts that Bruce suffered from leprosy. Eczema, motor-neurone disease, cancer or a series of strokes have also been suggested as explaining Bruce's symptoms; see M. H. Kaufman and W. J. MacLennan, 'King Robert the Bruce and Leprosy', *Proceedings of the Royal College of Physicians of Edinburgh*, 30 (2002), 75–80.

65. *ER*, i, 176, 213, 238 and *ad indecim* for almonds and rice, ginger, galangal, pepper, mace, nutmeg, saffron, sugar, salt, verjuice, vinegar and olive oil; Rawcliffe, *Leprosy in Medieval England*, 205–51.

66. Prestwich, *Edward I*, 556–7.

67. *The Bruce*, 320–1, 780.

68. W. C. Jordan, *The Great Famine: Northern Europe in the Early Fourteenth Century* (Princeton, NJ, 1996), ch. 4; S. DeWitte and P. Slavin, 'Between Famine and Death. England on the Eve of the Black Death: Evidence from Paleoepidemiology and Manorial Accounts', *Journal of Interdisciplinary History*, xliv (2013), 51–4.

69. Proctor, 'Perfecting Prevention', 102: 'Robert the Bruce, who risked many dangers by eating moray eels which are by nature like lampreys ... caught in muddy and corrupt waters (the River Leven at Cardross?)'. For royal purchase of eels and lampreys including seven barrels for Cardross, see *ER*, i, 118, 119, 135, 140, 148, 157, 192, 195, 200, 219, 226.

70. H. Jardine, 'Extracts from the Report Made by Henry Jardine, Esq., His Majesty's Remembrancer in Exchequer, Relative to the Tomb of King Robert Bruce and the Church of Dunfermline, Communicated to the Society on 10 December 1821', *Archaeologia Scotica: Transactions of the Society of Antiquaries of Scotland* (1822), ii, 435–55.

71. In fact several different faces – one a scarred, bald leper (produced by allowing the artist 'licence' based on the 'knowledge' that Bruce had leprosy), another a clear-skinned, well-coiffed, square-chinned type; the latter face reconstructed by Edinburgh University Dental School was used for the Pilkington-Jackson statue of Bruce unveiled at the Bannockburn heritage site in 1964; see V. Møller-Christensen and R. G. Inkster, 'Cases of Leprosy and Syphilis in the Osteological Collection of the Department of Anatomy, University of Edinburgh, with a Note on the Skull of King Robert the Bruce', *Danish Medical Bulletin*, 12 (1965), 11–18; *Scotsman* (Edinburgh), 27 November 1996, 'The Bruce's Face Lives Again', in I. MacLeod and B. Hill, *Heads and Tales: Reconstructing Faces* (National Museums of Scotland, 2001), 35–44; M. Vanezis, 'Forensic Facial Reconstruction Using 3-D Computer Graphics: Evaluation and Improvement of its Reliability in Identification', unpublished PhD, University of Glasgow (2007), 42; M. H. Kaufman, 'Analysis of the Skull of Robert the Bruce', *History Scotland*, 8, 1 (January/February 2008), 22–30. And see Glasgow University's 2014 facial reconstruction project at: https://www.gla.ac.uk/news/archiveofnews/2016/december/headline_503481_en.html, accessed 27/4/18.

72. I. Fraser, 'The Tomb of the Hero King: The Death and Burial of Robert I, and the Discoveries of 1818–19', in R. Fawcett, ed., *Royal Dunfermline* (Edinburgh, 2005), 155–77, at 156–7, 172–5.

73. Simpson, 'The Heart of Robert I: Pious Crusade or Marketing Gambit?', 173–86.

74. S. Boardman, 'Dunfermline as a Royal Mausoleum', in R. Fawcett, ed., *Royal Dunfermline* (Edinburgh, 2005), 139–54, at 150.

75. P. Chalmers, *Historical and Statistical Account of Dunfermline* (2 vols, Edinburgh, 1844–59), i, 136–9; P. Yeoman, 'Saint Margaret's Shrine at Dunfermline Abbey', in Fawcett, ed., *Royal Dunfermline*, 79–88, at 80 (plan).

76. *Chron. Bower*, vii, 45.

77. Ibid., 35. Fordun's source might have seen Robert's tomb before the high altar, but as it blocked performance of the liturgy the tomb was later moved to the aisle (where Bower saw it), leaving behind only a slab covering the coffin. The tomb of Bishop Sinclair (d.1337) in Dunkeld Cathedral had to be moved from directly before the high altar as it obstructed the priests; see R. D. Oram, 'Bishops' Tombs in Medieval Scotland', in M. Penman, ed., *Monuments and Monumentality across Medieval and Early Modern Europe* (Donington, 2013), 185.

78. A. Erlande-Brandenburg, *Le Roi Est Mort: Étude sur les funérailles, les sépultures et les tombeaux des rois de France jusqu'à la fin du XIIIe siècle* (Paris, 1975), 81–5; P. Binski, *Westminster Abbey and the Plantagenets: Kingship and the Representation of Power 1200–1400* (London, 1995), ch. 3, 96–9, 103–23; R. Fawcett, 'Dunfermline Abbey Church', in *idem*, ed., *Royal Dunfermline*, 27–64, at 32 (plan), 51–2.

79. *ER*, i, pp. cxxi–cxxiv, 176, 193, 213–14; A. Fenton, ed., *Angels, Nobles and Unicorns: Art and Patronage in Medieval Scotland* (Edinburgh, 1982), 32 (C15); Fraser, 'Tomb of the Hero King', 156–7 (images), 170–2.

80. *Chron. Bower*, iv, 251.

81. Sir Joseph Ayloffe, 'An Account of the Body of King Edward the First, as it Appeared on Opening his Tomb in the Year 1774', *Archaeologia*, 3 (1775), 376–413.

82. J. Gregory, 'Exhumation and Re-interment of Robert Bruce', *Quarterly Journal of Science, Literature and the Arts*, 9 (1820), 138–42.

83. *Vetera*, 244–5, nos 480–1, 485; *CPL*, ii, 289, 291.

84. *Oeuvres de Froissart*, ed. Lettenhove, xvii, 30–1. Or Froissart muddled the date of Queen Elizabeth's funeral after her death on 26 October 1327.

85. Although on 23 June 1329 Randolph as Guardian was at Berwick to hand over the first peace indemnity payment (*CPR, Edward III, 1327–30*, 404).

86. *ER*, i, 215, 297.

87. Ibid., 176, 193, 215, 221, 243, 255. There is no indication that David Bruce was present.

88. M. Penman, 'A Programme for Royal Tombs in Scotland? A Review of the Evidence, c.1093–c.1542', in *idem*, ed., *Monuments and Monumentality across Medieval and Early Modern Europe*, 243–5.

89. The intensifying visual presence of Scotland's royal arms may also explain the appearance by 1329 of a pet lion in the king's household, perhaps, as Edward III later quipped to Philip VI, 'lions never harm a true king' (*ER*, i, 277; Bloch, *The King's Touch*, 148).

90. A. M. Morganstern, *Gothic Tombs of Kinship in France, the Low Countries and England* (Pennsylvania, PA, 2000), 3–8 and chs 4–5, 7.

91. Penman, 'A Programme for Royal Tombs in Scotland?', 246–7.

92. *ER*, i, pp. cxxi–cxxiv, 213–14, 221 (gold leaf from Newcastle and York), 243; Erlande-Brandenburg, *Le Roi Est Mort*, 81–5. And see Ian Fraser of Historic Environment Scotland's *Lost Tomb of Robert the Bruce* digital recreation on display in Dunfermline Abbey Church.

93. J. Burden, 'Rewriting a Rite of Passage: The Peculiar Funeral of Edward II', in N. F. McDonald and W. M. Ormrod, eds, *Rites of Passage: Cultures of Transition in the Fourteenth Century* (Woodbridge, 2004), 13–29; Phillips, *Edward II*, 550–60. Robert I's tomb was thus certainly not akin to the bronze effigy erected to Henry III in 1290 or the unadorned monumental box of Edward I, both in Westminster Abbey.

94. *ER*, i, 288.

95. Ibid., 450–1.

96. *Chron. Bower*, vii, 45–51. Compare this to Edward III's tomb epitaph: 'Here lies the glory of the English, the flower of past kings,/The model of future kings, a merciful king, the peace of the people,/Edward III fulfilling the jubilee of his reign,/Invincible panther, powerful as Maccabeus in war./While he lived in good fortune, his kingdom in goodness found new life./ He ruled valiantly, now let him be in heaven, a celestial king' (Morganstern, *Gothic Tombs of Kinship*, 117–19).

## Conclusion: Bruce Kingship and the Legacy of Scotland's Wars, c.1286–c.1329

1. *Chron. Bower*, vii, 47–51.

2. It is similar to the *Commendatio Lamentabilis in Transitu Magni Regis Edwardi*, eight laments for Edward I written circa 1307 that also idealised royal cooperation with a supervisory political community; see B. Weiler, 'The *Commendatio Lamentabilis* for Edward I and Plantagenet Kingship', in C. Given-Wilson, A. Kettle and L. Scales, eds, *War, Government and Aristocracy in the British Isles, c.1150–c.1500: Essays in Honour of Michael Prestwich* (Woodbridge, 2009), 114–30.

3. S. Mapstone, 'Bower on Kingship', and J. B. Voorbij, 'Bower's Use of Vincent of Beauvais', in *Chron. Bower*, ix, 260–80 and 321–8; J. Watt, 'Spiritual and Temporal powers', in J. H. Burns, ed., *The Cambridge History of Medieval Political Thought, c.350–c.1450* (Cambridge, 1988), 397–423; A. Rigaudière, 'The Theory and Practice of Government in Western Europe in the Fourteenth Century', in Jones, ed., *NCMH*, vi, 17–34; J. Watts, *The Making of Polities: Europe, 1300–1500* (Cambridge, 2009), 131–48, 254–6; J. P. Canning, *Ideas of Power in the Late Middle Ages, 1296–1417* (Cambridge, 2011), chs 1–3.

4. Prestwich, *Edward I*, 556–67; J. R. Strayer, *The Reign of Philip the Fair* (Princeton, NJ, 1980), *passim*; S. Kelly, *The New Solomon: Robert of Naples (1309–1343) and Fourteenth-Century Kingship* (Leiden, 2003), ch. 7.

5. *Barbour's Bruce*, i, 39–45; *The Bruce*, 14–30; *Chron. Scalacronica*, xlv–xlvii, 57 ('chronicles of his deeds'); *The True Chronicles of Jean le Bel, 1290–1360*, trans. N. Bryant (Woodbridge, 2011) ('the history commissioned by King Robert himself').

6. *Chron. Bower*, vii, 51–7.

7. *The Bruce*, 65, 73, 117, 133, 125, 397, 463, 537. A sixteenth-century manuscript of Fordun's chronicle contains an appended ballad naming Bruce as a Tenth Worthy; see A. McKim, ed., *Blind Harry, The Wallace* (Edinburgh, 2003), xiii, xx n19.

8. R. J. Goldstein, *The Matter of Scotland: Historical Narrative in Medieval Scotland* (Lincoln, NB, 1993), chs 5–7; C. Edington, 'Paragons and Patriots: National Identity and the Chivalric Ideal in Late Medieval Scotland', in D. Broun, R. J. Finlay and M. Lynch, eds, *Image and Identity: The Making and Re-making of Scotland through the Ages* (Edinburgh, 1998), 69–81; S. Foran, 'A Great Romance: Chivalry and War in Barbour's Bruce', in C. Given-Wilson, ed., *FCE*, vi (Woodbridge, 2010), 1–26.

9. The aftermyth of Robert Bruce deserves full study with a start made in M. Penman, 'Reputations in Scottish History: King Robert the Bruce (1274–1329)', *Études Écossaises*, 10 (2005), and *idem*, 'Robert Bruce's Bones: Reputations, Politics and Identities in Nineteenth-Century Scotland', *International Review of Scottish Studies*, 34 (2009), 7–73.

10. *RRS*, v, 178–97, plates at 179, 182.

11. Barrow, *Robert Bruce*, 351–80; R. Nicholson, *Scotland: The Later Middle Ages* (Edinburgh, 1974), 109–13; A. Grant, *Independence and Nationhood: Scotland, 1306–1469* (Edinburgh, 1984), 120–30; M. Brown, *The Wars of Scotland, 1214–1371* (Edinburgh, 2004), 224–6. By contrast, the English Crown created five new earldoms in Ireland circa 1315–29 and Edward II's frequent promotion of his favourites to high rank was highly provocative; see K. J. Stringer, 'States, Liberties and Communities in Medieval Britain and Ireland (c.1100–1400)', in M. Prestwich, ed., *Liberties and Identities in the Medieval British Isles* (Woodbridge, 2008), 16–21; B. Davis, 'Lordship in the British Isles, c.1320–c.1360: The Ebb Tide of the English Empire', in Given-Wilson, Kettle and Scales, eds, *War, Government and Aristocracy in the British Isles, c.1150–1500*, 158–60; R. R. Davies, *Lords and Lordship in the British Isles in the Late Middle Ages*, ed. B. Smith (Oxford, 2009), 21–4.

12. M. Hicks, *Bastard Feudalism* (London, 1995), 27–33; Penman, *David II*, 48 (1332, with the earls of Mar and Moray, Bruce of Liddesdale, Murdoch of Menteith and Alexander Fraser killed), 50–1 (1333, claiming Guardian Archibald Douglas of Lothian, William Douglas, Alexander Bruce, earl of Carrick, John Campbell, earl of Atholl, and the earls of Lennox, Ross and Sutherland), 136–7 (1346, claiming the earls of Moray and Strathearn, Marischal Robert Keith, Constable Gilbert Hay and at least twenty other named nobles).

13. A. Grant, 'Service and Tenure in Late Medieval Scotland, 1314–1475', in A. Curry and E. Matthew, eds, *Concepts and Patterns of Service in the Later Middle Ages* (Bristol, 2000), 170, 177–9; *idem*, 'Franchises North of the Border: Baronies and Regalities in Medieval Scotland', in Prestwich, ed., *Liberties and Identities in the Medieval British Isles*, 155–199, at 157–9, 167, 169, 173, 193–6.

14. *RPS*, 1308/1; *RMS*, i, App. i, no. 38.

15. Barrow, *Robert Bruce*, 372–6; *RRS*, v, 48–54.

16. S. Reynolds, 'Fiefs and Vassals in Scotland: A View from Outside', *SHR*, lxxxii (2003), 187–92.

17. By 1330 no account from the burgh of Wigtown had been rendered for 'seven terms', and the sheriff's recordable activity halted with Robert I's death (*ER*, i, 113, 181, 186–90, 195, 204, 303).

18. *RRS*, v, 785–6 (maps); N. A. T., Macdougall, *James IV* (2nd edn, East Linton, 1997), 282–7.

19. Penman, *David II*, chs 1–2; Brown, *Wars of Scotland*, ch. 11.

20. *SP* and *ODNB*, *ad indecim*, for these families. The same can be said of key English border families such as the Nevilles and Percies; see A. King, 'War, Politics and Landed Society in Northumberland, c.1296–c.1408', unpublished PhD, University of Durham (2001), 83–5, 256–9.

21. *RPS*, 1318/4–5, 1318/8, 1318/12.

22. M. Brown, *Disunited Kingdoms: Peoples and Politics in the British Isles, 1280–1460* (Harlow, 2013), 73; D. Carpenter, 'Scottish Royal Government in the Thirteenth Century from an English Perspective', in M. Hammond, ed., *New Perspectives on Medieval Scotland, 1093–1286* (Woodbridge, 2013); A. Taylor, *The Shape of the State in Medieval Scotland, 1124–1290* (Oxford, 2016).

23. C. R. Backman, *The Decline and Fall of Medieval Sicily: Politics, Religion and Economy in the Reign of Frederick III, 1296–1337* (Cambridge, 1995), xi, 24, 196, 243–4; C. Michaud, 'The Kingdoms of Central Europe in the Fourteenth Century', in Jones, ed., *NCMH*, vi, 743–4.

24. K. Pennington, 'Law, Legislative Authority and Theories of Government, 1150–1300', in Burns, ed., *Medieval Political Thought*, 424–53; A. Taylor, '*Leges Scocie* and the Lawcodes of

David I, William the Lion and Alexander II', *SHR*, lxxxviii (2009), 207–88; *idem*, 'The Assizes of David I, King of Scots, 1124–53', *SHR*, xci (2012), 197–238.

25. Lord Cooper, ed., *Regiam Majestatem & Quoniam Attachiamenta* (Stair Society, Edinburgh, 1947); *Scottish Formularies*, 1–121; *RRS*, v, 258–61.

26. B. Guenée (trans. J. Vale), *States and Rulers in Later Medieval Europe* (Oxford, 1985), ch. 8; Watts, *Making of Polities*, 23–34; S. Bagge, *From Viking Stronghold to Christian Kingdom: State Formation in Norway, c.900–c.1350* (Copenhagen, 2010), 11–14.

27. Duncan, *Kingship, ad indecim*, 'Scottish Church'; J. Watt, 'The Papacy', in Abulafia, ed., *NCMH*, vi, 158–63; P. N. R. Zutshi, 'The Avignon Papacy', in Jones, ed., *NCMH*, vi, 653–9; P. Herde, 'From Adolf of Nassau to Lewis of Bavaria, 1292–1347', in Jones, ed., *NCMH*, vi, 515–41; Watts, *Making of Polities*, 49–73, 118–22.

28. A. A. B. McQueen, 'Parliament, the Guardians and John Balliol, 1284–1296', in K. M. Brown and R. J. Tanner, eds, *Parliament and Politics in Scotland, 1235–1560* (Edinburgh, 2004), 29–50.

29. J. R. Maddicott, *The Origins of the English Parliament, 924–1327* (Oxford, 2010), 277–95, 332–58.

30. *ER*, i, 120 (barley for the Lent parliament at Holyrood, 1328), 121 (wine undrunk from the same assembly).

31. *RPS*, 1318/1.

32. See Appendix, adding fifteen or sixteen possible assemblies to those listed in *RPS*.

33. *RPS*, 1318/1–29; *RMS*, i, App. i, no. 59 (petition of the men of Galloway, 1324, for exemption from summary royal justice), and App. ii, nos 692–710 (seventeenth-century notes of petitions to parliaments).

34. E. A. R. Brown, 'Reform and Resistance to Royal Authority in Fourteenth-Century France: The Leagues of 1314–1315', in *idem, Politics and Institutions in Capetian France* (Great Yarmouth, 1991), 109–37; W. H. TeBrake, *A Plague of Insurrection: Popular Politics and Peasant Revolt in Flanders, 1323–1328* (Philadelphia, PA, 1993), 1–14; E. B. Fryde, 'The Financial Polices of the Royal Governments and Popular Resistance to them in France and England, c.1270–c.1420', in *idem, Studies in Medieval Trade and Finance, Vol. I* (London, 1983), 824–60, at 831–43.

35. G. L. Harriss, *King, Parliament and Public Finance in Medieval England to 1369* (Oxford, 1975), chs 2–4; Maddicott, *Origins of the English Parliament*, 333–58.

36. R. Bartlett, *The Making of Europe: Conquest, Colonisation and Cultural Change, 950–1350* (London, 1993), chs 11–12; W. Prevenier, 'The Low Countries, 1290–1415', in Jones, ed., *NCMH*, vi, 570, 575–7; S. C. Rowell, 'Baltic Europe', in Jones, ed., *NCMH*, vi, 719, 721; P. Linehan, 'Castile, Navarre and Portugal', in Jones, ed., *NCMH*, vi, 620–34; Michaud, 'The Kingdoms of Central Europe in the Fourteenth Century', 735–6, 743–4, 756–7; A. Forey, 'The Crown of Aragon', in Jones, ed., *NCMH*, vi, 596–7, 611–13; Backman, *The Decline and Fall of Medieval Sicily*, ch. 1; Kelly, *The New Solomon*, 5–8 and ch. 4; P. Engel, *The Realm of St Stephen: A History of Medieval Hungary, 895–1526* (London, 2005), chs 7–8.

37. J. P. Canning, 'Law, Sovereignty and Corporation Theory, 1300–1450', and J. Quillet, 'Community, Counsel and Representation', in Burns, ed., *Medieval Political Thought*, 454–76 and 520–73; Rigaudière, 'The Theory and Practice of Government', 38–41; Watts, *Making of Polities*, 270–81.

38. *RPS*, 1326/2.

39. Ibid., 1326/1.

40. Ibid., 1328/1.

41. Penman, *David II*, 170–2.

42. *The Bruce*, 749.

43. Maddicott, *Origins of the English Parliament*, 299–325, 332–66.

44. 'The Scottish King's Household and Other Fragments', ed. M. Bateson, *Scottish History Society Miscellany*, vol. ii (Edinburgh, 1904), 31–43; D. A. Carpenter, ' "The Scottish King's Household" and English Ideas of Constitutional Reform', part of *The Breaking of Britain: Cross-Border Society and Scottish Independence, 1216–1314* project, http://www.breakingofbritain.ac.uk/blogs/feature-of-the-month/october-2011-the-scottish-kings-household/.

45. *Parliamentary Texts of the Later Middle Ages*, ed. N. Promay and J. Taylor (Oxford, 1980), 91; W. C. Weber, 'The Purpose of the English *Modus Tenendi Parliamentum*', *Parliamentary History*, 17 (1998), 149–77.

46. *RPS*, 1315/1, 1318/3–4, 1318/15, 1318/23, 1318/26, 1318/29, 1323/7/4, 1328/1.

47. Contra Taylor, 'The Assizes of David I', 229. Under David II, who would require repeated parliamentary consent to raise taxes or customs to pay his annual ransom instalments, legislation would be recorded as 'agreed and assented by the three communities there present', 'expressly granted and also publicly proclaimed by the king in the said parliament at the instance of the three communities' or 'ordained and decreed by the said assembled and chosen three communities'; see M. Penman, 'Parliament Lost – Parliament Regained? The Three Estates in the Reign of David II, 1329–71', in Brown and Tanner, eds, *Parliament and Politics in Scotland, 1235–1560*, 74–103, at 90.

48. P. Binski, *Westminster Abbey and the Plantagenets: Kingship and the Representation of Power 1200–1400* (London, 1995); Kelly, *The New Solomon*, ch. 3 ('Piety'); G. Klaniczay (trans. E. Pálmai), *Holy Rulers and Blessed Princesses: Dynastic Cults in Medieval Central Europe* (Cambridge, 2002), 298–330; W. C. Jordan, *A Tale of Two Monasteries: Westminster and Saint Denis in the Thirteenth Century* (Oxford, 2009). And see T. Turpie, *Kind Neighbours: Scottish Saints and Society in the Later Middle Ages* (Leiden, 2015).

49. *CDS*, ii, no. 1827. And see now A. Ruddick, *English Identity and Political Culture in the Fourteenth Century* (Cambridge, 2013), esp. ch. 6.

50. *The Bruce*, 608–14.

51. *ER*, i, 255, 277, 450; *Chron. Bower*, vi, 367–75; F. Lachaud, 'Liveries of Robes in England, c.1200–c.1300', *EHR*, cxi (1996), 279–98; A. Ailes, 'Heraldry in Medieval England: Symbols of Politics and Propaganda', in P. Coss and M. Keen, eds, *Heraldry, Pageantry and Social Display in Medieval England* (Woodbridge, 2002), 83–105, at 85; B. A. McAndrew, *Scotland's Historic Heraldry* (Woodbridge, 2012), 24–32.

52. *Chron. Bower*, vii, 85 ('The double-dealing of King Edward [III]'); Edington, 'Paragons and Patriots'; M. H. Brown, 'The Development of Scottish Border Lordship, 1332–58', *HR*, lxx (1997), 1–22.

53. M. Vale, *The Origins of the Hundred Years War: The Angevin Legacy, 1250–1340* (Oxford, 1990), 244–52; Ormrod, *Edward III*, 82–3.

54. S. Boardman, 'Coronations, Kings and Guardians: Politics, Parliaments and General Councils, 1371–1406', in Brown and Tanner, eds, *Parliament and Politics in Scotland, 1235–1560*, 102–22.

55. R. J. Tanner, *The Late Medieval Scottish Parliament: Politics and the Three Estates, 1424–1488* (East Linton, 2000), *passim*; J. E. A. Dawson, *Scotland Re-Formed, 1488–1587* (Edinburgh, 2007), chs 1–3.

56. Barrow, *Robert Bruce*, 213.

# Acknowledgements

I would like to thank a number of people for materials, ideas and thought-provoking challenges relating to Robert I. Any errors of fact or interpretation which remain are very much my own.

I owe a substantial debt to my Stirling medievalist colleagues, Richard Oram and Alasdair Ross, and to Norman Macdougall, Michael Brown (St Andrews) and Stephen Boardman (Edinburgh), for discussions and references touching on many of the events, individuals and themes within this work. I am also grateful to colleagues for advice in relation to particular themes and documents: to the late Geoffrey Barrow (Emeritus, Edinburgh), Archie Duncan (Emeritus, Glasgow) and Dauvit Broun (Glasgow) for early critique of my work on the 'Soules conspiracy' – and to Dauvit for exchanges on a Bruce letter to Edward II; to Alexander Grant (Lancaster), Cynthia Neville (Dalhousie) and Elizabeth Ewan (Guelph) for early discussion of royal piety; to Roland Tanner, Alastair Mann (Stirling) and the other members of the original *Records of the Parliaments of Scotland to 1707* project for exchanges on Bruce councils and parliaments; to Frédérique Lachaud (Metz) for collaboration on the comparative study of succession; to Andy King (Southampton) for advice on northern England and Gray's *Scalacronica*; to David Simpkin (Birkenhead) on military matters; to Timothy Newfield (Princeton) and Philip Slavin (Kent) for environmental context (which I also owe to Richard and Alasdair at Stirling); to Richard Fawcett (St Andrews) for his expertise in relation to Bruce's tomb; to Alice Taylor (King's College London) for an early look at her work on medieval law reform; to my several fellow members of the Bannockburn Academic Advisory Panel to the National Trust for Scotland – Ted Cowan, Tony Pollard, Michael Prestwich, Fiona Watson and Richard Oram – for back-and-fore on Bruce's victory; and to my postgraduate students Amanda

Beam, Muir Shaw, SangDong Lee and Lucy Dean, whose work has questioned many aspects of this period. Stirling undergraduates and teachers of history have also contributed much to my reassessment of Robert's reign and I thank the cohorts of students who have taken courses since 2000 on the Wars or returned to Stirling for seminars.

I must also acknowledge assistance received at several repositories: the National Library of Scotland (Edinburgh), the National Records of Scotland (Edinburgh), the Royal Commission of Ancient and Historic Monuments of Scotland (Edinburgh), the British Library (London), the National Archives (Kew), the Archives Nationales and Bibliothèque Nationale of France (Paris), Durham Cathedral Muniments, Canterbury Cathedral Archives, and the special collections of St Andrews, Edinburgh and Stirling Universities. I am also very grateful for research funding from a number of bodies: the British Academy, the Institute of Historical Research, the Carnegie Trust, the Strathmartine Trust and the Hunter Memorial Trust. I owe much, too, to the support staff of History and Politics at Stirling. My great thanks also to the staff at Yale University Press: in particular to Heather McCallum for her advice and the opportunity to publish alongside the *English Monarchs* series; and to Richard Mason for his invaluable editorial input.

Finally, my parents, Catherine and Alan, have as ever been supportive in all possible ways, as have my in-laws Frank, Grazyna and Irena. Many thanks, too, to my sister, Alix, for timely pep-talks, and to my family generally for putting up with(out) me. The real medal for that of course belongs to my better half – Angela McDonald – who as a doctor of Egyptology understands the pressures of modern academia. Without her encouragement, humour, walkie-talkies with our dog Rosie and film choices throughout, this would not have been possible.

# Index

Abell, Adam, monk of Inchaffray/Kelso, chronicler (1530s) 219
Aberdeen, 52, 75, 84, 100, 210, 219, 247–8, 252, 286, 291, 298, 317, 349 n127, 352 n83, 358 n61, 360 n108, 364 n76, 375 n13, 378 n104, 379 n115, 381 n8, 397 n144
  bishop of 160, 162, 198, 210, 219, *see* also Cheyne, Henry; Kinninmonth, Alexander de
  retaken by Scots (1308) 107–8
  sheriff of 85, 223–4
  shire 4, 74, 85, 223, 234, 244, 246, 256, 289, 293, 296, 318, 363 n44/46, 364 n70, 365 n90/97, 381 n37, 393 n36, 397 n130
Aberdour, barony (Fife) 257
Aberlemno, thanage (Angus) 262
Abernethy, Sir Alexander 72, 76, 82, 85, 100, 109, 121, 126–30, 267, 359 n75, 366 n107
Abernethy, family/lordship 27, 234
Abernethy, Sir Hugh 27, 342 n67
Abernethy, Sir William 216
Aboyne, thanage (Aberdeenshire) 99, 168, 248–9, 278
Airth, Hugh of 138, 140, 163
Alexander I, King of Scots (r.1107–24) 305
Alexander II, King of Scots (r.1214–49) 17, 21, 35, 50, 83, 172, 186, 195, 198, 229, 245, 251, 255, 271, 272, 301, 357 n29
Alexander III, King of Scots (r.1249–86) 61, 83, 95, 109, 111–12, 114, 116, 182, 196, 215, 234, 245, 248, 270–1, 305, 350 n24, 357 n29, 373 n110, Plate 2

death (1286) 3, 20–1, 22, 316
children/issue 14–15, 17, 21, 26, 28, 46
homage to England (1251, 1278) 16, 32, 50, 68
succession plans (1281, 1284) 21–5, 28, 89–90
Alexander, Prince of Scotland (d.1284) 21, 22
almonds 264–5, 392 n182, 401 n65, *see also* 'king's dish', rice
Alnwick castle (Northumberland) 268, 279, 282
Amersham, Walter de, English Chancellor of Scotland (1296–7) 47
Angus, earldom or region 78, 114, 133, 153–4, 183–4, 196, 204, 206, 223, 225, 227, 234, 261–3, 267, 278, 286, 289, 311, 337 n6, 369 n29/31
  earls of, *see* Stewart, John of Bonkle; Umfraville: Gilbert d', Gilbert d', and Robert d'
animal pandemic 9, 40, 149, 166, 211–12, 227, 231, 237, 261, 286, 304, 321, 326, 378 n92, 381 n14, 393 n33, Plate 21b), *see also* cattle
Annan, burgh (Dumfriesshire) 64, 70, 71, 85, 131, 132
Annandale, (Bruce family) lordship 13–18, 41, 43, 49, 56–60, 63, 66, 68–9, 72, 98, 101, 103, 121–5, 156, 178–9, 205, 213, 216, 220, 225, 234, 298, 307, 314, 340 n38, 351 n40, 282 n92, 399 n20
  forfeited by Scots 44 (1296), 351 n38 (1302)
  granted to Thomas Randolph (c.1312) 124, 135, 147, 255, 363 n46
  inherited by RB (1304) 78–9, 86, 89

inquest on its liberties (1304) 78–9, 316, 354 n135
men of refuse to follow RB (1297–1302) 54, 64
Antrim (Ireland) 19, 103, 104, 157, 165, 294
'Appeal of the Seven Earls' (1290–1) 30
Applegarth, church (Annandale) 66
Aquinas, Thomas 310
Aquitaine, duchy of (France) 137, 218, 219, 250, 252, 263, 288
Aragon 6, 254, 259; James II, king of (r.1291–1327) 254
Arbroath (Forfarshire), abbey/abbot of 70, 75, 99, 106, 173, 182–3, 205, 227, 239, 251, 255, 268, 284, 291, 307, 326, 346 n53/55, 370 n56, 372 n109, 375 n13, 376 n57, 384 n111, 386 n31, 397 n138
  Abbot, Henry 346 n55; John 105, 109–10, 121, see also Bernard
  'Declaration of' (1320) 181, 200, 209, 212–22, 224–6, 228–9, 232, 282, 304, 323, 350 n25, 364 n76
  dedication to St Thomas (Becket) 17–18, 46, 55, 104, 131, 139, 186, 234, 299, 331
  houses RB's Chancery (1308–9) 105–6, 109, 131–2, 119–21, 123–4, 167–8, Plate 13
  tomb of William I at, enhanced by RB 167–8 (1315), 239 (1322), 373 n110
Ard, Sir Christian del (of the Aird, Invernessshire) 259
Ardnamurchan (Argyllshire), lordship 102
Ardrossan, Fergus of 165, 222
Argentein, Sir Giles d' (d.1314) 143, 310
Argyll, bishop of 19, 113, 128–9, 162, 201, 219, 245, 259–62, 280, 292, 297–9, 315; Bishop Andrew 251, 255, 399 n17
Argyllshire 3, 19, 52, 59, 100, 102, 111, 116, 123, 140, 153, 163, 165, 246, 251, 387 n62, 398 n164
Aristotle 310
army, English 65, 66, 119, 170, 172, 179–80, 182, 202, 203, 238,
  1296 campaign/at Berwick and Dunbar 44
  1297 campaign/at Stirling Bridge 56
  1298 Falkirk campaign 59
  1303–4 campaign 75
  1310 campaign 121–3
  1314 campaign/at Bannockburn 136–41
  1319 campaign/at Berwick siege 207–8, see also Myton

1322 campaign 236, see also Old Byland
1327 campaign/Weardale 281
army, Scottish 3, 65, 66, 73, 121, 170, 172
  1297 at Stirling Bridge 56
  1298 at Falkirk 59
  1314 at Bannockburn 140
  1315–18 on Irish campaign 165
  1327 in Weardale campaign 281
Arran, isle of 19, 26, 105, 114, 245, 297
Arthur, King of Britain 20, 105, 235, 311
Arundel, earl of 125, 127, 172, 178
Assisa Regis David (Scots law treatise, c.1318–20s) 155, 195, 316, 369 n39
Atholl, earldom of 3, 52, 101, 108, 114, 128, 129, 133, 153–4, 168, 178, 196, 198, 244–6, 295, 311, 337 n 6
  earls of Atholl, see Campbell, John; Strathbogie: David, David and John
Athy, Sir John d', English Admiral 188, 201
Avignon (Papacy) 61, 110, 157, 171, 175, 177, 179–81, 212–19, 226, 246, 248–50, 259, 263, 291, 306, see also Papacy, Rome
Ayr 54, 57, 99, 104–5, 123, 125, 132, 157, 168, 236, 245, 248, 286, 291, 298, 302, 353 n95, 361 n145, 385 n134, 399 n24
  1315 parliament at 134, 152, 159–65, 322
  castle 51, 57, 59, 70, 72, 75, 92, 119, 120, 124, 132, 204, 353 n94, 361 n145
  sheriff 27, 35, 38–9, 47, 60, 66, 74, 81, 84–5, 227, 292, 316, 342 n87, 352 n70
  shire 13, 18, 26, 52, 54–6, 70, 84, 99, 105–6, 128, 161–2, 171, 183, 221–2, 236, 244, 263, 353 n95, 372 n92, 374 n40, 389 n104, 391 n181

Baddeby, Alexander 115–16, 161, 247, 371 n72
Badenoch (Moray), lordship 100, 114, 128, 133, 152, 196, 224, 234, 256, 278, 337 n6, 375 n12
Baker, Geoffrey le, English chronicler 13
Balfour, Sir David 369 n24; Sir Michael 178
Balliol, Sir Alexander of Cavers 72, 82
Balliol, Edward, pretender King of Scots (r.1332–56) 4, 15, 31, 37, 250, 261, 274–5, 278, 289, 292, 312, 320, 370 n49, 380 n132, 382 n59, 383 n82, 396 n110
  birth (1283) 15, 28, 157
  marriage plans in Franco-Scottish treaty (1295) 42

Balliol, Edward (*cont.*)
  as English captive (1296–c.1313) 45, 53,
    65–6, 71–2, 80, 86, 136, 157–8, 162,
    175, 200 348 n124, 352 n98
  in household of Thomas earl of Norfolk
    202–3
  and 'Soules conspiracy' (1318–20) 202,
    203–5, 207, 213, 216–17, 219, 221,
    225–8, 240
  invades Scotland (1332) 178, 223, 227,
    269
  crowned at Scone (1332), 295, 310, 327
Balliol, family 170, 312, 314
Balliol, Sir Henry 169
Balliol, Sir John (d.1268), lord of Barnard
    Castle and Galloway 15, 215
Balliol, Sir John (d.1314), lord of Barnard
    Castle and Galloway/John I King
    of Scots (r.1292–6) 4, 82, 87, 90,
    105, 153, 161, 199–200, 202–3, 205,
    217, 223, 229, 239, 241, 244–5, 249,
    251, 257, 267, 286, 292, 306, 316,
    318–19, 323
  as English crown servant 15
  during interregnum (1286–90) 21, 23–4
  collusion with Bishop Bek (1290) 30–1
  in Great Cause (1291–2) 33–6
  inauguration (1292) 38, 96
  homage to Edward I (1293) 38, 68, Plate
    7
  as King of Scots 38–47
  and side-lined by Scots council of
    twelve? (1295) 42
  captured by Edward I – deprived as
    'Toom Tabard' (1296) 46
  diplomacy on behalf of (1298–1302)
    49–50, 52–3, 57, 59, 60–3, 64–9, 73
  released to Papacy (1299) 62
  transferred to France (1301) 69–71
  renounced by 'Declaration of the Clergy'
    (1309–10) 94, 111–12
  death in Picardy 157
Balliol of Urr and Redcastle, family 65
Balliol, Sir William 60, 92
Balmerino (Fife), abbey/abbot 178, 397
    n152
Balmyle, Nicholas de (d.1319), bishop of
    Dunblane, Chancellor 29, 66,
    105–6, 113, 179, 200, 214, 360
    n101, 380 n7
Balvenie castle (Moray) 106
Banff 75, 230, 286, 291, 360 n102
  castle 119, 120
  sheriff 85, 106, 107, 108, 224, 231
  shire 99, 107, 233, 234, 247, 259, 291,
    299, 360 n113

Bannockburn, battle of (1314) 181, 185,
    188, 199–200, 204, 222, 225–6, 238,
    249, 270, 279, 283, 290, 302, 307,
    311, 326–8, 330, 364 n76, 368
    n106/123, 367 n135/142/144, 375
    n13
  casualties 142–3
  consequences 1–5, 149–51, 164, 165,
    158–9, 162, 164, 166, 169, 171,
    174–5, 314–17
  day 1, 23 June 1314 141–2, Plate 14
  day 2, 24 June 1314 142–3
  encounter set (1313–14) 135–9
  English army at 136–41
  saints' relics at 106, 139, 142, 152–3, 186
  Scottish army at 140–1
  terrain at 141, Plate 14
Barbour, John, archdeacon of Aberdeen,
    poet/chronicler, author of *The Bruce*
    (1371–5) 93, 126, 141, 159, 166,
    173, 177–8, 330, 355 n146, 360
    n118, 365 n79, 367 n140/142, 368
    n150, 368 n19, 380 n149, 386 n8,
    394 n40, 395 n91, 397 n158
  distorts events 4, 13, 16, 36, 88–9, 102–5,
    107, 130, 135–6, 140, 185, 207–9,
    221, 225–7, 237–8, 269, 279–82,
    300–1, 303, 304, 310–11, 320, 327
  his sources 4, 88, 93, 101, 135, 137, 164,
    185, 209, 225, 320, 355 n141
  Stewart patronage of 5–8, 18–19, 313,
    323
Barclay, Sir David 111, 116, 179, 210, 224,
    266–7, 383 n78, 386 n31
Barclay, family 154, 163, 313
Barclay, Sir Hugh 247
Barclay, Sir Walter (sheriff of Aberdeen)
    108, 223, 224, 247
Barons' Wars (England, 1260s) 15, 29, 49,
    217, 319, 324, 342 n95, 345 n30,
    361 n147
barony, a royal grant in free (franchise/
    liberty) 3, 116, 161, 168, 177, 196,
    220, 233, 313, 374 n9, 396 n128, *see
    also* regality
Baston, Robert, English poet 143, 181, 327
Bathgate, barony (West Lothian) 161,
    204–5, 277
Beaton, Pàdraig, RB's doctor 257
Beaumont, family 204
Beaumont, Sir Henry de (d.1340) 141, 178,
    180, 240, 267, 279, 285, 289, 290,
    294–5, 365 n80, 386 n35, 389 n115,
    397 n132, 398 n167
Beaumont, Louis de, bishop of Durham
    180, 284, 386 n35

Beauvais, Vincent of 310

Bek, Anthony, bishop of Durham (d.1310) 30–1, 36, 58, 123, 348 n119

Bel, Jean le, Hainault chronicler (c.1290–1370) 8, 16, 150, 279, 281, 301, 307, 392 n11

Belhelvie (Aberdeenshire) 247

Ben, James, bishop of St Andrews (1328–32) 210, 258, 291

Ben Cruachan, battle of (1308/9, 'Pass of Brander') 107, 256

Benedict XI, Pope (1303–4), *see* Papacy

Benderloch (Argyllshire) 246, 297, 298, 387 n65

Benedictine, Chapter General 267, 274

Bernard (d.1331), abbot of Arbroath, Chancellor, bishop of the Isles/ Sodor 5, 8, 110, 113, 116, 121, 131–2, 138, 155, 158, 167–8, 170, 179, 200, 210, 214–15, 234, 262–3, 273, 287, 297–8, 302, 306, 318, 331, 348 n106, 364 n70, 365 n90, 368 n11, 371 n68, 373 n110/131, 380 n146, 388 n77, 391 n176
   loses abbacy of Kilwinning (1297) 55
   becomes Chancellor (1307–8) 55, 105
   becomes abbot of Arbroath (1309–10) 55, 109, 120, 124, 362 n19
   becomes bishop of Isles (1328) 104, 255–6, 291
   writes verse chronicle of RB's reign 107, 118, 130, 142, 355 n141

Berwick (-upon-Tweed) 4, 31, 40, 43, 49–50, 60, 71, 84, 92–5, 100–1, 121–3, 126, 274, 279, 281, 283, 286–7, 290–5, 301–2, 325–8, 343 n114, 345 n43, 348 n119, 351 n39, 368 n11, 372 n103, 375 n33, 380 n149, 383 n92, 385 n123, 387 n48, 390 n131/144, 394 n57, 395 n101, 396 n105, 402 n85, *see also* parliament (Scottish)
   attempted by RB (1312) 130; (1316) 169
   castle 44–5, 64, 72, 90, 119, 124, 136, 166, 179, 182, 184–5, 196, 205
   English siege (1319) 200, 206–8, 209, 210
   Great Cause at (1291–2) 33–7
   RB rebuilds (1318-) 185–6, 201–2, 211, 213, 219–20, 226, 231, 233–4, 236–7, 241–4, 252, 263–4, 300, 317, 376 n54, 379 n109
   retaken by Scots (1318) 137–8, 143, 164, 167, 170–1, 173, 177–90, 193, 196, 197
   sacked by Edward I (1296) 44–5, 90

sheriff of 185
   shire 100, 115, 116, 133, 150, 170, 181, 187, 234, 247, 262, 291, 535 n113, 362 n9, 373 n123, 380 n142, 390 n141, 396 n104
   wedding of David Bruce at (1328) 291–4

Betoigne, Sir David de, of Ethiebeaton (Angus) 100, 154, 369 n40, 379 n118, 382 n59

Bickerton, family (Annandale retinue) 25, 342 n74, 361 n141

Bickerton, Sir John 25

Bickerton, Sir Walter 98, 116

Biggar, Sir Nicholas, claimant to throne (1291–2) 35

Birgham, treaty of (1290) 28–30, 38, 61, 196–7, 217, 272, 322, 323

Bisset, Baldred, cleric, envoy to papacy (c.1299–1302) 61–2, 66–7, 74, 109, 181, 216, 232, 350 n24

Bisset, Sir Walter 85

Bisset, Sir William of Upsetlington 82, 284

Bisset of Aboyne, family 85

Bisset of Antrim, family 104, 157, 165

Blackness castle (W. Lothian) 71

Blount, family 154

Blount, Stephen, clerk 262

Blount, Sir William 262, 391 n170/171/173, 398 n159

Boece, Hector, chronicler (1465–1536) 219, 379 n115

Bohemia 6, 321

Bohun, de, Henry de (d.1314) 141, 327, 330, Plate 14, *see also* Hereford, earl of

Boniface VIII, Pope (1294–1303), *see* Papacy

Bonville, Sir John 230

Boroughbridge (Yorkshire) 184, 207, 236
   battle of (1323) 227, 386 n8

Boscos, de, family (Annandale retinue) 19, 363 n46, 372 n92, 399 n20

Bothwell castle (Lanarkshire) 2, 70, 138, 143, 245, Plate 15

Boutetort, Sir John de 151, 157 (Admiral), 163, 166

Bower, Walter, abbot of Inchcolm (d.1449), chronicler, author of *Scotichronicon*, 7, 50, 88–90, 143, 195, 221, 266, 269, 310, 355 n149, 375 n26
   reproduces Irish Remonstrance of 1317 181
   and RB consecration of St Andrews (1318) 186
   and RB's killing of Comyn (1306) 88–90

Bower, Walter (*cont.*)
  and RB's tomb, Dunfermline Abbey
    305–6, 308
  and 'Soules conspiracy' (1320) 227
Boyd, family 19, 313, 314
Boyd, Sir Robert of Kilmarnock 84, 85, 92,
    98, 102, 103, 111, 165, 220, 298,
    361 n147, 382 n57, 385 n139
  granted Noddsdale 99, 131, 161
Brabazon, Roger, English Chancellor 31
Brechin, bishop of 25, 29, 38, 75, 98, 113,
    220, 233, 234, 352 n75, 363 n46,
    365 n90/97, 369 n24, 385 n139,
    386 n31, 390 n147
Brechin, castle 75, 369 n31
Brechin, Sir David de (d.1320) 63, 100,
    126, 187, 196, 204, 267, 377 n81
  executed/forfeited for role in 'Soules
    conspiracy' (1320) 216, 222–3, 225–7
Bren, Llwywelyn (d.1318) 169
brieves 154–5, 163, 172, 233–4, 315, 323,
    369 n35, 376 n54, 378 n102/104,
    390 n142/145, 393 n38, 396 n118,
    397 n152
  1318 parliament legislation concerning
    194–8
Broun, Alexander 222–4
Broun, family 222, 314
Broun, Richard 222
Broun, Thomas 222
Broun, William 222
*Bruce, The*, poem (1371–5), *see* Barbour,
  John
Bruce, Alexander (RB's brother, d.1307) 18,
    49, 74, 81, 97, 98, 102, 104–5, 131,
    357 n34, 372 n92
  Cambridge graduation (c.1303) 4, 74
  Dean of Glasgow 49, 81, 97, 367 n34
  envoy to Ireland (1306) 104
  executed (1307) 131
Bruce, Alexander (Edward Bruce's
    illegitimate son, d.1333) 164, 168,
    221, 262, 280, 365 n98, 369 n31
  birth (c.1312–14) 136
  death 403 n12
  place in royal succession 136, 160, 198,
    277
  planned role in Carrick/Galloway 299,
    314
  pretender (1344) 399 n24
Bruce, Christina (RB's sister, d.1356–7) 98,
    103, 109, 126, 135, 151, 158, 161–2,
    201, 233, 257, 269, 296, 306, 355
    n159–60, 368 n13, 392 n18–19
  captured (1306) 103
  exchanged (1315) 515, 158

  granted Garioch (1315) 161–2, 201, 233,
    296
  marries Sir Andrew Murray (1326) 269
Bruce, David, RB's son and successor, *see*
  David II
Bruce, Edward (RB's brother, d.1318), lord
    of Galloway, earl of Carrick, High
    King of Ireland (r.1315–18) 75, 98,
    102, 104, 114, 120, 125–6, 130, 132,
    150, 152, 268, 280, 299, 360 n124,
    365 n90/97–8, 366 n106, 368 n11,
    370 n62, 372 n92, 375 n12/27, 384
    n102, 387 n59, 395 n79
  upbringing 15, 18–19
  in English royal household (c.1302–4)
    20
  in Inverurie campaign (1308) 106–7
  made Lord of Galloway (c.1309–12)
    110, 124
  made earl of Carrick (c.1313) 135, 328,
    330
  and Atholl marriage (c.1312) 135–6,
    138, 140–1, *see also* Bruce,
    Alexander (d.1333); Strathbogie,
    Isabel
  and 1315 act of succession 157–62
  invasion of Ireland (1315) 158–69
  1316 Irish campaign 171–6, 177, 179,
    182
  contact with Welsh (1316) 173
  1318 Irish campaign 187–90
  death at Faughart and consequences 4,
    190, 191–2, 196, 198, 200–2, 206,
    225, 229, 239, 244, 255, 311–12,
    314
Bruce of Annandale (and Carrick), family
    13–37
Bruce, Isabel (RB's sister, d.1358), queen
    (mother) of Norway 28, 35, 43, 129,
    192, 377 n80
Bruce, John (RB's son, d.1326) 252, 265–6,
    267, 312, 325, 328, 331, 388 n92–3
  birth (1324) 234, 243, 249–50
  death 268, 271
Bruce, Margaret (RB's daughter, d.1346)
    167, 191–2, 254, 279, 377 n79
Bruce, Marjorie (RB's daughter, d.1317)
    49, 55, 66, 72, 98, 191, 204, 322,
    364 n55
  birth of son, Robert 170
  captured (1306) 2, 103, 114, 126, 133,
    135, 139, 150
  death (1317) 174
  exchanged (1315) 151, 158
  marries Walter Steward (1315) 160–1,
    165

Bruce, Mary (RB's sister, d.1323), 98, 126, 135, 198, 249, 278, 306, 366 n106, 373 n112
and Atholl lands 168, 244
captured (1306) 103
exchanged (1315) 150–1, 158, 363 n55
marries Sir Alexander Fraser (1316) 168, 244
marries Sir Neil Campbell 102, 161
Bruce, Matilda (RB's daughter, d.1357) 234, 377 n79
Bruce, Maud (RB's sister, d.c.1329) 98, 249, 306, 364 n55, 371 n69
captured (1306) 103, 126, 135
exchanged (1315) 151, 158
marries Hugh Ross 161
Bruce, Neil (RB's brother, d.1306) 18, 87, 98, 102–3, 296
Bruce, Sir Richard (RB's uncle, d.1286), 14, 20, 25
Bruce, Robert II (d.c.1194), of Annandale 17
Bruce, Robert III (d.c.1191), of Annandale 18
Bruce, Robert IV (d.1226x33), of Annandale 14
Bruce, Robert V (RB's grandfather d.1295), of Annandale, the Competitor 5, 49, 51, 53, 54, 68, 84, 89–90, 112, 114, 134, 135, 188, 215, 340 n38, 342 n81
and Turnberry Band (1286) 25–6
disputes Maid of Norway's succession (1286) 13–30
and talks with Edward I/Norway (1289–90) 27–8
raises troops and sends 'Appeal of the Seven Earls' (1290–1) 29–30
and succession hearings (1290–1) 31–41
resigns kingship claim (1292) 36–7, 344 n139
death 43
Bruce, Robert VI (RB's father, d.1304), earl of Carrick 5, 90, 97, 229, 317, 340 n34, 342 n76, 351 n40
Carrick marriage and children (1272) 13–20
during Interregnum (1286–90) 21–4
during 'Great Cause' and under King John (1291–6) 25, 28, 35
denied vassal kingship (1296) 38, 45
death (1304) 78
as keeper of Carlisle (1296) 44, 48, 55, 57
loyal to Edward I (1296–1304) 40–1, 44, 47–9, 53–5, 57, 58, 60, 67, 71, 73, 76

resigns Carrick (1292–3) 36, 39
submits to Edward I (1296) 43
Bruce, **Robert** VII (d.1329), earl of Carrick (1293–1306), **Robert I, King of Scots** (r.1306–29)
*Thematic*:
character 9, 309–11, 327–31
dealings with council/parliament 317–24
epitaph 308–10
historiography of his reign 4, 32, 36, 61, 86–91, 215–17, 232, 337–8 n21–2/28–9, 339 n3, 351 n43, 396 n105
illegitimate children 400 n62
ill-health and cause of death 16, 107, 131, 138, 175, 191, 232, 236, 257, 262, 263–5, 266, 273, 276, 278, 281, 285–6, 290, 293, 296–302, 302–4, 331, 397 n135/158, 398 n8; and leprosy 302–5; skull and modern facial reconstruction 306, 401 n71
and law/justice 315–17, 353 n89/94/115, 354 n123, 362 n18
military skills 310–11, 326–8
patronage 311–15, *see also* patronage
piety 8, 55–6, 70, 91, 139, 142, 149–50, 167–8, 169–70, 185–7, 233–4, 264, 292, 296–302, 300–2, 310, 311, 316, 324–6, 329, 331, *see also* relics, saints
relationship with Edward Bruce 107, 110, 114, 124–5, 132, 134–6, 138, 160, 162, 164–5, 173–4, 179, 188
sisters' marriages and issue 102, 161, 168, 244, 269
succession 111, 113–14, 125, 132–5, 139, 157–62, 162, 167, 170–1, 174–5, 190–3, 198–9, 201, 217–18, 232–3, 240, 249–50, 257, 268–70, 287–8, 299, 316, 318, 321–3, 325, 328–9, 343 n126, 371 n66–7, 388 n94
*Chronological*:
birth (1274) 13–14
childhood and education 5, 13–20
early piety 17–19
fosterage to 'Gael' 18–19, 24
'bachelor' in Edward I's household 20, 29, 31–2, 34, 36
becomes earl of Carrick (1293) 36
homage to King John (1293), 39
marriage to Isabella of Mar (c.1293) 39
aids Edward I's conquest of Scotland (1296) 44–8
and 'Ragman' rolls (1296) 45–8, 288, 396 n125
rebellion under influence of Bishop Wishart (1297) 48–54

Bruce, Robert (*cont.*)
  resubmission to Edward I (1297) 48, 54,
    55–6
  (not) at battle of Falkirk (1298) 58–9
  as Guardian for King John (1298–1300)
    59–64
  resubmission (1301–2) 58, 65, 67, 69–73,
    78–9, 89, 93
  in Edward I's service (1302–4) 73–4
  marries Elizabeth de Burgh (1302) 72, 74
  inherits Annandale etc (1304) 78–9
  'Cambuskenneth Bond' with Bishop
    Lamberton (1304) 79–80, 89
  at March 1305 Westminster Parliament
    81–2
  kills John Comyn of Badenoch (1306)
    58, 86–91, Plate 9
  raises support and takes throne (1306)
    86–90
  inauguration or coronation? (1306) 5, 53,
    58, 92–5, 142
  excommunication (1306–8) 41, 90, 96,
    103, 106, 125
  exile (1306–7) 19, 98–104
  returns to Scotland (1307) 104
  guerrilla warfare (1307–8) 105–7
  first Parliament, St Andrews (March
    1309) 110–16
  and Scottish Church Council (1310)
    118–20
  and Edward II's 1310 campaign 120–4
  and Ordainer's crisis (1311–12) 124–8
  patronage and assembly (1311–12)
    128–33
  takes English garrisons (1311–12) 130–2
  October 1313 parliament: succession
    133–6; ultimatum to Scottish
    opponents 136–8, 151
  Bannockburn campaign (1314) 138–44
  kills de Bohun (1314) 141, 327
  takes part in raids into England
    (1314–15) 150–1, 156–7
  November 1314 parliament and act of
    forfeiture 150–6
  prepares for invasion of Ireland (1315)
    157–65
  April 1315 Ayr parliament (act of
    succession) 159–63
  Irish campaign (1315–16) 165–71
  and earl of Fife's submission (1315) 160,
    167
  Irish campaign (1316–17) 171–6
  and Thomas earl of Lancaster 172,
    179–80, 208
  recapture of Berwick and papal
    intervention (1317–18) 177–85

excommunication (1318–29) 175, 177,
    179, 185, 188, 190, 204–5, 212–13,
    214, 217, 218, 228, 243, 246, 249,
    250, 251, 253, 259, 263, 283, 287,
    289, 301, 302, 306, 320, 325, 328,
    359 n93, 400 n43
  defeat in Ireland (1318) 186–90
  and Dec. 1318 Scone parliament (act of
    succession, legal reforms, rumour-
    mongering, military service)
    190–202
  defense of Berwick (1319) 203–8
  Balliol plot or 'Soules conspiracy'
    (1318–20) 202–7, 211–27
  papal summons and 'Declaration of
    Arbroath' (1319–20) 213–19
  peace talks (1320–1) 227–34
  letter to Edward II (Oct. 1320) 229–30,
    384 n99, 395 n97
  Lancaster and Hereford rebellion (1322)
    235–6
  1322 English campaign and 'Chapter of
    Myton' 237–8
  and peace with Andrew Harcla (1323)
    239–41
  and 13-year-truce of Bishopthorpe with
    Edward II (1323) 242–3
  and birth of sons (1324) 243, 247–50
  and plans for Western approaches
    (1321–4) 243–7
  and peace talks (1324) 251–6
  and James Douglas 'Emerald charter'
    (1324) 252–3
  forfeits Ranald MacRuaridh (1325)
    259–62
  makes treaty of Corbeil with France
    (1326) 258, 263, 266–8
  at Tarbert (1326) 260
  and act of Succession (1326) 268–70
  and parliamentary grant of tenth for life
    (1326) 270–3, 286, 289, 292–3
  breaks Anglo-Scottish truce (1327)
    275–82, Plate 25
  in Ulster (1327) 280–1
  and Weardale campaign (1327) 281–2
  concludes Anglo-Scots peace treaty of
    Edinburgh-Northampton (1328)
    282–94
  and royal finances (1328–9) 283, 286,
    290–3 (1327–9)
  and son's wedding (1328) 293–4
  in Ulster (1328) 294–5
  and western approaches (1329) 296–9
  makes Whithorn pilgrimage (1329)
    297–9
  testament (1329) 300–1

death (7 June 1329) 302
burial/tomb 3–4, 153, 248, 258, 264, 266,
    300–2, 305–8, 325, 393 n32, 401
    n77, 402 n92–3, Plate 27a)
heart pilgrimage to Holy Land 300–2,
    305, 307, 399 n39, Plate 27b)
Bruce, Robert (RB's natural son, d.1332) of
    Liddesdale and Clackmannan,
    133–4, 221, 227, 262, 266, 269, 314,
    367 n148, 374 n9, 382 n57, 394
    n59, 398 n159
accuses Donald earl of Mar of treason
    (1332) 278
awarded Liddesdale 230, 290
death 313, 403 n12
pension (£500) 267, 271
Bruce, Thomas (RB's brother, d.1307) 17,
    18, 87, 98, 102, 105, 372 n92
envoy to Ireland (1306) 104
executed 131
Bruges (Flanders) 233, 290, 293, 307
Buchan, earldom 15, 100, 111–12, 114,
    230, 240, 256, 279, 290, 311, 315,
    337 n6
forfeiture and division by RB 129, 133,
    153–4, 158, 196, 224, 245, 248
'heirship' of (1308) 107–8
Buittle, lordship (Galloway) 15, 229, 257
castle 24, 125, 127, 130, 346 n62
Burgh, Elizabeth de, Queen of Scots
    (r.1306–27) 66, 98, 100, 103, 151,
    159–60, 260–1, 262, 265, 296,
    305–6, 322, 357 n47, 354 n54–5,
    372 n94, 398 n4, 402 n84
captured (1306) 103, 126, 133, 135,
    139
death 285–6
exchanged (1315) 2, 151, 158
marries RB (1302) 72, 74
pregnancies 160, 167–8, 174, 191, 232–3,
    247, 249–50, 388 n77
Burgh, Richard de, Earl, see Ulster, Richard
    de Burgh
burghs/burgesses 43, 82, 125, 190, 193, 211,
    247, 248, 286, 291, 298, 300,
    316–17, 322, 323, 354 n120, 397
    n145
Burgh Convention, Dundee (1325) 262
Burgh Convention, Edinburgh (1328)
    287
Burgh Convention, Stirling (1326?) 271
Burgh-by-Sands (Cumberland) 76, 105
Burgundy 6, 36
Bute, isle of 26, 102
Butler, Sir Edmund, Justiciar of Ireland
    173–4

Butler, of Scottish royal household 201,
    220, see also Menteith, Sir John;
    Soules, Sir William

Cadzow, barony (Lanarkshire) 158, 245
Caerlaverock castle (Dumfriesshire) 66,
    105, 125, 127, 131, 223, 225
Caerlaverock, William de 222, 223
Caithness, bishop 108, 111, 129, 152,
    162, 293
Caithness, earldom 107, 111, 233, 268,
    364 n76;
Caithness, Magnus, earl of (and Orkney)
    216
Cambridge 49, 74, 310
Cambuskenneth Abbey/abbot
    (Stirlingshire) 34, 79, 124, 140, 141,
    163, 266, 268, 273, 307, 311, 366
    n126, 367 n134, 369 n32, 390 n142,
    383 n21, Plate 17
Nov. 1314 parliament at 1–5, 7, 114,
    136, 149–56, 159, 197, 271, 320,
    Plate 18
'Cambuskenneth Bond' (1304) 1–2, 79–80,
    89, 93, 94
Campbell, Sir Arthur of Ardscotnish
    245–6, 260, 299, 387 n65
Campbell, Colin (Neil's son) 158, 189
Campbell, Donald 216, 246, 260, 262, 290,
    361 n126, 369 n28–9
Campbell, Dougal (Neil's brother)
    129, 245, 246, 262, 298
Campbell, Duncan 260, 297–8
Campbell, family 19, 104, 129, 140, 158,
    165, 166, 192, 245, 246, 251, 261–2,
    278, 307, 313, 314, 315
Campbell, John (Neils' son, d.1333), earl
    of Atholl, 102, 154, 161, 168, 198,
    244, 249, 269, 277, 278, 387 n58,
    403 n12
Campbell, Sir Neil, of Lochawe (d.1316) 3,
    158, 198, 245, 246, 262, 282, 297,
    362 n7, 367 n140, 370 n55
aids RB's escape (1306) 102
and Atholl lands 154, 161
death 168
marries Mary Bruce 102, 150, 161
Campbell, Nigel 116, 361 n126, 369 n24
Canmore dynasty (MacMalcolm) 3, 284
Canterbury, Archbishop 54, 55, 61, 118,
    125, 180
Canterbury, Cathedral Priory 17, 34, 40,
    43, 46, 62, 67, 72, 104, 123, 128,
    132, 182, 253, 299, 340 n33, 351
    n44, 365 n89, 376 n63
'Quitclaim' of (1189) 51, 68, 272

Canterbury, Cathedral Priory (*cont.*)
  RB grant of rings for altar (1302?) 74,
    340 n34
Cardross, (RB's manor house 1325-,
    Dumbartonshire) 131, 233, 245,
    260-1, 266, 285, 292, 294, 296, 299,
    302, 303, 362 n153, 391 n159, 395
    n81, 397 n158, 398 n6, Plate 24
Carlisle, Bishop John de Halton of 55, 99,
    138, 237
Carlisle (Cumberland) 15, 17, 41, 43, 47,
    65, 71, 88, 104, 119, 144, 150-1,
    164, 167, 171, 188, 204, 208, 225,
    228-9, 236-8, 242, 268, 280, *see also*
    Harcla, Andrew
  besieged by Scots (1315) 166
  Robert Bruce VI as keeper of Carlisle
    (1296) 44, 48, 55, 57
  RB's oath of loyalty at (1297) 46
Carlisle, family (Annandale retinue) 19,
    363 n46, 399 n20
Carrick, Adam of Kilconquhar, earl of
    (d.1271) 14
Carrick, Christina de 365 n98
Carrick, earldom 3, 5, 13-19, 25, 39-40, 43,
    49, 54, 56, 59-60, 66, 69-70, 73-4,
    78, 89-90, 98, 103, 104, 106, 122,
    136, 138, 140, 158, 165, 171, 175,
    192, 196, 221, 223, 238, 257, 269,
    291, 293-4, 297-9, 307, 314-16,
    351 n38, 359 n78, 393 n21
  attained by Bruces (1272) 14
  earldom's lands in Ireland 15, 165
  forfeited by Scottish parliament 44
    (1296), 351 n38 (1302)
  resigned to RB by father (1293) 36
  RB grants to Edward Bruce (1313) 135
Carrick, earls of, *see also* Bruce: Alexander
    (d.1333); David (II); Edward,
    Robert VI (d.1304); Robert VII
    (d.1329)
Carrick, family (Bruce retinue) 19
Carrick, Gilbert de 39, 114
Carrick, Marjorie, Countess of (RB's
    mother) 14, 17, 19, 26
Carrick, Neil, earl of (d.1256) 14, 19, 26
Carrick, Neil de 298 (RB's natural son?);
    son John 298
Carrickfergus, castle (Ireland) 173, 177,
    201, 294
  besieged by Edward Bruce (1315-16)
    166-7, 171
Carruthers, family (Annandale retinue) 19
Castile 6, 259, 321
castles, Bruce tactics towards 106, 124, 127,
    130-3, 137-8, 210, 243, 260-1

cattle 123, 127, 138, 150, 166, 184, 207,
    210, 282, 304, 378 n92, 386
    n17/20
  outbreak of cattle plague (1319-)
    211-12, 227, 237-8, 321, 326
Celestine V, Pope (1294), *see* Papacy
Chamberlain (Scottish) 125, 158, 161,
    168, 244, 262, 271, 273, 278, 324,
    *see also* Fraser, Sir Alexander;
    Lindsay, William; Peebles,
    Robert de
Chancellor/Chancery (Scottish) 5, 47, 55,
    98, 104, 105, 110, 120-1, 154, 158,
    162, 167, 171, 182, 187, 190, 195,
    218, 220, 248, 258, 262, 268, 273,
    288, 291, 316-17, 323, 324, *see also*
    Bernard, abbot of Arbroath;
    Twynham, Walter de
Charles IV, King of France (1322-8) 242,
    243, 254, 259, 261, 275, 276, 282,
    287-8, 392 n187
  alliance with Scotland (1326) 258, 263,
    267-8, 274, 283, 287-8, 322,
    323, 328
  death 287-8
  war of St Sardos with England (1324-5)
    250, 252
Charteris, Thomas, clerk 248, 290
Chester, earldom of 14, 254, 339 n9
Cheyne, family 224
Cheyne, Henry, bishop of Aberdeen 34, 85,
    113, 129, 160, 212, 214, 220, 248,
    256, 379 n115, 386 n31, 388
    n75/77
  pardoned by RB (1318/23) 198-200,
    246
Cheyne, Sir Reginald of Duffus 76, 82,
    85, 107, 129, 198-9, 200, 216,
    224, 388 n75
church, Scottish (*Ecclesia Scoticana*) 28,
    33-4, 44-5, 66-7, 96, 99, 112, 115,
    120, 149, 152-3, 155, 162, 175,
    189-90, 193, 205, 211, 214-15,
    218, 252, 255-6, 293, 305, 315,
    317-18, 325
  'special daughter' of Rome (1192-) 7,
    50-1, 61, 113, 217, 232
Church Council, Papal 73, 110-13, 115,
    179, 193
Church Council, Scottish 50, 115, 322,
    323, 329, 354 n120, 361 n130
  at Dundee (1310) 119-20
  at Edinburgh (1328) 286-7
  at Perth (1321) 233
  at Scone (1325) 258
  at Stirling (1326?) 272-3

chronicle(r)s 4, 7–8, 13–16, 32–3, 36, 44–5, 50, 57, 61, 65–9, 86–9, 97, 101, 125–6, 130, 139–43, 150, 159, 165, 207–8, 219, 221–4, 226, 232, 302, 308, 325, 338 n33, 355 n141, *see also* Bel, Jean le; Bower, Walter; Fordun, John de; Froissart, Jean; Gray, Sir Thomas; Guisborough, Walter of; Lanercost; Wyntoun, Andrew de; *Vita Edwardi Secundi*
  lost history/poetry of RB's life and reign 4, 16, 88, 150
Clackmannan, castle 131, 183, 269, 333, 342 n78, 374 n9
Clackmannanshire 292, 299, 363 n153, 387 n52
  sheriff of 116, 292
Clare, Thomas de of Thomond 25
Clement V, Pope (1305–14), *see* Papacy
Cleveland (Yorkshire) 236, 282
Clifford, Sir Robert (d.1314) 54, 57, 100, 122, 125, 126, 141, 143, 151, 359 n96
Clifford, Sir Robert (d.1344) 235, 386 n9
climate 8, 40, 51, 64, 78, 82, 107, 120, 133, 138, 141, 149, 163–4, 166, 178, 212, 227, 272, 304, 321
Cluny, barony (Aberdeenshire) 249, 278
Clyde, river 66, 245, 292
Coigners, Geoffrey de 97, 367 n33
coinage 320–1
Coldingham priory (Berwickshire) 183, 294, 300, 353 n115, 395 n101, 396 n104/111
  claimed by Dunfermline Abbey (1318–) 247, 274, 284, 394 n42
community (of the realm) 5–7, 23, 25, 29–30, 33, 42, 53, 56, 65–6, 77, 79–80, 83–4, 94, 100–19, 152–3, 156, 159–61, 174–5, 190–2, 195, 199, 215–18, 232, 251, 275–6, 278, 283, 287, 290, 311–12, 315–19, 329, 402 n2
Comyn, Alexander, earl of Buchan, Guardian (d.1289) 23, 27, 215, 296
Comyn, Sir Edmund of Cavers 128
Comyn, family and affinity 14–15, 21, 24, 26–31, 33–5, 38–9, 47–9, 52–3, 58, 63, 81, 84–5, 93, 99–100, 114, 126, 135, 140, 153–4, 222–4, 248, 271, 286, 292, 312, 314
Comyn, Sir John, lord of Badenoch, Guardian (d.1302) 23, 27, 30, 33, 53, 215

Comyn, Sir John, of Badenoch (d.1306) 53, 92–3, 96, 100, 106, 127–8, 141, 212, 317, 329–30, 340 n38, 352 n78, Plate 9
  heir to Balliols 37, 53, 80
  Guardian (1298–1300) 59–65, 67, 69, 73
  accuses RB and Bishop Lamberton of St Andrews of treason (1299) 60, 62–4
  victory at Roslin (1303) 74
  negotiates Scots' surrender (1304) 75–9, 83–5
  kingship deal with Bruce? (1306) 89–90
  killed at Dumfries by RB (1306) 5, 86–91
Comyn, John, of Badenoch (d.1314) 128, 134, 140, 143
Comyn, John, earl of Buchan (d.1308) 34, 44–5, 57, 59–60, 61, 63, 65, 67, 73, 80, 82–4, 89–90, 100, 129, 222, 248
  defeated at Inverurie by RB (1306) 107–8
Comyn, Sir Robert (d.1306) 87–8, 212
Comyn, Sir Walter of Kilbride (d.1314) 143, 363 n55
Comyn, Walter, earl of Menteith (d.1258) 200, 215; daughter Isabella 200
Comyn, William, bishop of Brechin 25, 29, 34, 38
Comyn, William, rector of St Mary's of the Rock (St Andrews), chronicler? 56, 58, 88, 347 n79, 355 n153
conciliar(ism) 7, 80, 318
Conor, battle of (Ireland, 1315) 168
Constable, hereditary royal household office of 3, 140, 290, *see* Hay, Gilbert
Copeland (Cumberland) 127, 150, 237
Corbeil, treaty of (Franco-Scottish, 1326) 4, 258, 263, 267–8, 274, 283, 287–8, 322, 323, 328
Corbridge (Northumberland) 123, 127
coronation, rite of 4, 68, 81, 118, 187, 249, 269–70, 278, 288, 305, 306, 324, 325, 356 n22/24, 357 n29/30/34, 393 n22, Plate 8
  RB in 1306? 95–7
Corrys, family (Annandale retinue) 19, 363 n46, 399 n20
councils, Scottish, *see* parliament (Scottish)
Coupar-Angus Abbey/abbot (Angus) 34, 83, 109, 172, 206, 266, 268, 278, 331, 346 n59, 354 n127, 373 n140, 379 n115, 392 n185, *see also* St Malachy
Courtrai, battle of (Flanders, 1302) 73, 151
Crabbe, John, engineer 207

Craigie (Fife) 116, 231

Crail (Fife) 279, 286, 291

Crambeth, Matthew de, bishop of Dunkeld
(d.c.1309) 33, 41, 43, 63, 66, 73, 80,
83, 84, 98, 113

Crawford, Hugh 223

Crawford, Sir Reginald 47, 85, 105, 162,
372 n92

Cressingham, Hugh de, English Treasurer
of Scotland (1296–7) 46, 51, 52, 53,
56, 57

Cromarty (Sutherland) 75, 116, 168, 247
sheriff of 168, 292
thanage of 168, 247, 259, 292

cross-border landholding 14, 43, 45, 66, 70,
82, 115, 126, 151–2, 156, 229, 240,
253, 255, 256
and 1328 peace 283–5, 288–9, 294,
299–300, 315, 327

crusades 2, 14, 26, 40, 79, 99, 110–11, 177,
187, 204, 232, 250, 300, 326, 339
n12
Bruce family and (1271–2) 15, 17–18
Edward I and (1271–4) 17–18, 31, 301
Philip IV of France and 110–11
Philip V of France and 215
Pope John XXII and 175, 214, 218
Robert I and 2, 79, 305, 307, 325

Cullen (Banffshire), church of St Mary's
230, 233, 285, 286, 291, 296

Culross Abbey (Fife) 131, 139, 186, 198,
237, 307, see also St Serf

Cumberland/Cumbria 8, 15, 17, 33, 40, 43,
45, 52, 56, 69, 75, 78, 105, 128, 138,
150, 156, 163, 205, 210, 229, 237,
239, 241, 254, 274, 282, 284, see also
tribute

Cumnock (Ayrshire) 74, 128

Cunningham, Sir James 230

Cunningham, lordship (Ayrshire) 74, 92,
221, 314, 369 n26
granted to Stewarts (c.1326) 192

Cupar (Fife) 171–2, 286
castle 101, 361 n141

customs (laws/institutions/government) 6,
7, 21, 22, 28–9, 30, 34, 54, 77, 83,
118, 155, 173, 272, 291, 315, 316,
317–24

customs (trade tariffs) 170, 186, 197, 231,
232, 241, 247, 248, 252, 258, 263–4,
270, 271, 274, 300, 320, 390 n144

Dalrigh, battle of (1306) 102

Dalswinton lordship (Dumfriesshire) 86,
110, 234
castle 92, 130

Dalton, Thomas de, bishop of Galloway
(d.1326) 238–9, 244, 255, 384 n106
appointed with Bruce support (1294) 41

Dante, Allighieri 11, 320

Darel, Sir Edmund 207

David, earl of Huntingdon (d.1219), 14, 17,
22, 23–5, 60, 71, 90, 119, 204, 249

David, Prince of Scotland (d.1281) 21, 22

David I, King of Scots (r.1124–53) 18, 22,
25, 82, 155, 229, 255, 284, 325, 387
n40, 400 n57
and Dunfermline Abbey 3, 131, 249,
305–6, 357 n29
as occupant of 'RB's grave' at
Dunfermline 306
a saint 3, 249
and Scots law 83, 195, 378 n94

David II (Bruce), King of Scots (r.1329–
71), son and successor of RB/
Robert I 4, 16, 19, 306, 307, 325,
328, 331, 338 n33, 340 n38, 383
n78, 385 n141, 388 n92–4, 390
n151, 394 n57, 396 n105, 398
n159/8, 402 n87, 405 n47
birth (1324) 4, 248–50, 252
coronation (1331) 269–70, 306, 356 n22
as earl of Carrick (1326–) 269, 271–2
marries Joan of England at Berwick
(1328) 291–4
tensions with nobles as king 135, 227,
240, 243, 260, 266–8, 277–8, 281,
283, 285–90, 297–9, 312–14, 323,
329, 397 n130, 403 n47
troubled succession 377 n79, 388 n45,
399 n24

'Declaration of Arbroath' (6 May 1320)
181, 200, 222, 224–6, 228, 229, 232,
282, 304, 323, 350 n25, 364 n76
authorship 215, 220, see also
Kinninmonth, Alexander
content 209–19
impact 219–21

'Declaration of the Clergy' (1309/10) 73,
110–13, 120, 160, 215, 218

'Declaration of the Nobility' (1309) 73,
110–11, 218

Denmark 6, 321

Derry, battle of (Ireland, 1318) 189

Dervorguilla, Countess of Galloway
(d.1290) 23, 24, 31, 34

Deskford, barony (Banffshire) 259

Despenser, family 179, 235, 267, 274–5,
379 n111

Despenser, Hugh the Younger, Chancellor
of England, earl of Winchester 210,
236, 242

Dingwall (Rossshire), thanage 108–9, 234, 292

Dischington, family 154

disinherited, the (nobles forfeited by RB) 126, 157–9, 175, 178, 204, 219–27, 230, 240, 253, 267, 274–5, 278, 396 n105/106/110, *see also* Beaumont, Henry; Ferrers; Macdougall, Alan and John; Macdowall, Dougal; Percy, Henry (d.1381); Stafford, Ralph; Strathbogie, David (d.1326) and David (d.1335); Umfraville, Gilbert d' (d.1381), Ingram and Robert; Wake, Thomas; Zouche

created by act of forfeiture (1314) 151–2
excluded from 1328 peace 283–5, 288–9, 294–5, 299–300
and 'Soules conspiracy' (1320) 200, 203, 205, 225
support Edward Balliol's invasion (1332) 310, 312, 315, 323, 327

Donald III, King of Scotland (r.1093–4, 1094–7) 90

Donydouer, Stephen, English Chamberlain of Scotland (1309) 115, 172, 177

Douglas, Archibald (James's brother), Guardian (1332–3) 227, 248, 280, 290, 382 n57, 403 n12

Douglas, Archibald (James's natural son) 384 n102

Douglas, family 4, 284, 311, 313, 389 n112

Douglas, Sir/Lord James, the Good (d.1330) 3, 54, 111, 130, 314, 320, 360 n108, 367 n131, 369 n24, 370 n62, 371 n68/78, 373 n131, 375 n31, 377 n81, 381 n9/22/23, 384 n102, 385 n139, 386 n31, 388 n84, 390 n137, 391 n176, 396 n104, 397 n158, 398 n159

joins RB (1306–8) 98, 106–7
re-takes Roxburgh (1314) 137
at Bannockburn 140, 143
regular witness to royal acts 174, 290, 293–4, 298, 302, 307
raids England (1315–) 150, 158, 166, 169, 225, 227, 229–31, 235–8, 248, 256–8, 260, 274, 276, 278
Guardian? (1317) 173
victory at Lintalee (1317) 178
and Berwick campaigns (131719) 181–2, 184–5, 187, 205–7, 209–11, 213–14, 216
made warden of Marches/Forest (1320) 220–2
granted 'Emerald charter' (1324) 213, 252–3, 313

to collect Galloway justice teinds 251
named as future Guardian in acts of succession (1318/1326) 191, 268–9
and Weardale campaign (1327) 280–2
recovers English lands (1328–9) 284, 300
takes RB's heart to Holy Land (1329–20) 301
death in Spain 399 n39

Douglas, Sir William (d.1297) 38, 52–5

Douglas, William (James's son, d.1333) 365 n98, 403 n12

Douglas, Sir William of Lothian 301

Douglasdale 252

Downie (Angus), thanage 116

Dryburgh Abbey/abbot (Peeblesshire) 171, 376 n64

Dublin (Ireland) 157, 164, 169, 171, 173, 177, 187–9, 371 n86

Duffus (Moray) 106, 107, 129

Dumbarton 72, 120, 132, 134, 158, 220, 233, 245, 285, 291, 292, 391 n159, 399 n17
castle 27, 51, 63, 75, 84, 95, 100, 114, 117, 132, 201, 227, 346 n62, 371 n82
sheriff of 134, 223, 245
shire 18, 131, 184, 231, 260, 266

Dumfries 79, 86–7, 90, 92, 125, 131, 132, 150, 156, 163, 223, 229, 286, 291, 353 n95, 354 n133, 355 n149/160, 369 n26/32
castle 69, 75, 86, 87, 92, 127, 130
Greyfriars church 5, 86–91, 106, 207, 355 n149, Plate 9
sheriff of 24, 46, 79, 86, 292
shire 98, 110, 205, 207, 210, 213, 220, 223, 225, 230, 233, 234, 252, 280, 290, 295, 297, 354 n133, 357 n33, 360 n108, 363 n46, 368 n8, 369 n26, 376 n57, 382 n57, 389 n104, 399 n27

Dun, Thomas, Scottish sea captain 132, 173, 187–8, 376 n49
captured (1317) 187–8, 376 n49

Dunaverty castle (Argyllshire) 92, 102–3, 245, 365 n3, 358 n69

Dunbar
battle of (1296) 44, 45, 47, 109, 204
castle 2, 15, 44, 138, 143, 390 n133
earldom of (March) 111, 124, 133, 205, 223, 337 n6

Dunbar, Patrick, IV earl (d.1186) 284

Dunbar, Patrick VI earl (d.1289) 27, 34, 43, 47, 48, 342 n81
seals Turnberry Band (1286) 25–6

Dunbar, Patrick VII earl ('of March')
  (d.c.1308) 72, 83, 84, 90, 100
  loyal to Edward I (1296) 43, 47
Dunbar, Patrick VIII earl (d.c.1340?)
  220–2, 234, 256, 266, 281, 284, 314,
  327, 348 n118, 352 n75, 368 n149,
  368 n18, 369 n29, 371 n68, 373
  n131, 376 n64, 377 n81, 382 n52,
  388 n84, 395 n101
  betrays 'Soules conspiracy' (1320) 219,
    220–2, 226
  helps Edward II escape Bannockburn
    (1314) 143
  helps take and defend Berwick for RB
    (1317–19) 152, 162–3, 179, 181–2,
    184, 187, 196, 207, 210, 214, 216
  loyal to Edward II 124, 126, 136, 138,
Dunblane, bishop of 110, 210, 214, 255,
  293, 363 n44/46, 381 n32, 388 n77
Dundalk (Ireland) 173, 189
Dundas (Lothian) 206, 231
Dundee 75, 82, 100, 114, 123, 138, 170,
  236, 258, 263, 286, 287, 291, 302,
  348 n114, 375 n12, 397 n144
  castle 60, 67, 119, 124, 128, 130, 183,
    204, 222, 224, 225, 262, 379 n116
  falls to Scots (1312) 124
  RB's 1313 parliament ultimatum 2,
    132–3, 135–6
  Scottish Church Council (1310) 119–20
Dundrennan Abbey (Kirkcudbrightshire)
  284, 295, 299
Dunfermline, Abbey/abbot (Fife) 20, 33–4,
  123, 154, 178, 186, 191, 227, 232–3,
  236, 244, 257, 266, 284, 300, 317,
  326, 342 n78, 352 n75/76, 354
  n127, 357 n29, 361 n143, 365
  n90/97, 367 n134, 368 n19, 375
  n30, 376 n54, 385 n123/125/137,
  398 n4, 400 n43, Plates 26, 27, see
  also St Margaret
  Abbot Hugh 132
  Abbot Robert of Crail 138
  Abbot Alexander de Ber 292–3
  Benedictine Chapter meeting (1326)
    267, 274
  Edward I resident at (1303–4) 76
  John de, clerk of Liverance 298
  Lady Chapel at 306
  parliament at (1296) 43
  royal mausoleum at 3, 46, 153, 285,
    305–6, 325
  RB at 116, 152, 167–8, 247, 270
  RB's children born at 249, see also Burgh,
    Elizabeth de, pregnancies
  RB's tomb 4, 131, 153, 248, 305–7

Dunipace (Stirlingshire) 307
Dunkeld, bishop of 100, 109, 110, 120, 139,
  178, 220, 233, 264 n70
Dunoon (Argyllshire) castle/constabulary
  245, 255
Duns, Park of (Berwickshire) 171, 185
Duns Scotus, John (d.1309?), cleric/
  academic 80
Dunstaffnage castle (Argyllshire) 107, 116,
  245, 246
Dunstanburgh castle (Northumberland)
  205, 268
Dunyvaig castle (Argyllshire) 104
Dupplin, battle of (1332) 313
Durham 17, 35, 44, 46, 123, 139, 156, 167,
  172, 180, 182, 202, 236, 239, 242,
  248, 254–5, 274, 281, 284, 287, 294,
  340 n30, 385 n4, 395 n101, 396
  n104/111
  County 170, 307, 386 n17; pays truce
    tribute to Scots 127, 150, 166, 184,
    282
Durham, bishop of 17, 30, 31, 172, 202,
  236, 239, 248, 254, 282, 385 n4, 385
  n35, see also Beaumont, Louis de;
  Bek, Anthony; St Cuthbert
  daughter house, Coldingham Priory 183,
    274, 284, 294, 300

Eaglesham, William de, archdeacon of
  Lothian (1315–24) 66
d'Eauze, Cardinal 178–82, 188
Edgar I, King of Scotland (r.1097–1107)
  284
Edinburgh 33, 75, 120, 124, 163, 181, 207,
  220, 234, 243–4, 263, 281, 285–7,
  291, 294, 300, 327, 391 n162, 396
  n114/126, 397 n144
  castle 2, 46, 50, 64, 69, 70, 88, 123, 169,
    206, 237, 272; retaken by Thomas
    Randolph (1314) 137–8
  parliament (or council) at: 169–70
    (1316); 180–1 (1317); 234 (1321);
    284–90, 323, 396 n128, 404 n30
    (1328, Holyrood)
  Scottish royal records/muniments kept
    at 354 n121, 378 n104
Edinburgh-Northampton, Anglo-Scottish
  peace treaty of (1328) 4, 18, 48, 126,
  240–1, 253, 272, 276, 312, 315, 323,
  396 n105/122, 397 n135
  concluded at Holyrood 282–94, 296
Edmund ('Crouchback'), prince of England
  (d.1296) 14, 15
Edward I, King of England (r.1272–1307)
  5, 110–12, 115, 121, 126, 134, 139,

151, 154–5, 157, 165, 177, 181, 185,
188, 200–1, 213–14, 217, 222, 224,
241–2, 251, 256, 271, 288, 301–4,
306, 310, 316, 322, 324, 330, 341
n54/56/60, 349 n140, 375 n33, 379
n122, 399 n41, 402 n93, 402 n2,
Plates 2, 7
crusade (1271–4) 17–18, 31, 301
Scottish succession and 'Process of
Norham' (1291) 13–17, 20, 23,
25–33, 35, 188
and 'Great Cause' 31–7
invades Scotland (1296) 44–6
seizes Scottish records/muniments/relics
(1296) 46–7
and Scots rebellion 1297 49–62
and political crisis in England (1297–8)
56–7
in Falkirk campaign (1298) 57–9
and 1301 reply to Papal bull *Scimus Fili*
(1299) 61–2, 64–76
and RB's resubmission (1301–2) 58, 65,
67, 69–73, 78, 79, 89, 93
and reconquest of Scotland (1303–4)
74–6
winters at Dunfermline Abbey (1303–4)
76
distrust of RB (1304–6) 75–84
and 1305 Westminster parliament 81–3
and Ordinance for government of
Scotland (1305) 83–5, 94, 96–8,
100, 102–3
reaction to death of John Comyn of
Badenoch (1306) 86–7, 90–1,
93–4
treatment of Bruce supporters/family
(1306–7) 98–103
death 104–5
model for RB as king 46, 76, 78, 81–3,
318–20, 327, 329
Edward of Caernarfon, Edward II, King of
England (r.1307–27) 192, 196,
209–10, 214–17, 221–3, 226,
228–33, 303, 308, 318, 320, 326–8,
359 n96, 362 n15, 364 n56/66, 367
n107/111/117/123, 369 n27, 370
n49, 374 n145, 375 n21, 379 n111,
382 n44, 384 n106, 385 n141, 386
n11/36, 388 n99, 389 n130, 395
n77, 398 n167
planned marriage to Maid of Norway
(1290) 27–30
service in Scottish wars (1300–6) 20,
74–6, 69, 73–6, 81–2, 98
at feast of Swans (1306) 98
accession (1307) 107, 111, 113

coronation (1308) 118; plans for second
with 'Holy Oil' of Becket (1318)
187
marriage to Isabella of France (1308) 73,
359 n96
1310 campaign 118–24
and Piers Gaveston 110, 118–23, 124–7,
364 n57
tensions with Thomas earl of Lancaster
(1310–11) 121, 122, 125, 127
and Ordainers/Ordinances 125–38
in civil war (1312) 124–7
and RB's ultimatum (1313) 136–7
and Bannockburn campaign (1314) 1–3,
8, 28, 136–44, 150, 151
tensions with Thomas earl of Lancaster
(1315–19) 150, 156–7, 159, 162,
164, 166–7, 169–70, 172, 175, 177,
179–80, 182–4, 187; reconciled
(1319) 188–9, 203, 208
reaction to Bruce invasion of Ireland
(1315–18) 169, 173–4, 187–8, 373
n121
and Berwick siege (1319) 202–8
and 'Soules conspiracy' for Balliol
(1318–20) 162–3, 190, 199–201,
202–7, 219, 224–5
and Papal censures of RB (1317–) 188,
204–5, 212, 218, 243, 250, 259,
390 n152
and Lancaster/Hereford rebellion (1322)
227–8, 234–6
in 1322 campaign 235–8
and Bruce-Harcla peace 239–42
takes 13 year Anglo-Scottish truce
(1323) 242–3
and Anglo-Scottish peace talks (1324)
243, 252–6
Anglo-French war of St Sardos
(1324–5) 250, 252, 258, 260–3,
267–8
invasion of Isabella and Mortimer
(1326) 274–5
deposition and death (1327) 275–82
Edward of Chester, Duke of Aquitaine
(1325), Edward III, King of
England (r.1327–77) 48, 134–5,
207, 224, 283, 287, 295–6, 299–300,
307, 326, 391 n170, 392 n11, 393
n27, 394 n62, 397 n132, 398 n165,
402 n89
tensions between Edward II and Isabella
261, 263, 267, 269
deposition of Edward II (1326–7) 274,
276, 277, 279–82
accession (1327) 276

Edward of Chester (*cont.*)
  and Weardale campaign (1327) 280–2,
    Plate 25
  and 'shameful peace' with RB (1328) 293
  letters of recognition of Scottish
    sovereignty (1328) 288–9
  supports Edward Balliol and
    disinherited (1332-) 223, 285, 310
Eleanor of Castile, queen of England
  (d.1290) 31
Elgin (Moray) 44, 75, 108, 123, 129, 133
  cathedral 290
Elphinstone (Lothian) 206, 233
English government of Scotland
    (occupation regime) 45, 47, 48,
    48–9, 51–2, 57, 59, 77, 80–1, 84–6,
    262, 271, 273, 352 n70
Eric II, King of Norway (d.1299) 21, 27,
    28, 35, 40, 43, 192, 377 n80
Eskdale (Dumfriesshire) 114, 131, 205
Estates-General (French) 73–4, 112
exchequer, Scottish royal 8, 18, 24, 35, 115,
    143, 154, 163, 186, 194, 244, 257–8,
    260, 264–5, 267, 270–1, 286, 304–5,
    311, 322–3 327, 396 n114, 397 n144
  accounts intromitted (1327–9) 290–3
  audit 133, 161, 165, 236, 250–1, 263,
    290, 296–7, 324, 375 n13
  Frescobaldi/Bardi loans? 393 n31/32
  'king's deposit', Lochleven (1327) 272
excommunication, *see also* interdict
  of RB 1306–8: 41, 90, 96, 103, 106, 125
  of RB 1317–29: 175, 177, 179, 185, 188,
    190, 204–5, 212–14, 217–18, 228,
    243, 246, 249, 250–1, 253, 259, 263,
    283, 287, 289, 301–2, 306, 320, 325,
    328, 359 n93, 400 n43

Falaise, Anglo-Scottish treaty of (1174) 18,
    46, 51, 68
Falkirk, battle of (1298) 57–9, 62, 139, 140,
    149
famine 9, 71, 107, 122, 209–10, 238, 261,
    286, 304, 321, 326
  1290s: 40
  1315–18: 141, 149, 158, 163–4, 166, 169,
    171, 174–5,
Faughart, battle of (Ireland, 1318) 4, 135–6,
    189, 190, 192, 199, 201, 209, 211,
    220, 268, 312, 326
Fenton, John 216, 223
Ferincoskry, thanage (Sutherland) 108–9,
    234
Ferrers, family 114, 153, 161, 204, 231
Ferrers, Sir Henry 295
Ferrers, Sir William 206

feud 196, 292, 378 n104, 397 n147
feu-ferme 213, 271, 300, 317
Fieschi, Cardinal 178–82, 188
Fife, Duncan earl of, Guardian (d.1289) 23,
    28, 30, 34, 342 n87
  murdered by Sir Hugh Abernethy
    (1289) 27
Fife, Duncan, earl of (d.1353) 95, 112, 144,
    152, 154, 163, 206, 213–14, 216,
    220, 223–4, 234, 256, 266, 284, 289,
    314, 368 n19, 385 n139, 386 n31,
    388 n77/84
  affinity (1332) 383 n82
  daughter Isabella 277, 394 n58
  declines battle? (1323) 178
  earldom promised to Robert Steward? 277
  joins Edward Balliol and disinherited
    (1332) 178, 196, 198–9
  marries Mary de Monthermer (c.1307)
    134, 172, 186, 192
  submits to RB (1315) 160, 167, 170
Fife, earldom/region 17, 25, 27, 40, 46, 76,
    78, 83, 109, 111, 116, 131, 133–5,
    140, 167, 175, 200, 223, 226, 244,
    266, 286, 289, 291, 337 n6, 368 n19,
    394 n58
Fife, Isabel of, Countess of Buchan, 95, 97,
    103
Fifeshire 224, 289
  sheriff of 178, 267, 383 n78
Fitz Gilbert, Sir Walter 152, 158, 244–5,
    367 n148, 370 n58, Plate 19
  surrenders Bothwell castle and Hereford
    earl to RB (1314) 143
Fitz Marmaduke, Sir Robert 167
Flanders/Flemish 6, 40, 54–6, 58, 137, 151,
    157, 163, 175, 207, 218, 230, 233,
    246, 259, 293
  Count Guy of 22
  Count Louis of 241
  Count Robert of 241
  marriage treaty with Scots (1281) 22, 24,
    31, 34, 37, 42
  peace with England (1323) 241–2
  rebellion against tax in (1323–8) 321
Fleming, family 19, 313
Fleming, Sir Malcolm of Biggar and
    Kirkintilloch (earl of Wigtown,
    1341-) 102, 158–9, 298, 313, 398
    n159, 399 n24
*Flores Historiarum*, English chronicle 86–7
Fochabers (Banffshire), thanage 128
Fordoun (Angus) 186
Fordun, John de (d.c.1388), chronicler
    (collator of *Gesta Annalia I* and *II*
    of *Chronica Gentis Scotorum*) 7, 14,

36, 42, 45, 50, 56, 58, 67, 88–90, 95, 102, 122, 174, 181, 212, 221, 269, 305, 310, 341 n63, 388 n8, 401 n77, 402 n7

forests 18, 40, 109–10, 183–4, 206, 220, 231, 247, 260, 262, 266–7, 271, 278, 340 n39, 360 n104, 375 n38, 381 n162, 391 n162, 396 n126, 399 n20
 RB appointed keeper of northern forests for Edward I (1304) 75, 82, 107, 354 n116/129

Forfar 109, 234, 239, 286, 291
 castle 100, 105, 109, 360 n118
 sheriff 60, 109, 391 n117
 shire 60, 109–10, 154, 257, 262–3, 271, 278, 291, 299

forfeiture, act of (Nov. 1314) 2, 3, 4, 99, 136, 151–5, 197, 244, 271, 311, 337 n6, Plate 18

Forres (Moray) 116, 123

Forth, river 75, 95, 119, 121, 128, 137, 138, 141, 155

Fortingall, lordship (Perthshire) 101, 128, 168

fosterage 18–19, 24, 164, 341 n46

Foullarton, family 154

France/French 14, 25, 27, 97, 119–21, 127, 132–3, 137, 151, 172, 175, 215, 218–19, 228–32, 303, 307–8, 311, 318, 325, 328, 338 n33, 392 n11, see also Charles IV; Isabella of France; Louis X; Philip IV; Philip V; Philip VI
 alliance with Scotland (1295) 41–3, 46, 48, 50–2, 54, 57, 59, 62, 64–7
 alliance with Scotland (1326) 267–8, 276, 287–8
 custody of John Balliol (1301–14) 69–74, 77, 111
 letter to Scots (1309) 110–11
 peace with England (1302) 73
 royal succession in 192, 371 n67
 tax revolts in (1314–15) 321
 war of St Sardos (1324–5) 238, 241–2, 246, 250, 252–4, 257–9, 261, 263, 274

Franciscans (Irish) 164, 173, 183

Fraser, Sir Alexander of Philorth (d.1333) 99, 108, 111, 129, 158, 247–9, 262–3, 273, 278, 360 n108, 361 n126/141, 369 n31, 373 n112, 403 n12
 appointed Chamberlain (c.1319) 210
 marries Mary Bruce (c.1316) 168
 oversees Atholl 168, 170, 192, 198, 214, 216, 224, 244
 son Sir John 249, 278, 373 n112

Fraser, family 34, 48, 85, 98, 154, 307, 313

Fraser, Sir Simon of Oliver Castle (d.1306) 67, 74, 75, 76, 79, 80, 99, 101, 103, 358 n53
 at battle of Roslin (1303) 74
 captured and executed 103

Fraser, William, bishop of St Andrews, Guardian (d.1297) 21, 23, 25, 27, 38, 41, 49, 50, 66
 denounced by Bruce of Annandale (1291) 34
 warns Edward I about Bruce and Balliol (1290) 29–31

Frendraught, Sir Duncan de 84, 85, 99, 106–7, 203, 224, 360 n108

Frere, William de, archdeacon of Lothian (1310) 66

Froissart, Jean, Flemish chronicler (c.1337–c.1405) 8, 307, 402 n84

Frosterley, marble (County Durham) 167, 239, 248, 307

Furness Abbey (Lancashire) 170, 237, 386 n16

galloglass 19, 26, 104, 106, 165, 173, 188, 189

Galloway, Alan, lord of (d.1234) 24

Galloway, bishop of 34, 41, 47 (Thomas de Dalton), 113, 238–9, 244, 254, 255, 293, 299, see also Whithorn
 archdeacon of, Gilbert 239

Galloway, lordship 3, 14–15, 23, 34, 58, 62, 63, 66, 69, 74, 82, 86, 100, 105, 107, 153, 157, 171, 173, 196, 203, 222–3, 226, 229, 238–9, 244, 251, 279, 289, 292, 297, 299, 337 n6, 377 n67, 389 n105, see also Balliol, John; Bruce, Edward; Dervorguilla, Countess of Galloway
 Alan, Lord of 24, 389 n105
 attacked by Bruces (1286) 24, 26
 attacked by Edward Bruce (1308–12) 110, 360 n124
 granted to Edward Bruce (1308/1312) 122, 124–5, 131, 133
 intended for Alexander Bruce? 314, 315
 men of, appeal to: Alexander II (1234) 389 n105; Edward I (1305) 82, 193; RB as king (1324) 251, 404 n33
 Thomas, Lord of 65

Garioch, lordship (Aberdeenshire) 15, 27, 35, 85, 107, 215, 247, 269, 277, 278, 337 n6, 386 n28
 granted to Christina Bruce (1315) 161–2, 201, 233, 296

Garmoran, lordship (Argyllshire) 259–60
Gascony (France) 41, 42, 82, 126, 254, 259, 261, 276, 288
Gaveston, Piers, earl of Cornwall (d.1312) 110, 118–20, 124–6, 364 n57
  and 1310 campaign 121–3
  executed 127
Gilsland (Westmorland) 209–10
Glasgow, burgh 93, 184, 245, 250, 285, 297
  bishop of 21, 32, 49–50, 55, 70, 81, 93, 94, 113, 115, 139, 158, 172, 177, 180, 184, 201, 205, 213, 214, 217, 225, 230–1, 245, 250–1, 255, 258, 285, 293, 297, 303, 370 n58, 380 n142, 381 n23, 390 n145, see also Donydouer, Stephen; Lindsay, John; Wishart, Robert
  cathedral 55, 70, 94, 158, 172, 370 n58
  RB absolved at (1306) 94
Glen Trool, skirmish (1307) 105
Glenarm, Larne (Ireland) 15, 165
Glenbreackerie (Argyll) 245
Glencarnie, Sir Gilbert de 85, 128, 162, 203, 256, 360 n102, 379 n118, 382 n59, 383 n69
Glencoe, lordship (Argyllshire) 102
Glendochart, lordship (Perthshire) 101, 128, 168, 183
Glenluce Abbey (Wigtownshire) 299
Gloucester, earls of (de Clare, lords of Thomond) 14, 19, 20, 31, 34, 36, 72, 76, 143, 151, 394 n158, see also Monthermer, Ralph de
  Gilbert de Clare, earl of (d.1314) 88–9, 135, 140, 141
  killed at Bannockburn 143
Gordon, Sir Adam (de), of Huntly 83, 84, 92, 152, 314, 327, 366 n111, 371 n78, 377 n81, 386 n20
  appeals to Edward II (1313) 136
  defects to RB (c.1313–14) 163, 181, 207
  delivers 'Declaration of Arbroath' to Avignon (1320) 219–20
  granted Strathbogie lordship 198, 231, 248, 278
Graham, Sir David 63, 79, 128, 216, 223, 233, 245, 261, 266, 371 n69, 398 n159
  accuses Malcolm Wallace (and RB) of treason (1299) 63
  exchanges Cardross with RB (1325–6) 245, 261
Graham, family 34, 154, 313
Graham, Sir John 114, 210, 216, 223
Graham, Patrick 216, 223, 24
Gray, Sir Thomas senior (d.c.1344) 20, 87,
141, 282, 355 n139, 361 n141, 365 n80 n97, 386 n20/24
Gray, Sir Thomas junior (d.1369), Northumbrian chronicler (Scalacronica) 8, 16, 20, 34, 45, 55, 62, 87–8, 130, 141–3, 150, 178, 184, 199, 206, 221, 225, 235, 281–2, 285, 288, 296, 394 n58
'Great Cause', Scottish succession hearings (1291–2) 13, 23, 31–7, 43, 49, 50, 51, 61, 65, 70–1, 94, 134, 157, 181, 188, 199, see also Norham, 'Process'
Greencastle (Ireland) 171, 295
Gruffudd, Rhys ap (d.1335) 275, 294, 395 n77
Guardians, Scottish 23–31, 35, 49–51, 56, 60–7, 69, 72, 75, 77, 80, 84, 89, 94, 106, 174, 177, 191, 199, 225, 254, 268, 285, 290, 292, 299, 300, 306, 312, 316, 318–19, 322–3, 329, 378 n95
  six elected (1286) 23–4
  William Wallace (1298) 57
  RB and John Comyn of Badenoch (1298) 59
  Bishop William Lamberton (1299) 63
  Ingram d'Umfraville (1300) 65
  John Soules (1301) 66
  John Comyn of Badenoch (1303–4) 76
  James Douglas and Walter Steward (1317) 173
  Thomas Randolph (1329–32) 269
  Donald earl of Mar (1332) 278
  Archibald Douglas (1332–3) 227
  Andrew Murray (1335–8) 269
Guines de, family 153
Guisborough (Yorkshire) 8, 16, 17, 43, 86, 340 n30
Guisborough, Walter of, English chronicler 8, 48, 51, 53–6, 59, 86–7, 119

Haddington (Lothian) 35, 182, 198, 206, 263, 286, 291, 379/109
Hainault (Low Countries) 6, 268, 302, 321, 370 n49, 391 n11
Hainault, Phillipa of, queen of Edward III of England 267, 276, 279, 281, 392 n11
Hainault, Count William of, aids Isabella and Mortimer (1326) 246, 267–8, 276, 392 n11
Hakon IV, King of Norway (r.1217–63) 158, 356 n24
Hakon V, King of Norway (r.1299–1319) 129
Halidon Hill, battle of (1333) 313

Haltwhistle (Northumberland) 18, 123, 284, 299, 384 n111

Hamelin of Troup, Banffshire, family 85, 108, 223, 234

Harbottle castle (Northumberland) 184, 210, 385 n138

Harcla, Sir Andrew, sheriff/earl of Carlisle (d.1323) 144, 204, 208, 262, 386 n33/36, 387 n39, 396 n116
    defeats Hereford/Lancaster (1322) 236, 238
    defends Carlisle (1315) 166–7
    peace with RB (1323) 239–42
    executed 242

Hartlepool (Yorkshire) 166, 184, 236

Hartness, lordship (Yorkshire) 15

harvest failure 40, 56–7, 78–9, 138, 141, 156, 163–4, 166, 171, 189, 211–12, 227, 271, Plate 21a), see also famine

Hastings, Sir Edmund 71, 85, 101, 114, 200, 370 n58; son, John 200

Hastings, family 161, 204, 341 n72

Hastings, Lord John 71–2

Hastings, Sir John, claimant to throne (1291–2) 35–6

Hastings, Sir Robert 60, 63

Hatfield Regis (Essex) 13–14, 17, 18, 78, 79, 253, 256, 389 n119

Hawick, barony (Roxburghshire) 230, 290

Hay of Errol, family 313, 320

Hay, Sir Gilbert of Errol (d.1333) 360 n108, 361 n126/147, 363 n44/46, 364 n70, 369 n24/28/31/33, 371 n68/78, 380 n146, 385 n139, 388 n84, 391 n176, 403 n12
    loses office to David Strathbogie, earl of Atholl (1312) 127–8; restored (1314) 140, 150, 153, 158, 170, 179, 181, 184
    regular witness to royal acts 150, 210, 214, 216, 220, 230, 233, 278–9, 290, 298, 302
    son Sir Nicholas 233, 256
    supports RB from 1306, appointed Constable 3, 83, 99, 102, 108, 110, 138

heart, RB's to Holy Land (1329–30) 305, 307, 325

Henry, earl of Northumbria (d.1152) 25, 229, 255

Henry I, King of England (r.1100–35) 400 n57; his queen, Matilda, daughter of Malcolm III 400 n57

Henry II, King of England (1154–89) 46, 50, 182, 187

Henry III, King of England (1216–72) 15, 17, 29, 42, 55, 96, 215, 350 n24, 402 n93

Hereford, earl of, Humphrey de Bohun (d.1322), 13, 31, 34, 76, 103, 121, 125, 127, 140, 158, 180, 207, 381 n11, 383 n92
    captured after Bannockburn (1314) 43–4
    rebellion with Lancaster, collusion with RB (1322) 227, 235–6, 238

Hermitage castle (Liddesdale) 205, 230, 274

Hexham burgh/priory (Northumberland) 127, 349 n130

historiography (of RB and Wars) 4, 32, 36, 61, 86–91, 215–17, 232, 337–8 n21–2/28–9, 339 n3, 351 n43, 396 n105

hobelar 19, 72, 123, 208, 236, 238, 363 n34

Holland 6, 321

Holland, Floris, Count of 34, 35

Holm Cultram priory (Cumberland) 17, 78, 229, 237, 340 n30

Holy Roman Empire/Emperor 6, 33, 42, 68, 216–17
    Henry VII of Luxembourg, Emperor (d.1313) 310, 318

Holyrood Abbey/abbot (Lothian) 34, 120, 237, 244, 286, 288, 289, 290, 317, 323, 326
    Abbot Simon de Wedale 244, 346 n59, 372 n109, 396 n128, 397 n135
    parliament at (1328) 284–90, 323, 396 n128, 404 n30

Holywood Abbey (of St Congall, Galloway) 229, 384 n102

Hospitallers, order of Knights (of St John) 156

Hothum, John de (bishop of Ely) 177, 207, 210

Hungary 6, 321, 325

Huntingdon, earldom of 14, 17, see David 'husbandmen' of Scotland 79, 82, 193, 211

Imperial law 21, 33, 36, 191, 226, 311

inauguration, Scottish royal 46, 52–3, 93–5, 167–8

Inchaffray Abbey/abbot (Perthshire) 98, 138, 139, 181, 183, 184, 219, 246, 305, 331, 358 n59, 359 n82, 376 n52, see Maurice, abbot of Inchaffray

Inchcolm Abbey/abbot of (Forth) 7, 139, 181, 305

Inchinnan, shrine (Renfrewshire) 303

Inchmahome, priory (Menteith) 109, 120

Inchmartin, Sir John de 83, 84, 216
Inchture (Forfarshire) 124
indemnity (war damages from Scots to
    English) 229, 261, 286
  £20,000 (1328) 272, 283
  40,000 merks (1323) 240
  tax of tenth for 'peace contribution'
    (1328–31) 286–7, 289, 291–4, 300,
    323, 397 n156, 398 n166, 402 n85
Innermessan (Wigtownshire) 238
Innerpeffray, Sir Malcolm 130
inquest (legal, landed) 116, 124, 133,
    154–6, 161–2, 167, 170–1, 178, 185,
    187, 192–7, 210, 230, 233, 236, 244,
    246, 262, 266, 273, 287, 315–17,
    353 n95, 354 n135
  Annandale (1304) 78–9
  Buchan (c.1315) 158
  Carrick (1293) 39
interdict, Papal on Scotland (1318–29) 185,
    187, 204–5, 213–14, 217, 218, 228,
    259, 283, 296, 301, 306, 325, 328,
    see also excommunication
Inverkeithing (Fife) 167, 178, 232, 234,
    236, 248, 286
Inverkip castle (Renfrewshire) 75, 92
Inverlochy castle (Invernessshire) 106, 107
Inverness 52, 128, 133, 252, 271, 286, 291
  castle 75, 106
  Scoto-Norse treaty of (1312) 129
  sheriff of 108, 292
  shire 100, 267, 397 n147
Inverurie (Aberdeenshire), battle of (1308)
    107–8
Ireland/Irish (Sea) 41, 64, 66, 70–2, 75, 82,
    116, 119–20, 123–4, 132, 136, 215,
    217, 224, 236, 238, 242–5, 260–1,
    275, 342 n76, 372 n92, 377 n69,
    395 n79/81, see also Faughart;
    O'Néill, Domnal; Remonstrance of
    the Irish Princes to Papacy (1317);
    St Malachy; Ulster, earldom of
  Bruce/Carrick family connections with
    15, 18–19, 24–6, 165
  Edward Bruce as High King (1315–) 19,
    167, 177–9, 181–2, 184
  Franciscans of support Scots 164,
    173, 183
  invasion by Edward Bruce (1315) 3, 6,
    167–71
  motives and preparation for Bruce
    invasion (1315) 157–65, 312,
    314–15, 328, 330
  RB in (1327/1328) 280–2, 287, 294–5,
    303
  RB letter to (1306) 103–7

Scots' campaign in (1316–17) 171–6
Scots defeated at Faughart (1318)
    186–90, 202, 206, 211
Irvine (Ayrshire) 54–6
Irvine, Sir William 247
Isabella of France, Queen of England
    (r.1308–27) 73, 126, 137, 219, 307,
    359 n96, 385 n141, 386 n24, 392
    n11, 398 n166
  and the disinherited (1327–8) 274–5,
    279, 285, 289, 294–5
  invades England with Mortimer,
    Edward of Chester and Hainault
    forces (1326) 274–5, 276–7, 282,
    286
  negotiates with Charles IV for Edward
    II (1325–6) 258–9, 263–4, 267
  negotiates with Scots at Berwick (July
    1328) 293–4, 296
  targeted by Scots (1322) 207, 238
  and Valois succession in France (1328)
    288–90
Isles (or Sodor, including Man), bishop of
    34, 104, 152, 162, 201, 219, 239,
    254, 297–8
  Bishop Alan 251, 255
  Bishop Bernard 291, 297–8, see also
    Bernard
  Bishop Gilbert 239, 255–6, 298, 386 n16

James I, King of Scotland (r.1406–37) 314,
    396 n122
James IV, King of Scotland (r.1488–1513)
    253, 314
Jedburgh (Roxburghshire),
  abbey/abbot 33, 172, 178, 255, 284, 300,
    352 n75, 354 n127, 385 n139, 389
    n125, 392 n185, 396 n102
  castle 59, 124, 200, 220, 222, 234, 236
  forest 150, 252
Joan, princess of England, queen of David
    II of Scotland 269, 286, 287, 289,
    297, 385 n141, 396 n105
  wedding to David Bruce (1328) 291–4
John I, King of England (r.1199–1216) 165
John I, King of Scotland (r.1292–96), see
    Balliol, John
John XXII, Pope (1316–34), see Papacy
Judas Maccabeus 81, 89, 217, 232, 309,
    311, Plate 5
justice 3, 178, 193–8, 238, 243–4, 247, 251,
    252, 257, 270–1, 310–11, 315–17,
    329, 378 n104
justiciar 47, 52, 84, 86, 92, 117, 154–5, 210,
    220, 222, 230–1, 246, 256, 289,
    314–15, 391 n176, 397 n130

Keith, Sir Alexander 85, 162
Keith, Sir Edmund 108
Keith, Sir Edward 108, 216, 233–4, 252, 256, 361 n126, 396 n128
Keith, family 313, 315, 320
Keith, Sir Robert, Marischal (d.1343–4) 3, 63, 67, 76, 83–5, 352 n75, 360 n104, 361 n126/147, 362 n154, 363 n41/44, 364 n170, 365 n90/97, 369 n24, 370 n62, 371 n68/78, 373 n131, 377 n81, 390 n146, 381 n23, 385 n139, 386 n31, 392 n12, 398 n159
   appointed hereditary Marischal (1308) 110, 116, 138
   defects to RB (c.1309) 108
   envoy to France (1326) 258, 263–4
   'justiciar of Scotia' (1310) 117, 155
   regular witness to royal acts 210, 214, 216, 220, 230, 279, 290, 298, 302
   role at Bannockburn (1314) 140, 142
   service in raids and Berwick campaign (1315–19) 150, 158, 162, 170, 174, 179, 181, 184–5, 187, 203, 206–7
   tailzie of family lands (1324) 252, 256
   to tutor Bruce princes (1325–) 257
Keith, Sir Robert, Marischal (d.1346) 252, 256, 403 n12
Kells, battle of (Ireland, 1315) 168
Kells, church of (Galloway) 239
Kelso Abbey/abbot (Roxburghshire) 34, 55, 70, 119, 204, 219, 230, 284, 385 n139, 386 n31, 389 n125, 396 n102
Kenilworth castle (Warwickshire) 275–6
Kildare (Ireland) 169, 280
Kildrum (Lanarkshire) 120, 228
Kildrummy castle (Mar) 102–3, 277
   held by RB for Edward I (1304–5) 75, 85
Kilmarnock, lordship (Ayrshire) 84, 85
Kilwinning, Abbey/abbot (Ayrshire) of 55–6, 70, 99, 119, 220, 348 n107, 372 n92, 399 n17, see also Bernard
Kincardineshire 109, 168, 223, 247, 248, 256, 262, 278, 292
'king's dish', of RB at Melrose Abbey (1325–) 263–4, 300, 307, 392 n188, see also almonds; rice
Kingston, Sir John de 64–5, 69, 85
Kinkell (Garioch) 215, 296
Kinloss Abbey (Moray) 75, 116, 371 n70
Kinninmonth, Alexander de 232, 291, 296, author of 'Declaration of Arbroath' (1320?) 215, 220, 229
   bishop of Aberdeen (1329–) 318, 381 n37

Kinninmonth, John de, bishop of Brechin 233
Kinnoul (Perthshire) 277
Kinross, burgh 3
Kinrossshire 3, 131, 154, 247
Kintyre, lordship (Argyll) 19, 26, 51, 92, 102, 104, 105, 159, 166
   granted to Robert Stewart (c.1321–4) 246
   held by Angus Og MacDonald (1306?) 102
   sheriff/sheriffdom of 38 (James Steward, 1293–6), 245, 246, 292, 297, 299
Kirkandrews, barony (Dumfriesshire) 220, 280, 290, 368 n8
Kirkcaldy, burgh 232
Kirkcudbright(shire) 66, 298
Kirkintilloch, lordship (Dumbartonshire) 99, 102, 159
Kirkmichael (Dumfriesshire) 231
Kirkpatrick, Sir Humphrey 233
Kirkpatrick, Sir Roger de 86, 150, 203, 210, 363 n46, 385 n139, 399 n20
Kirkpatrick, Sir Simon 207
Kirkpatrick, Sir Thomas 207
Knapdale, lordship (Argyll) 26, 114, 245, 379 n122, 399 n17
knighting 39, 98, 142, 149, 276, 327

de Lacy, family 168, 188, 189, 280
Lamberton, Sir Alexander 216
Lamberton, William, bishop of St Andrews (d.1328) 34, 152–3, 174, 179, 181, 206, 210, 318, 355 n153, 363 n46, 364 n70, 365 n90, 371 n68, 376 n58, 377 n81, 384 n109, 385 n139, 386 n31, 388 n77, 395 n101
   appointed by Wishart/Wallace (1297) 50, 57, 347 n79
   Guardian-in-chief (1299–1300) 63–5, 89
   suspected by Comyns (1299–1300) 61, 63, 65
   and Papal/French diplomacy (1299–1302) 59, 66, 69, 73–4
   'Cambuskenneth Bond' with RB (1304) 1–2, 5, 79–80, 83–5, 89–90, 93
   at RB's enthronement (27 March 1306) 93–7
   captured by English (Aug. 1306) 93, 97, 98
   paroled to 1309 parliament (St Andrews)/1310 Scottish Church Council (Dundee) 113, 116, 119–20

Lamberton, William (*cont.*)
  on parole from England (1306–c.1312)
    101, 103, 105, 109, 132, 140
  and consecration of St Andrews
    cathedral (1318) 185–6
  summoned to Rome (1318–20) 212,
    213–14, 220
  envoy to peace talks (1320s) 232, 242,
    250–1, 255–6, 258, 260,
  death 291, 297 n138
Lanarkshire 47, 60, 70, 99–100, 120, 137,
  158, 169, 221, 234, 256, 278, 286,
  299
  sheriff of 51, 52, 291–2, 316, 342 n87,
    352 n70
    Bruces as 27, 47, 53
    Hazelrig (d.1297) 84
    RB as (1304–5) 75, 81, 84
    Sir Walter Logan of Hartside 84–5,
      349 n126
Lancaster, earldom of 76, 254
Lancaster, Henry earl of (d.1328) 274, 276,
  290, 295, 385 n4, 386 n8, 398 n167
Lancaster, Thomas earl of (d.1322) 139,
  227–8, 242, 274, 373 n138,
  Plate 21c)
  Berwick siege (1319) 203, 205, 207–8
  death 236
  and English Council (1315–) 150,
    169–70, 172, 179
  kills Gaveston (1312) 127
  peace with Edward II (7–9 Aug. 1318,
    treaty of Leake) 188–9
  rebellion with Hereford (1322) 235–6
  rumoured collusion with RB (1317) 172,
    180, 182–4, 187
  talks with RB (1321) 208, 212, 234–5
  tensions with Edward II (1310–11)
    121–2, 125
Lanercost, chronicle of 8, 33, 40, 46, 52, 56,
  92, 104, 124, 127, 150, 156, 166,
  169, 183, 207, 209–10, 235, 237,
  275, 276, 281, 288, 344 n12, 346
  n52, 347 n89, 377 n72, 383 n82
Lanercost, priory (Cumberland) 8, 33, 40,
  52, 104
Largs, battle of (1263) 26
Larne (Ireland) 15, 172, 294
*Laudabiliter*, Papal bull (1155) 181–2, 375
  n26
Lauder, Sir Robert of the Bass 185, 242,
  256, 371 n78, 373 n116, 391 n176,
  398 n159
  justiciar of Lothian 230–1
law, Scottish, codification of 6, 7, 16, 83,
  154–6 (1314–18), 192–7 (1318

  parliament), 251, 311, 315–17, 318,
  320, 378 n96/102–3, 379 n109, *see
  also Assisa Regis David; Regiam
  Majestatum*
Leake, treaty of (1318) 188
Leinster (Ireland) 173
Lennox, Malcolm earl of (d.1333) 34, 39,
  56, 83, 138, 140–1, 352 n70, 360
  n108, 362 n44 n46, 364 n70, 365
  n90/97, 371 n68, 375 n13, 403 n12
  regular witness to royal acts 159, 165,
    184, 216, 223, 228, 231, 234, 245,
    256, 278
  as sheriff of Clackmannan (1309) 116
  as sheriff of Dumbarton (1318/21)
    200–1, 233
  supports RB and aids RB's escape (1306)
    98–9, 102, 104, 106, 111
leprosy (and RB) 302–5, 341 n59, 400
  n53/57/58/64
Leslie, Andrew 216
Leslie, family 249
Leslie, Sir Norman 85, 108
Lesmahagow priory (Lanarkshire) 70, 119,
  170, *see also* St Machutus
Libaud, Piers 169, 206, 373 n116
Liddesdale, lordship 3, 150, 156, 158, 198,
  213, 230, 278, 280, 290, 314, *see also*
  Bruce, Robert (d.1332); Soules,
  William
  castle 205, 225
Lindores, priory (Fife) 17, 41, 119, 362
  n154
Lindsay, Sir Alexander (d.1309) of
  Barnweill, Crawford and the Byres
  54, 55, 79, 85, 95, 98, 102–3, 111,
  115, 117
  with RB at Dumfries (1306?) 355 n149
Lindsay, Sir David of Barnweill 102, 117,
  210, 216, 223, 230
Lindsay, family 313, 315
Lindsay, James 116, 158
Lindsay, John, cleric, rector of Ratho (W.
  Lothian), elect/bishop of Glasgow
  158, 180, 186, 214, 375 n22, 390
  n142, 381 n23, 387 n41, 399 n17
  Glasgow provision settled with Anglo-
    Scots truce (1323) 220, 225, 230–1,
    234, 241
  recognises crown's control of
    ecclesiastical temporalities (1325)
    258
  resigns Dumfriesshire barony of
    Staplegordon to RB (1320) 213
Lindsay, Sir Philip 158, 213, 370 n44
Lindsay, Sir Simon 158, 225, 234, 370 n44

Lindsay, William, cleric, rector of Ayr, Chamberlain (1309) 115–16, 155, 158, 161, 227, 231, 367 n148, 375 n22

Linlithgow (W. Lothian) 33, 69, 71, 75, 121, 291
  captured by Scots (1313) 137

Lintalee, skirmish (1317) 178

Linton (Lothian) 204–5

lion rampant 307, 327, 402 n89

Livingston, Sir Alexander 137

Llywd, Sir Gruffudd, suspected of contact with Scots in Ireland (1316–18) 173

Loch Broom (Sutherland) 116

Loch Doon castle (Carrick) 14, 92, 103

Loch Lomond (Dumbartonshire/ Argyllshire) 102, 159

Loch Tay (Perthshire) 101–2

Lochaber, lordship (Argyllshire/ Invernessshire) 100, 114, 128, 133, 135, 140, 292, 337 n6, 364 n71
  RB grants to MacDonalds (c.1306–8?) 102, 129, 256
  RB grants to Thomas Randolph within Moray regality (1312/1324) 129, 256

Lochindorb castle (Banffshire) 75, 106

Lochleven, priory (Kinross) 101, 131, 154, 186, 247, 274, see also St Serf

Lochmaben castle (Annandale) 14, 59, 64, 66, 69, 75, 81, 86, 131, 205, 207, 239, 272, 399 n20

Logan, Sir Walter of Hartside 95, 98, 349 n126, 359 n72; sheriff of Lanark (1304–5) 84–5

Logie, Sir John, of Strathgartney (d.1320) 200, 222, 230, 231

London 15, 35, 45–6, 68–9, 88, 103, 125, 127, 144, 182, 184, 224–5, 235, 250, 275

Longforgan, barony (Perthshire) 85, 162

Lorn (Argyllshire) 26, 38, 100, 153, 245–6, 251, 337 n6, 379 n122

Lothians 100, 116–17, 122, 142, 155, 169–70, 178, 183, 187, 196, 206, 220, 231, 256, 281

Loudon Hill, skirmish (1307) 105

Louis IX, King of France and St. (r.1226–70) 14, 325

Louis X, King of France (r.1314–16) 157, 192, 370 n49

Lubeck (Germany) 233

Lucy, Sir Anthony de (d.1314) 144
  son Sir Anthony 225, 267

McCan, Donald 107

McCan, family (Galloway) 83, 126

MacDomnaill, family (Ireland) 19, 66, 72, 104, 107–8, 120, 245, 246, 256, 292, 314, 315

MacDonald, Alexander of Islay 19, 26, 102

MacDonald, Alexander, son of Alexander of Islay or Angus Og (?) 102, 189

MacDonald, Angus Mór 38, 40
  seals Turnberry Band (1286) 25

MacDonald, Angus Og 102, 104–5, 166, 261
  as 'lord of Kintyre' (1306?) 102
  assumes control of family (1318) 201

MacDonald, 'Donald of Islay' 107, 111, 157, 189, 372 n92
  at 1309 St Andrews parliament 102

MacDonald of Islay, family 51–2, 92–3, 112, 121, 126, 128–9, 132, 140, 153, 159, 165, 168, 365 n3, 358 n67–8

MacDonald, John, first Lord of the Isles (d.1387) 102, 249, 261

Macdougall, Alan of Argyll 203, 223, 382 n59

Macdougall, Alexander of Argyll 34, 84, 111, 114, 363 n34
  at 1309 St Andrews parliament 107, 112

Macdougall of Argyll/Lorn, family 26, 38, 52, 72, 93, 100, 166, 246, 261, 278, 289, 312

Macdougall, John of Argyll (d.c.1316) 106, 112, 116, 128, 159, 165, 173, 223, 363 n34, 372 n95, 379 n118/122
  Admiral for Edward I/II in Irish Sea (1309–16) 107, 123, 157
  defeated by RB/MacDonalds at Ben Cruachan (1308) 107
  defeats RB at Dail Righ (1306) 102, 103
  takes Isle of Man (1315) 157

Macdowall, Dougal 82, 126, 153, 165, 203, 278, 289, 359 n72, 382 n59
  captures Thomas and Alexander Bruce (1307) 105
  surrenders Dumfries (1313) 131
  surrenders Isle of Man/Rushen (1313) 132, 372 n95

MacDuff of Fife, family 40

MacLean of Duart, family
  Donald and Neil 260

MacMalcolm dynasty, see Canmore

MacNaughton, Alexander 260

MacQuillan, Malcolm, keeper of Dunaverty castle (Argyllshire) 105, 365 n3

MacRuaridh, Alexander 189

MacRuaridh, Christina 'of the Isles' 260, 359 n82, 365 n98
   aids RB 1306–7 104
MacRuaridh of Garmoran, family 19, 52, 63, 72, 92, 103, 107–8, 140, 165, 245–6, 259–61, 278, 292, 314–15
MacRuaridh, Ranald 260–1 (forfeited 1325), 391 n166
MacRuaridh, Ruaridh 246, 259–60
MacSween, family 104
Magna Carta (1215) 29, 216–17, 319, 324
Maineri, Maino, Milanese surgeon-physician to RB (1327–9) 264–5, 304, 392 n188, 400 n53, 401 n69
Malcolm III, King of Scotland (r.1058–93) 3, 233, 305, 307, 325
Malcolm IV, King of Scotland (r. 1153–65) 25, 266
Malherbe, Sir Gilbert 200, 222
Man, Isle of 120, 126, 158, 162, 165, 216, 237, 239, 243, 255, 279–80, 287, 314, 372 n95, 376 n49, 377 n67
   granted to Thomas Randolph (1312–13, 1316/1324) 132, 171, 255
   retaken by John Macdougall (1315) 157
   retaken by Scots (c.1317–18) 178–9, 184, 188–9, 197, 200
   taken by Edward I (1290) 28
   taken by Scots (1313) 132
   taxed by Randolph (1329) 293, 298–9
Mandeville, Henry de, steward of Ulster (1327–8) 280, 296–7, 398 n164
   indenture with RB (1327) 280
Mar, Donald earl of (d.c.1297) 27–30, 34, 35, 39, 43, 48, 134, 345 n19
Mar, Donald earl of (d.1332) 27, 271, 275, 289, 314, 327, 364 n55, 394 n57, 396 n128, 398 n167
   death 402 n12
   natural son, Thomas Balliol? 20, 394 n62
   place in succession 201, 269
   possible return to Scotland (1319?) 201, 204
   raised in England 79–80, 98, 103, 134–5, 151, 159
   raises support in Wales for Edward II (1327) 276–7, 284
   refuses to leave Edward II (1315) 160, 201, 204
   returns to Scotland (1327) 279–80, 295, 299, 312
   suspected of Balliol sympathies while Guardian for David II (1332) 278
   ward of RB (1304–5) 75, 85
Mar, earldom/family 107, 111, 133, 191–2, 234, 248–9, 271, 307, 337 n6

Mar, Gartnait earl of (d.c.1302) 39, 52, 57
Mar, Isabella of, first wife of RB (d.c.1296) 2, 39, 49, 133–4
March, days of (Anglo-Scots border tribunals, 1323–) 239–40, 243, 274, 287
March, earls of, see Dunbar: earldom of; Patrick IV, VI, VII, VIII
Margaret, Maid of Norway, Lady of Scotland (1286–90) 21–4, 26–30, 49–50, 112
Margaret, Princess of Scotland (d.1283) 21, 22
Margaret, Queen of England 97
Margaret of England, Queen of Scots (d.1275) 46
Marischal, hereditary, Scottish royal household
   office of 3, 116, 252, see Keith, Robert
Marshall, Adam de of Hilton 115, 161
Marshall, Edmund de 230
Marshall, family 247
Marsilius of Padua 310
Maubuisson, Sire Odard d', French envoy 218
Mauley, Sir Edmund (d.1314) 143
Maurice, abbot of Inchaffray 98, 101, 142, 200; as bishop of Dunblane 246, 248, 266
Maxwell, Eustace 223
Meath (Ireland) 168, 173, 189, 295
Mellifont Abbey (Ireland) 173, 374 n146
Melrose Abbey/abbot (Roxburghshire) 17, 33, 52, 73, 83, 89, 114, 117, 122–3, 317, 326, 340 n30, 342 n95, 351 n53, 354 n127, 371 n70, 375 n14, 381 n28, 385 n139, 389 n125, 390 n142/144, 391 n181, 392 n183/185, 400 n43
   Abbot William de Fogo 172
   burnt by English (1322) 238
   patronage from RB 186, 227, 229–30, 252, 284, 290
   RB assigns justice teinds to rebuild (1325) 258, 274, 279
   RB at 170, 172, 179, 183 (Christmas 1317), 263, 266
   RB's heart to be buried at 300–1, 325, Plate 27b)
   RB's 'king's dish' at (1325–) 263–4, 300, 307, 392 n188
Melton, Archbishop, of York 207–8, 209, 229
Menteith, Alan earl of (d.1309) 25, 48, 51, 61, 63, 98, 103, 199; daughter Mary 200

Menteith, earldom 25–6, 109, 111–12, 114,
120, 133, 153, 192, 199–201, 222,
231, 245–6, 277–8, 292, 337 n6,
351 n39, 361 n142, 394 n58
Menteith, family (Stewart) 313–15
Menteith, Sir John de, of Knapdale and
Arran (d.c.1323) 95, 100, 103, 116,
134, 138, 140, 158, 165, 166, 172,
184, 206, 213, 361 n142/147, 362
n7, 265 n97, 369 n31, 370 n62, 377
n81, 384 n116
captures William Wallace (1305) 84,
200
defects to RB (c.1308) 114
guardian of Menteith 200, 216
royal Butler 201
sheriff of Dumbarton 134, 200–1
Menteith, Sir John de, of Arran and
Knapdale, 206, 227, 233, 242, 260,
262, 297, 387 n62
granted Strathgartney (c.1320–3) 222,
230–1, 245
sister Joanna 278
Menteith, Murdoch of (d.1333) 167, 231,
259, 297, 327, 379 n116/118, 384
n116, 387 n62, 388 n77, 398 n164,
399 n17, 403 n12
betrays 'Soules conspiracy' to RB
(c.1318–20) 199–201, 203, 211,
221–2, 224, 226–7
granted Menteith (c.1320) 235, 245–6
Menzies, Sir Alexander of Weem 85, 98,
101, 108, 128, 130, 168, 256, 313,
360 n108, 364 n67/70, 365 n97,
371 n74
Menzies, Sir Thomas 216
Methven, battle of (1306) 101
Methven, lordship (Perthshire) 277
Middleton, Sir Gilbert (d.1318) 180, 182,
184, 375 n21, 376 n43
military services 99, 109, 116, 125, 128–9,
158, 161–3, 184, 202, 205–7, 220,
230–1, 236, 245, 248, 252, 260, 299,
314, 393 n27, see also ships
archers 58, 63, 73, 115, 121, 141, 142,
161, 162, 170, 207, 208, 233, 262,
267, 271, 278, 297, 313, 372 n92
weaponshows (wappinschaw) 202
mint 185, 252, see also coinage
Mitford castle (Northumberland) 184
Modus Tenedi Parliamentum, English
political tract 324
Montefichet, Sir William de 233, 242
Montfort, Simon de, earl of Leicester
(d.1265) 29, 43, 342 n95, 350 n24,
366 n123

Monthermer, Mary, Countess of Fife, 134,
167, 277, 284
Monthermer, Ralph de, earl of Gloucester
122, 125, 128, 134, 144, 151
Montrose (Forfarshire) 46, 121, 223, 29
Moravia, Adam de, bishop of Brechin 390
n147
Moravia, David de, bishop of Moray
(d.1326) 63, 80, 98, 108, 113, 129,
256, 262, 349 n132, 363 n19, 364
n69, 365 n90 n97
death 287
founds seed of 'Scots College', Paris 259
preaches 'crusade' against England
(c.1307) 99, 326
summoned to Avignon (1319–20) 210,
212, 214
Moray, bishop of 293; Pilmuir, John de
287, see also Moravia, David de
Moray, earldom of 3, 30, 44, 75, 107, 120,
133, 135, 171, 178, 230, 256, 311,
see also Randolph, Thomas
RB creates Randolph regality (1312)
128–9, 364 n69
Moray, Sir William de 236, 363 n46
More, Sir Adam of Rowallen (Ayrshire)
298, 302; William 161
Moreville-de Quinci, (Galloway)
inheritance 153, 279, 295
Morham, Sir Herbert 67
Morham, Sir Thomas 158, 171, 216, 383
n69
mortality rates (due to war, disease, famine)
40, 78, 174, 211–12, 257, 321
Mortimer, Roger of Wigmore, Lieutenant
of Ireland (d.1331) 126, 174, 188–9,
267, 285–6, 289, 290, 294–6, 373
n121, 374 n145, 398 n166
deposes Edward II with Isabella 274–82
Morvern, lordship (Argyllshire) 102
Mowat, family 168, 314
Mowat, Sir William of Cromarty 203, 210,
216, 381 n23
killed defending Norham (1327) 225, 282
in 'Soules conspiracy' (1320) 225
Mowbray, Alexander 223, 224, 383 n70,
385 n136
Mowbray, family 221–2, 223–4 (and
affinity), 314
Mowbray, Sir Geoffrey of Barnbougle 25,
34
Mowbray, Sir John 81–4, 10, 222, 235, 383
n69, 386 n9
Mowbray, Sir Philip (d.1318/20?) 126, 182,
187, 196, 205, 206, 224, 226, 370
n41, 377 n81, 387 n59

Mowbray, Sir Philip (*cont.*)
  keeper Stirling Castle for Edward II
    (1313–14) 138, 143, 222
  killed at Faughart (1318?) 165, 224
Mowbray, Sir Roger (d.1320) 179, 216,
  222–4, 226, 230, 231, 232, 234, 248,
  277
  corpse tried by RB in 'Black Parliament'
    (1320) 222
Munster (Ireland) 173, 280
Murray, Sir Alan 216
Murray, Sir Andrew, Guardian (d.1338)
    158, 213, 225, 277–9, 306, 369 n24,
    371 n73, 397 n145
  Guardian for David II (1332, 1335–8)
    269, 278, 393 n32
  marries Christina Bruce (1326) 161–2,
    269, 392 n18–19
  royal Pantler 269
  sons John and Thomas 269
Murray, Sir Andrew, rebel leader 1297
    (d.1297) 52, 56, 269
Murray, Sir Andrew of Avoch and
    Bothwell 34, 52, 342 n87
Murray, family 48, 98, 143, 224, 307, 313,
    315
Murray, Sir Maurice, earl of Strathearn
    (d.1346) 403 n12
Murray, Sir Walter 165
Musselburgh (E. Lothian) 232
Myton, battle/'chapter of' (1319) 207–8,
    209, 327

Nairn (Moray) 106, 108, 128, 292
Naples 6, 321, 325, *see* Robert, King of
    Naples
Neville's Cross, battle of (1346) 313
Newbattle Abbey/abbot (Lothian) 183,
    213, 215, 218, 220, 284, 346 n59
Newcastle 38, 70, 71, 84, 93, 119, 127, 138,
    150, 164, 167, 170, 172, 178, 180,
    182, 202, 210, 229, 230, 231, 237,
    238, 242, 262, 283
Nine Worthies, the 311, 402 n7
Nithsdale, lordship (Dumfriesshire) 86,
    110, 135, 205, 220, 314
Noddsdale, lordship (Ayrshire) 99, 220,
    298, 314
Norfolk, Thomas earl of 135, 202–3, 275,
    370 n49
Norham, castle (Northumberland) 30, 49,
    50, 61, 127, 150, 225, 268, 386 n20
Norham, 'Process' of succession hearings at
    (1291) 31–3, 35, 188
Norway 21, 26, 28, 35, 39, 40, 50, 96, 103,
    165, 192, 222, 307, 341 n61, 344
    n10, *see also* Eric II; Hakon IV;
    Hakon V; Bruce, Isabel; Margaret,
    Maid of Norway
  marriage treaty with Scotland (1281) 22,
    42
  treaty with France (1295) 43
  treaty of Inverness with Scotland (1312)
    129
North Berwick (East Lothian) 152
Northallerton (Yorkshire) 184, 238
Northburgh, Roger 151 (keeper English
    privy seal)
Northumberland/Northumbria 3, 15, 31,
    43, 47, 56, 123–4, 127, 138, 150,
    156, 166, 170, 184, 203, 205, 225,
    229, 238, 254–5, 274, 282, 284, 299,
    301, 395 n91, 396 n104, *see also*
    tribute

oaths 94, 125, 162, 170, 190, 217–18, 268,
    276, 318, 371 n76
  English coronation (1308) 118, 323–4
  RB to Edward I on relic of St Thomas
    (1297) 48, 54, 55
  Scottish 'coronation' (1306?) 95, 323–4
O'Brien, family 174
Ó Conor, family 19, 104, 189
Ó Donnell, family 19, 104
Ó Néill, Domnall, King of Tyrone 173–4,
    177, 189
  invites RB to take High Kingship of
    Ireland (1314–15) 164
  supports Edward Bruce in *Remonstrance
    of Irish Princes* (1317) 181–2
Ó Néill (of Tyrone), family 19, 104, 164,
    173, 189, 371 n86
Ogilvy, family 154, 313
Old Byland, battle of (1322) 238, 250, 252
Oliphant, family 154, 263, 313
Oliphant, Sir William (d.1313) 80, 132, 360
Oliphant, Sir William 206, 216, 223, 233,
    263, 266–7, 369 n31, 391 n175
Ordainers/Ordinances (English
    parliamentary opposition 1309–22)
    119–32, 150–1, 157, 177, 179, 183,
    228, 237, 321, 324, 369 n27
Ordinance for Government of Scotland
    (1305) 155, 271
Orkney 103, 119, 128, 129, 364 n70
  Earl Magnus (and of Caithness) 216,
    364 n76, 376 n57
overlordship, of Scotland (homage for
    Scotland to kings of England)
    38–9, 43, 46, 61, 72, 75, 77, 94, 157,
    205, 216, 231, 241, 253–4, 256, 283,
    287, 396 n122, Plates 2, 7, *see also*

Canterbury Cathedral Priory, 'Quitclaim' of (1189); Falaise, treaty of (1174); Norham, 'Process' (1291)
1174–89: 50–1, 68, 272
1251: 32, 50, 68
1278: 16, 32, 68
1291–92: 18, 30–1, 32–3, 36, 68
Oxford 7, 29, 49, 139, 310, 367 n142

Paisley Abbey (Renfrewshire) 19, 99, 106, 116, 279, 357 n41, 370 n58, 371 n82, 385 n139
Papacy/Pope 6–8, 22, 50, 53, 59, 95–7, 109, 113, 115, 119–21, 127, 132, 136, 164–5, 193, 210, 216, 229, 231, 241, 254, 256, 258, 275, 293, 305–7, 311, 318, 321, 331, 364 n56, 389 n125, *see also* Avignon; excommunication; interdict; 'Declaration of Arbroath'; 'Declaration of the Clergy'; 'Declaration of the Nobility'; Papal tenth; Rome
  Benedict XI (1303–4) 80
  Boniface VIII (1294–1303) 47, 57, 61–2, 65, 67–8, 73–4, 80, 99, 112, 264, 310
    clashes with Philip IV of France 73, 80, 310
    declares Papal Jubilee (1300) 65
    *Scimus Fili* bull (1299) and custody of John Balliol (1299/1301) 57, 61–2, 65–9, 71–2
  Celestine V (1294) 42
  Clement V (1305–14) 80, 82, 96, 99, 106, 110–13, 126, 136, 137, 157
  John XXII (1316–34) 157, 172, 177, 181–2, 187–9, 200, 212, 214, 215, 232, 249, 255, 259, 296, 310, 375 n29, 389 n130, 392 n12
    censures RB and Scotland (1318) 175–86
    and 'Declaration of Arbroath' (1320) 217–18, 227–8
    grants kings of Scots rite of coronation (1329) 325
    styles RB as 'king of Scots' to Edward II (1324) 250
    summons RB and his bishops (1319) 213, 219
Papal tenth (or Church or Crusading tenth, *St Peter's Pence*) 40–1, 47, 51, 61, 63, 65, 73, 78, 99, 251, 345 n19, 346 n59, 357 n42
  annates 361 n139
  old extent (*antiquo taxio*, papal tax rate in Scotland of c.1240s–60s) 270, 272–3, 320–2, 393 n36

Paris 43, 61–3, 65–7, 73, 157, 172, 218, 246, 250, 254, 258, 263, 276, 293, 307
Paris, John of 310
Paris, University of 36, 80, 259, 264 and 390 n151
parliament (English),
  general 47, 77, 79, 81, 83, 118, 123, 127, 156, 236, 287, 377 n86, 378 n90
  Westminster unless otherwise stated:
    Jan. 1292 31
    Sep. 1293 40
    Jun. 1294 40, 41
    Sep. 1302 77, 81
    Mar. 1305 81–3, 115, 251, 319, 354 n116
    Sep. 1305 83–4
    Apr. 1309 119
    Oct. 1309 (York) 119
    Feb. 1310 119
    Aug. 1311 123
    Aug. 1312 128
    Dec. 1312 137
    Oct.–Dec. 1313 137
    Sep. 1314 (York) 150–1
    Jan. 1315 (York) 157
    Jan. 1316 (Lincoln) 169, 170
    Jul. 1317 179–80
    Mar.–Jun. 1318 183
    Oct.–Nov. 1318 (York) 188–90, 202
    Aug. 1321 235
    May 1322 (York) 237
    Nov.–Dec. 1322 (York) 238, 240
    Sep. 1327 (Lincoln) 282
    Feb./May/Jul. 1328 (York) 283, 285, 289
parliament (Scottish) or councils,
  general 4–5, 33, 41, 67, 87, 94, 103, 155, 214, 272–3, 290, 297, 300, 303, 315, 317–24, 326, 329, 378 n95, 394 n59, 396 n118, 405 n47
    Apr. 1284 (Scone) 21–4
    Apr. 1286 (Scone) 21, 23–5
    May 1291 (Norham) 30
    Feb. 1293 (Scone) 38
    Aug. 1293 (Stirling) 39
    Jul. 1295 (Stirling) 42
    Feb. 1296 (Dunfermline) 43
    Mar. 1296 (Stirling) 44
    Aug. 1296 (Berwick) 47–8
    Mar. 1298 (?) 57
    council Aug. 1299 (Peebles) 60–3, 64–5, 86

parliament (Scottish) (*cont.*)
  May 1300 (Rutherglen) 64–5
  Feb. 1302 (Scone) 351 n38, 352 n83
  Sep.1302 (Aberdeen) 352 n83
  Mar. 1304 (St Andrews) 78, 110, 318
  May 1305 (Scone) 83, 89
  council, Oct. 1308 (Auldearn) 108–9
  Mar. 1309 (St Andrews) 102, 110–16,
    132, 152, 157, 160, 161, 325, 360
    n125
  council Apr. 1312 (Inchture) 124
  council Apr. 1312 (Dundee) 124
  council Mar. 1313 (Scotlandwell) 131–2
  Oct. 1313 (Dundee) 2, 132, 133–8
  Nov. 1314 (Cambuskenneth) 1–5, 7, 114,
    136, 149–56, 159, 197, 271, 320,
    Plate 18
  Apr. 1315 (Ayr) 134, 152, 159, 65, 322
  Mar. 1316 (Edinburgh) 169–70
  council Sep. 1316 (Cupar) 171–2
  Jun. 1317 (Scone) 178–9
  Sep. 1317 (Edinburgh) 180–1
  Jul./Aug. 1318 (?) 187
  Dec. 1318 (Scone) 4, 153, 155, 162,
    190–202, 211, 219, 226, 246, 292,
    315–16, 319–20
  council Jan. 1319 (Berwick?) 205
  council Nov. 1319 (Berwick) 210–11
  council Mar. 1320 (Newbattle) 213, 215,
    218–19
  Aug. 1320 (Scone, 'Black Parliament')
    219, 221, 226–7, 320
  Jul. 1321 (Scone) 233–4
  council Sept. 1321 (Edinburgh) 234
  Jul.–Aug. 1323 (Scone) 199, 243–6
  council Mar.–Apr. 1324 (Berwick)
    249–50
  council Nov.–Dec. 1324 (Berwick)
    251–2, 254–7
  Mar. 1325 (Scone), 257, 259, 261, 263
  council Mar. 1326 (Scone?) 267
  Jul. 1326 (Stirling) 258, 268–73, 286,
    319, 322
  council Mar. 1327 (Stirling) 279
  Mar. 1328 (Holyrood) 284–90, 323, 396
    n128, 404 n30
  Nov. 1331 (Scone) 269–70, 323
  Aug. 1332 (?) 278
  Feb. 1352 (Scone) 323
  chronological listing (1306–29)
    Appendix 332–3
patronage (RB's grants) 267, 270, 277–9,
    282, 337 n9, 360 n108, 375 n38, 381
    n8–9/22, 382 n57, 384 n114–16,
    387 n52/58, 389 n104, 391 n173,
    396 n128, 399 n25/27, 403 n11

  after coronation/in flight (1306) 98–100,
    108–10
  1307–9: 111–14
  after first parliament (1309) 114–16, 120
  1312–13: 128–9, 131–2, 133, 135, 143
  after act of forfeiture (Nov. 1314) 149,
    153–4, 158–62, 165, 167–9, 171–2,
    183, 187, 192, 198,
  after death of Edward Bruce (1318)
    200–1, 205–7
  after 'Soules conspiracy' (1320) 210, 213,
    220, 225, 226–7, 229–31, 233–4,
    236, 243–9, 312
  after birth of sons (1324) 251, 251–2,
    254–6, 258–65, 312
  nature of 8, 311–15, 320, 326, 328
peace (indenture/talks) 67, 73, 120–3,
    125–7, 203, 205, 250–1, 259, 262,
    267–8, 272, 276, 279, 312, 315, 362
    n7, 365 n101, 384
    n99/109/111/118, 387 n39, 389
    n115, 396 n105/116/122
  of Amiens (Anglo-French, 1302) 74
  Anglo-Scots after Bannockburn
    (1314–15) 150–1, 156, 158, 164
  Anglo-Scots after siege of Berwick
    (1319) 210–11, 214–15
  Anglo-Scots (at Bamburgh, 1321)
    227–33, 236, 238
  Anglo-Scots (at York, 1324) 241–3,
    252–7
  Anglo-Scots (Edinburgh-Northampton,
    1328) 282–300, 303
  Anglo-Scots negotiated by papal legates
    (1318–19) 170, 175, 177–8, 183,
    188
  Anglo-Scots with Andrew Harcla
    (1323) 239–40
Peebles 64–5, 76, 86, 243, 286, 292,
    329–30
  shire 115, 161, 169, 170, 247, 301–2, 369
    n26, 281 n23
  war council at (Aug. 1299) 60–3
Peebles, Robert de, clerk, Chamberlain 277,
    287, 291
pension (annuity) 223, 234, 248, 252,
    263–4, 267, 270–1, 274, 298,
    300, 313
Percy, family 204, 403 n20
Percy, Sir Henry (d.1314) 47, 54, 100, 103,
    105, 123, 125, 126
Percy, Sir Henry (d.1352) 262, 279, 280,
    282, 283–5, 287, 289–90, 294, 295,
    346 n62, 397 n132
  claim to Scottish lands recognised by RB
    (1328) 285

Perth 29–30, 33, 46, 59, 82, 109, 114,
119–20, 122, 125, 158, 193, 222,
224, 230, 233–4, 264, 286, 291–2,
327, 356 n27, 375 n13, 396 n114,
397 n144
retaken by RB or David earl of Atholl
(1312?) 129–30
shire 27, 76, 78, 85, 100, 101, 130, 134,
152, 159, 162, 168, 170, 178, 206,
244, 267, 277, 298, 364 n67, 370
n56, 379 n115
petitions (to parliament/Crown) 82–4,
114–15, 124–5, 153–4, 192–3, 195,
273, 284, 300, 319–31, 324, 396
n106
by 'captains and men of Galloway' 82,
193, 251, 389 n105, 404 n33
Philip III, King of France (r.1270–85), 288
Philip IV, King of France (1285–1314) 57,
61–2, 64–5, 96, 119, 126, 132, 134,
136–7, 151, 241, 267, 288, 364 n56
alliance with Scotland (1295) 41–3
clashes with Boniface VIII 73–4, 80, 310
death 157
takes custody of John Balliol (1301)
69–71
writes to RB and Scots (1309) 73,
110–12
Philip V, King of France (r.1316–22), 172,
192, 215, 218, 228, 232, 242
Philip (Valois) VI, King of France
(r.1328–50), (Valois), 288, 307,
402 n89
piety (RB's) 8, 55–6, 70, 91, 139, 142,
149–50, 167–8, 169–70, 185–7,
233–4, 264, 292, 296–302, 310, 311,
316, 324–6, 329, 331, see also
pilgrim(age), relics, saints
(individually listed)
pilgrim(age) 17, 34, 65, 91, 232, 239, 250,
274, 292, 297–9, 300–1, 325, 340
n30
heart to Holy Land (1329–30) 300–2
Pluscarden priory (Invernessshire) 123
Poland 6, 316, 321
Pontefract (Yorkshire) 180, 182
Ponthieu (France) 218, 254
prices 40, 211–12, 272, 371 n80
prise 29, 54 (wool maltot), 82, 100, 119,
193, 251, 273, 289, 298, 322, 375
n30, 392 n2, see also purveyance
Prendergast, Sir Henry of Akeld/
Kirknewton 284, 396 n104
propaganda 105, 110–17, 164–5, 173,
190–1, 195, 215–18, 268–70, 302–3,
305, 327, 328, see also 'Declaration';

'Ragman' rolls; 'Remonstrance of
the Irish Princes'
Prudhoe (Northumberland) 123
purveyance 51, 110, 119, 125, 163, 322
Pylche, Alexander 108

Queensferry (Lothian-Fife) 227, 234
Quo Warranto, English legal hearings 31

'Ragman' rolls (1296) 45–8, 51, 288
subsequent 'ragman' style submissions of
loyalty 84, 111, 152, 161, 162, 181,
218–19, 268, 342 n74, 396 n125
raids (Scots into northern England) 2–3,
45, 56–7, 75, 122, 123–4, 127, 132,
148 (Map 4), 150, 156–7, 163–4,
166, 169, 170–1, 179, 182, 184,
205–11, 213, 236, 272, 276, 278–80,
321, 330, see also tribute
Ramsay, family 154, 163
Randolph, 'Black Agnes', Countess of
Dunbar 389 n133
Randolph, John, earl of Moray, lord of
Annandale and Man (d.1346) 135,
179, 249, 365 n98, 375 n31, 376
n49, 377 n81, 378 n103, 380 n146,
403 n12
Randolph, Thomas, earl of Moray, lord of
Annandale and Man (d.1333) 365
n98, 373 n92, 403 n12
Randolph, Thomas, lord of Nithsdale,
Annandale and Man, earl of Moray
3, 98, 130, 135, 137, 361 n126, 363
n46, 365 n90/97, 397 n136/158,
398 n159, 398 n2, 399 n20, 402
n85, Plate 20
knighted by RB (1306?) 357 n38
captured (1306) 101
defects to RB (c.1309) 103, 110
granted Nithsdale (1309)110
appointed 'king's lieutenant between
Forth and Orkney' (1310) 119–20
granted Annandale (1312) 124–5
granted Moray in regality (1312) 128–9,
135; confirmed (1316); 171
confirmed (1324) 256; 257–60,
263–4, 268–9, 311, 313, 320
granted Isle of Man (1313) 132, 171,
255
takes Edinburgh castle (1314) 137–8
role at Bannockburn (1314) 140–1
regular witness to royal acts 152, 154–5,
158, 248–52, 274, 276, 280, 368 n9,
369 n29, 370 n62, 373 n131/135,
385 n123/139, 386 n31, 387 n48,
390 n137/141, 392 n12,

Randolph, Thomas (*cont.*)
  and acts of Succession (1315; 1318; 1326) 161–5; 191, 193; 218–20
  in Ireland (1315–18) 164, 166, 168–70, 173–4
  role after Bannockburn (1314–20) 178–9, 182, 184–5, 187–9, 207, 209–11, 213–14
  made 'Lieutenant South of Forth' (1319) 205–6
  role in 1322 campaign 216, 230, 235–9
  envoy to Avignon (1324) 246, 259
  envoy to Paris (1325–6) 258, 267, 307
  dedicates chantry at Elgin to RB and St Thomas (1328) 290
  negotiates Anglo-Scots peace (1328) 282–94, 297–300, 302
  assumes power for ill RB (1328–9) 278–9, 298
  Guardian for David II (1329–d.1332) 257, 269, 285, 292, 299–300, 306
ransom 2, 127, 143–4, 207, 225, 250, 252, 323
Rathenach (Banffshire), thanage 128
Rathlin island (Ireland) 103, 280, 395 n80, Plate 11
Ratho, barony (W. Lothian) 161, 180, 204–5, 277
Rattray, Eustace de 223–4
Redcastle, barony (Forfarshire) 66, 262, 279, 290, 369 n31
regality, a royal grant in free (franchise/liberty) 120, 128–9, 194, 196–7, 213, 248, 252, 256, 257, 273, 311, 312, 378 n103, *see also* barony
*Regiam Majestatum* (Scots law treatise c.1318–22?) 7, 155–6, 195, 209, 316, 369 n39, 378 n92/94
relics 3, 8, 17, 47–8, 55, 70, 76, 78, 94–7, 101, 187, 190, 233, 257, 268–70, 301, 366 n123/125, 371 n76, *see also* saints
  'Black Rude' of St Margaret 288, 295, 398 n165
  True Cross 46, 60, 139, 209, 247, 284, 288, 295, 303, 325–6, 366 n123, 400 n56
'Remonstrance of the Irish Princes' to Papacy (1317) 177–8, 181–2, 215, 217, 375 n27
Renfrew (Renfrewshire), barony 299, 303
resettlement, RB's of Scotland (1306–29) 2–5, 8, 146–7 (Maps 2, 3), 161–2, 175, 192–7, 200–1, 211, 226, 232–3, 240, 243–7, 251–2, 258, 262–3, 277–8, 290–2, 328, 337 n6, *see also* patronage

Restenneth Priory (Forfarshire) 234, 236, 268, 375 n13, 388 n93
  John Bruce buried at (1326) 234, 268, 388 n93
rice 264–5, 401 n65, *see also* almonds; 'king's dish'
Richard I, King of England (r.1189–99) 50
Richmond, John of Brittany, earl of, lieutenant of Scotland (1305) 76, 84–6, 93, 95, 231, 238, 267, 282, 385 n4, 389 n115
Richmond (Yorkshire) 150, 170, 236
Rievaulx Abbey/abbot (Yorkshire) 17, 279, 295, 340 n30, 384 n99, 386 n22
Robert, King of Naples (r.1309–43) 310–11
Robert I, King of Scotland, *see* Bruce, Robert VII
Rome 30 61–2, 65, 67–8, 73–4, 80, 186, *see also* Avignon; Papacy/Pope
Rome, Giles of 145, 310
Ros, Sir Godfrey de 84, 161
Roslin, battle of (1303) 74, 76
Ross, bishop of 34, 108, 113, 293
  Roger de Ballinbreich, bishop 259
  Thomas de Dundee, bishop 129, 259
Ross, earldom 100, 128
  Euphemia (queen of Robert II of Scotland) 179, 375 n12
Ross, family 313, 314, 315, 385 n134
Ross, Hugh, earl of (d.1333) 168, 247–8, 256, 259, 266, 277, 290, 292, 307, 360 n113, 361 n126, 366 n106, 369 n24, 371 n69, 397 n145, 403 n12
  granted Buchan lands 111, 129, 224, 248
  marries Maud Bruce (d.c.1329) 161
  submits to RB (1308) 108–9, 313
  supports Balliol/Comyns 72, 76, 80, 82, 84, 90, 100
Ross, Isabel 136, 179
Ross, John 109, 129, 224, 249
Ross, William, earl of (d.1274) 34, 38, 48
Ross, William, earl of (d.1323) 320, 352 n75, 360 n113, 361 n147, 363 n44 n46, 365 n90, 366 n106, 371 n69, 397 n130
  at Bannockburn (1314) 140
  patronage from RB (1314–23) 152, 161, 168, 179, 192, 216, 224–5, 234, 248
  role for RB (1308–23) 82, 103, 111, 114, 129–30, 136
  sheriff of Skye (1293) 26, 38, 245
  submits to Edward I (1302–3) 72
  submits to RB (1308) 108–9, 313
  truce with RB (1307) 106–7
Ross, William, earl of (d.1372) 161, 261

Rothesay island/castle (Argyllshire) 75, 92, 255

Rothiemay, barony (Banffshire) 231, 259

Roxburgh 33, 63, 69, 71, 82, 126, 133, 137, 158, 286, 291, 327
  castle 2, 40, 51, 55, 60–2, 75, 124, 128, 136, 196, 204, 279, 281, 391 n161
  retaken by Scots (1314) 137
  sheriff: Ingram d'Umfraville (1299) 63; James Douglas (1319) 220
  shire 17, 18, 63, 85, 99, 133, 138, 158, 163, 169, 172, 187, 220, 221, 230–1, 258, 262, 284, 290, 373 n123, 382 n57, 383 n68, 384 n115

Rushen castle (Isle of Man) 132

Rutherglen (Lanarkshire) 64, 107, 158, 286, 303

Ruthven castle (Perthshire) 106


saints 3, 8, 17, 104, 106, 138–9, 149, 164, 186–7, 190, 241, 302–3, 326, 331

St Andrew 38, 46, 94, 96, 106, 139, 142

St Andrews (Fife) 33, 44, 59, 88, 89, 90, 102, 131 132, 152, 158, 159, 233, 305, 325–6, 393 n33
  bishop 1, 7, 14, 33, 44, 46, 56–7, 59, 78, 88–90, 94, 96, 102, 106, 131, 139, 142, 158–9, 205, 217, 233, 259, 293, 302, 309, 324–6, 366 n125, 381 n37, 393 n33/36, see also Ben, James; Fraser, William; Lamberton, William
  consecration of cathedral (5 July 1318) 185–6, Plate 22
  diocese vacancy: 50, 57, 347 n79 (1297); 291, 297 n138 (1328)
  parliament at: 78, 110, 318 (1304); 110–16 (1309)
  prior(y) of 34, 132, 278, 365 n90/97, 376 n58, 386 n31, 396 n102

St Brendan 70, 104

St Brigit (of Larne) 172, 251, 374 n140

St Columba (of Iona/Dunkeld) 104, 139, Plate 12a)

St Congall (of Holywood, Galloway) 229

St Convall 56, 303

St Cuthbert (of Durham) 17, 35, 44, 46, 98, 139, 167, 241, 284, 302, 340 n30, 395 n101

St Denis (France) 307

St Duthac (of Tain) 103, 109, 234, 385 n134

St Edward the Confessor (King of England, r.1042–66) 44, 46–7, 118, 253, 325

St Fillan 139, 302, 326, 331, 366 n125, Plate 12b)
  aids RB escape (1306) 100–2

St George 44

St John, Sir John de 69, 76, 86, 350 n31

St John the Baptist 159, 241, 249, 290, 302

St John of Beverley 44, 98, 139, 209, 241

St Kentigern (Mungo) of Glasgow 49, 70, 94, 97, 104, 139, 186, 234, 241, 247, 302–3, 346–7 n72, 356 n9, 387 n40, 400 n58

St Kessog 159

St Louis of Anjou 325

St Machutus (or Malo, of Lesmahagow) 70, 91, 169–70, 302, 350 n36

St Magnus (Orkney) 129, 364 n76

St Malachy (at Clairvaux/Armagh) 17, 91, 172–3, 206, 302, 331, 371 n86, 373 n140

St Margaret (d.1093, Queen of Malcolm III, King of Scotland) 3–4, 21, 39, 46, 49–50, 76, 97, 101, 131, 137, 139, 152, 302–3, 306–7, 325–6, 331, 337 n15, 341 n59, 346 n56, 366 n125, 400 n57/58, Plate 26, see also Dunfermline
  'birthing serk' relic 167, 232–4, 247–8, 342 n78

'Black Rude' of 288, 295

St Ninian (of Whithorn) 17, 41, 91, 104, 139, 156, 239, 241, 297, 299, 302, 303, 331, 366 n125, 375 n27, 400 n58
  church of, at Bannockburn 141
  RB pilgrimage to shrine of at Whithorn (1329) 297–9

St Palladius 186, 376 n57

St Sardos, war of (Aquitaine, 1324–5) 250, 252

St Serf 247, 326, 362 n153, 376 n57
  Abbey/shrine at Culross 131, 139, 186, 198, 237, 307
  chapel at Cardross (RB's viscera interred at, 1329) 301–2
  Priory at Lochleven 8, 131

St Stephen (of Hungary) 325

St Thomas (Becket of Canterbury) 34, 40, 51, 68, 91, 94, 98, 123, 186–7, 210, 239, 241, 253, 302, 303, 307, 326, 346 n55, 350 n10, 356 n9, 359 n95, 365 n89, 367 n142, 370 n58, 376 n63, 387 n40, 392 n2, Plate 12c)
  Arbroath abbey dedicated to 17–18, 55, 105, 110, 131, 139, 168, 173, 179, 219, 234, 299, 331, Plate 13
  Bruce family veneration of 17–18
  Edward I dies on Translation feast of (7 July 1307) 104–6

St Thomas (*cont.*)
  Edward I worships him at Applegarth
    (Annandale, 1300) 66
  invoked in 'Remonstrance of the Irish
    Princes' (1317) 182
  invoked by Scots at Bannockburn (1314)
    106, 142
  John Balliol's muniments gifted to
    Canterbury (1299) 46, 62
  Randolph chantry at Elgin dedicated to
    (1328) 290
  RB oath on relic of (1297) 46, 48, 54,
    55–6
  RB offers rings to Canterbury altar
    (c.1302) 46, 74, 340 n34
  Scotlandwell (Lochleven) dedicated to
    101, 138
St Waltheof (of Melrose) 325
St Winnin 56, 104, 326, 387 n40
Salisbury, treaty of (1289) 27–8
  John of 310
*Scimus Fili* (Papal bull, 1299) 61–2, 65,
    66–7, 68, 72
Scone Abbey/abbot (Perthshire) 4, 34, 52,
    75, 93–8, 124, 210, 229, 233, 245–8,
    275, 277, 317, 326, 368 n11, 391
    n162, 392 n2, 394 n59, Plate 10, *see
    also* coronation; parliament (Scottish)
  inauguration stone 46, 81, 95–6, 253,
    256, 288, 295, 356 n15
  John Balliol enthronement (1292) 38
  RB enthronement (1306) 5, 53, 58, 92–5,
    142
Scotlandwell (Kinrossshire) 101, 138
*Scottish King's Household, The*, English text
    (c.1292–6) 324, 344 n5
scrofula (and 'royal touch') 303, 400 n53
Scrymgeour, Sir Alexander, royal standard
    bearer 60, 67–8, 98–9, 183, 359 n72
Scrymgeour, family 154
Scrymgeour, Sir Nicholas 183, 248, 282,
    375 n38
Segrave, Sir John de 76, 121–2, 144
Selkirk
  castle 71, 75, 122, 196, 363 n40
  forest 55, 60, 75, 101, 122, 123, 150, 252,
    284
  shire 99, 169, 205, 291, 373 n123
Seton, Sir Alexander, of Seton 216, 230, 234,
    237–8, 242–3, 248, 256, 298, 327,
    369 n24, 372 n92, 381 n25, 398 n159
  in Berwick campaign (1317–18) 152,
    165, 181–2, 184, 187, 196, 203,
    205–7, 210
  defects at Bannockburn (1314) 141–3,
    206, 367 n140

granted Lothian lands/leadership
    (1319–) 206, 231, 233, 384 n114
  service in Ireland (1315–18) 372 n92
  sheriff of Berwick (1319) 185
  supports RB (1306–7) 142, 367 n140
Seton, Sir Andrew 216
Seton, Sir Christopher (d. 1306) 87, 98,
    103, 355 n139, 359 n72
  brother John 98, 103
  chapel to, dedicated to Holy Cross, at
    Dumfries by wife Christina Bruce
    (1324) 257, 355 n160
Seton, family 313
sheriffs (Scottish) 14–15, 24, 26–7, 35, 38,
    47, 53, 60, 63, 79, 86, 106, 108–9,
    116, 123–4, 130–1, 134, 154, 163,
    166, 168, 178, 185, 190–7, 201–2,
    220, 223–4, 244–7, 261–2, 267, 271,
    273, 279, 297–8, 311–12, 315–16,
    323–4, 352 n70, 353 n95, 379 n122,
    383 n78, 403 n17
  accounts intromitted to exchequer 291–3
  RB as sheriff of Ayr and Lanark
    (1304–5) 75, 81, 84
ship 4, 92, 102–3, 104, 123, 157, 163, 173,
    187–8, 201, 207, 236, 294, 298,
    Plate 4, *see also* military services
  galley or 'birling service' 3, 19, 120, 129,
    132, 158, 166, 184, 245, 260, 297,
    299, 313
  piracy 274, 394 n40
  RB's 'great ship' and Randolph's ship at
    Cardross 260
Sicily 6, 68, 316, 321
Sinclair, family 313
Sinclair, Sir Henry, bailie of Caithness 84,
    170, 216, 223, 230, 233, 256, 266–7,
    364 n70 n76, 365 n97, 374 n9
Sinclair, William, bishop of Dunkeld 113,
    120, 210, 212, 214, 256, 258, 266,
    327, 365 n98, 371 n68, 384 n109,
    385 n139, 386 n31, 388 n77,
    401 n77
  defends Fife against invasion (1317) 178
  provision supported by RB (1311) 109,
    366 n107
Sinclair, Sir William 262
Siward, Sir Richard 76, 86, 92, 354 n133
Skerries, battle of (1316, Ireland) 169
Skye, isle lordship/proposed sheriffship of
    26, 38, 245
Somerville, family 204
Somerville, Sir Thomas 204, 366 n111
Somerville, Sir William of Liston,
    Bathgate and Ratho 204–5
'Soules conspiracy' (c.1318–20) 3, 4, 162–3,

190, 219, 224–5, 238, 240, 271, 312, 315, 328, 383 n88, *see also* Umfraville, Ingram d'; Soules, William

precipitated by death of Edward Bruce (1318) in support of Edward Balliol 199–207

smashed in 'Black Parliament' (Aug. 1320) 219, 224–5

Soules, family 215, 220

Soules, Sir John, Guardian for King John (1300–4, d.c.1310) 39, 63, 66, 67, 69–70, 77, 80, 81, 89, 199, 350 n13, 353 n99

auditor for Bruce of Annandale (1291–2) 34

embassy to France: 43 (1295); (1302–3) 73–4

Soules, Sir John, of Torthorwald and Kirkandrews (d.1318) 150, 152, 165, 199, 220, 368 n8

killed at Faughart 189

Soules, Sir Nicholas 215

Soules, Sir William, of Liddesdale (d.1322?) 34, 152, 156, 158, 169, 189, 223, 226, 230–1, 233, 314, 366 n111, 383 n92, 386 n28, *see also* 'Soules Conspiracy'

brother Thomas 203, *see also* Soules, John (d.1318)

Butler (1319) 201, 220

father William 220

gaoled (1320 but escaped, killed at Boroughbridge (1322?) 227

snubbed by RB patronage (1318–20) 199, 203–7, 210, 213, 216, 220–1

Spalding, Peter de 183–5, 206, 380 n149

betrays Berwick to RB (1318) 183

Sprouston, barony (Roxburghshire) 221, 230, 290

Stafford, Sir Ralph de 280, 295, 396 n110

Standfordham (Northumberland) 203, 380 n134

Stanhope Park (Co. Durham) 281

Staplegordon, barony (Dumfriesshire) 158, 213, 220, 357 n33, 369 n26

Stirling 18, 33, 39, 67, 75, 89, 131, 133, 136–44, 156, 206, 251, 278–9, 291, 319, 368 n3, 391 n162, Plates 14, 17

battle of (1297) 56, 58, 59, 149, 188

castle 1, 2, 61, 64, 78–80, 124, 130, 136, 138, 141, 143, 222–4, 263, 352 n76, Plate 14

New Park 141–2

parliament at (1326) 258, 268–73, 286, 319, 322

sheriff of 85, 163

shire 159, 200, 223, 225, 244, 248, 384 n114

Stewart, Sir Alan 161

Stewart, Sir Alexander of Bonkle (d.1319) 34, 143, 152, 154, 171, 181, 204, 366 n111, 369 n29, 373 n131, 375 n14

defects to RB (1314) 138

son John made earl of Angus by RB 134, 262

Stewart, Sir James (Steward) (d.1309) 5, 62–3, 65, 67, 73, 161, 329, 346 n62, 348 n106, 351 n53, 353 n99, 361 n147, 370 n58, 371 n78

death 116

envoy to France (1302–3) 73–4

Guardian (1286) 23–6, 30, 34, 38–9

marries sister of de Burgh of Ulster 51

rebels with Wishart, Douglas and RB (1297) 51–6, 57, 59

sheriff of Kintyre 38, 51

sheriff of Ayr 35, 38

son Andrew 93, 98

submits to Edward I: 51 (1296); (1297) 54–5; (1304) 77; (1306) 103

supports RB (1306–7) 80–1, 89, 102–4, 111

Stewart, family, hereditary Stewards of Scottish royal household 4, 19, 26, 52, 166, 255, 292, 295, 297, 307, 311, 313–14, 320, 394 n58

Stewart, Sir James of Durisdeer 280

Stewart, John of Bonkle, earl of Angus (d.1333) 134, 262, 278, 281, 369 n29, 394 n62

Stewart, Sir John, of Jedburgh (d.1298) 25, 34, 54

Stewart, Sir John of Jedburgh (d.1318) 99, 165, 189, 205–6

Stewart, Sir John of Kyle (Robert III, King of Scotland, r.1390–1406) 249, 253, 329, 388 n94

Stewart, Robert (RB's grandson) (Steward (1327)), Robert II, King of Scotland (r.1371–90) 174, 227, 240, 279, 289–90, 307, 329, 369 n31, 375 n12, 387 n50, 394 n58,

birth (1316) 170

expectancy of earldom of Fife 167, 277

granted Cunningham 192

granted Kintyre 102, 246, 299

granted Methven 277

granted Renfrew 299

granted Roxburghshire baronies 231, 384 n115

Stewart, Robert (*cont.*)
  recognised as heir presumptive: 190–1
    (1318); 268–9 (1326)
  tensions with David II 277, 299, 323,
    388 n94, 399 n24
Stewart, Thomas, earl of Angus (d.1363)
    394 n62
Stewart, Walter Balloch, earl of Menteith
    (d.1294) 26, 27, 34, 35, 51, 84,
    399 n17
Stewart, Sir Walter (Steward) (RB's
    son-in-law, d.1327) 3, 98, 280, 370
    n58/62, 373 n131, 385 n139, 386
    n31, 387 n62, 388 n84, 390 n137
  Barbour invents his division at
    Bannockburn (1314) 140
  in Berwick campaigns (1318–19) 174,
    178–80, 185, 192, 206–7
  death 279
  Guardian with James Douglas (1317) 173
  marries Marjorie Bruce (1315) 161, 204
  patronage from RB 116, 129, 152, 158,
    160, 165–7
  regular witness to royal acts 210, 213–14,
    216, 220–1, 230–1, 236, 245–6, 256,
    265, 277–8
Stewart of Bonkle, family 25, 225, 227,
    313, 315
Stewart of Menteith, family 25, *see also*
    Menteith: Alan; Alexander; John;
    John; Murdoch
Stewartry (Steward family lands) 54, 59,
    75, 98, 106, 140, 165, 260–1
Stracathro (Angus) 46, 75
Straiton, Sir Alexander 216
Strath'an (Aberdeenshire) 153, 234, 278,
    364 n69, 385 n136
Strathbogie, David, earl of Atholl (d.1326)
    27, 107, 160, 178, 224, 238, 244,
    314, 364 n71, 365 n80/90/97, 369
    n27, 375 n12, 379 n118, 383 n70
  and Balliol conspiracy (1320) 203–4
  Bruce-Atholl marriage (1312) 126,
    128–9, 133–7
  defects back to Edward II (1314) 3, 140,
    153
  defects to RB (1312) 127–8
  takes Perth (1312?) 130
Strathbogie, David, earl of Atholl (d.1335)
    140, 160, 278, 289, 295, 365 n80,
    394 n58/64
  deal with Edward III and Robert
    Steward over Fife (1335) 135
Strathbogie, Isabel (betrothed of Edward
    Bruce) 27, 160, 198, 226, 299,
    375 n12

betrays 'Soules conspiracy' (1320?) 221–2
jilted by Edward Bruce (1313–14) 135–6
secures lands for her son, Alexander
    Bruce 164, 168, 221, 262, 280, 365
    n98, 369 n31
Strathbogie, John, earl of Atholl (d.1306)
    76, 80, 84, 85, 109, 224, 234, 364
    n67
  alliance with Bruces and Mar (1286–90)
    26–30, 34–5, 43, 48, 52, 57, 60–1
  distrust of Comyns (1299) 65
  executed 103
  supports RB as king (1306) 98–102
Strathbogie, lordship 107, 114, 128, 153,
    163, 234, 271, 278, 337 n6
  granted to Adam Gordon 198, 231, 248
Strath Braan (Perthshire) 134, 152
Strathearn, Agnes Countess of 200, 221–2,
    223, 365 n79
  and 'Soules conspiracy' (1320) 200,
    221–2
Strathearn, earldom 101, 130, 133, 140,
    168, 178, 203, 314, 315
Strathearn, Malise (VI) earl of (d.c.1317)
    34, 76, 80, 103, 140, 220, 221
  captured with Perth (1312) 130
  forced to submit by RB (1306) 100, 358
    n59
Strathearn, Malise (VII), earl of (d.c.1325)
    179, 198–200, 216, 220, 223, 256,
    262, 266, 278, 365 n79, 388 n77,
    394 n5
  gifted title by RB (1312–14) 140
  sheriff of Perth 130
Strathearn, Malise (VIII) earl of (forfeited
    1343) 394 n58, 397 n159
Strathfillan (Perthshire) 101
Strathgartney, lordship (Perthshire) 200,
    222, 231, 245
Strathord (Perthshire) 134, 152, 170
succession, royal 2, 34–6, 53, 59, 61–2,
    65–6, 71, 80, 87, 90, 111, 113–14,
    125, 132–5, 139, 316, 318, 321–3,
    325, 328–9, 343 n126, 371 n66–7,
    388 n94, *see also* 'Great Cause'
  act of Scottish (1284) 21–4, 27, 32
  act of Scottish (1315) 157–62, 167,
    170–1, 174–5
  act of Scottish (1318) 190–3, 198–201,
    217–18, 232–3, 240, 249–50, 257
  act of Scottish (1326) 4, 268–70, 287–8,
    299
  English (1290) 31
Sully, Henry, Grand Butler of France 238,
    242, 250
Sutherland, earldom 107, 108, 130

Sutherland, William, earl (d.1330) 30, 34, 109, 111, 112, 216, 306, 377 n79, 403 n12
    grandson John (d.1351) 388 n94
    son William marries RB's daughter, Margaret (c.1346) 306
Swans, feast of (Westminster 1306) 98
Sweden 6, 321
Sweetheart abbey (Galloway) 52, 62, 284
syphilis 304–5

Talbot, family 104
Tange, Andrew, English clerk 188, 208, 231
    edits records of 'Great Cause' (1315) 157
Tarbert castle (Argyllshire) 162, 245–6, 298–9, Plate 23
    John de Lany, keepers' account (1325–6) 245, 260
    RB at: 159, 166 (1315); 260–1 (1325), 297 (1329)
tax 40–1, 51, 54, 65, 78, 137, 185, 251, 258, 261, 263, 277–9, 282, 298, 318, 321–3, 329, 344 n161–7, 376 n54, 381 n28, see also Papal tenth
    for Berwick's walls 213–14
    king's tenth for lfe (1326) 270–2, 286–93
    peace contribution (1328) 272, 286–93
    verus valor (1366–) 393 n36
Templars, Order of Knights (disbanded by Papacy 1312) 113, 120
thanage (royal demesne) 99, 110, 116, 123, 128, 129, 166, 168, 234, 247, 262, 312, 342 n74, 360 n113
    RB policy of alienation as king 109, 271
Thomond (Ireland) 14, 165, 173
Thorinborne, Patrick 223; Thomas 223
Tibbers castle (Dumfriesshire) 86, 92, 103, 110, 130
Torthorwald, family/lordship of (Dumfriesshire) 19, 220, 233, 340 n38, 368 n8
Tottenham (London) 14
tournament 20, 29, 149, 207, 282, 288, 327, 396 n126
trade 41, 233, 241, 246
Tranent, barony (Lothian) 206, 231, 238
tribute (payment for truce from Scottish raids) 119, 124, 136, 138, 150, 166, 170–1, 174, 178, 179, 184, 205, 237, 272, 279, 282, 374 n152, 385 n4, 396 n116, see also Durham, County; Cumberland; indemnity; Northumberland; Westmorland
truce (indenture/talks) 64, 66–7, 106–7, 122–3, 132–3, 136, 150–1, 166–7, 169–70, 172, 175, 177–9, 182, 184,

188, 205, 228, 231–2, 234, 236, 250, 253, 255–6, 259, 263, 267, 272–6, 279, 283, 286, 362 n9, 373 n138, 386 n36
Anglo-French of Asnières (1302) 70
Anglo-Scottish (Feb.–Nov. 1309) 110, 116, 119–20
Anglo-Scottish (1319–21) 210–12, 214, 219
Anglo-Scottish (1323–36) 241–5
tuberculosis 303
Tungland abbey/abbot (Galloway) 34
Turnberry Band (1286) 25–7, 38, 79, 342 n81
Turnberry castle (Carrick) 13–14, 25, 58, 69, 70, 105, 294, 297, 298, 339 n3, Plate 3
Tweng, Sir Marmaduke 144, 151, 368 n150
Twynham, Walter de, canon of Glasgow, Chancellor (1328–) 210, 232, 258, 291, 298, 302, 398 n159
Tynedale (Northumberland) 3, 31, 156, 182, 205, 215, 370 n41
Tynemouth (Northumberland-Co. Durham) 211, 238

Ulster, earldom of (Ireland) 2, 19, 103, 132, 164–5, 166, 169, 173, 174, 188, 271, 280, 307
Ulster, Richard de Burgh, earl of (d.1326) 55, 119–21, 141, 159, 161, 165, 166, 271, 280, 342 n76, 352 n78, 362 n7, 367 n138
    and 1302–4 English invasion of Scotland 72, 75
    daughter's marriage to RB (1302) 66, 72, 74
    death 260–1
    defeated by Edward Bruce at Conor (1315) 168
    sister's marriage to James Steward (c.1296) 51
    suspected during Bruce invasion of Ireland (1315–17) 173
    and Turnberry Band (1286) 25–7
Ulster, William de Burgh, earl of (d.1333) 280, 395 n79
    installed by RB in Ulster (1328) 294
Umfraville, Gilbert d', earl of Angus (d.1307) 34, 43, 47
Umfraville, Gilbert d', earl of Angus (d.1381), 262, 271, 278, 312
Umfraville, Sir Ingram d' 34, 38, 60–70, 73, 77–8, 100, 121, 126, 128, 158, 196, 204, 216, 314, 353 n99, 383 n86
    and Balliol plot (1318–20) 219, 222–7

Umfraville, Sir Ingram (*cont.*)
  captured at Bannockburn (1314) 143
  escapes to England (1321) 226
  replaces RB as Guardian (1300) 65
Umfraville, Robert d', earl of Angus
      (d.1325) 100, 123, 126, 153–4, 203,
      222, 225, 238, 289, 348 n119, 370
      n58, 394 n64
  captured at Bannockburn (1314) 143
*Unam Sanctum,* Papal bull (1302) 73, 310,
    *see also* Papacy, Boniface VIII;
      Philip IV
Upsetlington (Berwickshire) 32, 82, 284,
    395 n104
Urquhart castle/lordship (Invernessshire)
    52, 75, 106, 259
Urr, barony of (Galloway) 66, 279, 290

Valence, Aymer de, earl of Pembroke
      (d.1324) 75–6, 100–5, 118, 125–7,
      167, 170, 172, 175, 177, 180, 182,
      200, 210–11, 235, 242, 359 n96,
      360 n121, 374 n8, 382 n59
  at Bannockburn (1314) 143
  at Berwick siege (1319) 207
  defeated by Douglas at Old Byland
      (1322) 238
  death 389 n115
  joins Ordainers (1310) 121
  leads talks with Scots (1326) 229–30
  lieutenant of Scotland (1306–7) 106
Valence, William de, earl of Pembroke 37
Vienne (Papal Church Council 1310/12)
      110, 112, 113, 115, 120, 179, 361
      n131
  Archbishop of, papal envoy 228–9
de Vipont, family 116, 361 n126
*Vita Edwardi Secundi,* English chronicle 8,
      125–6, 141–3, 149, 163, 177, 183,
      187, 203, 205, 208, 252–5, 256
  clerk Walwayn, John de, author? 125

Wake, family 114, 204
Wake, Sir Thomas 275, 280, 285, 289, 290,
    294–5, 397 n132
Wales 20, 56, 58, 64, 70, 82, 105, 121,
      164–5, 168–9, 177, 188–9, 211,
      235–6, 261, 280, 282, 330, 373 n145
  Edward Bruce letter to Welsh (1315)
      173
  Donald of Mar and Rhys ap Gruffudd,
      raise Welsh support for Edward II
      (1327) 275, 294, 395 n77
  Llywd, Sir Gruffudd Llywd suspected of
      contact with Scots in Ireland
      (1316–18) 173

revolt (1284) 31–2, 34
revolt of Madog ap Llywelyn (1294–5)
      41–2
Wales, Gerald of 310
Wallace, Sir William, Guardian (d.1305) 5,
      65, 76–80, 200, 269, 348 n114, 349
      n142, 354 n123
  appointed Guardian (1298) 57
  brother Sir Malcolm Wallace supports
      RB (1299) 62–3, 223
  captured and executed 84
  defeat at Falkirk (1298) 58
  historic tradition of relationship with RB
      (1298) 58–9
  rebels against England (1297) 52–63
  reaction to Wishart, Steward, Carrick
      rebellion (1297) 55
  victory at Stirling Bridge (1297) 56
Walsingham (Norfolk) 35
Warenne, John de, VI earl of Surrey
      (d.1304), lieutenant of Scotland 30,
      44, 45, 47, 51, 55–7
Warenne, John de, VII earl of Surrey 122,
      127, 182, 207, 238
Wark (-on-Tynedale), castle/lordship 3, 43,
      97, 150, 156, 184, 268
Warkworth castle (Northumberland) 282
Warwick, earl of 44, 76, 121, 125,
      127, 139
Weardale (Co. Durham) 123, 280–2
      (campaign, 1327), 327
Wemyss, Sir David, sheriff of Fife 178, 216,
      224, 289, 383 n82
Wemyss, family 163
Wemyss, Sir Michael 224, 383 n82
Westerker/Westerkirk (Dumfriesshire)
      204, 210, 220, 230–1, 369 n26
Western Isles 18–19, 24, 26, 52, 59, 70, 111,
      119, 140, 157, 164, 172, 255,
      259–61, 280, 294, 296–9, 315, 330,
      *see also* Campbell, family; Menteith,
      family; MacDonald of Islay, family;
      Macdougall of Argyll/Lorn, family;
      MacRuaridh of Garmoran, family;
      Ross, family; Tarbert castle
  RB in exile in (1306–7) 102–4
  RB's policy towards 129, 166, 244–6,
      251, 260–1, 278, 292, 297–9, 314
Westminster, Abbey 16, 29, 31, 34, 40,
      46–7, 54, 77, 96, 98, 118–19, 121,
      125, 127–8, 204, 221, 251, 253–4,
      275–7, 295, 306, 319, 402 n93,
      Plate 2, *see also* parliament
      (English)
  1305 parliaments and Ordinance for
      government of Scotland 81–5

Westminster, Palace 35, 81, Plate 5
Westmorland 123, 127, 156, 205, 210, 254, 256, 282, *see also* tribute
Whithorn, bishop of 41, 201, 219, 293, 340 n30, 366 n125, 399 n27, *see also* Dalton, Thomas de; Galloway, bishop of
  Cathedral Priory 17, 139, 156, 238–9, 255, 262, 290, 297–9, 304, 326, 331, 357 n42, 366 n125, 375 n27, 399 n27/8, *see also* St Ninian
Wigtownshire 14, 24, 47, 244, 257, 279, 286, 290, 292, 297–9, 315, 403 n17
William I the 'Lion', King of Scotland (r.1165–1214) 14, 18, 21–2, 34, 46, 51, 68, 167–8, 239–40, 249, 272, 303, 342 n81, 373 n110, 386 n31
William I, the Conqueror, King of England (r.1066–87) 233
Winchelsey, Archbishop of Canterbury 54, 55, 61, 62, 118, 125, 132
Winchester 20, 29, 98, 341 n56, Plate 6
Wiseman, Sir William 108, 111, 361 n108 n147
Wishart, Robert (d.1316), bishop of Glasgow 2, 5, 41, 43, 74, 89, 175 186, 241, 318, 329, 353 n115, 356 n11, 365 n55, 366 n107, 373 n135
  Guardian (1286) 21, 23–4, 29–30, 32
  at 'Process' of Norham (1291) 33, 61
  auditor for Bruce of Annandale (1291–2) 33
  influences RB to revolt with Steward, Douglas, Wallace and Murray (1297) 48–53
  submits with RB, Steward and Douglas at Irvine (1297) 54–5, 57, 59, 62–3
  exiled by Edward I for 3 years (1304) 77, 80
  at Wesminster parliament for Scots with RB and John Mowbray 81–3

absolves RB of Comyn's murder (1306) 93–4
  role in RB's enthronement (1306) 94–7, 98–9
  captured (1306) 101, 103, 106, 109, 113, 120
  exchanged (1315) 1, 151–2, 158
  death 172
wool 40, 51–2, 54, 137, 185, 231, 233, 241, 258, 264, 300, 392 n185
Writtle, lordship (Essex) 13–14, 17, 18, 78, 79, 115, 256, 284, 389 n119, Plate 1
  possible RB birthplace (1274) 13, 339 n5
  RB seeks restoration (1324?) 253, 339 n6
Wyntoun, Andrew de, Prior of St Serf's, chronicler (*Original Chronicle*, c.1410–20) 1, 8, 90, 320, 355 n146, 371 n66

Yolande de Dreux, queen of Scotland (r.1285–6) 22, 24, 26, 27, 28, 342 n78
York 41, 58, 81, 115, 124–7, 139, 156, 172, 203, 208, 209, 229–30, 244, 280, 303, 384 n106, 386 n28, 395 n91, *see also* parliament (English)
  Anglo-Scots peace talks at (1324) 251–6
  shire 8, 15–17, 25, 115, 138, 170, 182, 184, 207, 235, 238, 242, 253, 254, 274, 279, 342 n74, 384 n99, 385 n4, 396 n102, 396 n125

Zealand (Low Countries) 321
Zouche, Sir Alan 206, 275
Zouche, family 153, 161, 204, 231, 285, 295, 396 n110
Zouche, Sir William 279–80, 287